Lucy Becker - Carol Frain - Karen Thomas

GRAMMAR MATRIX

LETTER TO STUDENTS

Dear Student,

WHY IS GRAMMAR MATRIX USEFUL?
- It helps you to reflect on the grammar patterns and structures of the English language from A1 to B2+ levels of the Common European Framework of Reference for Languages.
- It gradually introduces the rules from the easiest to the most difficult, in a clear, comprehensible way with the help of tables and maps.
- It offers a wide range of examples taken from the language in use and its various registers.
- It gives answers to common areas of confusion and doubt thanks to the **FAQ** section (Frequently Asked Questions) and to the FOCUS boxes.
- It offers hundreds of exercises and activities, each with a level of difficulty indicated from • (easiest) to •••• (most difficult), so that you can pace your learning.
- It is a flexible grammar book that you can use in conjunction with your textbook to learn or revise at home or at school.
- It can be used to prepare for International certification exams, such as Preliminary or First Certificate.
- The version with keys is perfect for self-study.

HOW IS GRAMMAR MATRIX ORGANISED?
In **GRAMMAR MATRIX** you will find:
- **21 units** on a comprehensive range of grammar points; each unit is divided into **four lessons** followed by a **Round Up** section with more detailed studies and revision exercises, and a **Reflecting on Grammar** section, which is a test of your knowledge of grammar;
- An initial **Basics** section from **Unit 1** to **Unit 6**, to help you to learn and/or revise the basic elements of English grammar (verbs *be* and *have*; articles; nouns, etc.);
- **Revision**, **Exam Practice** and **Self-Check** sections for self-evaluation every three units;
- **Visual Grammar** specially designed for an inclusive learning approach;
- An appendix with sections on *Irregular Verbs, Punctuation, British / American English, Phonetics* and *Grammar Words*;
- A detailed index to help you to find topics easily;
- Extra material online, including simplified activities for learners with special needs.

WHO WROTE IT?
GRAMMAR MATRIX has been written by a team of experienced authors who are aware of the challenges students have to face when learning English. Because of its status as a global language, English is constantly evolving. This results in many learners feeling that they can never gain a thorough grasp of it. However, English is based on simple grammar concepts, or 'matrices': once you understand them, you can write and speak in English with precision and accuracy.
Take the GRAMMAR MATRIX challenge and see the difference it makes to your English!
This is the challenge we would like you to face.

CONTENTS

GRAMMAR MATRIX

Mind Maps — p. 8

BASICS SECTION
A1–A2

UNIT 1 — Nouns and articles — p. 11
- **Lesson 1** Regular and irregular plural nouns — 11
- **Lesson 2** Countable and uncountable nouns — 14
- **Lesson 3** The indefinite article *a / an* — 16
- **Lesson 4** The definite article *the* — 19
- **Round Up 1** — 22

UNIT 2 — Personal pronouns + verb *be* — p. 26
- **Lesson 1** Subject pronouns — 26
- **Lesson 2** Verb *be* — 28
- **Lesson 3** *There is / There are* — 32
- **Lesson 4** Question words — 34
- **Round Up 2** — 38

UNIT 3 — Adjectives — p. 42
- **Lesson 1** Demonstratives: *this / that / these / those* — 42
- **Lesson 2** *Some / any / no / none* — 44
- **Lesson 3** Qualifying adjectives and adjectives of nationality; order of adjectives — 46
- **Lesson 4** Numbers and dates — 48
- **Round Up 3** — 52
- **Revision and Exams 1** — 56
- **Towards Competences / Self Check 1** — 60

UNIT 4 — Verb *have* + possessives — p. 62
- **Lesson 1** Verb *have* – positive form — 62
- **Lesson 2** Verb *have* – negative and interrogative forms — 63
- **Lesson 3** Possessive adjectives and pronouns — 66
- **Lesson 4** Interrogative *whose* and the possessive case — 68
- **Round Up 4** — 72

UNIT 5 — Imperatives, present simple, adverbs of frequency, time expressions, object pronouns, connectors — p. 76
- **Lesson 1** The imperative — 76
- **Lesson 2** Present simple — 77
- **Lesson 3** Adverbs of frequency and expressions of time — 81
- **Lesson 4** Object pronouns and some conjunctions — 83
- **Round Up 5** — 86

3

UNIT 6 -ing form and present continuous   p. 90

Lesson 1 -ing form	90
Lesson 2 Present continuous	91
Lesson 3 Present continuous vs. present simple	96
Lesson 4 Verbs + -ing and verbs + infinitive	100
Round Up 6	102
Revision and Exams 2	106
Towards Competences / Self Check 2	110

MAIN SECTION

UNIT 7 Prepositions (A2–B1)   p. 112

Lesson 1 Prepositions of time	112
Lesson 2 Prepositions of place	114
Lesson 3 Other prepositions / Verbs with two objects	117
Lesson 4 Adjectives and verbs followed by prepositions	119
Round Up 7	124

UNIT 8 Past simple and past continuous (B1–B2)   p. 128

Lesson 1 Verb *be* – past simple	128
Lesson 2 Regular and irregular verbs – past simple	129
Lesson 3 Uses of the past simple, time expressions and time sequencing, *used to…*	133
Lesson 4 Past continuous, time clauses with *When / While*	136
Round Up 8	140

UNIT 9 Present perfect and past perfect   p. 144

Lesson 1 Present perfect simple: *ever, never, recently, today…*	144
Lesson 2 Present perfect simple: *just, already, yet…* / Present perfect vs. past simple	147
Lesson 3 Present perfect simple and continuous / How long…? *for* / *since…*	151
Lesson 4 Past perfect simple and continuous	159
Round Up 9	164
Revision and Exams 3	168
Towards Competences / Self Check 3	172

UNIT 10 Adverbs and quantifiers   p. 174

Lesson 1 Adverbs of manner and other adverbs	174
Lesson 2 Adverbs of degree	177
Lesson 3 Indefinite adjectives and pronouns to express large quantities	180
Lesson 4 Indefinite adjectives and pronouns to express small quantities	183
Round Up 10	186

UNIT 11 Comparisons — p. 190

- **Lesson 1** Comparative adjectives — 190
- **Lesson 2** Comparative structures using *less … than* and *not as … as* with adjectives — 194
- **Lesson 3** Superlative adjectives — 196
- **Lesson 4** Comparative and superlative of adverbs, comparatives with nouns and verbs — 200
- **Round Up 11** — 204

UNIT 12 Adjectives and pronouns — p. 208

- **Lesson 1** Indefinite pronouns made with *some, any* and *no* — 208
- **Lesson 2** Distributive adjectives and pronouns; *both, most, all; everybody, everything…* — 211
- **Lesson 3** Reciprocal pronouns: *each other / one another*; correlative conjunctions: *both… and… / either… or…*; compound words with *–ever* — 214
- **Lesson 4** Reflexive pronouns; *one, ones* — 217
- **Round Up 12** — 222
- **Revision and Exams 4** — 226
- **Towards Competences / Self Check 4** — 230

B1–B2+
UNIT 13 Modal verbs to express ability, possibility and volition — p. 232

- **Lesson 1** Characteristics of modal verbs; *can / could* and verbs that express similar concepts — 232
- **Lesson 2** Modal verb *may / might* — 235
- **Lesson 3** Modal verb *will / would*; verbs *want* and *wish* — 238
- **Lesson 4** Conditional forms *would like, would prefer, would rather* — 243
- **Round Up 13** — 246

UNIT 14 Modal verbs to express obligation and necessity — p. 250

- **Lesson 1** Modal verb *must* and verb *have to* — 250
- **Lesson 2** *Need to… / don't need to… / needn't…; be to…* — 253
- **Lesson 3** *Shall / should; ought to..; had better…* — 255
- **Lesson 4** *Be obliged / compelled / forced to…; be due; be bound to…*; verb *owe* — 258
- **Round Up 14** — 260

UNIT 15 The future — p. 264

- **Lesson 1** Different types of future tenses; the future with the present continuous and the present simple — 264
- **Lesson 2** The future with *going to…* — 267
- **Lesson 3** The future with *will* — 269
- **Lesson 4** Future continuous; future perfect — 273
- **Round Up 15** — 276
- **Revision and Exams 5** — 282
- **Towards Competences / Self Check 5** — 286

UNIT 16 — Conditional sentences and *if*- clauses — p. 288

- **Lesson 1** Present and past conditionals — 288
- **Lesson 2** Type 0 and Type 1 conditional sentences — 291
- **Lesson 3** Type 2 and Type 3 conditional sentences — 293
- **Lesson 4** Use of modal verbs in conditional sentences — 297
- **Round Up 16** — 302

UNIT 17 — Passive forms — p. 306

- **Lesson 1** The present passive — 306
- **Lesson 2** The past passive — 309
- **Lesson 3** The passive form in the future and with modal verbs — 312
- **Lesson 4** Personal and impersonal passive form; *have / get something done* — 315
- **Round Up 17** — 320

UNIT 18 — Relative clauses — p. 324

- **Lesson 1** Relative pronouns in defining relative clauses — 324
- **Lesson 2** Relative pronouns in non-defining relative clauses — 328
- **Lesson 3** Other relative pronouns and adverbs: *what, all that, where, when…* — 330
- **Lesson 4** Relative clauses expressed by the present or past participle; verbs of perception — 332
- **Round Up 18** — 336
- **Revision and Exams 6** — 340
- **Towards Competences / Self Check 6** — 343

UNIT 19 — Direct speech and reported speech — p. 346

- **Lesson 1** Verbs *say* and *tell* — 346
- **Lesson 2** Indirect speech: giving orders and expressing statements in the present that are still true — 348
- **Lesson 3** Indirect speech: statements that were true in the past — 351
- **Lesson 4** Reported speech: questions — 354
- **Round Up 19** — 358

UNIT 20 — Connecting clauses — p. 362

- **Lesson 1** Adversative and concessive clauses — 362
- **Lesson 2** Reason, consecutive and purpose clauses — 365
- **Lesson 3** Time clauses; sequencing adverbs; linking words to build an argument — 367
- **Lesson 4** Other conjunctions; causative verbs — 370
- **Round Up 20** — 374

UNIT 21 — Word order, phrasal verbs, word formation — p. 378

Lesson 1	Word order in positive and negative sentences; inversion of verb and subject	378
Lesson 2	Questions and short answers; question tags; *So do I / Neither do I*	380
Lesson 3	Word formation; prefixes and suffixes	385
Lesson 4	Phrasal verbs	390
Round Up 21		394
Revision and Exams 7		398
Towards Competences / Self Check 7		402

Visual Grammar — p. 404

Visual Grammar Answer Keys — p. 420

Appendix — p. 421

British English / American English main grammatical differences	421
International Phonetic Alphabet (IPA)	422
Punctuation Marks	423
Moods, Tenses and Aspects	424
Modal verbs – Tenses	425
Conditional Sentences	426
Conjugation of an irregular verb	427
Main irregular verbs	428

Grammar Words — p. 430

Index — p. 434

Index of Tables — 438

Student's book Answer Keys — p. 439

Symbols

MATRIX + The symbol Matrix + indicates further expansion of topics and related exercises.

Dots show the level of difficulty for each exercise:

 – easy   – medium  – difficult  – advanced

THE WORDS OF GRAMMAR
Nouns, articles and verb cluster

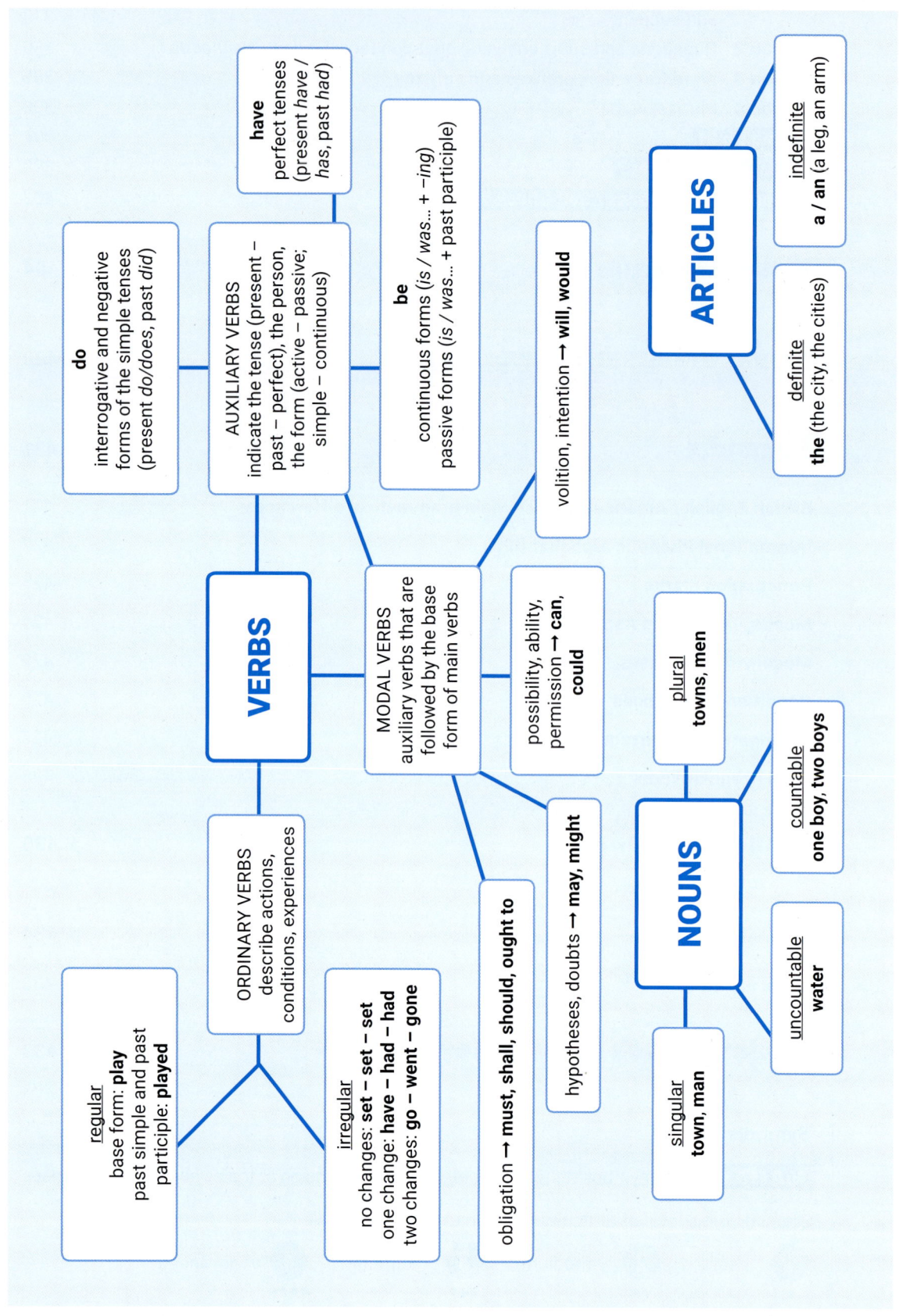

Adjectives and pronoun cluster

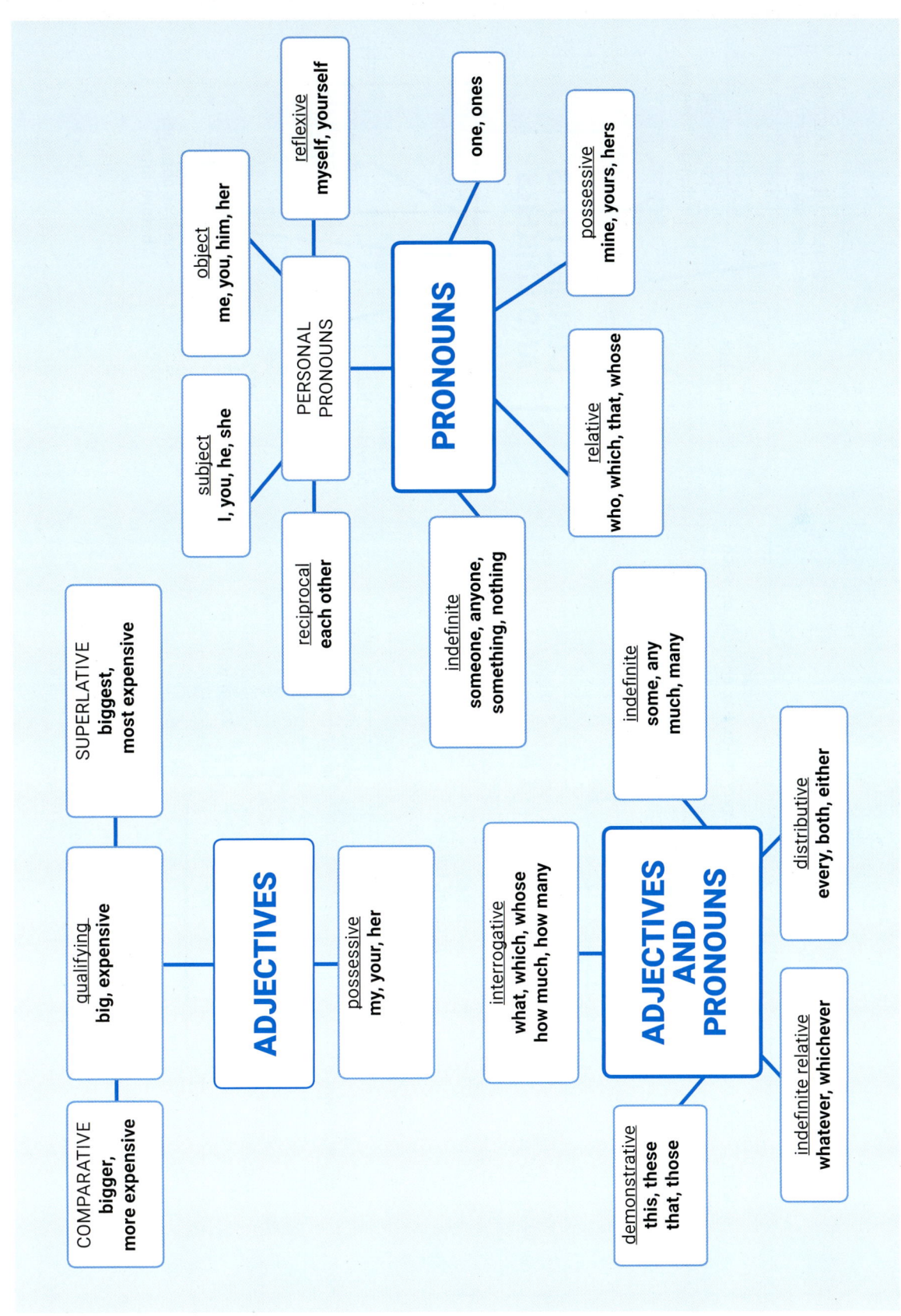

Adverbs, connectors, linkers and preposition cluster

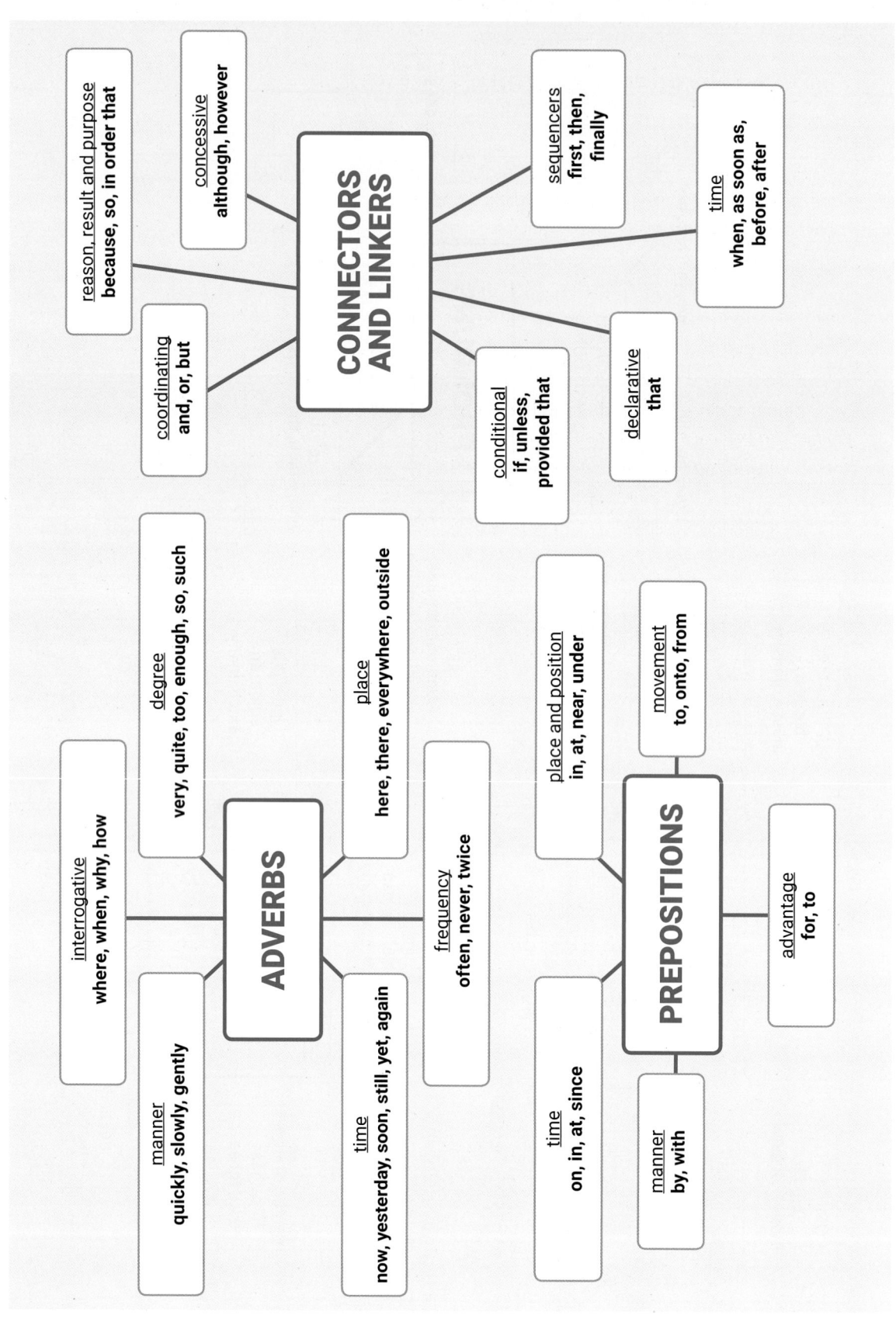

GRAMMAR MATRIX BASICS

UNIT 1 Nouns and articles

LESSON 1 Regular and irregular plurals

Formation of the plural

- To make the plural form of a noun, we usually add an **–s** to the singular form:
  street → street**s**   computer → computer**s**   file → file**s**
- If the noun finishes with **–s**, **–sh**, **–ch**, **–x** or **–z**, we add **–es**:
  bus → bus**es**   dish → dish**es**   watch → watch**es**   box → box**es**   buzz → buzz**es**
- If the noun ends in a consonant + **–y**, we form the plural with **–ies**:
  cherry → cherr**ies**   city → cit**ies**   story → stor**ies**

  If, however, the noun ends in a vowel + **–y**, the plural is formed by adding **–s**:
  day → day**s**   key → key**s**   toy → toy**s**
- Most nouns ending in **–f** or **–fe** form the plural with **–ves**:
  wolf → wol**ves**   leaf → lea**ves**   knife → kni**ves**
  Exceptions: roof**s**, chief**s**, gulf**s**, cliff**s**, chef**s** and a few others.
- Many nouns ending in **–o** make the plural by adding **–es**:
  potato → potato**es**   tomato → tomato**es**   hero → hero**es**
  In other cases we only add **–s**:
  kilo**s**, video**s**, photo**s**, zoo**s**
  Or both forms are possible:
  volcano**es** / volcano**s**, mango**es** / mango**s**, mosquito**es** / mosquito**s**

1 Write the plural form of each noun in the correct column.

shelf   boy   strawberry
branch   country
wish   half   volcano
calf   party   orange
wife   roof   lorry
match   glass   novel
echo   lady   drink
library   fox   life   thief
earphone   baby   ray

–s	–es	–ies	–ves

2 Rewrite the sentences in the plural.

1 The school is closed today.   Schools ....
2 It's an old church.   They're ....
3 That cliff is dangerous.   Those ....
4 The shop is open now.   The ....
5 Where's my key?   Where ....
6 It's a great city.   They're ....
7 This story is true.   These ....
8 A car is parked in the street.   Two ....

3 Complete the texts with the correct form (singular or plural) of the nouns below.

wall   singer   shelf   bed   book   poster   actor

In my bedroom there's a bookcase and some ¹.......................... which are full of ².......................... . On the ³.......................... over my ⁴.......................... there are ⁵.......................... of my favourite ⁶.......................... and ⁷.......................... .

armchair   table   sofa   meal   chair

In the living room there's a ⁸.......................... and two comfortable ⁹.......................... where we sit in the evenings. There's also a large ¹⁰.......................... and six ¹¹.......................... . We usually have our ¹².......................... there.

4 Complete the text with the correct plural form of the words below.

cherry   strawberry   city   bus   cliff   tomato   potato

I live by the coast in a cottage near some ¹.......................... . I have a large garden and I grow my own fruit and vegetables. I grow ².......................... and ³.......................... , onions and beans and I have some fruit trees which produce ⁴.......................... and apples. I also grow ⁵.........................., which are delicious with sugar and cream. I like living in the country. I don't like ⁶.......................... and it is easy to get into town because there are a lot of ⁷.......................... every day.

Irregular plurals

Some nouns have irregular plural forms:

man → men	ox → oxen	goose → geese
woman → women	tooth → teeth	mouse → mice
child → children	foot → feet	louse → lice

| penny → pence |
| person → people (But *people* meaning 'nation' has the plural *peoples*.) |

Other nouns use a single form for both singular and plural:

sheep   fish   deer   dice   means   series   species

5 Complete the sentences with a plural form from the table above.

1 Mr and Mrs Sherwood have three .... : Gemma, Ian and Matt.
2 That's 85 .... , please.
3 It's a sunny day and lots of .... are having a break from work in the park.
4 Men and .... haven't always had the same rights.
5 .... are big white birds with yellow beaks.
6 .... , rats and squirrels are all rodents.
7 Buses are a common .... of transport in towns and cities.
8 We need two .... to play this game.
9 I like the tropical .... in your aquarium.
10 She wears size 10 shoes. She has really big .... !

Nouns used only in the plural form

Some nouns are only used in the plural, for example:

clothes	goods	binoculars
trousers	earnings	contents
shorts	savings	outskirts
pyjamas	scissors	remains
vegetables	glasses	surroundings

! These nouns are always used with a plural verb!
'Where **are** my pyjamas?' '**They're** on your bed.'

FAQ

Q: In a music magazine, I saw the sentence **The group are on tour in Italy. Group** is a singular noun, so why is **are** used rather than **is**?

A: **Group** is a collective noun and can be considered singular (when considering the whole) or plural (in the sense that it is made up of different individual parts). The pronoun used to substitute the noun may be **it** or **they**, and the possessive adjective is usually **their**. Other collective nouns include **team, staff, audience, army, family, government, band, class**.

Q: Why do people say **The United States of America is a big country?** Isn't it a plural noun?

A: **The United States** is a federal state, forming a single nation, so the main idea is that of a single entity and the noun is used in the singular.

6 Complete the sentences with *is* or *are*. Sometimes both options are possible.

1 The scissors .... in the top drawer.
2 The Rolling Stones .... playing at the O2 Arena tonight.
3 Your shorts .... in the wardrobe and your new T-shirt .... on your bed.
4 The USA .... in the central part of North America.
5 All my savings .... in a bank account.
6 The government .... debating an important law today.
7 The team .... going to celebrate this evening.
8 Our staff .... all busy at the moment. Please hold.
9 My pyjamas .... under the pillow.
10 The United Arab Emirates .... a very rich state.
11 The audience .... mostly students.
12 His team .... in the 1st division.
13 Her glasses .... over there.
14 Their earnings .... enormous!

LESSON 2 Countable and uncountable nouns

Countable and uncountable nouns

- Countable nouns describe objects that can be counted and that therefore have a singular and a plural form:
  one car / two cars, one bike / two bikes…
- Uncountable nouns have only a singular form
  bread, rice…
- Many uncountable nouns refer to items of food and drink (*water, flour, milk, sugar…*) or to materials (*glass, wood, paper, cotton…*).
- Abstract nouns are also uncountable:
  love, hope, fear, imagination…

1 Write C next to the countable nouns and U next to those that are uncountable.

wool ....   lemon ....   egg ....   ice ....   window ....
butter ....   bottle ....   beauty ....   sandwich ....   snow ....
chair ....   wine ....   silver ....   tea ....   rain ....
juice ....   peace ....   plastic ....   biscuit ....   gold ....

Do not use the indefinite articles **a / an** in front of uncountable nouns!
NOT: ~~a water~~, but **some water**, or **a bottle / a glass of water**
To express the exact amount of a substance, use:
- a unit of measurement: *a kilo of flour, a pint of beer*
- the name of the container: *a jar of honey, a cup of tea*
- one part of the whole: *a slice of bread, a bar of chocolate*

2 Write *some* or *a / an*.

.... oil   .... bread   .... sweets
.... butter   .... artichoke   .... tomato sauce
.... apple   .... banana   .... mayonnaise
.... onions   .... food   .... sugar

3 Match the two halves of the expressions.

1 a slice of	A salt
2 a jar of	B tea
3 a pinch of	C chocolate
4 a cup of	D cake
5 a glass of	E sugar
6 a bar of	F water
7 a packet of	G yoghurt
8 a tub of	H marmalade

1 ....
2 ....
3 ....
4 ....
5 ....
6 ....
7 ....
8 ....

4 Write the words from exercise 2 in the correct column, then add the names of other food and drink.

a jar of	a bottle of	a kilo of	a bag of	a packet of	a slice of

 Do not use the definite article **the** before uncountable nouns to talk about things in general or before abstract nouns!
I like chocolate.
Gold is a precious metal.
Patience is a great virtue.

FAQ

Q: In a café, I heard someone ask **'Three coffees, please'**. If **coffee** is an **uncountable** noun, why is it used in the plural?

A: Coffee can be used as a countable noun to mean 'a cup of coffee'. Rather than say **Three cups of...**, it's shorter to just use the name of the drink.

Focus

There are nouns which are used in the plural in some languages but are uncountable – and therefore singular – in English. Common examples are:
furniture, hair, homework, information, money, luggage, news, business, advice.

Verbs and pronouns referring to these nouns are always singular:

Here's my luggage. NOT: *Here are...*

This is today's news. NOT: *These are...*

How much money do you need?
NOT: *How many...?*

We haven't got much homework today.
NOT: *...many homeworks.*

Her hair is beautiful! NOT: *...are beautiful.*

Is this your luggage?

15

5 Complete the sentences with the words below and the correct verb form (*is* or *are*).

information   news   homework   business   furniture   hair   luggage   teas

1 My .... really long. I want to have it cut.
2 Today's maths .... quite difficult. I can't do most of the exercises!
3 The .... they give us when we start college .... always really useful.
4 'Where's your ....?' 'It .... at the hotel.'
5 The .... on at 10 pm. There is a report about the situation in Syria.
6 IKEA .... nice and modern.
7 .... good! Our profits are up 10% this year!
8 Here .... two .... and here's the milk.

LESSON 3   The indefinite article *a / an*

- The indefinite article **a / an** is used before singular countable nouns to describe an undefined thing or person, an example of a class of things, or to mention something for the first time.
- **A** is used before singular nouns beginning with a consonant, voiced **h**, **w** and **y**:
  a cat   a house   a window   a year
- **An** is used before nouns starting with a vowel or a silent **h** sound:
  an appointment   an only child   an English lesson   an hour

FAQ

Q: Which words begin with a silent **h** sound?

A: Only **hour**, **heir / heiress**, **honour**, the adjective **honest** and its derivatives **honourable** and **honestly**.

Q: Why do people say *a university, a union, a European citizen*? Shouldn't there be the article **an** before words starting with a vowel?

A: These are exceptions. Words that begin with the /j/ sound are used with the article **a**, just like those which begin with consonants.
On the other hand, look at these examples: *an FM radio station*, *an X-ray machine*. **An** is used because in the alphabet **f** is pronounced /ef/ and **x** is pronounced /eks/.

1 Complete with *a* or *an*.

1 .... elephant
2 .... yellow car
3 .... interesting book
4 .... window
5 .... horror film
6 .... uniform
7 .... underground station
8 .... hundred
9 .... art gallery
10 .... hotel
11 .... honest man
12 .... iceberg
13 .... important event
14 .... watch
15 .... unit
16 .... woman
17 .... yacht
18 .... heir
19 .... horse
20 .... hour
21 .... SMS

Focus

English uses the indefinite article to talk about things we have (or haven't) got available to use:
I've got an umbrella. NOT *I've got the umbrella.*
I haven't got a watch. NOT *I haven't got the watch.*

The indefinite article is also used with the names of professions:
My father is an engineer. I'm a teacher.

A third use of the indefinite article is with illnesses:
I've got a sore throat / a cough / a temperature / a stomachache...

Note the use of the article **a / an** in the following expressions:
- *frequency:* three times a day, once a month
- *speed:* 50 km an hour
- *price:* ten euros a kilo
- *time:* half an hour

English uses the indefinite article in expressions with **what** and **such**:
What a day! What a great champion!
It's such a shame! He's such a nice boy!

FAQ

Q: What's the difference between **a pair of...** and **a couple of...?**

A: A pair of... is used for two matching objects such as *a pair of shoes / glasses / boots...*
A couple of... means two, or not many more, for example *a couple of friends, a couple of drinks.*

2 Choose the correct option.

1 Sorry, I haven't got **a / an / the** pen with me.
2 My brother is **a / an / the** interpreter.
3 What **a / an / the** fantastic match!
4 I've got **a / an / the** bike so I cycle to school every day.
5 A hundred miles **the / a / an** hour! You're going too fast!
6 I've got **the / a / an** very bad headache today.
7 I go running in the park twice **an / a / the** week for half **the / an / a** hour.
8 An apple **the / a / an** day keeps **the / a / an** doctor away!
9 It's such **a / the / an** bad time at the moment. Can I talk to you later?
10 **A / The / An** race is nearly finished.
11 I've got **a / the / an** sore throat.
12 What **a / the / an** great idea!
13 The baby has got **a / the / an** termperature. Let's call the doctor.
14 It was such **an / the / a** amazing concert. You should have come.
15 Have you got **the / a / an** umbrella? It's raining.
16 Those apples are quite expensive – £3 **a / an / the** kilo!

FAQ

Q: Can I use *one* instead of the article *a / an*? For example, is it better to say *I've got one cat* or *I've got a cat*?

A: There's not much difference between the two sentences. *I've got a cat* is more common. *One* is used to answer a specific question relating to numbers such as 'How many brothers or sisters have you got?' 'I've got one sister and one brother.' Alternatively the adverbs *only* or *just* are used to say no more than one, just one.

Q: I once wrote *Matthew is a my friend*. Why did the teacher mark it wrong?

A: Because the article is never used before a possessive adjective. We can say *One of my friends* or *A friend of mine*. For the plural, we can say *Some of my friends*.

! Never use **a/an** before a plural noun!
He's wearing black trousers. NOT *He's wearing a black trousers.*
He's got broad shoulders. NOT *He's got a broad shoulders.*

---

3 Complete the sentences with *one* or *a / an*.

1 What .... terrible experience!
2 Just .... bag of crisps, please, not two.
3 'How many children have you got?' 'I've only got ...., David. He doesn't like being .... only child!'
4 We've got three pets – .... dog and two cats.
5 I need .... pair of jeans and .... couple of white T-shirts.
6 I saw Tom about half .... hour ago.
7 I only need .... apple to make the smoothie.
8 .... of my uncles lives in California.
9 .... good friend of mine won an important prize last week.
10 It was such .... embarrassing situation!

4 Read the sentences. Write *correct* if they are right and correct those that have one or more mistakes.

1 I need a pair of black trousers. ....
2 Why don't we go for a walk? It's beautiful day. ....
3 Serena is at home because she's got cough. ....
4 Do you have an high temperature? ....
5 There's a hotel at the end of the road. ....
6 I'm going out with a couple of friends tonight. ....
7 What an horrible day! So many things to do! ....
8 Mike, a your friend's on the phone! ....
9 Sheila has got a brown hair and a brown eyes. ....
10 A friend of mine is waiting for me at the bus stop. ....

5 Complete the paragraph with *a / an* or *one*.

My best friend is ¹.......... bank employee. She's ².......... elegant woman. She's tall and slim with blonde hair and green eyes. She often wears ³.......... pair of trousers and ⁴.......... silk shirt to work. But in her free time she likes to wear casual clothes and ⁵.......... comfortable pair of trainers.

She's married but, unlike me, she only has ⁶.......... child while I have three. That's probably why she is much more elegant than me.

LESSON 4 The definite article *the*

In English, there is only one definite article: **the**. However, the way that the article is used means that it is not as simple as it looks!

The article **the** is used before singular and plural nouns to indicate precise people or things that are known to the listener, or which have already been mentioned. Compare:
Take **a** chair. (any chair)
Put **the** chair in the corner. (that particular chair)
There's **a** concert at eight o'clock tonight.
The concert starts at eight o'clock.

The article **the** is also used before:
- nouns of which there is only one:
  the sun, the moon, the world, the queen, the king, the president...
  Peter is the new team captain.
- nouns made specific by the use of the prepositions **of** or **in**:
  the inhabitants of Morocco
  I like the photos in your blog.
- nouns followed by a relative clause containing **who**, **which** or **that**:
  The people who live next door are really nice.
- names of musical instruments:
  I can play the piano quite well.
- ordinal numbers:
  The third day in December is a Monday.
- superlative adjectives:
  He's the greatest player in the team.
- names of peoples:
  the Chinese, the British, the French
- adjectives used as nouns:
  the young, the rich

1 Write *the* before nouns describing a unique person or thing. In the other cases, write *a / an*.

1 ...... equator
2 ...... bird
3 ...... fish
4 ...... South Pole
5 ...... Earth
6 ...... insect
7 ...... uniform
8 ...... Queen
9 ...... minister
10 ...... Prime Minister
11 ...... Pacific Ocean
12 ...... world
13 ...... American President
14 ...... Pope
15 ...... actress
16 ...... North Sea

2 Complete the sentences with *the* or *a / an*.

1 .... capital of Argentina is Buenos Aires. It's .... very big city.
2 They have .... son and .... daughter. .... boy is .... vet and .... girl is .... engineer.
3 Sonia is .... very tall girl. Actually, she's .... tallest girl in .... school.
4 Show me .... video of your wedding. I'd really like to see it.
5 .... sun goes down at about five o'clock in winter.
6 This is .... most important thing of all. Write it down, please.
7 My brother plays .... guitar and .... flute. He's .... very musical person.
8 My birthday's on .... 21ˢᵗ of September.
9 What are .... ingredients in the recipe?
10 .... good friend is someone who can keep .... secret.

FAQ

Q: It's not easy to know when to use the definite article **the** and when to use the indefinite article **a / an**. I often mix them up and there are several mistakes of this kind in my homework…

A: Try this method. Think about bingo or a lottery game.
a / an represents one of the balls spinning around the wheel;
the is the ball that is drawn. So:
a / an → one of many objects, an undefined number, not one number in particular
the → that particular object, a defined object
For plural nouns, on the other hand, keep this basic concept in mind:
plural noun without the article → a whole category of objects, in general
the + plural noun → precisely those particular objects

 The is not used before:

- plural nouns used to mean 'in general':
  I like sweets. NOT *the sweets*
- abstract nouns: *peace, happiness, love, nature…*
  Happiness is a walk in the park on a sunny day. NOT *The happiness is…*
- names of meals: *breakfast, lunch, dinner…*
  Lunch is at one o'clock today. NOT *The lunch is…*
- names of sports: *tennis, basketball, baseball…*
  I play football three times a week. NOT *I play the football…*
- school subjects: *maths, biology, chemistry…*
  Physics is my favourite subject. NOT *The physics is…*
- possessive adjectives and pronouns: *our teacher, their lessons, your school…*
  Your sandwiches are ready. NOT *The your sandwiches…*
  'Whose book is it?' 'It's mine.' NOT *…the mine.*

3 Complete the sentences by writing *the* where necessary. Write the symbol // where it is not necessary.

1 I love .... animals – .... horses are .... my favourite animals.
2 .... pandas that live in .... zoo have a new baby!
3 Mr Randall is .... new maths teacher.
4 Mum likes .... flowers. Let's give her a bunch of .... roses.
5 'Can you play .... guitar?' 'No, I can't, but I can play .... drums.'
6 .... woman who lives in that house is a famous singer.
7 Are you going to play .... basketball at .... weekend?
8 .... lunch is ready! Everybody go to .... kitchen!
9 'Is this .... your bike?' 'No, it isn't, ... mine is blue.'
10 .... Italians love .... good food. Some of .... best chefs in .... world are Italian.

To talk about an entire species, of an animal or plant for example, we can either use the article **a / an** or **the** before the singular noun. A third option is to use the noun in the plural with no article:
The gazelle runs very fast. / A gazelle runs very fast. / Gazelles run very fast.

4 Choose the correct option. Sometimes two options are possible.

1 **A / An / The** hyena is **a / an / the** animal that lives in many African countries.
2 **A / An / The** Indian elephant is smaller than **a / an / the** African elephant.
3 **A / An / The** cactus is a plant that grows in the desert.
4 **A / An / The** wombat is **a / an / the** typical Australian animal.
5 **A / An / The** lion is **a / an / the** wild animal.

 Be careful with the use of the article with geographical names!

MATRIX +

The	No article
mountain ranges (the Alps)	single mountains (Mont Blanc)
archipelagos (the Hawaiian Islands)	single islands (Malta)
rivers (the Nile)	lakes (Lake Superior)
seas and oceans (the North Sea, the Pacific Ocean)	cities (London)

FAQ

Q: Why is it **Germany, Italy, France,** but **the USA**?

A: The article is only used before the names of plural states (**the United States, the Netherlands**) or when the name includes the word **Kingdom, Republic** or **Federation** (**the United Kingdom, the Czech Republic, the Russian Federation**…).

5 Complete the sentences by writing *the* where necessary. Write the symbol // where it is not necessary.

1 Paris is .... capital city of .... France.
2 .... highest peaks in .... world are in .... Himalayas.
3 .... USA is between .... Atlantic Ocean to .... east and .... Pacific Ocean to .... west.
4 .... Sardinia and .... Sicily are .... two largest islands in .... Italy.
5 .... Mississippi is .... longest river in .... American continent.
6 'Is Kate from .... Netherlands?' 'No, she's from .... Belgium.'
7 .... Lake Garda is in .... north-east of .... Italy.
8 .... Thames is the river that runs through .... London.

6 Correct the mistakes in these sentences.

1 The mathematics is my favourite subject.
2 There's a good film on at cinema this week.
3 The quiz starts at the 7.30.
4 Jason plays drums.
5 Eleanor loves the nature.
6 I don't like the tennis.
7 These are the your sandwiches.
8 Sardinia is the beautiful island.

ROUND UP 1

1 Complete the sentences with the plural form of one of the words below.

wife   half   life   leaf   shelf   thief   knife   loaf

1 Strangely, all three of the actor's former .... are having lunch together in a restaurant.
2 In the first scene of the film *Autumn in New York*, there are trees with yellow ....
3 The cook in this sushi bar uses very sharp .... to cut the fish.
4 Thousands of .... are at risk in this TV series, but the hero will save everyone.
5 How many .... of bread shall I buy for the party?
6 The books you need are on the two top .... of this bookcase.
7 Cut the peaches into .... and fill them with crumbled macaroons. The dessert will be delicious!
8 I was relaxing in the park when I saw two .... stealing a car.

2 Complete the sentences with *is* or *are*.

0 The scissors ...*are*... in the drawer.
1 My favourite rock band .... in town.
2 My pyjamas .... on the bed.
3 The men .... in the square.
4 All my savings .... in this bank.
5 The goods .... in the truck.
6 The goose .... in the pond.
7 My hair .... too long.
8 The trousers .... over there.
9 Your homework .... quite difficult.
10 The information .... very interesting.
11 Where .... my scissors?
12 My luggage .... in the hall.

3 Decide if the underlined word is singular (S) or plural (P).

1 There are only three <u>species</u> of big cat in our city zoo. ....
2 The <u>headquarters</u> of that film studio are outside our town. ....
3 Working in a cafè is a popular <u>means</u> of earning money for students. ....
4 Are you going to watch the new cartoon <u>series</u> on TV? ....
5 The actor had an accident at a dangerous <u>crossroads</u>. ....
6 The <u>media</u> can deeply affect our lives! ....

MATRIX +

Some words of Greek or Latin origin make their plurals according to the rules of Greek or Latin:
curriculum → *curricula*, *medium* → *media*, *criterion* → *criteria*, *phenomenon* → *phenomena*, *stimulus* → *stimuli*, *antenna* → *antennae*, *crisis* → *crises*, *thesis* → *theses*, *analysis* → *analyses*, *hypothesis* → *hypotheses*

While other words from the same origins make their plurals following the rules of English, that is by adding **–s** or **–es**.
gymnasium → *gymnasiums*, *dogma* → *dogmas*, *genius* → *geniuses*

A few words have both forms:
fungus → *fungi* / *funguses*, *formula* → *formulae* / *formulas*, *matrix* → *matrices* / *matrixes*

4 Complete the text with the plural form of one of the words below. All the words come from Matrix +.

medium   hypothesis   fungus   analysis   criterion

Some rare ¹............................ have attacked a precious old painting in the local art gallery. A few famous painters have come up with some different ²............................ about the cause of this attack. They all agree that further ³............................ are needed to decide the ⁴............................ of the restoration works. All the local ⁵............................ are publishing articles about the painting because it is one of the main tourist attractions of the area.

5 Read the dialogue and choose the correct option.

Ann   How ¹*many / much* flour do you need for the cake, Bettie?
Bettie Not ²*much / many*. Only 300 grams. And we don't need ³*much / many* apples either.
Ann   How ⁴*much / many*?
Bettie Only three. What else do we need?
Ann   ⁵*A / An* glass of milk and ⁶*some / a* jam.
Bettie Okay. We can start now.

6 Complete the expressions with one of the words below.

a bottle of   a box of   beer   chocolate   a drop of
a slice of   a jar of   a cup of   paper   bread

1 .... coffee
2 .... marmalade
3 a sheet of ....
4 a loaf of ....
5 .... meat
6 .... Champagne
7 a pint of ....
8 a bar of ....
9 .... oil
10 .... biscuits

MATRIX +

Some uncountable nouns such as **business**, **hair**, **damage** or **paper** can also be used as countable nouns, and so have a plural form, with a change of meaning, e.g. *a business, a hair, a paper, damages*:
They set up a successful business last year.
My son is allergic to cat hairs.
Can I have today's paper, please?
They are liable for damages of £2,000.

 7 Complete the pairs of sentences using the word given. Use the singular form as an uncountable noun and the plural as a countable noun.

1 **EXPERIENCE**
  A This pilot has had a lot of .... flying planes.
  B I had some wonderful .... in New Zealand last winter.

2 **BUSINESS**
  A Mark has decided to leave his job and go into ....
  B In spite of the crisis, a number of new .... are setting up in this area.

3 **DAMAGE**
  A The car driver will have to pay .... of up to £ 5,000 for bumping into the school.
  B The twister caused quite a lot of ....

4 **FISH**
  A This .... is delicious. It's cod, isn't it?
  B The children saw lots of little .... swimming in the shallow water.

5 **COFFEE**
  A 'How many .... did we order?' 'Four.'
  B 'Would you like some more ....?' 'No, thanks. I'm fine.'

6 **GLASS**
  A The ball hit the window and shattered the .... while the family was having dinner.
  B There were lots of empty .... on the table after the party.

8 Complete the expressions with *a / an* or *the*.

1 .... moon   11 .... conference
2 .... mammal   12 .... world
3 .... fish   13 .... ostrich
4 .... South Pole   14 .... elephant
5 .... Earth   15 .... actress
6 .... artichoke   16 .... EU
7 .... sky   17 .... sun
8 .... Queen   18 .... Union Jack
9 .... minister   19 .... yell
10 .... Prime Minister   20 .... yolk

9 **Complete the sentences with *the* or *a / an*.**

1. Take a chair. Take .... red chair near .... desk.
2. .... capital of Morocco is Rabat. It's .... big city.
3. He has two pets, ... rabbit and .... hamster. .... rabbit is white and .... hamster is brown.
4. Sonia is .... tallest girl in our class.
5. The Coliseum is .... biggest amphitheatre I've ever seen.
6. .... sun sets at about five in winter.
7. There's .... full moon tonight.
8. I really like .... biscuits your mother has made.

MATRIX +

The article **the** is also used in the following cases:
- with plural surnames to mean a married couple or an entire family:
  the Wades   the Baileys
- with acronyms for organisations of different kinds:
  the WWF (Worldwide Fund for Nature), the UN (United Nations), the EU (European Union)
- before nouns of places such as **garden**, **park**, **cinema / movies**, **theatre**, **mountains**, **country / countryside**, **seaside**, **office**, **swimming pool**, both as a direct object of a verb of movement to a place (**to the...**) and as a direct object of a stative verb (**in the..., at the...**):
  They usually go to the seaside in summer.
  Why don't we buy a cottage in the mountains?
  I love spending my free time in the garden.
  We always walk to the office together.

Reflecting on grammar

Study the rules and decide if the following statements are true or false.

		True	False
1	The plural form of all nouns is made by adding **–s** to the singular form.		
2	Some nouns do not have a singular form.		
3	All nouns have a different form for the plural.		
4	Abstract nouns are uncountable.		
5	Nouns such as *luggage* or *money* are used in the plural form.		
6	Use the article **an** before words beginning with a /j/ sound like *yacht* or *university*.		
7	There is no difference between the use of **a pair of...** and **a couple of...** .		
8	You do not use the definite article before plural nouns used to mean 'in general'.		
9	Possessive adjectives are always preceded by an article.		
10	Articles are not used before the names of lakes.		

GRAMMAR MATRIX BASICS

UNIT 2 Personal pronouns + verb *be*

LESSON 1 Subject pronouns

The subject forms of personal pronouns are as follows:

Singular
I (always with a capital letter)   you   he   she   it

Plural
we   you   they

- The pronoun **he** is used instead of the name of a male person: *my brother / Harry → he*
- **She** replaces a female person: *my sister / Ellen → she*
- **It** replaces the name of a thing or an animal: *my diary / the rabbit → it*
- The pronoun **they** replaces a plural noun, and is used for people, things or animals: *the children / Tony and Jo / the books / my dogs → they*

FAQ

Q: When talking about my dog, is it better to use the pronoun **it** or the pronoun **he**, since it's a male dog?

A: Generally speaking, we use **he** for a boy and **she** for a girl when we speak about our pets. For example: *I've got a cat. She's black and white.* On the other hand, if we don't know the animal's gender we use the neutral pronoun **it**.

Q: When someone is introduced to me in England, I say **Nice to meet you**, so I'm using the familiar form. Shouldn't I use the polite form?

A: No, there is no polite form in English. We always use the pronoun **you** when talking to people directly - both friends and people we don't know well.

1 Read the sentences and choose the correct pronoun.

1. Rebecca is French. **He / She** comes from Paris.
2. Robert is my new classmate. **She / He** is very nice.
3. Tina and I are best friends. **We / They** are always together.
4. Sam and Mark are very tall. **You / They** play in the basketball team.
5. Do **you / we** like my jacket? **She / It** is new and **it / she** was a real bargain.
6. You and Emma go to the same school. Are **you / we** in the same class, too?
7. These are good history books. **It / They** are about Napoleon.
8. Here's the article about cyber-bullying. **He / It** is very interesting.
9. Carol and Sue live next door to each other. **They / We** both work at the same supermarket.
10. Have a look at our online catalogue, Dave. **You / It** will find it very useful.

The pronoun *It*

The pronoun **It** is very commonly used in English. It is used in a range of impersonal expressions, such as:

It's all right. / It's okay.   It's late. / It's early.   It's time to go to bed.   It's great to be here!

It is also used in the following cases:
- to say the day, date and time: *It's Tuesday, the 3rd of February.   It's four o'clock.*
- to talk about the weather: *It's raining.   It's cold.*
- to talk about distance and travel time: *It's 150 km from here.   It takes two hours.*
- to give a price: *It's three pounds fifty.*
- to answer the phone or the front door: *It's Miss Collins speaking.   'Who is it?' 'It's me, Sarah.'*
- to ask about who someone is: *'Who's that over there?' 'It's Mr Jones, my art teacher.'*

Focus

In English, we must express the subject in sentences. The most common subjects are nouns or personal pronouns:

My teacher's nice.   I'm tired.   You're late.   He's happy.

The subject pronoun may only be omitted in coordinate clauses with **and**, **but** or **or**, if the subject pronoun is the same as the subject in the main clause.

We usually watch TV or listen to music after dinner.
I meet my friends and go to the cinema on Sundays.

> ! Never use a noun followed by a pronoun: the pronoun replaces the noun, so... either one or the other!
> *My mum's at home now.* NOT ~~My mum she's~~ at home now.
> *Simon and Fiona are cousins.* NOT ~~Simon and Fiona they're~~ cousins.

2 **Complete the sentences with personal pronouns.**

1 .... is a beautiful girl. And .... is very clever, too.
2 .... are Uncle George and Aunt Carol. .... live in Chester.
3 .... am a very sensitive person. .... can't stand arrogant people.
4 Karl and Thomas are brothers. .... are twins.
5 Bob, come on! .... are late for school as usual.
6 I love designer clothes, but .... are so expensive!
7 This is my friend Tom. .... is staying with us for the weekend.
8 My sister and I get on very well. .... help each other a lot.
9 Pleased to meet you, Ms Blake. .... must be the new web designer, right?
10 Meet Morris, our receptionist. .... will help you during your internship.
11 Have you seen Suzie, my cat? .... is missing again!
12 Wendy and Mike, can .... organise the tickets for the concert, please?
13 My brother and I are very alike, but .... don't get on very well.
14 'Kate and I won the dance competition last night!' 'That's wonderful, ...'re such great dancers!'

3 Match the questions to the answers.

1 How much is a Coke?
2 How far is it to the Lake District?
3 How long does it take to get there?
4 What's the time, please?
5 What day is it today?
6 How about going to the seaside?
7 What's the weather like?
8 Who's that over there?

A It's Thursday, the 11th of May.
B It's hot and sunny.
C I think that's a great idea!
D It's one pound thirty.
E It's a friend of mine.
F It's a quarter past nine.
G It takes about an hour.
H It's about two hundred miles.

1 ..... 2 ..... 3 ..... 4 ..... 5 ..... 6 ..... 7 ..... 8 .....

4 Put brackets around the pronoun when it can be omitted. Cross it out (x) when it really mustn't be used.

0 We start work at 9 a.m. and (we) finish at 5.30 p.m.
1 My dad he always gets back home very late.
2 Ann likes cooking but she hates cleaning the kitchen.
3 On Saturdays they go shopping or they see their friends.
4 John and Kylie they have a lot of common interests.
5 Marion plays computer games or she reads a book in her spare time.
6 The film it starts at 8.30 and it ends at eleven o'clock.
7 I love Japanese food but I don't like Indian food. It's too hot and spicy.
8 Mr Ross leaves home at 7.30 every morning and he takes a bus to his office.
9 Jason he is late as usual.
10 Karen doesn't play the piano but she sings beautifully.
11 The children they go to the playground every afternoon.

5 Circle the correct option.

1 'What's the weather like?'
   '**He's** / **It's** cold and cloudy.'
2 'How much **'s** / **is** that jacket?' 'It's £27.'
3 **You're** / **They're** Mr Ross, right?
4 'What day is it today?' '**It's** / **Is** Friday.'
5 '**Is** / **Who's** that boy over there?'
   '**Is** / **He's** Tom, the new student.'
6 'You are late as usual!' 'That's not true. **I'm** / **You're** never late!'

LESSON 2 Verb *be*

→ Visual Grammar page 404

Verb *be* – positive form

The verb **be** has three forms: *am*, *is*, *are*.
There is a full form and a short form.

Full form	Short form
I am	I'm
You are	You're
He is	He's
She is	She's
It is	It's
We are	We're
You are	You're
They are	They're

It's so cute!

The short form is very common, both in spoken and written English. It can also be used when the subject is a singular noun that doesn't end in **–s**: *Kate's a nice girl.*   *My dad's a great cook!*

UNIT 2

1 Write sentences using the correct form of the verb *be*.

1. Camilla / a nice old lady
2. Brian / thirsty
3. Jack and Debbie / our next-door neighbours
4. The dog / outside in the garden
5. Mark and I / cousins
6. My parents / on holiday in Spain
7. I / very tired tonight
8. You / really funny

2 Complete the sentences with *am / is / are* using the short form where possible. Do not use the short form if the subject is formed by two nouns or by a plural noun.

1. You .... 16 years old, but you look younger.
2. It .... a trendy jacket.
3. Tom and Jerry .... my cats.
4. She .... my younger sister, Lucy.
5. He .... a successful businessman.
6. Mark .... a very young musician. He .... only 11.
7. They .... from Scotland, but they live in London.
8. We .... here on holiday.
9. I .... interested in modern art.
10. My friends .... crazy!

3 Complete the sentences with one of the words or phrases below.

thirsty   sleepy   hot   in a hurry   right   scared   cold   hungry

1. I'm .... Can I have some water, please?
2. Why are you running? You're always ....
3. You're .... , this is the best place to be on holiday!
4. I'm .... Close the window, please.
5. I'm .... of spiders! Especially the black hairy ones.
6. I'm very .... Can I have something to eat?
7. I'm so ....! It must be the jetlag.
8. It's .... in here. Turn the heater off.

4 Complete the text with the correct form of *be*.

Hi, my name [1].............. Sam. I [2].............. a student at Bath University. My brother [3].............. here too. We [4].............. both sportsmen. He [5].............. good at swimming and I [6].............. good at running. Bath [7].............. a great place to study. The campus [8].............. five minutes away from the centre by bus. My parents [9].............. from near here, so they [10].............. often here to visit us!

Verb *be* – negative form

Full form	Short form
I am not	I'm not
You are not	You aren't
He is not	He isn't
She is not	She isn't
It is not	It isn't
We are not	We aren't
You are not	You aren't
They are not	They aren't

This isn't my dog.

! The short form is very common in the negative form too. To be more emphatic, we can use the form **You're not, He's not, We're not…** For example: *'I think Roland's French.' 'He's not French, he's Belgian!'*. Note that you can't say *I amn't*.

5 **Rewrite the sentences using the short form of the negative.**

1 We're ready for the test. ....
2 They're at home now. ....
3 It's too late! ....
4 Aman is at school today. ....
5 I'm afraid of the dark. ....
6 She's 17 years old. ....
7 My parents are at work. ....
8 I'm very good at maths. ....

6 **Complete the sentences with the positive or negative form of *be*. Use short forms where possible.**

1 You .... a bad player. You can play quite well!
2 Your eyes .... brown, they're green.
3 I .... on a diet. I want to lose some weight.
4 We .... friends and we go to the same school.
5 Claire and I .... sisters. We're cousins.
6 Karen .... British, she's Australian.
7 Mr and Mrs Taylor .... from York. They're from Leeds.
8 These jeans aren't blue. They .... black.

7 **Complete the text with the appropriate positive or negative form of the verb *be*.**

Sam and Phil [1]............. students at a comprehensive school in London. Sam [2]............. 16 and Phil [3]............. 17. They live in London, but they [4]............. English. Sam [5]............. Irish, and Phil [6]............. from Scotland. I [7]............. a good friend of Sam and Phil's even if I [8]............. at their school. We often see each other in the afternoon after school because we [9]............. in the same football team.

Verb *be* – interrogative form and short answers

When forming questions, the verb **be** precedes the subject.

Are you...?	Is he / she / it...?	Are you / we / they...?
Yes, I am.	Yes, he / she / it is.	Yes, we / you / they are.
No, I'm not.	No, he / she / it isn't.	No, we / you / they aren't.

Short answers

Short answers are formed as follows:
Yes, + pronoun + *am / is / are.*
No, + pronoun + *'m not / isn't / aren't.*

In positive answers, the verb is always in the full form, while in negative answers the short form is usually used:
'Is your room on the first floor?' '**Yes, it is.**' NOT Yes, ~~it's~~.
'Is it a large room?' '**No, it isn't**. It's quite small.'
Note that *No, he / she / it's not* and *No, we / you / they're not* are also possible.

Negative – interrogative form

Aren't we / you / they...?
Isn't he / she / it...?

'**Aren't you** happy?' 'Yes, I am!'
'**Isn't it** a good idea?' 'Yes, it is.'

Note that **Am I not**...? does not have a short form.
'**Am I not** good?' (**Aren't I good?** is also possible) 'Oh yes, you're very good!'

8 Complete the questions using the verb *be*.

1 ...... Sara at school today?
2 ...... they on holiday on Tuesday?
3 ...... we here tomorrow?
4 ...... I late?
5 ...... she at the dentist's?
6 ...... you American?

9 Complete the questions and short answers.

1 '...... they at home today?' 'No, they ....'
2 '...... she here tomorrow?' 'Yes, she ....'
3 '...... we happy?' 'No, we .... !'
4 '...... I part of this class?' 'Yes, you ....'
5 '...... he out?' 'Yes, he ....'
6 '...... it red?' 'No, it ....'

10 Write positive or negative questions using the prompts and the verb *be*. Then write short answers.

0 your son / a teenager
   Is your son a teenager? .... No, *he isn't* .... He's 22 years old.

1 Matthew / Susan's cousin
   .... ? Yes, ...

2 he / not / a good singer
   .... ? Yes, ...

3 your children / at school / today
   .... ? No, ... They're on holiday.

4 your sister's name / Claire
   .... ?   Yes, ...

5 Chris and Daniel / twins
   .... ?   No, ... Chris is older than Daniel.

6 Bob and Edward / not / good friends
   .... ?   Yes, ...

11 Write suitable questions for these answers.

1 '...?'   'No, you aren't short, Ann. You're quite tall.'
2 '..................................... in here?'   'No, I'm quite cold. Close the window, please.'
3 '..................................... of the dark?'   'Yes, quite. Switch on the light, please.'
4 '...?'   'No, my sister is terrible at maths.'
5 '...?'   'Sisters? No, Claire and I are cousins.'
6 '...?'   'On the first floor? No, Peter's office is on the second one.'
7 '...?'   'Mark? No, John has got a sister, he hasn't got any brothers.'
8 '...?'   'Yes, very. Can I have a sandwich, please?'

LESSON 3 There is / There are

→ Visual Grammar page 414

There is / There are

Positive	**There is** a / an / some…	**There are** some…
Negative	**There isn't** a / an / any…	**There aren't** any…
Interrogative	**Is there** a / an / any… ?	**Are there** any… ?
Short answers	Yes, **there is**. No, **there isn't**.	Yes, **there are**. No, **there aren't**.

When we introduce the existence of something for the first time, we use the structure **There is / are** and put the real subject after the verb: **There is a new restaurant in Hill Street** NOT ~~A new restaurant is in Hill Street~~.

There is (abbreviated to **There's**) can be followed by a singular countable noun (**There's** *a party tomorrow.*) or by an **uncountable** noun (**There's** *some cheese* in the fridge.).
There are is followed by a plural noun (**There are** *some photos* of the concert on my blog.).

FAQ

Q: I've heard people say: **In my bedroom, there's a wardrobe, a desk and two chairs. Why is it there's** and not **there are**, given that it's about several things?

A: When there's a list of things, we start with **There is…** if the first item in the list is singular, as in the sentence you heard. If the first item is plural, we start with **There are…**, for example **There are two chairs, a desk and a wardrobe.**

Here / There

Here is an adverb of place. It means 'in this place' and is used for something or someone close to the speaker:
Here's your seat.   Here are your bags.
Where's my pen? Oh, here it is.

Here you are or **Here's…** is an expression used when we give something to someone:
Here's your change.   'Can I have the bill, please?' 'Sure. Here you are.'

There is an adverb of place too and it's used for something or someone which is at a distance from the speaker:
There's your car!
Where's David? Oh, there he is!

 If the person or thing is a noun, it goes after the verb in the sentence. If, however, it is a pronoun, it goes before the verb:
Here **are** <u>your keys</u>.   Here <u>they</u> **are**.

1 **Complete the sentences with *there's*, *there are*, *there isn't* or *there aren't*.**

1 .... a very good film on Channel 5 tonight. I want to see it.
2 .... a washing machine in my flat, but there's a launderette nearby.
3 .... a sofa and two armchairs in the living room.
4 .... two beds and two desks in our bedroom.
5 .... any milk in the fridge. We must get some.
6 .... any glasses in the cupboard. They're all in the dishwasher.
7 .... a large living room, but .... a study in my house.
8 .... any plants on the balcony. I want to buy some.

2 **Complete the questions with *Is there* or *Are there*. Then complete the short answers.**

0 <u>Is there</u> .... a park near your house?   Yes, <u>there is</u> .... It's just opposite my house.
1 .... any parks around here?   Yes, ... There's one over there.
2 .... a station in your village?   No, ... But there's a good bus service.
3 .... any ATMs in the town centre?   Yes, ... Three or four.
4 .... a supermarket near here?   No, ... , but there are some shops.
5 .... a hospital around here?   Yes, ... The Milford Hospital.
6 .... any restaurants nearby?   No, ... Just a couple of pubs.

3 **Complete the sentences with *here* or *there*.**

1 Where's the car? Oh, ... it is – next to that red car.
2 Where are my keys?! Ah, ... they are – in the bottom of my bag.
3 Where's Mark? Ah, ... he is – I can see him outside.
4 Thanks for buying my lunch. ....'s the money.
5 You're at the front – ah, ...'s your seat.
6 'Can I have the results?' 'Sure, ... you are.'

Asking if someone is there

To ask about where someone is, we can say, for example **Is John here?** (close to the speaker) or **Is John there?** (at a distance from the speaker) NOT ~~Is there John?~~
The answer is **Yes, he is. / No, he isn't**.

Look at this, too: '**Are your parents there?**' '**No, they aren't. They're out.**'

To ask how many people there are, we say **How many of you are there?** and we answer, for example **There are four of us.** (or **There's four of us.**) NOT ~~We are in four.~~

Note too: **How many of us / How many of them are there?**

4 Underline the mistake in each sentence, then rewrite the sentences correctly.

0   <u>Is here</u> Simon?   *Is Simon here?*
1   Here's a great match tomorrow.   ....
2   There are one table and four chairs in the kitchen.   ....
3   'Is there your brother?' 'No, he's at work.'   ....
4   'There is a room for tonight?' 'Yes, there is.'   ....
5   Here it is your bill.   ....
6   How many of you there are?   ....
7   There are any tickets left?   ....
8   There's two bags on the table.   ....

LESSON 4 Question words

Question words (or **wh–** words), are found at the beginning of a sentence. The main ones, that is pronouns, adverbs and interrogative adjectives, are as follows:

To ask about…

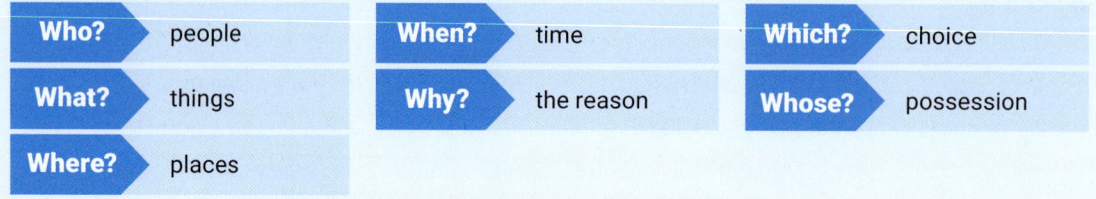

Who?	people	When?	time	Which?	choice
What?	things	Why?	the reason	Whose?	possession
Where?	places				

What can either be used as a pronoun or an adjective, followed by a noun:
What's your email address?
What kind of music do you like?

Which can also be either a pronoun or an adjective. **Which** is usually used when there is a limited choice, whereas **what** is used when the choice is larger:
Which subject do you prefer? Maths or science?
What's your favourite subject? (of all the subjects)

Remember! To answer a question with **Why?** you use **Because**.
'Why are you late?' 'Because the bus was late.'

1 Match the questions to the answers.

1 What are you buying?
2 Where are they going?
3 Who's that boy?
4 When are you coming to see me?
5 Which one is your bicycle?
6 Why are you so late?
7 Which of these jackets do you prefer?
8 Whose book is this?

A He's Paul, our new classmate.
B Because I missed the bus.
C The red one over there. It's new.
D It's my book.
E Some food and drink for the party.
F I like the red leather one.
G Maybe next Saturday.
H They're going home.

1 ..... 2 ..... 3 ..... 4 ..... 5 ..... 6 ..... 7 ..... 8 .....

Interrogative words with *How...?*

Another interrogative adverb is **How**?
How is used as part of several other expressions, for example:
- **How much?** to ask about the amount of an uncountable noun or a price
- **How many?** to ask about the amount of a countable noun
- **How old?** to ask about age
- **How long?** to ask about the length of time something takes
- **How far?** to ask about distance
- **How often?** to ask about frequency

2 Complete the questions with a suitable question word.

1 .... is your English teacher?   I think she's nearly 60.
2 .... does it take you to go home?   About 15 minutes.
3 .... students are in your class?   Twenty-five.
4 .... is this skirt?   It's £25.
5 .... are you so unhappy?   Because I got a D in maths.
6 .... is your school from here?   It's about 500 metres.
7 .... is your birthday?   It's on 5th January.
8 .... are you and your family?   We're all very well, thanks.
9 .... is Mr Smith?   He's in his office.
10 .... do you practise?   Three times a week.

 Wh– words always appear at the beginning of questions.

Focus

If the question contains a preposition, it is usually placed at the end of the question in English:

Who is this <u>for</u>?
Who are you going on holiday <u>with</u>?
Where do they come <u>from</u>?
What is it <u>about</u>?
Which computer are you working <u>on</u>?

FAQ

Q: Someone once asked me: **What's your school like?** and I answered: **I like it very much.** Then I realised that the question didn't mean 'Do you like your school?', but rather was asking a general question about the school. Why isn't the question **How is your school?**

A: Questions using **What... like?** are used to ask for a description of someone or something. **Like** is a preposition in this case. You could have answered, for example: **It's a big school. It's old / modern...**

Another example of this type of question is **What's your family like? (It's a big family – two brothers, a sister...)**, whereas **How is your family?** is a question about the health of your family. (**We're all very well, thanks** is a possible answer.)

3 Write questions using the prompts, then match them to the correct answers.

1 like / what's / house / your / ?
2 you / talking / to / are / who / ?
3 the / what's / like / weather / ?
4 is / how / now / Peter / ?
5 your / like / sister / what's / ?
6 from / are / you / where / ?
7 are / talking / about / you / what / ?
8 is / this / for / present / who / ?

A It's very cloudy. It's going to rain.
B He's much better, thanks.
C She's quite tall and she's got long hair.
D It's a small semi-detached house.
E We're from Mexico.
F We're talking about music.
G It's for Mum. It's her birthday tomorrow.
H I'm talking to Grandma.

1 ..... 2 ..... 3 ..... 4 ..... 5 ..... 6 ..... 7 ..... 8 .....

4 Write suitable questions for the answers.

1 .... ? My family's pretty small. Only me and my mum.
2 .... ? John is only at home in the afternoons.
3 .... ? The party is at the youth club.
4 .... ? Mr Blackwell? He's my ICT teacher.
5 .... ? My favourite food is pizza.
6 .... ? It's 347 998532.
7 .... ? Silvia's from Rome.
8 .... ? There are 20 people.
9 .... ? I think I've got about £20 in my wallet.
10 .... ? Carol? She prefers the black car.

Question words about size

Other interrogative expressions containing **how** are:

How high?	for distance from top to bottom (mountains, shelves,...)	**How wide?**	for distance from side to side (a road, a lake)
How tall?	for people, columns, narrow objects, buildings, trees	**How long?**	for distance from beginning to end
How deep?	for distance from surface to bottom (the sea, a lake)	**How big?**	for mass or surface area

Focus

When answering these questions in English, the numerical information goes first, followed by the adjective:
'How tall is Brian?' 'He's **1.70 m** tall.'
'How long is the Eurotunnel?' 'It's **50 km** long.'

Remember!
How long? is also used to ask about duration.
How long does it take to get to your house?

5 Match questions and answers.

1 How high is Mount Everest?
2 How long is the Mississippi River?
3 How deep is Loch Ness?
4 How big is the Isle of Wight?
5 How tall is your brother?
6 How wide is this table?

A 80 cm
B 380 km^2
C 1.75 m
D 227 m
E 3,734 km
F 8,848 m

6 Match the questions in exercise 5 to the answers (A–F).

A It's 80 cm wide.
B It covers an area of 380 km^2, nearly 150 square miles.
C Its deepest point is 230 m (755 ft). (ft = feet)
D He's nearly 2 m tall.
E It's approximately 3,730 km long (2,320 miles).
F It's 8,848 m (29,029 ft), it's the world's highest mountain.

1 .....
2 .....
3 .....
4 .....
5 .....
6 .....

ROUND UP 2

1 **Rewrite the sentences replacing the nouns that are underlined with the corresponding pronouns.**

1 <u>Phil and Josh</u> are both from Newcastle. ....
2 <u>Silvia</u> is 16 years old. ....
3 <u>East Side Comprehensive</u> is a big school. ....
4 <u>Peter</u> is Swedish. ....
5 <u>Jim and I</u> are friends. ....

2 **Complete the dialogue with suitable subject pronouns.**

A Look at that girl! What's her name?
B ¹............'s Erica.
A Erica? Is ²............ English?
B No, ³............'s Italian. ⁴............'s here with a group of Italian students on a school exchange visit.
A Are ⁵............ here on a European project?
B Yes. ⁶............'s Erasmus Plus.
A Are ⁷............ part of it?
B No. ⁸............ 'm not. ⁹............ 'm too young. ¹⁰............ 's for people in Year 12.

3 **Rewrite the sentences using *there is* / *there are*.**

0 A lot of people are on the beach today. — *There are a lot of people on the beach today.*
1 A lamp and a book are on my bedside table. ....
2 Three cans of orangeade are in the fridge. ....
3 A new boy is in my class this year. ....
4 A lot of books are in your rucksack! ....
5 Only 12 students are in the class today. ....
6 A lot of good songs are on my MP3 player. ....

4 **Complete the text with the correct positive or negative form of *be*.**

Sam and Thomas ¹............ colleagues at Barkley's Bank in Newcastle. Sam ²............ 26 and Thomas ³............ 30. They live in Newcastle now, but they ⁴............ English. Thomas ⁵............ Scottish and Sam ⁶............ American.

I ⁷............ a good friend of Sam's even if I ⁸............ in the same office. I work as an accountant for a big kitchenware factory just outside Newcastle. We often meet at the weekend because we ⁹............ in the same five-a-side football team.

5 **Complete the text with the correct form of *be*. Add a subject pronoun where necessary.**

Having a family around you ¹............ a wonderful feeling. I think ²............ very important to ³............ with your family. The family ⁴............ the centre of your life. The people in your family ⁵............ always there to help you if ⁶............ in trouble and to share good times when ⁷............ happy. Your mother ⁸............ probably the person who ⁹............ closest to you when ¹⁰............ small, but your brothers and sisters ¹¹............ more important when you get older.

6 Each sentence contains a grammar mistake. Find it and rewrite the sentence correctly.

1 Susan and I am students in this school.
   ....

2 Janet is 15 and her twin brothers is 20.
   ....

3 – Who are that man?   ....
   – She's my uncle.   ....

4 – Is you a member of the drama club?   ....
   – Yes, I'm.   ....

5 Thomas and his friend is taking part in the school tennis tournament.
   ....

6 The student's room are on the first floor.
   ....

7 I know that policeman. She's a friend of my brother's.
   ....

8 Is we going to the cinema tonight?
   ....

7 Complete the dialogue with the missing words.

At the restaurant

Man   Is ^{0} *there* a table for two, please?
Waiter Yes, sir. ^{1}.......................... one, by the window.
Man   Can we see the menu, please?
Waiter Of course. Here ^{2}.......................... .
Man ^{3}.......................... any vegetarian dishes?
Waiter Yes, there ^{4}.......................... some, on page 3.
Man   Great! Umm… I'll have the couscous with vegetables.
Woman   And I'll have the tomato soup.
Waiter Okay, thank you.

   (A few minutes later)

            ^{5}.......................... you are, couscous with vegetables and your soup, madam.
Man   This is delicious! What about your soup?
Woman ^{6}.......................... very nice.
Man   Would you like anything else?
Woman   No, I'm fine.
Man   Okay. Can we have the bill, please?
Waiter Sure, ^{7}.......................... your bill. ^{8}.......................... £16.75.
Man   Here ^{9}.......................... . Thank you.
Waiter And ^{10}.......................... your change, sir.

8 Complete the mini-dialogues with the missing words.

1 'Is your father at home in the evenings?' 'Yes, ... is.'
2 '............. Mrs Basset your maths teacher?' 'No, she .... She's my history teacher.'
3 'How .... is your home from the town centre?' 'About 2 km.'
4 'Why .... Marion at school today?' 'Because .... is ill.'
5 'Who's that girl?' '............. my sister Tricia.'
6 '............. you at home tonight?' 'No, I'm ....'
7 'What's your town ....?' 'It's small but pretty.'
8 '.............'s your brother?' 'He's fine, thank you.'

MATRIX +

Study the difference in use between **it's** and **that's**. **It's...** usually introduces a new piece of information, while **That's...** is used to comment on what has been said. **That** actually refers back to the thing that has been said:

It's time to go. (announces something that the interlocutor does not know)
So it's time to go. That's too bad! (**That** refers to the previous sentence, to the need to leave.)
A holiday in Greece? That's great!

9 Match sentences 1–6 to sentences A–F.

1 I'm eating lots of vegetables these days.
2 I'm taking a short break.
3 Look! That's Henry's mum!
4 It's only two degrees!
5 Where's Marcia's house?
6 It costs £20.

A That's good! You need one.
B That's expensive!
C It's a long way from here.
D That's good for you!
E That's cold!
F No, it's his sister!

1 ..... 2 ..... 3 ..... 4 ..... 5 ..... 6 .....

10 Complete the second sentence so that it has a similar meaning to the first sentence, using the word given. Do not change the word given. You must use between two and five words, including the word given.

1 In my opinion, inviting Susan to the party is not a good idea.

   IT   In my opinion, ... idea to invite Susan to the party.

2 I think arguing with your family is very upsetting.

   TO   I think .... argue with your family.

3 That's Mum's favourite vase, so don't break it!

   BECAUSE   Don't break that vase .... favourite!

4 Yes, I agree that going to the cinema this evening is a good idea.

   OKAY   Yes, ... me if we go to the cinema this evening.

5 Mum says eating fish is good for me.

   IT   Mum says .... to eat fish.

6 What you just said was the nicest thing anyone's ever said to me!

   THAT   .... anyone's ever said to me!

11 **Complete the dialogues with *it's* or *that's*.**

1 'Who's on the phone?' '………… Peter.'
2 '………… very cold in this room.' 'Oh, dear. ………… too bad. There's a meeting in here in a quarter of an hour.'
3 'Shall we eat out tonight?' '………… a good idea.'
4 'Shall we go?' 'No, ………… only half past four.'
5 '………… three miles to the station.' 'Is it? ………… too far to walk.'
6 'Jean isn't coming to the party.' '………… a shame! She's so funny.'
7 'This grey suit, sir? ………… £350.' 'Oh, dear. ………… too expensive!'
8 '………… a shame the Giants aren't playing.' 'Yes, that would have been great.'

12 **Complete the questions using the correct *wh–* word or phrase.**

1 '………………… wrapping paper is there?' 'Three metres. It's enough for this big present.'
2 '………………… emails are there in the in-box?' 'Thirty. Dear me!'
3 '………………… is the new receptionist?' 'Twenty-five. He's quite young.'
4 '………………… are you late?' 'Because I missed the bus.'
5 '………………… is everybody?' 'At the office Christmas party. Let's go too.'
6 '………………… is your birthday?' 'Tomorrow.'
7 '………………… are you today?' 'Fine, but still a bit tired.'
8 '………………… is that over there?' 'That's Chloe. She's my cousin.'
9 '………………… is your car?' 'The old blue one over there.'
10 '………………… is your dad?' 'Only about 1 m 60. He's quite short, really.'

Reflecting on grammar

Study the rules and decide if the following statements are true or false.

		True	False
1	There are three subject pronouns for the third person singular of the verb.		
2	There are three subject pronouns for the third person plural of the verb.		
3	The verb **be** has three forms in the present simple.		
4	The interrogative form of **be** is made by changing the intonation of the voice, without changing the order of the words.		
5	The short form of **be** is not used very much in spoken English.		
6	The answer to the question *Are you ready to go?* is *Yes, I'm.*		
7	The expressions **there is / there are** agree grammatically with the first noun in the list.		
8	The sentence *There are a bottle of champagne and six glasses* is correct.		
9	**Not there is** is the negative form of **there is**.		
10	**Wh–** words do not always appear at the beginning of questions.		

GRAMMAR MATRIX BASICS

UNIT 3 Adjectives

LESSON 1 Demonstratives: *this / that / these / those*

| this | that | these | those |

This and **that** are used with singular nouns.
These and **those** are used with plural nouns.
This and **these** are used to indicate people or things that are near the speaker.

That and **those** are used to indicate people and things that are distant from the speaker.

I like this T-shirt.

I like these trainers.

Do you like that hoodie?

Do you like those jeans?

1 🎧 02 Look at the picture and complete the dialogue using suitable demonstratives: *this*, *that*, *these*, *those*. Then listen and check.

Katie Look at [0] *these* hats! They're great!

Tom Yes, they're cool! And look at [1] .... striped socks. I love them!

Katie And what about [2] .... T-shirts here in the front? They're fantastic!

Tom Mmm, yes. And [3] .... trousers at the back are funny! I would definitely wear them!

Katie They really go with [4] .... jacket over there.

Tom Yes – what a great outfit!

Katie The only thing I don't like much is [5] .... skirt near the trousers.

Tom No, it's a bit bright. Let's go in and buy something.

Katie Yes! Cool!

A demonstrative can have the function of an adjective when it is followed by a noun:
That man is my uncle.
These children are four years old.

Or it can function as a pronoun:
This is for you.
Those are my friends.

Demonstratives are often used to:
- introduce someone:
  'This is my brother Steve.' *'Hello, Steve.'*
- ask who someone is:
  'Who's that?' *'It's Jim'.*
- introduce oneself, for example on the phone:
  This is Mrs Jones speaking.

FAQ

Q: When are the expressions **This one** or **That one** used?

A: The pronoun **one** replaces a singular noun. It is used with **this** or **that** when choosing between two or more items. For example: 'Which is your bag?' 'This one.'

Q: Does the pronoun **ones** exist too?

A: Yes, **ones** replaces a plural noun and is used with **these** or **those**. For example: 'Which shoes do you prefer?' 'These ones.'

2 Complete the sentences with *this* or *that*.

1 ………..'s my new car over there.
2 Mr Burnet, ………… is Ms Cooper, our new editor.
3 Which is your bag, this one or ………… one over there?
4 Who's ………… nice-looking boy near the door?
5 Good morning. ………… is Howard Preston speaking.
6 'What's …………?' 'My new hat. Don't you like it?'
7 '………… is Carol. She's from England.' 'Nice to meet you.'
8 'Is ………… you, Phil?' 'Yes, it's me.'

3 Reorder the words and write sentences.

1 new / a / student / school / He's / this / in / .
....
2 good / is / This / news / !
....
3 are / These / mobile phones / our / .
....
4 a / idea / That's / great / !
....
5 me / Give / magazines / please / those / . / ,
....
6 all / need / I / That's / .
....
7 is / This / my / friend / best / .
....
8 are / those / Who / two / guys / there / over / ?
....

4 Complete the sentences with *this*, *that*, *these* or *those*.

1 'Which apples would you like, madam?' '………… ones over there. The red ones.'
2 'Who are ………… children in the hall?' 'They're Mr Benson's children.'
3 ………… here are Tom's school books. They aren't mine.
4 'Are you sure ………… aren't your glasses?' 'Of course. Look! I can't see anything with ………… ones!'
5 'I really like ………… T-shirt you're wearing.' '………… one? It's really old!'
6 'Could you put ………… flowers in ………… vase over there, please?' 'Yes, of course.'

LESSON 2 Some / any / no / none

➡ **Visual Grammar page 416**

	Countable plural	Uncountable
+	There are **some** tomatoes.	There's **some** bread.
−	There aren't **any** tomatoes.	There isn't **any** bread.
?	Are there **any** tomatoes?	Is there **any** bread?

To talk about a certain number or an indefinite quantity of something, we use **some** in positive sentences, and **any** in negative and most interrogative sentences (not all! See FAQ below).

Some and **any** may be used as adjectives before plural nouns or singular uncountable nouns. They can also be used as pronouns:
'Are there any eggs?' 'Yes, there are **some**.'
'Is there any sugar?' 'No, there isn't **any**.'

> ❗ We use the indefinite article **a** / **an** before singular countable nouns.
> Compare *Have you got any brothers?* (plural) with *Have you got a brother?* (singular).

1 Complete the sentences with *some* / *any* or *a* / *an*.

1 'Is there .... butter in the fridge?' 'No, there isn't ....'
2 Here's .... money to pay the bills.
3 There isn't .... match today, but there's one tomorrow.
4 We have .... good friends in the USA.
5 'Have you got .... street map?' 'Yes, here you are.'
6 I haven't got .... English dictionary.
7 Are there .... exams at the end of the school year?
8 We need to buy .... bread for dinner.

2 Write six sentences in your notebook using the words in the table.

There's	a	important meeting	just round the corner.
		good news	on this island.
	an	fruit	in the kitchen.
		post office	this morning.
There are	some	children	in today's paper.
		fantastic beaches	in the playground.

FAQ

Q: Why is *some* used in a question like *Would you like some tea?*? Isn't *any* needed in questions?

A: In actual fact, **some** is also used in questions when we make an offer or request, and in all cases when we expect a positive answer. **Any**, on the other hand, is used when we ask for information. Compare, for example:
Can I have some milk? → I ask for milk, and I expect the answer to be yes.
Have we got any milk? → I want to know if there is any milk, I don't know what the answer will be.

3 Write O if the questions in these mini-dialogues are offers, R if they are requests and I if they ask for information. Then complete the questions with *some* or *any*.

1 A Can I have .... milk with my coffee? B Yes, sure. ....
2 A Would you like .... sugar in your tea? B No, thanks. ....
3 A Can you get me .... oranges from the supermarket? B Okay. How many? ....
4 A Are there .... good shops in this street? B I don't know really. ....
5 A Have you got .... new friends on Facebook? B Yes, a lot! ....
6 A Do you want .... more juice? B Yes, please. ....

> Look at these examples:
> There is**n't any** cheese. → There**'s no** cheese.
> There **aren't any** tomatoes. → There **are no** tomatoes.
>
> Both sentences have the same negative meaning. Use **any** in sentences with a negative verb and **no** in sentences with a positive verb.
>
> Instead of **no** + noun, you can use the pronoun **none**:
> 'Is there any flour?' 'No, there's **no flour**.' → No, there's **none**.
> 'Are there any carrots?' 'No, there are **no carrots**.' → No, there are **none**.

FAQ

Q: I heard the sentence:
There isn't any rice left.
Let's buy some. What does left mean?

A: **Left** is the past participle of the verb **leave**, and the idea here is that there is no more rice, no rice remaining.
Left with this meaning can also be found in positive sentences:
There's some left.
or in questions:
Is there any left?

4 Complete the sentences with *any*, *no* or *none*.

1 Are there .... questions? No? Let's go on, then.
2 There's .... more time. Hand in your papers now, please.
3 Sorry, there isn't .... ice cream left.
4 'Can I have some lemonade?' 'Sorry, there's .... left. We finished it yesterday.'
5 There's .... cheese in this sandwich. I don't like it without cheese.
6 'Have we got .... eggs?' 'Let me see. No, we've got .... left, I'm afraid.'
7 So there are .... tweets from the Prime Minister today. That's strange!
8 'How many "likes" does your video have?' 'It doesn't have .... so far.'

FAQ

Q: I've seen the word **any** used in affirmative sentences, too. How come?

A: In positive sentences, **any** has the meaning 'whatever', 'practically every' or 'no particular (one)':
Come any time. (= It doesn't matter what time).
'Which sandwich would you like?' 'Any. I don't mind.' (= Practically all the sandwiches are fine, I don't have a preference.)

! It's not easy to remember when to use **some**, **any** and **no**. Try this method. Think of the particles in an atom: protons, neutrons and electrons. **Some** has a positive meaning, like the electrical charge of a proton; **any** is like a neutron, neither positive nor negative; **no** has a negative meaning, like an electron. This is the basic concept that will help you make the right choice on a case-by-case basis.

5 🎧 **Complete the mini-dialogues using *some* or *any*. Then listen and check.**

1. **A** Mum, can I go out tonight?
   B Yes, okay, but you mustn't come back late.
   A Don't worry. I'll be home by ten. Er... and can I have [1]............. money?
   B Well, I haven't got [2]............. cash, but you can ask Dad.

2. **A** Is there [1]............. fruit left? I want to make [2]............. fruit salad.
   B Yes, there are [3]............. apples, [4]............. peaches and [5]............. grapes, but there aren't [6]............. pears.
   A Never mind. [7]............. kind of fruit will do.

3. **A** What kind of novels do you like reading?
   B [1]............. type – adventure, love stories, thrillers... I love all kinds of novels.

4. **A** There isn't [1]............. paper in the printer. Can you get [2].............? It's in the drawer on the left.
   B Ah, yes, here you are. Is there [3]............. ink in the cartridge?
   A Yes, there's still [4]............. left.

LESSON 3 Qualifying adjectives and adjectives of nationality; order of adjectives

Qualifying adjectives

	singular	plural
masculine	a **shy** boy	some **shy** boys
feminine	a **shy** girl	some **shy** girls
neuter	an **interesting** museum	some **interesting** museums

Qualifying adjectives are used to describe people or things. They are invariable, that is they never change from singular to plural or from masculine to feminine.
When they qualify a noun, they always come before the noun and never follow it:
It's a modern flat.   I don't like arrogant people.
When used predicatively, they may be found after the verbs **be**, **get**, **look**, **seem**, **feel** and other verbs of perception:
I'm tired.   I feel great.   Sally looks sad.   It's getting dark.

Focus

Study the position of an adjective used as a predicate with the verb **be** in questions:
Is Jennifer Irish?
Are the students worried about the exam?
As you can see, in English the adjective follows the subject in this case.

1 Underline the adjective in each line. Then reorder the words to write logical sentences.

1. a / day / hot / today / it's / .
2. is / there / my / village / small / church / a / in / .
3. these / comfortable / are / chairs / ?
4. looks / the / house / big / square / abandoned / the / in / .
5. are / children / in / there / some / young / park / the / .
6. tower / view / the / is / from / fantastic / the / .
7. famous / expensive / restaurant / this / is / ?
8. is / a / clothes shop / new / there / the / on / street / main / .

2 Some of these sentences contain a mistake. Find the mistakes and write correct sentences.

1. There are two bigs computer labs in our school.
2. Is ready your brother for his final exam?
3. Fatima is a good student.
4. The school building looks big, but there are only 20 classrooms.
5. Are happy your parents with your school results?
6. Mr Ross always gives speeches interesting.
7. Some youngs boys are playing in the park.
8. This is an amusing TV series.

Adjectives of nationality

Apart from a few exceptions, nationality adjectives are made from the names of the relative countries or continents plus a suffix.
Here are the most common suffixes.

−an / −ian		−ish		−ese		different	
Italy	Italian	Sweden	Swedish	China	Chinese	France	French
Germany	German	Britain	British	Portugal	Portuguese	Greece	Greek
Canada	Canadian	Denmark	Danish	Japan	Japanese	Holland	Dutch
Europe	European	Scotland	Scottish	Senegal	Senegalese	Switzerland	Swiss
Australia	Australian	England	English	Congo	Congolese	Wales	Welsh
Brazil	Brazilian	Turkey	Turkish	Sudan	Sudanese	Pakistan	Pakistani

In English, nationality adjectives are always written with a capital letter. Nationality adjectives used without the article generally become nouns and mean the language of the nation:
I love English.   I don't speak French.
Putting **the** before the nationality adjective means 'the people of that country':
The Dutch speak English as a second language.

Order of adjectives

When two or more adjectives refer to a noun, those expressing opinion usually precede more descriptive adjectives. This chart shows the most commonly used order:

indefinite / possessive	opinion	size	age	shape	colour	origin	material
a	lovely	small	new	round	white	Chinese	cotton
some	nice	large	ancient	square	red	African	gold
my	expensive	huge	old	circular	blue	American	silver
your	famous	tall	young		green		wood

She's a famous Italian writer.
Do you like my ancient Chinese pearl earrings?
I bought two lovely small rectangular Persian rugs.

47

3 Look at these items from an antique shop. Write a brief description for each object using the prompts.

0 silver / small / teapot / antique
A small, antique, silver teapot
1 porcelain / fruit bowl / Chinese / blue and white
2 painting / abstract / oil / large
3 wooden / neoclassical / French / chest of drawers
4 old / five / Italian / silver / coffee spoons
5 paperweight / Venetian / white and violet / glass

4 Complete the sentences using the adjectives in the correct order.

1 The girls are wearing .... jackets. (leather / American / black / expensive)
2 Here's a .... elephant for your collection. (ebony / valuable / African / old)
3 Why don't you buy that .... dress? (simple / cotton / green)
4 Let's sit around this .... table. (plastic / dark green / oval)
5 The new teacher is a .... man. Everyone likes him! (young / Canadian / tall / handsome)
6 His girlfriend has got .... hair. (blonde / long / straight)
7 There's a .... spider in my bedroom. (black / big / horrible)

LESSON 4 Numbers and dates

Cardinal numbers

All numbers (except **one**, obviously!) are followed by plural nouns:
five children, ten pence, seven days, 12 months, four seasons...

Numbers between 13 and 19 end in **–teen** *thirteen, fourteen...*:
Multiples of ten end in **–ty** *twenty, thirty...*:
Multiples of ten and single numbers are joined to hundreds with **and**:
168 → one hundred **and** sixty-eight
2,340 → two thousand three hundred **and** forty

FAQ

Q: I know that teenagers are young people between the ages of 13 and 19, because those are the numbers ending in **teen**. I've also heard people talking about **tweenagers**. Who are they?

A: **Tweenagers**, or **tweens**, are young people between the ages of about ten and 12 years old. The word comes from **between**. In this case they are between childhood and adolescence.

1 Match the prices expressed in numbers and in words.

1 £223.50   .... A eighty one pounds and thirty pence
2 £243.15   .... B two hundred and forty-three pounds and fifteen pence
3 £44   .... C sixty-five pounds
4 £65   .... D eighteen pounds and forty pence
5 £81.30   .... E forty-four pounds
6 £18.40   .... F two hundred and twenty-three pounds and fifty pence

Focus

In English, commas are used to separate thousands, and a full stop is used to separate decimal numbers from whole numbers. Decimal numbers are read one by one:
10,000 → *ten thousand*   3.14 → *three point one four*
100 = *a hundred / one hundred*   1,000 = *a thousand / one thousand*
1,000,000 = *a million / one million*   1,000,000,000 = *a billion / one billion*
Hundred, thousand, million and *billion* preceded by a number do not take a plural **–s**.
An **–s** is added when the meaning is several, an indefinite number. In this case, the noun is followed by **of**.
six hundred metres   BUT   *hundreds of metres*
four thousand people   BUT   *thousands of people*

2 Circle the correct option.

1 Shhh… I'm counting!… **two hundred twenty-five / two hundred and twenty-five**.
2 This precious watch cost several **hundreds / hundred** of pounds.
3 Nearly five **thousands / thousand** people were at the concert last night.
4 **Thousands / Thousand** of people were cheering the rock star.
5 About four **millions / million** people watched the *Master Chef USA* final last Saturday.
6 This jacket is really expensive. Look: **two and hundred five pounds / two hundred and five pounds**.
7 There are eight **hundreds thirty-three / hundred and thirty-three** students in our school.
8 255 divided by a hundred is **two point fifty-five / two point five five**.
9 **Thousand / Thousands** of people died in the tsunami.
10 **Two thousands and seven / Two thousand and seven** people ran in the half-marathon last month.

Ordinal numbers

Most ordinal numbers are formed like this: **cardinal number + th = ordinal number**
four → fourth   six → sixth   ten → tenth   eleven → eleventh
But: *first   second   third*   and therefore *twenty-first, twenty-second, twenty-third, thirty-first*, etc

Be careful with the spelling of the following:
fifth   eighth   ninth   twelfth
twentieth   thirtieth   fortieth   and so on for all multiples of ten.

Ordinal numbers are often preceded by the article **the**:
the second prize   Queen Elizabeth I (the first)   King Henry VIII (the eighth)
Ordinal numbers are also written in an abbreviated way, for example: *10th, 21st, 22nd, 23rd…*

FAQ

Q: Since we have to do mathematics in English, how do we read fractions?

A: The top number, or numerator, is expressed by a cardinal number. The bottom number, the denominator, is expressed by an ordinal number in the singular or plural:
¼ *one fourth / one quarter*
⅔ *two-thirds*
⅗ *three-fifths*
But: ½ *one half*

3 Write the ordinal numbers in words.

1. Yesterday was our 20th (..........................) wedding anniversary.
2. My hotel room is on the 5th (....................) floor.
3. What was life like in the 13th (...............................) century?
4. When's your 16th (...................................) birthday?
5. This cathedral dates back to the 12th (..............................) century.
6. He came 2nd (............................) in the race. It was his best time ever.
7. Alaska is the 49th (................................) state of the USA and Hawaii is the 50th (..............................).

Dates

In English, the date is expressed by ordinal numbers used in the short form:
7th July (the seventh of July)   **31st May** (the thirty-first of May).

FAQ

Q: I received a letter from the United States where the date was written: **03/06/2016**. But it meant the 6th of March, not the 3rd of June. This is confusing...

A: In American English usage, the month comes first followed by the day, for example: **September 7th (09/07)**, **May 31st (05/31)**. It's important to remember this!

Years

The year is usually expressed as follows:
1565 fifteen sixty-five   *1992* nineteen ninety-two
2018 twenty eighteen or two thousand and eighteen

Careful!   221 B.C. → two hundred and twenty-one (before Christ)
            210 A.D. → two hundred and ten (Anno Domini = after Christ)
            1600 → sixteen hundred   1605 → sixteen hundred and five or sixteen-oh-five

In the twenties / thirties... of the 20th century (meaning the decades)

4 Write the short form of the date, adding (Am.) for American English usage and (Br.) for British English.

1. June the ninth, twenty sixteen
   June 9th, 2016 (Am.)
2. The first of January, two thousand
   ....
3. The twenty-third of April, two thousand and five
   ....
4. March the seventeenth, nineteen sixty-nine
   ....
5. July the fourth, Independence Day
   ....
6. The ninth of November, two thousand and eleven
   ....
7. The thirtieth of January, twenty fourteen
   ....
8. January the first, New Year's Day
   ....

5 Write the fractions in numbers.

1. two-ninths = ...
2. four-sevenths = ...
3. four-fifteenths = ...
4. seven-eighteenths = ...
5. five-eighths = ...
6. three-fifths = ...
7. six-seventeenths = ...
8. two-elevenths = ...

Focus

The number 0 is written in different ways in English:

- for temperatures, we use **zero**:
  It's quite cold today. It's ten degrees below zero.

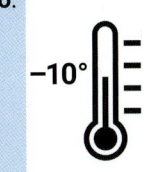

- in maths we use **nought** or **zero** (in American English):
  0.58 → nought point five eight

- for phone numbers we use **zero** or **oh**:
  Susan's phone number is 171 3400518 → one seven one, three four double oh five one eight.

- for sports results, we usually use **nil**:
  Leicester has just won three goals to nil.

- in tennis scores we use the term **love**:
  The score in this game is thirty love.

6 You have to report the following information. Write how you would say the 0 in each case.

1. In Helsinki it is −12°C.
   In Helsinki it is twelve degrees below ....

2. It's 40−0 to Murray.
   It's forty .... to Murray.

3. It's 2−0 to Chelsea.
   It's two .... to Chelsea.

4. James Bond is a 00 agent.
   James Bond is a double .... agent.

5. He got 0 / 10 in the test.
   He got .... out of ten in the test.

6. The first answer in the quiz is 0.21.
   The first answer in the quiz is .... point two one.

7. Our room number is 202.
   Our room number is two .... two .

8. The diameter of the hole is 0.65 cm.
   The diameter of the hole is .... point six five centimetres.

9. My mobile number is 07793 294546.
   My mobile number is .... double seven nine three, two nine four five four six.

! Study how to say the following mathematical expressions and percentages:

Four out of five of the boys in the class like playing football.
Twenty-five percent of the kids go to school by car.
Jimmy scored ten out of ten in the test, he got all the answers right.
This week there's twenty percent discount on electrical appliances in the local supermarket.

ROUND UP 3

1 **Rewrite the sentences in the plural.**

1. This is my friend. ....
2. That is his dog. ....
3. This is our sister. ....
4. That is your student. ....
5. That is their car. ....

2 **Complete the sentences with *some* or *any*.**

1. I haven't got .... money with me. Could you lend me .... ?
2. There's .... interesting information on this website.
3. Have you got .... news from the German school?
4. .... students are working on a project about the history of the EU.
5. Our school hasn't got .... Erasmus partners in Italy.
6. 'Are there .... teachers in the staff room?' 'No, they're all in their classrooms.'
7. 'Have you got .... blue pens?' 'Yes, we have .... in this box.'
8. The children don't have .... computers in their class.
9. We live in a very small town. There aren't .... hotels, but there are .... lively pubs.
10. There isn't .... housework to do today.

MATRIX +

Study the expressions:
none of us (= not a single person in our group)
none of you (= not a single person in your group)
none of them (= not a single person or thing in their group)
none of these (= not a single thing among these)
none of those (= not a single thing among those)
none of my friends (= not a single friend of mine)

The expression **none of...** can be followed by a verb in the singular or the plural:

*None of these people **works** / **work** in a factory.*
*None of us **is** / **are** going to the cinema tonight.*

3 **Complete the sentences with *no* / *none*.**

1. 'Can I have a French magazine, please?' 'Sorry, there are .... left.'
2. We were lucky. We found .... difficulties in carrying out this project.
3. Great! There are .... lessons tomorrow.
4. .... of them arrived in time.
5. There are .... good restaurants in this little town.
6. .... sensible person would behave like that.
7. .... of the local museums are open today. It's a national holiday.
8. 'Did any students hand in their reports yesterday?' 'No, sorry. ....'

MATRIX +

Some, **any** and **no** are also used in the following special ways.
Some + singular countable noun has the meaning 'a certain', 'a non-specific':
They live in some village in this valley.

Some before a numeral means 'about', 'more or less':
The nearest hospital is some 30 km from here.

Any and **no** are used as adverbs before comparatives and the adjective **good**. A verb in the **–ing** form may follow:
Is it any better after a hot cup of tea?
Was it any good talking to your principal?

No + adjective + noun means 'not at all', 'not in the least':
I'm no great singer.

No is also used to express prohibition:
No smoking in the school premises.

4 Underline the mistake in each sentence, then rewrite the sentences correctly.

1 No shops aren't open today. It's a holiday.
   ....

2 I haven't no homework to do for tomorrow.
   ....

3 'Are there any restaurants in this street?' 'No, there aren't none.'
   ....

4 Not any patients are allowed in this area.
   ....

5 None journalists can get into the room.
   ....

6 It's no any use crying over spilt milk.
   ....

7 The airport must be any 20 miles from here.
   ....

8 We're some good at painting. We're really hopeless!
   ....

5 Complete the sentences with the correct noun or adjective.

1 My friend Sintija lives in Helsinki, but she isn't .... She was born in Latvia from .... parents.

2 Montreal is a cosmopolitan .... city where people speak English and French.

3 There's a .... girl in my class. She arrived from Thailand two months ago.

4 Helen is in Austria because she wants to improve her .... She needs it for her job.

5 Brussels is the capital city of .... and the seat of the Council of ....

6 Van Basten comes from .... He's Dutch.

6 Choose the correct option: A, B or C.

1 ……… are allowed in these rooms.
  A None visitors   B No visitors   C No visitor

2 'Is there any tea in the teapot?' ' No, ……… .'
  A there's none   B there's some   C there's no

3 ……… museums are open in town today because it's Monday.
  A Not any   B None   C No

4 I haven't got ……… homework for tomorrow.
  A any   B no   C some

5 I need a ……… table for my garden.
  A new square plastic   B plastic new square   C square plastic new

6 '………' 'No, I think he's Spanish.'
  A Is Scottish the new receptionist?   B Is the new Scottish receptionist?
  C Is the new receptionist Scottish?

7 Steve was born on ……… January.
  A 12nd   B 12th   C 12rd

8 Joanne lives on the ……… floor.
  A fiveth   B fifeth   C fifth

9 ……… of mobile phone buyers are under 18.
  A One third   B One threeth   C One threerd

10 The company invested two ……… pounds to renovate its old factories.
  A billions   B billion   C milliards

11 It's really cold tonight. It's five degrees below ……… .
  A nought   B nil   C zero

12 Chelsea FC is winning three goals to ……… .
  A nil   B nought   C love

13 ……… my family live in the United States.
  A A half   B Half   C The half

14 Nadal is leading in the final set by three games to ……… .
  A zero   B nil   C love

MATRIX +

Basic mathematical operations

Addition
5 + 8 = 13 → five plus eight equals thirteen / five and eight is thirteen

Subtraction
12 − 4 = 8 → twelve minus four equals eight / four from twelve is eight

Multiplication
4 x 5 = 20 → four multiplied by five equals twenty / four times five is twenty

Division
32 ÷ 4 = 8 → thirty-two divided by four equals eight / four into thirty-two is eight

More complex mathematical operations

Exponents and exponential functions

base → 3^2 ← exponent

4^2 → four squared equals sixteen / four to the second power equals sixteen

7^3 → 343 seven cubed equals three hundred and forty-three / seven (raised) to the third power equals three hundred and forty-three

Exponential statement

$y = b^x$ → y equals b raised to the xth power

Roots

$\sqrt{16} = 4$ → the square root of sixteen equals four

$\sqrt[3]{90} = 4.48$ → the cubic root of ninety is approximately four point four eight

index → $\sqrt[3]{64}$ ← argument of the radical / radicand
radical symbol →

Logarithms and logarithmic functions

$\log_2 (8) = 3$ → logarithm base two of eight equals three

$$\log_6 (216) = 3$$

base ↗   ↑ argument

Logarithmic statement

$\log_b (y) = x$ → logarithm base-b of y equals x

Reflecting on grammar

Study the rules and decide if the following statements are true or false.

		True	False
1	The plural form of **that** is **these**.		
2	When I ask a question to make an offer or ask to have something, I use **some** and not **any**.		
3	**Any** is never used in affirmative sentences.		
4	**No** is accompanied by a verb in the negative form.		
5	The expression *None of us are ready* is incorrect.		
6	In questions with the verb **be** used as a predicate, the adjective precedes the noun.		
7	Nationality adjectives always begin with a small letter in English.		
8	The adjectives in the following sentence are in the correct order: *Have you seen the amazing new French science-fiction film?*		
9	I received a letter with this date: 03.21.2016. It's from New York.		
10	All ordinal numbers are formed by adding **–th** to the cardinal number.		

Revision and Exams 1 (UNITS 1 – 2 – 3)

1 **Complete the email with *a / an* or *the*. Use the // symbol when no article is needed.**

From: **Asta** astalas@gmail.com
To: **Julie** julieb99@yahoo.com

Hi Julie!
I'm Asta, your new key pal. My teacher gave me your email address. She says we can do an e-twinning project this year.

I'm 16. I'm Lithuanian and I live in Vilnius, ¹............. capital city of ²............. Lithuania. Do you know where ³............. my country is? It's in ⁴............. north-east of Europe, near ⁵............. Russia and ⁶............. Poland. It isn't big, but it's ⁷............. interesting country on ⁸............. Baltic Sea.

I'm ⁹............. student at secondary school and I study ¹⁰............. English. I like ¹¹............. languages and I like travelling.

Tell me about yourself and send me ¹²............. photo. You'll find ¹³............. photo of ¹⁴............. my city cathedral in ¹⁵............. attachment.

Write soon,
Asta

2 **Complete the text with the correct form of the verb *be*.**

Things ¹............. different in my family these days. I ²............. a member of a big family now and I ³............. an only child any more. My dad and Maria ⁴............. married now, so she ⁵............. my new step-mother. And there ⁶............. three children in Maria's family: Ann, Emma and Luke. We all live together in their big house in the country. We have a lot of fun and we ⁷............. all good friends. I think it ⁸............. great being part of a big family!

3 **Complete the text using the words below. Be careful: nouns must be in the plural form and the verb *be* must be conjugated.**

ox   sheep   cow   be (x3)   duck   goose   deer   bush

In the first scene of the movie, two ¹........................... are pulling a cart along a country path. It all seems peaceful and quiet, but the scene changes and you see a field with some ²........................... and ³........................... standing still in an unnatural silence. In the pond of a farm nearby, there ⁴........................... some ⁵........................... and ⁶..........................., but they are not moving – they're just floating on the water, absolutely still, as if they were frozen. Two ⁷........................... with big antlers are hiding behind some ⁸........................... and they are not moving either. There ⁹........................... a gloomy atmosphere, as if something terrible were going to happen. ¹⁰........................... you curious to see what happens? Go and see the movie this weekend, it's quite scary!

56

4 For questions 1–12, choose the answer (A, B or C) which you think fits best according to the text.

I like living in ¹...... little town. ²...... everything I need and everything I like doing.
I'm ³...... journalist and all I need for my work is ⁴...... computer and ⁵...... Internet connection. Here all the houses have broadband, so I can easily work from home.
⁶...... a railway station with lots of trains to and from London from early morning to late in the evening. About ⁷...... of the inhabitants work or study in London.
I like to take some exercise in my free time. There ⁸...... some gyms and a sports centre in town, but there isn't ⁹...... indoor swimming pool. There's a theatre too. Every winter, there's a drama festival that goes on for over two weeks. ¹⁰...... of the performances are really good and attract lots of people from nearby places.
In the evenings, I usually go to my favourite pub on the High Street. ¹¹...... of the other pubs have the same kind of 'vintage' atmosphere as The Crown and Anchor. The landlord is a good friend of mine and ¹²...... of the patrons are too. We really enjoy spending time together.

1	A	that	B	this	C	any
2	A	There are	B	There isn't	C	There's
3	A	//	B	the	C	a
4	A	the	B	some	C	a
5	A	an	B	a	C	//
6	A	There are	B	There's	C	There isn't
7	A	three-fourth	B	three-fours	C	three-quarters
8	A	aren't	B	are	C	is
9	A	any	B	an	C	a
10	A	Some	B	No	C	Every
11	A	None	B	No	C	Some
12	A	some	B	none	C	any

5 Complete Janet's email to her friend Irene using the adjectives in brackets in the correct order. Sometimes you will need to decide which adjectives to use in which gaps.

Hi Irene,
I've been surfing the net and I've just seen some ¹.. clothes on sale on a ²........................... website. (popular, trendy, great)
There are ³.. jackets that cost only £20.00. They are ⁴..........................., aren't they? (cheap, eco-leather, colourful)
And the T-shirts! ⁵..........................., ... or ...., ... T-shirts at the ⁶........................... price of £1 – yes, one pound! – each. (cotton, white, black, incredible, long-sleeved)
I wanted to buy a really ⁷... miniskirt, but my mum said no. (denim, short, tight)
But she let me buy a ⁸... dress. It's ⁹........................... for the summer! (fantastic, blue, low-necked, long)
I'm sending you the link to the website.
There's a ¹⁰...
.... dress that you'll love.
(evening, glittery, long)
Let me know.
Janet

6 Complete the text with the correct form of the verbs *be* or *have*.

Welcome to Snowdonia National Park

Snowdonia National Park ¹..................... vast areas of natural beauty and unique scenery. Its Welsh name can ²..................... translated as 'the place of the eagles'.

The park, which covers 838 square miles, ³..................... one of the three natural parks found in Wales and the oldest one, being designated as one in 1951. The area of the Snowdonia National Park ⁴..................... so much to offer to visitors that if you are visiting it for the first time, you will wonder why it took you so long to do it.

The landscape ⁵..................... breathtaking and unique. There ⁶..................... nine mountain ranges here and they cover over half of the national park's surface. Some of the peaks ⁷..................... over 3,000 feet (915 m).

Snowdonia offers first-class accommodation in a number of hotels and bed and breakfasts.

FOR MORE INFORMATION, PLEASE PHONE 01766 770274 OR SEND AN EMAIL TO park@snowdonia-npa.gov.uk.

7 Complete the text with the word which best fits each gap. Use only one word in each gap.

The British Isles

The British Isles ¹..................... an archipelago in ²..................... north-west of Europe. Great Britain is ³..................... biggest island. It ⁴..................... surrounded by the English Channel, ⁵..................... North Sea, the Irish Sea and the Atlantic Ocean. Ireland is ⁶..................... other big island of the archipelago. Northern Ireland belongs to the United Kingdom, like England, Scotland and Wales. ⁷..................... rest of the island is ⁸..................... independent country, called the Republic of Ireland.

⁹..................... Pennines are the backbone of England, while the Thames ¹⁰..................... the most important river, which flows through ¹¹..................... country from west to east. The Shannon is the longest river in Ireland. The biggest lake in Scotland ¹²..................... Loch Lomond, but the most famous is Loch Ness because of Nessie, the monster which is said to live in its dark deep water.

Preliminary (PET) | Reading Part 5

8 For questions 1–10, choose the answer (A, B, C or D) which you think fits best according to the text.

My brother is self-sufficient. He doesn't have ⁰..*a*.. job and lives in ¹...... cottage in the country where he grows all his own vegetables. In spring, there are ²...... lettuces in his garden, but there aren't ³...... tomatoes. In summer, there ⁴...... tomatoes, but ⁵...... lettuces. He also has ⁶...... fruit trees with cherries and plums, but ⁷...... apple trees. There ⁸...... any cherries at the moment, but there are ⁹...... plums. He always gives me ¹⁰...... when I visit him.

0	A the	B an	C (a)	D /
1	A an	B a	C /	D the
2	A none	B some	C the	D any
3	A no	B any	C none	D some
4	A are	B haven't	C isn't	D aren't
5	A no	B any	C some	D none
6	A any	B the	C none	D some
7	A some	B no	C any	D none
8	A are	B have	C aren't	D haven't
9	A some	B no	C any	D none
10	A any	B no	C none	D some

First (FCE) | Reading and Use of English Part 2

9 For questions 1–10, read the text below and think of the word which best fits each gap. Use only one word in each gap.

English, an international language

English is spoken in many parts of ⁰ *the* .... the world and is the official language in various International institutions, like ¹.......................... United Nations. ².......................... is also considered the language of science, commerce and technology and it is used in international aviation and navigation.

Here are the countries where English is spoken today:

³.......................... people speak it as their mother tongue, for example in ⁴.......................... USA, Britain, Ireland, Australia, New Zealand, most of Canada and ⁵.......................... of the Caribbean countries.

Some people speak it as ⁶.......................... official language; this means that nearly everybody understands it and ⁷.......................... speak it in government offices, the media and education. Examples of this are India, Singapore, Kenya and South Africa.

And a lot more people speak it as ⁸.......................... foreign language, because they learn it at school or at university.

But why is English so important? One reason is historical. Great Britain was the centre of an enormous empire in ⁹.......................... 19th century, and English was the language of her colonies all over the world. Another reason is linked to the economic and cultural prestige that the United States acquired in ¹⁰.......................... 20th century – and still has today – in the field of science and technology.

Towards competences

You are about to take part in a cultural exchange with an Australian school. Your teacher has asked you to write a short presentation about yourself for your host family. Talk about things that you like and don't like, your hobbies, mention any allergies or special requests you may have. Complete the form that your teacher has given you.

Australia 🇦🇺 School exchange

Presentation for your host family

_____
_____
_____
_____

Sign here _____

Stick your photo here.

Self Check 1

Circle the correct option. Then check your answers.

1. There are still some ……… on that tree.
   A leafs   B leaves   C leavs

2. The ……… are standing near the jewellery shop.
   A policewomens
   B policewoman
   C policewomen

3. Where ……… the scissors?
   A is   B are   C aren't

4. Listen! This is an interesting ……… .
   A news   B piece of news   C new

5. The crossroads near our office ……… very dangerous. Lots of accidents happen there.
   A aren't   B is   C isn't

6. The latest ……… are very reliable.
   A analyses
   B analysis
   C analysises

7. Oh no! There are dog ……… on the sofa again. Why can't he sleep in his basket?
   A hair   B hairs   C haires

8. My wife ……… .
   A does the nurse
   B is the nurse
   C is a nurse

9. I haven't got ……… umbrella with me.
   A an   B the   C a

10. Jeff plays ……… violin very well.
    A //   B a   C the

11. ……… breakfast is served on the terrace.
    A The   B A   C //

12. Spain is in ……… south-west of Europe.
    A the   B //   C a

13. Paul and I are good friends. ……… work in the same office.
    A You   B They   C We

14. ……… ten pounds fifty.
    A There's   B It's   C Is

15. Jane ……… from England. She's Australian, from Melbourne.
    A is   B aren't   C isn't

16. Can I have a glass of water, please? I'm really ……… .
    A hungry   B hurry   C thirsty

17. Kirsty and I ……… in a hurry because it's late.
    A am   B are   C is

18. Strange! There ……… any lights in this room.
    A are   B aren't   C isn't

19. Your room is 203. ……… your key.
    A Here
    B There is
    C Here is

20. There ……… a new smartphone and a special watch in that shop window. Let's go in and ask how much they are.
    A are   B aren't   C is

21. ……… 'No, she's out.'
    A 'Is your sister there?'
    B 'Is there your sister?'
    C 'Is here your sister?'

22. ……… is your favourite ice-cream flavour? Chocolate or vanilla?
    A How   B What   C Which

23. 'How ……… is it from the station to your office?' '500 metres.'
    A long   B far   C much

24. 'How ……… is that bridge?' '150 metres.'
    A long   B much   C deep

25. 'What's the hotel like?'
    A 'It's small and cosy.'
    B 'I like it very much.'
    C 'I don't like it at all.'

26. I like ……… trousers over there.
    A those   B this   C that

27. Is there ……… street map of London?
    A some   B a   C any

28. Can I have ……… salt, please?
    A some   B a   C any

29. There isn't ……… ink left in the printer cartridge.
    A some   B any   C no

30. There are some ……… in our town. There are concerts every week.
    A greats venues
    B venues greats
    C great venues

31. 'Have you got ……… relatives in China, Liu?' 'Yes, I've got three cousins.'
    A some   B any   C the

32. It's ……… good playing squash twice a week and having two hamburgers after each match.
    A no   B any   C some

33. He studied at ……… university in the south of the country.
    A no   B some   C any

34. ……… with her new job?
    A Susan is she happy
    B Is happy Susan
    C Is Susan happy

35. Look at that lovely ……… ……… ……… table by the window!
    A small, round, wooden
    B wooden, small, round
    C round, wooden, small

36. My daughter likes ……… cats very much.
    A soft, white, Persian
    B Persian, white, soft
    C soft, Persian, white

37. There are ……… people at the concert tonight.
    A seven hundreds and fifty
    B seven hundred fifty
    C seven hundred and fifty

38. Claire was born on ……… March.
    A 22rd   B 22nd   C 22th

39. The temperature today is five degrees below ……… .
    A nought   B nil   C zero

40. 'What's the ……… root of 25?' 'It's five.'
    A cubic   B square   C checked

Assess yourself!

- **0 – 10** Study harder. Use the online exercises to help you.
- **11 – 20** OK. Use the online exercises to practise things you don't know.
- **21 – 30** Good, but do some extra practice online.
- **31 – 40** Excellent!

GRAMMAR MATRIX BASICS

UNIT 4 Verb *have* + possessives

LESSON 1 Verb *have* – positive form

→ **Visual Grammar page 405**

The verb **have** has two forms: **have** and **has** (for the third person singular). It is often reinforced by the word **got**, especially in the short form. This usage is more common in British English.

Full form	Short form
I have got	I've got
You have got	You've got
He has got	He's got
She has got	She's got
It has got	It's got
We have got	We've got
You have got	You've got
They have got	They've got

Remember!
It is also possible to use the short form **has got** (**'s got**) when the subject is a noun, but the short form of **have got** (**'ve got**) is only possible with pronouns (**we**, **you**, **they**), and not with nouns:
John's got an appointment.
My dad's got an old guitar.
But NOT *The boys've got a football.*

FAQ

Q: Could I use the short form without **got**, for example *I've no money*?

A: Yes, it's possible, but not in the third person singular. That's because the short form of **has** (**'s**) could be confused with the short form of **be** (is → **'s**). We can't say, for example *He's no money*. The alternatives are *He has no money* or *He's got no money*.

Q: And could I use the full form with **got**? To say, for example, *I have got one ticket*.

A: Yes, of course, although the short form is more common.

The verb **have** is used to talk about:
- things that belong to us: *I've got a new car*.
- family relationships: *Simon's got a sister*.
- a person's physical characteristics: *She's got beautiful dark eyes*.
- illnesses and injuries: *I've got a cold*.

1 Rewrite the sentences, using the short form where it is possible.

1 My mother has got a part-time job.
2 They have got some relatives in Australia.
3 My cousins have got a kitten.
4 You have got great talent!
5 My brother has got a degree in physics.
6 She has got a very large house.
7 We have all got black hair in my family.
8 Julie has got a fantastic voice.

2 Reorder the words and write sentences.

1. has / hair / my / long, / straight / sister / .
   ....
2. got / bad / headache / I've / very / a / .
   ....
3. have / I / tattoo / left / on / arm / my / a / .
   ....
4. two / for / tickets / we've / concert / got / the / .
   ....
5. hotel / pool / has / our / an / got / indoor / .
   ....
6. dad / your / has / good / of / sense / humour / a / .
   ....
7. have / we / a / dog / black / big, / got /.
   ....
8. got / your / phone / I've / number / .
   ....

Verb *have* with other meanings

The verb **have** can have other meanings, such as 'do', 'take', 'buy', 'eat' or 'drink'. In these cases, it is never followed by **got**. Here are a few examples:

have breakfast / lunch / dinner / supper
have tea / coffee / fruit juice
have a snack / a sandwich
have a bath / a shower (Am.E.: take a bath / a shower)
have a break / a holiday
have a rest / a nap / a lie-in
have fun / a good time (= enjoy)
have a party / a meeting (= organise, arrange)
have a walk / a bike ride / a boat trip (= go for...)

! When we want to know what is wrong with a person, we do not say **What have you got?** but **What's the matter?** or **What's the matter with you?** or **What's wrong with you?**

3 Some of these sentences contain a mistake. Underline the mistakes and write the sentences correctly.

1. Adam's spiky hair. ....
2. I've got a new coat. ....
3. She's got a shower every morning. ....
4. The children've blue eyes. ....
5. Dad's got a rest in the afternoon. ....
6. Have got a good time at the party! ....
7. They have milk and cereal for breakfast. ....
8. We often have lunch in a café. ....

LESSON 2 Verb *have* – negative and interrogative forms

Negative form

We usually use the short form of the negative of the verb **have**, reinforced by **got** *(have not got → haven't got)*.

I / you / we / they	have not got	he / she / it	has not got
	haven't got		**hasn't got**

FAQ

Q: I've got an American friend who always says **I don't have a clue**. Why doesn't he say **I haven't got a clue**?

A: The negative form of **have** can also be **don't have**. Actually, in American English, this is the most commonly used form.

> ❗ When we use the verb **have** with a different meaning from 'possess' (see list on previous page), the negative forms are always formed using **don't** and **doesn't** in the third person singular:
> *I don't have a big breakfast in the morning.*
> *She doesn't have lunch at school.*

1 Complete the sentences with *have got*, *has got*, *haven't got* or *hasn't got*.

1. Rachel is blonde. She .... dark hair.
2. I usually cycle to school because I .... a car.
3. Their house .... a big garden with lots of flowers.
4. Melinda? No, she .... any children.
5. George .... long hair and he often ties it up in a pony tail.
6. They .... tattoos on their arms. I don't like them!
7. We .... a lot of books at home. We need to build some more shelves!
8. Bob .... two lovely dogs, but he .... any cats.

2 Rewrite the sentences in your notebook in the negative form.

1. I've got some warm clothes with me.
2. She's got a present for you.
3. The students have a break at 11 o'clock in the morning.
4. He's got a lot of contacts on social media.
5. They have a holiday in July.
6. She usually has tea for breakfast.
7. My mother's got blue eyes.
8. We've got tickets for the match.

3 Write sentences using the prompts.

0. Susan / country house (✗) / flat in the town centre (✓)
   Susan hasn't got a country house, but she has got a flat in the town centre.
1. My bedroom / balcony (✗) / French windows (✓)
   ....
2. The village / a post office (✓) / a bank (✗)
   ....
3. I / trees in my garden (✗) / lots of flowers (✓)
   ....
4. We / enough money for a pizza (✗) / enough for a couple of sandwiches (✓)
   ....

Interrogative form

In questions, the verb **have** comes before the subject. The word **got** is usually used as well.

Have I / you / we / they got... ?
- Yes, I / we / you / they have.
- No, we / you / they haven't.

Has he / she / it got... ?
- Yes, he / she / it has.
- No, he / she / it hasn't.

Short answers

Short answers are formed as follows:

| Yes, + pronoun + **have / has** | No, + pronoun + **haven't / hasn't** |

In affirmative short answers, the full form of the verb is always used, whereas in negative short answers, the short form is usually used. **Got** is never used in short answers:
'Have you got your tablet?' 'Yes, I have.'
'Has Karen got a motorbike?' 'No, she hasn't.'

Negative interrogative form

Haven't ▶ I / you / we / they got… ?

Hasn't ▶ he / she / it got… ?

'Haven't you got your key?' 'Yes, I have!'
'Hasn't your mum got a sister?' 'No, she hasn't.'

The negative interrogative form is usually used to check information.

When the verb is used with a different meaning from 'possess', questions are always formed with **do / does**:
Do you usually have a bath or a shower?

In American English, all questions with **have** are formed as follows, including those with the meaning of 'possess'.
Do you have… ? / Does he have… ?
Do you have a new email address?

Questions can start with a **Wh–** word *(what, where, when, why…)*:
Why have you got that big smile on your face? What do we have to eat?

4 **Match questions and answers.**

1. Have you got any plans for tonight?
2. Has Ben got any good video games?
3. It's heavy! What have you got in your bag?
4. Have we got time to catch the next train?
5. Have you got any good music on your MP3 player?
6. Have you got any pink clothes?

A My clothes and a lot of books.
B Yes, but we must hurry.
C No. I hate pink!
D No, I haven't. Have you got any ideas?
E Yes, he has. I sometimes borrow them.
F Yes, I have. Lots of rock and pop.

1 …… 2 …… 3 …… 4 …… 5 …… 6 ……

5 **Write the questions from exercise 4 using American English.**

1 *Do you have any plans for tonight?*
2 ....
3 ....
4 ....
5 ....
6 ....

6 **Write sentences using *have got* in the positive, negative and interrogative forms. Use the words given.**

1 My house / solar panels on the roof.
2 I / not / time to chat. I'm busy at the moment.
3 'Peter / a big family / ?' 'Yes, he / four children.'
4 'What car / you / ?' 'I / a hybrid car. It's very cheap to run.'

5 London / a population of over 8.3 million. ....

6 We / not / much money. We must find an ATM. ....

7 'you / any preferences for your room?' 'I'd like a non-smoking one, please'.
....

8 'your school / a big playground / ?' 'No, but it / a very big gym.'
....

9 'you / any hand luggage, madam / ?' 'I / only this handbag.'
....

10 We / not / any bread / but / we / some breadsticks.
....

LESSON 3 Possessive adjectives and pronouns

The possessive adjectives are as follows:

my name	**our** names
your name	**your** names
his name	**their** names
her name	
its name	

Possessive adjectives

- are invariable. That means that they do not change according to the gender of the noun, or whether the noun is singular or plural: *my father   my mother   my brothers   my sisters*
- are not preceded by any other determiner, such as an article, demonstrative or indefinite adjective:
  our school NOT *the our school*
  this friend of mine NOT *this my friend*
  a cousin of mine or *one of my cousins* NOT *a my cousin*
  some of your books or *some books of yours* NOT *some your books*

For the third person singular, possessive adjectives refer to and agree with the possessor:
Tony's office → **his** office (male)   **Sandra's** office → **her** office (female)
the bird's cage → **its** cage (neuter, used for animals and things)

> ❗ Be careful not to confuse: **You're** *a friend* with **Your** *friend…*
> **He's** *a friend.* with **His** *friend…*   **It's** *a nice photo.* with **Its** *photo…*

Possessive adjectives are sometimes strengthened by the use of **own**:
Each shop has got its own brand.
Was it his own idea?

Possessive adjectives show who an items belongs to:
This book belongs to me. → *It's my book.*

Focus

In English, possessive adjectives are also used with:
- parts of the body: *I've broken my leg.   She writes with her left hand.*
- clothes: *Take your coat!   He's wearing his black jeans.*

1 Circle the subject in 1–6, then find the possessive adjective that matches it in A–G.

0 (I)'m Tom, the new waiter.
1 So you're from Pakistan.
2 Zimbabwe is an African country.
3 Mr Johnson's our maths teacher.
4 Kate is my best friend.
5 We live in a high building.
6 My uncle and aunt like travelling

A Its capital is Harare.
B in their camper van.
C (My) surname's Brown.
D Our flat's on the eighth floor.
E Is Urdu your mother tongue?
F Her brother Ben is at college.
G His tests are always very difficult.

0 ..C..   1 .....   2 .....   3 .....   4 .....   5 .....   6 .....

2 Complete the sentences with the correct possessive adjective.

1 The boys have got .... own room.
2 What have you got in .... hand?
3 That building's got a big dish on .... roof.
4 Is she wearing .... hat with the flowers on it?
5 Oh no! I haven't got .... sunglasses.
6 He still can't stand on .... own two feet!
7 We've come in .... own car.
8 What are .... names, girls?

3 Each sentence contains a mistake. Rewrite the sentences correctly.

1 The his house is on Darwin Road.
2 Emma's got a little brother. He's name's Harry.
3 This farm belongs to my grandparents. It's your farm.
4 She's wearing his new red dress.
5 The hamster isn't in our cage!
6 My diary has got flowers on it's cover.
7 I often have sleepovers at the my friend's house.
8 John and Simon have his own fitness instructor.
9 Karen's got a sister. She's name is Davina.

Possessive pronouns

Possessive pronouns are used when the noun they refer to is not expressed: *It's mine*.
Like possessive adjectives, they are invariable and are never preceded by a determiner:

mine	hers
yours	ours
his	theirs

Instead of a pronoun, we can use the adjective + **own**: *Is it yours?* → *Is it your own?*

4 Circle the correct option.

1 Don't touch. They're not **your** / **yours**!
2 Give me **your** / **yours** mobile number and I'll give you **my** / **mine**.
3 This isn't Mark's notebook. **His** / **Hers** has got a red cover with **his** / **her** initials on it.
4 They've got an Audi, so that Mercedes certainly isn't **ours** / **theirs**.
5 I think this bag belongs to Fran. Yes, I'm sure it's **her** / **hers**.
6 My boyfriend's coming to the party tonight. What about **yours** / **your**?
7 My parents' house is opposite the station and **our** / **ours** is behind it.
8 About half of smartphone users check **their** / **theirs** phones several times an hour.

LESSON 4 Interrogative *Whose* with the possessive case

Whose is used to ask about possession and who things belong to.
Whose may be an adjective, that is, followed by a noun, or it may be a pronoun:
Whose mobile phone is this? (adj.) / *Whose is this mobile phone?* (pron.)

To answer a question beginning with **whose**, we can use the name of the possessor + **'s** (possessive case) or a possessive adjective or a possessive pronoun:
*It's **Olivia's**.*
*It's **her** mobile phone.*
*It's **hers**.*

1 Reorder the words to write each question in two different ways.

0 socks / are / these / whose / ? *Whose are these socks? / Whose socks are these?*
1 scooters / those / whose / are / ? ....
2 is / coat / that / whose / ? ....
3 is / whose / number / telephone / this / ? ....
4 are / suitcases / whose / those / ? ....
5 this / whose / magazine / is / ? ....
6 that / whose / is / idea / ? ....

2 Match the answers to the questions in exercise 1.

[0] They're David's socks.
[ ] Does it finish with double eight? It must be John's.
[ ] The blue scooter is my brother's. The other one belongs to his friend.
[ ] I don't know. No one has claimed them so far.
[ ] Which one? The brown leather coat? It's Mark's.
[ ] It's her idea! What do you think? Is it good?
[ ] It's not mine. I don't read stuff like that. Someone left it on the seat.

Focus

The **possessive case** (or genitive) is used to express possession. It is formed as follows:
name of the possessor + **'s** + the thing that is possessed (without the article!):
Adam's car

In English, remember that the name of the possessor always precedes the thing possessed:
my daughter's school

The possessive case can also be used to express family relationships:
my mother's cousin   your sister's husband

! When the possessor is a regular plural noun ending in **–s**, we only add the apostrophe:
my parents' bedroom
the Students' Union
But: *the children's toys* (irregular plural not ending in **–s**)

When the possessor is a singular name ending in **–s**, we usually add **'s**:
James's friend
Charles's car

But with names or surnames of famous people, we usually add only the apostrophe (see page 75).

When the same thing belongs to two or more people, we add **'s** only to the final name:
Sheila and Frank's room
Tom and James's video games (the same video games, that belong to both boys)
But:
Tom's and James's video games (different video games for each boy)

The **possessive case** is used when the possessor is:

- a person or animal:
  Sarah's garden
  the bird's cage
- an indefinite pronoun referring to a person:
  no one's land
  someone's bag
- a group of people:
  the band's name
  the company's headquarters

However, when we talk about a thing, the two nouns are put together without adding an **'s**, as if the first noun is an adjective:
the state capital
the US President (see page 386)
Alternatively, we can add the preposition **of**:
the pages of the book
the lid of the pan

We can also use the **possessive case** with:

- expressions of time:
  a week's holiday
  today's newspaper
  tomorrow's weather forecast
  an hour's walk
- names of places:
  London's traffic
  the world's top insurance company
  Chicago's tallest building

3 **Rewrite the underlined words using the possessive case.**

0 We're reading the plays of Ibsen in our literature lessons. *Ibsen's plays*
1 I'm having a holiday of a week next month. ....
2 Can I have the email address of your brother, please? ....
3 I'm not allowed to go into the bedroom of my brothers. ....
4 I think this is one of the best songs of Amy Winehouse. ....
5 The tricks of the clowns are quite funny. ....
6 I love the paintings of Van Gogh! ....
7 The office of the principal is on the ground floor. ....

4 **Rewrite the expressions so that they are shorter, putting the two nouns together.**

0 the lessons of maths → *the maths lessons*

1 the walls of the kitchen
2 the charger of the laptop
3 the cap of the pen
4 the cover of the book
5 the handle of the door
6 the legs of the table
7 the screen of the computer
8 the remote control of the TV
9 the top of the tree

5 **Rewrite the sentences using the possessive case.**

0 Jenny has an Alsatian dog. — Jenny's dog *is an Alsatian.*
1 My mother has got a white bicycle. — My mother's ....
2 This computer belongs to my father. — It's ....
3 My girlfriend has got beautiful eyes. — My girlfriend's ....
4 These backpacks belong to the guides. — These are ....
5 Kate's got a new smartphone. — Kate's ....
6 Charlie has a very good computer. — Charlie's ....

FAQ

Q: Why are the names of shops sometimes followed by 's? For example, Macy's in New York?

A: Because the name **shop** or **store** is understood. In the same way, the names of **cathedrals**, **restaurants**, **salons**, **(doctor's) surgeries** and similar places are also understood, for example:
We visited St Paul's (cathedral).
She's at the hairdresser's (salon).

Q: Can the word **house** also be understood?

A: Yes, it certainly can:
I had a sleepover at Helen's (house).

6 Complete the sentences with one of the words below.

chemist's   doctor's   greengrocer's   dentist's   baker's   Rino's   St Peter's   my friend's

1 Last night we had dinner at .... , a new Italian restaurant
2 I'm going to the .... to buy some aspirin.
3 Did you go to .... when you were in Rome?
4 I don't feel very well. I must go to the ....
5 I spent the afternoon at .... We did our homework together.
6 Try the .... on Green Street. They bake great bread.
7 Why don't you go to the .... if you have a toothache?
8 I usually buy my vegetables at an organic .... near my house.

Double genitive

The indefinite articles (**a**, **an**), numbers (**two**, **three**, ...), indefinite adjectives and pronouns (**some**, **many**, **a few**...) and demonstrative adjectives (**this**, **that**, **these**...) cannot be directly followed by the genitive or possessive case. In these cases, a double genitive or double possessive construction is used, as follows:

*a friend **of** Tom's* or *one **of** Tom's friends* (NOT ~~a Tom's friend~~)
*some photos **of** Janet's* or *some **of** Janet's photos* (NOT ~~some Janet's photos~~)
*three books **of** the children's* or *three **of** the children's books* (NOT ~~three children's books~~)
*this movie **of** Spielberg's* (NOT ~~this Spielberg's movie~~).
With demonstrative adjectives, this is the only possible form.

As you can see from the examples, the double possessive takes its name from the the fact that it uses both the preposition **of** and the genitive **'**s.

7 Rewrite the underlined parts of the sentences using the double genitive. Remember to keep the meaning of the original sentence.

0 A sister of Brenda moved to Germany last year.   *One of Brenda's sisters*
1 Two neighbours of the Smiths' come from Pakistan. ....
2 A colleague of my brother is coming to visit. ....
3 Many selfies of John's are on Facebook. ....
4 A friend of the Browns' is a very good golf player. ....
5 Four birthday presents of my cousin's were baseball caps! ....
6 A cousin of Peter's is moving to Canada. ....
7 Some stamps of my father's collection are very rare. ....

8 Study the family tree and complete the sentences using the possessive case to express the relationships between the family members.

```
            Joe ─┬─ Alice
      ┌──────────┴──────────┐
Albert ─┬─ Maddie         Daphne ─┬─ Jack
       Ann                        Mark
```

1 Mark is .... nephew.
2 Alice is .... mother.
3 Albert is .... son.
4 Ann is .... daughter.
5 Maddie is .... daughter-in-law.
6 Mark is .... grandson.
7 Joe is .... father-in-law.
8 Joe and Alice are .... grandparents.
9 Albert is .... husband.
10 Daphne is .... wife.

9 Seven of these sentences contain a mistake. Find and correct them.

1 The greengrocer's near my house sells very nice fruit.   ....
2 I usually have two week' s holiday in July.   ....
3 If you go to London, you must visit St Paul's.   ....
4 Where are the childrens' backpacks?   ....
5 Is James's brother a friend of Thomas?   ....
6 This isn't today's newspaper. It's yesterdays'.   ....
7 I'm going to Peggy's to study history this afternoon.   ....
8 Two UK's top attractions are the Tower of London and Windsor Castle.   ....
9 My office is five minute's walk from the bus station.   ....
10 The team's new coach is Mr Russel.   ....
11 One man's heaven is another man's hell. *(Proverb)*   ....
12 *Knockin' on Heaven's Door* is a Bob Dylan's most famous songs.   ....

10 Complete the sentences with the words and phrases below.

your father's   bicycles   Peter's and John's   girlfriend   Mrs   car   house   some of   students'
Mary and Lucy's   son   one of

1 .... Moulay is Bilal's mother.
2 This is my grandparents' old ....
3 Mr Murray's .... is parked on the other side of the street.
4 Sarah is Tom's ....
5 That is the staff room and this is the .... cafeteria.
6 The children's .... are in the garage.
7 James is Sheila and Frank's ....
8 This is .... bedroom.
9 These are .... bedrooms.
10 Simon is .... Rick's best friends.
11 .... Brenda's photos are published on *National Geographic*.
12 That friend of .... is very nice.

ROUND UP 4

1 Write as many logical sentences as possible with the words in the table.

SUBJECT	VERB	OBJECT	OTHER COMPLEMENTS
I		big responsibilities	
We		three sons but no daughters	
They		a movable roof	
Wimbledon Centre Court		a new email address	in my new job
Robert		some crisps	in our packed lunch
The black rhino	have got	a funny hat	for tomorrow
That girl	has got	a gigantic horn	in my contact list
That man		a lot of homework	in her hand
This mini-van		a beard and a moustache	
A dice		six hundred names	
The Statue of Liberty		eight seats	
		six faces	
		a torch	

2 Complete the text with the correct present simple form of the verbs *be* or *have*.

Steve [1]............. married and [2]............. two children, a boy and a girl. The boy, Jimmy, [3]............. 12 years old and the girl, Christine, [4]............. ten. Steve [5]............. the manager of a big computer shop in town, while his wife, Barbara, [6]............. a doctor at the local hospital. They [7]............. a lovely house in the centre, not far from the shop and the hospital. The house [8]............. a fairly big back garden where they often [9]............. barbecues with friends. They [10]............. a dog too, a golden retriever that loves running in the garden and loves sleeping next to the fireplace in the living room even more.

3 Write negative sentences with *have* using the given words. Be careful! You can't always use the form *haven't / hasn't got*.

1 They / lunch / at home / on weekdays.
....

2 I / a new car. This is my old one.
....

3 Sheila / an umbrella / with her.
....

4 The company / a new sales manager. Mr Jones is still the Chief Buyer.
....

5 We / a sandwich / for lunch / at the weekend.
....

6 That man / a pass. Stop him!
....

7 My parents / a walk / in the evening. They're far too lazy.
....

8 I / a cold. Why are you asking?
....

9 Mark / breakfast at home. He usually goes to a café next to his office.
....

10 Oh dear! I / my wallet with me. Can you lend me some money?
....

> **MATRIX +**
>
> When the verb **have** means *take*, *eat* or *drink* rather than 'possess', it is considered an action verb and so may also be used in the continuous form:
>
> *She's having a shower.   I'm having a cup of tea.*
>
> In the imperative, **have** is used for offers or as a kind of greeting:
>
> *Have a biscuit!   Have a nice day.*

4 Read the sentences and say what the function of *have* is in each: P (possessive case or family relationship), A (action), O (offer), G (greeting).

1 Have a cool drink! It's so hot today! ....
2 That lady's got a beautiful pearl necklace. ....
3 Bye! Have a nice evening and don't come back too late. ....
4 The flat has got two balconies overlooking the park. ....
5 We're having a great time at the seaside. We won't be back till next week! ....
6 Richard hasn't got a brother. He's an only child. ....

5 Use the verb *have* to write suitable questions, offers, invitations or greetings for each sentence.

1 ....?
   No, I don't. I always have a shower.
2 ...., sir.
   Thank you. I'm sure I'll enjoy staying in this hotel.
3 ....?
   No, not measles. Gwen's got chicken pox.
4 ....?
   I've got two sandwiches and an apple in my packed lunch.
5 ....
   Thank you. Your biscuits are delicious, but I've already had a lot.
6 ....?
   Yes, I am. I'm having a break after writing for two hours.
7 Let's ....
   No, please. Not a walk again! I'm really tired.
8 ....?
   Not any more! How can I have a rest if you are around?

6 Complete the mini dialogues with *Whose* and a suitable possessive adjective or pronoun.

1 **Ellen** Are you sure this is [1].......... umbrella, Brad?
  Brad Yes, it must be [2].......... . It's red and blue, exactly like [3].......... . [4].......... else could it be?
  Ellen Well, it could be Sara's. [5].......... is also red and blue and it's near [6].......... desk.
  Brad But Sara's not here today. And anyway it's raining, so I'll take it.

2 **Receptionist** Can I have [7].......... passports, Mrs and Mr Smith?
  Mrs Smith Here you are. This is [8].......... and this is [9].......... .
  Receptionist Thanks. And this is [10].......... key. Are those suitcases [11]..........?
  Mrs Smith No, they're not [12].......... . [13].......... luggage is still in the car. Could you send a porter, please? This is [14].......... car key.
  Receptionist Sure. Which is [15].......... car?
  Mrs Smith The green Jaguar just outside the door.

7 **Each of these sentences contains a mistake. Underline them and rewrite the sentences correctly.**

1 Has Pat usually a snack during the break? ....
2 This is not mine tablet. It's Peter's. ....
3 Jason must be at home. That's her bicycle in the garden. ....
4 Don't wait for me. I'm going to the dentists' and I'll be back late. ....
5 Let's print the students's reports before the end of the lesson. ....
6 Why don't we read a Dickens' novel this year, Miss Pearson? ....
7 'Whose those cars are?' 'I don't know. But they're parked outside our house.' ....
8 Some my friends are coming for dinner tonight. ....

8 **Complete the second sentence so that it has a similar meaning to the first.**

1 Are you wearing one of your father's ties?
  Are you wearing a .... ?
2 A nephew of mine is moving to Australia next month.
  One .... to Australia next month.
3 They painted the walls of the kitchen bright yellow.
  They painted the kitchen ....
4 A neighbour of my sister's has a beautiful German shepherd called Rex.
  One .... called Rex.
5 Some toys of the children's are still in the garden. Let's pick them up before it starts raining.
  Some of .... garden. Let's pick them up before it starts raining.
6 The room door was locked.
  The door ....
7 James lives next to one of his best friends.
  James lives next to a ....
8 Some of Thomas's neighbours are having a barbecue in the garden.
  Some neighbours ....

9 **Complete the text with possessive adjectives and pronouns.**

We are visiting some friends of ¹.......................... in Scotland next June. ².......................... house in the Highlands is quite small but warm and comfortable. Doug is a teacher in the village primary school. Most of ³.......................... students are the children of farmers – called crofters in this region. ⁴.......................... wife Fyfa works at the local post office. ⁵.......................... is a part-time job because she needs to look after ⁶.......................... children. There are three of them, all under seven, and ⁷.......................... main occupation is running around ⁸.......................... grandad's croft. ⁹.......................... grandma is an excellent cook and makes lots of cakes for ¹⁰.......................... grandchildren.

10 Complete the sentences with the most suitable words.

1 I have a terrible toothache. I'm going to the .... this afternoon.
2 I always buy organic fruit and vegetables at the .... in the square.
3 Are you going to the ....? Can you buy some bread for me, please?
4 There's a .... on the corner, but we never go there because we're vegetarian.
5 I have flu. Could you please go to the .... and buy some paracetamol for me?
6 You must go to the .... Your hair is really too long.

MATRIX +

We have seen that plural nouns ending in **–s** only take the apostrophe in the possessive case. As well as this, classical names or surnames of famous people ending in **–s** also only take the apostrophe, even if they are singular:
Euripedes' life
Jesus' miracles
Dickens' novels

11 Complete the sentences with the words in brackets. Use the possessive case.

1 .... are collected in this volume. (Sophocles / plays)
2 We're all meeting at .... (St James / Park)
3 Did you read .... ? (Dickens / biography)
4 The one on the left is .... (Prince Charles / residence)
5 Is this .... ? (Mr Fox / desk)
6 .... is only 14. (Douglas / son)

Reflecting on grammar

Study the rules and decide if the following statements are true or false.

		True	False
1	The verb **have** is always followed by **got**.		
2	The present of the verb **have** has two forms.		
3	With the verb **have**, we never use the auxiliary **do** in the negative and interrogative forms.		
4	The sentence *I haven't got breakfast in the morning* is correct.		
5	Possessive adjectives can be preceded by demonstrative and indefinite adjectives.		
6	For the third person singular, possessive adjectives refer to the possessor.		
7	Possessive pronouns can be preceded by the definite article.		
8	All possessive pronouns except for *mine* end in **–s**.		
9	The sentences *Whose house is this?* and *Whose is this house?* are both correct and mean the same thing.		
10	The sentence *A friend of my husband's often has lunch with us* is correct.		

GRAMMAR MATRIX BASICS

UNIT 5 Imperatives, present simple, adverbs of frequency, time expressions, object pronouns, connectors

LESSON 1 The imperative

	Positive	Negative
Second person singular and plural	Turn right.	Don't turn left.
First person plural	Let's turn right.	Let's not turn left.

In English the imperative has the same form in the second person singular and plural. The positive form of the imperative is the same as the base form of the verb. To be more emphatic, we can add **do** at the beginning of the sentence:
Do think about it!

The negative form takes **don't** or **do not** before the verb:
Don't touch it!

- In the second person, the imperative is used to give orders, instructions or advice to one or more people:
  Do this.

  or to tell someone not to do something:
  Don't do this.

- In polite requests, the imperative is often used with **please** or **will you**?
  Come here, please.
  Take the dog for a walk, will you?

- It is also used for
  invitations: *Come and see me tomorrow.*
  offers: *Have some crisps.*
  wishes: *Have a good time!*

The first person plural form of the imperative is formed with **Let's** (**Let us**) + the base form of the verb.

The negative form (which is not very common) is **Let's not** + the base form of the verb. It's used to make suggestions:
Let's do something together.
Let's not do this.

1 Circle the correct option.

1 Claire, **give** / **let's give** that pencil back to your friend.
2 Please, **sit** / **let's sit** down here, Ms Pearson.
3 **Wait** / **Don't wait** here to be seated.
4 Here… **don't have** / **have** a cup of tea.
5 **Don't** / **Let's** go to the new store. It's great!
6 **Don't** / **Let's** even think of buying that necklace. It's too expensive.
7 **Enjoy** / **Let's enjoy** your holiday!
8 **Let's go** / **Let's not go** out tonight. It's too cold and wet.

2 Complete the sentences with the positive (+) or negative (−) form of the imperative. Choose from the verbs below:

walk   remember   turn   write   sit   read   jump   be   tell   lie

1 (+) .... down when the bus is moving and (−) .... up and down!
2 (−) .... in the sun at midday. You may get sunburned.
3 (+) .... down this street for about 50 metres and then (+) .... left.
4 (+) .... this novel during the summer and then (+) .... a review of it in about 300 words.
5 (−) .... anyone. It's a secret.
6 (−) .... late tomorrow and (+) .... to bring your equipment.

3 Complete the suggestions using the positive (+) or negative (−) imperative in the first person plural. Choose from the verbs below.

buy   make   work   play   watch   have   go

1 (+) .... a cake for Mum's birthday.
2 (+) .... in groups to study for the exam.
3 (−) .... food here. It's really expensive. (+) .... to the market.
4 (−) .... this film. I've already seen it and it isn't very good.
5 (+) .... another game. I want to win this time.
6 Aren't you hungry? (+) .... something to eat.

LESSON 2 Present simple

→ Visual Grammar pages 406–407

Positive form

| I / you / we / they | work |
| he / she / it | works |

The positive form of the **present simple** is the same as the base form of the verb. It is the same for all persons except the third person singular, where we add an **−s** to the base form.

Be careful with the following spelling rules:

- if the verb ends in **ss, sh, ch, x, o**, we add **−es**, for example:

  pass → passes, wish → wishes, catch → catches, fix → fixes, go → goes

- if the verb ends in **y** preceded by a consonant, the **y** is replaced by **−ies**, for example:

  try → tries   but stay → stays (no change because the y is preceded by a vowel)

1 Write the third person singular of the verbs below in the correct column.

kiss   play   cry   study   do   wash   watch   mix   like
marry   prefer   tidy   find   pass   reply   ask   say   hurry

−s	−es	−ies

2 Write sentences using different subjects, as in the example.

0 I play volleyball.   Sara *plays volleyball, too.* ....
1 I study Russian.   Thomas ....
2 My sister goes to university.   I ....
3 I live in Manchester.   My cousin ....
4 My mother loves antique furniture. I ....
5 She gets up at seven o'clock.   I ....
6 I miss my friends.   He ....
7 I watch a lot of TV.   My boyfriend ....

3 Complete the sentences using the present simple of the verbs in brackets.

1 Pippa ………………… her room every Saturday morning. (tidy)
2 Tom ………………… hockey three times a week. (play)
3 Dad always ………………… the car at the weekend. (wash)
4 Chris ………………… his homework in the evening. (do)
5 My brother ………………… to work early in the morning. (go)
6 David ………………… the bus nearly every morning. (miss)
7 Maria always ………………… on time. (arrive)
8 She often ………………… up late in the evening. (stay)

Negative form

| I / you / we / they | don't work |
| he / she / it | doesn't work |

! In the negative form, we use **do not** or the short form **don't** between the subject and the base form of the verb. In the third person singular, we use **does not** or the short form **doesn't**.

Short forms are the most commonly used, while full forms are used when we want to be emphatic:
We do not know him.
Do can be used for emphasis even in positive sentences: *We do know him.*

4 Choose the correct options.

1 Liz doesn't **checks / check** emails at the weekend.
2 My father **don't wears / doesn't wear** a suit and a tie on Sundays.
3 The twins **don't go / not go** to the gym in the evenings.
4 My brothers **don't study / they not study** after dinner.
5 Danny **gets not / doesn't get** up early on Sunday mornings.

5 Rewrite the sentences using the negative form.

1 Frances dances very well.
   …………………………………………………
2 She likes romantic novels.
   …………………………………………………
3 We have lunch at school.
   …………………………………………………
4 They work in a hospital.
   …………………………………………………
5 Catherine plays the violin.
   …………………………………………………
6 We go shopping on Mondays.
   …………………………………………………
7 The film starts at 9.00.
   …………………………………………………
8 He goes to work by car.
   …………………………………………………

6 Complete the sentences using *don't* or *doesn't* and one of the verbs below.

go (x2)   watch   work (x2)   play   have

1 James ………………… breakfast.
2 My sister works in an office, she ………………… to university.
3 Rosie ………………… tennis.
4 My parents ………………… often ………………… TV in the evening.
5 I ………………… in a shop. I'm a vet, so I work in a surgery.
6 'You ………………… to work on Saturdays, right?' 'Yes, that's right. I ………………… at weekends.'

Interrogative form and short answers

Do I / you / we / they work?	• Yes, I / you / we / they do. • No, I / you / we / they don't.
Does he / she / it work?	• Yes, he / she / it does. • No, he / she / it doesn't.

To form questions, **do** or **does** precedes the subject and the base form of the verb.

To form short answers, we use **Yes** or **No** followed by the subject pronoun and the auxiliary **do / does** in the positive or negative form.

To make a negative question, we put **do** or **does** + **not** before the subject:
Don't you like this painting?
Doesn't Tom work with you?

Questions starting with a **Wh–** word have the following structure:
Wh– word + **do / does** + base form of the verb + ?
Where do you live?
What does he want?
When do they start work?

7 Complete the questions with *do / does* and write short answers.

1 .... you have free wi-fi?
Yes, ...

2 .... Mark live near the school?
No, ...

3 .... the children like the zoo?
Yes, ...

4 .... your father speak Spanish?
Yes, ...

5 .... you and your friends go jogging every day? Yes, ...

6 .... she play a musical instrument?
No, ...

7 .... you know the password?
No, ...

8 .... they like going to parties?
No, ...

8 Reorder the words and write questions.

1 do / When / you / do / homework / your / ?
....

2 does / Where / come / your best friend / from / ?
....

3 music / What / of / kind / do / like / they / ?
....

4 does / How much / that / cost / smartphone / ?
....

5 Which / do / like / you / song / best / ?
....

6 have / you / What / do / breakfast / for / ?
....

9 Match the questions in exercise 8 to the correct answers.

☐ A I have yoghurt and fruit.
☐ B They like heavy metal.
☐ C We usually do it in the evening.
☐ D I prefer the first one.
☐ E He comes from the Philippines.
☐ F About £100.

10 Complete the questions for these answers.

1 'What .... on Sundays?' 'We usually get up at 9.00.'

2 'How ....?' 'I go to work by car.'

3 'Who .... Michael .... with the housework?' 'His mum.'

4 'Where ....?' 'I usually meet my friends at the park.'

5 'When .... abroad?' 'I go abroad in the summer. We have a house in Spain.'

6 'Why .... with her grandparents?' 'Because her parents are in Dubai at the moment.'

Uses of the present simple

The **present simple** is the tense that is used for:
- fixed times, such as the arrival and departure times of means of transport, office opening and closing times, and the start and finish time of events:
  The train leaves at 7.35 and arrives at 9.25.
- habitual actions:
  I usually check my emails in the evening.
- facts that are always true, including scientific and universal truths:
  The sun rises in the east.
- situations that do not change, such as where a person lives or what occupation they have:
  I live in Italy, but I work in Switzerland.

FAQ

Q: I work as a shop assistant, but I have a fixed-term contract, so it is not a permanent job. And at the moment I'm living at my cousin's house. To talk about this situation, should I still use the present simple?

A: If you want to make it clear that this situation is temporary, you should use the present continuous: **I'm working as a shop assistant. I'm living at my cousin's.** And maybe add **at the moment** (see pages 94–95).

The **present simple** is also used with verbs that express:
- likes and preferences: **like, love, prefer, hate**
  I like rap, but he prefers jazz.
- mental activity: **know, remember, understand, mean**
  I don't know what you mean.
- your will: **want, wish**
  I want to go home.
- opinion, agreement and disagreement: **think, believe, agree, disagree**
  What do you think?
- possession: **own, belong, have**
  My family owns and runs a small restaurant.
- the senses: **feel, sound, look, smell**
  This cake looks nice. And it smells nice, too.

11 Decide if the sentences are correct (✓) or incorrect (✗). Correct those that are incorrect.

1 Water freeze at 0°C and boil at 100°C. ....
2 The museum closes at 6.00 pm. ....
3 The match doesn't starts at three o'clock. ....
4 This laptop don't belongs to the teacher. ....
5 What you think of this plan? ....
6 Her voice sounds weak tonight. ....
7 I doesn't agree with you. ....
8 Sam hates going shopping. ....
9 Do they want to eat out tonight? ....
10 He doesn't believes his team can win today. ....
11 Does he wants to go to the cinema with us? ....
12 The Earth takes 365 days to go round the Sun. ....

LESSON 3 Adverbs of frequency and expressions of time

Adverbs of frequency

To say how often an action happens, we use **adverbs of frequency**:

always
usually
often
sometimes
occasionally
seldom / rarely
never

always	usually	often	sometimes	occasionally	seldom / rarely	never
100%	80%	60%	30%	20%	10%	0%

Position of adverbs of frequency

The structure of a sentence with the **present simple** and an adverb of frequency is as follows:

- **Positive sentences: subject + adverb + verb**

  I **never** use my car to go to work.
  I **always** take the bus.

  ! However, in sentences with **be**, the adverb follows the verb: I am **always** hungry at this time of day.

- **Negative sentences**:
  subject + **don't / doesn't** + adverb + verb

  I don't **usually** get up late on Sundays.

- **Interrogative**:
  (**Wh– word**) + **do / does** + subject + adverb + verb + ?

  When do you **usually** have a break?
  Do you **ever** come to this hotel?

FAQ

Q: I've often heard sentences such as **I go to concerts sometimes.** Or even **Sometimes I go to concerts.** Shouldn't it be **I sometimes go to concerts**?

A: All three sentences are correct. **Sometimes** is a 'mobile' adverb, which may also be positioned at the beginning or end of a sentence.

1 Rewrite the sentences putting the adverb in the correct position.

1. We meet for a drink after work. (occasionally)
   ....
2. My brother is at home in the evening. (never)
   ....
3. Where do you have lunch? (usually)
   ....
4. He listens to classical music. (sometimes)
   ....
5. I don't go to the theatre. (often)
   ....
6. They are at school in the morning. (always)
   ....
7. My friend eats meat. (rarely)
   ....
8. We see each other at weekends. (never)
   ....

2 Add adverbs of frequency so that these sentences are true for you.

1. I go to the market on Saturday morning.
2. I am at home in the mornings.
3. I play tennis at the weekend.
4. I sleep till late on Sunday morning.
5. I go to the theatre with my friends.

3 Reorder the words to make sentences.

1 seldom / They / piano / lessons / have / in / morning / the / .
2 often / Internet / surfs / the / Greg / in / evening / the / .
3 This / is / train / time / on / usually / .
4 Mum / Does / come / late / from / back / ever / work / ?
5 sometimes / Jill / works / at / weekend / the / .

How often…? and time phrases

We can answer the question **How often…?** with an adverb of frequency or one of the following time phrases expressing frequency:

every day / week / month…

on Saturdays / Sundays… (days of the week with a plural **–s** ending, meaning every Saturday / Sunday)

at the weekend

once…
twice…
three / four times…
a day / month / year…

These time expressions usually appear at the end of the sentence:

'**How often** do you have a piano lesson?' 'I have a piano lesson **once a week**, on Tuesday afternoon.'

4 Match questions and answers.

1 Do you ever play sports during the week?
2 Does the supermarket open before eight?
3 How often do you go to the cinema?
4 How often does Dan come back from college?
5 When do you usually visit your grandparents?
6 Do you ever have a lie-in on Sunday mornings?

A Yes, but only on Wednesday mornings when it opens at 7.30.
B Every weekend! He's quite lucky.
C About once a month, but I watch lots of films on TV.
D Yes, quite often, especially in winter.
E Yes, I train with my team twice a week.
F On Sundays. We often have lunch together.

1 ….. 2 ….. 3 ….. 4 ….. 5 ….. 6 …..

5 Write at least six logical questions using the words in the table.

Where How much How What time When How often	do does	these shoes the post office the yoga course your parents the bus this book this machine you the shops	stop? leave? cost? work? open? start? practise? close?

……………………………………………
……………………………………………
……………………………………………
……………………………………………
……………………………………………
……………………………………………

6 Replace the underlined words with an expression showing frequency, as in the example.

0 Matt works out in the gym <u>on Tuesdays and Thursdays</u>. → *twice a week*
1 I go to school <u>from Monday to Friday</u>. ………
2 We go to the beach <u>in July and September</u>. ………
3 My parents go on a cruise <u>in May</u>. ………
4 I meet my friends <u>on Monday, Tuesday, Wednesday, Thursday, Friday, Saturday and Sunday</u>. ………
5 Take these tablets <u>in the morning and in the evening</u>. ………
6 We get our school report <u>in January, June and December</u>. ………
7 We have a maths test <u>on the 4th, 10th, 16th and 27th of each month</u>. ………

LESSON 4 Object pronouns and some conjunctions

Subject	I	you	he	she	it	we	you	they
	↓	↓	↓	↓	↓	↓	↓	↓
Object	me	you	him	her	it	us	you	them

The position of **object pronouns** is:

- after a verb:
  Why don't you love me?
- after a preposition, for example **with, for, to, at** :
  I want to be with you.
  I'm waiting for them.

Focus

In English, the object pronoun is always separate from the verb, even if it is pronounced as if it were a single word: *Tell him...   Give me...*
The object pronoun always follows the verb In English:
I know her.

1 Complete the sentences with object pronouns.

1 I like that jacket. Do you like ....?
2 Those jeans are nice. I want to try .... on.
3 We're going home now. Are you coming with .... ?
4 'Are you writing to Tom?' 'No, I'm not writing to ....'
5 Look! That's Angela. Let's call ....
6 Here's a present for .... , Louise. Happy birthday!
7 Peter and Bev? I'm going to meet .... at the pub right now.
8 I'm going shopping in a minute. Do you want to come with .... ?

2 Reorder the words to make sentences.

1 talking / Are / to / you / me / ?
2 present / Here's / a / you / , / Dad / for / !
3 her / I / know / very / don't / well / .
4 like / I / very / it / much / .
5 They / us / are / with / coming / .
6 for / Can / please / wait / you / me / , / ?

3 Replace the underlined nouns with subject or object pronouns.

1 <u>Lucy</u> is going to meet <u>her uncle</u> at the airport.
2 Do you want to play with <u>me and my friend</u>?
3 Give <u>this notebook</u> to <u>Sarah</u>, please.
4 <u>John</u> wants to buy <u>this T-shirt</u>.
5 Who's going with <u>Harry</u>? <u>Harry</u>'s got a big car.
6 Listen to <u>your mother</u>! <u>Your mother</u>'s probably right.
7 Where are <u>my glasses</u>? I can't find <u>my glasses</u>.
8 Can you meet <u>my friends</u> at the station? <u>My friends</u> are arriving at 2.00.

Conjunctions

To link two or more elements within a phrase, or two **clauses** within a sentence, we use **conjunctions**, also known as **connectors**.

The most common conjunctions are:
and   but   or
so   because

And is used to add one element to another:
I speak English and French.

But is used to contrast one element with another:
I speak English, but I don't speak French.

Or gives an alternative:
You can have a cake or a sandwich.

So introduces a consequence:
I've missed the bus, so I'll be late for school.

Because gives a reason:
I'm late because I missed the bus.

4 Choose the correct options.

1 Please stop here **because / so / and** that's my house.
2 They like studying together **because / so / but** they meet at my house every day.
3 I usually have a shower in the morning **but / and / or** then I have breakfast.
4 Can you make me a cup of tea **so / or / but** a hot chocolate, please?
5 Do your maths homework now **so / or / but** we can go out later.
6 We often watch a film **but / so / or** a quiz after dinner.
7 Do you really want to have both chocolate cake **or / and / so** ice cream?
8 Don't sit on that chair **so / but / because** it's broken!

5 Complete the sentences with suitable conjunctions.

1 I sometimes have bacon .... eggs for breakfast.
2 Gary plays baseball, ... he can't play basketball.
3 We're late, ... we'd better take a taxi.
4 We can go to the cinema .... stay at home .... watch a video.
5 Let's meet at 3.00 .... 3.30. What time is best for you?
6 Fish .... chips is typical English street food.
7 We can't visit the museum now .... it's closed on Mondays.
8 I'm putting on weight, ... I want to go on a diet.

6 Join the two sentences with a suitable conjunction.

0 My friends have a beautiful house. They also have big garden.
My friends have a beautiful house and a big garden.

1 Go to the science lab quickly. Your teacher is waiting for you.
....

2 Would you like an apple? Would you prefer an orange?
....

3 Come before five. We can have a nice chat this way.
....

4 Steve is a nice boy. He's a bit lazy.
....

5 My son helps me at home. He can't cook though.
....

7 Complete the dialogue with suitable object pronouns or conjunctions from those below.

them (x5)   him   me   because   and (x3)   so   or   but

Sarah The German guys are arriving in two weeks' time for the school exchange, remember?

Sam Oh yes, that's right.

Sarah Are you going to host any of ¹............................ , Sam?

Sam Yes, I'm going to host a boy called Hans. I saw ²............................ in a video he sent ³............................ . What about you, Sarah?

Sarah No, I'm not hosting anyone ⁴............................ we don't have a spare room, ⁵............................ mine is too small for two beds.

Sam We are going to organise a welcome party for ⁶............................ , aren't we, Sarah?

Sarah Sure. On Friday night. ⁷............................ not at the school. We're going to have the party at the youth club.

Sam Great! ⁸............................ who's going to meet ⁹............................ at the airport?

Sarah I am. My dad's got a minibus ¹⁰............................ we're going to drive ¹¹............................ to their host families' homes.

Sam Why don't we take ¹²............................ bowling one night?

Sarah Good idea. ¹³............................ we can go for a pizza ¹⁴............................ to the cinema another day.

8 Complete the passage with the missing words. They can be pronouns (both subject and object), possessive adjectives, conjunctions or prepositions.

Liz doesn't like school much, ¹............................ she likes weekends! On Saturdays ²............................ doesn't get up early ³............................ she often stays out till late on Friday night. When she goes downstairs ⁴............................ about ten, she makes ⁵............................ own breakfast ⁶............................ her parents usually go shopping in the morning. ⁷............................ favourite shopping place is the big street market ⁸............................ the main square, ⁹............................ they leave home around nine and hardly ever come back before midday.

After breakfast, Liz phones her friends ¹⁰............................ invites ¹¹............................ round for coffee. ¹²............................ best friend Violet often stays for lunch too ¹³............................ both her mother ¹⁴............................ her father work all day Saturday.

Violet ¹⁵............................ Liz go out together in the afternoon, ¹⁶............................ they don't go to market; they prefer the big department store in the High Street. There they find ¹⁷............................ favourite clothes and make up, ¹⁸............................ they don't always buy ¹⁹............................ , they often only try ²⁰............................ on.

ROUND UP 5

MATRIX +

Orders and prohibitions

- Orders, requests and prohibitions may be expressed with the imperative form of the verb, but may also be expressed in other ways:

    Listen carefully! → *You must listen carefully. / It is important that you listen carefully. / It is important for you to listen carefully. / It is essential that you listen carefully.*
    Wait for me please! → *Can you please wait for me?*
    Don't cross here! → *You mustn't cross here. / You can't cross here.*
    On road signs and notices → *No entry. / No smoking. / No fishing.*

Advice, offers and suggestions

- Advice may be expressed using a verb in the imperative form, but may be given in other ways:

    Don't be shy. Always try. → *You shouldn't be shy. You should always try.*

- To offer something:

    Have a cup of tea! → *Will you have a cup of tea? / Would you like a cup of tea? / Do you want a cup of tea? / How about a cup of tea?*

- Suggestions may be made using the imperative (**let's...**), but also in other ways:

    Let's go skating! → *Why don't we go skating? / How about going skating? / What about going skating? / Shall we go skating?* Also see page 280.

1 Write sentences with the same meaning using the imperative form or a different phrase from the box above.

1. You must always wear gloves and a mask.
   ....
2. You can't park your car here.
   ....
3. Will you have some coffee?
   ....
4. How about going to the leisure centre?
   ....
5. Why don't we have an ice cream?
   ....
6. You should read this novel. It's really good.
   ....
7. It is important that you read the instructions before you start.
   ....
8. Why don't we talk about it?
   ....
9. You should never give up.
   ....
10. Can you please come here?
    ....

2 Match the sentence halves in a logical way.

1 Don't eat
2 Always close
3 Come here
4 Put the lid
5 Wear
6 Carry your key
7 Go
8 Please don't
9 Give it
10 Stop

A the door of the fridge.
B with you at all times.
C away!
D be angry!
E all the biscuits.
F immediately!
G on the pan.
H warm clothes. It's cold.
I shouting!
J back to me, please.

1 ..... 2 ..... 3 ..... 4 ..... 5 ..... 6 ..... 7 ..... 8 ..... 9 ..... 10 .....

3 Say if the following statements are orders (O), prohibitions (P), advice (A), offers (OF) or suggestions (S).

1 Don't touch the leaves of that plant. They are poisonous! ....
2 I think you should be more optimistic. ....
3 Why don't we drive to the coast at the weekend? ....
4 Have a biscuit! ....
5 Take the dictionary from the top shelf! ....
6 Would you like something to drink? ....
7 Let's walk to the station. It's a nice day! ....
8 No fishing in this pond! ....
9 Paul should be more active. He's too lazy. ....
10 Do you want another blanket? It may be cold tonight. ....
11 Read the instructions before using this appliance. ....
12 Shall we visit the photo exhibition now? ....

4 Match the road signs to the instructions.

1 Don't drive faster than 20 mph.
2 Give priority to vehicles from opposite direction.
3 No overtaking.
4 Motor vehicles aren't allowed in this street.
5 You can't turn right.
6 No U-turns.
7 You can't stop here.
8 Turn left ahead.
9 No entry.
10 No cycling.

1 ..... 2 ..... 3 ..... 4 ..... 5 ..... 6 ..... 7 ..... 8 ..... 9 ..... 10 .....

5 Write the questions (*Yes / No* questions or *Wh–* questions) in the present simple for these answers.

1 .... ?
Yes, I do. I have piano lessons every Monday.

2 .... ?
No, she doesn't. She never eats meat. She's vegetarian.

3 .... ?
Yes, they do. They spend a few days in the Alps every summer.

4 .... ?
I study Spanish as a foreign language.

5 .... ?
We have basketball practice three times a week.

6 .... ?
I prefer the blue dress.

7 .... ?
My sister works in a hospital. She's a nurse.

8 .... ?
My parents? They live in Canada.

9 .... ?
We often go jogging at the weekend.

10 .... ?
No, we hardly ever go to the theatre because there isn't one in our little town.

11 .... ?
No, we never go to the mountains in summer.

12 .... ?
The Sales Manager's office? It's on the third floor.

13 .... ?
In the evening? My grandfather watches TV.

14 .... ?
We go to the cinema once a week. We like it!

6 Complete the dialogue with the words below.

can sign   you say   Get me (x2)   give me   Why don't you   go and see   Turn down

Sarah Rob! I'm thirsty. ¹.. a cola!

Rob   Please.

Sarah ².. a cola, please.

Rob   Okay, lazy sister. Here you are.

Sarah The doorbell's ringing. Rob, ³.. who it is.

Rob   It's DHL. A parcel for you.

Sarah I'm watching a film. You ⁴.. for delivery.

Rob   All right. […] Here's your parcel. […] Don't ⁵.. thank you?

Sarah Oh, yeah… ⁶.. the music, Rob! I can't hear the film. And I hate that band!

Rob   No, they're cool… Now, ⁷.. the remote. I want to watch the news.

Sarah ⁸.. watch the news on your tablet? I'm watching the TV.

Rob   Sarah, you're horrible!

7 **Complete the dialogue using the verbs below in the present simple positive form.**

catch (x2)   get up   say   work   go (x2)   finish   like   sleep   prefer

Dawn A proverb ¹............................ 'The early bird ².............................
the worm.' But you always ³............................ till nine or ten in
the morning!

Matt And I still ⁴............................ lots of worms! I'm an owl.
I ⁵............................ working in the evenings and I always
⁶............................ to bed very late. The firm for which I
⁷............................ is quite flexible on working hours luckily.
The important thing is that I ⁸............................ my work on time.

Dawn My brother is just like you. He usually ⁹............................ after
nine and ¹⁰............................ to bed at 1 or 2 a.m. But I
¹¹............................ the early hours. I have a lot more energy
in the morning.

8 **Complete the dialogue with the correct subject and object pronouns.**

Tom We love this band. Do you like ¹............................?

Linda Yes, I do. I think ²............................ are great.

Tom So why don't you go to the concert with Dave and ³............................ next week?

Dave Come on, join ⁴............................!

Linda Sorry, ⁵............................ can't come to the concert with ⁶............................ . I'm working for my
exam.

Tom Oh well, we'll tell ⁷............................ all about it when we get back!

Reflecting on grammar

Study the rules and decide if the following statements are true or false.

		True	False
1	The first person plural of the imperative form is made using **Let's…**		
2	There are two different forms of the imperative for the second person singular and plural.		
3	The positive form of the present simple is the same for all persons.		
4	The present simple is used to talk about habitual actions and situations that are always true.		
5	The negative form of *He knows* is *He doesn't knows*.		
6	**Always** is the opposite of **never**.		
7	In a positive sentence, adverbs of frequency usually go after the verb.		
8	The pronouns **you** and **it** may be both subject and object pronouns.		
9	Orders can only be expressed with the imperative.		
10	The conjunction **so** introduces a consequence.		

GRAMMAR MATRIX BASICS

UNIT 6 –ing form and present continuous

LESSON 1 –ing form

As a verb form, when we talk about the **–ing** form, it's the same as talking about the present participle or the gerund:
*I saw a man **walking** up and down the street.* (This means the same as saying that **the man was walking**.)
*I bought a lot of stuff in the sales, **spending** very little money.* (This means **and we spent**.)

It is usually formed by adding the suffix **–ing** to the base form of the verb:
eat → eating, look → looking,
study → studying, play → playing

Note the following spelling variations:

- We cut the final **–e** if it is not pronounced:
  hope → hoping, come → coming
  BUT: see → seeing, be → being (The final **–e** is pronounced.)

Note: In some verbs we keep the final **–e** even when it is silent to avoid confusion:
dye → dyeing

- We double the final consonant with:
  – verbs of one syllable, which end with a single consonant preceded by a single vowel:
  stop → stopping, sit → sitting
  BUT: beat → beating, meet → meeting (two vowels),
  send → sending (two consonants)
  – verbs of two syllables where the stress falls on the second syllable, and which end in a single consonant preceded by a single vowel:
  refer → referring, admit → admitting
  BUT: offer → offering (The stress falls on the first syllable.)
  repeat → repeating (two vowels in the second syllable)
  adopt → adopting (two final consonants)

- The final diphthong **–ie** is changed into **–y**:
  lie → lying, tie → tying, die → dying

FAQ

Q: I once wrote the word **traveling** and the computer marked it as a spelling error. How come?

A: Your computer was almost certainly set up for British English spelling. **Traveling** is correct in American English, but in British English, verbs that end in **–l** preceded by a single vowel double the **l**, so you should have written **travelling**. The same is true for **counsel → counselling** (UK) / **counseling** (USA). But **feel → feeling** (double vowel).

1 Write the *–ing* form of the verbs.

put	....	watch	....	leave	....
write	....	enter	....	answer	....
read	....	ask	....	lie	....
dance	....	hit	....	think	....
live	....	try	....	behave	....
stay	....	marvel (USA)	....	work	....
transmit	....	commit	....	suffer	....
refer	....	wait	....	stop	....
dye	....	type	....	change	....
play	....	paint	....	copy	....
rise	....	get	....	shout	....

The –**ing** form can be used as:
- a verb, with **be** in the progressive or continuous form → *It's raining.* (See Lesson 2 below.)
- a noun (or verbal noun) → *Swimming is my favourite sport. I like swimming.*

As you can see, when used as a noun, the –**ing** form can be either the subject of a sentence or the object of another verb:
Finding *a job is not easy.* (subject)
I hate **watching** *horror films.* (object)

- an adjective → *It's an **interesting** magazine. They're having an **exciting** holiday in the Caribbean.*

2 Underline the –*ing* form in these sentences and write V where it functions as a verb, N where it functions as a noun and A where it is an adjective.

0 The children are <u>playing</u> video games as usual. V
1 Playing tennis is one of his favourite activities. .....
2 I'm having a geography lesson in a few minutes. .....
3 She really loves working out in the gym. .....
4 Oh dear! That's such a heartbreaking story! .....
5 We're leaving for Paris next week. .....
6 That is shocking news. .....
7 Congratulations! You're doing a really great job. .....
8 Most people are interested in learning English. .....

3 Reorder the words and write logical sentences.

1 is / Dad / exotic / cooking / an / meal / tonight / .
   ....
2 hobby / Knitting / is / favourite / Rachel's / .
   ....
3 I / drawing / enjoy / painting / and / .
   ....
4 performance / so / Her / disappointing / was / !
   ....
5 really / Japanese / is / challenging / Learning / .
   ....
6 moving / is / a / film / This / deeply / .
   ....

LESSON 2 Present continuous

→ **Visual Grammar pages 408–409**

Positive form

We use the **present continuous** to describe actions that are happening at the moment of speaking or around the time of speaking:

The boys and girls are chatting in the students' room.
Mr Reeds, the new customers are waiting in the hall.
Susan is working a lot this week.

The positive form of the **present continuous** is constructed as follows:

I	am	–*ing* form of the main verb
He / She / It	is	
We / You / They	are	

Since the **present continuous** is formed with the auxiliary **be**, this tense also has a short form, which is more commonly used than the full form:

I'm	–*ing* form
He's / She's / It's / Jack's	
We're / You're / They're	

91

1 Complete the sentences with the present continuous of the verbs in brackets.

1. The students .... maths exercises for tomorrow's test. (do)
2. Alice .... a nice T-shirt. (wear)
3. Tom .... breakfast right now. (have)
4. Some people .... in the street. (walk)
5. Kate .... TV. (watch)
6. John and Harry .... football in the park. (play)
7. Jasmine .... dressed for the party. (get)
8. I .... a text to my friend in the UK. (write)
9. We .... some food for tonight. (buy)
10. Mark .... his girlfriend. (text)

2 Complete the sentences with the positive form of the present continuous of the verbs below. Where possible, use the short form.

stay   study   file   run   talk   lie   have (x2)   leave   work

1. The secretary .... some documents.
2. My brother .... at San Francisco State University.
3. The President .... to Congress right now.
4. The students .... to their class because they're late.
5. The ship .... New York harbour.
6. We .... in the sun.
7. My friends .... at a four-star hotel by the sea.
8. I'm sorry. Ms Sunis .... lunch at the moment. She can't talk to you right now.
9. Dad is busy right now. He .... dinner.
10. Sam .... on the roof. He can't talk to you on the phone.

Negative form

The **negative form** of the present continuous corresponds to the negative form of **be**:

| subject | am / is / are | not | –ing form |

The short form is the most commonly used form in the negative, too:
I'm not watching TV.
He isn't playing with the children.
We aren't leaving now.
I'm sorry you aren't having a good time.
They aren't working today.

3 Rewrite the sentences from exercise 2 in the negative form. Make all necessary changes.

1. ....
2. ....
3. ....
4. ....
5. ....
6. ....
7. ....
8. ....
9. ....
10. ....

4 Reorder the words to write negative sentences in the present continuous.

0 we / take / any photos
   We aren't taking any photos.
1 Julie / read / a magazine
   ....
2 My parents / meet / their friends
   ....
3 You / study / history
   ....
4 They / drink / tea
   ....
5 Ben / play / football
   ....
6 I / go / to the park / this afternoon
   ....
7 They / file / documents
   ....

5 Complete the sentences using the positive or negative form of the present continuous of the verbs below.

play (x2)   study (x2)   enjoy   go   cook   write   sleep   come

1 I .... maths, I .... history because I have a test tomorrow.
2 Kate? No, she definitely .... tennis. She hates it.
3 The twins .... tonight – James is making the main course and Steve is making dessert.
4 I .... the party at all. I don't know anybody here, and the music is awful.
5 Can you turn down the music? The children ....
6 I .... on my computer! I .... really .... an email to my German key pal!
7 We .... to the cinema tonight. Our friends .... for dinner and I'm cooking paella.

Interrogative form

In the **interrogative form**, there is also a correspondence with the verb **be**. **Yes / No** questions are answered with **short answers**:

Are you going out?
• Yes, I am.
• No, I'm not.

Is he / she / it going out?
• Yes, he / she / it is.
• No, he / she / it isn't.

Are you / we / they going out?
• Yes, we / you / they are.
• No, we / you / they aren't.

Am / Is / Are + subject + **–ing** form + ?
'Are you cooking dinner?' 'Yes, I am.'
'Is Dan coming home late tonight?' 'No, he isn't.'

Negative interrogatives are formed as follows:
Aren't / Isn't + subject + **–ing** form + ?
Aren't they working this afternoon?
Isn't Mum having a rest?

As you can see from the table, **short answers** are formed in exactly the same way as for the verb **be**. (See page 31)

Wh– questions are usually formed by putting the **question word** before the verb **be**:
Question word + **am / is / are** + subject + **–ing** form + ?
What am I doing here?
Why are you talking so loud?

6 Match questions and answers.

1. What are the children doing?
2. Where's Jack posting his photos?
3. Why are you spending hours on your computer?
4. Why are they laughing so loudly?
5. What are you doing?
6. Are you playing offline?

A Because I'm looking for my old school mates.
B I'm chatting with my friend.
C No, I'm playing online.
D On all the social networks!
E They're playing upstairs.
F Because they're watching a funny film.

1 ..... 2 ..... 3 ..... 4 ..... 5 ..... 6 .....

7 Write questions and short answers in the present continuous using the prompts.

0 Paula / talk to Phil on the phone? Yes.
Is Paula talking to Phil on the phone?
Yes, she is.

1 your brother / sleep / on the sofa? Yes.
....

2 Jo and Tamsin / act / in the school play? Yes.
....

3 she / not watch / TV / tonight? Yes.
....

4 they / have breakfast / now? No.
....
....

5 Tom / not iron / his shirts? No.
....
....

6 you / not study / for your test tomorrow? Yes.
....
....

7 the train / leave / in ten minutes? No.
....
....

8 Rob / take part / in the tennis tournament? Yes.
....
....

8 Write questions for these answers.

0 *Aren't you working today* ....? Working? No, it's my day off.
1 ....? Staying at home? No, we're going for a walk this afternoon.
2 ....? Yes, we're going out. We're going to a concert.
3 ....? Yes, I am listening to my favourite rock band!
4 ....? Tom? No, I'm not chatting with him.
5 ....? Because we don't have any homework today, Mum.
6 ....? They're running because the train is leaving.
7 ....? I'm playing with my little sister.

> **Uses of the present continuous**
>
> The **present continuous** is the tense used to talk about actions taking place at the moment of speaking. It is also used:
>
> - when speaking on the phone:
>   *I'm studying right now, Ann. I can't chat with you.*
>
> - when describing a scene or a picture:
>   *The person in the middle is sitting on a chair.*

> In these functions, the **present continuous** is often used with adverbs or expressions of time such as:
> **now** or **right now**
> **at the moment**
> **at present**

It is also used to talk about:

- an action that has started but is not yet finished, even if it is not happening at the moment of speaking:
  She's taking a course in business and administration.
- temporary activities, describing things that are different from what we usually do:
  I'm working at the school cafeteria this month.
- frequently repeated actions, which often annoy the speaker:
  He's always playing video games and not doing anything else and that annoys me.
- a definite arrangement in the near future:
  We're leaving tomorrow at 5 pm.

> When expressing future arrangements, the **present continuous** is generally used with adverbs and time expressions such as:
> **tonight**
> **tomorrow**
> **next week / month / summer…**
> Often, the precise time is mentioned → **tomorrow at four o'clock**

9 Match each sentence to its use.

1. We're meeting the counsellor tomorrow morning at ten.
2. Two people are walking in the rain. They're holding a big umbrella.
3. Mark is attending a painting course this term.
4. Sorry, Fran. I'm driving. I'll ring you back later.
5. This week Rebecca is standing in for a colleague in the new office in Marlowe Road.
6. He's always looking at his mobile phone, even when we're having lunch together.

A Speaking on the phone
B Speaking about a temporary activity, different to what we usually do
C Describing a picture
D Talking about an annoying action
E Talking about an action in progress at this time
F Talking about a definite arrangement in the near future

1 ..... 2 ..... 3 ..... 4 ..... 5 ..... 6 .....

10 Complete the sentences with the words below.

tonight   right   these   next   tomorrow   this   always   nowadays

1. Laura is .... chatting with Ann during the lessons. It's so annoying.
2. 'Are you going to the cinema ....?' 'Yes, we're meeting at 8.30 outside the cinema.'
3. We're really working hard .... days.
4. They're spending their holidays in Spain .... summer.
5. I'm going out .... now. Can you call me later?
6. Alice is only working in the mornings .... week, so she's free in the afternoons.
7. Technology is changing rapidly ....
8. Our friends are leaving for Sardinia ....

11 A detective is watching the guests in the entrance hall of the Excelsior Hotel, and looking for a suspect. Complete his thoughts with the verbs below.

sit   talk   wait   drink   call
carry   run   not walk   walk

So... someone tall... Look at that man near the lift. He's tall. He ¹.......................... probably .... for someone, maybe the elegant lady who ².......................... to the receptionist. Could he be the thief? But there's another tall man. He ³.......................... in that armchair and ⁴.......................... a cup of tea. He looks like a businessman, but who knows...

The young man who ⁵.......................... a heavy suitcase is the porter, but he isn't tall. And who's that lady ⁶.......................... towards the door? She ⁷.......................... simply ...., she ⁸.......................... to the door! She seems to be in a hurry. Wait a minute. The message says that a tall *person* is the thief, not a tall man. She ⁹.......................... a taxi right now. I must stop her!

LESSON 3 Present continuous vs. present simple

Compare the different uses of the **present simple** and the **present continuous**.

The *present simple* is used to talk about:	The *present continuous* is used to talk about:
• habitual actions that are repeated frequently: *I do yoga from six to seven on Friday evenings.*	• actions happening at the time of speaking: *I'm doing yoga right now.*
• actions that are part of a daily routine: *She usually wakes up at seven.*	• temporary actions that are different to a routine: *She's waking up at five today because she's getting the 6.15 train to Edinburgh.*
• fixed or permanent situations: *Ben is an architect. He works for a big building company.*	• temporary situations: *He's working in Dubai this winter. They're building a luxury hotel there.*
• scientific facts that are always true: *Water boils at 100°C.*	• actions that are happening now: *The water's boiling. Add the spaghetti, please.*

1 Circle the correct option.

1. **I'm spending / I spend** my holidays in France this year.
2. **Do you collect / Are you collecting** ancient coins?
3. **You're always making / You make always** a mess when you cook! It's so annoying!
4. Darren **does not go / is not going** home this weekend.
5. We **visit / are visiting** St Paul's Cathedral today.
6. They **are usually eating / usually eat** a packed lunch.
7. Lily **works / is working** for a big company. She's got a permanent job as an assistant manager.
8. David **watches / is watching** cartoons now.

2 Complete the sentences using the present simple or the present continuous of the verbs below.

cook   read (x2)   cycle   do   drive   shine   set   rain

1. I usually ……………… historical novels, but I ……………… a great thriller at the moment.
2. Mum usually ……………… the cooking, but it's her birthday today, so Dad ……………… her a special dinner.
3. John generally ……………… to work, but today it ……………… a lot, so he ……………… to the office.
4. The sun always ……………… on this island.
5. Look! The sun ……………… behind the mountains. How lovely!

3 Complete the dialogue using the present simple or the present continuous of the verbs in brackets. Then listen and check.

Steve Hello, Helen. Nice to see you!

Helen Hello, Steve. Nice to see you too!

Steve ¹……………… you still ……………… in that nice little flat in the town centre? (live)

Helen Well, no. I ²……………… in the country now. (live)

Steve In the country? What ³……………… there? (you, do)

Helen Well, my husband and I ⁴……………… a farm. We ⁵……………… crops – wheat, oats, rye – and we have fruit trees. (run, grow)

Steve So you're a farmer now. That's a big change from before, isn't it?

Helen Yes, but this month I ⁶……………… in town because we ⁷……………… a farmshop near the station. (stay, open)

Steve Great! Are you free tomorrow evening?

Helen Yes, I think so. Why?

Steve You ⁸……………… dinner with me and my family so you can tell us everything about your new life! (have)

Helen Okay, Steve, that sounds great! Can I invite my husband too?

Steve Of course!

Action verbs and stative verbs

Action verbs – **read, swim, drive**… – may be used both in the **present simple** and the **present continuous**.
I always read in the evenings before I go to sleep.
We are reading Shakespeare's tragedies at school this term.

Stative verbs, that is those that do not express an action, are not normally used in the continuous form. As well as the verbs listed on page 80 (Unit 5 Lesson 2), these include verbs of involuntary perception like **see** or **hear**, which are normally used with the modal verb **can**:
Can you see those people over there?
Can you hear this noise?

A few verbs expressing feelings and emotions, like **feel**, **hope** or **hate** may be used in both the simple and continuous forms:
I don't feel very well.
I'm not feeling very well today.
I hope you like my cake.
Doctors are hoping to find a better cure for cancer.
I hate memorising poems.
I'm hating this poem.

Some verbs are used in one form or the other with a change of meaning. When used in the continuous form, they express an action, while in the simple form they express a mental state:
think → to express an opinion: *I think it's a good idea.*
think → to reflect: *I'm thinking about his suggestions.*
enjoy → to like: *We enjoy skiing.*
enjoy → to amuse oneself, to have a good time: *I'm enjoying this party.*
see → to understand: *I see what you mean.*
see → to have an appointment to see someone: *I'm seeing the dentist tomorrow morning at nine.*
remember → to have a memory of something: *I remember the house where I lived as a child.*
remember → to recall: *We are remembering our early school days.*

4 **Circle the correct option.**

1 I **can't hear** / **am not hearing** what you're saying. Can you speak more clearly, please?
2 Sarah **enjoys** / **is enjoying** her holiday in Spain.
3 I **hate** / **am hating** rainy weather.
4 He **doesn't mind** / **is not minding** doing the washing-up.
5 We **see** / **are seeing** Dan tomorrow morning to organise our work schedule.
6 **Do you like** / **Are you liking** this film?
7 **Do you think** / **Are you thinking** study holidays are a good way to improve your English?
8 Dad **is having** / **has** a shower right now.
9 Kim **knows** / **is knowing** everything about her favourite group.
10 **Do you want** / **Are you wanting** a new mobile phone?
11 **Are you remembering** / **Do you remember** John? He was at primary school with us.
12 **I hate** / **I'm hating** this film. It's so violent! I don't want to watch any more.
13 **I enjoy** / **I'm enjoying** swimming in the sea, but I don't like swimming in a pool.
14 'What **do you think** / **are you thinking** about?' 'My exam tomorrow. I'm quite anxious.'

5 **Complete the dialogue with the present simple or present continuous of the verbs in brackets.**

A What ¹... of? (you, think)

B My old school mates.

A Why?

B Well, ²... Mark Robson? (you, remember)

A No, I ³... him. (not know)

B Mark is one of my old schoolmates. He ⁴... in Dubai (live) and we ⁵... on a new project now after 20 years. (cooperate)

A ⁶...with Edward? (not, usually work)

B Yes, but now he ⁷... his honeymoon on the French Riviera. (enjoy)

On the next page you will find a summary of the different uses of the present simple and the present continuous.

PRESENT TENSES
Uses of the present simple and the present continuous – Summary

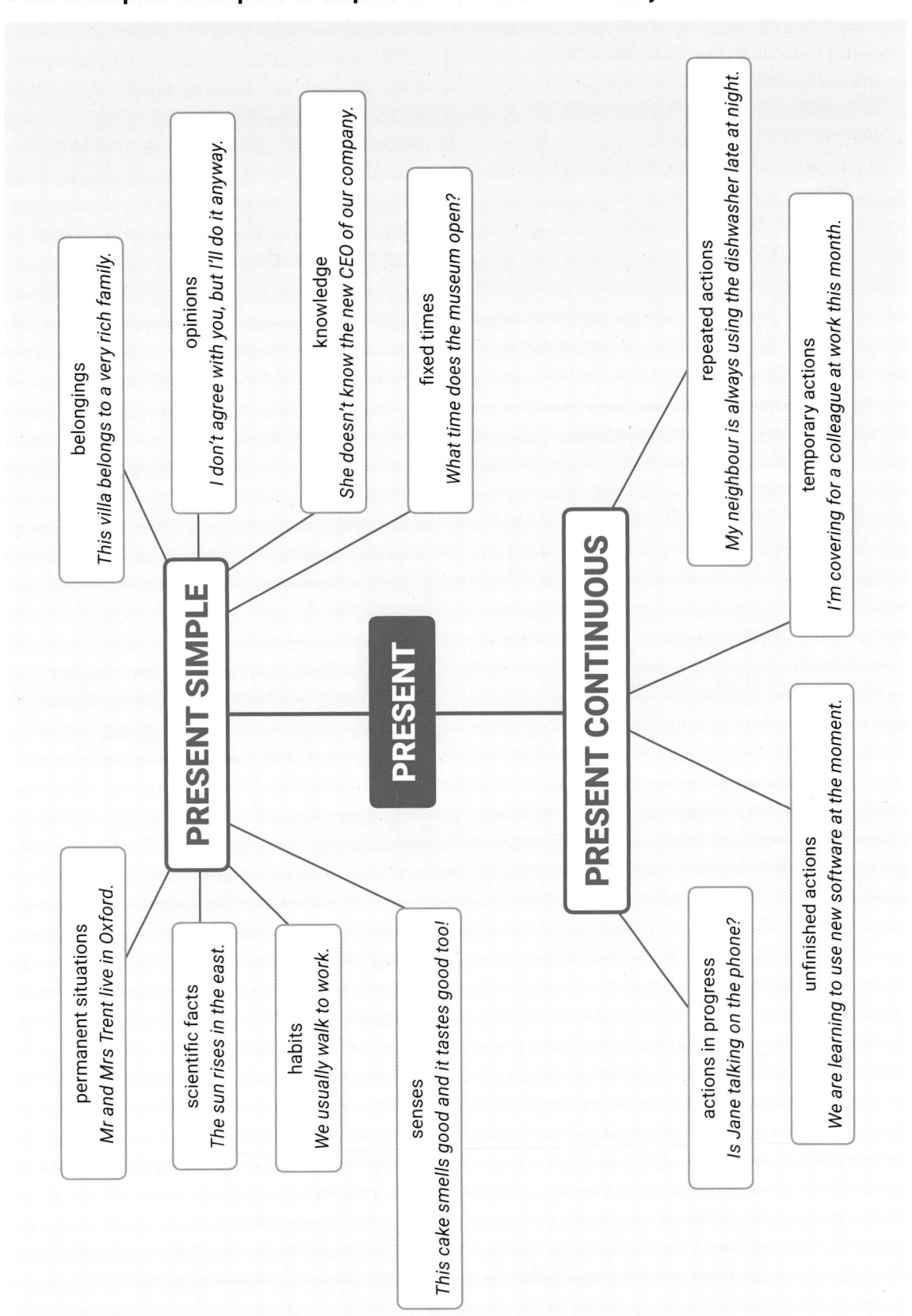

PRESENT

PRESENT SIMPLE

- **belongings**
  This villa belongs to a very rich family.
- **opinions**
  I don't agree with you, but I'll do it anyway.
- **knowledge**
  She doesn't know the new CEO of our company.
- **fixed times**
  What time does the museum open?
- **permanent situations**
  Mr and Mrs Trent live in Oxford.
- **scientific facts**
  The sun rises in the east.
- **habits**
  We usually walk to work.
- **senses**
  This cake smells good and it tastes good too!

PRESENT CONTINUOUS

- **repeated actions**
  My neighbour is always using the dishwasher late at night.
- **temporary actions**
  I'm covering for a colleague at work this month.
- **actions in progress**
  Is Jane talking on the phone?
- **unfinished actions**
  We are learning to use new software at the moment.

GRAMMAR MATRIX BASICS — UNIT 6

99

LESSON 4 Verbs + –ing and verbs + infinitive

We have already seen the different uses of the **–ing** form as a verb, a noun and an adjective (see Unit 6, Lesson 1). Often the **–ing** form of a verb follows another verb.

The **–ing** form of the verb is used after the following verbs:

- the verb **go**, to express the practice of some sporting or leisure activities:
  go skiing   go fishing   go dancing
- verbs expressing likes, dislikes and preferences:
  like   enjoy   love
  prefer   don't mind
  hate   can't stand
  loathe   dislike
  I prefer swimming to skiing.
  She doesn't mind walking the dog.
  I hate getting work phone calls in the evening.

> ! When we talk about a particular situation, **love**, **like**, **hate** and **prefer** are followed by the infinitive form, rather than the **–ing** form:
> *I like reading.* (in general)
> *I like to read before I go to sleep.*
>
> Both **I'd like** and **I'd love** are always followed by the infinitive:
> *I'd like to go to New Zealand and find a job there.*
> *We'd love to try the new Japanese restaurant.*

- verbs expressing starting, continuing or finishing:
  begin / start
  continue / keep / keep on / go on
  finish
  stop
  give up
  Let's start eating our lunch.
  Why don't you finish writing your essay?

Start, **begin** and **continue** can be followed by the infinitive with no change in meaning:
It's starting to snow.

A few verbs can be followed by both forms, but the meaning changes:

Stop + **–ing** form → no longer continue to do something
Stop talking.

Stop + infinitive → to stop doing an activity in order to do something else
Let's stop to fill up the car.

Try + **–ing** form → to experiment, try something for the first time
Try eating more fruit and you'll feel better.

Try + infinitive → to make an attempt or effort to do or get something
I tried to learn some Chinese before I left for Beijing.

Remember + **–ing** form → to keep an image in your memory of a past person, place or event
I remember playing cards with Granny when I was a child.

Remember + infinitive → to not forget to do something, to actually do what you have to do
Remember to see Mr Blake at ten this morning.

Forget + **–ing** form → to not be able to remember something that happened in the past
I forgot talking to the manager.

Forget + infinitive → to not remember to do something that you should do
Did you forget to see the manager?

Other verbs followed by the **–ing** form include:
admit
avoid
consider
deny
fancy
imagine
miss
postpone
practise
risk

1 Circle the correct option.

1. We'd like **to eat** / **eating** out from time to time.
2. Try to give up **smoking** / **to smoke**. You'll feel much better.
3. Avoid **getting** / **to get** into trouble this year!
4. Please, go on **to talk** / **talking** about the history of this town. It's interesting.
5. Can't you consider **moving** / **to move** to another country?
6. They tried **eating** / **to eat** fried ants when they were in China!
7. Do you miss **to work** / **working** at the bank now that you've retired?
8. I want to stop **having** / **to have** some lunch. I'm so hungry.
9. She admitted to **drive** / **driving** without a licence.
10. They don't mind **helping** / **to help** their parents with the washing-up.

2 Complete the sentences with the infinitive or the –ing form of the verbs below.

meet (x2)   drink   have   eat   learn   watch   ski   sing   wash

1. Stop .... so much junk food and you'll feel better.
2. Can't we stop here .... some lunch?
3. I must remember .... Jack at the café after work.
4. I forgot .... Jack yesterday. I should have seen him at three.
5. They hate .... romantic films.
6. I can't stand .... the dishes.
7. Why don't we go .... in the Alps in December?
8. Try .... some Spanish before your holiday in Ibiza.
9. Please, keep .... , Diana. You have a wonderful voice.
10. Why don't you finish .... your milk?

3 Each of these sentences contains a mistake. Underline it and rewrite the sentences correctly.

1. Keep to work hard and you'll get a promotion.
2. I'd love touring the Australian outback.
3. He denied to steal the gold necklace.
4. I'd like talking to the manager, please.
5. My son always avoids to help with the housework!
6. Don't forget buying some bread for tonight.
7. Do you miss to live in a big city?
8. I always stop buying the newspaper on my way to work.
9. I often fancy to tour Iceland in the summer.
10. Why don't we stop here having breakfast?

4 Complete the passage with –ing form or the infinitive of the verbs below.

wake up   be   tell   say   run (x 2)   do   avoid

All of my friends keep [1]............................ me that I have to do some exercise. They say that I shouldn't be so lazy and I should try [2]............................ early and go [3]............................ . But I hate [4]............................ , especially in the early morning. I'd like [5]............................ more active, but I am in my late fifties and I must remember [6]............................ doing too many aerobic activities. I don't mind [7]............................ some gardening in good weather, but my friends say that watering the plants is not enough to keep fit. They forget [8]............................ how tiring things such as weeding the garden or cutting the grass can be.

ROUND UP 6

MATRIX +

Other uses of the infinitive

We have seen that the infinitive (**to** + base form) is used after verbs that express volition (**want**, **would like…**) and many other verbs (**decide**, **hope**, **try…**). It is also used:

- to express purpose or intention:

  I went there to meet them.
  I'm going to tell you a story.
  His aim was to earn as much money as possible.

- to express the result of something, with **too** + adjective or adjective + **enough**:

  It's too cold to go out.
  I wasn't close enough to hear what they said.

- after **where, how, what**:

  She has no idea where to go.
  Do you know how to fix this bike?
  He didn't know what to say.

- after some adjectives such as **determined, sorry, free, happy, glad, pleased, sad**:

  I'm sorry to hear that.
  I'm determined to finish this job.
  Feel free to call me any time.
  I'm glad to be here!

- in impersonal expressions such as:
  It's time to… , It's good / nice / great to… , It's a good idea to… , It's too late to… , It's never too late to… , It's important to…

- as the subject or object of a sentence, with a use that is similar to the **–ing** form:

  To err is human; to forgive, divine. (Alexander Pope)
  I like to paint flowers.

! **To** can also be used by itself, the verb being understood, if it is easy to understand:
He asked me to join them, but I said I didn't want to. (understood: *join him*)
'Would you like to go?' 'Yes, I'd love to!' (understood: *go*)

---

1 Complete the sentences using the verbs below in the infinitive form.

talk   abandon   play   become   find   give   leave   go   get up   see   buy   do

1 He wants ………………… a job abroad.
2 They were so angry they refused ………………… to us.
3 They threatened ………………… the conference.
4 We can't afford ………………… on holiday this summer.
5 I decided not ………………… a diesel car.
6 I'm learning ………………… the guitar.
7 What are you planning ………………… next weekend?
8 He offered ………………… me a lift in his car.
9 They were so sad ………………… !
10 He's determined ………………… the mayor.
11 It's seven o'clock. It's time ………………… !
12 It's nice ………………… you again.

On the next you will find a summary of the different uses of the *–ing* form.

Uses of the –ing form – Summary

–ing FORM

- **NOUN VERB** (Verbal noun, to indicate an activity) used as
  1) the subject of a sentence → *Living alone is not too bad after all.*
  2) the direct object of a sentence → *I love meeting up with old friends.*
  3) the indirect object of a sentence (after a preposition) → *She dreams of going to live in the USA.* (see Unit 7 Lesson 4)

- **PRESENT PARTICIPLE** used
  1) as an adjective → *Complete the following sentences.*
  2) in place of a relative clause → *There are three roads leading off the roundabout.*

- **GERUND** used
  1) after a verb, to show how the action is performed: *She looked up, smiling at you.*
  2) with the auxiliary *be* in the continuous form: *The baby is crying.*

FAQ

Q: Why do I find the expression **coming soon** for a film that is about to be released?

A: The rest of the sentence is understood: **The film is coming soon.** It's a phrase in the present continuous for something that is scheduled for the near future.

2 Complete the sentences with the *–ing* form of the verbs below.

act   cook   rise   smoke   bully   talk   cry   raise   dance

1 She failed the exam and came home ....
2 I hope .... will be banned everywhere! It really harms our health.
3 The syllabus offers .... and .... as optional activities. Lots of students take them.
4 .... is becoming a more and more popular hobby. Lots of TV programmes teach you how to make really tasty meal.
5 Cases of depression are .... among young adults.
6 We need to take some kind of action against .... It has become a big problem in our school.
7 They are .... funds for their campaign. They need £50,000.
8 I saw him .... on the phone.

3 Mrs Johnson has a son who never helps around the house. Read the passage and complete it with the infinitive or *–ing* form of the verbs in brackets.

Mrs Johnson is a busy woman. She's a nurse and she never stops
¹........................... (work), either in the hospital or in her home. She doesn't mind ²........................... (cook), but she doesn't like ³........................... (clean) at all, so she would like her teenage son, David, ⁴........................... (help) her sometimes. But David always avoids ⁵........................... (help) with the cleaning. He stays in his room and promises ⁶........................... (help) later, but he never does. To make David help, she has to threaten ⁷........................... (stop) his pocket money.
Mrs Johnson's husband doesn't help much in the house either. He sometimes offers ⁸........................... (employ) someone ⁹........................... (help) with the housework, but she says she doesn't like to have a stranger in the house. 'I can't imagine ¹⁰........................... (pay) someone to do the jobs you boys should be doing,' she says.

4 Read the email and circle the correct option.

Dear Jack,
How are you? I'm on holiday in sunny California. I ¹ **am staying / stay** in a great hotel in Santa Barbara. I ² **am going / go** to the beach every morning and I ³ **lie / am lying** in the sun for hours. I ⁴ **don't swim / swim not** a lot though, because the water of the ocean is quite cold. But tomorrow I ⁵ **go / am going** surfing for the first time in my life. I ⁶ **am looking / look** forward to it.
What ⁷ **do you do / are you doing** in cold and foggy England? ⁸ **Do you study / Are you studying** hard? Let me know!
Carol

5 **Complete the text with the present simple or continuous of the verbs in brackets.**

Mr Robson is 55 years old. He ¹............................ (live) in Nottingham and he ²............................ (work) for a big company in the area. He's the sales manager. He ³............................ (get) to work in his car, driving about half an hour. He ⁴............................ (start) work at nine in the morning and usually ⁵............................ (finish) at 5 pm. Before he ⁶............................ (get) home, he usually ⁷............................ (go) to a pub near his house where he ⁸............................ (meet) his friends every evening. He's married to Sylvia and they have a son, Peter.

Peter is 25 and is unemployed at the moment. He ⁹............................ (look) for a job, but it isn't easy to find a good one. He ¹⁰............................ (stay) at a friend's house in London at the moment because there are more job opportunities there. He ¹¹............................ (not have) a routine because every day is different. Tomorrow he ¹²............................ (have) an interview at 11 am in the City, so he ¹³............................ (get up) quite late. After the interview, he ¹⁴............................ (go) to eat in a Thai restaurant in the area with a couple of friends. He isn't married, but he ¹⁵............................ (date) a girl called Jennifer. This weekend they ¹⁶............................ (go back) to Nottingham because he ¹⁷............................ (want) to introduce Jennifer to his parents.

6 **Analyse these sentences and say whether the –ing form is used as a noun verb (NV), a present participle (PP) or a gerund (G).**

1 Playing rugby is becoming more popular in our country. ....
2 After doing the housework, Sheila often goes out for a coffee with her friends. ....
3 There are a few people sitting in the waiting room. ....
4 They aren't walking home, they are taking the bus. ....
5 Please answer the following questions. ....
6 Jane entertained the guests speaking about her journeys around Africa. ....

Reflecting on grammar

Study the rules and decide if whether the following statements are true or false.

		True	False
1	The **–ing** form of the verb **try** is **trying**.		
2	The **–ing** form can have the function of a noun, a present participle or a gerund.		
3	The present continuous is formed with the auxiliary **have** + the **–ing** form of the main verb.		
4	The present continuous is used to talk about actions that are part of a daily routine.		
5	A future action that has already been planned can be expressed with the present continuous.		
6	Temporary actions are usually expressed with the present simple.		
7	The present simple is used to express universal or scientific truths.		
8	Stative verbs are not normally used in the continuous form.		
9	**Love, like** and **hate** can never be followed by an infinitive form.		
10	The sentence *I miss talking to you* is correct.		

Revision and Exams 2 (UNITS 4 – 5 – 6)

1 Complete the passage using the second person singular imperative form of the verbs below.

ride   admire   discover   not forget   observe   rent   finish

Greece
The Thessaloniki Waterlands

¹.............................. the beautiful waterlands of Thessaloniki, just a few kilometres away from the city centre. Start from Chalastra and go along the Coastal Bank up to the Lighthouse of the Axios Delta. ².............................. a bike and ³.............................. the beautiful rice fields which are everywhere. ⁴.............................. by the salt marshes and ⁵.............................. the rare species of birds you can see. ⁶.............................. your trip at the Lighthouse of the naval Army of the Thermalikos Gulf and ⁷.............................. to try the local food along the way!

2 Complete the leaflet using the imperative form of the verbs below. They may be in the positive or negative form.

take   keep   use   put   remember   leave   smoke   forget

Park Rules

- ¹........................... our park clean!
- ²........................... plastic bags on the ground after picnics. ³...........................! They take ten to twenty years to decompose.
- ⁴........................... recyclable containers and ⁵........................... them home with you.
- ⁶........................... your food leftovers into the special bins for organic materials. We use them to fertilise the soil.
- ⁷........................... in the park. ⁸........................... that cigarette butts take up to five years to decompose!

3 **Complete the dialogue using the correct form of the present simple, present continuous or imperative of the verbs in brackets.**

Teacher ¹............................ a few problems with your grammar, Kate? (have)

Kate Yes, I ²............................ making the same mistakes. I never ³............................ the rules. (keep, remember)

Teacher When you ⁴............................ a new rule, ⁵............................ some sentences with it. ⁶............................ about yourself: this ⁷............................ you to remember it better. (learn, write, write, help)

Kate Okay. I ⁸............................ that now. I ⁹............................ sentences with the imperative, the present simple and the present continuous. I ¹⁰............................ about my habits and about what I ¹¹............................ at weekends. (try, write, talk, do)

Teacher You see, you ¹²............................ the tenses correctly now because you ¹³............................ interested in what you ¹⁴............................ . (use, be, say) Well done!

4 **Read the text about two women who do the same job in two different places and complete it using the present simple of the verbs below.**

work   live   send   organise   sleep   do   pass   start   have   go (x2)   meet

Patricia lives in London, and Marion ¹................................ in Chicago, Illinois, USA. They ²............................ from their homes for the same firm, an Italian shoe manufacturing company. They ³................................ the orders, ⁴................................ the invoices and ⁵................................ shipments for the European and American markets. They often ⁶................................ the same things but not at the same moment. Local time in London is six hours ahead of Chicago, so when Patricia ⁷................................ work in London in the morning, it's night in Chicago and Marion ⁸................................ . When Patricia ⁹................................ lunch, Marion starts work in Chicago. In the afternoon London time, which is morning in Chicago, they are both on their computers and sometimes they have video conferences. And when Patricia ¹⁰................................ to bed, Marion is sometimes still on her computer or has just finished working. Patricia and Marion ¹¹................................ once a year, in June, when they ¹²................................ to Italy for the annual conference at their company's headquarters.

107

5 Reread the text in the previous exercise and write what Patricia and Marion are doing at different times of the day. Use the present continuous of the verbs in brackets.

1 It's seven o'clock London time. Patricia ………………… while Marion ………………… still ………………… . (get up / sleep)
2 It's 1.30 pm London time. Patricia ………………… lunch while Marion ………………… work. (have / start)
3 It's four o'clock London time. Patricia and Marion ………………… both ………………… . Patricia ………………… some invoices and Marion ………………… a big shipment to San Diego, California. (work / pass / organise)
4 It's five o'clock London time. Today they ………………… a video conference. (have)
5 It's 11 pm London time. Patricia ………………… to bed, while Marion ………………… still ………………… on the latest orders (go / work).
6 This year, Patricia and Marion ………………… on June 9th at the company's headquarters in Milan. They ………………… forward to it! (meet / look)

6 This is part of a leaflet about the Victoria and Albert Museum in London. Read and complete the text using the correct form of the present simple, present continuous or imperative of the verbs in brackets.

The Victoria and Albert Museum is the world's leading museum of art and design. Its collections [1]………………… (span) two thousand years of art in virtually every medium, from every part of the world. Besides the permanent collections on show, the museum [2]………………… (offer) a number of temporary exhibitions on every aspect of applied arts. Presently, you can visit a very interesting exhibition about footwear and another one about Indian jewellery.
The V&A is also a very active educational centre. It [3]………………… (offer) courses, workshops and evening events, as well as free tours and lesson-planning resources for schools and colleges.
On one of the current courses, professional goldsmiths [4]………………… (teach) how to make jewellery. If you are interested, [5]………………… (enrol) now because the course will only last till the end of March.
The museum [6]………………… (open) at 10 am and [7]………………… (close) at 5.45 pm with a late evening on Fridays till 10 pm.
As they [8]………………… (carry out) repairs at the main entrance this month, the main information desk is closed. Also the Members Desk [9]………………… (be) located in Room 50 in this period.
[10]………………… (visit) the V&A website for any information you need.

Preliminary (PET) | Writing Part 3

7 Here's part of an email that you've received from your English friend. Read the email and write an answer in no more than 100 words.

> ... And guess where I am now? Swimming in the Mediterranean off the coast of Santorini! It's fantastic. The sun shines every day and I spend most of the day lying on the beach and swimming. This afternoon I'm hiring a scooter to go around the island.
>
> What are you doing this summer? Are you having fun? Tell me about it!
>
> Susan

First (FCE) | Reading and Use of English Part 2

8 Read the text and complete it with the word which best fits each gap. Use only one word in each gap.

¹............................ you know what most European teenagers have in common? They all own a smartphone. They use ²............................ for a number of purposes, ³............................ they hardly ever make phone calls. They chat with friends on social networks, surf the Internet, ⁴............................ photos, make selfies.

Teenagers don't have many technological gadgets now ⁵............................ they use their smartphones for everything. They ⁶............................ write many text messages either because they are always connected via their 3G or 4G Internet connection.

Thirty-five percent of European teenagers also own a tablet and study or ⁷............................ homework with it. But when they write a lot, they still prefer using a computer with a keyboard ⁸............................ it is much easier.

Only about 20 percent of teenagers own a digital camera; they are amateur photographers, ⁹............................ they want to have the best equipment possible.

When it comes to playing video games, nearly 90 percent declare they have a console ¹⁰............................ 50 percent of them also play video games on their computers.

Towards Competences

The local tourist board where you live has asked you to prepare a leaflet about your area. It should describe a day's itinerary, including the main attractions and suggesting places to eat that offer local specialities.

Don't forget to include opening and closing times, and a map showing the itinerary and photos of major attractions. You can use a template like the one in the picture.

Exercise 1 of this revision section may help you (page 106).

Self Check 2

Circle the correct option. Then check your answers at the end of the book.

1 What ……… for breakfast?
   A have you usually got
   B do you usually have
   C have you usually

2 Tom and Sheila ……… a nice cottage in the country.
   A has got   B have   C 've got

3 Sonia ……… a snack in the afternoon.
   A don't have
   B hasn't got
   C doesn't have

4 'Have you got a cat?' 'Yes, ……… .'
   A I have   B I've got   C I've

5 I ……… right. This is not Baileys & Co's invoice.
   A have   B am   C do

6 '……… hungry?' 'No, not really.'
   A Are you   B Have you   C Do you have

7 'Whose bag is this?' 'It's ……… .'
   A my   B mine   C the mine

8 'Is that Mike's mobile phone?' 'No, it isn't ……… .'
   A his   B his's   C hers

9 These are ……… bicycles.
   A the children's   B the childrens'
   C the children

10 I'll have ……… next month.
    A a holiday of week   B a weeks' holiday
    C a week's holiday

11 ……… is coming to London next week.
    A One Daniel's friend
    B One of Daniel's friends
    C One friend of Daniel

12 Carol Sheer is the new sales manager. ……… office is on the top floor.
    A She's   B Hers   C Her

13 ……… are on my desk.
    A Some your documents
    B Some of your documents
    C Some of the your documents

14 ……… some salad. It's good for you.
    A You have   B Have you   C Have

15 ……… go out now. It's too hot!
    A Don't let's   B Let's not   C Let not

16 Gloria and I always ……… to work every day to keep fit.
    A cycles   B are cycling   C cycle

17 ……… the late show start at 10 pm?
    A Does   B Is   C Do

18 .... a break in the afternoon.
   A We haven't often got
   B We don't have often
   C We don't often have

19 Where .... your shoes?
   A do you buy usually
   B do you usually buy
   C you usually buy

20 .... skiing in winter?
   A Are you usually going
   B Do you go usually
   C Do you usually go

21 'How often .... your emails?' 'Once a day.'
   A do you check   B are you checking
   C check you

22 Stop! The sign says '......... entry'. We can't drive in there.
   A Don't   B No   C Mustn't

23 Luke and I are going shopping. Do you want to come with ....?
   A me   B our   C us

24 Ruth wants to try paragliding .... she is going to the mountains this weekend.
   A because   B so   C but

25 I love .... in the sun on the beach.
   A lying   B lieying   C lieing

26 Most of my friends are constantly .... their mobiles when we are in a restaurant together. It's so annoying!
   A checking   B check   C checked

27 Why .... so loud? I'm not deaf.
   A do you talk   B are you talking
   C don't you talk

28 Water .... at 0°C.
   A freezes   B is always freezing
   C freeze

29 Start .... without me. I'll be home late from work today.
   A eat   B to eating   C eating

30 I'm here .... the Personnel Manager. I have an appointment at ten.
   A meeting   B for meet   C to meet

31 We have no idea what .... tonight. Any suggestions?
   A doing   B to do   C do

32 'Do you fancy .... to the swimming pool this afternoon?' 'Yes, good idea.'
   A going   B to go   C go

33 We .... at home in the winter.
   A are often staying   B often stay
   C stay often

34 'Are you free tomorrow afternoon?' 'No, it's Friday and .... yoga on Friday afternoons.'
   A I always do   B I'm always doing
   C I'm always having

35 'What's that noise? .... video games?' 'Yes, as usual.'
   A Do the kids play
   B Don't the kids play
   C Are the kids playing

36 '......... a lie-in on Sundays?' 'No, my mum always gets up before eight.'
   A Do you all have
   B Have you all got
   C Are you all having

37 She .... dancing.
   A don't like   B doesn't likes
   C doesn't like

38 .... to music is so relaxing!
   A Listen   B Listening   C To listening

39 'Let's play squash tomorrow evening.' 'No, I don't want .... Let's go for a walk and relax.'
   A it   B playing   C to

40 We're all so happy .... you here again.
   A seeing   B to see   C for seeing

Assess Yourself!

0 – 10	Study harder. Use the online exercises to help you.
11 – 20	OK. Use the online practice exercises to practise things you don't know.
21 – 30	Good, but do some extra online.
31 – 40	Excellent!

GRAMMAR MATRIX MAIN

UNIT 7 Prepositions

LESSON 1 Prepositions of time

Fixed time	Duration	Start / End	Start	Finish	Before / After
at on in	for during over between ... and	from ... to	since	until till in within by	before after

The prepositions **in**, **on**, **at** are used before objects that express fixed times:
'When?' 'In December. / On Monday.'
'At what time?' 'At three o'clock.'

In is used with:
- the date expressed in years → *in 2015, in the year 34 BC*
- centuries → *in the 20th century, in the 21st century*
- seasons → *in winter, in the summer*
- months → *in January, in March*
- parts of the day → *in the morning, in the afternoon, in the evening, in the middle of the day*

On is used with:
- days of the week → *on Monday, on Sunday* (also: *on Monday morning / afternoon...*)
- dates expressed with the day → *on 7th June, on December 9th 2016*
- 'special' days → *on my birthday, on Christmas Day*
- parts of the day, when preceded by an adjective → *on a cold morning, on a dark rainy night*

At is used with:
- times → *at eight o'clock, at half past ten, at lunchtime, at dinnertime*
- holiday periods → *at Christmas, at the weekend* (also: *on the weekend*)
- the following expressions: *at night, at dawn, at sunset*

1 Circle the correct option.

1. The Industrial Revolution started **in / on** the 18th century.
2. I often read **in the / at** night. The house is so quiet then.
3. I like having a lie-in **on / in** cold rainy mornings.
4. Do they often go for a walk **at / in the** afternoon?
5. **In / At** summer, we often wake up **at / on** dawn and go running in the park.
6. Why don't we meet **on / at** lunchtime?
7. We generally stay at home **in / at** the weekend and relax in our garden.
8. I love sitting on the beach **at / on** sunset watching the seagulls.

2 Complete the sentences with the correct preposition. Choose between *in*, *on* and *at*.

1. The exams start ...... 18th June this year.
2. We usually go on a skiing holiday ...... Christmas.
3. My sister's birthday's ...... April 4th.
4. Naomi was born ...... the year 2000.
5. They sometimes go to Spain ...... summer.
6. I often play video games ...... the evening.
7. Shall we meet ...... four o'clock at my house?
8. Where are you going ...... New Year's Day?
9. Are you meeting Mrs Ferns ...... Monday?
10. I don't like getting up early ...... the morning.
11. Mozart was born ...... the 18th century in Salzburg, Austria.
12. I was born ...... the summer – my birthday is ...... July.

The preposition **for** is used to show a length of time → *'How long did you walk for?' 'We walked for two hours.'* But: *'How long have you been walking?' 'We've been walking for two hours.'* → Action still in progress → we use the present perfect (see Unit 9 Lesson 3)

during / **over** and **between… and…** describe a period of time, all through it → *During the day / the night / the week…   Over the weekend   Between the 3rd and the 5th of August*

The prepositions **from… to…** give a start and finish time for the action → *from 2 to 4 pm*
from Monday to Friday
from 2010 to 2013

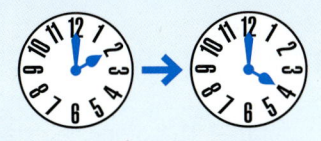

since expresses the time at which the action started. This action usually continues into the present → *'How long have you lived in England?' 'We've lived in England since 1999.'* This is an action that is still continuing into the present, so we use the present perfect.

until or **till** precede the time the action finishes → *I waited till dawn.*

in or **within** (which is more formal) express the period within which the action will finish → *I'm coming back in a week.   You have to hand in your project within three days.*

by expresses the precise moment in time (hour, day …) within which the action needs to be completed → *Please deliver the goods by 16th May.*

before / **after** at an earlier / later time → *Come back before midnight. Don't come back after midnight.*

3 Circle the correct option.

1 **In** / **On** July 2015 we were in Milan **for** / **since** a couple of days to visit Expo.
2 I usually read the newspaper **after** / **within** lunch.
3 'He should be here **in** / **by** an hour or so.' 'Oh I see. **By** / **Between** five o'clock, then.'
4 My son stayed with an American family **from** / **between** January to June last year.
5 I couldn't put this book down. I kept reading it **for** / **since** hours, **until** / **after** I finished it.
6 He sleeps **before** / **during** the day and works **in** / **at** night.
7 Please try to be here **by** / **from** eight o'clock, when we open the shop.
8 Where have you been **over** / **within** the weekend?
9 The goods should arrive **till** / **within** two weeks.
10 I waited **by** / **until** four o'clock but he didn't turn up.

4 Complete the sentences by choosing the correct preposition from those below.

from… to   since   for   between   by   during   before   in

1 Have you been working .... long?
2 We're going to have a holiday sometime .... June and August.
3 They work .... Monday .... Thursday and have a long weekend.
4 I never wake up .... the night. I sleep like a log.
5 John has been picking fruit .... seven o'clock this morning. He's dead tired.
6 You have to hand in your essay .... Thursday 13th April at the latest.
7 Mr Jackson is not here. He'll be back to work .... a week.
8 The theatre opens half an hour .... the show.

5 Find the mistakes in these sentences and correct them.

1 I often study in night.
2 Are you free on Monday to five from six?
3 What do you usually do at Christmas Day?
4 We have to hand in our essays within next Monday.
5 We like sleeping until late at Sundays.

LESSON 2 Prepositions of place

Prepositions indicating place and position

Prepositions indicating place and position tell us where something or someone is. They follow stative verbs such as **be, stay, live, stop, lie, stand, sit**, but also **land** and **arrive**.

The main ones are:
in, which is usually followed by the definite article **the** (**in the mountains**, **in the garden**...), except in the expressions **in bed, in hospital, in town** and a few others.

It shows:
- that something or someone is inside a place → *It's in the box.*
- where a person lives → *I live in Highbury Road in Chester.*
- the geographical location of a place → *Penzance is in Cornwall, in the south-west of England.*

at → This preposition is usually followed by the definite article **the** (**at the seaside, at the theatre**...), except in the expressions **at home, at work, at school / college / university** and a few others.
The preposition shows that something or someone is at a certain geographical point or in an open, not enclosed, space → *She's at the bus stop.*

> ! We use **at** when we also use the street number in an address:
> *I live **in** Brompton Road.* BUT: *I live **at** 25 Brompton Road.*

on → This preposition expresses the idea that something stands or lies on a surface or faces on to something → *It's on the table / It's on the lake / on the coast…*

under / below → in a lower position
over / above → in a higher position than something, without touching it

FAQ

Q: I heard the expression **They live on a farm**. Why **on** and not 'in a farm'?

A: The use of **on** means that the people both live and work on the farm, where they carry out all the related activities. Other examples: **The students live on a campus. / Most Native Americans live on reservations.**

1 Complete the sentences with the correct preposition. Choose from *on / in / at / over*.

1 The icon of the file you're looking for is .... the desktop.
2 The Statue of Liberty stands .... Liberty Island, ... the entrance of New York harbour.
3 The Hawaiian Islands lie .... the Pacific Ocean.
4 We live .... Pearson Street, ... number 19.
5 Edinburgh castle is .... top of a hill.
6 There's an LED lamp .... my desk and another one .... my bed.
7 We're spending a week's holiday .... the mountains .... Wales.

To talk about the position of one thing in relation to something else, or to a point of reference, we use the following prepositions:

near / close to   next to / beside (for elements which are in close proximity to each other)
far from   off (to express remoteness and detachment)
from (to express distance)
in front of (before, like the people in a queue)
opposite (facing something or on the other side of something)
behind (at the back of something)
between (in the middle of two elements)
among (in the middle of more than two elements)
around / round (surrounding something, like in a circle)
along (from one end to the other end of something, generally something long)
ahead of (further forward in space than something)

2 Complete the sentences with a suitable preposition. Choose from: *from / next / between / opposite / around / off / along / in front / behind / among*.

1 I usually sit .... to my friend Nora in the science class.
2 There are lots of shops .... the main road.
3 The village where I live is not far .... Nottingham.
4 The children are walking in a line, one .... of the other.
5 The Roman wall is all .... the town of York.
6 Great Keppel Island lies .... the coast of Queensland, near the Tropic of Cancer.
7 The travel agency is .... Lloyd's Bank and a restaurant.
8 They're our new neighbours. They've just bought the house .... ours.
9 The photographer made Sara stand .... me in the school photo because she's much taller than me.
10 He wandered .... the other guests at the party, feeling shy as he didn't know anyone.

Prepositions indicating movement

These prepositions indicate movement from or towards a point of reference. They follow verbs of movement such as **go**, **come**, **walk**, **drive**, **cycle**, **return** or **come back**. The main prepositions are:

to shows movement towards a place
→ *We're going to school / to the park.*
Also: *Have you ever been to France?*

! The word **home** does not take the preposition **to** → *We're going home.*

Points of the compass do not take **to** either → *Go west / north / south / east.*

into expresses entrance into a closed place or a street
→ *We're going into the supermarket. Turn left into that street.*

from expresses movement from a place, origin or source
→ *We're coming back from the office.*

Other prepositions of movement include:

out of
Get out of here.

away from
Go away from here.

past
Go past the flower shop.

over
He climbed over the wall.

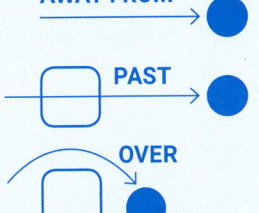

FAQ

Q: What prepositions are used with means of transport? Why do we say **get on the bus** but **get into the car**?

A: **Get on** is used for the train, the plane, the bus and means of transport with two wheels, because we go upwards to enter them, whereas we **get into** the enclosed space of a car. On the other hand, we use **get out of** for a car and **get off** for the other means of transport, for example **We're getting off the plane just now.**

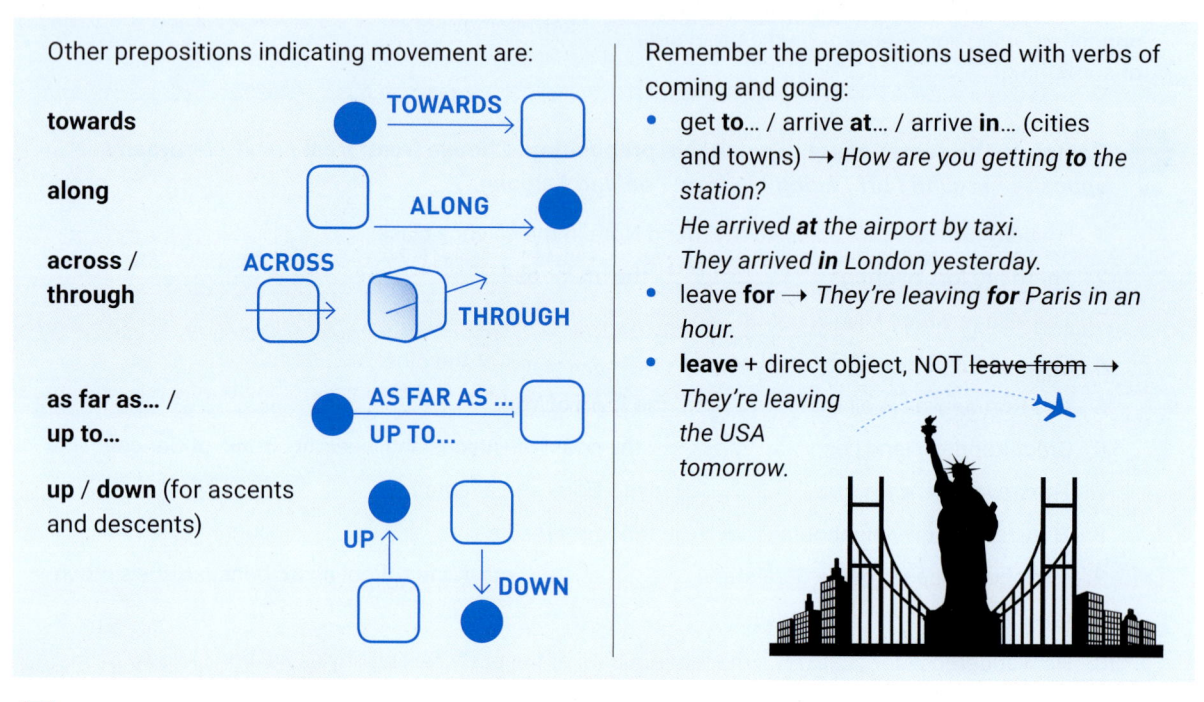

Other prepositions indicating movement are:

- towards
- along
- across / through
- as far as… / up to…
- up / down (for ascents and descents)

Remember the prepositions used with verbs of coming and going:

- get **to**… / arrive **at**… / arrive **in**… (cities and towns) → How are you getting **to** the station?
  He arrived **at** the airport by taxi.
  They arrived **in** London yesterday.
- leave **for** → They're leaving **for** Paris in an hour.
- **leave** + direct object, NOT ~~leave from~~ → They're leaving the USA tomorrow.

3 Circle the correct option.

1. Would you like to go **to / into** the office by bus or by underground?
2. Let's get **into / on** this bus. It goes straight **to / at** the station.
3. My brother is going **to / in** France on business.
4. Go **past / over** the chemist's and turn right. The flower shop is on your left.
5. Sam is leaving **for / to** New York in an hour.
6. Are you leaving **from / ---** Edinburgh tomorrow?
7. Let's go for a walk **along / past** the river bank.
8. Get **out of / off** the bus at the next stop.

4 Complete the sentences using the correct preposition. Choose from: *out of / from / along / at / up to / into / away from / to / through / for / as far as*.

1. My friend Ally comes .... Edinburgh.
2. My grandparents arrived .... my house this morning.
3. When are you leaving .... Greece?
4. Let's go for a stroll .... the beach. It's a nice walk.
5. The robbers got .... the house .... the window.
6. Read this survey .... page ten.
7. Move .... that crane. It may be dangerous.
8. This is not your room. Get .... here!
9. Have you ever been .... Scotland for your holidays?
10. Drive .... the next roundabout.

5 Prepositions of place are often used to give directions. Circle the correct option in the following street directions.

1 Go **towards / down** this road **as far as / until** the roundabout.
2 Turn right **into / from** Sutton Lane and take the first **at / on** the left.
3 Stop **to / at** the traffic lights and go **across / along** the square.
4 Get **off / out of** the bus **in / at** the next stop and walk **along / through** the main road.
5 Go **past / up** the bank and you'll see the post office **in / on** your left.
6 Excuse me. How do I get **at / to** the stadium, please?
7 Go **up / down** a hundred steps and you'll get a great view **for / from** the top.
8 Could you take me **in / to** my hotel, please? It's **in / into** Fairbank Avenue.
9 Drive **along / away** this road and you'll find the hospital at the end, on the right.
10 You should go **towards / onto** the station if you want to find a flower shop.

LESSON 3 Other prepositions / Verbs with two objects

The following prepositions are very common to introduce indirect objects:

with (+ person) → *I usually walk to school with Sara.*
(+ a means of some kind) → *Sign the form with a black pen, please.*

without (the opposite of with) → *I can't see without my glasses.*

by (+ a means of transport) → *I go to work by train / by tube / by car…*
BUT: **on** foot / **on** horseback.
If the means of transport is preceded by a possessive expression, we say: **on** my bike / **in** my mother's car

by (+ the agent as an object in the passive form) → *The film is directed by Spielberg.*
(see **Passive form**, Unit 17).

for (in favour of someone) → *We bought a present for Max.*
I would do anything for you.

of (+ material) → *It's made of cotton.*
(specifying details) → *The frame of my glasses is light and flexible.* But when someone possesses something, we say, for example, *Maria's house* (see **Possessive case**, page 68).

like (similar to) → *My smartphone is just like yours.*
What's the weather like?
She looks like her sister.

about (+ topic) → *The novel is about a young girl…*

except / but (for…) → *All the food was great except for the cake, which was not very nice.*
They all left quite soon but for Jason, who stayed a bit longer.

1 Complete the sentences with a suitable preposition.

1 Mum usually goes to work .... bus, but sometimes she goes .... foot.
2 'What's this old table made .... ?' 'It's made .... oak.'
3 'Isn't Jack at home?' 'No, he's out .... his motorbike.'
4 Here's an article you should read. It's .... job opportunities in Australia.
5 Look at you in this photo. You really look .... your mother.
6 The study .... rocks is called geology.
7 My class is going on a school trip .... the history teacher tomorrow.
8 The Shard, designed .... architect Renzo Piano, is the tallest building in London.
9 You're the person I want to be with. I can't live .... you.
10 Is this .... me? Wow! Thank you so much.

The preposition *to* with a double object

The preposition **to** introduces the person or things affected by the action → *You'd better talk to him. What have you done to your hair?*

Several verbs are followed by two objects: the direct object and the person affected by the action, for example 'give something to someone'. The most common verbs are **give**, **offer**, **lend**, **show**, **bring** (*carry towards the speaker*), **take** (*carry away from the speaker*), **send**, **tell**, **ask** and a few others.

In this case, the sentence can be formed in two ways:

1. **subject + verb + object + preposition *to* + person** → *I gave the keys to Brian.*
2. **subject + verb + person + object** → *I gave Brian the keys.*

The second construction is called **double object**: we bring forward in the sentence the person affected by the action, and the direct object (or thing) follows it. It's as if there were two objects because there is no preposition in the sentence.

If the object of the sentence is expressed by a pronoun and the person by a noun, or if there are two pronouns, we prefer the first construction → *I haven't got the keys. I gave them to Brian / I gave them to him.*

If, on the other hand, the person is expressed by a pronoun, we prefer the second construction: *I gave him the keys.*

Other verbs do not have a **double object** construction, but only a single object, that is: **verb + object + *to* + person**.
These verbs are, for example: **explain**, **introduce**, **dictate**, **report**, **deliver**, **suggest**, **propose**, **say** → *He's introduced his girlfriend to his parents.* (NOT: *He's introduced his parents his girlfriend.*)
She reported the news to everybody.

FAQ

Q: Does the word **object** in English grammar only mean a direct object?

A: No, it can mean any kind of object. A **direct object** does not usually have a preposition. An object with a preposition (**to**, **for**...) is called an **indirect object**. To be precise, the construction of a **double object** should be called a **direct double object**.

2 Tick (✓) the correct sentences and correct the mistake in the ones that are wrong.

1. Show me your notebook, will you? ☐ ....
2. Can you lend to me your credit card, Dad? ☐ ....
3. Dave gave a present to each of his nephews. ☐ ....
4. Samantha explained me her plans. ☐ ....
5. 'Take this basket to your grandmother,' said Little Red Riding Hood's mother to her daughter. ☐ ....
6. She introduced the new assistant to the manager. ☐ ....
7. Can you give him this document, please? ☐ ....
8. They offered to us a very good meal. ☐ ....
9. Why don't you dictate this letter to your secretary? ☐ ....
10. We will deliver our customers the goods in two weeks. ☐ ....
11. We must report the manager the theft. ☐ ....
12. Could you bring me a glass of water, please? ☐ ....

3 Rewrite the sentences using a double-object construction to replace the underlined words. This is not possible in two of the sentences. Identify which ones they are.

1 Can you give <u>a lift to my friend</u>, please?
2 Can you lend <u>this book to me</u>? I'd like to read it.
3 The teacher explained <u>the new rule to the students</u>.
4 Give <u>this paper to your sister</u>, please.
5 If you like, I'll show <u>my photos to you</u>.
6 They offered <u>a red rose to all the ladies</u>.
7 He said <u>something to the teacher</u>.
8 Have you sent <u>an email to Mr Wayne</u> yet?
9 My neighbour told <u>the news to everybody</u>.
10 The coach asked <u>their names to the players</u>.

LESSON 4 Adjectives and verbs followed by prepositions

Adjectives are often followed by prepositions, which in their turn are followed by nouns, pronouns or the **-ing** form of a verb which has the function of a noun (see page 91).

| adjective + preposition + noun or pronoun → *I'm good at maths. / I'm good at it.* | adjective + preposition + **-ing** form of the verb → *I'm tired of listening to the same old story!* |

Here are a few commonly used adjectives followed by their prepositions:

sorry	ABOUT	I'm **sorry about** the mistake.
worried		Are you **worried about** tomorrow's test?
surprised	AT	He was **surprised at** seeing her there.
good		I'm not very **good at** swimming.
disappointed	BY / AT / WITH	We were **disappointed by / at / with** the quality of the food.
qualified	FOR	Who's **responsible for** this mess?
responsible		James is not **qualified for** this job.
different	FROM / TO	The hotel was quite **different from / to** what I expected.
interested	IN	I'm not really **interested in** politics.
fond		She's very **fond of** her aunt.
afraid		I'm **afraid of** the dark.
scared	OF	She's **scared of** spiders.
tired		Aren't you **tired of** moving to different places every year?
aware		She's not **aware of** the importance of her new position.
keen	ON	My brother's **keen on** parachuting.
married	TO	He isn't **married to** Elisa, he's just **engaged to** her.
engaged		
angry		Don't be **angry with** him!
happy		I'm really **happy with** the exam results.
bored	WITH	I'm getting **bored with** being at home.
popular		Paul is very **popular with** his classmates.
satisfied		Are you really **satisfied with** this piece of writing?

1 Complete the sentences with a suitable adjective. Choose from: happy / keen / surprised / sorry / interested / good / angry / bored / popular / afraid / scared.

1 I'm not really .... on going to this concert.
2 .... about the wait! I hope it wasn't too long!
3 He was .... at hearing the good news.
4 'Are you .... with me?' 'No, why should I be?'.
5 The lead singer is very .... with girls!
6 I wish we didn't have to read this textbook. I'm really .... with it.
7 I'm not .... of spiders, but I'm .... of bats!
8 'Aren't you .... in sport?' 'Well, not really.'
9 I'm not very .... at skiing, I'm better at snowboarding.
10 The teachers are not .... with your behaviour at school.

2 Complete the passage with suitable prepositions.

Your problem is that you're always worried [1]............ silly things. You should be happier [2]............ your life. You're married [3]............ a good-looking man who's also clever and keen [4]............ sports like you. You have an interesting job and are very popular [5]............ your colleagues. Your days are very different [6]............ the dull routine lots of people have. So don't make me angry [7]............ you and stop complaining. Your father and I are both getting bored [8]............ your behaviour.

3 Find the mistakes in these sentences and correct them.

1 Aren't you surprised see me here? ....
2 My father is interested at learn how to surf the Internet. ....
3 Mr Higgins is really angry to his son because he has just broken the kitchen window. ....
4 I am very keen at English. ....
5 I am quite worried for the Spanish test. I haven't studied much. ....
6 I'm not very happy for my job. I would like a change. ....
7 Is she married with the new doctor? ....
8 Come on! You can't be scared with bugs. They're harmless. ....
9 She's always been very fond with her grandmother. She visits her every day. ....
10 We are really disappointed for the quality of this project. ....
11 Are you aware with all the risks involved in using chemicals? ....
12 He's responsible of the whole marketing department. ....

Prepositional verbs

As well as adjectives, many verbs are also followed by prepositions which introduce an **indirect object**. The sentence construction may be:

1 subject + verb + preposition + noun or pronoun → *They're talking about their friend. / They're talking about her.*
2 subject + verb + preposition + **–ing** form of the verb (verbal noun) → *I'm thinking of changing my job.*

FAQ

Q: I looked for the verb **ask** in the dictionary and I found three constructions: 1. **ask sth**, 2. **ask sb sth.**, 3. **ask sb about sth.** What do these abbreviations mean?

A: **Sth** is short for **something**, **sb** means **somebody**. So you could say, for example: **I asked a question.** (construction 1, direct object), **I asked John a question.** (construction 2, double object), **I asked John about the weather.** (construction 3, direct object + indirect object). Each verb usually has different constructions or **patterns**. If in doubt, check in a good dictionary.

Here's a list of very common verbs that are followed by one or more prepositions:

Agree with sb about sth / on doing sth → We agreed with them about the price.
Apologise to sb for sth / for doing sth → They apologised to the teacher for being late.
Apply for sth → I applied for the job but I didn't get it.
Approve of sth → I don't approve of his decisions.
Argue with sb about sth → They're always arguing with him about money.
Believe in sb / sth → Do you believe in our friendship?
Borrow sth from sb / sth → I borrowed two books from the library.
Care about sb / sth → I do care about the future of our planet.
Complain to sb about sth → He complained to the boss about his wage cut.
Depend on sb / sth → It depends on the weather.
Get used to sth / to doing sth → I'll never get used to waking up so early.
Hear from sb → Have you heard from them yet?
Laugh at sb / sth → Are you laughing at me?
Listen to sb / sth Listen to sb / sth → I enjoy listening to pop music. I enjoy listening to pop music.
Look after sb / sth → Who's going to look after the puppy?

Look at sb / sth → Don't look at me!
Look for sb / sth → We're looking for a new flat.
Look forward to sth / to doing sth → We're looking forward to meeting you.
Pay for sth → I'll pay for the bill!
Prepare for sth → Sue can't go out tonight because she has to prepare for her exam tomorrow.
Protect sb / sth from sb / sth → This spray can protect you from UV-rays.
Rely on sb → We all rely on you, Paul.
Shout at sb → Stop shouting at me!
Succeed in sth / in doing sth → She succeeded in having her first novel published.
Suffer from sth → My sister suffers from headaches.
Talk / Speak to sb about sth → Did you talk to him about your plan?
Thank sb for sth / for doing sth → I thanked them for their nice present.
Think of / about sb / sth → I'm thinking about my girlfriend.
Wait for sb / sth → Come on! We're waiting for you.
Worry about sb / sth → Don't worry about me.

---

4 Match the sentence halves.

1 Everybody is looking
2 You should think
3 What are you thinking
4 Who have you been
5 Talk to me later. I'm listening
6 I haven't heard
7 I'm getting used
8 You should apologise
9 My sister suffers
10 I really don't approve

A about other people a bit more.
B waiting for?
C to working the night shift.
D to the news.
E from my cousin for ages.
F of doing now?
G to your friend.
H for something better in life.
I of the way she dresses.
J from asthma caused by an allergy to cats.

1 ..... 2 ..... 3 ..... 4 ..... 5 ..... 6 ..... 7 ..... 8 ..... 9 ..... 10 .....

5 Circle the correct option.

1. I think we all agree **with / on / in** the importance of learning a foreign language.
2. We don't approve **for / about / of** your behaviour, Kate.
3. Have you heard **of / from / by** Tina recently?
4. I don't think Tom cares **about / with / of** anything except eating.
5. They finally succeeded **at / about / in** fulfilling their dream: going on holiday to New Zealand.
6. Why do you keep worrying **with / of / about** silly things?
7. Can you please thank your mum **of / for / to** the cake she made?
8. Do I have to pay **for / about / with** the excursion?
9. Are you waiting **to / for / with** the bus?
10. Who is looking **at / up / after** the children this afternoon?

6 Complete the sentences with the correct preposition.

1. Do you promise to think .... my proposal?
2. Do you know what they're talking ....?
3. Jenny usually looks .... her sister in the afternoon.
4. Do you agree .... me .... the importance of a healthy diet?
5. I hope I succeed .... getting my doctorate.
6. I borrowed this dictionary .... a friend.
7. He keeps worrying .... things that don't really matter.
8. Who paid .... the train tickets?
9. Don't ask me .... money. I haven't got any.
10. The hotel guests complained .... the manager .... the rooms.

7 Complete the sentences with the correct form of the verbs below.

ask   agree   get used   apologise   complain   shout   argue   thank   look   borrow

1. We want to .... the teacher about the arrangements for the exam.
2. I would like to .... to you for what I said yesterday.
3. I don't .... with you about the causes of the problem.
4. I can't .... to American coffee. It's too watery.
5. We are going to .... to the manager about our room. It's so dirty.
6. He always .... money from his sister.
7. Our neighbours are always .... about something. They keep shouting!
8. We are .... forward to receiving your initial order.
9. Why are you .... at me? I'm not deaf. You can speak quietly.
10. I'd like to .... you for hosting me. You have been very kind.

8 Choose the prepositional verb formed with *look* from the list below that can replace the verb in bold in each sentence.

look round   look at   look for   look after   look into   look up

1. We're going to **visit** an interesting archaeological site this afternoon. ....
2. We have to **care for** my daughter's dog while she's away. ....
3. I must **find** the meaning of this word in the dictionary. ....
4. The local police said they are **investigating** the problem. ....
5. We **examined** the paintings for a long time. ....
6. We **searched for** her lost bracelet everywhere. ....

To as a preposition and *to* as an infinitive

To is one of the most commonly used words in the English language. As a preposition, that it can be used:

- as an object for movement to a place → *go to work, get to the office*
- to introduce the person or thing affected by an action → *talk to sb, give sth to sb*
- in the expression **from... to...** → *from beginning to end, from London to Manchester*
- to give scores → *They won by three goals to two.*
- for the second term of comparison with the verb **prefer** → *I prefer cycling to walking.*
- after the adjectives **devoted, married, engaged, used / accustomed** (more formal) → *He's devoted to his family. We aren't used to this muggy weather.*

To in front of the base form of the verb is also an **infinitive marker**, highlighting the use of the infinitive. The infinitive is used especially after verbs that conceptually have a future time reference, for example:

- verbs of volition: **want, would like, decide, refuse** → *I want to go home. He decided to leave earlier. Would you like to join us for dinner? They refused to talk to us.*
- verbs that express future prospects or projects: **hope, plan, manage, learn, afford, need, arrange, expect, mean, agree, threaten, offer, promise** → *She hopes to start university in November. He expected to get a reward. I didn't mean to hurt you. We agreed to meet in the afternoon. We managed to arrive on time. I learnt to swim when I was three years old.*

The negative form of the infinitive is **not** + **to** + base form → *He promised not to say anything.*

FAQ

Q: Why do people say **I used to get up early**, but **I'm used to getting up early**, with the *–ing* form?

A: In the first sentence, the verb **use**, which expresses a past habit, is followed by the **infinitive with to**. In the second sentence, **used** is an adjective, followed by the **preposition to**. As we have seen, a verb that follows a preposition (**to, of, about, at...**) is always used in the *–ing* form. Here's another example where the preposition **to** is followed by the *–ing* form of a verb: *I'm looking forward **to going** to New York.*

9 Circle the correct option.

1. I'm getting used to **have** / **having** five hours' sleep a night.
2. I can't wait to **get** / **getting** the exam results.
3. He's tired of **waiting** / **wait** for her.
4. I'm thinking about **go** / **going** abroad next year.
5. We're looking forward to **see** / **seeing** you soon.
6. I'd like to **be** / **being** an engineer when I grow up.
7. Have you arranged to **meeting** / **meet** him?
8. I need to **find** / **finding** a little bit of courage.
9. I used to **be** / **being** very shy when I was little.
10. They're going to **play** / **playing** football tonight.
11. I can't afford to **go** / **going** on holiday this year.
12. I'm used to **work** / **working** the night shift now, but I found it very hard when I started.
13. She threatened to **tell** / **telling** his boss what he'd done.
14. I'm not accustomed to **be** / **being** spoken to like that.

ROUND UP 7

MATRIX +

Remember the following expressions with the preposition **in**:
- to be in prison / in hospital / in bed
- in the rain / in the sun
- in the middle of... in the centre of... → *While exploring Alaska, we found ourselves in the middle of nowhere.*

Expressions with the preposition **on**:
- on the right / left, on the way home, on the way back, on top of the hill
- on holiday, on a trip, on a cruise, on a diet, on TV

Remember too:
- in / on the corner   at / on the corner of... → *Write your name in the top left-hand corner.   Let's meet at the corner of Kearny and Grant Street.*
- at the front   at / on the back. BUT: in the front / in the back of the car / bus → *There's a garden at the back of the house.   She was sitting in the front of the car.*

1 Complete the sentences with the correct prepositions.

1. There's a newsagent's .... the corner of Columbus and Ocean Road.
2. I don't like sitting .... the front of the car. If I'm not driving, I prefer to sit .... the back.
3. There's a warehouse .... the back of the factory.
4. Your jacket is hanging .... the back of the chair near your desk.
5. I always meet Peter .... the way back from my office.
6. Are you going .... a school trip this year?
7. Mr Smith is .... holiday in the Seychelles.
8. Are you still .... bed? Come on! Get up! We can have a nice walk .... the sun this morning.
9. Did you know John is .... hospital? He fell off a ladder yesterday.
10. Look at that castle .... top of the hill! Isn't it beautiful?

2 Complete the sentences with the correct prepositions.

1. I will go, with or .... you!
2. I often go to school .... foot, even though it's quite a long way .... my house.
3. Today's history lesson was .... the Napoleonic wars.
4. Here's a little present .... the children.
5. This novel was written .... Stephen King.
6. Do you like going .... parties?
7. You'll never guess what happened .... me last night!
8. I can play badminton, but I'm not very good .... it.
9. There's a lovely park .... the centre of the town.
10. Fiona's not here – she's gone .... a Caribbean cruise.

3 Some of these sentences contain mistakes in the use of prepositions. Underline them and write them correctly.

1. I was born in 8th October 2005. ....
2. I don't like being home alone in the night. ....
3. We usually go in the mountains for a week on August. ....
4. I'm having a party at my house on Sunday. ....
5. I usually have a quick breakfast before I go to school. ....
6. I will be at home between four to five in the afternoon tomorrow. ....
7. We live at 16 Queen Victoria Road. ....
8. Go until the traffic lights and then turn to left. ....
9. A solar-powered plane landed in Hawaii after a five-day journey across the Pacific Ocean from Japan. ....
10. Do you often go jogging at morning? ....

4 Rewrite the sentences with a double object, without using *to*, as in the example.

0. They offered a cup of tea to their guest.
   They offered their guest a cup of tea.
1. He lent his mobile to his son.
   ....
2. Can you bring that magazine to me, please?
   ....
3. Give your email address to my secretary, will you?
   ....
4. They sent a lot of photos to us when they were in Australia.
   ....
5. Will you please give this book to your teacher?
   ....
6. We showed our new car to our friends.
   ....
7. He sent a beautiful present to his girlfriend for her birthday.
   ....
8. Take the paper to your dad.
   ....

MATRIX +

Other adjectives followed by a preposition

proud of… → I'm really proud of my son for winning the race.

ashamed of… → Don't be ashamed of asking for help.

bad / hopeless at… → I'm really hopeless at playing the piano!

embarrassed at / about… → You mustn't feel embarrassed at standing up and speaking out.

Other verbs followed by a preposition + the *–ing* form

forgive sb for doing sth → Please forgive me for being late.

suspect sb of doing sth → The maths teacher suspects one of his students of copying an exam paper.

dream of / about doing sth → I dream of going to live in New York.

accuse sb of doing sth → Maggie accused one of her classmates of bullying her.

congratulate sb on doing sth → I want to congratulate you on working so hard this year.

insist on doing sth → He always insists on paying for the taxi. (Be careful! He insists on <u>me</u> paying for the taxi.)

prevent sb from doing sth → My parents prevented me from having a tattoo.

feel like doing sth → I don't feel like going shopping today.

warn sb against doing sth → He warned me against driving too fast.

> The expression **It's worth / It isn't worth doing sth** means 'it's (not) useful or important to do something' → *It isn't worth working so hard.*
>
> **For + the –ing form** of the verb expresses the idea of the reason or motive for the action → *He felt bad for hurting her.* (also: ... because he had hurt her.)
>
> **By + the –ing form** of the verb expresses the way you can do an action or a condition placed on an action → *Delete the word by putting a cross through it.*   *You'll always be respected by respecting the others.* (also: ... if you respect the others.)

5 Read the text and choose the correct word (A, B, C or D) for each gap.

Whether you like it or not, adults are examples to young people. If you are a teacher or a parent, it is really important ¹...... your children ²...... succeeding in the things they do. If they feel you are proud ³...... them, they will want to achieve new things. If they are ⁴...... on doing something, however small or simple it is, it is important to show that you recognise it. If they are bad at ⁵...... something, they may feel embarrassed, and you must be prepared for them not succeeding ⁶...... everything. For example, my son is really bad at soccer, but I would not dream ⁷...... to force him to practise. None of us is good at doing everything, and we must forgive our children ⁸...... perfect. As Albert Einstein said, 'Everybody is a genius, but if you judge a fish by its ability ⁹...... a tree, it will live its whole life ¹⁰...... that it is stupid.'

'Look, Mum! I can swim!'

1	A	to congratulate	B	to congratulating	C	congratulate	D	congratulates
2	A	at	B	with	C	of	D	on
3	A	with	B	of	C	to	D	at
4	A	fond	B	keen	C	able	D	good
5	A	do	B	to do	C	doing	D	done
6	A	on	B	with	C	for	D	in
7	A	of try	B	to try	C	to trying	D	of trying
8	A	for not being	B	for being not	C	not to be	D	to be not
9	A	to climb	B	of climbing	C	to climbing	D	in climbing
10	A	to believe	B	believes	C	believing	D	for believing

6 Complete the sentences with the prepositions below.

about   for (x2)   of (x2)   to   at   like   by   on   with

1 He was sorry .... causing me trouble.
2 You'll never get anywhere .... being so rude to others!
3 He thanked me .... helping him.
4 I would never dream .... lying to you!
5 He insisted .... us going to stay with them.
6 John talked .... the manager .... employing more staff.
7 My cat is bad .... chasing birds. He's a lazy cat!
8 I don't feel .... cooking tonight. Let's go to a restaurant.
9 Are you aware .... the problems you're causing?
10 They weren't satisfied .... the accommodation they had found.

7 Complete the sentences with the correct verbs or prepositions.

1 Why are you .... me of hiding your school bag? Isn't it the one under your desk?
2 I must congratulate Mr Berenson, the sales manager, ... achieving great results this year.
3 Jason always feels .... at speaking to an audience – he's very shy.
4 Do you .... like going to the cinema tonight?
5 You shouldn't insist so much .... always being the group leader.
6 I'm really proud .... my students. They did a great project.
7 Ask .... help while doing group work. Don't be ashamed!
8 I often dream .... living by the sea.
9 Who is responsible .... quality control in this company?
10 This lotion should .... you from mosquitoes.

Reflecting on grammar

Think about the rules you learnt and say if these statements are true or false.

		True	False
1	We use the preposition **on** in front of months and seasons.		
2	**Till** and **until** are propositions of time and have the same meaning.		
3	**Under** is the opposite of **on**, **before** is the opposite of **after**.		
4	The sentence *I'm going to home with the bus* is correct.		
5	After a preposition, we can find a noun, a pronoun or the *–ing* form of the verb.		
6	The verbs **give**, **offer** and **show** can be used in a double-object construction.		
7	*The teacher explained us the lesson* is a correct sentence.		
8	With a double-object sentence, the object comes first, then the person.		
9	**To** is both a preposition and an infinitive marker.		
10	*I'm tired of studying* is a correct sentence.		

GRAMMAR MATRIX MAIN

UNIT 8 Past simple and past continuous

LESSON 1 Verb *be* – past simple

→ **Visual Grammar p. 410**

Positive form

The verb **be** has two forms in the past simple: **was**, **were**.
We use only the full form; there is no short form.
I was at home this morning.
We were at school yesterday.

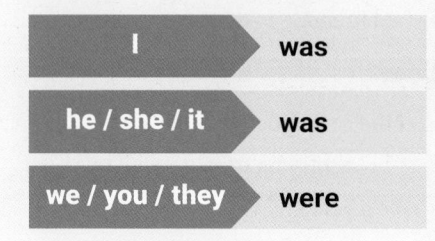

I	was
he / she / it	was
we / you / they	were

Negative form

The negative form can be:
- full:
  I / he / she / it was not
  we / you / they were not
- short:
  I / he / she / it wasn't
  we / you / they weren't

The short form is most frequently used → *It wasn't a good idea.*
They weren't at the stadium.

Interrogative form and short answers

Questions with **be** in the past simple are formed with:
Was I / he / she / it …?
Were we / you / they …?

Negative questions:
Wasn't I / he / she / it …?
Weren't we / you / they …?

Positive short answers:
Yes, + subject pronoun + **was / were**.
Negative short answers:
No, + subject pronoun + **wasn't / weren't**.
'Were the prices good?' 'Yes, they were. The sales were on.'
'Wasn't Luke at the party?' 'No, he wasn't.'

Wh– questions:
What was the weather like?
Why were you late?
When was your wedding anniversary?

REMEMBER:
There was / There were
There wasn't / There weren't
Was there…? / Were there…?
There were lots of people at the ceremony.
There wasn't enough time.
Was there a tennis court near the hotel?

Focus

We use the past simple of **be** to describe events completed in the past at a definite time:
He was at the restaurant when they called from the office.   They were at a party last night.

FAQ

Q: Why do you say **I was born…** to talk about your date and place of birth?

A: **To be born** is a verb only used in the passive. It means to come out of your mother's womb at the beginning of your life. It is obviously used in the past simple form. The question **Where and when were you born?** also uses the past simple of **be**.

UNIT 8

1 Listen and write what was or wasn't in the campsite where you were on holiday.

mini-market   playground   camper vans   tents   beach   restaurant   tourists

0 *There was a mini-market.*
1 ....
2 ....
3 ....
4 ....
5 ....
6 ....

2 Complete the sentences with the correct form of the past simple of *be*.

1 Don't put the blame on me. It .... my fault!
2 It .... a very exciting basketball game. The final score .... 86 to 84.
3 The weather .... very good, but we had a good time anyway.
4 There .... any good prizes in the raffle.
5 '............................ it a good weekend?' 'Yes, it .... fantastic.'
6 There .... a pool in the hotel, but there .... a beauty centre. I couldn't have a massage.
7 The wedding .... fabulous. There .... hundreds of guests. The location and the food .... just perfect.
8 '............................ you on the Continental flight to New York?' 'Yes, we ....'

3 Match the sentence halves.

1 The bus drivers were on strike yesterday,
2 There were some interesting statistics in yesterday's paper
3 There were so many good films on at the Multiplex last weekend
4 There was a terrible storm last night
5 The winner of 'Best of British' last year
6 The weather was really good last weekend,
7 The cave was dark and damp
8 There was a spectacular view

A that we couldn't make up our minds which one to see!
B was a young girl with a beautiful voice.
C so we decided to go to the lake.
D so there was a long queue for taxis.
E and there were long stalactites hanging from the roof.
F with strong wind, hail and thunder.
G from the top of the Empire State Building.
H about unemployment figures in Britain.

1 ..... 2 ..... 3 ..... 4 ..... 5 ..... 6 ..... 7 ..... 8 .....

LESSON 2 Regular and irregular verbs – past simple

→ Visual Grammar pp. 410–411

Positive form

There are **regular** and **irregular** verbs in English.

We form the past simple of regular verbs by adding **–ed** to the base form:
listen → listened   play → played   wait → waited   *They waited an hour.*

Irregular verbs have different past simple forms, which must be memorised, for example:
go → went   write → wrote   begin → began   have → had   *She had an important meeting yesterday.*

Sometimes the base form and the past simple are identical, for example **put → put**. A lot of common verbs are irregular, as you can see in the table on pages 428-429.
The past simple of both regular and irregular verbs has the same form for all persons.

| I / you / he / she / it / we / they | started |

| I / you / he / she / it / we / they | went |

> Pay attention to the following spelling rules when adding the ending **–ed**.
> - If the verb ends in **–e**, we add **–d**: like → liked   live → lived
> - We double the final consonant in:
>   – one-syllable verbs ending in one vowel + one consonant: **clap** → **clapped**
>   **rob** → **robbed**   BUT: **clean** → **cleaned** (two vowels)
>   **rent** → **rented** (two consonants)
>   – two-syllable verbs with a stress on the second syllable, ending in one vowel + one consonant: **prefer** → **preferred**   **omit** → **omitted**
>   BUT: **offer** → **offered** (stress on the first syllable)   **repeat** → **repeated** (two vowels in the second syllable)   **adopt** → **adopted** (two final consonants)
>   – verbs ending in **–el** preceded by a single vowel (in British English):
>   **travel** → **travelled** (USA: **traveled**)   BUT: **peel** → **peeled** (two vowels)
> - Verbs ending in a consonant + **y** change the **y** into **i** before adding **–ed**:
>   **cry** → **cried**   **study** → **studied**   BUT: **stay** → **stayed** (vowel + **y**)

1 Write the past simple of these verbs. Use the table on pages 428-429 for the irregular verbs.

Regular verbs		Irregular verbs	
Base form	Past simple	Base form	Past simple
stop		have	
help		know	
play		leave	
shout		meet	
work		go	
try		tell	
refer		take	
quarrel (UK)		read	
submit		come	
move		speak	

2 Complete the sentences with some of the past simple verbs from exercise 1.

1 Sam ………………… basketball when he was at college and was quite good.

2 I ………………… my old friend Dave on my way to work this morning.

3 My neighbours ………………… so loudly last night that I was going to call the police!

4 I ………………… for a transport company in London until May, then I ………………… to work in New York.

5 I ………………… a lot of books when I was on holiday in July.

6 I ………………… and I ………………… again, but I couldn't solve the problem. It was way too difficult for me.

7 They ………………… the 54 bus to the stadium last Saturday.

8 We ………………… a big breakfast this morning, so we aren't hungry now.

9 My teacher ………………… me a lot when I was having problems with my exam preparation.

10 He ……………… his application and CV to the Human Resources Manager.

3 Complete the story of a journey that an English family posted on their blog. Use the past simple of the verbs in brackets. They are all irregular except one. Which one?

We ¹........................... a fantastic holiday in Australia last summer. (have) We ²........................... a flight to Sydney via Singapore, where we ³........................... a six-hour stopover. (take, have) We ⁴........................... to Sydney at 11 am local time and we ⁵........................... a bit strange for the first few days because of jet lag. (get, feel)

We ⁶........................... five days in Sydney and ⁷........................... the Opera House, the Harbour Bridge and all the beautiful sights of the bay. (spend, see) After that, we ⁸........................... north in a mini-van and ⁹........................... the fantastic beaches of Queensland, past Brisbane then up to the Capricorn Islands. (drive, see) Then we ¹⁰........................... to Darwin, on the north coast, and ¹¹........................... the outback in a jeep, stopping at Ayers Rock, or Uluru, as the Aborigines call it. (fly, cross over) We ¹²........................... lots of unusual animals on our trip – dingos, kangaroos, wombats and snakes. (come across) It ¹³........................... really an unforgettable journey. (be)

Negative form

The past simple negative has a **full form** and a **short form** (the latter is much more frequently used):

Full form: subject + **did** + **not** + base form of the verb:
I did not know the answer.

Short form: subject + **didn't** + base form of the verb:
We didn't go to the theatre.

Interrogative form

Questions in the past simple are formed with:
Did + subject + base form of the verb + ...?
Negative questions:
Didn't + subject + base form of the verb + ...?
Short answers:
Positive: Yes, + subject pronoun + **did**.
Negative: No, + subject pronoun + **didn't**.
'Did you like the show?' 'Yes, I did.'
'Didn't they give you an answer?' 'No, they didn't.'
Wh– questions start with a question word:
Wh– word + **did** + subject + base form of the verb + ...?
What did you do at the weekend?
Where did you see him?

4 a Last night, Mr and Ms Steel spent a quiet evening at home. Complete the sentences with the positive form of the first verb and the negative form of the second.

1 Mr and Ms Steel .... at home last night, they .... their friends. (stay, meet)

2 They .... dinner at home, they .... to a restaurant. (have, go)

3 They .... a film on TV, they .... to the cinema. (watch, go)

4 They .... to bed early, they .... late. (go, stay up)

b On a different evening, Mr and Ms Steel went out with friends. Rewrite the sentences from exercise 4a using the negative form of the first verb and the positive form of the second.

1 ....
2 ....
3 ....
4 ....

5 Complete the past simple questions and short answers using the verbs in brackets.

1 '………………… you ………………… the concert?' 'Yes, ………………… . It was great.' (enjoy)

2 '………………… Tom ………………… in the last cricket match?' 'No, ………………… . He was ill.' (play)

3 '………………… they ………………… by coach?' 'No, ………………… . They went on the train.' (travel)

4 '………………… she ………………… last Saturday?' 'Yes, ………………… , but only in the morning.' (work)

5 '………………… you ………………… a good time at summer camp?' 'No, ………………… . It was a bit boring.' (have)

6 '………………… Rob ………………… home late last night?' 'Yes, ………………… . He came home at 9.30.' (come)

6 Reorder the words and write questions or negative sentences in the past simple.

1 didn't / We / at all / the / film / like / .

2 buy / Did / you / a / train ticket / return / ?

3 this morning / you / emails / check / Didn't / your / ?

4 didn't / go out / last night / with / She / Thomas / .

5 she / get up / Sunday / Did / late / on / ?

6 do / didn't / yesterday / our homework / We /.

7 the / same story / he / repeat / over and over / Did / again / ?

8 so early / They / didn't / to leave / want / the party / .

7 Complete the dialogues with appropriate Wh– questions using you. Then listen and check.

1 **A** ………………………… that lovely bag?
   B I bought it at Kensington market last week.
   A ………………………… for it?
   B You won't believe it... I only paid £3!

2 **A** ………………………… at the weekend, Dave?
   B I went to Brighton, on the south coast of England.
   A ………………………… with?
   B I went with my wife and the kids, and a friend of mine.
   A ………………………… get there?
   B We took the car. It was a couple of hours.

3 **A** Hi, Simon. How nice to see you! …………………………?
   B I got here yesterday morning. And I'm leaving tonight.
   A Really? It's just for a short stay, then.

4 **A** ………………………… in the USA?
   B I studied at Stanford University.
   A ………………………… there?
   B I studied politics and economics, then I got a Master's in business administration.

5 **A** So you were in Paris last week. ………………………… there?
   B Oh, I visited the Louvre for a whole day. I went up the Eiffel Tower and I saw the Tour de France on Sunday.
   A That was lucky! ………………………… your trip?
   B I booked it online – the flight, the hotel and everything. I found a very good last-minute offer.

LESSON 3 Use of the past simple, time expressions and time sequencing, *used to*...

The past simple is the verbal tense for narratives in the past. It refers to situations or events which started and finished in the past. Use it for:

- **past experiences** → *I got a good mark in yesterday's maths test.*
- **historical events** → *The Normans came to England in 1066.*
- **biographies** → *William Shakespeare was born in 1564 in Stratford-upon-Avon and died in the same place in 1616, on the same day of his birth, 23rd April.*
- **tales and fables** → *Cinderella had two wicked step-sisters.*
- **reports, news items** → *The car didn't stop at the red light and crashed into a van coming the other way.*
- **questions about when, at what time, where... something happened** → *When did you go to the bank? What time did you get up this morning?*

Usually the time when an event happened is mentioned unless it is obvious. In a past simple sentence these time expressions or time clauses can be used:

- this morning / this afternoon
- yesterday / the day before yesterday
- last night
- last week / month / year...
- two / three... hours / days ago
- a long / short time ago
- in December
- in 2013
- on June 4th
- at two o'clock
- in the 20th century
- when I was young / a child / six years old

The time expressions or time clauses usually appear at the end of the sentence:
I started reading this book three hours ago.
I got up early this morning.
Or they can appear at the beginning of the sentence:
When I was young, I lived in Scotland.

> **!** Note: *The last time I saw her was in March.*
> The same idea can be expressed with the adverb **last**:
> *I last saw her in March. / I saw her last in March.*

Focus

In some languages, the English past simple corresponds to a variety of tenses. The imperfect in your language may be similar to the past simple but also to the past continuous or **used to...** (see pages 135–136). The present perfect in your language may correspond to the English past simple or to the English present perfect (see page 144).

1 Circle the correct option. Focus on the verb tense and the time expression.

1. I went to Liverpool on business **next** / **last** Friday.
2. Our teachers **give** / **gave** us a lot of homework every weekend.
3. The club usually **opens** / **opened** at nine, but it **opens** / **opened** at ten last Sunday.
4. Some of my classmates play basketball **on** / **last** Wednesdays.
5. They spent the evening in a pub **last** / **every** Saturday.
6. Sam phoned me at 12 **yesterday** / **last** night.
7. We had an English test three days **long** / **ago**.
8. I didn't see him in his office **this** / **last** morning.
9. Ken left for Sydney the day **before yesterday** / **yesterday before**.
10. I finished work very early **last night** / **yesterday night**.

2 Complete the sentences with a time expression so that they are true for you.

1 It last rained heavily ....
2 The last time I went on a trip was ....
3 I saw a really good film ....
4 I got a present ....
5 I bought some new clothes ....
6 I got a Tweet or an SMS ....
7 I had a haircut ....
8 The last time I got a bad mark was ....
9 I last sent a postcard ....
10 The last time I took a train was ....

Time sequencing

Events in a story are usually narrated in chronological sequence. Instructions, for example in a recipe, are also given in sequence. We use adverbs or phrases to show the time sequence and we usually place them at the beginning of a paragraph.

Sequencing
- First / First of all
- Then
- After that
- Next
- Finally / In the end

! Note the difference between **then** and **after**. **Then** is an adverb and must be used on its own as a linking word between two clauses:
I did my homework, then I went out with my friends.

After is a preposition and is followed by a noun or a pronoun:
I went out after dinner.
He helped me fix my bike. After that, he mowed the lawn and cleaned my garage.

The same is true of **first** (adverb) and **before** (preposition). → *First I went shopping, then I had lunch.*
(NOT: Before I went shopping, after I had lunch.)   *I went shopping before lunch.*

After and **before** can also be used as conjunctions introducing a subordinate clause (subject + verb) or a verb in the –ing form:
We started eating dinner only after my father arrived.

We waited for my father to arrive before we started eating dinner.
After giving him the prize, we had a little party.
I went jogging in the park before having breakfast this morning.

3 Complete the text with sequencing words: *then / finally / first / after*.

Last Monday was a busy day for me. I got up very early. [1]............. having a quick breakfast, I left home in a hurry. [2]............. I went to the bank to get some cash, [3]............. I met George at the tube station and we took a train to Gatwick Airport. We waited for our German colleague Hans, who was arriving from Frankfurt, there. [4]............. saying hello to him, we helped him with his luggage and [5]............. we set off for the centre of London. Hans had a lot of bags, so we took him to his hotel [6]............. . [7]............. he left his luggage at the concierge, we drove to the Congress Centre where our meeting was scheduled. We stayed there till 7 pm. [8]............. , we all went for dinner in a good restaurant in the area.

4 Tell the story of an excursion you went on. Show the sequence of the events by using *first*, *then*, *after that / next*, *finally*. Use the *past simple* of the verbs below.

visit the cathedral   have lunch in a fast-food restaurant
go around the shops and buy gifts   have coffee and drive back home

Last Saturday, we went on a trip to Canterbury. ....
....
....
....

5 Reorder the instructions for this recipe. Pay attention to the words and phrases indicating the sequence.

TO MAKE GOOD CHOCOLATE–CHIP COOKIES, FOLLOW THIS SIMPLE RECIPE.

You need: 125 g butter, 50 g sugar, 150 g self-raising flour, 175 g plain chocolate, one egg.

After weighing all the ingredients, put them on the table and start working.

- [ ] Then bake in the oven for 15 to 20 minutes until the cookies are golden brown.
- [ ] Finally, put them on a wire rack to cool.
- [ ] Then break up the chocolate into small pieces and put them into the mixture.
- [ ] After greasing a baking sheet, put about 20 teaspoonfuls of the mixture onto it.
- [ ] When the butter and sugar mixture is light and fluffy, beat in the egg and slowly add the flour.
- [ ] First pre-heat the oven to 180°C.
- [ ] To make the dough, mix the butter and sugar together.

Used to

We use **used to** + base form of the verb to talk about habits in the past, especially when they were different from present habits. **Used to** is the same for all persons → *I used to go sailing when I was your age.*
We used to go camping every summer.
There used to be a statue in the square.

Negative forms and questions are the same as for the past simple (see page 131):

Negative: subject + **didn't** + **use to** + base form of the verb
→ *My mother didn't use to put on make-up when she was my age.*

Questions: Did /Didn't + subject + **use to** + base form of the verb + ...? → *'Didn't he use to work abroad?' 'Yes, he did. But he's retired now.'*

Wh– questions: *Wh–* word + did / didn't + subject + **use to** + base form of the verb + ? → *'Where did they use to go fishing?' 'In the little lake near their farmhouse.'*

6 Reorder the words and write sentences.

1 your / Did / brother / use to / a boy scout / be / ?
2 dye / Jane / her hair / used to / red / she / when / was / younger / .
3 used to / long hours / I / study / when / was / at college / I / .
4 mobile phones or / didn't / use to / MP3 players / We / have / .
5 a youth hostel / used / My family / to run / the / town centre / in / .
6 you / did / use to / Where / go dancing / in / old days / the / ?

7 Complete the text with the positive or negative form of *used to*, as appropriate.

Christmas is always a festive time, but lots of things have changed since I was a child. When I was little, I remember we [1]........................... (have) a real Christmas tree in the living room – now we have an artificial one. We [2]........................... (not buy) Christmas cakes or puddings, my grandmother [3]........................... (make) them. My sister and I [4]........................... (hang up) a stocking where Santa Claus could put our presents. We [5]........................... (not sleep) much on Christmas Eve because we were always very excited. We [6]........................... (not have) a party at school, but we [7]........................... (act) in a Nativity play and we [8]........................... (sing) Christmas carols at church.

8 Complete the second sentence so that it has the same meaning as the first one.

1 There was a fountain in this park.
   There used ....

2 We wore a uniform in primary school.
   We used ....
   when we ....

3 Before I went out, I closed all the windows and switched off the lights.
   I went out after ....

4 First I helped my grandma with the shopping, then I went skateboarding in the park.
   Before going ....,
   I helped ....

5 After driving five hours, my husband stopped at a service area.
   My husband drove ....
   before ....

6 When I was little, my father always helped me with my homework.
   My father used ....
   when ....

7 I last missed a day's work two years ago.
   The last time ....

8 The last time I was in bed with flu was during the Christmas holidays three years ago.
   I was last ....

LESSON 4 Past continuous, time clauses with *When* / *While*

We form the past continuous with the past simple of **be** followed by the **–ing** form of the main verb.

Positive: Subject + **was** / **were** + **–ing** form of the verb

I was practising for my piano exam.

Negative: Subject + **wasn't** / **weren't** + **–ing** form of the verb

The baby wasn't sleeping.

Questions: Was / **Were** + subject + **–ing** form of the verb + ...?

Were you having a good time at the party?

Negative questions: Wasn't / **Weren't** + subject + **–ing** form of the verb + ...?

Wasn't she dating Rob at that time?

Short answers: Yes, + subject + **was** / **were**.
No, + subject + **wasn't** / **weren't**.

'Was it snowing?' 'Yes, it was.'
'Were they wearing uniforms?' 'No, they weren't.'

Wh– questions: Wh– word + **was** / **were** + subject + **–ing** form of the verb + ...?

What were you doing?
Where was she going?
Why were you crying?

We use the past continuous to:
- talk about an action which was happening at a specific moment in the past and continued for some time → *I was watching a film at nine o'clock last night.*
- talk about actions which were gradually developing in the past. We use **get** + adjective in this case. → *It was getting dark.   I was getting tired.*
- talk about actions which were repeated over a period of time and were rather annoying, usually with the adverb **always** → *They were always talking nonsense.*
- set the scene or the context of a story → *The wind was blowing and not a soul was walking in the street.*

The past continuous is used mainly with action verbs, but sometimes also with verbs like **feel, hope, enjoy, hate** → *I wasn't feeling very well.   We were enjoying our meal.   I was hating that place!*

1 **Where were these people yesterday afternoon? What were they doing? Match the sentence halves.**

1 Patrick was at a club in Dublin.
2 Gerald was in the Sahara desert.
3 Mark was on a train to Bristol.
4 Clare was on a golf course in Stratford.
5 Kate was at a street market in London.
6 Mario was at a language school in Oxford.
7 Sarah was at home with her grandmother.
8 Peter was at the stadium with his dad.
9 Sheila was on a cruise on the Baltic Sea.
10 Agnes was behind the counter in her café.

A She was teaching her how to surf the Internet.
B She was making coffees and teas for her customers.
C She was buying some second-hand clothes.
D They were watching a great rugby match.
E He was riding on a camel among the dunes.
F She was learning how to play with her instructor.
G He was taking the Preliminary exam.
H He was having a party with his friends.
I He was reading the newspaper.
J She was lying in the sun on the upper deck.

1 .....   2 .....   3 .....   4 .....   5 .....   6 .....   7 .....   8 .....   9 .....   10 .....

2 **Complete the dialogues with the past continuous of the verbs in brackets. Then listen and check.**

1 **A** .... you .... your blue dress at the wedding? (wear)
   B No, I wasn't. I .... my long black skirt and pink top. (wear)

2 **A** .... your brother .... your car around town yesterday morning? (drive)
   B No, I don't think it was him. He .... at home. (study)

3 **A** What .... you .... on Sunday at around ten o'clock, Tom? (do)
   B At ten? Er... I .... in the garden, I guess. (work)

4 **A** Why .... the kids ....? (argue)
   B Because Mark .... a lot of noise while Jim .... TV. (make, watch)

5 **A** I .... fast, Officer. (not drive)
   B Oh yes, you were. You .... at nearly 80 miles per hour. And the limit is 60 miles on this road. (go)

Time clauses with *when* and *while*

When and **while** are conjunctions which introduce time clauses.

We use **when** to introduce an action (in the past simple) that happened while another action was in progress (in the past continuous):

> subject + past continuous + **when** + new subject + past simple
> ↓ ↓
> main clause   subordinate clause

My mother <u>was reading</u> in her room **when** her friend from France <u>called</u> her on Skype.
I <u>was making</u> a cake **when** somebody <u>rang</u> at the door.

We use **while**, or **when**, to introduce an action that was in progress (in the past continuous) when something happened (in the past simple):

> subject + past simple + **while** or **when** + new subject + past continuous
> ↓ ↓
> main clause   subordinate clause

I <u>entered</u> the conference room **while / when** the delegates <u>were debating</u> an important issue.
The cars <u>stopped</u> **while** all the runners in the marathon <u>were leaving</u> the stadium.

We also use **while** to talk about two or more actions in progress at the same time, with the past continuous in both the main clause and the subordinate clause.

> subject + past continuous + **while** + new subject + past continuous

Peter was listening to music **while** his brother was playing video games. (It is also possible to say: Peter was listening to music **and** his brother was playing video games.)

> **!** Note that **when** is more frequently used than **while**. We use **when** both for completed short actions and for actions in progress. We use **while** only for longer background actions in progress.
>
> The order of the clauses can be reversed, with the subordinate clause coming first, followed by the main clause. In this case, a comma is added before the main clause:
> *When my sister arrived, we were all watching a football match on TV.*
> *While I was working on my computer, the light suddenly went off.*

FAQ

Q: I know a nursery rhyme which says:
As I was going to St Ives, / I met a man with seven wives, / Each wife had seven sacks, / Each sack had seven cats, / Each cat had seven kits: / Kits, cats, sacks and wives, / How many were going to St Ives?
Why does it start with **as**? Shouldn't we say **while** or **when**?

A: In this case, the conjunction **as** has the same meaning as **while**. But what is the answer to the riddle *How many were going to St Ives?* In case you don't know it, the answer is **one**: only the person who is speaking was going to St Ives. All the others were going in the opposite direction!

3
Read the text about a famous historical event in the United States. Insert the missing sentences at the appropriate points. Write only the letter.

A She was sitting there
B was the beginning of a long struggle
C and he was standing.
D She was going home after a day's work.
E no one took the bus
F but she refused.
G everybody walked to work

On the evening of December 1st 1955, an Afro-American woman called Rosa Parks got on a bus in Montgomery, Alabama. ¹ [D] All the seats at the back of the bus were taken, so she took a seat in the front, which was reserved for white people. ² [A] when a white passenger got on the bus. He couldn't find a free seat ³ [C] . The bus driver asked Rosa to give her seat to the white man ⁴ [F] . So the driver called the police and she was arrested. This episode ⁵ [B] called 'The bus boycott'. From that day, all the Afro-Americans living in Montgomery stopped using the bus as a form of protest against the segregation laws between black and white people. Every day, for 12 months, ⁶ [G] and ⁷ [E] any more. Finally, in December 1956, the Supreme Court in Washington stated that segregation on buses was illegal. It was the first great victory for the civil rights movement in the USA and for its leader, Reverend Martin Luther King.

4
Write sentences with the same meaning. Start all the sentences with *While*.

1 I was walking in the street when I saw a bad accident.
   ....
2 We were all cheering when a group of hooligans invaded the football pitch.
   ....
3 They were going home when they saw an old friend getting off the bus.
   ....
4 The actors were getting ready for the shoot when the director suddenly left.
   ....
5 I was doing my homework while my friend was waiting for me in the hall.
   ....
6 I was talking to the English teacher when the principal came into the library.
   ....
7 We were having a drink when a band started playing folk music.
   ....
8 The exam students were still writing when the final bell rang.
   ....

5
Past simple or past continuous? Complete the sentences with the correct form of the verbs in brackets.

1 When I .... down a country road, I .... two deer behind a bush. (cycle, see)
2 A delicious smell .... from the kitchen where Dad's apple pie .... (come, bake)
3 The burglar .... to break the lock when the alarm .... (try, go off)
4 When I .... the front door, I .... a strange noise coming from the garden. (open, hear)
5 She .... when her cat .... on her bed and .... her .... (dream, jump, wake up)

ROUND UP 8

1 **Read the text and complete it with the correct form of the past simple of *be*: *was / wasn't, were / weren't*.**

Most people lived in small villages in the countryside in the 15th century, either in farmhouses or in cottages. A typical cottage of Tudor times ¹............................ very small. The walls ²............................ made of wood, mud and straw. The roof ³............................ often made of straw too, it ⁴............................ called 'thatched' roof. The windows ⁵............................ small and sometimes there ⁶............................ any windows at all, just a door. There ⁷............................ a kitchen downstairs and one or two bedrooms upstairs. The beds ⁸............................ quite short because people ⁹............................ very tall then. There ¹⁰............................ always a fireplace in the kitchen with a spit to roast meat. There ¹¹............................ a toilet – people washed themselves and their clothes outside in a stream or in a big basin in the kitchen when it ¹²............................ cold. People often lived together with their animals – chicken, sheep and goats – so the floor ¹³............................ very clean. In fact, there ¹⁴............................ a tiled floor, just dried mud covered with straw.

2 **Complete Shakespeare's biography with the past simple of the verbs below.**

study   be   not go   become   have   be born   retire   leave
found   write   buy   die   start   marry

William Shakespeare, often called the English national poet, is considered the greatest dramatist of all time. He ¹............................ in Stratford-upon-Avon in 1564. He ²............................ in Stratford at the local grammar school, but he probably ³............................ to university. In 1582, when he ⁴............................ only 18 years old, he ⁵............................ Anne Hathaway, who was 26. They ⁶............................ three children: a daughter and twins. In 1586, Shakespeare ⁷............................ his native town to go to London, where he ⁸............................ an actor with the Company of the Lord Chamberlain's Men. In London, he ⁹............................ writing plays. He ¹⁰............................ many historical plays, tragedies, comedies and also sonnets.
With the Lord Chamberlain's Men, he ¹¹............................ the Globe Theatre, where his works were performed. When he was rich and famous, he ¹²............................ a large house in Stratford where he ¹³............................ in 1611.
Shakespeare ¹⁴............................ in 1616, on the same day of his birth, April 23rd, and was buried in the churchyard of Stratford Parish Church.

MATRIX +

Past habits

To talk about a habit we had in the past, we can use **used to** or alternatively **would** + base form →
I used to travel a lot when I worked as a sales rep. = I would travel a lot, when I worked as a sales rep.

3 Write sentence with the same meaning using *would* or *used to*.

0 The children used to drink a lot of orange juice.   *The children would drink a lot of orange juice.*
1 I used to cycle to my grandma's every Sunday. ....
2 We would learn nursery rhymes by heart when we were in primary school.
....
3 He used to work six days a week for his former company.
....
4 My mother used to cook fresh vegetables every day.
....
5 They would go to an organic market to buy local cheeses when they lived in Lincoln.
....
6 I used to walk a lot when I was younger. ....
7 She didn't use to take her sister with her. ....
8 My brother would ride a big red motorcycle when he was young.
....

4 Order these time expressions from the most recent (1) to the earliest (7).

☐ Two months ago   ☐ Last night   ☐ Last week   ☐ Three hours ago
☐ Five minutes ago ☐ Last year   ☐ Yesterday morning

5 Complete the dialogue with the missing words. Use the verbs in the past simple or past continuous.

Adam Hi, Jack. What were you doing when we ⁰ *had* (have) the blackout last night?

Jack I was at home with my wife. We ¹................................ (watch TV). What about you?

Adam I ²................................ (go back home) in my car. I ³................................ (wait) at the traffic lights when all of a sudden all the lights ⁴................................ (go out).

Jack It ⁵................................ (be) really bad. It ⁶................................ (last) so long!

Adam Yes, nearly four hours. When I ⁷................................ (get back home), I just ⁸................................ (go to bed).

Jack Yes, so did I. With no electricity, there's nothing much you can do!

141

6 **Complete the text with the past simple of the verbs in brackets.**

The origin of coffee is lost in the timeless legends of the Middle East. What we know for sure is that coffee beans ¹............................ (spread) from Ethiopia to Yemen around 1400 and ²............................ (not reach) Europe until the 17th century. At that time, all the coffee ³............................ (come) from Arabia. However, thanks to the Dutch merchants, coffee cultivation ⁴............................ (begin) in the Americas. It ⁵............................ (spread) quickly to the West Indies, but the country where it ⁶............................ (grow) best was Brazil. Between 1850 and 1900, other Latin American countries ⁷............................ (develop) extensive coffee plantations. Around 1900, commercial coffee growing ⁸............................ (start) in central Africa thanks to the British, but the area only ⁹............................ (become) a major source of coffee after World War II.

7 **Complete the dialogue with the correct past form of the verbs below.**

do   check   have   get (x2)   hear   meet (x2)   sleep   walk   be (x3)   enjoy   leave
see   know

John   Have I called you at a bad time? ¹............... you ....?
Irene No, I ²............... my emails. When ³............... you .... back from Rome?
John   I ⁴............... back two days ago.
Irene ⁵............... you .... your business trip?
John   Well, yes. I ⁶............... various interesting meetings. And there's something more. Guess who I ⁷............... in Rome!
Irene How should I know? Who ⁸............... you ....?
John   While I ⁹............... to the hotel, I ¹⁰............... somebody I ¹¹............... sure I ¹²............... . It ¹³............... Peter. Do you remember him? He ¹⁴............... at university with us, but then he ¹⁵............... with his family and we never ¹⁶............... of him again.
Irene Peter? Yes, I remember him. What ¹⁷............... he .... in Rome?
John   Well, he lives there. He's a journalist with *Il Tempo*.

8 **Complete the text with the appropriate words. Write only one word in each gap.**

I went ¹............................ Neil's party last Saturday. There ²............................ about 30 people there and we ³............................ a great time. The party ⁴............................ in the garden of his parents' house, the same place where we ⁵............................ to play when we were children. There were a ⁶............................ of tables with the food, while the drinks were in big buckets full of ice. Before dinner, we all chatted with one another because most of us hadn't seen each other for a long time. ⁷............................ Neil was grilling steaks on the barbecue, his wife was frying chips in a huge deep-fat fryer. Not the healthiest food ever, but we all enjoyed it when it was ready.

⁸............................ dinner, Jason got his old guitar out of his car and started playing and singing old songs. ⁹............................ the party was getting a bit too nostalgic, Neil put on some lively music and we all ¹⁰............................ till dawn.

9 Complete the text with the past simple or the past continuous of the verbs in brackets. Sometimes you have to use the negative form.

What a terrible night! I ¹............................ (sleep) in my bed, when the telephone ²............................ (ring). I ³............................ (answer) immediately, but I ⁴............................ (hear) anything on the other side, just a strange sound, like a cat mewing. I ⁵............................ (put) the telephone down and I ⁶............................ (try) to go to sleep again, but it ⁷............................ (ring) again and again and again. I could only hear the same strange sound and nothing else. After an hour like this, I ⁸............................ (decide) to call the police. While I ⁹............................ (dial) the number, I ¹⁰............................ (see) a light in my garden. Someone ¹¹............................ (walk) there and ¹²............................ (search) the garden with a torch. At that point, I was really scared. When the police officer ¹³............................ (answer) the phone I ¹⁴............................ (whisper), so as not to be heard by the person in the garden and I ¹⁵............................ (try) to explain what ¹⁶............................ (happen). While I ¹⁷............................ (wait) for the police to come I ¹⁸............................ (hide) behind the curtains of my bedroom window to watch what the person ¹⁹............................ (do). While the reassuring sound of the police siren ²⁰............................ (get) nearer, I ²¹............................ (hear) a banging at the door…

10 Now write your own ending for the story.

Reflecting on grammar

Think about the rules you learnt and say if these statements are true or false.

		True	False
1	The past simple of **be** has two forms.		
2	There isn't a short form for *I was*.		
3	Irregular verbs form the past simple by adding **–ed**.		
4	The sentence *She didn't learnt anything* is correct.		
5	We use the past simple for actions which are still in progress at the moment of speaking.		
6	We use **used to** to talk about habits we had in the past.		
7	A time sequence usually ends with the adverb **then**.		
8	The sentence *First I had breakfast, after I read the newspaper* is correct.		
9	We use the past continuous for actions in progress at a specific moment in the past.		
10	We never use the past continuous in a clause starting with **when**.		

GRAMMAR MATRIX MAIN

UNIT 9 Present perfect and past perfect

LESSON 1 Present perfect simple: *ever, never, recently, today...*

→ **Visual Grammar pages 412–413**

The **present perfect simple** (from now on we will call it simply the **present perfect**) is formed with the auxiliary verb **have** followed by the past participle of the main verb.

How is the past participle formed?

REGULAR VERBS	IRREGULAR VERBS
By adding the ending **–ed**: finish**ed**, start**ed**, paint**ed**... It's the same form as the past simple.	Each verb has its own form. Sometimes it's the same as the base form or the past simple form: *found, come, cut*, but often it has a different form: *been, spoken, written*. You will find a list of irregular verbs on page 472. The past participle is shown in the third column.

Positive, negative and question forms

> **Positive**
> **Full form:** subject + **have** / **has** + past participle
> **Short form:** subject + **'ve** / **'s** + past participle (this form is more common if the subject is a pronoun)

We have finished (We've finished) at last.
She has arrived! (She's arrived!)
The children have had their lunch.

> **Negative:** subject + **have not (haven't)** / **has not (hasn't)** + past participle form of the verb

I haven't been very well.
He hasn't bought a paper today.

> **Interrogative: Have / Has** + subject + past participle... + ?

> **Negative interrogative: Haven't / Hasn't** + subject + past participle... + ?

> **Short answers: Yes,** + subject + **have** / **has**.   **No,** + subject + **haven't** / **hasn't**.

'Have you seen Dad anywhere?' 'No, I haven't.'
'Hasn't she passed her driving test?' 'Yes, she has.'

> **Wh– questions: Wh–** word + **have** / **has** + subject + past participle... + ?

Where have you been?   What have you bought?

Focus

In English, the auxiliary verb of the present perfect is always **have** (**I have gone, we have come back**).
Remember the present perfect of the verb **be**: **I / You / We / They have been   He / She / It has been**
I've been here for two hours.
She's been our general manager for ten years.

FAQ

Q: Sometimes I've heard **He's been to...** and other times **He's gone to...** to talk about someone being in a place. Is there a difference or can I choose either form?

A: There's a difference. If you say, for example, **He's been to South Africa**, it means that the person has been to South Africa and now he has returned home. On the other hand, if you say **He's gone to South Africa**, it means that the person is still there.

1 Complete the sentences with the present perfect of the verbs in brackets. Use the short form.

1 Oh no! I .... my wallet with all my credit cards. (lose)
2 We .... any new shrubs in our garden this year. (not plant)
3 I .... skiing a few times, but I'm just hopeless at it! (try)
4 Emma .... to a new flat near the city centre. (move)
5 I'm sorry, Miss Trevor. I .... my English homework today. (not do)
6 Stop being silly. I .... enough of your stupid antics. (have)
7 You .... the plants. Look – their leaves are all dried up. (not water)
8 We .... always .... this band. They play great music. (like)
9 Josh, you .... the dishes! They're all in the sink where they were last night! (not wash)
10 '........................... , sir?' 'No, you .... the menu yet.' (order, bring)

2 🎧08 Complete the questions with the verbs in the present perfect, match them to the answers, then listen and check.

1 .... you .... your emails? (check)
2 Your bag's heavy! What .... you ....? (buy)
3 .... the new teacher ....? (arrive)
4 .... they .... any new houses here? (build)
5 .... you .... Kate? (see)
6 Why .... Mum .... all this food? (cook)

A No, I haven't.
B Yes, I have.
C Lots of fruit and veggies.
D No, he hasn't.
E We're having a dinner party tonight.
F Yes, at the end of the street.

1 .....   2 .....   3 .....   4 .....   5 .....   6 .....

3 Circle the correct option.

1 Sally, you look wonderful! Have you **been** / **gone** to the hairdresser's?
2 Where have you **been** / **gone**? You're 15 minutes late and the lesson's started.
3 Do you know where Bill's **gone** / **been**? His motorbike isn't in the garage.
4 My friend Julie has just **been** / **gone** to India. She brought me back this beautiful silk sari.
5 Liza's **gone** / **been** to the doctor's. I hope she feels better when she comes back.
6 The boys have **been** / **gone** camping. They'll be back on Sunday.
7 Beth? She's **been** / **gone** to the mountains like every weekend. You know she's mad about trekking.
8 My husband's **been** / **gone** to the bank. There's something strange on our statement. I hope it's just a mistake and he can sort it out.
9 What a beautiful suntan! Where have you **been** / **gone**?
10 Haven't you **been** / **gone** to the gym this afternoon? The instructor has just called.

Some uses of the present perfect

The structure of the present perfect has an equivalent in many languages, although its use in English is more limited. It may be defined as a 'bridging tense' between the present and the past, an 'up to now' tense or a 'today' tense.

It is usually used to talk about actions that happened at some time in the past, especially actions that have a present result which we can see now or is relevant now.

1 We have run out of petrol.

2 John has broken his arm.

3 Dad has painted the front door.

Here are some more examples:

I've sold my car and I've bought this one. Do you like it? (The new car is here to be seen.)

The Millers have moved into the flat next to ours. (I don't say when it happened, but underline the fact that now they live here.)

The present perfect is also used to:

- talk about experiences, ask and say if something has ever happened, often with the adverbs **ever / never / always** → *'Have you ever tried paragliding?' 'I've never tried it, but I'd like to.'*

  Sometimes, you can also find the adverbs **before** or **so far** at the end of the sentence → *I've never been on a plane before. This is my first flight. Nothing has happened so far.*

- talk about things that have happened recently, using the adverbs **recently / lately** → *We've had quite a lot of rain recently.*

- say that something has happened **today**, **this week**, **in the last few days**, that is, during an unfinished period of time → *I've been very busy in the last few days.*

> ❗ However, if we talk about actions that happened **yesterday**, **last week** or during a definite time in the past, we must use the past simple, not the present perfect (see page 133) → *I was very busy last week.*

4 Complete the sentences with *ever* or *never*.

1 **A:** Have you .... been to Berlin? **B:** Yes, quite a lot. My aunt lives there.
2 Has anyone here .... had a part in a musical?
3 This is the best party I've .... been to.
4 We've .... stayed in a five-star hotel.
5 I've .... slept in a treehouse, but I'd like to.
6 I've .... heard anything like that. It's a very strange story.

5 **Reorder the words and write sentences.**

1 son / has / My / never / lived / before / on his own / .
   ....

2 ever / Have / thought / moving / you / of / abroad / ?
   ....

3 picture / never / such a / I've / seen / beautiful / !
   ....

4 you / any / done / so far / research / Have / ?
   ....

5 all day / It's / today / been / hot and / sunny / .
   ....

6 have / never / there / been / We / .
   ....

7 your / Has / match / team / this / won / a / so / far / year / ?
   ....

8 worked / restaurant / She / never / in / has / a / before / !
   ....

6 **Match the sentence halves.**

1 I haven't seen the weather forecast today.
2 The children haven't put their toys away.
3 Matt has posted some photos of the baby today.
4 I've been to Rome many times in the last few years.
5 My parents have never been on a cruise.
6 I've eaten a lot in the last few months.
7 I haven't been very well lately.
8 Lily has gone to New York on a business trip.

A Do you want to see them on my mobile phone?
B I'm putting on some weight, I'm afraid.
C She's coming back tomorrow.
D They're still all over the living-room floor.
E They're going on one next week for their 20th wedding anniversary.
F I don't know what the weather's going to be like.
G I'm going again in April.
H I'm going to hospital for a check-up tomorrow.

1 ..... 2 ..... 3 ..... 4 ..... 5 ..... 6 ..... 7 ..... 8 .....

LESSON 2 Present perfect simple: *just, already, yet…* / comparison between the present perfect and the past simple

The present perfect is also used in other cases which all have an impact on the present. In particular, it's used to:

- talk about things which have just happened, using the adverb **just** between the auxiliary **have** and the past participle of the main verb → *They've just come home from school. They've just got married.*

147

- ask whether something has been done or not, for example for a check list like this one, to remember to do some things before a trip:

• turn off heating   • water plants   • get passports   • weigh hand luggage

Have you turned off the heating? — Yes, I have.
Have you watered the plants? — Yes, I have.
Have you got the passports? — Yes, I have.
And have you weighed the hand luggage? We're flying low cost. — No, I haven't. You do it!

Often questions of this kind are used with the adverb **yet** (at the end of the sentence) or **already** (after the subject) → *Have you had lunch yet?* (a question with a 'neutral' tone) / *Have you already had lunch?* (a question with a surprised tone)

- talk about something that has **already** been done, using the adverb **already** between the auxiliary **have** and the past participle or talk about something that has not yet been done, with **yet** usually at the end of the sentence → *I've already fed the dog. I haven't taken him for a walk yet.*

In negative sentences, we can find **still... not** rather than **not... yet**. The use of **still** implies that the action should have already taken place (with a tone of voice that conveys 'What? Haven't you done it yet?') → *You still haven't taken your medicine... Do it now, you must keep to the times.*

Read these examples, too:
I haven't read this book yet. (neutral tone) / *I still haven't read this book.* (I meant to do it, but I haven't managed it yet.)

> ! In American English, sentences with **just**, **already** and **yet** use the past simple, not the present perfect as in British English.
>
> | UK 🇬🇧 | USA 🇺🇸 |
> |---|---|
> | • I've just seen her. | • I just saw her. |
> | • I've already done everything. | • I already did everything, |
> | • Have you heard from her yet? | • Did you hear from her yet? |

1 Complete the gaps with *just / already / yet / still* (British English).

1 **A:** Hi. Am I calling at a bad time? **B:** No, I'm at home. I've .... come back from work.
2 He's been away ten days and I .... haven't received a message from him.
3 James has .... found a new job in the bank. He's starting next week.
4 **A:** Have the boys come back from the gym .... ? **B:** No, not ....
5 The coach has .... stopped at a motorway service area and everyone is getting out.
6 Oh no! The baby has .... woken up and his milk isn't ready ....
7 The teacher hasn't given us back our tests ....
   (*Two days later*) She .... hasn't given them back to us!
8 No, thanks. I don't need your dictionary, I've .... done the translation.
9 Have you .... finished your homework? I can't believe it.

2
Write six sentences in the present perfect, choosing an item from each column.

SUBJECT	AUXILIARY	ADVERB	PAST PARTICIPLE	OBJECT
We	have	just	written	this film.
They			read	a flight to New York.
I		already	seen	bungee jumping.
My sister			played	the xylophone.
He	has	never	booked	my history project.
She			tried	this novel.

3
Fran is preparing a party in her garden for her son. Look at her notes. She has done some things (✓), but she hasn't done other things yet (X). Write sentences with *already* or *not... yet*, as in the example.

- call Steve's mum to see if he's coming ✓
- buy some bags of sweets for the kids ✓
- decorate the birthday cake X
- put the marquee up in the garden X
- organise some games ✓
- ask Martha for some more chairs X
- buy some balloons and party hats ✓

0 *Fran has already called Steve's mum to see if he's coming.*
1 ....
2 ....
3 ....
4 ....
5 ....
6 ....

4
Match the questions and answers.

1 What a lot of washing-up! Let me help!
2 Have you told your mum about your exam results yet?
3 Has John already gone to the airport?
4 Where have you been? Shopping?
5 Now, where have I put the car keys?
6 Have you seen my glasses anywhere?
7 Haven't you done your homework yet?
8 Has Diana got back from Spain yet?
9 Who did you say you've just seen?
10 It's only eight o'clock. Have the kids already gone to bed?

A Yes, and I've just bought this dress.
B Yes, they were tired!
C Yes, I've just put them on your bedside table.
D No, not yet. She'll be angry with me when she hears I've failed.
E Yes, she's just arrived. She said she loved Barcelona!
F Jude Law, that famous actor. He was sitting next to me on the tube!
G Don't worry. I've already put a lot of it in the dishwasher.
H No, I'm going to do it now, I promise.
I You've probably left them on the kitchen table.
J Yes, he wanted to get there a bit ahead of time.

1 ..... 2 ..... 3 ..... 4 ..... 5 ..... 6 ..... 7 ..... 8 ..... 9 ..... 10 .....

FAQ

Q: In my language, I usually only use one past tense when I speak. But it's not like that in English. How do I know when to use the present perfect and when to use the past simple?

A: Try this method. Think about the things you want to say as if they were files on your computer. If the file is closed and filed in a folder, use the past simple. But if the file is still open or is on your desktop, use the present perfect. This means:

completed experience, which happened at a precise time in the past (filed document) → **past simple**

past experiences that are still relevant now (closed files on your desktop) or experiences that began in the past but are not yet finished (open documents) → **present perfect**.

For this last use, called the 'duration form', go to page 151.

5 Present perfect or past simple? Circle the correct option.

1 My family **lived** / **have lived** in Wales before they **came** / **have come** to London over two years ago.
2 We **were** / **have been** in San Francisco for a week now. We're enjoying it!
3 I **have got up** / **got up** later than usual yesterday morning. I **have had** / **didn't have** anything important to do.
4 We **have lived** / **lived** on this farm for a long time. We really like living in the country.
5 I **have read** / **read** three books so far this week. This one is my favourite.
6 She **hasn't been** / **wasn't** very well recently. She should talk to the doctor.
7 I **have had** / **had** a lot of interviews, but I still **haven't found** / **didn't find** a good job.
8 I **stayed** / **have stayed** at a very good hotel when I was in Tokyo.
9 We **haven't had** / **didn't have** time to meet Peter when we **were** / **have been** in London on business.
10 **Have you ever been** / **Were you ever** to Kenya?

6 Reorder the words to make correct sentences. Write PS next to the sentences with the past simple and PP next to those with the present perfect.

1 tidied / haven't / I / yet / bedroom / my / .
   ....
2 tidied / She / bedroom / Saturday / her / last / .
   ....
3 Louise / from / France / yet / back / got / Has / ?
   ....
4 did / Louise / back / get / France / When / from / ?
   ....
5 just / who / Guess / seen / have / I / town / in / !
   ....
6 saw / an / friend / mine / I / old / of / last / theatre / at / night / the / .
   ....
7 brother / has / My / already / graduated / from / school / high / .
   ....
8 graduated / I / year / from / high / last / school / .
   ....

7 Complete the sentences with the present perfect or the past simple of the verbs in brackets. The adverbs or time expressions in bold will help you decide.

1 We .... (have) dinner at a Mexican restaurant **last night**. The food .... (be) excellent. .... (**ever** / try) tacos?
2 We are in London! We .... (**already** / do) lots of things: **yesterday** we .... (go) to the National Gallery and we .... (see) the Changing of the Guard. We .... (not visit) the British Museum **yet**. We're going today.
3 We .... (**just** / get back) from summer camp. We had a great time there.
4 '............... (book) the flight **yet**?' 'Yes, I .... (do) it **last night**.'
5 I .... (**already** / buy) the presents for most people, but I .... (**still** / not buy) one for my sister.
6 **Last year**, I .... (not go) on holiday, but **this year** I .... (**already** / be) to the seaside twice.
7 I .... (**never** / be) to the stadium to watch a football match.
8 Mark .... (**just** / phone). He .... (arrive) at the hotel **two hours ago**.

8 Write short dialogues using the prompts.

1 Mark .... ? (visited the Tate Modern)
  Julie .... (Yes)
  Mark .... ? (When / go)
  Julie .... (yesterday afternoon)
2 Adam .... ? (been camping)
  Rick .... (Yes)
  Adam .... ? (like)
  Rick .... (Yes / great experience)
3 Brad .... ? (been to Australia)
  Frances .... (twice)
  Brad .... ? (stay long)
  Frances .... (two weeks the first time – three weeks the second time)
  Brad .... (cities / visit)
  Frances .... (Sydney and Melbourne)

LESSON 3 Present perfect simple and continuous / *How long…?* for / since…

The duration form with the present perfect simple

A particular use of the present perfect simple is the so-called 'duration form up to the present'.

It is used for actions that began in the past and continue into the present (and are therefore unfinished). The duration of the action is shown either using the preposition **for** + the period of time or using the preposition **since** + the starting point of the action:

I've lived in England for three years.
I've lived here since December 2015.

1 Write the expressions of time in the correct column.

... ten minutes   ... yesterday   ... March 2015   ... two years   ... last month   ... an hour
... last week   ... five o'clock ... 1998   ... centuries   ... a long time ... ages

FOR	SINCE
ten minutes	yesterday
two years	March 2015
an hour	last month
last week	five o'clock
centuries	1998
a long time	we got married
ages	

FAQ

Q: I once wrote **I've lived in this town since when I was born**, but the teacher marked it wrong. What's the problem with my sentence?

A: **Since when** is not correct. **Since** can be used as a conjunction and means 'from the time when', so we don't add **when**. A clause introduced by **since** uses a verb in the past simple, so the use of tenses in that case is correct.

2 Write the verbs in the present perfect simple, then complete the gaps with *for* or *since*.

1. The Wilsons .... (live) next door to us .... the summer of 2010. They're a nice family.
2. Kylie .... (be) in Greece .... last Monday. She says she's having a great time there.
3. I .... (know) my music teacher .... years, ... I started playing the guitar.
4. I .... (want) to see the mountains in Nepal .... I was a child, when I saw a documentary about Everest on TV.
5. We .... (live) in this house .... we got married in 2003.
6. Bill .... (own) this shop .... a long time. He's doing good business.
7. I .... (be) a teacher of English .... 1980. I .... (teach) generations of students .... nearly forty years.
8. Claire and Tom .... (work) together in the same office .... ten years now, ... Tom moved to London from Yorkshire.

The present perfect simple is used in the duration form when the main verb is not an action verb (also called a dynamic verb). It is used with:

- stative verbs, like **be**, **live**, **stay** → *I've been here for an hour.*
- verbs that express possession, like **have**, **own** → *They've owned the shop for two years.*
- verbs that express mental states or feelings, like **know**, **want**, **love** → *She's known him for a long time.*

152

With an action verb, such as **work**, **play**, **run...**, we usually use the present perfect continuous (see page 154).

'How long have you been playing video games?' 'I've been playing for an hour.'

The duration form with negative and interrogative sentences

Negative form

The present perfect simple is used with the duration form in the negative with all verbs, both action verbs and stative verbs, when it refers to situations or actions that have not happened for some time:

> subject + **haven't** / **hasn't** + past participle + **for** / **since...**

I haven't been to New York for ten years.
She hasn't played the piano for a long time.

Interrogative form

- Yes / No questions, to ask if a situation has lasted for a certain amount of time:

> **Have** / **Has** + subject + past participle + **for** / **since...** + ?

'Have you been here for a long time?' 'No, I haven't. I've just been here for a couple of weeks.'

- Questions with **How long** or **Since when**:

> **How long** / **Since when** + **have** / **has** + subject + past participle... + ?

'How long have you had this car?' 'I've had it for a long time. It's quite old.'
'Since when have you known Jennifer?' 'Since last Saturday. I met her at a party.'

> ❗ If, on the other hand, you want to ask when something happened (questions with **When**), you must use the past simple, because you are asking about a specific time in the past:
> 'When did you meet Jennifer?' 'I met her last Saturday.'

3 🎧 **Complete the dialogue with the verbs in brackets in the present perfect or the past simple. Then listen and check.**

A How long [1].......................... Bruce for? (know)

B Bruce? I [2].......................... (know) him since we were at primary school together, so that means about 20 years. We've been close friends ever since.

A And when [3].......................... last .... him? (see)

B Well, I [4].......................... (see) him a couple of weeks ago. He [5].......................... (come) to my house with his wife.

A Really? I didn't know he was married. When [6].................................. ? (get married)

B He got married in June. Ellen, his wife, is really nice.

A How long [7]................................ each other? (they, know)

B Not that long. They [8].......................... (meet) in January and decided to get married six months later. He says they [9].......................... (be) in love since they first met!

A It was love at first sight, then!

B By the way, [10].......................... (hear) from Sara?
I [11].................................. (not hear) from her for ages.

A Yes, she's just emailed me from Tanzania. She [12].......................... (be) there for six months working with a charity.

B How interesting!

4 Complete the second sentence so that it has a similar meaning to the first sentence. Use the words given.

1 The last time I was in New York was ten years ago.
I haven't been to ....

2 We last had dinner in a restaurant on my birthday.
We haven't ....

3 I haven't had a long holiday since the summer of 2016.
The last time ....

4 I have owned this Harley Davidson for three years.
I bought ....

5 I started being a Manchester City fan when I was five years old.
I've been ....

6 They've been best friends for a long, long time.
They became .... ago.

7 He went to a club at 11 last night and stayed there until 2 am.
He was .... for .... last night, from .... to ....

8 We last had a heavy snowfall in the winter of 2014.
We haven't ....

9 Carol met Richard in 2011 and they got married a year later.
Carol and Richard .... 2011 and .... 2012.

10 The last time they played tennis together was last year.
They .... last year.

Present perfect continuous

All tenses have two forms: simple and continuous. This characteristic of the English tense system is called its **aspect** and it indicates both whether the action happens repeatedly or a single time and whether it is completed or still in progress.

We have already seen the difference between the present simple, which is used for habitual actions, repeated over time, and fixed situations (see page 80) and the present continuous, which is used for actions in progress and temporary actions (see page 95). We've also seen the difference between the past simple, which is used for completed past actions (see page 133), and the past continuous, which is used for for actions happening around a certain time in the past (see page 137).

As you already know, the continuous form is expressed with the auxiliary **be** followed by the present participle, or **–ing** form, of the main verb:
present continuous → verb **be** in the present simple plus **–ing**: *I'm waiting* (now)

past continuous → verb **be** in the past simple plus **–ing**: *I was waiting* (then)

The present perfect continuous will therefore have the verb **be** in the present perfect: *I've been waiting* (continuously up to now)

Positive: subject + **have / has been** + **–ing** form of the verb

Interrogative: (Wh– word) + **have / has** + subject + **been** + **–ing** form of the verb + ?

Negative: subject + **haven't / hasn't been** + **–ing** form of the verb (not a very common form)

The use of this tense conveys the idea of a continuous, prolonged action lasting into the present. We often find it used with adverbial expressions like **all day / all day long, all night, all week**, etc.

'What have you been doing today?' 'We've been studying all day.'

> While the continuous form of the present perfect indicates a process, the simple form highlights the final result of the action:
> **He's been chopping** wood all morning.
> Look! **He's chopped** over twenty large trunks.

5 Students and teachers in a school have spent the morning doing different activities and have produced different results. Look at the table and write sentences as in the example.

	PROCESS	RESULT
students in Class 4	work in groups	make a PowerPoint presentation about bioenergy
Mr Reed	teach Class 3	design a school web page
students in Class 2	read their study notes	revise things for their exams
the ICT teacher	tutor a small group	learn InDesign
our English class	look at the present perfect	do this exercise
the headteacher	write end-of-term reports	nearly finish all the reports
Mrs Seath	revise French irregular verbs	read out a list of difficult verbs

0 *The students in Class 4 have been working in groups. They have made a PowerPoint presentation about bioenergy.*

1 ....

2 ....

3 ....

4 ....

5 ....

6 ....

The duration form with the present perfect continuous

The present perfect continuous with **for** or **since** is often used to talk about how long an action lasts, following the rules described on page 152:
'How long have you been running?' 'I've been running for a couple of hours.'
Remember!
The present perfect continuous is used:
- when there is an action verb
- in positive or interrogative sentences
- if the action is still in progress or has just ended and its results are visible now.

6 Choose the correct sentence, A or B.

1. A How long have you been in this school?
   B How long have you being in this school?
2. A I've been in this school for two years.
   B I've been in this school since two years,
3. A He's been slept since three o'clock
   B He's been sleeping since three o'clock.
4. A I've lived in Johannesburg for five years before I moved to London.
   B I lived in Johannesburg for five years before I moved to London.
5. A My brother hasn't driven a pick-up since he was in the army.
   B My brother hasn't been driving a pick-up since he was in the army.
6. A We have been working for this firm since 2013.
   B We are working for this firm since 2013.
7. A I've been having this bicycle for ten years.
   B I've had this bicycle for ten years.
8. A I haven't been seeing her for ages.
   B I haven't seen her for ages.

7 Complete the first part of the sentence by putting the verb in brackets in the present perfect continuous. Then match sentences 1–8 with sentences A–H.

1. I .... French for two years, (learn)
2. I .... since seven o'clock. (work)
3. We .... for you for ages. (wait)
4. We .... for hours. (walk)
5. Mr Simmons .... maths in my school since 2005. (teach)
6. I .... to find a job for months, (try)
7. She .... the harp in this orchestra for three years. (play)
8. I .... for my piano exam for weeks. (practise)

A Why are you always late?
B He's a really good teacher.
C but I still haven't got one!
D but I still don't speak it fluently.
E She plays very well!
F I'm really tired.
G I'm ready now.
H Let's have a rest now.

1 ..... 2 ..... 3 ..... 4 ..... 5 ..... 6 ..... 7 ..... 8 .....

8 Write the questions for these answers.

1. Since when .... ?
   I've been singing in the school choir since the beginning of the year.
2. Has .... there?
   Yes, it's been raining all afternoon. And it's been raining hard!
3. How long .... the kids .... ?
   They've been playing all afternoon.
4. .... you .... chemistry?
   No, I've been studying physics actually. We have a test tomorrow.
5. How long .... for?
   We've been eating since 2 pm – it's a big dinner!
6. What kind of music .... you .... to ?
   I've been listening to a live concert of The Rolling Stones!
7. What .... this afternoon?
   I've been cleaning the house.
8. Since when .... on your computer?
   I've been working since nine this morning and I'm quite tired now.

9 Complete the second sentence so that it has a similar meaning to the first sentence using the words given.

1. I started working on this project five days ago and still haven't finished.
   I've ....
   for ....

2. It's seven o'clock now. Peter has been working out in the gym since five.
   Peter ....
   for ....

3. I have told you many times how to behave! Why don't you ever listen to me?
   I've been ....
   over and over again ....

4. It started snowing at 9 pm. It's midnight now and it's still snowing.
   It's been ....
   for .... ,
   since ....

5. The boys started swimming an hour ago and are still in the pool. They've been training for their next event.
   The boys have ....
   for ....
   for their next event.

10 Complete the dialogues using the correct form of the present perfect simple or continuous of the verbs in brackets. Then listen and check.

1. **A** .... you already .... , Ben? (order)
   B Yes, I have actually.
   A You didn't wait for me? Oh well, what .... you .... ? (order)
   B Lasagne. It's great here.
   A OK. I'll have the same.

2. **A** What .... you .... at home all day? (do)
   B I .... and .... and .... TV. It's been a lazy day! (sleep, read, watch)
   A What .... on TV? (watch)
   B I .... my favourite series – *Doc Martin!* (watch)
   I love watching TV on a rainy day like this.

3. **A** Mum's in a cooking mood today, she .... all afternoon! (cook)
   B What .... she .... ? (cook)
   A She .... some really nice things: chocolate muffins, flapjacks and shortcake! (make)
   B Yum!

4. **A** You .... from that book for hours. (not look up) What .... you .... about? (read)
   B An international spy ring. I .... nearly .... it now. (finish)

5. **A** .... you ever .... white-water rafting, Rachel? (try)
   B No, never! And nor would I like to. Have you?
   A Yes, I go rafting on the river with an instructor every Sunday. It's good fun!
   B Very adventurous!

PRESENT PERFECT
Uses of the *present perfect simple* and *continuous* – Summary

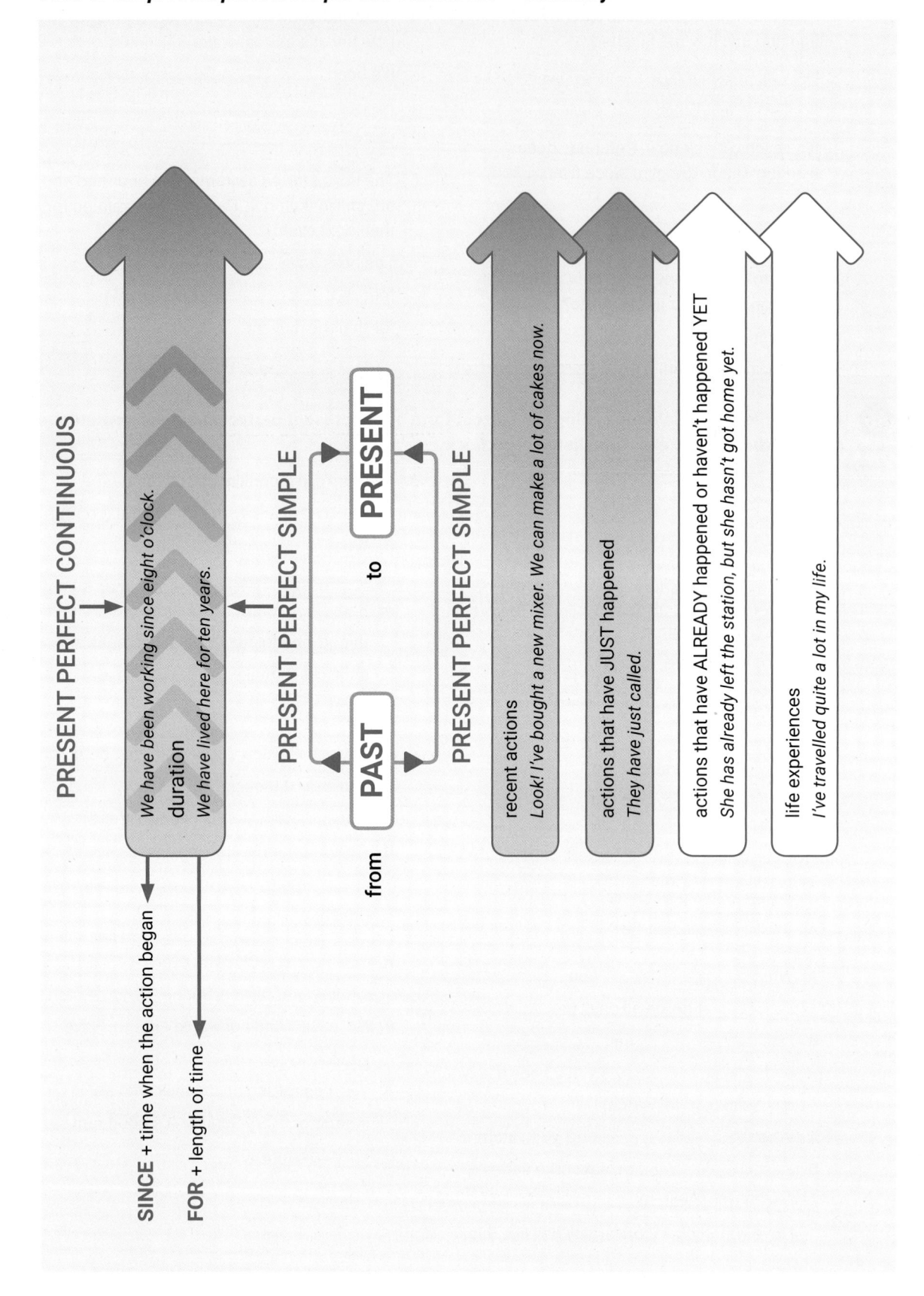

PRESENT PERFECT CONTINUOUS

We have been working since eight o'clock.

duration

We have lived here for ten years.

SINCE + time when the action began
FOR + length of time

PRESENT PERFECT SIMPLE

from **PAST** to **PRESENT**

PRESENT PERFECT SIMPLE

recent actions
Look! I've bought a new mixer. We can make a lot of cakes now.

actions that have JUST happened
They have just called.

actions that have ALREADY happened or haven't happened YET
She has already left the station, but she hasn't got home yet.

life experiences
I've travelled quite a lot in my life.

LESSON 4 Past perfect simple and continuous

Past perfect simple

The past perfect simple (which from now on we will simply call the past perfect) is formed with the auxiliary **had** for all persons, followed by the past participle of the main verb.

Positive, negative and interrogative forms

> **Positive**
> **Full form:** subject + **had** + past participle (**–ed** ending for regular verbs or the third part of the paradigm for irregular verbs)
> **Short form:** subject + **'d** + past participle (the least common form)

They had already left when we got there.

> **Negative:** subject + **had not (hadn't)** + past participle

We hadn't been there before.

> **Interrogative: Had** + subject + past participle... + ?
> **Negative interrogative: Had** + subject + **not** + past participle... + ? or **Hadn't** + subject + past participle

> **Short answers: Yes**, + subject + **had**.
> **No**, + subject + **hadn't**.

'Had she made a mistake?' 'No, she hadn't.'
'Hadn't he passed his final exam?' 'Yes, he had.'

> **Wh– questions: Wh–** word + **had** + subject + past participle... + ?

Where had they been?
What had she said?
How long had he had that job?

Focus

In some languages, the auxiliary verb used in the past perfect is **have** with transitive verbs and **be** with intransitive verbs, while in English, the auxiliary verb for the past perfect is always **had** (**I had had, I had gone, they had arrived**).

Remember!
Past perfect of the verb **be:** I / You / He / She / It / We / They had been
Past perfect of the verb **have:** I / You / He / She / It / We / They had had

Some uses of the past perfect

The past perfect (or pluperfect as it is sometimes known) has an equivalent tense or tenses in many languages. It is a tense used to describe actions that preceded other actions in the past, when these are expressed with the past simple. It's the tense that means 'already happened before'. In fact, it is often used with the adverb **already**:

*The police arrived quickly, but the robber **had already escaped**.* (*The robber had already escaped before the police arrived* → previous action)

The **past perfect** is often found:

- in the main clause following a subordinate time clause introduced by the conjunctions **When** or **Before** or by the expression **By the time**. The subordinate clause uses a verb in the past simple.

  When he called her, she had already crossed the road and couldn't hear him. (*When he called...* → subordinate clause with the past simple; *she had already crossed...* → main clause with the past perfect)

  Before it got dark, they had mowed the lawn and watered the garden.
  By the time my parents got home, we had cleaned the house.

- in a subordinate clause introduced by **After** or **Till / Until**. In these cases, the main clause has a verb in the past simple.

After he had spoken to the students, the principal turned to the door and left the class. (*After he had talked...* → subordinate clause with the past perfect; *the principal turned...* → main clause with the past simple)

She didn't want to leave until everybody had finished eating.

- in indirect speech, when the reporting verb (**say** or **tell**) is in the past simple and what is being reported happened previously (see page 351):

They said they had already bought everything we needed.
I told her I had been there before.

1 Tick ✓ the sentence (A or B) that has the same meaning as the original sentence.

1 My friend tried to ring my mobile soon after I had switched it off.
  - A I switched off my mobile before my friend tried to ring.
  - B My friend tried to ring before I switched my mobile off.

2 Mr Connelly couldn't ring my mobile because he had lost my phone number.
  - A Mr Connelly couldn't find my phone number so he didn't ring me.
  - B I had never given Mr Connelly my mobile phone number so he couldn't ring.

3 My daughter had learnt to read before she started primary school.
  - A My daughter learnt to read soon after she started primary school.
  - B My daughter learnt to read, then she went to primary school.

4 By the time all the students were seated, the teacher had already handed out all the test papers.
  - A The teacher had started handing out the test papers before all the students were seated.
  - B The teacher waited for all the students to be seated, then handed out all the test papers.

5 Matthew went to work for a non-profit organisation as soon as he had finished university.
  - A After finishing university, Matthew went to work for a non-profit organisation.
  - B Matthew started working for a non-profit organisation, then finished university.

6 By the time Jack finished his homework, he had already eaten two sandwiches.
  - A Jack finished his homework, then ate two sandwiches.
  - B Jack ate two sandwiches while he was doing his homework.

2 Complete the gaps with the verbs in the past simple or past perfect simple.

1 I arrived late at the venue and the conference .... already .... (begin)
2 The traffic on the motorway was so bad last night that I .... home at half past eleven, when everybody .... already .... to bed. (get, go)
3 After Mary .... her breakfast, she met her friend and .... to school. (eat, walk)
4 When I .... the fridge, I found out that someone .... all the beer. (open, drink)
5 Fiona's birthday was in July, but her mum .... already .... her a present three months before. (buy)
6 Our cousins .... to see us in Italy last summer. We .... them since they left for Buenos Aires in 1998. (come, not see)
7 I was so happy! I .... never .... an A in a maths test before. (get)
8 As soon as Jim read the exam questions, he knew that he .... enough. (not study)

Past perfect continuous

The past perfect continuous is formed with the past perfect of the verb **be** followed by the **–ing** form of the main verb: *I **had been** waiting.* (continuously up until then)

> **Positive:** subject + **had been** + **–ing** form of the verb
> **Negative:** subject + **hadn't been** + **–ing** form of the verb (not a very common form)
> **Interrogative:** (Wh– word) + **had** + subject + **been** + **–ing** form of the verb + ?

The use of this verb tense expresses the idea of a continuous action, which was lasting up to a certain time in the past and which was still continuing or had just finished. It is used in particular:

- when talking about past events, to describe an action that had been continuously happening previously. Often the sentence contains expressions of time like **all day**, **all afternoon** or similar:

It had been raining all day and we were looking forward to a little bit of sunshine.
My uncle arrived at last. We had been waiting for him all morning.

Focus

The past perfect continuous does not have an equivalent tense in all languages, so these aspects can be expressed in a slightly different way in other languages.

3 Join the two parts of the sentence so that they make sense. Then complete them using the past perfect simple or the past perfect continuous form of the verbs in brackets.

1. Yesterday I found the book I .... (look for).
2. Tom started doing his homework at ten o'clock.
3. Tina started working in a shop when she was 18.
4. My father .... retired for a couple of years (be)
5. When Miss Bradshaw said her name,
6. Before my daughter took her final exam,
7. Ben .... cartoons for two hours (watch)
8. We .... for hours without a break (drive)
9. They .... the house for hours (tidy)
10. The party .... (already / finish)

A. By 11, he .... half of it. (do)
B. when he decided to start a new business.
C. she .... an advanced ICT course. (attend)
D. It was in a drawer.
E. when his mum told him to switch off the TV.
F. when we finally stopped at a motorway service area.
G. I remembered I .... her before. (meet)
H. By the age of 20, she .... a promotion. (have)
I. when Philip turned up.
J. because their parents were about to come home from their holidays.

1 ..... 2 ..... 3 ..... 4 ..... 5 ..... 6 ..... 7 ..... 8 ..... 9 ..... 10 .....

The duration form with the past perfect simple and continuous

Just as the present perfect is used to express the duration of an action up to the present moment (see page 151), so the past perfect is used to express the duration of an action up to a moment in the past.

In particular, it is used for situations or actions which lasted for a period of time or had just finished at a certain time in the past. The beginning of this time period is often given (with the preposition **since**) or the duration indicated (with the preposition **for**).

- The past perfect simple is used with verbs that are not action verbs and with all kinds of verbs in the negative form:

  He <u>had been</u> mayor <u>for two years</u> when he was ousted in a bribery scandal.

  The tenor <u>hadn't sung for some time</u> because his voice was a little hoarse.

- The past perfect continuous is only used with action verbs in the positive and in the interrogative forms:

  When I entered the theatre in the evening, the actors told me they <u>had been rehearsing since one o'clock</u>. They were exhausted.

  How long <u>had you been training</u> when I saw you on the track the other day?

  We <u>had been training for a few minutes</u>. We had just started.

4 Circle the correct option.

1. Sara found the glasses she **was** / **had been** looking for all morning.
2. The gold medallist **had been** / **was been** training for months before she won the event.
3. As soon as he had finished writing emails, he **went** / **had gone** for a run in the park.
4. His wife was exhausted because she **had** / **has** been doing household chores all day.
5. A group of teenagers **had been shouting** / **had shouted** in the street when the police arrived.
6. Jane **had been hoping** / **used to be hoping** to get a job interview for months – when she finally did, it was for a job she really hated.
7. What **have** / **had** you been doing here? What's all this mess?
8. Joanne fell asleep during the lecture because she **had been** / **was** walking all day to visit as much as she could of the city.
9. When their parents **got** / **had got** home, the kids had already tidied up after the party.
10. Lucy **was** / **had been** studying for months for her anatomy exam and she got a top mark in the end.

5 Complete the text with the correct form of the verbs in brackets: past simple, past perfect simple or past perfect continuous.

Jessica, my grandmother's helper, ¹............................ (not be) to her native country, Ecuador, for four years when she finally ²............................ (have) a chance to go back last summer. She ³............................ (look forward) to it for a long time. As soon as she got there, she ⁴............................ (visit) her parents and all of her relations, including a new nephew and a niece she ⁵............................ (never meet) before. Her family ⁶............................ (organise) a welcome party for her. She ⁷............................ (stay) with her parents for a whole month and, when it was time for her to go, everybody ⁸............................ (be) upset. My grandmother was happy when Jessica got back. She ⁹............................ (miss) her when she ¹⁰............................ (be) away.

PAST TENSES
Use of past tenses – Summary

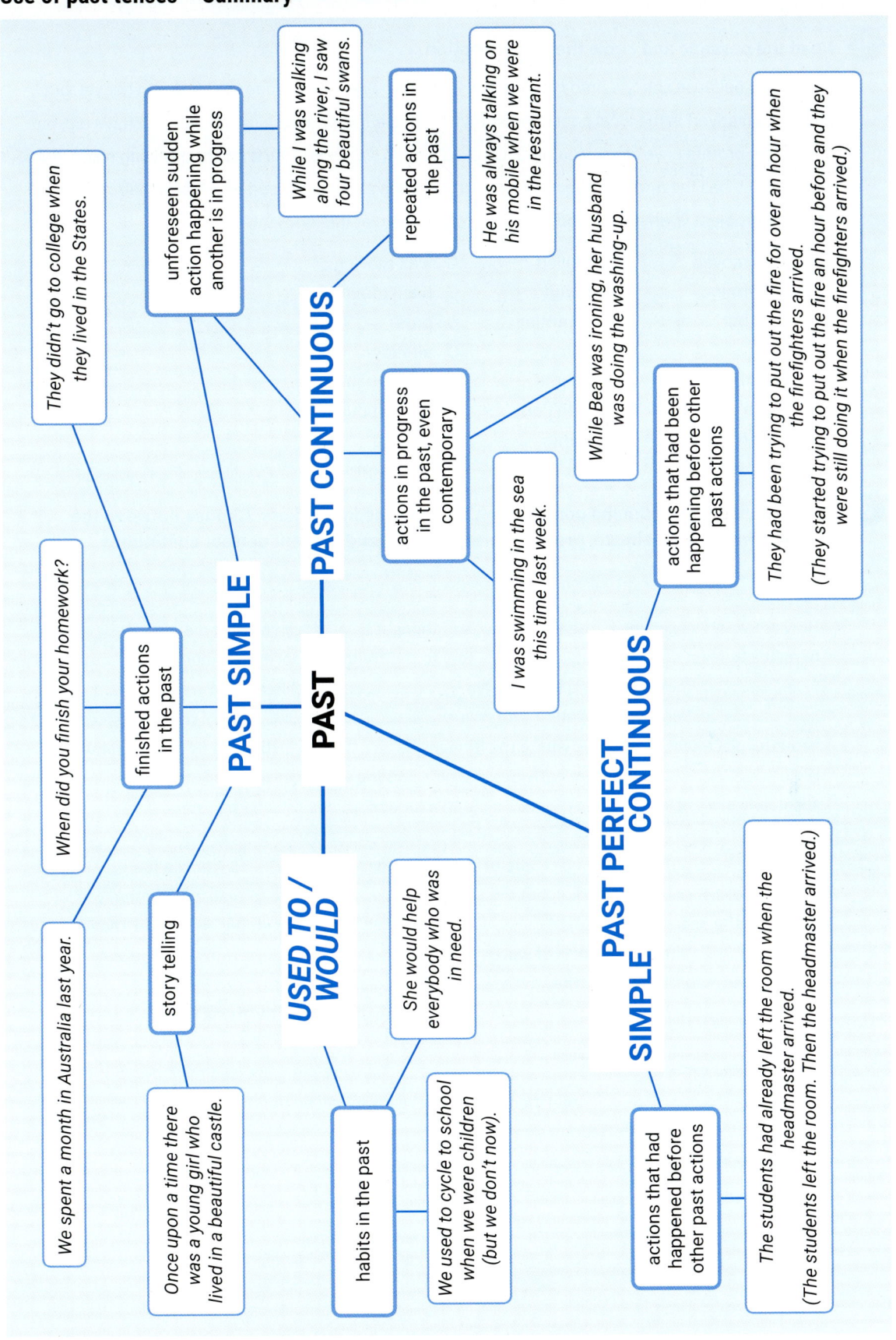

PAST branches into: **PAST SIMPLE**, **PAST CONTINUOUS**, **USED TO / WOULD**, **PAST PERFECT SIMPLE**, **PAST PERFECT CONTINUOUS**.

PAST SIMPLE
- **finished actions in the past**
  - They didn't go to college when they lived in the States.
  - When did you finish your homework?
  - We spent a month in Australia last year.
- **story telling**
  - Once upon a time there was a young girl who lived in a beautiful castle.

PAST CONTINUOUS
- **unforeseen sudden action happening while another is in progress**
  - While I was walking along the river, I saw four beautiful swans.
- **repeated actions in the past**
  - He was always talking on his mobile when we were in the restaurant.
- **actions in progress in the past, even contemporary**
  - I was swimming in the sea this time last week.
  - While Bea was ironing, her husband was doing the washing-up.

USED TO / WOULD
- **habits in the past**
  - She would help everybody who was in need.
  - We used to cycle to school when we were children (but we don't now).

PAST PERFECT SIMPLE
- **actions that had happened before other past actions**
  - The students had already left the room when the headmaster arrived.
  - (The students left the room. Then the headmaster arrived.)

PAST PERFECT CONTINUOUS
- **actions that had been happening before other past actions**
  - They had been trying to put out the fire for over an hour when the firefighters arrived.
  - (They started trying to put out the fire an hour before and they were still doing it when the firefighters arrived.)

GRAMMAR MATRIX MAIN — UNIT 9

ROUND UP 9

1 **Read the passage and circle the correct option.**

Jo's happy because she ¹...... into her new flat yesterday. She ²...... anyone to share with her yet, but she ³...... an advert in the local paper and she's ⁴...... had a few phone calls about it. The flat's big, but Jo and her brother have already painted it and Jo's mum ⁵...... some curtains for the living room last week. Jo ⁶...... all the furniture she needs yet, but she has already decided which armchairs she ⁷...... . The only problem is, she ⁸...... enough money to buy them at the moment.

1 A has moved   B moved   C was moving
2 A has found   B found   C hasn't found
3 A has put   B is putting   C puts
4 A yet   B before   C already
5 A was buying   B bought   C has bought
6 A hasn't bought   B didn't buy   C doesn't buy
7 A has wanted   B wants   C wanted
8 A get   B got   C hasn't got

2 **Complete the email with the correct form of the verbs in brackets. Choose between the present simple, past simple, present perfect simple and present perfect continuous.**

Hi Sarah,
How are you? I've got some free time today, so I thought I would tell you how we are getting on here. It's the first time we ¹........................... (be) to the south of France and I must say it ²........................... (not disappoint) us at all. We ³........................... (be) here for a week and ⁴........................... (already / see) quite a lot. We ⁵........................... (just / come back) from a beautiful place called La Turbie, where the Romans ⁶........................... (build) a beautiful monument. We ⁷........................... (get) there early this morning and the view over the sea ⁸........................... (be) absolutely incredible. We ⁹........................... (eat) a lot of delicious fish and had some amazing wine there too!
We wandered around the town a couple of days ago and I ¹⁰........................... (buy) a few French books at the street market, but I ¹¹........................... (have) time to read any of them yet – even on the beach we ¹²........................... (always / find) something else to do! They ¹³........................... (teach) all sorts of water sports here – I ¹⁴........................... (never / feel) so energetic before! Yesterday they even ¹⁵........................... (get) me to ride a jet-ski, but I soon ¹⁶........................... (give up) – it is one of the most terrifying things I ¹⁷........................... (ever / do).
Well, I'd better go now. Paul ¹⁸........................... (already / get) dressed to go out, but I still have to. He ¹⁹........................... (tell) me I need to be ready in half an hour! We ²⁰........................... (book) a table at a small restaurant on the beach.
See you soon!
Emma

3 Complete the text with the correct form of one of the verbs below. Choose between the past simple, past continuous and past perfect.

look   find   live (x2)   come   ask   can   break   throw   imagine

When I was a child, I ¹............................ in an old house in the country. One summer, while I ²............................ around the attic for old things, I ³............................ across a big old wooden box under a pile of curtains. I immediately imagined I ⁴............................ the treasure from some famous robbers who ⁵............................ in the house centuries ago. The box was locked. I ⁶............................ open it, so I ⁷............................ my elder brother to come and help and he tried to open it with a screwdriver.

He tried and tried, and we heard the sound of metal objects rattling around inside. We ⁸............................ all the jewels inside the box: long pearl necklaces, diamond rings, golden coins. Suddenly, the lock ⁹............................ and the box sprung open… Inside were the old, battered pots and pans used by our great-grandparents that my mother ¹⁰............................ away because they were too old.

MATRIX +

As you have seen, the present perfect continuous is rarely used in the negative form because the action did not take place and therefore could not have been continuing.
However, it is used in sentences which are not really negative but could be formed with a positive verb with the same meaning:
The kids haven't been playing for long. Let them stay at the park a bit longer. → *The kids have been playing for a short time.*

4 Complete the second sentence so that it has a similar meaning to the first using the word given. Do not change the word given.

1 He has been studying for three hours and he's beginning to feel tired.
   STARTED   He .... ago and he's beginning to feel tired.

2 We were standing talking when the robbery happened.
   WHILE   .... talking, the robbery happened.

3 I've never walked farther than I did yesterday.
   EVER   Yesterday it was the farthest ....

4 Marion started her project at the beginning of the week and she hasn't finished yet.
   SINCE   Marion .... the beginning of the week.

5 The shops opened before we got to the shopping centre.
   WHEN   .... to the shopping centre, the shops ....

6 The performance started before we got to the theatre.
   ALREADY   When .... , the performance ....

7 Henry hasn't been waiting for long. Why is he complaining?
   SHORT   Henry .... Why is he complaining?

8 We haven't been working out much this week.
   LITTLE   We .... this week.

165

5 **Complete the text with the past simple or the past perfect of the verbs in brackets.**

As soon as I ¹............................ (get) home last night, I ²............................ (realise) that something strange ³............................ (happen). I was sure someone ⁴............................ (break) into my flat. I ⁵............................ (open) the living-room door and immediately I saw that things ⁶............................ (move). I ⁷............................ (leave) my laptop on the table and, when I looked, it ⁸............................ (be) on the floor! I ⁹............................ (clear up) everything in the kitchen before I ¹⁰............................ (leave) for the weekend, but now there were dirty plates and glasses in the sink. I ¹¹............................ (phone) my sister because I thought maybe she ¹²............................ (be) there while I was away… but, no, she hadn't. It's a complete mystery!

6 **Complete the text with the correct past tense of the verbs in brackets.**

I ¹............................ (decide) to go to London for the day. I ²............................ (not have) much money. I ³............................ (go) to the ticket office and ⁴............................ (buy) a day return to London. Since I ⁵............................ (have) 40 minutes to wait for the train, I ⁶............................ (decide) to buy a newspaper and have a coffee. Then I ⁷............................ (go) to the platform, where the ticket inspector ⁸............................ (ask) to see my ticket. I ⁹............................ (can not) find it anywhere. I ¹⁰............................ (search) everywhere for it. 'I'm sorry, Inspector,' I ¹¹............................ (say), 'but I ¹²............................ (lose) my ticket.' 'That's too bad,' he ¹³............................ (say), 'you can't get on the train without a valid ticket.' The train ¹⁴............................ (come) and the train ¹⁵............................ (leave) without me. Eventually, I ¹⁶............................ (find) my ticket in my inside jacket pocket, so I ¹⁷............................ (catch) the next train. On the train, I ¹⁸............................ (go) to the buffet car, where I met an old friend. He ¹⁹............................ (ask) me how I ²⁰............................ (be) and I ²¹............................ (tell) him that I ²²............................ (lose) my ticket and ²³............................ (miss) the last train. 'But, 'I ²⁴............................ (say), showing it to him, 'I ²⁵............................ (find) it now!'

7 **Complete the text with the past simple, the past perfect (simple or continuous) and the present perfect (simple or continuous) of the verbs in brackets.**

I remember my first day at work quite clearly. I ¹................................ (have) a job interview two weeks before for the position of Digital Manager. I had mixed feelings about whether I would get the job, as I felt the guy who ²................................ (interview) me didn't like me that much. He was very serious. However, a week later I ³................................ (receive) a letter saying that the job was mine. I was happy. I ⁴................................ (look) for a job for over three months and I knew I had the right qualifications and skills.

On my first day, I ⁵................................ (arrive) in good time and they ⁶................................ (take) me to see the director of the company. He was quite a serious, intimidating man who ⁷................................ (not show) much emotion, but he was welcoming and professional.

My team were hard-working and I ⁸................................ (feel) very at ease with them. And now? I'm still working here. I ⁹................................ (work) here for over 25 years and I ¹⁰................................ (be) very happy all that time.

8 Complete the text with the correct past tense of the verbs in brackets.

When I ¹............................. (arrive), the post office ²............................. (already / close). Shame, because I ³............................. (have) to send an urgent parcel. It ⁴............................. (be) the new model of our famous mixer, and our clients in Spain ⁵............................. (wait) for it. It ⁶............................. (be) a Friday evening and the post office would only reopen on Monday morning.
While I ⁷............................. (go) back home, I was quite upset. My boss ⁸............................. (tell) me to hurry up and deliver the parcel just two hours earlier, but I ⁹............................. (want) to finish writing some urgent emails. And now I had to explain to him that the parcel still ¹⁰............................. (not leave).

9 Complete the text with the correct past tense of the verbs in brackets.

Last week, Luke and Alice ¹............................. (dance) in a Latin American dance competition. They ²............................. (practise) for six months before they ³............................. (take part) in the competition. They ⁴............................. (be) very good. While they ⁵............................. (wait) for their turn, they ⁶............................. (talk) to their friend Mathilda, who ⁷............................. (be) in the audience.
She ⁸............................. (never / see) them dance before. In fact, Luke and Alice ⁹............................. (never / dance) in front of anyone before the competition.
After everyone ¹⁰............................. (perform), the judges ¹¹............................. (announce) the winners.
Luke and Alice ¹²............................. (win)! Alice said she ¹³............................. (never / be) so happy before.

Reflecting on grammar

Reflect on the rules and say whether the following statements are true or false.

		True	False
1	The present perfect is formed with either the auxiliary verb **have** or the auxiliary verb **be**.		
2	The present perfect is used for actions that are complete in the past and do not affect the present.		
3	The present perfect has exactly the same rules in both British and American English.		
4	The sentence *I have just washed the dishes* is correct.		
5	The sentence *We have moved to our new house last week* is wrong.		
6	The duration form can be expressed both with the present perfect simple and continuous.		
7	The sentence *We've been here since yesterday* is correct.		
8	The expressions *How long...?* and *Since when...?* mean exactly the same thing.		
9	The sentence *He's been waiting for us since three days* is correct.		
10	The past perfect is often found in a main clause accompanied by a subordinate clause introduced by **when**, **before** or **by the time**.		

Revision and Exams 3 (UNITS 7 – 8 – 9)

1 Circle the correct option.

Jim Emma!
Emma Yes, Jim. What's the matter?
Jim Can you give me a lift? Mark's not going to work and I don't want to get the bus.
Emma Alright, get [1] **on / into** the car. Are you going [2] **to / in** the university?
Jim Yes, I'm going to a different department to my usual one, but I'll tell you where to go. Drive [3] **down / from** this road. Not so fast. Slow down!
Emma What shall I do when I get [4] **in / to** the crossroads?
Jim Turn left [5] **into / in** Darwin Street. Darwin was a famous…
Emma I know who Darwin was…
Jim Well, the applied physics department is [6] **on / at** the end of the street [7] **on / at** the left. It's next [8] **of / to** the astrophysics department…
Emma Okay, now can you get [9] **off / out of** the car, Jim? I'm really late for work.

2 Roy Brooks, an American businessman, and his girlfriend have disappeared. A police officer is writing a report about what Roy had done the last time he was seen. Transform the text from the present to the past using suitable tenses, and making any other necessary changes (*this* → *that*, etc).

Roy Brooks gets up at 9.00 on Monday 11th May 2015 and has breakfast on the terrace of his penthouse overlooking the bay. He usually has a big breakfast, but this morning he only has a cup of green tea.

He feeds his dogs, two giant black Schnauzers, and plays with them for half an hour. After washing and getting dressed, he leaves home at about 11.00 and drives to his office downtown. At 11.30, he parks his car in his office parking lot and takes the elevator to the 27th floor, where his secretary greets him with a cup of coffee.

He doesn't have any lunch today. At 3.00, a South American man goes into Roy's office and they talk for about an hour. Just before the man leaves the office, Roy is shouting some words in Spanish. When the man leaves, Roy is visibly upset and makes a few telephone calls.

At 6.00, he takes a taxi to The Fox and Hunter, a fashionable bar on Columbus Avenue, where his girlfriend Linda is waiting for him. They have a Martini, leave the bar and walk to a nearby Chinese restaurant, Chow Mei. They have dinner there and Roy talks to the Chinese restaurant manager for quite a long time. At 10.30, a driver they have never seen before picks them up and drives them towards the harbour.

3 Circle the correct option.

When we saw Debbie, she ¹ **had been sitting** / **sat** on the same chair in the same café for over an hour. She ² **had** / **has** been waiting for Mark, but he hadn't turned up. She ³ **was** / **has been** half worried and half furious with him. She ⁴ **was** / **had been** calling him on his mobile for the last 20 minutes, but it was switched off.

'You know, he used to be late most of the time in the past, but lately he ⁵ **has always been** / **always was** on time,' she said.

We ⁶ **reminded** / **used to remind** her that he often forgot to recharge the battery of his mobile, so he was probably stuck somewhere and was not able to call her.

We sat at Debbie's table and waited with her. While we ⁷ **had been chatting** / **were chatting**, Debbie's phone rang. It was Mark, at last! But where was he?

4 Complete the text with the past simple of the verbs in brackets.

A SHORT HISTORY OF YORK

York ¹........................ (become) important during Roman times when the Romans ²........................ (establish) a permanent fortress in AD 71. The fortress was the largest military garrison in the north and ³........................ (house) 6,000 soldiers.

When the Romans ⁴........................ (withdraw) from Britain, the fort and the town ⁵........................ (fall) under Anglo-Saxon rule and York ⁶........................ (become) the capital of the independent Kingdom of Northumbria. The Vikings ⁷........................ (be) the next group to rule the city in 866 and ⁸........................ (give) it the name of 'Jorvik'.

When the Normans ⁹........................ (invade) Britain in 1066, William the Conqueror soon ¹⁰........................ (establish) a presence in York, and over the next 300 years, the city ¹¹........................ (flourish), becoming the capital of the north and the second largest city in the country.

Between the 15th and the 17th centuries, the importance of the city ¹²........................ (decline), but with the restoration of the English monarchy, York ¹³........................ (enter) the period of Enlightenment with elegant new buildings, such as the Assembly Rooms, Assize Courts and numerous hospitals.

During the Industrial Revolution, York ¹⁴........................ (become) a major railway centre and this ¹⁵........................ (help) expand the manufacturing industry.

Today, although traditional manufacturing has declined, new industries have sprung up in the city and with nearly four million visitors a year, the tourist industry now plays a major role in the local economy.

Preliminary (PET) | Reading Part 3

5 Read the sentences about the Royal Pavilion in Brighton. Then read the text and tick column A if the sentence is true and column B if it is false.

                                                                                       A B

1. Marine Pavilion is the name of a neo-classical villa next to the Royal Pavilion.
2. George became king before they finished building the Pavilion.
3. Everybody liked the Pavilion when it was built.
4. The king liked hosting people at his Brighton residence.
5. Queen Victoria fell in love with the building at first sight.
6. She spent some time there alone with her husband.
7. The Royal Pavilion is closed three days a year.
8. In summer, visitors have one more hour to see the Pavilion.
9. The ticket office closes at 4.30 in October.
10. Groups don't need a reservation if they visit the Pavilion in winter.

Experience the extraordinary at the **Royal Pavilion**, an exotic palace in the centre of Brighton. Built as a seaside pleasure palace for George IV, this historic house mixes Regency grandeur with the visual style of India and China.

The Royal Pavilion started as a modest 18th-century lodging house. Architect Henry Holland helped George, Prince of Wales, turn his house into a neo-classical villa – known as the Marine Pavilion.

In 1815, George hired architect John Nash to redesign the building in Indian style. By the time the work was completed in 1823, George had become king. Though largely criticised at the time, today this building is the symbol of Brighton.

George enjoyed entertaining society guests. At the Royal Pavilion, he hosted gastronomic feasts in the Banqueting Room, and balls and concerts in the Music Room.

Queen Victoria first visited the Royal Pavilion in 1837 and felt it was a 'strange, odd, Chinese-looking place, both outside and inside'. She returned for a longer stay with her husband Albert and two children in 1842, and the upstairs chamber floor was adapted to accommodate the Queen and her family.

Today, the Royal Pavilion is open daily with the exception of Christmas Eve, Christmas Day and Boxing Day. From October to March, the visiting times are between 10 am and 5.15 pm, while they start half an hour earlier and finish half an hour later from April to September. Remember that in both periods, the last tickets are sold three-quarters of an hour before closing time.

As the Royal Pavilion is very busy in July and August, especially at weekends, they do not admit unbooked groups. Call this number for group bookings – 03000 290901 – and our booking team will give you a time slot for entry. Or visit the groups page on their website for more information.

Preliminary (PET) | Reading Part 5

6 Read the text and choose the correct word (A, B, C or D) for each gap.

Mirella has never ¹...... to England, but she ²...... writing to a young man called Tom, from Margate in the south of England. He ³...... Italian for five years now and really loves it. Last year, Tom ⁴...... three weeks in Verona, in the north-east of Italy, and ⁵...... a full-immersion course where no English was spoken. Mirella and Tom ⁶...... emails almost every day ⁷...... the past two months. Mirella is going to England ⁸...... and she ⁹...... a low-cost flight from Bergamo to Stansted, one of the London airports. She'll then get the train to Margate. It won't be Mirella's first time abroad. When she was a child, she ¹⁰...... spend every summer in the French Riviera.

1	A	gone	B	been	C	got	D	went
2	A	has recently started	B	started recently	C	did recently start	D	have recently started
3	A	studies	B	studied	C	has been studying	D	has studied
4	A	has spent	B	spent	C	has been spending	D	have spent
5	A	attended	B	has attended	C	did attend	D	attend
6	A	exchange	B	exchanges	C	are exchanging	D	have been exchanging
7	A	for	B	since	C	from	D	after
8	A	at July	B	next July	C	last July	D	on July
9	A	has booked	B	has been booking	C	books	D	is booking
10	A	used	B	has used to	C	used to	D	did use to

First (FCE) | Reading and Use of English Part 4

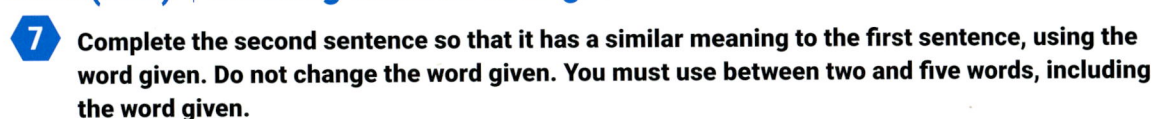

7 Complete the second sentence so that it has a similar meaning to the first sentence, using the word given. Do not change the word given. You must use between two and five words, including the word given.

0 It's ten o'clock and Maggie rang the dentist a few minutes ago.

    JUST   It's ten o'clock and Maggie .... *has just rung* .... the dentist.

1 We have lived near the Griffins for ten years.

    BEEN   The Griffins .... neighbours for ten years.

2 Dan and Brian were golf champions years ago.

    USED   Dan and Brian .... golf champions years ago.

3 I sat down at my desk as soon as I got into the office at 9 am. It's 1 pm and I'm still sitting here.

    HAVE   I .... at my desk for four hours.

4 Sam started cooking at ten and he was still cooking at 12.

    HAD   By 12 o'clock, Sam .... two hours.

5 Luke started watching his favourite cartoons hours ago and he's still watching them.

    FOR   Luke has been watching ....

6 We met Susan ten years ago.

    KNOWN   We .... years.

7 I tidied my room earlier, Mum.

    ALREADY   I .... room, Mum.

8 I saw your sister a few minutes ago.

    JUST   I ....

Towards competences

The local tourist office has asked your school to devote the English part of its website to information about your town. Your task is to write about the history of your city in approximately 250 words. Write your article and illustrate it with photos or period drawings.

Self Check 3

Circle the correct option. Then check your answers at the end of the book.

1. They used to have a family reunion once a year, usually ……… Christmas.
   A on   B at   C in

2. I usually switch my mobile off ……… night.
   A during   B at   C in

3. We would like to receive the goods ……… May 20th.
   A within   B in   C by

4. He lives ……… 10 Ramsay Lane, not far from my mother's house.
   A on   B at   C in

5. She generally goes to work ……… her colleague's car.
   A by   B on   C in

6. Hurry up! I'm waiting here ……… the rain and I haven't got an umbrella with me!
   A at   B under   C in

7. The President was sitting ……… the back of the car next to his wife.
   A in   B on   C at

8. The police warned us ……… driving along the mountain road in the snow.
   A by   B from   C against

9. Why don't you offer ……… in your restaurant?
   A to him a job   B him a job   C a job him

10. We got bored ……… staying at home and decided to go for a walk.
    A by   B at   C of

11. I remember ……… to the park every afternoon when I was a child.
    A to walk   B walking   C walk

12. 'What are you looking ………?' 'My wallet. I may have left it at Helen's house.'
    A for   B after   C at

13. ……… you stay at home last weekend?
    A Have   B Are   C Did

14. My cousin ……… his leg last Sunday while skiing.
    A breaks   B broke   C broken

15. 'What ……… at the party last night?' 'My new red dress.'
    A were you wearing   B have you worn
    C have you been wearing

16. Tom ……… a meal at the restaurant when he got an urgent phone call.
    A ordered   B has been ordering
    C was ordering

17. She ………… why her son was always late for dinner.
    A didn't understood   B didn't understand
    C understood not

18. Dad ……… to work when we lived in Hastings.
    A used to walk   B used to walking
    C would to walk

19. They ……… their summers in Wales when they were younger.
    A used to spending   B would spend
    C would to spend

20 .... 'No, but I'll finish it tomorrow.'
   A 'Have you finished your project yet?'
   B 'Have you ever finish your project?'
   C 'Have you finished your project yesterday?'

21 Tess .... here for ten years now.
   A lived   B lives   C has lived

22 Our team .... a match recently.
   A has never win   B has won
   C never won

23 My brother .... a new flat in the town centre.
   A has bought   B have bought
   C has buyed

24 Dad has .... arrived home from work. He's having dinner now.
   A never   B just   C yet

25 'Have they had breakfast ....?' 'No, they are waiting for us. We're having breakfast together.'
   A already   B yet   C still

26 'Where's Benjamin?' 'He .... to the bank.'
   A has been   B has gone
   C has been going

27 Where have you ....? The film started ten minutes ago.
   A been   B gone   C stayed

28 We're really worried. Ann hasn't ....
   A got home yet.   B already got home.
   C ever got home.

29 '......... did you arrive in Italy?' 'Two years ago.'
   A How long   B Since when   C When

30 Miles has been driving .... six hours and he's feeling quite tired now.
   A since   B from   C for

31 '......... have you had this computer?' 'For three years.'
   A Since long   B How much time
   C How long

32 'Have you .... tried free climbing?' 'Are you joking? I'm terrified of heights.'
   A just   B ever   C yet

33 'What's the matter with you? You look exhausted.' '......... for over an hour.'
   A I've been run   B I've been running
   C I ran

34 Poor Paula! She .... the dishes for an hour. She should buy a dishwasher.
   A has been washing   B has washed
   C washed

35 '......... have they lived in this village?' 'Since last August.'
   A Since long   B Since when
   C How often

36 When I got there, the library ....
   A had closed just
   B had already been closing
   C had already closed

37 Dan .... all afternoon, but a dog got into the flower beds and destroyed all of his work!
   A gardens   B had been gardening
   C was gardening

38 We were very late. .... we got to the airport, the boarding gate had closed and we had to wait for another flight.
   A As soon as   B After
   C By the time

39 The guests arrived before I .... cooking the dinner.
   A had finished   B was finishing
   C had been finishing

40 By the time the train got into the station, the passengers .... and moved towards the doors.
   A stood up   B were standing up
   C had already stood up

Assess yourself!

- **0 – 10** Study harder. Use the online exercises to help you.
- **11 – 20** OK. Use the online exercises to practise things you don't know.
- **21 – 30** Good, but do some extra practice online.
- **31 – 40** Excellent!

GRAMMAR MATRIX MAIN

UNIT 10 Adverbs and quantifiers

LESSON 1 Adverbs of manner and other adverbs

We use **adverbs of manner** to say how something happens or how something is done:
'How does she speak English?' 'She speaks fluently.'

We usually form adverbs by adding **–ly** to the corresponding adjective.
Will you please listen carefully?

adjective	adverb
quick	quickly
slow	slowly
clear	clearly
short	shortly

Study these spelling variations:

adjectives ending in –y	y → i	lucky happy	luckily happily

But: *shy* → *shyly* and **not** ~~shily~~

adjectives ending in –ple, –ble, –tle	–ply, –bly, –tly	simple, irritable, gentle	simply, irritably, gently
adjectives ending in –al, –ul	–ally, –ully	central careful	centrally carefully
adjectives of one syllable ending in a silent –e	remove the –e	true	truly

But: *pure* → *purely*   *safe* → *safely*   *rude* → *rudely*

> ❗ A few adjectives also end in **–ly**: **lovely**, **friendly**, **silly**, for example.
> In these cases, the adverbial form is expressed by saying **in a ...... way**:
> *She talked to me in a friendly way.*
> *Don't behave in a silly way.*

1 Transform the adjectives below into adverbs and write them in the correct column of the table.

angry   possible   easy   soft   comfortable   lazy   probable   quick   lucky   political   beautiful
cheap   free   honourable   idle   social   impressive   practical   incredible   whole

smartly	hungrily	notably	ideally	truly

174

Adverbs and adjectives

Adverbs of manner usually go after a verb, but they can also modify an adjective, a past participle or another adverb:

adverb + adjective	This beach is **really beautiful**.
adverb + past participle	I'm **absolutely overwhelmed** by its beauty.
adverb + adverb	Tourism is developing **incredibly slowly** in this area.

> ❗ When verbs of perception (**look, smell, sound, feel...**) are used intransitively, they are followed by an adjective and not an adverb:
> This cake smells *delicious*! NOT ~~deliciously~~
> It sounds *good*. NOT ~~well~~

Not all adverbs end in **–ly**. Some have the same form as the adjective:

	adjective	adverb
hard	It's **hard** work.	He works **hard**.
fast	He's a **fast** runner.	He runs very **fast**.
straight	She's got **straight**, blonde hair.	Go **straight** on along this road.
early	I had an **early** start this morning.	I woke up **early** this morning.

Be careful of the irregular form **good → well**:
He's a **good** cook. He cooks very **well**.

> ❗ Not all adverbs ending in **–ly** are adverbs of manner; some are adverbs of frequency, like **rarely** and **usually**, others are adverbs of degree, like **fairly** and **extremely**. Look too at: **generally, especially, mainly**.

FAQ

Q: If **hard** is used both as an adverb and an adjective, then what does **hardly** mean, which I've often heard used?

A: Hardly is also an adverb, from the word **hard**, but with the meaning *almost not* or *almost none*:
She has hardly any free time these days. She's very busy.

Adverbs with two forms and different meanings

Like **hard / hardly**, there are also other adverbs with two forms and two different meanings:

high	highly
Look at that kite. It's flying really high!	Business in this country is highly competitive.
late	**lately**
Sorry for being late.	Have you seen David lately?
near	**nearly**
The exam date is drawing near.	It's nearly ten o'clock.
fine	**finely**
Good job! You're doing fine.	Chop the herbs finely.

2 Adjective or adverb? Circle the correct option.

1. James can't type very **good** / **well**. For this position we need a person who types **quick** / **quickly**.
2. 'Have I spelt your name **correctly** / **correct**?' 'Yes, it's **perfect** / **perfectly**.'
3. The assistant did a very **good** / **well** job.
4. Her essay is too **simple** / **simply**. I don't think she will get a good grade.
5. She looked **beautiful** / **beautifully** in that evening dress.
6. This coffee smells **deliciously** / **delicious**. Can I have some?
7. It's been a **hard** / **hardly** week. I've **hardly** / **hard** seen anyone.
8. Andrea Bocelli sang **wonderful** / **wonderfully** during his latest concert.

3 Rewrite the sentences inserting the adverbs below in the correct position.

totally   terribly   seriously   happily   highly   incredibly   ~~carefully~~

0. Everything has been planned for the trip.
   Everything has been carefully planned for the trip.
1. The computer system was damaged by a virus.
2. Harrison Ford is unrecognisable in this film.
3. Your lasagne is good. You always cook it well.
4. It's improbable that they will be here tomorrow.
5. Dear me! It's late. I must hurry up.
6. They have been married for over 20 years.

4 Which adverbs correspond to the adjectives below? Complete the sentences with the correct adverbs.

good   fast   hard   quiet   careful   easy

1. The manager left the room ………………… , without saying anything else.
2. Ian studied very ………………… for his final exam.
3. The editor checked the essay ………………… before publishing it.
4. Nicole didn't feel very ………………… , so she took an aspirin and went to bed.
5. Irene understood everything quite ………………… .
6. He had an accident because he was driving too ………………… .

5 Complete the sentences with the adjectives below or the corresponding adverbs.

late   lucky   correct   easy   delicious   different   angry   careful   hard   friendly   good

1. ………………… nobody was badly hurt in the accident.
2. Sally looks very ………………… . I ………………… recognised her at the supermarket yesterday.
3. I don't know why, but James talked to us ………………… .
4. ………………… I haven't been feeling ………………… .
5. Our new neighbours are very nice and we often have a ………………… chat over the garden fence.
6. I ………………… get bored. I need something new every day.
7. Listen ………………… , please.
8. Most students answered the test questions ………………… .
9. That cake you made tasted really ………………… . Can you make another one soon?

LESSON 2 Adverbs of degree

We use **adverbs of degree** to modify the meaning of a qualifying adjective or adverb, and either make it stronger or weaker. Adverbs of degree usually precede the adjective or adverb to which they refer. Here are the most common ones in degree order:

+ +	**too** old
+	**very** / **really** old
+ −	**fairly** / **quite** / **rather** old
−	**not very** old
− −	**not** old **at all**

The most common **intensifiers**, which strengthen or increase the degree of an adjective, are: **too**, **very**, **really**, but also **extremely** and **absolutely**. **Definitely**, on the other hand, is used with a verb:

The film was too long.
It's a very interesting book.
It was a really nice day.
She's extremely patient.
You're absolutely right.
I definitely remember texting him about the meeting.

Too can be further reinforced by adding **much**, **way** or **far**:

It's much too late to ring him up.
They spend way too much money on clothes.
This silk shirt is far too expensive for me.

The most commonly used **mitigators**, or modifiers that lessen the degree of an adjective, are: **fairly, quite, rather, pretty, enough, not very, not at all**.

- **Fairly** is used a lot with adjectives and adverbs that have a positive meaning and to express approval:

    Today's test was fairly easy. (and I'm happy about that)

- **Quite** is used with adjectives and adverbs, and also with verbs:

    Her new hairstyle is quite nice.
    Quite surprisingly, they didn't finish before midnight.
    They quite enjoyed the show.

Focus

Look at the position of the indefinite article when there is a noun in the sentence → *It was **quite a good** concert.* NOT ~~a quite good concert.~~

- **Rather** implies a slight sense of criticism or disappointment. It can also indicate that something is unusual or better than expected, and is a surprise:

    Yesterday's training session was rather hard. (even too hard for me)
    The band's new concert was rather long. (and I didn't like that)
    He's just got his licence but he drives rather well. (that's unusual and it surprises me)

    It's also used before a verb: *I rather like it.*

    Look at the position of the indefinite article when there is a noun in the sentence:
    *A lot of people thought it was **rather a success**, but not me.* (only a noun is present)
    *It's **a rather difficult** question. / It's **rather a difficult** question.* (adjective + noun)

- **Pretty** is used only with adjectives and adverbs, usually in an informal context:
  We had a pretty good time at the party.
  She can sing pretty well.
- **Enough** is used with adjectives, adverbs and verbs and normally follows them in the sentence:
  You aren't old enough to drive a car.
  He doesn't speak fluently enough.
  We haven't trained enough for the match.
  However, if there is a noun in the sentence, **enough** goes first → *We don't have enough tables.*

> Study these examples:
> *We don't have enough big tables.* → *enough* modifies *tables*.
> *We don't have big enough tables.* → *enough* modifies *big*

- **Not very** and **not at all** are used in negative sentences:
  What you said is not very interesting.
  I'm not at all happy about it. (Also: *I'm not happy at all...*)

FAQ

Q: I once heard: 'Are you sure?' 'Yes, definitely.' What does that mean exactly?

A: **Definitely** means that there is no doubt about it.
Here's another example:
You look tired, you definitely need a break.

1 Reorder the words to write meaningful sentences.

1 quite / I / had / a / in / good / yesterday's / result / test / .
   ....

2 perfect / performance / absolutely / was / Their / .
   ....

3 We / quite / last / watched / an / film / night / enjoyable / .
   ....

4 but / It's / late / the / still / shop / is / rather / open / .
   ....

5 pretty / can / They / well / dance / .
   ....

6 everybody / there / for / chairs / Were / enough / ?
   ....

7 The / was / fairly / a / building / hotel / modern / .
   ....

8 what / This / holiday / is / expensive / way / package / for / it / too / offers / .
   ....

2 Complete the sentences with the correct adverb of degree below.

not at all   not very   enough   rather   fairly   too (x2)   extremely

1 The room was .... crowded, so they left and went into the garden.
2 Our primary school teacher was .... patient with us. She often lost her temper.
3 The boss is .... satisfied with their work. They will have to do it all over again.
4 Her latest novel is .... good – much better than his previous one, I must say.
5 This film is .... violent. I'm not going to watch it to the end.
6 I knew her .... well, but we were not really close friends.
7 I can't believe it! It's .... good to be true.
8 This room isn't big .... for all these people.

'Strong' adjectives

With 'strong' adjectives, which already have their own superlative meaning, we don't use the adverbs of degree **very**, **fairly**, **rather** and **too**. Instead, we use adverbs like **really** and **absolutely** or **quite**, which in this sense has the meaning *completely*.

Here are some examples of 'strong' adjectives: **huge**, **awful**, **wonderful**, **amazing**, **great**, **impossible**, **essential**:

The party was absolutely great. NOT ~~very great~~
The food was really awful. NOT ~~fairly awful~~
You're quite right. NOT ~~very right~~

3 Write the adjectives below in the correct column.

ugly   happy   excited   marvellous   scared   nice   astonishing   sad   furious   cold   freezing
fantastic   nervous   angry   frantic   afraid   horrible

basic meaning	strong meaning

Adverbs + verb

Some adverbs of degree modify the meaning of the verb that follows them: **nearly**, **almost**, **hardly**, **scarcely**, **barely**, **just**, **only**:

She almost fainted when she saw him.
He was so tired he could barely keep his eyes open.
It was so foggy that we could hardly see the road.
They just sat down without saying a word.
We only need a few more glasses.

Very much and **a lot** follow the verb or the verb + object:
I like reading a lot.
I like reading detective stories very much.

So and **such a** intensify meaning in exclamatory sentences. Look at the sentence constructions they are used with:
so + adjective or adverb
such a / an + adjective + noun
*It's **so cold** today!*
*It's **such a cold** day!*
A consecutive clause, indicating the result, often follows these intensifiers, introduced by **that** → *It was so cold / such a cold day that we couldn't even go skiing.*

4 Circle the correct option.

1. The English test was **so / such** difficult that nearly all the students failed it.
2. Hardwell's music was **very / really** fantastic.
3. I **quite / fairly** like drawing and painting.
4. It was **quite a hard / a quite hard** match, but we won in the end.
5. It sounds **absolutely / too** incredible, but George Clooney is shooting a film in my town.
6. That horse was **really / very** amazing – he won every race!
7. What a goal! He's **such a / so** great player!
8. I'm two metres tall and the hotel bed is not **enough long / long enough** for me.

5 Reorder the words and write logical sentences.

1. had / We / really / a / holiday / nice / summer / last / . ...
2. The / was / big / so / we / got / that / lost / palace / . ...
3. quite / He / good / is / a / actor / . ...
4. It / enough / warm / to / isn't / the / swim / lake / in / . ...
5. such / It's / a / dog / cute / little / . ...
6. rather / day / It's / dull / a / autumn /. ....

6 Each sentence contains a mistake. Underline them and rewrite the sentences correctly.

1. He's enough old to cook his own meals.
   ....
2. It's a so exciting thriller. It keeps you on edge until the end.
   ....
3. I could hard understand what she was saying.
   ....
4. The view from the hotel terrace is very amazing.
   ....
5. We bought a quite cheap dishwasher but it broke after a couple of years.
   ....
6. My son likes a lot cooking.
   ....

7 Complete the sentences with the adverbs below.

much   quite   hardly   too   so   really

1. Are you sure that the show tickets aren't .... expensive?
2. I was .... moved during the ceremony that I could .... speak.
3. Mark was .... embarrassed when he got his award.
4. It was .... late when we got to the restaurant, but it was still open.
5. He got good results in the test. I'm surprised, because he doesn't usually study ....

LESSON 3 Indefinite adjectives and pronouns to express large quantities

Large quantities

a lot of / lots of / plenty of	in front of plural countable nouns and singular uncountable nouns	mostly in positive sentences
much	in front of singular uncountable nouns	mostly in negative and interrogative sentences
many	in front of plural countable nouns	

See page 14 for the definition of countable and uncountable nouns.

We use the indefinite pronouns and adjectives in the table to talk about large quantities.

A lot of is used in positive sentences but also in negative and interrogative sentences in informal language:
There's a lot of noise in this room.
A lot of people visit the museum every weekend.
There aren't a lot of people in the queue.

As a pronoun, we use **a lot** and **plenty** (without **of**) → *'How many stamps have you got?' 'I've got a lot.'*

Lots of and **plenty of** are more colloquial expressions:
There's lots of / plenty of room for everyone.

Even more informal are the expressions **a load of** / **loads of**, which are especially used in spoken language:
I've got loads of homework for tomorrow.

Much and **many** are mainly used in questions and negative sentences:
We haven't got much money. Let's get some from the ATM.
Have we got many eggs?

With the word **times**, we usually use **many**, even in positive sentences:
I've been there many times.

1 Complete the sentences with *a lot of*, *much* or *many*.

1 There are .... new apps coming out tomorrow.
2 There aren't .... tomatoes, but there's .... lettuce there to make a salad.
3 I haven't got .... money with me. Let's go to the bank first.
4 'Have you got .... CDs?' 'No, I haven't got .... now.'
5 You need .... cocoa to make these cookies – about 300 grams.
6 This fruit loaf isn't fattening because there isn't .... butter in it.

Questions

To ask about quantity or the number of an item, we use the following expressions:

| **How much** + singular uncountable nouns | *How much luggage have you got?* |
| **How many** + plural countable nouns | *How many seats do we need for the meeting?* |

How much and **How many** can also be used as pronouns:
How much / How many do you need? (the noun is understood)

When we want to show that there is an excessive quantity of something, we use the adverb **too**:

too + adjectives	*It's too hot today.*
too much + singular uncountable nouns	*There's too much traffic on the motorway today.*
too many + plural countable nouns	*There are too many cars in the town centre.*

Too much and **too many** can also be used as pronouns:
That's too much!   There are too many.

2 Circle the correct option.

1. It's true. **Too / How** many cooks spoil the broth.
2. It's **much / too** cold in here. Let's close the windows.
3. The police officer wants to know how **many / much** people live in this building.
4. Don't buy too **much / many** bread. We're all on a diet!
5. The streets are **too / too much** busy today. I'll take my bike.
6. Don't give the kids too **many / much** sweets. They'll spoil their teeth.
7. Don't tell me! It's **too / too much** good to be true.
8. How **many / much** money do you need for the school trip?
9. Don't put all that flour in the bowl. That's way too **much / many**!
10. How **much / many** information can you fit on that memory stick?
11. It's **too much busy / too busy** in town today. Let's come back another day.
12. Are you **too / too many** tired to help me?

Other adjectives and pronouns expressing quantity

Other adjectives and pronouns that express quantity are:

enough	There's enough paper in the printer. (There's a sufficient quantity of paper.)
most	Most students live in this area. (The majority of the students…)
all	All the seats were taken. (Not even one seat was vacant.)
	'Anything else?' 'No, that's all, thanks.' (I don't need anything else.)

FAQ

Q: Can I say both *Most plants in this garden are tropical* and *Most of the plants in this garden are tropical*?

A: Yes, both forms are correct. But if we talk about things and people in a general sense, without going into detail, we use only **most**: She likes *most vegetables*.
If there's a pronoun, we always use **most of**: As *most of you* know, we have a new colleague.

Be careful of the construction with **enough**:

enough + noun	There were enough handouts for everyone.
adjective + enough	The room was big enough for all the participants.
verb + enough	I have enough to do today.

FAQ

Q: I've heard sentences like *I've had plenty.* or *We saw plenty of him.* I don't think **plenty** means *a lot* here.

A: In actual fact, when **plenty** is used in an informal register, it can also have the meaning of *enough*, as in the two sentences that you mention. The first means 'I've had enough', and the second means 'We've seen enough of him, even too much'. In both cases you could also say: *I've had enough. We saw enough of him.*

3 Circle the correct option.

1. Does Sam have **many / much / lots** CDs by Jason Derulo?
2. We haven't got **lots / many / plenty of** new Facebook friends.
3. Have you got **much / many / loads** free time in the evening?
4. I can't speak **lot of / much / many** languages, only English and Italian.
5. There's **plenty of / too many / most** food for ten people.
6. **All / Most / Plenty** the candidates are ready for the exam to start.
7. **Lot / Most / Much** of the class want to do a cultural exchange with a German school.
8. We haven't **plenty / enough / many** money for a meal in that posh restaurant.
9. Let's book that hotel – there are **much / loads of / plenty** things to do there.
10. Have you got **plenty / much / enough** money to buy a new car yet?

4 Reorder the words and write logical sentences. Be careful of the position of *enough*.

1. aren't / There / enough / for / sandwiches / these / all / people / .
   ....
2. enough / The / room / isn't / big / the / party / for / .
   ....
3. have / film / seen / enough / of / this / We / .
   ....
4. studied / He / enough / pass / hasn't / this / to / test / .
   ....
5. Harry / enough / isn't / to / his own / old / credit card / have / .
   ....

5 Complete the sentences with suitable adverbs.

1. There aren't .... restaurants in this area.
2. I'm new in this school and I don't know .... of my colleagues.
3. In the conference hall there aren't .... chairs for all the participants.
4. How .... money do you have on your credit card?
5. There are too .... car parks in this town, but not .... playgrounds.
6. I know .... of the songs on this album, but not .... of them.

LESSON 4 Indefinite adjectives and pronouns to express small quantities

Small quantities

little	in front of singular uncountable nouns
few	in front of plural countable nouns
a little	in front of singular uncountable nouns
a few	in front of plural countable nouns

We use the indefinite adjectives and pronouns in the table to talk about small quantities:

I'm sorry but I've got **little** information about this topic.

There are **few** folders left. We must buy some.

Here's **a little** money.

Note the differences between **little** / **a little** and **few** / **a few**.
Little = not much **Few** = not many (there's the idea of not enough, of scarcity)
There's little milk. I can't make a milkshake.
She feels lonely because she knows few people here.

A little / **A few** = some, a small number (the words have a positive meaning)
There's a little milk. We can make a milkshake.
She moved here only last month but she's already got a few friends.

1 Complete the sentences with *little*, *a little*, *few* or *a few*.

1 She works a lot, even at the weekend, so she has ………………… time for her family.
2 She never works at the weekend because she wants to have ………………… time for her family.
3 Have a sandwich. There are ………………… on the table.
4 I can't make an apple pie. There are just ………………… apples.
5 Look! There are ………………… people in the garden. What are they doing?
6 Hurry up! We have ………………… minutes left before the train leaves.
7 I've already put ………………… salt in the soup but maybe it's not enough.
8 You'll get ………………… help from her. She's such a selfish girl.

A bit (of) / **a little bit (of)** are more colloquial expressions often used instead of **a little**:
Can I have a bit of sugar in my tea, please?
'Would you like some milk too?' 'Just a little bit.'

Small quantities can also be expressed with **not much** and **not many**, or with the adverb **only** or **just** before **a little** or **a few**:
I didn't have many chances. = I only had a few chances.

Very small quantities are expressed with **very little**, **very few** and **hardly any**.
I know very little about New Zealand.
Very few people live in this village.
We have hardly any petrol in the tank. Let's stop to fill up.

For 'zero quantity', we use the expressions **not any**, which is both an adjective and a pronoun; **no**, which is only an adjective; and **none**, which is only a pronoun.
'Have you got any more tickets for tonight's show?' 'I'm afraid we've got no tickets left. / …we've got none left.'
(see page 45)

2 Circle the correct option.

1 'Have you got **a few** / **a little** coins in your pocket?' 'No, **any** / **none** at all.'
2 The President doesn't have **many** / **much** power in my country.
3 In Italy, there's **few** / **hardly any** interest in cricket.
4 Very **few** / **little** English students learn ancient Greek today.
5 I only have **a few** / **a little** money left. Let's get some from the ATM.
6 There are **a lot of** / **a little** stars in the sky tonight. It'll be a beautiful day tomorrow.
7 Just **a little** / **a few** people have a lot of responsibility in our company.
8 **Not many** / **Not a few** tourists visit this museum even though it's really worth it!
9 There are **very little** / **hardly any** tea bags left. Can you put some on the shopping list, please?
10 I wanted to buy a ticket for the Rihanna concert, but there were **none** / **no** left.

3 Circle the correct option.

1. Oh dear! Let's stop at the service station. We've got ...... petrol left.
   A much   B little   C few   D a lot of

2. I'm working hard. I don't have ...... time to go out with my friends.
   A a lot   B many   C little   D much

3. We can't make a cheesecake. There isn't ...... cottage cheese in the fridge.
   A many   B any   C few   D some

4. Venice is a unique city so ...... tourists visit it every year.
   A very   B a lot   C lots of   D few

5. I'm quite happy to live in this town. People are friendly and I have already made quite ...... friends here.
   A a little   B a few   C much   D lots

6. Jim doesn't like living in Los Angeles. He has only got ...... few friends there.
   A much   B any   C a   D very

7. We have hardly ...... time.
   A some   B any   C little   D much

8. I've taken ...... of photos!
   A many   B loads   C lot   D much

4 Complete the second sentence so that it has the same meaning as the first one.

1. We have little information about the facilities in this town.
   We haven't got .... about the facilities in this town.

2. There are two little lakes outside the town, but at this time of year the water is too cold to swim in.
   There are two little lakes outside the town, but at this time of year the water isn't .... to swim in.

3. I know there aren't many ethnic restaurants.
   I know there are only ....

4. There's little traffic except for the rush hour.
   There isn't .... except for the rush hour.

5. It's a quiet town so there is hardly any traffic at this time.
   It's a quiet town so there isn't ....

6. I don't want you to take any risks while you're diving.
   I want you to .... while you're diving.

7. The rhythm of the music was so irresistible that everyone started to dance.
   The music had .... to dance.

5 Fill in the gaps with a suitable quantifier. Choose from:

very little   few   a little (x2)   much   many (x2)   no   a few

1. He can speak English, French, Japanese and .... German.

2. There were very .... people at the conference. Pity, because it was very interesting.

3. There's still .... ink in the printer.

4. When we got back home from our holidays, there was .... to eat in the fridge so we ordered a meal from the Chinese take-away.

5. We didn't visit .... museums when we were in Paris.

6. There isn't .... sugar in my coffee.

7. There weren't .... supporters at the stadium last Saturday.

8. There were .... flowers in the garden, but not many.

9. There was .... point in continuing, as nobody was listening.

ROUND UP 10

MATRIX +

Intensifying adverbs

We have already seen that **very** and **really** are used to strengthen the meaning of an adjective or adverb. There are other words that do this in colloquial language, such as **just**, **awfully**, **amazingly**, **terribly**, **totally** and **incredibly**:

Everything's just fine!   She was terribly late.   It's totally useless!

We can also use **thoroughly** and **utterly**, although these are more formal:
I'm thoroughly confused.   You look utterly exhausted!

Mitigating and diminishing adverbs

To lessen the degree of an adjective or adverb, as well as **fairly**, **rather**, **quite** and **pretty**, we can use **slightly** or **a bit / a little** → *It's slightly different.   He was a bit worried.*

1 Complete the sentences with a suitable adverb of degree from those below. More than one adverb is possible in some cases.

very   quite   too   absolutely   such   really   so   at all   a bit   rather   slightly   just

1 This coffee is .... strong! I can't possibly drink it.
2 You're .... good at chess! You always beat me.
3 They're .... right! There's nothing we can say.
4 The test was .... easy. I think I got it right.
5 Yesterday was .... a lovely day! We had a .... nice walk.
6 She was not .... lucky this time!
7 They weren't successful .... !
8 This problem is just .... more difficult than the other one.
9 She's just .... overweight, but not very.
10 My new shoes are nice, but they're .... uncomfortable.
11 You're .... hopeless! How can you play .... badly?

2 Complete the sentences with the best adverb of manner below.

quietly   fluently   unfortunately   luckily   enthusiastically   straight   beautifully   hard   well

1 Sit down .... and concentrate on your work.
2 Go .... ahead and then turn right.
3 My father speaks German ....
4 She's a great dancer. She dances ....
5 .... we still have plenty of time!
6 My son is doing incredibly .... in his new school.
7 They're studying really .... this term.
8 The maths teacher didn't speak very .... about her class.
9 I'm sorry to tell you that .... you have failed the test again.

MATRIX +
Indefinite quantifying adjectives and pronouns

Little is both an indefinite adjective or pronoun and a qualifying adjective.
A little followed by an uncountable noun means 'a small amount' → *I've got a little money.*
A little followed by a singular countable noun mean 'a small' → *I've got a little dog.*

> ❗ **Small** and **little** have a slightly different meaning. **Small** is used for people, animals and objects of a small size. **Little**, on the other hand, is used for animals or people of a young age who will grow in the future → *I have a little brother. He's two years old.   My sister is a small girl.*

As well as **many** and **a lot of**, for large numbers we can also use the indefinite adjective **several**, which is more formal → *There are several foreign students this year.*

Quite is often used before **a few** and **a lot** in colloquial language → *Quite a few people were waiting at the bus stop.   He used to spend quite a lot of time in France.*

All is used with uncountable nouns, plural nouns and expressions of time (**all day**, **all night long**, **all week**) → *They've lost all their money.   I like all kinds of music.   I worked all day.*

In front of a plural noun, we use **all the...** or **all of the...** if the clause is qualified with more details:
→ *We liked all (of) the songs they sang last night.*

All is also used as a pronoun → *They've all worked hard. / All of them have worked hard.   She bought tickets for us all.*

The whole means 'all, the entire thing' and is generally used with a singular countable noun → *They ate the whole cake!*

---

3 Complete the sentences with *all / all of / all the / the whole*.

1 Not ………………… people you invited are coming.
2 He didn't want to hear ………………… story. It was long and boring.
3 There are people going in ………………… directions.
4 Please be quiet! ………………… you!
5 Do you really know ………………… these people?
6 I stayed at home ………………… day yesterday because I wasn't very well.
7 I love this album – I know ………………… the songs on it by heart.
8 ………………… class is going on the trip – no one is staying behind.

4 Reorder the words and write logical sentences.

1 too / It's / true / good / to / be / . …………………………………………………………………
2 salt / too / There's / much / in / soup / the / . …………………………………………………
3 coffee / There / sugar / in / enough / isn't / my / . ……………………………………………
4 too / noise / in / much / room / this / There's / . ………………………………………………
5 The / are / on / too / shops / the / first / day / of / the / sales / crowded / . ……
6 here / are / too / There / people / many / today / . ……………………………………………
7 got / money / I / enough / haven't / ticket / the / for / . ………………………………………
8 enough / table / isn't / This / large / . …………………………………………………………

5 Complete the dialogue with the words below.

How many   finely   How much   gently   enough   delicious   some (x3)
a little   any   slowly

Fiona What are you doing, Mum?
Mum I'm making ¹............................ chocolate-chip cookies.
Fiona Cookies? Great! Can I help you?
Mum Sure. Get ²............................ chocolate, please.
Fiona ³............................ do you need?
Mum 175 grams.
Fiona We've got a whole 200, gram bar, so that's ⁴............................ . Do you need ⁵............................ butter?
Mum Yes, 125 grams. And now eggs…
Fiona ⁶............................ eggs do you need?
Mum Just one. And 150 grams of flour.
Fiona One egg and ⁷............................ flour. Here you are. Anything else?
Mum Yes, I need ⁸............................ sugar, about 50 grams.
Fiona Here. What should I do now?
Mum Chop the chocolate ⁹............................ while I'm creaming the butter and sugar.
Fiona Okay. What next?
Mum Beat in the egg. And now add the flour ¹⁰............................ . Mix ¹¹............................ .

30 minutes later

Mum You can take the cookies out of the oven now, Fiona. They're ready.
Fiona Mmmm… They smell and look ¹²............................ .

6 Complete the text with the adverbs or quantifiers below. Some of them may be used more than once.

a few   a little   very   much   fairly   very much   any   actually

Karen is ¹............................ pleased because she has just moved into her new flat in Chelsea. It hasn't got ²............................ furniture, but she has brought ³............................ essential things from her parents' house. She's got a bed and a ⁴............................ big table, but she hasn't got ⁵............................ chairs yet, so she has to sit on the bed. She has already painted the walls because she didn't like the old colour ⁶............................ and she has hung a few pictures up. She's ⁷............................ optimistic and she's planning to have a party when she has somewhere for her guests to sit. In fact, she's invited ⁸............................ friends to come round next weekend. The flat doesn't ⁹............................ belong to Karen. She has rented it for a year and her parents have given her ¹⁰............................ financial help because she doesn't work.

7 Fill in the gaps with the words and phrases below.

especially   quite a   a few   all   quite   all of us   completely   the most   rather   a bit
definitely   whole   slightly   so few

Have you ever been on holiday in February? I'm spending ¹............................ days in the French Riviera because a friend has got ²............................ big house in the hills and has invited me for her birthday. There are five of us, and we all come from different European countries. ³............................ are French teachers and we are making ⁴............................ of this opportunity to speak French ⁵............................ day long. The village where we are is ⁶............................ small, but it's always ⁷............................ crowded in summer, whereas at this time of year there are ⁸............................ visitors that it looks quite different. It's ⁹............................ sad sometimes, ¹⁰............................ in the late afternoon when the sun starts setting and the ¹¹............................ atmosphere changes ¹²............................ . We are often the only people walking along the silent streets and lanes, which makes us feel ¹³............................ uneasy. In spite of the amazing beauty of the landscape, we all ¹⁴............................ prefer a holiday in the summer.

8 Read the text below. Use the words given in capitals at the end of some of the lines to form a word that fits in the gap in the same line.

The natural display of varying colours in the Arctic sky is one of
Iceland's biggest tourist sights. ¹............................ it's rather   FORTUNATE
²............................ , so visitors should try a few times to be sure they can see   PREDICT
the Northern Lights. But what are they? The Northern Lights refer to one
of the most ³............................ wonders of the world, the aurora borealis, a   AMAZE
⁴............................ and flickering display of colours most   GLOW
⁵............................ seen in the northern hemisphere. The colours you see   COMMON
are caused by gases in the air, ⁶............................ a mixture of oxygen and   MAIN
nitrogen.

Reflecting on grammar

Reflect on the rules and say whether the following statements are true or false.

		True	False
1	All words ending in **–ly** are adverbs.		
2	All adverbs of manner end in **–ly**.		
3	After the verbs **smell, sound, look, feel**, we use adjectives like **great**, and not adverbs.		
4	*There were hardly any people at the conference* means that there were lots of people at the conference.		
5	**Too** is used in front of an adjective or adverb.		
6	**Enough** is used in front of an adjective or after a noun.		
7	The sentence *It's a very fabulous landscape* is correct.		
8	**Little** and **few** are used with a negative meaning about small quantities.		
9	The sentence *We haven't got much time* is incorrect.		
10	The question *How many passengers were on the bus?* is correct.		

GRAMMAR MATRIX MAIN

UNIT 11 Comparisons

LESSON 1 Comparative adjectives

→ Visual Grammar page 418

When we want to compare the characteristics of two things or people, we use **comparative adjectives**. Comparative adjectives are used to say that one thing is more important, more interesting etc than another, that is, it has a greater degree of a certain quality. Comparative adjectives are formed in different ways according to the number of syllables in the adjective.

more + adjective	adjective + *–er*
adjectives with three or more syllables *more difficult, more popular, more expensive*	**adjectives with just one syllable** *older, smaller, colder* Be careful with the spelling variations: • adjectives ending in **–e** just add **–r**: *nice → nicer, large → larger* • adjectives ending in a single vowel + a consonant double the final consonant: *hot → hotter, thin → thinner*, BUT: *cheap → cheaper* (two vowels)
two-syllable adjectives *more famous, more recent, more careful*	**two-syllable adjectives ending in –y** *easy → easier, happy → happier* Be careful: the **y** changes to an **i** before adding **–er**.

Some two-syllable adjectives can have both forms, for example those ending in **–ow**, **–er**, **–le**, plus a few others like **quiet**, **friendly**, **polite**, **common**, **stupid**...: *more narrow / narrower, more clever / cleverer, more gentle / gentler, more quiet / quieter, more friendly / friendlier*

1 Write the comparative form of the adjectives below in the correct column. Be careful: some double the final consonant.

healthy   tall   intelligent   slim   dry   smart   dangerous   heavy   cheap   interesting   hot
trendy   successful   bright   important   lucky   beautiful   pretty

Adjective + *–er*	Adjective + *–ier*	*More* + adjective

2 Use the adjectives from exercise 1 in both the basic form and the comparative form to describe the pictures, as in the example.

0   *This diamond is bright. The other one is brighter.*

1   ....

2   ....

3   ....

4   ....

5   ....

6   ....

The structure of a comparative sentence

The second term of comparison, that is, the second item of the two that are compared, is introduced by **than** → *Exercise 1 is easier than exercise 2.*

Than may be followed by:

- a noun or pronoun → *My cousin is younger than me.*
  Be careful: the object pronoun (**me**, **him**, **her**... see page 83) is more common in spoken language, whereas more formal language uses the subject pronoun followed by the auxiliary verb → *My cousin is younger than I am.*

- a secondary comparative clause → *The exam was harder than I thought.*

A comparative adjective can also be used attributively. Its position is always before the noun, as for any other adjective in the basic form (see page 46): *Manchester is a big city. It's a bigger city than York.*

Special types of comparison

- A special type of comparative expresses the idea that two changes happen together in a parallel way:

The + first comparative (+ subject + verb), **the** + second comparative (+ subject + verb)

The richer he gets, the meaner (he gets).
The greater the challenge, the greater the reward.
The older this wine gets, the better it is.

- If we compare two actions, the first is expressed by a verb in the infinitive (**to** + base form), the second just by the base form → *Sometimes it's quicker to cycle than go by car.*

- We can also use the comparative with two elements to express a superlative concept: **the** + comparative + **of...**

I bought the cheaper of the two dresses.
They took the shorter of the two roads.

3 Complete the sentences with comparative adjectives. Add *than* where it is needed.

1. The flight was .... we expected – it cost only £60. (cheap)
2. He isn't .... you. You can do just as well. (clever)
3. This test is .... the one we had last week. (difficult)
4. Try to be .... when writing in English. You've made a lot of spelling mistakes. (careful)
5. His second novel has been .... the first one. (successful)
6. The .... the food you eat, the .... you are. (healthy)
7. Today is a .... day .... yesterday. (warm)
8. I think it's .... to travel with a friend .... travel on your own. (nice)
9. I'll take the '0915 express', it's the .... of the two trains. (fast)
10. The .... you are to people, the .... people will be to you. (kind)

Much more... / A little more... / Getting more and more...

We have already seen how to intensify the meaning of the base form of adjectives, for example by using **very**, **quite** and other similar expressions (see Unit 10 Lesson 2).

- To intensify the meaning of a comparative adjective, we use the adverbs **much** / **a lot** or **far** / **way** (USA):

'Their room is very large'. 'Yes, it's much bigger than ours.'
Tom is a far smarter guy than Rick.

- To lessen the degree of a comparative, on the other hand, we use expressions like **a little** / **a bit** or **slightly**:

My dad is a bit more patient than my mum.

- Another way to increase the degree of a comparative is to use two of the same comparatives with the conjunction **and**. This expresses the idea of a gradual increase:

It's getting warmer and warmer.
Petrol is getting more and more expensive.

4 Complete the sentences with comparative adjectives preceded if possible by an intensifying adverb of your choice: *much*, *a lot* or *far*.

0. Today's English lesson was *much more interesting than* yesterday's. (interesting)
1. His latest film was .... than his previous ones. (exciting)
2. Christina is .... than the other girls in her class. (quiet)
3. It's getting .... and .... We'll soon be able to see the stars. (dark)
4. These trainers are .... but they're also .... than the others. (expensive, comfortable)

5 This summer has been .... than all the ones I can remember. (hot)

6 She's on a strict diet. She's getting .... and ....
every day. (thin)

Irregular comparatives

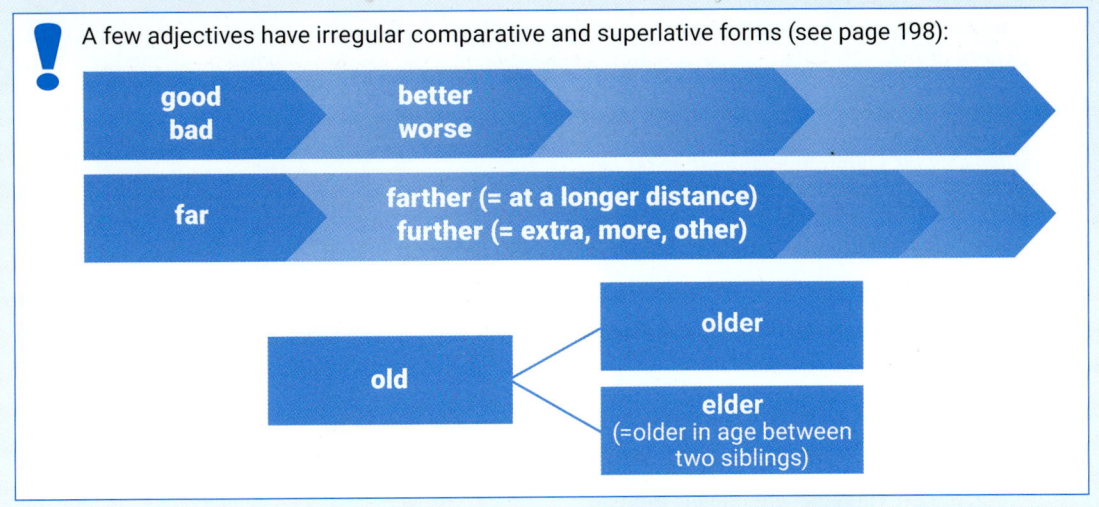

A few adjectives have irregular comparative and superlative forms (see page 198):

| good / bad | → | better / worse |

| far | → | farther (= at a longer distance) / further (= extra, more, other) |

| old | → | older |
| | → | elder (=older in age between two siblings) |

Yesterday the weather was bad, but today it is even worse.
Saturn is farther from the Sun than Venus.
For further information, call 0369382662.
Rachel is my elder sister. She's three years older than me.

I have to admit that my wife is a better skier than I am.

5 Write sentences comparing the two elements, as in the example. Choose between these adjectives: *good / healthy / relaxing / exciting / tiring / boring / expensive / cheap / nice / easy*. SInce it is your opinion, write *I think…* at the start of each sentence.

0 salad / French fries
I think salad is healthier than French fries, but French fries are much nicer!

1 living in a big city / living in the country
....
....

2 adventure films / comedies
....
....

3 cycling / walking
....
....

4 travelling by train / travelling by car
....
....

5 working in an office / working in the open air
....
....

6 doing yoga / going jogging
....
....

7 golf / football
....
....

193

LESSON 2 Comparative structures using *less than* and *not as... as* with adjectives

The comparative structure using *less than*

The comparative using **less than** is used when we want to compare one thing with another that is <u>less</u> important, less useful, etc, in other words to express a lesser degree of a certain quality.

It is formed with the adverb **less** in front of all adjectives (containing one, two or more syllables). The second term of the comparison is introduced by **than**, just like the structure with **more**:

> **less** + adjective + **than** + second term of comparison (noun or pronoun).

The sequel was less interesting than the first film.

Than can also introduce a secondary comparative clause:
Our holiday in the Bahamas was less exciting than we thought.

1 Write sentences with the same meaning, using *less* and an adjective with the opposite meaning, as in the example.

0 My car is an older model than yours. (recent)
My car is a less recent model than yours.

1 Mr Johnson's lessons are usually more interesting than Mr Riley's. (boring)
....

2 The blue coat is cheaper than the brown one. (expensive)
....

3 My suitcase is lighter than yours. (heavy)
....

4 This building is a more classical style than the other one. (modern)
....

5 Today it's cooler than yesterday. (warm)
....

6 This TV series is more boring than the one on Channel 4. (exciting)
....

7 It's unlikely to rain this afternoon. (likely)
....

Comparisons with *as... as*

We can compare two things or people to express the idea that one thing or person is **as...** interesting, important, etc **as** another, that is, that it possesses the same amount of a certain quality.

It is formed as follows:

> **as** + adjective + **as** + second term of comparison (noun or pronoun)

Houses in this area are as expensive as those in my town.

We can use the adverb **just** as an intensifier before **as** + adjective:
John is just as clever as his brother.

The 'comparison of equality', as it is called, is frequently used in the negative, as an alternative to the comparative of a lesser degree. In this case, the first **as** can be substituted by **so**:

Today it isn't as cold as yesterday. = Today it's less cold than yesterday.
The prices here are not so high as in the other supermarket.

2 Write comparisons using the words in brackets and the structure *as... as*.

1 (just / beautiful) She's .... her sister.
2 (busy) Luckily I'm not .... today .... I was yesterday.
3 (famous) Bob Dylan is .... Bruce Springsteen.
4 (interesting) This article is not .... the one in *TIME* magazine.
5 (exciting) The show was .... a cold rice pudding!
6 (just / good) Their latest concert was .... last year's.
7 (popular) The Rolling Stones were .... The Beatles in the 1960s.

3 Write positive or negative comparisons using (*not*) *as... as* and the adjective in brackets.

0 Joe: 1.70 m / Marion: 1.70 m (tall)
Joe is as tall as Marion.

1 Claire: 60 years old / Karen: 60 years old (old)
....

2 Today: 38 °C / Yesterday: 38°C (hot)
....

3 Blue jacket: £65.00 / Black jacket: £80.00 (expensive)
....

4 Their flat: 70 sq.m / Our flat: 100 sq.m (large)
....

5 The history book: 250 pages / The grammar book: 300 pages (big)
....

6 The Ohio river: 1,579 km / The Mississippi: 3,730 km (long)
....

7 The Breithorn: 4,164 m / Mont Blanc: 4,810 m (high)
....

8 Oxford: about 50 km from here / Salisbury: about 50 km from here (far)
....

4 Write sentences with the same meaning using the structure *not as... as*.

0 The oral exam was less difficult than the written one.
The oral exam wasn't as difficult as the written one.

1 Cross-country skiing is less risky than alpine skiing or snowboarding.
....

2 A small tent is less comfortable than a campervan.
....

3 This song is less famous than the others on her latest album.
....

4 Baseball is less popular in Italy than football.
....

5 She's been less successful in her career than her sister.
....

6 My scooter is less sporty than your motorbike.
....

LESSON 3 Superlative adjectives

→ Visual Grammar page 419

Superlative adjectives

When we want to compare the characteristics of a person or thing in relation to a group, we use a superlative adjective.

Superlative adjectives are used to say that a certain thing is the most important, the most interesting, etc, that is that it possesses the highest grade of a particular quality compared to the rest of the group. As with the comparative, seen on the previous pages, the superlative also has different forms depending on the number of syllables in the adjective.

The most + adjective	The adjective + *–est*
adjectives with three or more syllables *the most dangerous* *the most important* *the most expensive*	**adjectives with just one syllable** *the smallest, the tallest, the youngest* The spelling variations are the same as those you have seen for comparative forms (see page 190): • adjectives ending in **–e** add only **–st**: *wide* → *the widest, safe* → *the safest* • adjectives ending with one vowel plus one consonant double the final consonant before adding **–est**: *fat* → *the fattest, thin* → *the thinnest,* BUT: *cheap* → *the cheapest* (two vowels)
two–syllable adjectives *the most frequent* *the most careful* *the most secure*	**two–syllable adjectives ending in –y** *heavy* → *the heaviest, funny* → *the funniest* Be careful: the **y** changes to **i** before adding **–est**.

Some two-syllable adjectives can have both forms, for example those ending in **–ow**, **–er**, **–le**, plus a few others like **quiet**, **friendly**, **polite**, **common**, **stupid**...: *the most narrow / the narrowest, the most clever / the cleverest, the most stupid / the stupidest.*

Focus

The superlative is almost always preceded by the definite article:
This is the most important event of the year.

The expression **One of the** + superlative form is also very common → *Cricket is one of the most popular sports in England.*

1 Complete the sentences with *the* + the superlative form of the adjective in brackets.
Careful: one sentence does not take the article *the*.

1. New York's Central Park is one of .... urban parks in the USA. (large)
2. Yellowstone is .... National Park in the USA. (old)
3. One of America's .... national monuments is Waco Mammoth in Texas. (new)
4. Rotterdam is one of .... ports in Europe. (busy)
5. Robert is .... driver I know. He's never had an accident. (careful)
6. The Hilton is one of .... hotels in London. (exclusive)
7. Last summer I went to Jamaica. It was .... holiday of my life. (exciting)
8. The atom used to be considered .... particle which matter is made up of. (small)

The structure of a superlative sentence

After a superlative adjective, we usually find:

- an object introduced by **in**, if it is a place → *The Nile is one of the longest rivers <u>in the world</u>.*
- an object introduced by **of** in other cases, for example:
  - with an expression of time → *It's one of the best novels <u>of all time</u>.* (also: *It's one of the best novels <u>ever</u>.*)
  - with reference to a group → *He's the most generous <u>of all my friends</u>.*

We can also find a relative clause, with or without the pronoun **that**, and a verb in the present perfect, and sometimes the adverb **ever** → *It's one of the funniest films <u>that I've ever seen</u>.*

If the main clause has a verb in the past simple, the relative clause that follows will have a verb in the past perfect. → *She was the kindest person <u>I had ever met</u>.*

To strengthen a superlative, we can use the expression **by far**:
Today is by far the hottest day of the month. The temperature has reached 42°C.

FAQ

Q: When we talk about a superlative in English grammar, it always means a 'relative superlative', that is, relative to a particular group. I've never heard of an 'absolute superlative' in English. Does it exist?

A: In fact, there is no specific superlative form. To strengthen the meaning of an adjective, we can usually use the adverb **very**, even twice, or **way** in colloquial American English. → **very, very tall / way tall (USA)**.
We can also use the expression **most** + adjective → **It's most annoying.**
See also adverbs of degree in Unit 10 Lesson 2.

2 Complete the sentences with the prepositions *of* or *in*.

1. Aconcagua is the highest peak .... South America.
2. January is usually the coldest month .... the year.
3. Which is the biggest city .... India?
4. He was one of the greatest actors .... all time.
5. This is the most important event .... the musical season.
6. Bill Gates is one of the richest people .... the world.
7. He's the most talented student .... his school.
8. This is going to be the best day .... my life.
9. This is the most expensive house .... the whole city.

3 Reorder the words to write meaningful sentences.

1. most / This / is / exciting / one / of / the / matches / we / have / football / seen / ever / .
   ....

2. most / Mrs Ray / is / the / teacher / I've / ever / competent / met / .
   ....

3. This / best / is / the / ever / career / opportunity / by far / Jack / has / had / .
   ....

4. It's / moving / of / most / stories / one / I've / ever / the / read / .
   ....

4 Match the sentence halves, changing the verb to the present perfect or past perfect, as in the example.

0 My friend, Pat, is the most intuitive person
1 Last night's fireworks display was the most spectacular
2 This is the biggest pumpkin
3 This is the most comfortable armchair
4 It's one of the funniest stories
5 That was the steepest path
6 I'm having fun in Ibiza. It's the most exciting holiday
7 George thought that was the hardest exam

A they / ever / grow
B I / ever / hear
C we / ever / walk up
D I / ever / meet
E I / ever / have
F I / ever / try
G we / ever / see
H he / ever / take

0 *My friend Pat is the most intuitive person I've ever met.* **(D)**
1 ....
2 ....
3 ....
4 ....
5 ....
6 ....
7 ....

Irregular superlatives

As we have already seen for comparatives (see page 193), some adjectives have an irregular form either for both comparative and superlative, or superlative only.

| good / bad | → the best / the worst |
| far | → the farthest / the furthest |

old →
- the oldest
- the eldest (= the oldest in age between three or more siblings)

late →
- the last (= there won't be any more after this)
- the latest (= the most recent)

Anne and I are best friends.
This is the worst experience I've had in my entire life.
Since Pluto was named a 'dwarf planet', Neptune has been considered the farthest planet from the Sun.
John is our eldest brother. He's 24 years old.
The Tempest is Shakespeare's last work.
I read an interesting article in the latest issue of National Geographic.

5 Complete the sentences with a superlative adjective. Choose from the irregular forms of *good*, *bad*, *far*, *old*, *late*.

1 This is one of the .... restaurants I've ever been to – great food and excellent service.
2 Martin is the .... singer I know. He has no sense of rhythm and his voice is terrible!
3 Simon is Brian's .... friend. They've been good friends for a long time.
4 I think we should go to a beach that is nearer. Golden Beach is the .... from here.
5 My friend Lawrence is a good athlete. His .... time for the 100 metres is just over ten seconds.
6 You don't like this singer. Why do you have his .... CD?
7 My mother has three sisters who are younger than her. She's the .... in her family.
8 I'm leaving tomorrow. This is my .... day in New York.
9 This is the .... car I've ever had. It keeps breaking down, and repairing it has already cost me a fortune.
10 The Shetland Islands are .... north you can go in the UK.

Superlative forms with *least*

The superlative form with **least** is used to say that a certain thing is the least important, the least interesting, etc., that is, that it possesses a quality to a lesser degree compared with others. It is formed with **the least** before the adjective:

Flying with a low-cost company is the least expensive way to travel abroad.

6 Complete the sentences with the words in brackets. Use *the least* + adjective + noun.

1 (useful / thing) This is .... you've ever bought!
2 (exciting / match) This is .... I've ever watched.
3 (amusing / programme) It's .... we've ever seen.
4 (complicated / person) He's .... I've ever met.
5 (interesting / place) This is .... we have ever been to.
6 (popular / resort) This must be .... in the region.
7 (expensive / bag) This is .... they have in this shop.
8 (relevant / thing) It's .... I've ever heard.
9 (flattering / outfit) That's .... you've ever worn!
10 (impressive / attempt) His last jump was .... at clearing two metres in the high jump.

FAQ

Q: I've often heard the expression **Last but not least....** What does it mean, exactly?

A: It means that something or someone is **last** in order of time, but that *doesn't* mean that it is the **least** important.

Q: And when do we say **more or less**?

A: It's used with the meaning *approximately, about*. Here's an example: *It weighs ten kilos, more or less.*

LESSON 4 Comparative and superlative of adverbs, comparatives with nouns and verbs

Comparative of adverbs

The comparative of adverbs is formed in a similar way to adjectives (see pages 190 and 194).

For comparatives with **more**:

- we add the ending **–er** to one-syllable adverbs, which often have the same form as the adjectives, for example: **late, fast, high, long, hard**… → *later, faster, higher, longer, harder*…
- we use **more** for adverbs ending in **-ly** → *more slowly   more quickly*

For comparatives with **less**:

- we use **less** before the adverb → *less carefully   less fluenty*

The second term of the comparison or the secondary clause in the comparison are both introduced by **than** → *He's driving faster than usual.*
It took much longer than I thought.

Remember! To express the consequence of an action done in a certain way:

> **The** + first adverb of the comparison… , **the** + second adverb of the comparison…

The harder you study, the sooner you'll get your diploma.

For comparatives with **as… as…**:

- These are formed with **as… as…**, like adjectives → *This morning I didn't get up as early as I did yesterday.*

Superlative of adverbs

Superlatives also follow the same rules that we have seen for adjectives (see page 196):

- we use **the** and we add the ending **–est** to single-syllable adverbs → *the longest*
- we use **the most** for adverbs ending in **-ly** → *the most quickly*

The turtle is one of the animals that lives the longest.

I work the most quickly when I'm not under pressure.

Most, without the article **the**, is used to strengthen an adverb, and means 'extremely', 'massively' → *You behaved most stupidly!*

Adverbs with irregular comparative and superlative forms

well / badly	better / worse	best / worst

You dance better than he does. Actually, you dance the best of all.
I usually play badly, but yesterday I played worse than ever!

FAQ

Q: I read a sentence with the expression *as well as*, but it didn't mean 'just as good as…'. Does it have another meaning?

A: Yes. **As well as…** means *also, in addition to*. For example: *You can use my laptop as well as my tablet.*

1 **Circle the correct option.**

1 Tonight we're going to bed just as late **than / as** yesterday.
2 *Les Miserables* is one of the **longest / longer** running musicals ever.
3 You can get the floor cleaned **most / more** quickly if you use a robot.
4 The **later / latest** you arrive, the **longest / longer** the queue you'll find at the ticket office.
5 You can eat your lunch **more / most** slowly, we're not in a hurry.
6 'What time shall I come?' 'The sooner, the **best / better**.'
7 He jumped **higher / more high** than ever before. He broke his own record.
8 My father drives **less / least** carefully **than / as** my mother.
9 The **more / most** you tease him, the **more / most** likely he is to cry.
10 The **further / more far** you get from an object, the **smaller / smallest** it looks.

2 **Reorder the words to form sentences.**

1 as you / sure / I / run / I'm / as fast / can / .
....
2 I / This term / studied / as hard / last term / as / haven't / .
....
3 than / always / Paula / harder / everyone else / works / .
....
4 later / festival / this year / started / The film / .
....
5 higher / They / than / ever / climbed / before / .
....
6 longer / journey / usual / took / us / The last / than / .
....
7 quickly / speaks / the most / He / nervous / he's / when / .
....
8 you / The / earlier / leave, / the less / you'll / find / traffic / .
....

Comparatives and superlatives with nouns

For larger quantities and numbers, we use **more** and **the most**, which are comparative and superlative respectively for **much / many / a lot**.
For smaller quantities, we use **less** and **the least**, comparative and superlative of **little**.
For smaller numbers, we use **fewer** and **the fewest**, comparative and superlative of **few**.
So:

- the comparative structure with a singular uncountable noun or a plural noun is expressed by **more**, and the superlative by **the most**:

    I've had <u>more free time</u> since I retired from work.
    In the summer I have <u>the most free</u> time.
    I have <u>more friends</u> here than I had where I lived before.
    This is where I've had <u>the most friends</u> ever.

- The comparative and superlative with **less / the least** are expressed with:
  - **less / the least** + a singular uncountable noun:
    I've got <u>less money</u> than you.   No one has got much, but I've got <u>the least money</u> of all.
  - **fewer / the fewest** + a plural noun:
    You've made <u>fewer mistakes</u> than usual.   In this test you've made <u>the fewest mistakes</u> ever. Well done!
- The comparative structure with **as... as** is expressed with:
  - **as much** + singular uncountable noun + **as**:
    This week I haven't got <u>as much time</u> to train <u>as</u> last week.
  - **as many** + plural noun + **as**:
    There aren't <u>as many people</u> on the beach today <u>as</u> there were yesterday.

Comparative structures with verbs

After a verb we can find:

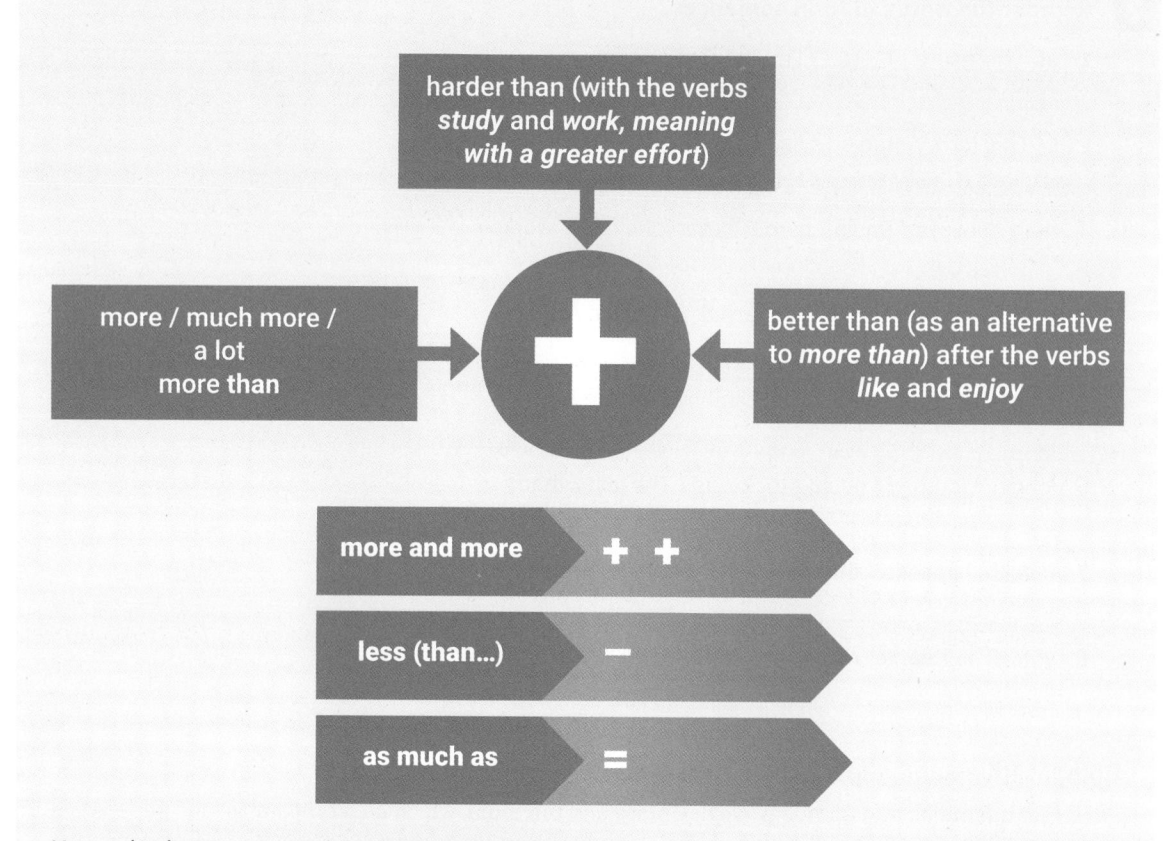

- harder than (with the verbs *study* and *work*, meaning *with a greater effort*)
- more / much more / a lot more than
- better than (as an alternative to *more than*) after the verbs *like* and *enjoy*

- more and more ++
- less (than...) −
- as much as =

He used to be very reserved, but he talks <u>a lot more</u> now.
I'm working much <u>harder</u> this month.
I like this song <u>better than</u> the other one.
You're eating <u>more and more</u> every day. Isn't that too much?
She looks sad. She's smiling <u>less than</u> usual.
I'm not spending <u>as much as</u> I used to. I'm trying to save some money.

Remember! Any more in negative sentences means 'no longer':
I can't play any more. (= I can play no longer.)
The hooligans got an ASBO. They can't cause any more trouble now. (= They can no longer cause trouble.)

3 Rewrite the sentences using *as much as...* or *as many as...*, as in the example.

0 Both the Robsons and the Wilsons have four children, two sons and two daughters.
The Robsons have as many children as the Wilsons, two sons and two daughters.

1 Yesterday we had 20 guests in our restaurant. Today we have 20 guests too.
....

2 We took a lot of time to clean the house and a lot of time to prepare dinner.
....

3 There are 50 seats in the conference room on the first floor and 50 in the one on the ground floor.
....

4 There are 12 fish in the aquarium and 12 fish in the pond.
....

5 Both Italy and Belarus got ten gold medals in the Baku 2015 European Games.
....

6 Both Paul and Lawrence collect elephant statuettes and they have 550 each.
....

4 Complete the sentences using the comparative with *more* (+), the superlative with *the most* (++), the comparative with *less* (–), the superlative with *the least* (– –) or the comparative with *as... as* (=).

1 People should be a bit more relaxed, there should be .... competition. (–)
2 I like this T-shirt .... the other one (+), but I like the blue one .... of all. (++)
3 The English teacher has .... patience .... the PE teacher. (–) The maths teacher has the .... patience of all. (– –)
4 I can't spend such a lot! I don't have .... money with me .... you have. (=)
5 In my class there are .... students .... in your class this year. (=)
6 Today I have .... homework .... usual. That's great! (–)
7 You've got a lot of luggage, but I've got .... you. (+)
8 These biscuits contain .... sugar and .... fat .... most others. (–) They're quite healthy.
9 I'm not spending .... you this month (=). I'm saving .... (+)
10 This year my son is getting .... rewarding marks .... he did last year. (+)
11 I have .... students this year in my courses .... I did last year (+), but my colleague Albert has got .... in the whole school. (++)
12 He has always got .... baggage of all, only a small backpack. (– –)

5 Fill in the gaps with a suitable comparative.

1 I enjoy eating out .... cooking – I hate doing the washing-up!
2 The .... time I spend with Tim, the .... I like him.
3 My holiday to Kos cost much .... my friend's holiday to the Caribbean, so I saved money.
4 There are .... reasons to shop around for your car insurance these days.
5 Karen studied .... Michelle all year, so it wasn't surprising when she got a better mark in the exam.
6 We like Italian food .... Chinese food. It's always really hard to choose!

ROUND UP 11

MATRIX +

Comparatives and superlatives with nouns – Summary

	a lot of	more	the most
with plural countable nouns and uncountable nouns in positive sentences	We had a lot of guests last summer. Annie earns a lot of money.	We had more guests than usual. Simon earns more money than her.	Last year we had the most guests ever. Jessica earns the most money of all.
	many	**more**	**the most**
with plural countable nouns in negative and interrogative sentences	I didn't have many friends then. Did you have many problems at the customs?	I don't have more friends than you. Did you have more problems than last year?	Which student had the most friends of all? When did you have the most problems?
	much	**more**	**the most**
with uncountable nouns in negative and interrogative sentences	Pete didn't have much time to train. Did they have much money?	Sam didn't have more time than Pete. Did they have more money than you?	Which player had the most time of all? Who had the most money?
	few / a few	**fewer**	**the fewest**
with plural countable nouns	There were few seats available. There are only a few biscuits left.	There will be fewer seats tomorrow night. And there are even fewer sandwiches.	This stadium has got the fewest seats of all. Who ate the fewest sandwiches?
	little / a little	**less**	**the least**
with uncountable nouns	Arlene has little patience with the children. We'll have a little time to go shopping.	I have got even less patience than Arlene. We'll have less time for shopping today.	Charlie has got the least patience of all. We had the least time for shopping last week.

1 **Circle the correct option. Check the table on the preceding page if you are not sure.**

1 Our new restaurant is doing very well. There are **many / much** customers every night, but tonight we've had **the most / the more** customers since we opened.
2 My little daughter usually gets **lots of / lot of** presents at Christmas, but this year she's got **the much / the most**!
3 There are only **a few / a little** tickets left for the concert. If you wait till tomorrow, there will be even **fewer / fewest** or none at all.
4 We can't buy all these things. We have very **little / less** money.
5 I like doing different things every day. I agree with the saying '**The less / The least** routine, **the more / the most** life'.
6 **More and more / Many and many** people are gathering in Trafalgar Square in London to celebrate the New Year.
7 It took me **less / fewer** than one hour to get to York.
8 Who signed **the most / the many** autographs? The film director or the main actor?
9 There are very **few / little** people who can play the piano as well as Margot.
10 If you have **fewer / less** than £100 in your account, you won't earn any interest.

MATRIX +

A few adjectives, called strong or 'ungradable' adjectives, do not have a comparative or superlative form, because they already have an absolute meaning. Here are a few examples:
full / empty, right / wrong, correct / incorrect, freezing / boiling, equal / unequal

But here is an exception, which is said sarcastically: *All animals are equal, but some animals are* **more equal** *than others*. The sentence comes from the famous novel *Animal Farm* by George Orwell.

The comparative and superlative are formed with **more** and **most**, just like polysyllabic adjectives when:

- the adjective is a **past participle** → **more bent   the most drunk   the most hidden**
  BUT: **the best known**
- the adjective ends with a suffix like **–less** or **–ful** → **harmless: more harmless, the most harmless, hopeful: more hopeful, the most hopeful**

2 **Complete the sentences with comparative or superlative forms.**

hidden   bent   known   harmless   hopeless   helpful   renowned   shaken

1 The tall pine tree was the ……………………… by the strong wind.
2 This type of snake is the …………………… . It isn't poisonous at all.
3 This is the ……………… place in the wood. Nobody will ever find you there!
4 That spoon is ………………… than ever! It was quite straight before you started messing with it.
5 This is one of the ………………………… novels by this author.
6 This is her …………………………… poem. We have all read it in school.
7 You're the …………………………… football player I've ever seen! You never score a goal!
8 He's usually …………………………… than his sister. He usually offers to do the washing-up.

3 Read the text and choose the correct word (A, B or C) for each gap.

Some people think that the quality of life in a small quiet town like the one where I live is ¹...... than in a big city. There aren't ²...... as ³...... go to work or school by bike, so the centre is quiet. A small town is generally ⁴...... than a big one, which is another reason why ⁵...... ten percent of the people living in cities have now chosen to move to ⁶...... . None of the people we've interviewed complain about the lack of opportunities in a town with ⁷...... 50,000 inhabitants. They all say that they can find whatever they want and they can easily reach ⁸...... big city if they want to see a new film release or theatre show.

1 A much better   B much best   C as good
2 A much cars   B many cars   C any cars
3 A few of the people B more of the people C most of the people
4 A less polluted   B not so polluted   C least polluted
5 A at last   B at least   C at most
6 A smallest places   B more small places   C smaller places
7 A no more than   B any more than   C none more than
8 A the nearer   B the most near   C the nearest

4 All these sentences contain a mistake. Highlight them and write the correct version.

1 Who jumped the farther in the last event? ....
2 Your girlfriend was the most elegant in all the girls at last night's party. ....
3 The most people communicate through social networks these days. ....
4 Please drive more carefuller than usual. There's a baby in the car. ....
5 Why didn't you study as hard than usual? ....
6 Always try to do your better. ....
7 I like this song as more than the other one. ....
8 Their later CD is much better than the previous one. ....
9 Which was the worse experience you've ever had, if I may ask? ....
10 Don't go any farthest. It could be dangerous. ....
11 The more people there are, the loudest you'll have to shout. ....
12 As harder as it seems, it will be worth it in the end. ....

5 Fill in the gaps with the superlative or the comparative of the adjectives and adverbs below.

late (x2)   good   long   old   young

Come to the concert tomorrow night. There will be ¹................. rock and hip–hop bands of our town with their ²................. songs. My ³................. brother is coming too when he finishes work, but not my ⁴................. brother because he's got a basketball match after school. Let's meet at 8.00. Don't be late as usual. The ⁵................. you get there, the ⁶................. we will have to queue up for the tickets.

6 Read the text and choose the correct word(s) (A, B, C or D) for each gap.

These are the outcomes of a survey which was carried out by a group of famous psychologists a few months ago. According to them, life is much ¹...... when people are ²...... and behave ³...... to each other. But too often people become ⁴...... when their life gets ⁵...... than before. The pace of life is getting ⁶...... every day and few people seem to be able to live ⁷...... these days. Even children don't seem to be ⁸...... they were. They watch ⁹...... television and eat ¹⁰...... food than previous generations, and generally live ¹¹...... . In their report, the psychologists underline the need to find a way to make everyone ¹²...... .

1	A nicer	B nicest	C nice	D nicely
2	A less happy	B happy	C more happy	D happily
3	A kind	B kindly	C less kind	D more kind
4	A more aggressive	B aggressiver	C aggressively	D most aggressive
5	A difficult	B difficulter	C difficulty	D more difficult
6	A fast	B faster	C fastly	D more fast
7	A calm	B calmer	C calmly	D calmest
8	A so carefree than	B carefreer than	C carefreest as	D as carefree as
9	A most	B much	C more	D the most
10	A badder	B worse	C worst	D baddest
11	A unhealthy	B unhealthiest	C unhealthier	D unhealthily
12	A more contented	B less contented	C as contented as	D most contented

Reflecting on grammar

Reflect on the rules and say whether the following statements are true or false.

		True	False
1	All two-syllable adjectives form the comparative with **more**.		
2	The second term of comparison for structures with **more** or **less** is introduced by **then**.		
3	The sentence *He's very younger than me* is correct.		
4	The comparative form of **bad** is **worse**, the superlative form is **worst**.		
5	The sentence *She is as old as me but looks much younger* is correct.		
6	When a TV series completely finishes, we say *This is the latest episode of the series*.		
7	**The farthest** is the superlative of **far**.		
8	The superlative form of an adjective with three syllables is formed by adding **–est**.		
9	The sentence *He's the eldest of two brothers* is correct.		
10	The sentence *This book is less interesting than the other one* is the same as saying *This book is not so interesting as the other one*.		

GRAMMAR MATRIX MAIN

UNIT 12 Adjectives and pronouns

LESSON 1 Indefinite pronouns made with *some*, *any* and *no*

→ **Visual Grammar page 417**

The indefinite pronouns made with **some**, **any** and **no** (see page 44) are the following:

	–THING	–BODY	–ONE	–WHERE
SOME–	something (+ / ?)	somebody (+ / ?)	someone (+ / ?)	somewhere (+ / ?)
ANY–	anything (+ / ? / –)	anybody (+ / ? / –)	anyone (+ / ? / –)	anywhere (+ / ? / –)
NO–	nothing (+)	nobody (+)	no one (+)	nowhere (+)

Compound pronouns with **–thing** refer to things.

We use **something**:
- in positive sentences → *I have something to tell you.*
- in questions that are offers → *Would you like something to eat?*
- in requests → *Can I have something to drink, please?*
- in questions when we expect a positive answer → *So, did you learn something?* (I really think and hope so)

We use **anything**:
- in 'neutral' questions, for information → *Did you buy anything in the sales?*
- in positive sentences where the meaning is 'any one thing (of many things)', 'whatever thing' → *You can have anything you like.*
- in sentences with the verb in the negative form → *I don't know anything about that.*

We use **nothing**:
- in sentences with a negative meaning, but with a positive verb → *We had nothing to eat.*
- as the subject of a sentence → *Nothing happened.*

Focus

In English we can only have one negative form in a sentence, so there are two possible structures:
1) **negative verb + compound pronoun with *any*** → I <u>don't</u> know <u>anything</u>.
2) **positive verb + compound pronoun with *no*** → I know <u>nothing</u>. NOT ~~I don't know nothing.~~

1 Complete the sentences with *something*, *anything* or *nothing*.

1 'Didn't they tell you ....?' 'No, they didn't.'
2 'Do you want .... to eat?' 'Yes, please.' 'What would you like?' '............................ you have in the fridge, I don't mind.'
3 There's .... to watch on TV this evening. Let's go out!
4 There's .... good and .... bad in all of us.
5 We have .... to do here now. Why don't we go somewhere else?
6 'Could we have .... to drink, please?' 'Yes, sure. Here's a glass of water.'
7 I don't like having .... to eat late at night – it gives me nightmares!
8 Have you got .... to tell me? Like how this window got broken?
9 There's .... better than spending the day pottering around at home.
10 I couldn't find .... about the news story on the internet.

Compound pronouns with **–body** and **–one** refer to people. They can be used interchangeably because they have the same meaning, e.g.: *Did you see anybody? / Did you see anyone?*

We use the pronouns with **–body** and **–one** following the same criteria as the pronouns with **–thing**.

> ❗ **Some** has a positive meaning, **No** has a negative meaning, **Any** has a 'neutral' meaning (see page 44).

Here are a few examples:
You must tell someone. (positive sentence)
Did you meet anyone from the management? (neutral question, for information)
It's so easy anybody can do it! (positive sentence, with the meaning 'any person, it doesn't matter who')
I didn't know anybody. = I knew nobody. (sentence with a negative meaning, but a single negative form)
Nobody knows. = No one knows. (sentence with a negative meaning and **nobody** / **no one** as subject)

2 **Circle the correct alternative.**

1. I've found **someone / anyone / something** who can help me with my homework.
2. Can **nothing / anyone / anything** here play a musical instrument?
3. There's **somebody / nobody / something** at the door. Go and see who it is.
4. When I got back home, the lights were on but **no one / anyone / someone** was there.
5. There isn't **anyone / someone / somebody** who knows how to fix my computer.
6. Did you meet **somebody / anybody / anything** you knew at the concert?
7. Is there **anything / anybody / nobody** I can do for you?
8. **Nobody / Nothing / Anything** is as important as a good education.
9. **Something / Somebody / No one** must have seen **anything / nothing / something** – the robbery happened in broad daylight!
10. There's **nobody / no one / nothing** that can be done to improve the situation, unfortunately.
11. 'Is there **anybody / no one / anything** I can do to help?' 'No, **something / nothing / anything**, thanks.'
12. That's **anything / nothing / something** that I've been wanting to learn for ages.

Compound pronouns with **–where** refer to places and follow the same rules of use as described above.
Let's go somewhere this afternoon. (positive sentence)
Did you go anywhere last weekend? (neutral question)
Put your bag anywhere you like. (positive sentence with the meaning 'in any place you like')
I didn't go anywhere. = I went nowhere. (sentence with a negative meaning)
Nowhere is like home. (**nowhere** is the subject of the sentence)

Focus

- You can often find an adjective after an indefinite pronoun: **something / nothing / anything...** + adjective.
  At your wedding you must wear something old, something new, something borrowed and something blue.
  There's nothing interesting on TV tonight.

- You can also find the adverb **else** after an indefinite pronoun: **something else, nothing else, nobody else, somewhere else**:
  'Do you need anything else, madam?' 'No, nothing else, thank you.'

3 Write the second sentence so that it has a similar meaning to the first one using the indefinite pronoun in brackets, as in the example.

0 There wasn't anyone in the hall. (no one) *There was no one in the hall.*

1 John told me nothing about what happened last night. (anything)
   ....

2 There was no one who knew the right answer. (anybody)
   ....

3 If we don't have a car, there isn't anywhere we can go. (nowhere)
   ....

4 We haven't bought anything for Emily's birthday yet. (nothing)
   ....

5 I have nothing new to tell you. (anything)
   ....

6 I saw nobody in town yesterday. (anybody)
   ....

7 We went nowhere at the weekend, we stayed at home. (anywhere)
   ....

8 Sorry, there isn't anything else I can do for you. (nothing)
   ....

4 Complete the sentences with the correct pronoun referring to things, people or places. Choose between those in the table on page 208.

1 .... is as important to me as my wedding ring.

2 Is there .... special you want to go tonight?

3 .... can dance as well as Kim. She's such a great dancer!

4 There is .... at the airport where you can leave your bags, so keep them with you.

5 Look. .... is walking down the street in a clown costume!

6 My brother is going to work .... in Australia soon.

7 Oh no! The fridge is empty. There isn't .... left.

8 We didn't know .... in this town when we came to live here.

9 I can't find my keys .... They must be .... in the house.

10 I hope there's .... nice to eat tonight. My husband has been cooking all day.

11 Jane was so unhappy. .... called her on her birthday.

12 'Is .... absent today?' 'No, Miss. We're all here.' 'Good. Let's start then.'

5 Each of these sentences contains a mistake. Underline it and rewrite the sentences correctly.

1 There must be something of wrong with the dishwasher. It doesn't work properly.
   ....

2 We aren't doing nothing special tomorrow night.
   ....

3 There wasn't someone waiting for us at the station. We had to take a taxi.
   ....

4 'Are you reading anywhere interesting these days?' 'Yes, a very good novel.'
   ....

5 'Is anything going to buy the food for the picnic?' 'Yes, I am.'
   ....

6 'Some cheese… some ham… Anything other?' 'No, thanks, that's all.'
   ....

7 Let's go anywhere tonight. I don't want to stay at home.
   ....

8 No, thanks. I don't want nothing to eat. I'm not hungry.
   ....

LESSON 2 Distributive adjectives and pronouns; *both, most, all*; *everybody, everything*...

Distributive adjectives refer to the elements of a group when we consider them separately, as individual items. They are usually followed by a singular noun and the singular form of the verb.

Each	Either
Each test has the same level of difficulty.	Come on Friday or Saturday. Either day is fine.
Every	**Neither**
Every student on this course gets a tablet to work on.	Neither answer is correct.

1. The boy ...... from London.
   A is   B are   **C were** ✓   D am
2. It ...... a dark and stormy night.
   A is   **B are** ✓   C were   D be

Every and **each** have a similar meaning. **Every** is only used as an adjective, whereas **each** can also be used as a pronoun, usually followed by **of** + a plural noun or pronoun. → *Each student / Every student / Each of the students* NOT *Every of the students*; *Each of us*, but NOT *Every of us*.

Either indicates one or other of two possible options. **Neither** indicates not one and not the other of two options. Both can also be used as pronouns, followed by **of** + a plural noun or pronoun. → *Either of these books / Either of them is available in the library.*
Neither of us went to Jane's party.

Study the two possible structures of a sentence with a negative meaning (not one and not the other). Note that there cannot be two negative elements:

neither + positive verb   or   *either* + negative verb

'Did you pass both exams?' 'Actually, I passed neither of them. / I didn't pass either of them.'

All these distributive structures can be followed by **one**, to strengthen the concept of each part of the whole being a single element (*each one of us, every one of the students, either one of you, neither one of them...*).

Both, most, all
There are other adjectives that refer to groups of elements when considered as a whole. These are usually followed by a plural noun and a plural verb.

The main ones are:

Both
Both novels are very good. (This novel and that novel...)
Most (see page 182).
Most children go to kindergarten when they're three or four years old. (Almost all...)
Note that the verb is plural! **All** (see page 182)
All the people in the room were well dressed. (Not one excluded)

Both, **most** and **all** can be used as pronouns, too, often followed by **of** + a plural noun or pronoun → *Most of the candidates passed their exams. Most of them soon found a good job.*
All of my friends joined the music club.

Note the use of **both** with personal pronouns:

subject pronoun (**we, you, they**) + **both** + verb

or

both of + object pronoun (**us, you, them**) + verb

I have a brother and a sister. <u>They both live</u> *in Berlin.* / <u>Both of them live</u> *in Berlin.*

With an auxiliary or modal verb (**be, have, can**...) **both** usually follows the verb:
<u>We were both</u> *worried.* BUT *Both of us were worried.*
<u>You have both</u> *read this book, haven't you?*

<u>They can both</u> *swim, can't they?*
If **both** is the direct object, the personal pronoun precedes it → *I saw two films. I liked* <u>them both</u>.

All can also be followed by a singular none in time expressions → *All day* (= from morning to evening). Note the difference with *Every day* (= on Monday, Tuesday, Wednesday...) *All year round* (= from January to December).

All can also be followed by an uncountable noun → *All the money you need*

1 Circle the correct option.

1 You can borrow **either** / **each** of my two bikes.
2 **Most of** / **Most** the people in the audience **was** / **were** journalists.
3 He gave me **all** / **every** the latest news about his family business.
4 You can't visit **both** / **either** exhibition. You don't have time.
5 'Where shall we go for our holidays? Malta or Greece?' '**Either** / **Neither**. I'd rather go to Sardinia.'
6 The two dogs are similar: they're **both** / **all** labradors.
7 I can't remember **neither** / **either** song. I'm not very musical.
8 They studied **all** / **every** day yesterday. They have an exam soon.
9 You can **both** / **all** come in the car with us. There's room for two more.
10 'Do you want strawberry or vanilla ice cream?' '**Neither** / **Either**, I don't mind.'
11 Don't be greedy – you can't have **both** / **all** the cake.
12 Don't take **each** / **all** day about it – we're waiting for you!

2 Complete the sentences with *both*, *each*, *either* or *neither*.

1 The school band had a lot of performances this year and .... one of them was a success.
2 If you like this skirt and the other one, why don't you buy them .... ?
3 .... candidate presented his/her CV and was interviewed by the human resources manager.
4 .... of the men is trustworthy. I can't really trust .... of them.
5 'Which film shall we see? This one or the other one?' 'I don't mind ...., they're .... good.'
6 'Which of these two books would you suggest for my 12-year-old son?' 'They're .... good, but this one's probably more popular with boys.'
7 You can't park on .... side of the road. This is a no-parking zone.
8 'Shall we go to the pub or the cinema?' '.................... . I'm too tired to go out tonight.'
9 'Can .... of you speak Spanish?' 'No, we can't.'
10 'Shall we meet on Saturday or Sunday?' '.................... I'm afraid. I'm busy all weekend'.

Compound pronouns and adverbs with *every*

Everybody / Everyone (pronoun)
Everyone said it was a great match. It's a shame I wasn't there!

Everything (pronoun)
Everything was ready for the party.

Everywhere (adverb)
There are people everywhere.

We always use a singular verb with **everybody** / **everyone** / **everything**:
Everybody likes this cake. It's delicious.

In spoken English, the agreement with a possessive form is commonly made with a plural form:
Everybody must have their money ready before getting on the coach. (Also *...his/her money ready...*, but this is less commonly used)

All of us / of you / of them... NOT *Everybody of us...*

3 Complete the sentences with *every*, *everybody* / *everyone*, *everything* or *everywhere*.

1 I go to work at seven o'clock .... day, including Saturdays.
2 Come on, ... ! It's time to go. Aren't you ready yet?
3 .... said the food was excellent.
4 We haven't seen .... yet – there are a few more places we want to go to.
5 Get organised! .... in its place and a place for ....
6 I knew most people at the party, but I didn't talk to ....
7 I'd like to buy .... in this shop. They have such fabulous clothes!
8 You say you've already been .... Well, I don't think that's possible!
9 .... employee attended the presentation of the company outcomes.
10 .... in the class was working hard when the principal opened the door.

4 Some of these sentences contain a mistake. Decide if the sentences are correct (✓) or incorrect (✗). Correct those that are incorrect.

1 Everyone I know like reading. ....
2 My friend is a shopaholic. He would buy everything he sees! ....
3 Everybody of them went to the same place for their holidays. ....
4 These souvenirs cost five dollars each. ....
5 There's free WiFi in every rooms of the hostel. ....
6 If you want everything, you may end up with nobody. ....
7 Everyone wants to have a good job which is well-paid. ....
8 Money is not everything! ....

5 Rewrite the sentences so that they have the same meaning, using a phrase with a pronoun or adverb to replace the underlined words.

1 We went <u>to all the possible places</u> when we were travelling in Argentina.
 ....
2 They interviewed <u>all the people</u> who had attended the course.
 ....
3 I did <u>all the possible things</u> to avoid him getting angry.
 ....
4 I'd like to play <u>this game and that game</u>.
 ....
5 <u>80%</u> of the students passed their entrance exams.
 ....
6 <u>100%</u> of the passengers said they enjoyed the journey.
 ....
7 <u>Not you or me</u> can make any difference.
 ....
8 You can't go <u>to any place</u>.
 ....
9 <u>The sales manager and the purchasing manager</u> spoke to the CEO yesterday morning.
 ....
10 <u>Not the doctor or the nurse</u> had seen the patient leave his room.
 ....

LESSON 3 Reciprocal pronouns *each other* / *one another*; correlative conjunctions *both... and...* / *either... or...*; compound words with *–ever*

Reciprocal pronouns

The reciprocal pronouns are **each other** and **one other**. They have a similar, reciprocal meaning.

We use reciprocal pronouns to indicate that two or more people do the same thing, interchangeably. In some languages, this relationship is expressed with a reflexive verb:

They love and respect each other. = He loves and respects her, she loves and respects him.
During the debate, everyone talked to one another at the same time. It was very confusing!

FAQ

Q: In a London pub, I saw a sign that said: **Yes, we do have free Wi-Fi, but don't forget to talk to each other.** Wouldn't it be more correct to say **to one another**? I know that **each other** refers to two people, whereas **one another** is used more generally, and refers to more people. Isn't that right?

A: Yes, that's right, that rule is correct, but in today's spoken English this is tending to disappear. **Each other** is the form that is most often used in colloquial language.

We can also use the possessive form with reciprocal pronouns: **each other's** / **one other's**:
We sometimes spend the weekend at one another's houses.

1 Use the prompts and write sentences with *each other* or *one another*.

0 The three brothers / not talk / for a long time
The three brothers haven't talked to one another for a long time.

1 Simon and Rachel / often / help
....

2 They / not listen / , all of them just went on talking.
....

3 Sally and I / send / birthday cards / for many years
....

4 My neighbour and I / often / look after / cats / when we're away
....

5 Mark and Fiona / be / madly in love
....

6 When we met at the airport, we / give / a big hug
....

Correlative conjunctions

Correlative conjunctions always appear in pairs within sentences, first one, then the other. They connect two balancing elements within a sentence.

> **Both... and....**: indicates both one and the other.
> <u>Both</u> my mum <u>and</u> my dad came to the college Open Day last week.
>
> **Either... or...**: means either one thing or the other.
> You can come to my house <u>either</u> now <u>or</u> later.
>
> **Neither... nor...**: expresses neither one thing nor the other.
> This colour is <u>neither</u> green <u>nor</u> blue.

> ❗ If **Either... or... / Neither... nor...** are the subject of the sentence, the verb is in the third person singular:
> Neither the cat nor the dog <u>lives</u> in the house.

We can also use these correlating conjunctions to link different clauses within a sentence:
You can either have lunch at home or grab a sandwich in the canteen.

Another set of correlating conjunctions that we can often find is **not only... but also...**:
She not only had a dessert but also a cup of hot chocolate.

Other constructions such as **as... as..., as much... as..., as many... as...** that we have seen in the unit on comparatives (see pages 194 and 202), are correlating constructions, as are **such... as..., so... as..., rather... than...** and others that we will see later on (see page 365).

I want an ice-cream and a lollipop.

No, you can't have both. You can have either an ice-cream or a lollipop.

2 Match the sentences halves.

1. No problem! You can use either
2. The boys both worked hard
3. We enjoyed both the concert
4. Neither the black and white dress
5. I not only went to the museum yesterday
6. Both the tourists and the guide were late,
7. You can have either the cheesecake
8. The school trip could be either to Barcelona
9. You can eat as much food
10. I answer as many

A nor the blue one is ready to wear.
B so the coach didn't leave on time.
C but also to the theatre.
D and had great fun at the baseball camp.
E as a hundred emails a day.
F 'each' or 'every' in this sentence.
G as you like for £10.
H or Prague. We'll see which one is more popular.
I or a muffin, but not both!
J and going backstage to meet the group.

1 ..... 2 ..... 3 ..... 4 ..... 5 ..... 6 ..... 7 ..... 8 ..... 9 ..... 10 .....

Compound Wh– words + ever

Compound **Wh– word** + **ever** are used as pronouns and adjectives, adverbs or conjunctions, expressing the idea of 'any one', 'it doesn't matter what, who, when, how or which one'. This construction is formed with the interrogative like **who** or **what** (see page 34) followed by **ever**. They have a similar use to compound words with **any–** in affirmative sentences (see page 208).

- **Whoever** → anyone / anybody / any person
  Whoever said so is a liar. (also: *Anyone who said so is a liar.*)

- **Whatever** → any / anything
  The expression is both an adjective and a pronoun: *Whatever decision you make, I'll be on your side.* (Also: *Any decision you make…*)
  You can have whatever you like. (Also: *You can have anything you like.*)

- **Whichever** (with a limited choice) → any / anything
  The expression is both an adjective and a pronoun: *Whichever way you look at it, it will never be the right thing to do.*

- **Wherever** → anywhere, in any place, to any place
  Wherever they go, they find new friends. (Also: *Anywhere they go to…*)

- **Whenever** → any time, every time
  Come whenever you like, I'll be waiting for you. (Also: *Come any time…*)
  Whenever it rains hard, the streets get flooded.

- **However** → any way, in every possible way, in whatever way
  However hard he tries, he will never please her.
  There's no dress code, you can dress however you want.

3 Complete the sentences with a compound Wh– word + *ever* from those below.

wherever (x3)   whoever (x2)   whatever (x3)   whenever

1 I will find them, ... they are.
2 .... follows me on Twitter is a friend.
3 I will do it, ... the consequences.
4 You can eat .... you like. It's all-inclusive.
5 .... you go, you'll find nice people.
6 Come and see us .... you have time.
7 I don't want to talk to anyone. .... calls me, please say I'm busy.
8 .... will be, will be. We can make no more changes now.

4 Rewrite the sentences using the words below. Remember to keep the meaning of the original sentence.

whichever   anywhere (x2)   whoever (x2)   anything   ~~whenever~~ (x2)   whatever (x2)   any time

0 Every time they meet, they have lots of things to talk about.
   Whenever they meet, they have lots of things to talk about.

1 Wherever you go on this island, you find people enjoying themselves.
   ....

2 You can go into any bars or restaurants wearing anything you like.
   ....

3 Just call me whenever you want.
   ....

4 Whatever I cook, he finds something wrong with it.
   ....

5 Anyone who touches my computer wouldn't dare do so again.
   ....

6 Any one of you who wants to work on this project should come to tomorrow's meeting.

....

7 Some cause happiness to every place they go, others anytime they go. (Oscar Wilde)

....

8 I take my tablet with me wherever I go.

....

9 Tell anyone who comes that I'm very busy these days.

....

10 Here's some money for your birthday. Buy anything you like.

....

LESSON 4   Reflexive pronouns; *one / ones*

Subject pronouns		Object Pronouns		Reflexive pronouns
I	→	me	→	myself
you	→	you	→	yourself
he	→	him	→	himself
she	→	her	→	herself
it	→	it	→	itself
we	→	us	→	ourselves
you	→	you	→	yourselves
they	→	them	→	themselves

As you can see, reflexive pronouns are formed with the possessive adjective (**my**, **your**, **our**) or the object pronoun (**him**, **her**, **it**, **them**) followed by **self** for singular persons, and **selves** for plural persons. **Oneself** is the indefinite or emphasising form of the reflexive pronoun.

Verbs + reflexive pronouns

We use reflexive pronouns when the action of the verb is directed towards the subject, that is, when the subject and the object are the same. Reflexive pronouns can be:

- the direct object of some verbs → *enjoy oneself, hurt oneself, help oneself*
- the indirect object, that is, preceded by a preposition → *think to oneself, say to oneself, make a fool of oneself*

> **!** If the verb is a phrasal verb, the reflexive pronoun comes between the verb and the particle: *Joan felt she had let herself down when she failed her driving test.*

FAQ

Q: I have a few problems when using the verb **enjoy**. I shouldn't always use the reflexive pronoun, is that right?

A: That's right. We use the verb in a reflexive way when we mean 'have a good time', for example, **They enjoyed themselves at the party.** But **enjoy** is also a synonym of **like**. In this sense it's followed by a direct object (noun, pronoun or **–ing** form of the verb) → **They enjoyed the party. / They enjoyed it very much. / They enjoyed dancing at the party.**

Focus

If the direct object is a part of the body, in English we always use the possessive pronoun (and NOT the reflexive pronoun) → *Wash your hands.* NOT *Wash yourself the hands.*
She cut her finger with a knife.

Compared to other languages, there are fewer reflexive verbs in English. However, English uses the structure **get** + adjective for expressions where some other languages use reflexive verbs → *get angry, get married, get ready, get dressed, get used, get drunk* and various others.

1 Match the sentence halves.

1 I cut   A cut itself on some glass in the park.
2 The baby cried   B look at herself in the mirror before she goes out?
3 Tess and Daniela   C myself chopping onions.
4 The dog   D a fool of yourself!
5 Are you   E to himself that he wouldn't go.
6 Can't she   F enjoyed themselves a lot at karaoke last night.
7 Don't make   G washing yourselves, kids?
8 He said   H when he saw himself in the mirror.

1 ..... 2 ..... 3 ..... 4 ..... 5 ..... 6 ..... 7 ..... 8 ....

2 Complete the sentences with a suitable reflexive pronoun.

1 You can't keep it to .... You should tell someone.
2 I said to .... , 'I mustn't get angry this time.'
3 Nobody understands how Paula hurt .... the other day.
4 I can't stand people who are always talking about ....
5 We enjoy .... a lot when we have a sleepover at each other's houses.
6 Jason made a fool of .... at the party last night. He got very drunk.
7 The cat meowed when it saw .... in the mirror.
8 Behave .... , girls! Don't be so loud!
9 We washed .... in the lake when we were camping.
10 Help .... to another drink.

3 Fill in the gaps in the sentences with the correct tense of the verbs below and a suitable reflexive pronoun.

cut   cheer up   wash   enjoy   tie   find   ask   scare   buy   hurt

1 Albert .... with a knife while carving a big piece of meat.
2 Thank you very much! We really .... at the party.
3 The dog .... in the river when we went for a walk.
4 She .... a very nice leather handbag in Florence.
5 Why don't you .... if you really want to go to university?
6 They .... stranded at the airport because of a strike.
7 He got very confused when trying to explain the instructions and .... up in knots.
8 Fortunately, I didn't .... when I fell off my bike.
9 They .... silly watching a horror film late at night.
10 Tania .... by eating a big box of chocolates.

Reflexive pronouns used as emphasising pronouns

We can use reflexive pronouns after a noun or pronoun to emphasise the idea of 'I, myself /you, yourself...' in person:

Did you make it yourself?   The President himself congratulated the Olympic champions.

By + reflexive pronoun = **alone**:

I'm often at home by myself.   Tom doesn't like working by himself. He prefers working in a team.

On + possessive adjective + **own** (in the sense of 'in an independent way'):

My daughter has lived on her own since she was 18.
He doesn't mind being on his own.

FAQ

Q: What does **self** mean, exactly?

A: **Self** is a noun that is used to refer to one person, as an individual. It appears in many compound words that are also used in other languages e.g. – **self service**, **self help**, **self conscious**, **self control**. The adjective **selfish**, which is the opposite of **generous**, also derives from the word **self**.

4 Complete the sentences with the missing words.

1 Dear me! Can't you iron your clothes on .... own?
2 When I was young I used to travel around Europe .... myself.
3 I would like my students to learn to think for ....
4 I hate playing video games by .... I like to play with my friends.
5 What? Did you leave little Henry by .... in the house?
6 My son is going to live .... his own next month.
7 She shouldn't always work by .... : Working in a team would be easier.
8 Come on! I'm sure you didn't make this amazing cake ....
9 I can't lift this box on my .... Can you help me, please?
10 My mum enjoys having time to .... , but it doesn't happen very often!

5 Rewrite the sentences using a reflexive pronoun. Remember to keep the meaning of the original sentence.

0 She likes to spend time alone.
   She likes to spend time by herself.

1 He was on his own all weekend.
   ....

2 They did it without any help.
   ....

3 You can work on your own today.
   ....

4 I travelled around France alone.
   ....

5 I have never sung solo before.
   ....

6 You can't leave a baby alone in the house!
   ....

7 He was able to run the firm single-handed.
   ....

8 I don't mind living on my own in my new flat.
   ....

9 Don't worry. She used to staying at home on her own.
   ....

10 Look at this beautiful cake! I decorated it without any help.
   ....

One / ones

We use the pronouns **one** / **ones** to avoid repeating a noun that has already been used a short time before or when it's clear what we are talking about, because the object is present and is mentioned in the sentence.

One replaces a singular noun, **ones** replaces a plural noun:
I like this racket, but I prefer the other one.
I don't like these shoes. The other ones are much nicer.

One / **ones** are preceded:

- by the definite article → *I'd like the one on the left.*
- by a demonstrative adjective → *I'd like this one here / those ones over there.*
- by the interrogative word **which** → *Which one / ones would you like?*
- by the expression **the other** → *Give me the other one / ones, please.*

One can also be preceded:

- by the indefinite article + an adjective → *I want to rent a new flat. I'd like a bigger one.*

Ones can also be preceded:

- by an indefinite expression (**some, any, no**) + an adjective → *I'd like some apples. Have you got any nice ones?*

6 Choose the correct pronoun.

1 I don't like this T-shirt. I prefer the red **one** / **ones**.
2 'Is this your hat?' 'No, it's the other **ones** / **one**.'
3 'Can you please pass me those books?' 'Which **one** / **ones**?' 'The **one** / **ones** on the top shelf.'
4 Eat this strawberry yogurt because the other **one** / **ones** has gone off.
5 Would you like these Italian shoes or the English **one** / **ones** over there?
6 Which painting do you like? This **one** / **ones** here or that **one** / **ones** over there?
7 My car keeps breaking down. I want to buy a more reliable **one** / **ones**.
8 I just got a new phone. It's **one** / **ones** of the latest **one** / **ones**.

7 Some of these sentences contain a mistake. Underline the mistakes and rewrite the sentences correctly.

1 Lisa must learn to control himself. ....
2 I don't like that jumper. I prefer the other one. ....
3 'I like those boots.' 'Which one do you mean?' ....
4 I always tell the children to wash themselves the hands before eating. ....
5 Tom convinced himself that he was right. ....
6 You will need to look after yourself! ....
7 We really enjoyed myself at the barbecue party. ....
8 Help yourself, guys! There's food for everyone. ....
9 The twins hurt theirselves when their treehouse fell down. ....
10 We need to ask ourselves if this is the right move for us. ....

8 🎧11 **Look at the picture and complete the dialogues with *one / ones* and the missing words. Then listen and check.**

1   **A:** Can I try this ¹............. on?
    B: Which ²............. do you mean?
    A: The ³............. in the middle.
    B: This one is too small for you. I'll get you a bigger ⁴............. .
    A: And how much are the ⁵............. underneath?
    B: The blue ⁶............. ? They're £50. But the ⁷............. on the right have 30% off. That's a good discount.

2   **A:** Why don't we buy a ⁸............. for tonight?
    B: Let's buy the small ⁹............. , the ¹⁰............. with apples. I'm on a diet.
    A: But there are six of us. And Jim doesn't like apples. I would buy the chocolate ¹¹............. .

9 🎧12 **Complete the mini-dialogues with the words below. Add *the*, *a / an* where necessary. Then listen and check.**

similar one   French one   best one   Which one   new one   another one

1   **A:** What do you think of Brad Pitt's latest film?
    B: I think it is .... of his career so far.

2   **A:** Oh no! The washing machine isn't working!
    B: Don't panic! Let's buy .... This one was old anyway.

3   **A:** What kind of cheese would you recommend?
    B: .... They're very good.

4   **A:** .... is your toothbrush?
    B: The one on the right.

5   **A:** Have another burger, Jack!
    B: Thanks, but I'm full to the brim. I couldn't possibly eat ....

6   **A:** Do you like this blue purse, madam?
    B: No, I've already got ....

ROUND UP 12

1 Complete the dialogue with the indefinite adjectives or pronouns below.

someone (x2)   everybody   some (x2)   all (x2)   no one   anyone (x3)   any

Drama teacher Hello, class 2D! Listen, please. We're going to put on a musical for the end of the school year and we need ¹............................ help.

Brian What kind of help?

Drama teacher First of ²............................ , we need ³............................ who can help with the costumes. Is ⁴............................ here good at sewing? ⁵............................? Well, never mind, I'll ask the people from another class. Are there ⁶............................ artists who can help with the scenery maybe?

Thomas I enjoy painting and doing things like that. I think I could help.

Drama teacher Sure, thanks. We also need ⁷............................ who can play a musical instrument.

Marion I play the piano.

Steve And I play the guitar but I'm not very good at it. Can I still help?

Drama teacher Yes, of course. We need ⁸............................'s help. And is ⁹............................ in the school choir? We need people who are good at singing. One, two, three, four… Great. This is a very musical class! And, last but not least, we have to write the invitation cards. Can ¹⁰............................ help with that?

Lisa I could make ¹¹............................ nice cards. I like graphic design.

Drama teacher Fine. Will you please give me ¹²............................ your names? I'll let you know…

2 Complete the sentences with the words below.

both… and   most   every   each (x2)   neither…nor   something   each other   nothing

1 .... my husband .... I have joined a yoga class. It's very relaxing.
2 .... of the students took part in the school exchange, but not all of them.
3 I've been thinking of you .... single day!
4 .... season has its own fruits.
5 I'm going to .... Greece .... Spain this year. I want to do .... different, so I've booked a trip to Iceland.
6 Come on, shake hands with .... and forget all about it!
7 .... gives you more comfort than a nice cup of hot chocolate.
8 .... of you should have a map of the city.

3 Complete the answers with *either* or *neither*.

1 'Do you like these two paintings?' 'Actually, I don't like .... of them. They're too dark.'
2 'You can have two bottles of shampoo for the price of one. Would you like these two?' 'No, ... of them, thanks. I bought some yesterday.'
3 'Could you give me his fax number or his email address, please?' 'I'm sorry I can't remember .... of them at the moment.'
4 'Which pub shall we go to? The Courage or the Red Lion?' '............................ of them. I have to work tonight.'
5 'Do you want to watch a comedy or an action movie?' '............................ of them. I want to finish reading this gripping detective story.'
6 'Do you think anybody could help me fix my laptop?' '............................ Paul or Jason. They're both very good at repairing computers.'

4 Each of these sentences contains a mistake. Find and correct them.

1 Every of these sentences contains a mistake. Find and correct it.
   ....
2 Most of the tourists who visit Juliet's house in Verona leaves a love message.
   ....
3 He's new here. He doesn't know nobody yet.
   ....
4 Everybody like this cake. It's very popular with my family.
   ....
5 All, clap your hands and give our host a warm welcome.
   ....
6 Either John and Jack must have left his coat behind.
   ....
7 You can have whenever you like, it's all free.
   ....
8 Whoever want to join me on my adventure is welcome.
   ....

5 Complete the sentences using compound words with *–ever*.

1 I take my laptop with me .... I go.
2 .... wants to meet me, tell them I'm very busy this morning.
3 Come .... you like. I'm free all day.
4 You can eat .... you like. It's an 'All you can eat' kind of restaurant.
5 .... I go in this little town I meet somebody I know.
6 I must have this beautiful leather handbag .... much it costs.

6 Match questions and answers.

1 Can you pass me those glasses, Ted?   A I'm sorry, I haven't got one with me.
2 Which trainers are most comfortable?   B The warm woollen ones. It'll be cold in the mountains.
3 Could you lend me an umbrella?   C It's a French blue one.
4 Which sweaters shall I pack?   D Try the ones on that shelf. They're very comfortable.
5 What sort of cheese is that?   E The white chocolate one.
6 Which cake would you like, Davina?   F The ones on the coffee table?

1 ..... 2 ..... 3 ..... 4 ..... 5 ..... 6 .....

7 Circle the correct option.

1 That boy and that girl are madly in love with ....
   A both   C one other
   B either D each other

2 .... Sam and Ann can help you. They're very good cooks.
   A Both   C Neither
   B Either D Each

3 Kathleen was so sad. .... of her Irish relatives phoned her on her birthday.
   A Neither C None
   B Nobody   D Either

4 We need .... warm clothes and trekking boots for the excursion.
   A both   C neither
   B either D none

5 Diana cut .... with a broken glass while washing the dishes.
   A her   C –
   B herself D her own

6 Good night and thank you. We have really enjoyed .... tonight.
   A us
   B our own
   C one another
   D ourselves

7 'Where can we buy this brand of perfume?' '......... you see this logo in the shop window.'
   A Whatever   C However
   B Wherever   D Whoever

8 Don't be sad! .... happens, I'll be here with you.
   A Whoever
   B Whenever
   C Whatever
   D However

9 Don't worry. You can call me .... time you like.
   A whenever C each
   B any   D some

10 'What would you like to eat?' '......... . I'm very hungry.'
   A However
   B Any
   C Anything
   D Whoever

8 Circle the correct option.

¹**Every / all** time I watch TV after dinner, I tend to fall asleep on the sofa ²**whatever / anything** the programme is. I may sleep for about twenty minutes, then I wake up and keep watching, but I always miss ³**everything / something**, so I start asking to ⁴**anything / whoever** is at home with me questions. I like action films quite a lot, but I often have to watch them twice because I miss over a quarter of ⁵**each / every** of them. Nowadays, with satellite TV, I can rewind to the point when I fell asleep and watch it again, but only if I'm at home on my ⁶**own / myself**. The problem is that if I have a nap, then I can't sleep ⁷**any more / anyone** until well after midnight, so I'm quite tired when I wake up in the morning.

9 Complete the gaps with a suitable word.

1 I've looked ...., but I can't find my sunglasses. They must be ...., though.

2 .... of the city centre is a pedestrian area, so there isn't much traffic.

3 I don't like working on my .... I prefer working in a team.

4 'Don't worry. You'll find your ideal partner one day. There must be .... somewhere who's looking for you.' 'Yes, but who? And .... ? I'd really like to know.'

5 .... you go, you'll find nice and friendly people.

6 Don't be selfish! Help one ....

7 There were only two exercises in the test, but they were .... very difficult. I doubt I'll pass it.

8 I'd like to go .... this afternoon, but I don't know where.

9 'Is there .... I could do for you?' 'No, thanks. I'm fine.'

10 'Do you need .... else?' 'No, ... else, thanks.'

10 Read this web page from the Sydney Opera House website and circle the correct options.

Welcome to Sydney Opera House

Around a quarter of Sydney Opera House performances are for kids under 12. Did you know that? Kids and families are welcome here all year round because there is a programme for ¹................ season. They can enjoy ²................ classics such as episodes from *Alice in Wonderland* or classical music shows suitable for introducing toddlers to classical music. ³................ you choose, your kids will find ⁴................ immersed in a unique classical music experience.

Treat ⁵................ and your kids at the Opera Bar or Opera Kitchen, in a quiet and relaxed atmosphere with the best harbour views.

⁶................ adult ticket includes coffee and a slice of cake. Children's tickets include a 'babychino', a small cappuccino with no coffee in it, while children under 12 months get free entry.

1	A	both	B	all	C	each	D	everything
2	A	–	B	themselves	C	themself	D	them
3	A	Whoever	B	Whenever	C	Whatever	D	Wherever
4	A	themselves	B	theirselves	C	them	D	ourselves
5	A	you	B	ourselves	C	–	D	yourself
6	A	All	B	Some	C	Each	D	Everyone

Reflecting on grammar

Reflect on the rules and say whether the following statements are true or false.

		True	False
1	It's correct to say *I don't know nothing about that*.		
2	Compounds with **any**, for example **anybody**, can be used in both positive sentences and in negative and interrogative sentences.		
3	Both phrases *Nothing else* and *Nothing other* are correct.		
4	**Each** and **Every** have similar meanings.		
5	**Both** refers to two people or things.		
6	**Most** + a plural noun is followed by a verb in the plural form.		
7	The indefinite pronouns ending in **–one** refer to things, while those ending in **–body** refer to people.		
8	It's correct to say *Everybody of us*.		
9	The meaning of **Whatever** is similar to that of **Anything** in positive sentences.		
10	Reflexive pronouns are all formed with possessive adjectives followed by **–self** or **–selves**.		

Revision and Exams 4 (UNITS 10 – 11 – 12)

1 Read the text and circle the correct option.

When my family moved to Bristol, ¹**none** / **any** of us was happy about it. ²**Both** / **As** my brother Dave ³**and** / **than** I had to leave our friends behind and we missed them.

Our new school was ⁴**quite** / **enough** small and there weren't ⁵**lot of** / **many** sports facilities, just a gym and an outdoor tennis court. ⁶**Neither** / **Either** Dave ⁷**or** / **nor** I enjoyed playing tennis but it was the only sport available. One day a new PE teacher started working at our school. He was ⁸**such a** / **a so** great tennis player that we ⁹**either** / **both** became very good and started to train every day. Now we represent our school in the county championships.

2 Read what Martha, a Canadian girl, says about her life in Italy. Complete the text with the appropriate superlative or the comparative form of the words below. Remember to add *the* and *than* where necessary.

far   long   exclusive   hot   good   mild   cold   dark   tasty   few

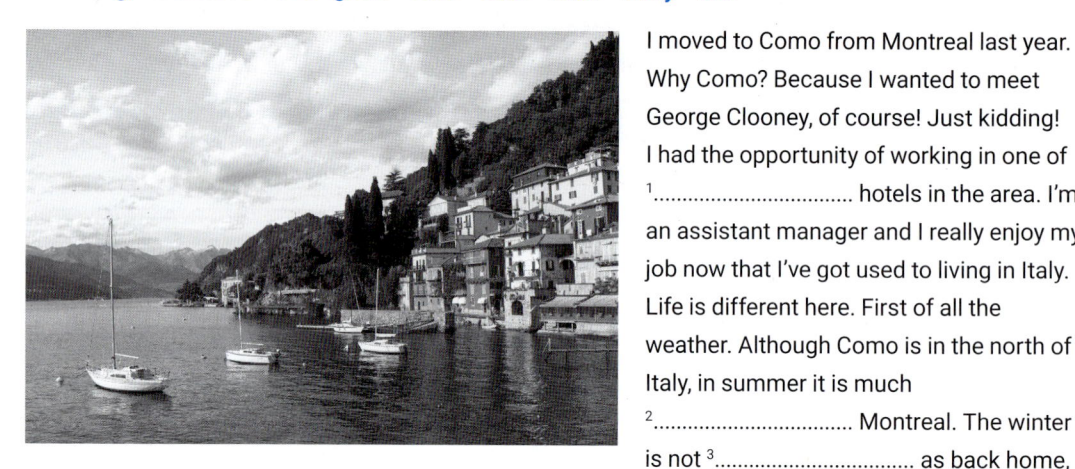

I moved to Como from Montreal last year. Why Como? Because I wanted to meet George Clooney, of course! Just kidding! I had the opportunity of working in one of ¹................................. hotels in the area. I'm an assistant manager and I really enjoy my job now that I've got used to living in Italy. Life is different here. First of all the weather. Although Como is in the north of Italy, in summer it is much ²................................. Montreal. The winter is not ³................................. as back home, and it is even ⁴................................. in nearby Milan. That's because Como is on a lake and the micro-climate here is different from that of other places which are ⁵................................. away from a big mass of water. What's more, winter days are ⁶................................. and ⁷................................. in Canada – but I miss the special light of Canadian spring.

Then the food. Italian food is much ⁸................................. and more varied than Canadian food. Our cuisine has certainly ⁹................................. dishes than Italian; still, I think that our *poutine* is one of ¹⁰................................. dishes in the world. What is it? French fries topped with fresh cheese curds and covered with brown gravy. A real treat!

3 Circle the correct option.

I know that ¹**everyone** / **whoever** always thinks I have a great time ²**everywhere** / **whenever** I go to Italy on business, but actually I don't! It's very hard work – one day I find ³**me** / **myself** on a train or plane going ⁴**somewhere** / **wherever** or in an office having a meeting. And I can tell you that there is ⁵**anything** / **nothing** more frustrating than discussing work when you know there's ⁶**something** / **whatever** beautiful to see in the next street! The problem is that you can't ⁷**either** / **both** work and play at the same time. However, there isn't ⁸**nothing** / **anything** nicer than sitting at a café in a nice square after a hard day's work.

4 Complete the dialogues with the words below.

best   faster   anyone   either   more   very   both   anything (x2)   herself   all

Alice Is there [1]............... here who could win a medal for our school in the town sports competition?
Ben Well, Mark can run very fast. He could do well in the 100 or 200 metres.
Alice But he can't win [2]............... because there are [3]............... runners in the other schools. What about long jump?
Ben Julie is [4]............... good at it. She won last year and she may win again this year.
Alice You're forgetting Sara. She's the [5]............... one in town in the high jump. She will win for sure.
Ben I still think that we have [6]............... chances in the long jump. Let's ask Julie.
Alice Hang on, I've just remembered – we can't ask Julie. She hurt [7]............... last week. She fell off her bike on her way to school.
Ben Oh no! Poor Julie! Did she break [8]............... ?
Alice No, but she hurt [9]............... her legs quite badly. She's got cuts and grazes [10]............... over them.
Ben That's terrible! Is there [11]............... we can do to help her?

how much   anything   ones (x2)   much   how many   many

Greengrocer Can I help you?
Lady Yes, please. Could I have those green apples over there?
Greengrocer Sorry, which [12]............... ?
Lady The green [13]............... next to the pears.
Greengrocer [14]............... would you like?
Lady Four, please… er, no, make it six.
Greengrocer [15]............... else?
Lady Yes, four bananas and something else for a fruit salad except pears. We don't like them very [16]............... .
Greengrocer What about kiwis? You don't need [17]............... of them. Three is enough.
Lady Alright. [18]............... is it altogether?
Greengrocer £6.50.

5 Complete the text with the adjectives and pronouns below.

himself   lots of   everybody (x2)   neither (x2)   each other (x3)   both

Bob and Jasmine were madly in love with [1]............... . [2]............... thought they would get married soon because they also shared [3]............... interests. [4]............... liked art and going to exhibitions. [5]............... enjoyed crowded places or loud music, so they never went to discos. They liked the same kind of food. They gave [6]............... the same kinds of presents. They were always together. [7]............... of them would go to a party on their own.
Their friends found them boring and stopped going out with them. After a few months, Bob and Jasmine got bored with [8]............... too and to [9]...............'s surprise they broke up. Last time I saw Bob, he was dancing in a crowded disco and seemed to be enjoying [10]............... very much. Life is strange, isn't it?

First (FCE) | Reading and Use of English Part 2

6 Read the text and think of the word which best fits each gap. Use only one word in each gap. There is an example at the beginning (0).

It was my ⁰......*last*........ day at the school where I had taught Art for 30 years. I was retiring the next day. ¹............................ my wife and my daughter came along to help me collect ²............................ of my stuff – books, notes, folders, etc. I was feeling ³............................ sad. ⁴............................ of my colleagues had already said goodbye, but I knew I would miss my students ⁵............................ of all. While I was collecting my things, ⁶............................ from the secretary's office turned up to tell me I should drop into the sports hall for a minute before leaving the school. When I got there, all my students were cheering and clapping. ⁷............................ of them wanted to shake my hand and thank me. My wife and daughter were just ⁸............................ touched as me by them. ⁹............................ said something nice – it was the ¹⁰............................ send-off I could have wished for.

Preliminary (PET) | Reading Part 5

7 Read the text and choose the correct word (A, B, C or D) for each space.

I have ⁰..*B*.. important to do on Monday. I'm meeting ¹...... from the local council to discuss recycling waste ²...... in our company. So far, ³...... has been putting ⁴...... into the same bin. It makes me cross because I recycle ⁵...... at home.

We want to convince the local council to give us ⁶...... bins to put ⁷...... they are needed. We also need ⁸...... bins in the courtyard to collect all the waste from the building.

We have already sent a letter to the council, but ⁹...... has replied. Two days ago, I called the office and asked to meet ¹⁰...... involved with urban waste.

0	A someone	B (something)	C somewhere	D anywhere
1	A someone	B nobody	C anybody	D somewhere
2	A proper	B property	C properly	D proper way
3	A everywhere	B everything	C everybody	D anything
4	A everywhere	B something	C nothing	D everything
5	A something	B everything	C everywhere	D somewhere
6	A any	B each other	C enough	D no
7	A everywhere	B nowhere	C somewhere	D anything
8	A biggest	B more big	C bigger	D the most big
9	A anybody	B everybody	C everyone	D nobody
10	A anyone	B noone	C anywhere	D anything

First (FCE) | Reading and Use of English Part 4

8 Complete the second sentence so that it has a similar meaning to the first sentence, using the word given. Do not change the word given. You must use between two and five words, including the word given. Here is an example.

0 I have never walked farther than I did yesterday.

FARTHEST Yesterday I walked ....*the farthest*............ ever.

1 The film crew is leaving Los Angeles tomorrow.

LAST Today is the .... in Los Angeles.

2 Nobody in the class is such a good dancer as Alice.

BEST Alice dances ....

3 Nobody in our family drives as fast as he does.

THE He is .... in our family.

4 There isn't anything John wouldn't do for us.

IS There .... wouldn't do for us.

5 I've got nothing suitable to wear to the party.

HAVEN'T I .... to wear to the party.

6 We quite like English cheddar and French camembert cheese.

MIND We don't .... or French camembert cheese.

7 The theatre is almost empty tonight.

LOT There are .... seats in the theatre tonight.

8 All of the students got their certificates.

STUDENT .... got his/her certificate.

9 The lift was too small for all of us to get into.

ENOUGH There .... for all of us to get into the lift.

10 The film was so funny that it became a big box-office hit.

SUCH It was .... that it became a big box-office hit.

Towards competences

The editor of your school magazine has decided to publish a special edition called *Comparisons*, which will also be sent to your partner school abroad. Your task is to write an article in English. You can choose a comparison between two people or two places that have had a particular influence on your life, explaining how and why. Your article should be 200–250 words long.

Self Check 4

Circle the correct option. Then check your answers at the end of the book.

1. She looks ……… in that dress.
   A beautifully   B beautiful
   C in a beautiful way

2. I hope Jack will cook tonight. He cooks ……… .
   A really good   B really nice
   C really well

3. I ……… recognised him when I saw him in hospital last week.
   A hard   B hardly   C difficult

4. Everybody thought the film festival was ……… success this year.
   A quite a   B a quite   C pretty a

5. There were over 150 people at the meeting and we didn't have ……… .
   A an enough big room
   B a big enough room
   C a big room enough

6. Oh dear! We're ……… late. Let's run!
   A very   B terribly   C totally

7. Don't ask Tom to sing on stage – he's ……… shy.
   A little   B lot   C very

8. It was ……… freezing this morning.
   A absolutely   B fairly   C very

9. I have to file ……… documents by the end of the week, Sara. Can you help me?
   A load of   B plenty   C loads of

10. ……… people wanted to buy tickets. They were all sold out by 2 pm.
    A Too much   B Too many
    C Too plenty of

11. ……… in the room already knew the speaker, so it was a good talk.
    A Plenty of the people
    B All people
    C Most of the people

12. They only sent out ……… invitations, so there weren't many people at the wedding.
    A a few   B little   C a little

13. You've eaten ……… melon. You're going to feel sick.
    A all   B the all   C the whole

14. 'Would you like some more cake?' 'Yes please, but just ……… .'
    A little   B a little bit   C a few

15. Vegetables are ……… than cheese or meat.
    A much healthy   B much more healthier
    C much healthier

16. The road was getting ……… and the bus driver was getting worried.
    A more narrow and more narrow
    B narrower and narrower
    C always more narrow

17. Wear your warm coat. Today it's ……… than yesterday.
    A much freezing   B much colder
    C more freezing

18. This is ……… the two villages.
    A the quieter of   B the quietest of
    C quieter than

19 Dan isn't ………. as Steve.
    A as cleverer   B as clever   C cleverer

20 A: Isn't this exercise ……… difficult than you expected?
    B: Yes, it's hard!
    A more   B less   C very less

21 The blue whale is ……… animal ever known to have existed.
    A the heavier
    B the most heavy
    C the heaviest

22 Mark is the most reliable ……… my friends.
    A of   B than   C from

23 Look at that man! He's ……… renowned surgeon in town.
    A the most   B the more   C the best

24 Which was the ……… journey of your life?
    A terriblest   B most ugly   C worst

25 Did you read the article about Rome in *Time* magazine's ……… issue?
    A last   B latest   C most late

26 Could I have ……… onions, please? I don't like them very much.
    A less   B the less   C fewer

27 Dad doesn't drive ……… mum.
    A as fastly as
    B as fast as
    C as fastest as

28 Irene lives ……… in the middle of the country.
    A somewhere   B anywhere
    C nowhere

29 We haven't spoken to ……… about the new project yet.
    A nobody   B somebody   C anybody

30 The people in the room were all talking to ……… and weren't paying attention.
    A each one   B anyone else
    C one another

31 Can I have something ……… to eat? I'm still very hungry.
    A else's   B other   C else

32 I have lunch in the same restaurant ……… day.
    A every   B all   C each one

33 Why don't we get a different pizza ……… and then we can share?
    A every   B each   C both

34 The school wants to give a tablet to ……… student in Year 6.
    A each   B some   C any

35 We invited Eric and Fiona, but ……… turned up.
    A either of them
    B neither of them
    C both them

36 Are you sure you can't find your jacket? Have you really looked for it ……… , even in the car?
    A somewhere   B nowhere
    C everywhere

37 What's that? It's ……… sweet ……… sour. It isn't a dessert. Anyway, whatever it is, I don't like it.
    A either… nor   B neither… nor
    C neither… or

38 ……… , tell them I'm out.
    A Whoever calls   B Whoever call
    C Whenever call

39 Are you sure you don't need any help? You can't always do everything ……… .
    A on yourself   B by yourself
    C by your own

40 The kids were really enjoying ……… at summer camp.
    A theirselves   B theirself
    C themselves

Assess yourself!

☐ **0 – 10**   Study harder. Use the online exercises to help you.

☐ **11 – 20**   OK. Use the online exercises to practise things you don't know.

☐ **21 – 30**   Good but do some extra practice online.

☐ **31 – 40**   Excellent!

GRAMMAR MATRIX MAIN

UNIT 13 Modal verbs to express ability, possibility and volition

LESSON 1 Characteristics of modal verbs; *can / could* and verbs that express similar concepts

General characteristics

The modal verbs, or **modal auxiliary verbs**, are:
can / could (to express ability),
may / might (to express possibility)
will / would (to express volition)
must, ought to, shall / should (to express obligation)

These verbs are used with other verbs to express ability, probability, obligation, volition and various other 'modalities' of meaning.

Modal verbs:

- do not add **–s** to the third person singular form → *She can speak four languages*.
- are followed by the base form of another verb → *You should try again*.
- are auxiliary verbs, so questions are formed with the modal + subject (*Can we stay here?*) and negative sentences are formed with the modal + **not** (or the short form **–n't**), without **do / does** or **did** (*You mustn't be late*).
- do not have an **–ing form** (present participle) or an **–ed form** (past participle), and therefore cannot be used in the continuous form or in compound tenses such as the **present perfect** or **past perfect**, nor can they be used with the **will** future or with the infinitive form. In these cases, other verbs are used instead of modals.

1 Each of these sentences contains a mistake. Underline the mistakes and correct them.

1 Sam cans ski well because his father is a ski instructor. ....
2 They might to arrive a bit late tonight. ....
3 Does he will go to university after secondary school? ....
4 You don't should go to bed so late every night! ....
5 Do we may hand in our assignment next week, Miss? ....
6 Joe can drives us to the restaurant. His car's bigger than ours. ....

Modal verb *can / could*

Positive and negative form
Present

Can is the only form in the present → *I / you / he / she / it / we / you / they can do it*.
Cannot or **can't** (more common in the contracted form) is the only form for the present negative → *I / you / he / she / it / we / you / they can't do it*.

Past / Conditional

Could is the only form for the past and the conditional → *I / you / he / she / it / we / you / they could do it*.
Could not or **couldn't** is the only negative form in the past and conditional → *I / you / he / she / it / we / you / they couldn't do it*.

Questions and answers of different kinds

Positive 'Can I do it?' 'Yes, you can. / No, you can't'.
'Could they help him?' 'Yes, they could. / No, they couldn't'.

Negative 'Can't you stay a bit longer?' 'No, I can't. Sorry'.
'Couldn't he come with me?' 'Yes, he could. Good idea'.

Wh– questions 'Where can I find the key?' 'It's in my bag'.
'What could you do for her?' 'Nothing much, I'm afraid'.

The modal **can** / **could** expresses:

- the possibility – or impossibility – of doing something because the circumstances allow it, or not:
  I can come and see you tomorrow. (It is possible for me to come...)
  I can't pay for everyone. I haven't got enough money.

  > ! **You can...** is very commonly used as an impersonal form, for example in a tourist brochure, to describe what visitors can do in a place → *You can go to the top of the tower or you can walk along the busy lanes of the town centre.*

- the ability – or inability – to do something
  He can ride a horse very well.   They can't solve this problem.

The same functions can refer to the past using **could** instead of **can**: *I could go and see them yesterday. I couldn't pay for everyone.   They couldn't solve this problem.*

The modal verb **can** / **could** is also used:

- to ask for permission (**can** in informal situations and **could** in formal situations) → 'Can *I have a look at your profile?*' 'Sure.'   'Could *I ask you a question?*' 'Yes, of course.' (Also: **May I ask you a question?**, another formal way of asking for permission). (See page 237).

- to request or order something, for example in a bar or a shop → 'Can *we have two of those sandwiches, please?*' 'Sure. Here you are.' (Also: *Could we have...?*)

- in the negative, to express disbelief about something that seems impossible → *Really? It can't be true. She couldn't have all that money!*

- in the conditional, for polite requests to other people to do something → *Could you please sign here?*

Generally speaking, remember that the conditional **could** belongs to a more formal register than **can**.

2 Complete the sentences with *can*, *can't*, *could* or *couldn't*.

1. Luke is a good swimmer, but he .... do the backstroke at all.
2. '.............. you ski when you were a child?' 'Yes, I .... I started skiing when I was three!'
3. We .... call on Sarah last night because we left the office quite late.
4. '.............. I use your mobile, Sam? I forgot mine.' 'Sorry, you .... The battery's flat.'
5. 'Excuse me, ... I have a doughnut and an orange juice, please?' 'Certainly. Here you are.'
6. Are you joking? That white Maserati .... be theirs. They .... afford such an expensive car.
7. '.............. you please fill in this form, sir?' 'Yes, of course. .... I have a pen, please?'
8. '.............. you go to the doctor's another day?' 'No, I have to go now. I need an urgent prescription.'
9. You .... do all that work in one day, it would be impossible for anyone.
10. '.............. we have two cups of tea, please?' 'Yes, of course.'
11. '.............. you talk to them?' 'Well, I tried to, but got no answer.'

3 Write questions for these answers.

1. .... No, I can't look after your dog today. I'm really busy.
2. .... No, he couldn't. He started walking when he was 15 months old.
3. .... Yes, I can help you paint the kitchen. When?
4. .... Yes, sir. Here's your coffee. And the milk.
5. .... No, you can't. My car is too fast and you aren't a good driver.
6. .... Which door? The garage door? Okay. Shall I lock it too?
7. .... Euston Station? Yes, go straight along this road for about half a mile.
8. .... No, they couldn't go on holiday last summer. They had a lot of work to do.

4 What function do these sentences express? Write P for possibility / impossibility, I for incredulity or disbelief, R for request and A for ability.

0. I'm not working, so I can go to Paul's house tomorrow. ..P..
1. Come on! Susan can't be 50. She looks so young. ......
2. Julie can't take part in the race. She's not very well. ......
3. Could you make a cake for my birthday? ......
4. They can dance the flamenco really well. ......
5. Dave, can I have a cheese sandwich, please? ......
6. I could play squash quite well when I was younger. ......
7. I couldn't see the exhibition. I was away on business. ......
8. It can't be Tom! He was so thin when I last saw him. ......

> **Substitute structures for the modal verb *can***
>
> Some verbs or verbal expressions can replace the modal verb **can** in the present, past and all tenses where **can** has no suitable form (present perfect, past perfect, infinitive, **–ing** form, future...).
>
> To express possibility, the replacement form is:
>
> - **be possible** used impersonally: *It is possible to do sth. / It is possible for sb to do sth.*
>
>   *Is it possible to get to the stadium on the tube? = Can you get to...?* (in the present tense you can use both forms)
>
>   *It won't be possible for you to join in.* (in the future tense you can only use this form)
>
> To express ability, the replacement forms are:
>
> - **be able to...**
>
>   *The lawn mower is still broken. I haven't been able to fix it.* (present perfect)
>   *Will you be able to get there by eight?* (**will** future)
>   *It was a shame that they weren't able to join in!* (past simple) Also: *...they couldn't join in.*
>
> - **manage to...** (do something complicated, with obstacles to overcome)
>
>   *I thought they had managed to qualify for the final!* (past perfect)
>
> To express permission, the replacement forms are:
>
> - **be allowed to... / be permitted to...** (more formal)
>
>   *I haven't been allowed to bring my dog in.* (this has not been granted to me – present perfect)
>   *You are permitted to carry only one piece of hand luggage on this flight.* (present, quite formal)

5 Rewrite the sentences using the tense and substitute words in brackets.

0 Could you see the latest exhibition at MOMA, Emma? (past simple – *manage to*)
   Did you manage to see the latest exhibition at MOMA, Emma?

1 I'm sorry I can't come to the conference next week. I'll be away on business. (*will* future – *be able to*)

2 I couldn't get to the top of the mountain. It was too hard for me. (past simple – *manage to*)

3 We can't park on this side of the road. (present simple – *be allowed to*)

4 Students can't smoke in the school grounds. (present simple – *be permitted to*)

5 Could you talk to the manager? (present perfect – *be able to*)

6 Can we see the house later this afternoon? (*will* future – *be possible*)

7 We can't enter the club. We aren't dressed properly. (*will* future – *be allowed to*)

LESSON 2 Modal verb *may / might*

Positive and negative form

Present
May is the only present form → I / you / he / she / it / we / you / they may arrive soon.
May not is the present negative form → I / you / he / she / it / we / you / they may not arrive soon.

Conditional
Might is the only conditional form → I / you / he / she / it / we / you / they might arrive soon.
Might not (or more rarely **mightn't**) is the negative conditional form → I / you / he / she / it / we / you / they might not arrive soon.

Questions and answers of different kinds
'**May** I use your Internet access, please?' 'Yes, of course. This is the password…'

'**Might your sister** know him?' 'Yes, she might. / No, I don't think so.'

The modal verb **may** / **might** is used to express the possibility of doing something – or that something happens – in the present or the future → *My father may be here soon.* (probable, not certain)

The choice of **may** (present) or **might** (conditional) expresses a greater or lesser degree of probability, but this is a subtle difference, so we can consider the two verbs to be almost equivalent → *'Do you think she may like this T-shirt?' 'Yes, I think she might like it.'*

May not or **might not** express the idea that something may not happen or that we are not sure if it will happen.

1 Write sentences with *may* (possible), *may not* (unsure) or *might not* (very unsure).

0 I'm unsure if Liz will arrive in time for the conference.
   Liz may not arrive in time for the conference.

1 It is possible that my favourite basketball team will win the championship this year.

2 It is possible that they will arrive any minute now.

3 It's very unsure that we will go on holiday with our parents next summer.
   ....

4 I'm unsure that I will be able to come to your graduation next week.
   ....

5 It's very unsure that the local council will organise a summer festival this year.
   ....

6 We're unsure that we will join the drama club this year.
   ....

As an alternative to **may / might**, to say that something may possibly happen, we can use:

- a verb in the present or future, together with the adverbs **perhaps, maybe, probably**:

  Perhaps they are not at home at this time. = *They may not be at home…*
  Look at the sky. It will probably snow today. = *It may snow today.*
  Maybe we will go to London for the weekend. = *We might go…*

> ! Look at the word **maybe**: if we divide it into two words, it is **may be**.

- the impersonal expression **It's likely / unlikely / not likely that…**:

  It's not likely that she will come.. (Also: **She's not likely to come.** It's the same meaning with a personal construction.)
  It's likely that it will rain later in the day. (Also: **It's likely to rain… / It will probably rain…**)

2 Write the second sentence so that it has the same meaning as the first one. Use the adverb in brackets.

0 I may not play the piano at the school concert. (unlikely)
   It's unlikely that I will play the piano…. / I'm unlikely to play the piano at the school concert.

1 Your brother may know our new colleague. (maybe)
   ....

2 They might spend next weekend in Paris. (perhaps)
   ....

3 Tom may leave early tomorrow morning. (likely)
   ....

4 Mary may want to go to the zoo next Sunday. (maybe)
   ....

5 Melanie might not go to John's party if you're not going. (unlikely)
   ....

6 Jim and I might visit the new museum on Saturday morning. (perhaps)
   ....

7 We may join the carnival tomorrow if it's sunny. (likely)
   ....

8 Ben may decide to retire next year. (probably)
   ....

9 We may not have time to go. (maybe)
   ....

10 My sister may join the yoga club. (likely)
   ....

May / might is also used:
- to ask permission (questions with **I** or **we** as the subject), as well as give or refuse permission in formal situations → *May I have your email address, please? You may go now.* (this expresses authority, 'I grant this to you').
There are verbs that can replace **may** in this context: **be permitted** or **be allowed** (see page 234). *I'm not allowed to go to the party.*

FAQ

Q: My mother told me that when she went to school, and wanted to leave the classroom, she had to ask: *May I go out please, Miss?*. If she had used *Can* instead of *May*, the question would have been impolite. Today, however, everyone is quite happy to say *Can I go out?*. Has the use of language changed?

A: It's true that **may** is used in more formal situations and in the past the relationship between teachers and pupils was more distant and detached. It's not like this today, and the use of **Can** is correct here, even if it belongs to a more informal register. However, we should never forget to use the word **please**, a key word in social relationships among speakers of English, today as much as yesterday!

- to express a wish, usually in written language → *May you live happily together forever and ever.*
- with the adverbs **as well** or **just as well**, to express the intention of doing something because there's nothing better to do, or because there's no reason not to do it → *It's only 5 am, but since he's wide awake, he may as well get up.*

I may as well get up.

It's already nine and she's not coming, so we might as well start without her.

I might just as well stay with you one more day. I won't be able to get home before Sunday, anyway.

3 Read the sentences and decide which function they express. Write **Pr** for probability, **Pe** for permission, **W** for wish, and **I** for intention to do something.

1. We may as well go to the cinema if it keeps raining. ......
2. She might not get to work tomorrow morning. She's not well. ......
3. Those guys over there might be Susan's friends. ......
4. I may just as well give up smoking if it's forbidden in so many places. ......
5. Long may she reign / May she defend our laws... (from *God Save the Queen*) ......
6. You may say I'm a dreamer, but I'm not the only one (from *Imagine* by J. Lennon) ......
7. May I use your tablet for a moment, please? I need to send an urgent message. ......
8. May all of your dreams come true! ......
9. My wife is bit tired of her job, so she might look for a part-time job next year. ......
10. May your days be merry and bright... (from *White Christmas* by I. Berlin) ......

4 Write the second sentence so that it has the same meaning as the first one. Use *may* or *might*.

0 Maybe I'll watch a new episode of my favourite TV series tonight.
I may watch a new episode of my favourite TV series tonight.

1 Perhaps my friends will organise a barbecue in their garden next Sunday.
....

2 Peter is not likely to marry Jane. They're so different.
....

3 Ted and Sue will probably enjoy their holiday in Florida.
....

4 It's possible that Greg will buy a new suit for the wedding.
....

5 We will probably join our friends in the pub tonight.
....

6 It's unlikely that Lily will leave Marshall. She still loves him.
....

7 It's possible that my father will give me some money to buy a present for Jenny.
....

8 The tourist guide is likely to organize an excursion to the island.
....

9 It's likely that Mr Ross will put off his lesson to next week.
....

10 It's unlikely that the twins will wear the same clothes at the wedding tomorrow.
....

LESSON 3 Modal verb *will* / *would*; verbs *want* and *wish*

Positive and negative forms

Present

Will is the only form of the present → *I / you / he / she / it / we / you / they will go.*
Will not (or the contracted form **won't**) is the only form of the present negative → *I / you / he / she / it / we / you / they won't go.*

Past / Conditional

Would is the only form of the past and conditional → *I / you / he / she / it / we / you / they would go.*
Would not (or the contracted form **wouldn't**) is the only form of the past and conditional in the negative → *I / you / he / she / it / we / you / they wouldn't go.*

Questions and answers of different kinds

Positive	'<u>Will you</u> dance with me?' 'Oh thanks. I'd love to. / No, thanks. I can't dance.'
	'<u>Would you</u> say I'm too thin?' 'No, I didn't mean that.'
Negative	'<u>Won't you</u> do what I tell you?' 'Well, I'm trying to.'
	'<u>Wouldn't she</u> marry him?' 'No, I don't think she would.'
Wh– questions	'<u>What would you</u> like with your tea? Cake or biscuits?' 'A piece of cake, please.'
	'<u>When would you</u> go there?' 'In the afternoon.'

The modal verb **will / would** is mainly used in the second person singular or plural to:
- offer something → '*Will you have an ice-cream?*' '*No, thanks.*'
- invite someone to do something → '*Will you come to my house this afternoon?*' '*Okay. What time?*'
- make a polite request → '*Will you open the window, please?*' '*Yes, certainly.*' (Also **Could you open...?** See page 233). This is a so-called 'rhetorical question': we are not asking the other person if they really want to open the window, but rather if they would do it for us, and we expect a positive answer. We could also say: **Open the window, please!**, using the imperative.

The same functions could also be expressed with **would** in the place of **will**, to be more formal → *Would you open the window, please?*

1 Ask suitable questions for each situation. Use *will* or *would*.

1 Invite a friend to have lunch with you today.
   ....
2 You ask Jack if he wants a sandwich.
   ....
3 You want the menu. Ask the waiter.
   ....
4 You want more salt. Ask Susan to pass you some.
   ....
5 You need some help to make dinner. Ask your son Harry.
   ....
6 Offer a drink to your friend.
   ....

Will / would is also used to express:
- strong will, especially a stubborn attitude, which provokes disapproval:
  – in the present → *My son always wants to have his own way. He just won't take my advice.*
  – in the past → *He wouldn't listen to me when I told him to find a better job.*
- past habits (only with **would**), often with the adverb *always* or other expressions of time with **every** (*every day / week*...). This usage is similar to that of *used to* (see page 135).
  When I was a child, I would always go to the cinema with my grandfather.

Remember! Will is the auxiliary verb used to express the future (see page 269) and **would** is used for the conditional (see page 288) of all verbs.

2 Match the sentences to the correct function.

1 They won't listen to me!
2 We would go for a bike ride every day when we lived in the country.
3 Will you close the door, please?
4 Will you have some tea, Max?
5 Will you go to the cinema tomorrow?

A Offer something
B Ask for something politely
C Disapprove
D Talk about habits in the past
E Invite somebody

1 ..... 2 ..... 3 ..... 4 ..... 5 .....

The verb *want*

The most commonly-used verb that is not a modal verb which expresses volition is the verb **want**. It is a regular verb – **wanted** is the past simple and the past participle. It is used especially in an informal register.

> ! Since it is not a modal verb:
> - it takes an **–s** in the third person singular → *She wants…*
> - it has a negative form with **don't / doesn't / didn't** → *I don't want… / He doesn't want… / We didn't want…*
> - it forms the interrogative with **do / does / did** → *Do you want…? / Does she want…? / Did they want…?*
> - it can be followed by a noun → *He just wanted some attention.*
> - it can be followed by a verb in the infinitive with **to** → *He wanted to get some attention.*

If we want someone else to do something, we use the construction **want someone to do something**:

subject + **want** + object (noun or pronoun) + verb in the infinitive with **to**

They wanted me to help, but I couldn't.
My parents want my sister to go to university, but she won't go.

3 Rewrite the sentences as in the example. Use the verb *want* in the positive or negative form.

0 **Mum:** Sarah, will you go to the shops and buy some cheese, please?
Mum wants Sarah to go to the shops to buy some cheese.

1 **Mr Hanley:** Ms Dell, please make an appointment with Ms Bradley on Tuesday morning.
....

2 **Our parents:** Tom, Claire, don't get back late tonight!
....

3 **John's mother:** Don't play video games all afternoon, John!
....

4 **Tess:** Please, invite David to your party, Nella.
....

5 **My brother:** Lend me ten pounds, please.
....

The verb *wish*

Wish is not a modal verb. It is a regular verb - **wished** is the past simple and the past participle. It is used to express wants or desires that are difficult to make a reality or which do not depend on us but on others. It also expresses dreams or regrets, referring both to ourselves and to others.

Wish has special constructions, such as **I wish I were…** (or *I wish I was…* in a more informal register); **I wish I had…**; **I wish I could…**; **I wish I knew…**

If the want or desire refers to a present situation, we use:

subject + **wish** + same or different subject + **past simple** of the verb

We wish we had more free time.
I wish it didn't rain so hard.

Or:

subject + **wish** + same or different subject + **could** + base form of the verb

With **could**, we underline the idea of being able to do something or knowing how to do something:

Jack wishes he could buy a motorcycle.
I wish you could pass your driving test.

4 Look at the pictures and complete the speech bubbles.

0 have some rain — *I wish we had some rain.*

1 be at home

2 hot

3 lie on a beach

4 have some snow

5 paint better

6 sing like her

If we want someone else to behave differently, we use:

subject + **wish** + new subject + **would** + base form

I wish you would listen to me sometimes!
His parents wish he would give up smoking.
(Also: **... he gave up smoking**, with the past simple, but with **would** we underline more the idea of an effort of will.)

If we are talking about a regret, with reference to a past situation, we use:

subject + **wish** + same or different subject + verb in the past perfect (**had** + past participle)

I wish you had never met him!
They wish they had accepted your offer. (They regret not having accepted it, but now it's too late to do anything about it.)

Wish is also used to express good wishes → *We wish you a Merry Christmas!*

5 Write sentences using the prompts to express desires that cannot become reality at the moment.

0 Laura / go trekking in Nepal
Laura wishes she could go trekking in Nepal.

1 We / our favourite team / win the championship
....

2 I / 10 cm taller
....

3 We / our neighbours / not so noisy
....

4 Dan / have a brand new car
....

5 I / my husband / more free time
....

6 Our teacher / retire / at the end of this school year
....

6 Write sentences expressing disappointment or regret using subject + *wish*.

0 I was so rude to Jack yesterday.
I wish I hadn't been so rude to Jack yesterday.

1 We weren't very lucky!
....

2 Ben and Karen went out trekking in the bad weather.
....

3 Dinah was wearing her gold necklace last night and she lost it.
....

4 Mike didn't go to university after secondary school.
....

5 I forgot the appointment with an important customer.
....

6 They all went to the club without me.
....

7 Match the sentence halves.

1 My friend Tom would always copy during tests.
2 He would arrive late for classes every day,
3 I wish I could stay here for a few more days,
4 I wish my mother could see me!
5 Would you help me put this bag on the luggage rack, please?
6 Would you join us for lunch?

A saying he had missed the bus.
B I've never looked so good in my life.
C It's too heavy for me to lift.
D He was such a cheat!
E We need to talk about the new office.
F but I have to go back to work tomorrow.

1 ..... 2 ..... 3 ..... 4 ..... 5 ..... 6 .....

8 What could these people say in each situation? Use *wish* and a verb in the appropriate form.

1 Tom's girlfriend is away and he misses her.
....

2 Sara's friends are going out tonight, but she has to stay at home.
....

3 Diane's feeling sick because she had raw fish last night.
....

4 Hilary regrets she didn't learn to ski when she was young.
....

5 Tina works in a supermarket, but her dream is to be a pop singer.
....

LESSON 4 Conditional forms *would like, would prefer, would rather*

To express wants and preferences, we often use conditional forms like **I would like**, **I would prefer** and **I would rather**.

Would like
This is the conditional form of the verb **like**. It is used to express desires or wants, like **want** and **wish**, but with differences of register (see page 240).
Remember: Would like has a more formal use than **want**.

Positive form
Would like can be contracted to **'d like**, only if the subject is a pronoun → *John would like to become a famous football player. He'd like to play for Manchester United.*

Negative form
Would not like is usually contracted to **wouldn't like** → *I wouldn't like to be there now!!*

Questions and different types of answers
Would / wouldn't always precedes the subject in a question:

Positive	'Would you like anything to drink?' 'No, thanks. Nothing for me.'
Negative	'Wouldn't you like to try this restaurant?' 'Yes, I'd love to.'
Wh– questions	'What would you like to do tonight?' 'I'd like to watch a film on TV.'

Look at the answers to **Yes / No questions**. We do not usually find short answers containing **I would / I wouldn't**, but rather expressions to accept or refuse an invitation or a suggestion: **Yes, please / No, thanks / I'd love to**.
Think about the answer **I'd love to** → **I would love to**. It's the conditional of the verb **love**. We use it when we want to express enthusiasm in accepting a suggestion or an invitation.

Remember: like the verb **want**, **would like** can also be followed by:
- a noun → *I'd like an organic multi-vitamin juice, please.*
- a verb in the infinitive form with **to** → *We'd like to visit not only the museum but also the temporary exhibition.*

> ! Be careful not to confuse **I'd like to...** with **I like + –ing**, for example: *I like visiting museums.* (See page 100)

Would like is used to:
- make an offer:

  'Would you like a milkshake?' 'Yes, please.' Also: **Will you have / Would you have a milkshake?** (See page 239) Or: **Do you want a milkshake?** for more informal use. (See page 240)

- ask and say what we would like or make a request, for example in a restaurant or a shop:

  'So, what would you like to eat, sir?' 'I'd like some chicken and potatoes.'
  (**What do you want...?** would not be appropriate in this context, because it is too familiar for an exchange between a waiter and a customer.)

If we want someone else to do something for us, we use the same construction that we saw with the verb **want**, i.e. **would like someone to do something**.
(See page 240):

> subject + **would like** + object (noun or pronoun) + infinitive form of the verb with **to**

We'd like our daughter to become a doctor.
I'd like her to give me another chance.

FAQ

Q: What's the difference between **I wish I had a car** and **I'd like to have a car**?

A: In the first sentence, the speaker dreams of having a car and we understand that there is some regret about not having one. It's as if the sentence were an exclamation followed by an exclamation mark: *I would like to have a car so much!*
The second sentence does not contain this idea, it simply expresses a desire, which can become a reality.

1 Match the sentences with the corresponding function.

1. Our teacher would like us to hand in our projects by Monday.
2. What would you like to drink, sir?
3. I'd like a cup of hot chocolate, please.
4. Would you like to join us at the club tonight?
5. I wish I had a house by the sea.
6. I'd like to have a motorcycle.
7. Would you like some chips, Liz?

A. Expressing wants that can be fulfilled
B. Expressing wishes
C. Offering
D. Inviting
E. Making a request
F. Collecting an order
G. Asking somebody to do something

1 ..... 2 ..... 3 ..... 4 ..... 5 ..... 6 ..... 7 .....

2 Complete the sentences with *would like* or *like*.

1. We .... going to the cinema. We often go on Friday night.
2. I .... to go to the cinema tomorrow. Will you come with me?
3. '........................... you .... to play a game of cards?' 'Yes, why not?'
4. He .... me to help him with his project, but I really can't this week.
5. We .... vegetables and we eat a lot of them, even though we aren't vegetarian.
6. '........................... you .... cartoons?' 'Not really, I prefer watching films.'

Would prefer to… / Would rather…

To express a preference between two things that we could do, we use the conditional expressions **I would prefer to…** or **I would rather…**.

- **I would prefer** (contracted form **I'd prefer**) is the conditional of the verb **prefer**, and is constructed as follows:

  > subject + **would prefer** + **to** + base form

  My wife would like to go on a cruise, but I'd prefer to go on a car trip.

  When the same subject indicates a preference between two things, the construction is:

  > subject + **would prefer** + **to** + base form + **rather than…** + base form

  I'd prefer to travel in a campervan rather than go by plane.

- **I would rather** (contracted form **I'd rather**) is formed with **would** and the adverb **rather** (see page 178), and is constructed as follows:

  > subject + **would rather** + base form

  I'd rather take a taxi than go by bus to the airport.

  In a question: *Would you rather have tea or coffee?*

  What would you rather do? Stay at home or go for a walk?

3 Complete the sentences with *would rather* or *would prefer*.

1 I .... to stay at home tonight. It's so cold and miserable out.
2 'What shall I cook for dinner?' 'Fish. Erik .... eat fish than meat.'
3 My parents .... go on a cruise this summer. They're fed up with the mountains.
4 Alan is tired. He .... not play five-a-side football this Saturday.
5 Mum .... to wear a suit to the wedding rather than a long dress.
6 I .... to take you to a good restaurant than have dinner at home.
7 We .... go to London this weekend.
8 I .... to work today and have a day off tomorrow.

4 Match the sentence halves.

1 Where would you like to go at the weekend?
2 What would you like for breakfast?
3 Would you like to go for a bike ride?
4 What would you like to be when you grow up?
5 Which way would you prefer to go?
6 Would you rather go home now or stay a bit longer?
7 Would you like some cake?
8 If you don't want to play tennis, what would you rather do?

A I'd like to be a chef.
B I'd like to go the country way.
C No, thanks. Just a cup of tea.
D I don't mind. Where would you like to go?
E I'd like to go for a walk on the seafront.
F I'd like some coffee and a blueberry muffin.
G Yes. Let's hire a couple of mountain bikes.
H I'd like to go home, please.

1 ..... 2 ..... 3 ..... 4 ..... 5 ..... 6 ..... 7 ..... 8 .....

5 Each of these sentences contains a mistake. Underline it and rewrite the sentence correctly.

1 I'd like that James washes my car. It's so dirty!
 ....
2 They would rather spending the weekend in London than at home doing gardening.
 ....
3 He would prefer go to a rock concert. He doesn't like house music very much.
 ....
4 Would you like coming to my birthday party next week?
 ....
5 'What would you like to drink?' 'I like a soft drink.'
 ....
6 Do we really have to go out with Ben and Louise? I had rather eat out you and me alone.'
 ....
7 Our instructor would like we trained three times a week.
 ....
8 It's so cold that I had prefer stay at home tonight.
 ....
9 'Would you like sitting on the terrace?' 'Oh yes, that would be nice.'
 ....
10 'Do you want a drink of water?' 'Well, er..., I'd rather to have some juice.'
 ....

ROUND UP 13

1 **Complete the sentences with the correct modal verb:** *can / could, can't / couldn't.*

1. All your dreams .... come true – you only have to work hard to make it happen.
2. They .... join us on the trip, they had work to do.
3. I .... stand all this noise any more. It's so annoying!
4. You .... believe all that he says. He often makes up his stories.
5. It .... cost all that money! It looks like an ordinary bag.
6. My daughter .... read and add up at an early age.
7. I just .... remember what Mum told me to do. I'll have to call her.
8. She .... sing beautifully. She has a fantastic voice.
9. I .... help you with your project if you need me to.
10. He .... do judo very well, he has a brown belt.

MATRIX +

Look at these examples:

The girl in the club can't have been Sara. She hates dancing. (= the girl in the club definitely was not Sara.)
They may have arrived by now. (= They are likely to have arrived by now.)

The structure **can't** + **have** + **past participle** is used to express a supposition or a logical deduction made at the time of speaking but referring to events in the past.

The structure **may** + **have** + **past participle** has the same usage.

2 **Complete the deductions referring to the past. Use the verbs below and the modals** *can't* **or** *may.*

go   hand in   be (x4)   finish   run   have   arrive

1. You .... that hungry at lunch time after all you had for breakfast.
2. They .... to the beach. The weather is gorgeous today.
3. That boy you saw in the pub .... Tom's brother. Tom's brother left for New York two days ago.
4. The car you saw in the accident .... Jason's car. His is blue and it's smaller.
5. My father .... in Boston by now.
6. The story they told you .... true. There are too many strange coincidences.
7. The conference .... , but let's try and go into the room anyway.
8. He .... some problems at work because he hasn't arrived yet.
9. Sara .... so fast. She must have cheated somehow.
10. Judith .... her written exam by now. I hope she passes because she's really worked hard.

MATRIX +

Note the expression **I can't help** + **–ing form** (Also: **I can't help but** + **base form**), which means "I can't avoid". → *I can't help thinking he's not being honest with me.* *I couldn't help laughing. / I couldn't help but laugh.* (= I couldn't avoid laughing.)

3 **Complete the second sentences so that it has the same meaning as the first sentence. Use the word given and don't change it.**

1 The film was so moving that I couldn't help crying most of the time.
   BUT   The film was so moving .... most of the time.

2 He couldn't help but tell her, although it was a secret.
   TELLING   He .... her, although it was a secret.

3 It's possible that they can help you, but I'm not sure.
   MIGHT   They ....

4 Perhaps I'll visit my American cousins next summer.
   MAY   I ....

5 It's unlikely that the witness recognised the thieves. They were wearing masks.
   CAN'T   The witness ....

6 Dinah would prefer to buy a notebook instead of a tablet.
   RATHER   Dinah ....

7 If only I could have more money!
   WISH   I ....

8 Jane regrets that she didn't learn to play an instrument when she was young.
   WISHES   Jane ....

9 It's likely that Terry is at home. That's her car over there.
   MAY   Terry .... That's her car over there.

10 Lucy would rather call a wedding planner to organise the ceremony.
   PREFER   Lucy ....

4 **Reorder the words to make logical sentences.**

1 do / you / Will / able / be / to / it / ?
   ....

2 won't / You / midnight / allowed / to / be / after / come back / .
   ....

3 haven't / been / They / to / go / allowed / .
   ....

4 You / calculator / not / be / allowed / to / may / use / your / .
   ....

5 has / She / time / to / get / managed / on / here / .
   ....

6 will / that / it / It's / snow / tonight / likely /.
   ....

7 I / be / know / if / I / don't / come / will / able / to / .
   ....

8 late / will / She / be / probably / .
   ....

9 about / you / Could / behaviour / horrible / talk / to / him / his / ?
   ....

10 might / They / be / to / help / able / to / the / catering / for / organise / garden / your / party / .
   ....

5 **Rewrite the sentences using the tenses and words in brackets.**

1 He can leave early tomorrow because there's a train at 6.30 am. (*will* future / able)
....

2 Visitors may only see the rooms on the ground floor. (past simple / allowed)
....

3 I could fix my bike on my own eventually. (past simple / able)
....

4 I can't stay out late in the evening. My dad's very strict about that. (*will* future / allowed)
....

5 I can't come, I'm sorry. I'm very busy tomorrow. (*will* future / able)
....

6 I see you could make this elaborated chocolate cake. It looks delicious. (present perfect / manage)
....

7 'Could you talk to Mr Bailey?' 'No, I couldn't.' (present perfect / able)
....

8 I can't park my car in front of the restaurant. (*will* - future / able)
....

9 We can't go to Sally's wedding next month. We're on holiday. (will - future / able)
....

10 They may go to the Halloween party. (past simple / likely)
....

6 **Use the prompts to write requests with *Will you…?* (informal) and *Would you…?* (formal).**

0 Your friend Liza / help you clear the garage
Will you help me clear the garage, please, Liza?

1 Your friend Ben / dig the garden
....

2 A passer-by / tell you where Castle Street is
....

3 A man at the post office / wait in the queue
....

4 Passengers / fasten their seat belts
....

5 Hotel guest / follow you to the lift
....

6 Your brother Steve / go to the football match with you
....

7 Your art teacher / go to the art exhibition with you
....

8 Customer / sign at the bottom of the form
....

7 **Rewrite the sentences as in the example.**

0   I'd like a new bike. (Dad / give me)
    I'd like Dad to give me a new bike.

1   She wants a big chocolate cake for her birthday. (her mum / make her)
    ....

2   I'd like to go on a cruise. (my parents / book me)
    ....

3   Bill wants a fancy-dress party. (his friends / organise)
    ....

4   My son would like a grant to study in Berlin. (the university / give him)
    ....

5   My brother wants my new laptop. (me / lend him)
    ....

6   The citizens want a new indoor swimming pool. (the city council / build)
    ....

FAQ

Q: In songs, I've often heard the word **wanna**. Does it have something to do with the verb **want**?

A: It certainly does. It's the contracted form of **want to**, a colloquial form used in American English, and to be avoided in written language: **I wanna go**. Note too the noun form **wannabe**, used in informal language for someone who 'wants to be', or rather wants to appear to be something they are not → *Your friend is such a wannabe!*

Reflecting on grammar

Reflect on the rules and say whether the following statements are true or false.

		True	False
1	Modal verbs are always followed by the **–ing** form of another verb.		
2	Modal verbs behave like auxiliary verbs.		
3	The modal verb **can** has a single past and conditional form: **could**.		
4	**Could** can be used to make polite offers.		
5	**Be able to** substitutes the modal verb **can** in various verb tenses, such as the future.		
6	**May / Might** is the modal verb that expresses certainty.		
7	The two sentences *He may come tomorrow* and *Perhaps he will come tomorrow* have a similar meaning.		
8	The verb **want** is not a modal verb. It's a regular verb.		
9	The sentence *I wish I have a sister* is correct.		
10	The conditional forms **Would like** and **Would prefer** are followed by another verb in the base form, like **Would rather**.		

GRAMMAR MATRIX MAIN

UNIT 14 Modal verbs to express obligation and necessity

LESSON 1 Modal verb *must* and verb *have to*

The modal verb **must** expresses obligation, necessity and prohibition.
It has only one form, which is present, and invariable for all persons. The negative form is **must not** or **mustn't**. Questions are formed by putting **must** before the subject. As for all modal verbs, it is followed by the base form of another verb.

> I / you / he / she / it / we / you / they must
> I / you / he / she / it / we / you / they mustn't
> Must I / you / he / she / it / we / you / they ...?

Questions in the first person (**Must I / Must we...?**) are used to ask for confirmation about something that in reality we don't want to do → *Must I really tidy my room?*
Must we really work next Sunday?

Questions in the second person (**Must you...?**) or with subjects in the third person, sound like an invitation to stop doing something annoying or unsuitable. → *Must you keep talking?*
Must they play such a violent videogame?

Must / mustn't is used to express

- an obligation imposed by others → *I must take these tablets twice a day. The doctor said so.*
- something felt as a duty → *I must be punctual. I must do my homework today.*

It's also used to

- gove advice, strongly recommend doing something → *You must see that musical. It's really fabulous!*
You must visit the new interactive museum. It's so interesting!
- say that something is forbidden or inadvisable (in the negative form) → *You mustn't smoke in here. See the sign?*
You mustn't miss the latest episode of the series. It's the best so far.

- give rules, usually using the impersonal form **You must / You mustn't** → *You must wear a uniform in this school. You mustn't wear shorts or sleeveless shirts to your classes.* (Also **You can't...** which is more widely used than **You mustn't...** in informal registers)

Must is also used to

- make a deduction based on evidence, to say that something is very likely
    - in the present:

    > **must** + base form of the verb

    → *He must be a New Zealander. You can tell from his accent.*
    This must be Jenny's bag. There's her mobile phone in it.

    - in the past:

    > **must** + **have** + past participle

    → *It must have been an easy test. Everybody finished well before the given time.*
    She must have forgotten her mobile at home. It rings but nobody answers it.

Have to... / Have got to...

The verb **have to...** or **have got to...** can replace **must** in the present, especially in the case of

- routine commitments → *I have to be at the office by nine every morning. / I've got to be at the office...*
- obligations imposed on us by others → *You have to pay in advance. / You've got to pay...*

Have to… (without **got**) is also used as an alternative to **must**
- in questions where we are reluctant to do something → *Do I have to come with you? Can't I stay at home?*

Since **must** is only present, for all other tenses we use **have to**, for example
- Past simple → *I had to wait for an hour. I didn't have to wait long.*

- **will** future → *You'll have to work hard next year. You won't have to work very hard.*
- Present perfect → *I've had to do a lot of work this morning. She's had to help her mum tidy the kitchen.*

> ❗ **Have to…** is <u>not</u> an auxiliary verb, so it takes **do**, **does** or **did** in questions or in negative sentences.

Mustn't… / Don't have to…

The negative form of **have to** (**don't / doesn't have to…**) does not have the same meaning as **mustn't**:

- **Mustn't** expresses prohibition → *You mustn't walk on the flower beds.*
- **Don't have to** expresses absence of necessity (**It's not necessary…**) → *You don't have to water the flowers every day. It's not very hot.* (it's certainly not forbidden, but it isn't necessary)

Compare:
You mustn't run in the school corridors!
You don't have to run. You still have plenty of time to catch the train.

1 Match the sentence halves.

1 You mustn't cross the street here.
2 You must get off at the stop after the bus station.
3 It must have been a hard exam.
4 The sea must be very rough.
5 The project needs to be finished by May 8.
6 We have to be home by five.

A Look at that boat – it's being tossed around a lot.
B It's dangerous.
C My parents are arriving.
D The museum's right there. You can't miss it!
E Only a few candidates passed.
F You've got to finish it for that deadline.

1 ….. 2 ….. 3 ….. 4 ….. 5 ….. 6 …..

2 Complete the second sentence so that it has a similar meaning to the first using the given word. Do not change the given word.

0 You mustn't park your car here. It's a restricted zone.
   CAN   You *can't park your car* …………………… here. It's a restricted zone.

1 He can't stay in bed late in the mornings.
   GET UP   He has …………………………………… in the mornings.

2 Talking in the library is prohibited.
   MUST   You …………………………………… .

3 Are you going to Greece with that heavy coat? You won't need it.
   BRING   You …………………………………… that heavy coat to Greece.

4 I already know about that. It's not necessary for you to tell me.
   HAVE You .... me. I already know about that.

5 Dictionaries must be available in each classroom.
   FIND Students .... dictionaries in each classroom.

6 You must hand in your essays on Friday.
   HAVE You .... on Friday.

3 Rewrite the sentences using the tense in brackets.

0 Mum mustn't cook tonight. We're going to take her out. (will- *future*)
   Mum won't have to cook tonight.

1 We have to carry a lot of books to classes. (*past simple*)
   ....

2 They don't have to hurry to catch their train. (*past simple*)
   ....

3 She has to work very hard to prepare for the exam. (will- *future*)
   ....

4 I have to buy a new car; mine is very old now. (will- *future*)
   ....

5 It must be love! (*past infinitive*)
   ....

6 He has to study all the irregular verbs for the test. (*present perfect*)
   ....

7 I have to mow the lawn every week. (*past simple*)
   ....

4 Match each sentence to the appropriate function.

1 You must see the exhibition in the castle. It's great!
2 You mustn't take photos in the museum.
3 Must we really write this essay for tomorrow morning?
4 I have to make coffee for my boss every morning at ten.
5 I must help them.
6 It must be late. All the shops are closing.
7 You must switch off your mobiles during the lectures.

A Ask for confirmation of something that you wouldn't do
B Oblige / order somebody to do something
C Express an obligation that you feel as a duty
D Make a supposition
E Say that something is forbidden
F Give a piece of advice
G Speak about routine committments

1 ..... 2 ..... 3 ..... 4 ..... 5 ..... 6 ..... 7 .....

5 Write appropriate questions to these answers.

1 ....? No, I don't have to. I only work from Monday to Friday.
2 ....? Yes, you must. The grass is too high.
3 ....? At work? No, I don't have to wear a uniform.
4 ....? You must hand in your project by Friday afternoon.
5 ....? No, sorry, you can't sit on these sofas.
6 ....? Yes, I have to. My old computer is not working any longer and I need a new one.

LESSON 2 Need to… / don't need to… / needn't…; be to…

As well as **have to** (see page 250), to express the idea of necessity, we can also use the verb **need**, a strange hybrid verb that can be used both as a main verb and as a modal verb in the negative and interrogative forms.

- In the positive form, **need** is used as a main verb, and therefore
  - it takes **–s** in the third person singular and is followed by **to** + base form → *She needs to be there by ten o'clock sharp.* (= It is necessary for her to be there…)
  - the past is formed by adding **–ed** → *He needed to have his own car for the job as a sales rep.* (= It was necessary for him to have…)
- In the negative, it expresses an absence of obligation, just like **don't have to…** It can be both a main verb and a modal verb. Look at the two possibilities:

Present I <u>don't need to</u> go. = I <u>needn't</u> go.
He <u>doesn't need to</u> go. = He <u>needn't</u> go.
The sentences are equivalent, so we can use them interchangeably.

Past 'Did you go there?' 'No, I <u>didn't need to</u> go.'
'Did you go there?' 'Yes, but I <u>needn't have</u> gone.'

In this case, the meaning is not the same. In the first example, it was not necessary, so I didn't do it. In the second example, I could have avoided doing it because it wasn't necessary.

When the verb has a passive sense, that is, to express the idea that something has to be done, the verb **need** can be followed either by **to** + base form or by the **–ing** form of the verb. → *Your car needs to be repaired. / Your car needs repairing.*

FAQ

Q: Can **Need** also be followed by a noun or pronoun?

A: Yes, of course. When it means 'be useful', **need** can be followed either by a noun (**I need your help**) or pronoun (**I need you**).
In this case, **need** is the main verb, so the negative and interrogative forms will be: **I don't need… / Do you need…?**
I don't need your help.   Does he need my help?

1 Complete the sentences using the verb *need* in the positive, negative or interrogative form.

1. Everybody ………………… to love and to be loved.
2. Thanks for lending me your book, I ………………… it any more now.
3. '………………… you still ………………… my pen?' 'No, thanks, I've just found mine.'
4. We ………………… to carry some heavy bags, so we'd better go in the car.
5. Janet ………………… to write her essay today. The deadline is tomorrow.
6. You ………………… have worried. Everything was okay in the end. *(modale)*
7. I ………………… to give him the good news. He had already heard about it.
8. She ………………… to rent a car, but she couldn't find her credit card.
9. '………………… you really ………………… to buy a new dress?' 'Not really, but this one's lovely.'
10. You ………………… work so hard. Get some rest and relax.
11. They ………………… some warm clothes when they go to Alaska.
12. Do you think the children ………………… some help with their science project?

2 Rewrite the sentences using *need*.

0 No booking is required.
   You *don't need to book* .

1 It may be necessary for you to reserve a table.
   You ....

2 It doesn't seem necessary for them to go.
   They ....

3 It is necessary to dry-clean this coat.
   This coat ....

4 You don't have to be there before nine o'clock.
   You ....

5 All passengers have to be informed about the safety rules.
   All passengers ....

6 It wasn't necessary to call the doctor for our mother.
   We ....

The verb *be to*...

As an alternative to **have to** (see page 250), we can use **be to...** in the following cases:

- to express 'bureaucratic' obligations, imposed by law or by an external authority. This is typically used in formal registers, particularly in written language.

  Each participant is to pay a £10 fee for insurance. (Also **...has to pay...** or **...needs to pay...**, less formally)

  Mr Johnson's will is to be read in the presence of all the heirs.

- to talk about official engagements, fixed itineraries and agreements. This is typically used in journalism.

  The US President is to arrive in Rio de Janeiro tonight. He is to continue his journey to Uruguay in the following days.

---

3 Complete the sentences with *be to* and the verbs below.

meet   be signed   talk   vote   show   get out

1 All passengers .... their passports at the check-in desk.
2 The British Prime Minister .... to the United Nations on Thursday.
3 The contract .... before tomorrow morning.
4 Senators .... on the new tax bill in tomorrow's session.
5 The First Lady .... a group of children during her charity campaign.
6 .... I .... of the car, Officer?

4 Complete the sentences with the positive or negative form of *have to, need, be to, must*.

1 I .... feed the hamster every day. My brother .... clean the cage.
2 You .... to pay in advance. You can pay later.
3 The British Prime Minister .... to come back from Brussel today.
4 You .... to read the contract before signing it.
5 Candidates .... leave the room as soon as they finish the test.
6 He .... some more money. He hasn't got enough.

LESSON 3 *Shall / should; ought to...; had better...*

Shall / should is a modal verb principally used to ask and give instructions, advice and suggestions.

Shall (negative form: **shall not** or **shan't**) is the form of the modal which is least popular in spoken language. It has almost disappeared from American English and has a rather limited use in British English, too.

- It was traditionally used to make predictions about the future with the first persons **I** and **we** → *This time tomorrow I shall be in London.*
  In modern English, we use the **will** future and its contracted form **'ll** for all persons → **This time tomorrow I will be / I'll be in London.** (see page 269).
- Another use of **shall**, which is 'out of fashion' nowadays, is giving orders or instructions in a formal register → *All passengers shall remain seated until the sign has been switched off.*

The main use of **shall**, especially in British English, is in first person questions (**Shall I / we...?**) with the following functions:

- ask for instructions about what to do → *'Shall we go straight on?' 'No, take the first turning on the right.'*
- offer to do something that we think is useful → *'Shall I switch on the light?' 'Yes, please, do.'*
- make a suggestion or ask others to make a suggestion → *'Shall we go to a club tonight? 'Yes, great idea.' / 'No, I'd rather go to the cinema.' 'What shall we do at the weekend?' 'Let's go and see Ian and Maggie.'*

Should is the conditional form of **shall**.
Positive and negative form
I / you / he / she / it / we / you / they should try.
I / you / he / she / it / we / you / they shouldn't try.
Questions and answers of various kinds
Positive: 'Should I wait for them?' 'No, you don't need to. They can go by themselves.'
Negative: 'Shouldn't you be studying at the moment?' 'Yes, Dad, you're right. I'll start now.'
Wh– questions: 'I'm in trouble. What should I do?' 'I really don't know!'

Should is more widely used than **shall**. It is used in the following situations:

- giving or asking for advice → *You shouldn't drink alcohol – certainly not at your age!*
  'What do you think? Should I go for it?' 'Yes, I think you should.'
- say what we think is the right thing to do → *We should recycle as much waste as we can.*
- say that something is probable, based on known facts. This is a similar deduction to that used with **must** (see page 250) → *They left three hours ago. They should be here by now. We've just passed Slough. We shouldn't be far from Windsor.*

> **!** **Should** is also used as an alternative to **shall** in questions:
> - to ask for instructions → *Should we turn left now?*
> - to offer to do something we think is useful → *Should I get you some food?*
> - to make a suggestion → *Should we go to the movies tonight?*

1 **Match the statements with the correct questions.**

1 It's a bit cold in here.
2 Come to dinner at 8 pm.
3 The baby's asleep on the sofa.
4 I'd like to know what the weather will be like tomorrow.
5 I'm quite hungry.

A Shall I switch off the radio?
B Shall I make you a sandwich?
C Shall I check for you on my smartphone?
D Shall I close the window?
E Shall I bring a dessert?

1 ..... 2 ..... 3 ..... 4 ..... 5 .....

2 **Match each question to one of the answers below. Be careful, there are two extra answers.**

Let's get some drinks and snacks.
Let's go to the Multiplex.
Take the number 15. It's quicker.
Would that blue coat suit you?
Would three o'clock be okay?
No, it's cold today.
You needn't cook tonight. I'll get pizza.
No, I've got some. Get some crisps.

1 Shall I take the bus or the tube? ....
2 What shall we buy for the party? ....
3 Shall I buy some popcorn? ....
4 Where shall we go tonight? ....
5 What time shall we meet? ....
6 What shall I make for dinner? ....

3 **Complete the second sentence so that it has a similar meaning to the first using *shall* or *should*.**

0 What about meeting for a chat and a coffee, Bridget?
Shall we meet for a chat and a coffee, Bridget?

1 You're supposed to be working at the moment.
....?

2 Do you think I need to bring a large bag?
....?

3 Why don't we watch this DVD?
....?

4 Do you think it's a good idea to give her some flowers?
....?

5 Why don't we ask Mark to our party?
....?

6 Do you think it is better for them to walk or take the bus?
....?

Ought to

This is a strange modal verb: it is the only one followed by **to** + base form. It has only one form and a conditional meaning:

Positive: I / you / he / she / it / we / you / they ought to try.
Negative: I / you / he / she / it / we / you / they ought not to / oughtn't to try.
Interrogative: Ought I / you / he / she / it / we / you / they try? (rarely used)

Ought to has the same uses as **should**, that is:
- giving advice:
*You oughtn't to eat so many sweets. Sugar is bad for your teeth.
You ought to eat more vegetables.*

- say what would be, or what would have been, the right thing to do: *She ought to apologise.*
In the past: *She ought to have apologised.*

- make a sugestion: *You ought to save some money for your next trip.*

- say that something is probable: *It's 11 o'clock. He ought to have finished by now.*

Had better

As an alternative to **should** and **ought to**, we can use the expression **had better** to give advice or make a recommendation. The expression is used informally.

Positive form:

subject + had ('d) better + base form

→ *You'd better hurry or you'll be late.*

Forma negativa:

subject + had ('d) better not + base form

→ *You'd better not say a word.* (= It would be a better idea if you didn't say a word.)

FAQ

Q: In a novel, I came across the expression **You'd better marry him.** I thought it was a conditional, that is, that **'d** was the contracted form of **would**, as in **I'd rather....** But I discovered that it's not the case.

A: No, you're right. **You'd better** means **You had better**. It's difficult to explain this grammatically: the **past simple** of **have** is used here with a conditional meaning. These are the oddities of English!

4 Choose the correct alternative.

1 I **had better** / **ought** / **shall** to give up smoking.
2 You **should** / **ought** / **have better** be more careful when driving.
3 You **ought** / **'d better** / **'ve better** tell him or he'll be very angry with you.
4 She **shouldn't** / **not ought** / **not shall** answer his emails.
5 They **have better** / **should** / **ought** study more if they want to pass their exams.
6 '**Shall I** / **Have I better** / **Ought** I switch off the lights?' 'Yes, please.'

5 Complete the sentences with *had better / had better not* or *ought / ought not*.

1 You .... wear a warm jumper. It's really cold out today.
2 You .... get up, Mark. It's late!
3 She .... to be more careful. She's always falling over.
4 You .... go out. There's a really bad storm!
5 We .... go skiing this weekend. There are warnings about avalanches.
6 You .... take your umbrella. It's going to rain.
7 They .... to go home until it stops snowing.
8 You .... apologise to your friend. Your behaviour has been awful!

LESSON 4 Be obliged / compelled / forced to...; be due; be bound to...; verb owe

To express the idea of strong obligation, as well as **must** and **have to** (see page 250) we can use two expressions with **be** + past participle of the verbs **oblige** and **compel**: **be obliged** and **be compelled**, which are practically synonymous.
To express the idea of an even greater constraint, we can use **be forced**.
These expressions all belong to a more formal register compared to **must** and **have to** and they are more common in written language.

> ❗ The verb that follows is preceded by **to**.
> **Be obliged / compelled / forced** have all the verb tenses, we just need to conjugate the verb **be**. For example:
>
> **Present**
> Thousands of people <u>are forced</u> to leave their countries every day because of war and persecution. (stronger than ...**must leave**...)
>
> **Past**
> One of the ministers <u>was compelled</u> to resign from office following a bribery scandal. (stronger than ... **had to resign**...)
>
> **Future**
> They <u>will be obliged</u> to accept the agreement. (stronger than: **They will have to accept**...)
>
> **Present perfect**
> My husband has lost his job so we <u>have been obliged</u> to sell our house.

Be due

To express the idea that something is expected to happen at a prearranged time, we can use the expression **be due**. It's used especially to talk about the arrival times of means of transport, deliveries and similar topics. The verb that follows is often just understood, rather than expressed.

The train from Lancaster is due (to arrive) in 15 minutes.
Delivery is due within the next few days.
The flight from Madrid was due (to land) at 4.50 pm, but it is delayed.

Be bound

To express the idea that something is destined to happen or will inevitably happen, we can use the expression **be bound**. The verb that follows is preceded by **to**.

It's bound to be so! (= I'm sure it's like that, it can't be otherwise.)
With her talent, she's bound to be successful. (Also: ...she's sure / certain to be successful).
He's drinking and driving every night – sooner or later he's bound to have an accident.

FAQ

Q: At home I have a CD of Simon and Garfunkel songs. One that I really like is called **Homeward bound**. What does it mean, exactly?

A: **Bound** in this case means 'directed towards', so in this case 'directed towards home'. If we look carefully, there is a connection between the meaning of 'directed' and 'destined for'. Think of Ulysses, who was **homeward bound** too - he was destined to return to Ithaca!

To owe
To express the idea that I'm in debt with someone both in terms of money and in a metaphorical sense (gratitude, for example) we use the regular verb **to owe** (simple past and past participle **owed**).
He owes me a lot of money, which I lent him a long time ago.
'How much do I owe you?' 'Fifty pounds.'
You've been of great help to me. I owe you a lot! (Also: I'm very grateful to you!)

1 Complete the sentences with the correct form of *be obliged / forced* **or** *be due*.

1 Yesterday's train delay .... to the storm.
2 He .... to learn Chinese for his job. He's having the first lesson today.
3 Last month Francine .... to resign and look for another job.
4 The bus .... in five minutes. Let's run!
5 Our plane .... to land in New York at 5 pm.
6 It's a sunny day, but I .... to stay in and study for the test.

2 Complete the sentences with the correct form of *be bound* **or** *owe*.

1 I .... you all I've ever had. You have been such a good friend!
2 She .... her classmate £7.50 for the cinema ticket.
3 He studied so hard that he .... to pass his science test.
4 How much do I .... you for the pizza and coke?
5 Things .... to go wrong if you don't listen to me!
6 They .... to win. They play so much better than the other team.

3 Complete the text with the words below. Be careful! There's one extra word.

alerted   due   will be obliged   been forced   compelled to   take off   owing

The hurricane is ¹.................................. to hit the eastern coast of the United States at the weekend. The population has already been ².................................. . All people living within five kilometres of the sea are ³.................................. leave their houses by Saturday morning. Airlines have ⁴.................................. to cancel all weekend flights that were due to land or ⁵.................................. from airports in the area. People travelling in the area ⁶.................................. to leave the coastal roads and drive along the motorways.

4 Match the sentence halves.

1 We were forced to abandon our house   A in two minutes. Hurry up!
2 They owe me   B a great actor!
3 I was compelled to   C his offer for the house.
4 Their flight is due to land   D at Heathrow Airport at 3 pm.
5 You are bound to become   E five euros for the taxi.
6 We'll be obliged to accept   F after the earthquake.
7 The train is due   G a career in politics.
8 Peter's bound to have   H tell him the truth.

1 .....   2 .....   3 .....   4 .....   5 .....   6 .....   7 .....   8 .....

ROUND UP 14

1 Look at the table on page 280 and write what function the following sentences express.

1. Shall we try the new Japanese restaurant?
   ....
2. You needn't bring your device. There'll be computers in the room.
   ....
3. They must be at home. The lights are on.
   ....
4. Can I leave earlier today, Ms Spencer?
   ....
5. Shall I go ahead along this road?
   ....
6. You ought to tell your father about your plans.
   ....
7. I'd like Jack to cut the grass.
   ....
8. We have to meet the manager every Monday morning.
   ....
9. They mustn't touch the old books on that shelf.
   ....
10. Could we have the menu, please?
    ....

2 Complete the sentences with the modal *must / mustn't* and one of the verbs below.

forget   fasten   leave   win   tell   tidy   drive   book   be   hurry

1. You .... lies!
2. Passengers .... their seat belts.
3. We .... this important match.
4. You .... your passport.
5. You .... slowly when it's foggy.
6. You .... your seats in advance.
7. I .... in the office by eight o'clock.
8. Students .... the school building without permission.
9. Emma .... her room. It's a real mess!
10. We're terribly late. We .... !

3 Complete the sentences with *have to* in the positive, negative or interrogative forms of the correct tenses.

1. She .... buy a new bike. Hers has been stolen.
2. We .... do a lot of work yesterday. We were really tired in the end.
3. I .... wait long. She arrived after five minutes.
4. .... you really .... get up at five o'clock every morning?
5. We .... sign all the documents before we could leave.
6. Everybody could speak English, so they .... use an interpreter in the meeting.
7. I .... find a new job. My firm has closed down.
8. We .... answer hundreds of emails today.

4 Complete the sentences with *must*, *don't have* or *should*. Then match the sentence halves.

1. We .... buy some food.
2. Tomorrow's my day off.
3. There's been an accident.
4. You .... see this musical.
5. I really .... clean the kitchen.
6. You .... to worry.

A It's fantastic!
B Everything's alright.
C I .... to go to work.
D The fridge is nearly empty.
E I haven't cleaned it for a week.
F We .... call an ambulance.

1 ..... 2 ..... 3 ..... 4 ..... 5 ..... 6 .....

5 Here are some rules for students attending a language school. Circle the correct option.

1 You **can** / **have to** drive to the school, but you **mustn't** / **don't have to** park your car in the teachers' car park.
2 You **mustn't** / **don't have to** eat in the multimedia lab, but you **can** / **can't** have a sandwich in the students' room.
3 You **can** / **must** buy your own books, but you **can't** / **don't have to** buy your own CDs.

6 Complete the sentences with *mustn't* or *don't* / *doesn't have* to and the verbs in brackets.

1 Your husband .... me to the station, I can take a taxi. (drive)
2 You .... on the ice, you could fall into the lake. (walk)
3 He .... a uniform for his job, but he must dress smartly. (wear)
4 Students .... school before the end of the lessons. (leave)
5 You .... the dishes tonight. I can do it tomorrow morning. (wash)

7 Complete the deductions referring to the past. Use *must* / *mustn't* and one of the verbs below.

win   have   cost   be   get up   be

1 Look how happy he is. He .... the competition.
2 They're still together. She .... his partner for at least ten years.
3 They .... a lot of money in the bank to buy that mansion.
4 Climbing that peak .... very hard. You look exhausted.
5 They're already here. They .... very early this morning.
6 Your ring looks very expensive. It .... at least £800.

8 Complete the second sentence so that it has a similar meaning to the first. Replace the words in italics with one of the following expressions: *must be, must have been, can't be, can't have*.

1 *Surely you didn't go* on holiday with no money?
   You ....
2 *I'm sure there's* a report on yesterday's athletics competition in the local newspaper.
   There ....
3 *I'm certain that he isn't* over 65. He's still working!
   He ....
4 *I assume that he is* fit, as he is a PE teacher.
   He ....
5 *I'm certain that there is* some coffee left. I bought it yesterday.
   There ....
6 *You definitely didn't recharge* the mobile phone battery last night: it's off already.
   You ....
7 *Surely she isn't* her mother: she's far too young.
   She ....
8 *I'm sure* the person who's just left is the new manager.
   The ....

9 **Complete the sentences with the appropriate words.**

1 You .... to know what to do before leaving.
2 'I .... you five pounds.' 'No, you don't .... me anything. Don't worry.'
3 I'm always under pressure. I .... really work less.
4 You'd .... not spend all your money, you .... save some.
5 We were .... to go back to work before the end of our holidays.
6 You .... to listen to what I have to tell you.
7 You .... to come in the early morning. You can come later.
8 The train was .... at 9.30 but it was late.
9 You're not .... to go into the theatre when the show has started.
10 'What .... we make for dinner tonight?' 'Let's make chicken salad.'
11 I'm not quite sure. .... I stay a little longer or .... I go straight away?
12 They were .... to abandon their farm because of the hurricane alert.

MATRIX +

We can use the modal **should** in a secondary clause introduced by the verbs: **advise**, **recommend**, **suggest**, **insist**.

Our teacher suggests that we should take the exam quite soon.
He insisted that I should have lunch with him.

This use is typical of British English and sounds quite formal. In spoken language, it's more common to say: **Our teacher suggests we take the exam… / He insisted I had lunch…** , without the modal **should** and omitting the conjunction **that**.

10 **Circle the correct option.**

Glen [1]...... ride his motorbike so fast. And he [2]...... wear his crash helmet all the time. If he [3]...... regulations like that, he [4]...... so many fines (*multe*).
His parents [5]...... his fines. If I [6]...... his mother, I [7]...... his motorbike in the garage for a week or two after each fine. I [8]...... him to find some kind of Saturday job too, so that he could pay his fines himself. If he [9]...... use his own money, perhaps he [10]...... learn to be a bit more careful.

1	A	had better	B	wouldn't	C shouldn't
2	A	had better to	B	hadn't better	C ought to
3	A	didn't ignore	B	ignored not	C wouldn't ignore
4	A	didn't get	B	wouldn't get	C ought not get
5	A	ought not to pay	B	had better pay	C shouldn't to pay
6	A	were	B	am	C would be
7	A	had better to lock	B	would lock	C ought to lock
8	A	had better make	B	should make	C would oblige
9	A	would be obliged	B	had better	C had to
10	A	must	B	would	C had

11 Complete the passage with the appropriate verbs or modal verbs.

Dear Janine,
I'm writing you from the garden of the Hotel Plaza! What am I doing here? I'm working. I've got a new job as junior receptionist. I started two weeks ago and I ¹................. say I'm enjoying what I'm doing.
I ²................. work six hours a day five days a week. Twice a month ³I .... work at the weekend. I ⁴................. wear a uniform but luckily I ⁵................. wear high-heeled shoes. I wouldn't be able to wear them for six hours, standing most of the time.
Anyway, you ⁶................. see the hotel. The hall is huge with wonderful liberty decorations and elegant furniture. The guests ⁷................. all be very rich because the rooms are extremely expensive.
Yesterday a famous French actress arrived. She was ⁸................. to come at about midday and lots of journalists were there but she didn't turn up until late in the evening when most of the journalists had left.

12 Find the mistakes and correct them.

1 Our bus is due arriving in the next few minutes. Hurry up!
....

2 They were forced leave their home because of the flood.
....

3 'How much owe I you?' 'Eight pounds.'
....

4 You'd better to come to work on time if you want to keep your job.
....

5 Tess suggested to have lunch together tomorrow.
....

6 You look tired. Shall I to cook for you tonight?
....

Reflecting on grammar

Reflect on the rules and say whether the following statements are true or false.

		True	False
1	The negative forms of **must** and **have to** can be used interchangeably because they have the same meaning.		
2	**Have to** is not a modal verb, so we need to use **do/does/did** in questions and negative forms.		
3	*You dont' have to…, You don't need to… e You needn't…* all have the same meaning.		
4	**Should** is the conditional form of the modal **shall**.		
5	The full form of **You'd better** is **You would better**.		
6	The expression **be due** is used to talk about owing money.		
7	The expression *It's bound to happen any time soon* is correct.		
8	The sentences *You'll be obliged to go* and *You'll be allowed to go* mean the same thing.		
9	The sentence *Their plane is due to land in ten minutes* is correct.		
10	**Ought** is the only modal verb followed by **to** + base form.		

GRAMMAR MATRIX MAIN

UNIT 15 The future

LESSON 1 Different types of future tenses; the future with the present continuous and the present simple

The three main ways of expressing the future are:

1. present continuous — They're leaving at 10 pm.
2. **going to...** — They're going to leave.
3. **will** future — I think they will leave soon.

Each of the three has its own parametres of usage and shades of meaning, depending on both the intention of the speaker and on the context. Often, it is possible to use more than one form in the same situation and the choice is subjective.

FAQ

Q: I always mix up these three types of future: whatever form I choose is never the correct one! How do I know which form to use?

A: As a general guide, try and ask yourself these questions when you need to choose which form to use:
- Is it an appointment that you have written in your diary? Has it already been planned? → **present continuous**
- Is it what you mean to do? → **going to...**
- Does what will happen not depend on you? Is it a prediction? → future with **will**

For more detailed explanations, which can help you decide which future to use on a case by case basis, check the mind map on page 275.

1 Which of the three forms of future is appropriate to each situation? Circle the correct answer.

1. The weather forecast says ...... at the weekend. (forecast)
   - A the sun is shining
   - B it will be sunny
   - C it's going to be sunny

2. I think Chelsea ...... the Cup. (prediction)
   - A is going to win
   - B is winning
   - C will win

3. ...... a party for my birthday. (intention)
   - A I will have
   - B I'm going to have
   - C I'm having

4. Grandma ...... on the five o'clock train. (planned action)
   - A is going to arrive
   - B will arrive
   - C is arriving

5. ...... to the dentist's at 11 o'clock. (appointment)
   - A I'm going
   - B I'm going to go
   - C I will go

6. ...... a trip to Scotland. (intention)
   - A I'm going to go on
   - B I will go on
   - C I'm going on

Present continuous for the future

As we saw in Unit 6 (see page 95), the future can be expressed with the **present continuous**, that is

subject + **am** / **is** / **are** + **–ing form** of the verb

to express

- actions, facts. or planned events, usually in the fairly near future → *We're playing an important match tomorrow.*
- personal commitments, decisions taken, for which something has been prearranged, for example the purchase of tickets, a seat reservation, an appointment at a fixed time... → *I'm going to the U2 concert on 4th September. I'm looking forward to it!*

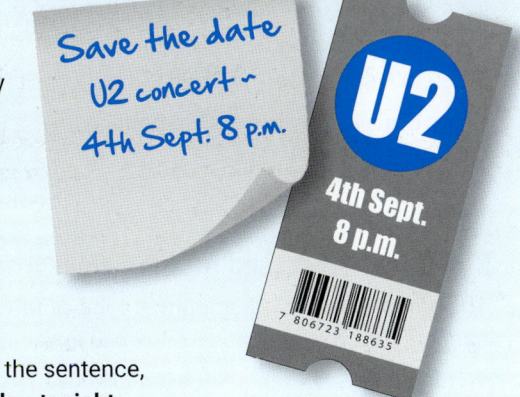

In these cases, there will be a future time expression in the sentence, for example: **in ten minutes**, **at six o'clock**, **later in the day**, **tonight**, **tomorrow**, **at the weekend**, **next week**... and similar expressions of this kind.

This use is common with verbs of movement, like **go**, **come**, **leave**, **arrive** → *'Are you coming to my house this afternoon?' 'Sorry, I can't. I'm meeting my aunt at the airport at four o'clock. She's arriving from Florida.'*

Save the date
U2 concert –
4th Sept. 8 p.m.

2 Use the prompts and write sentences and questions in the present continuous.

0   you / see / Mr Randall / after the meeting / .
    You are seeing Mr Randall after the meeting.

1   we / visit / the Tate Gallery / at three o'clock / .
    ....
    ....

2   you / go shopping / this afternoon / ?
    ....
    ....

3   I / have dinner / at a Greek restaurant / tonight / .
    ....
    ....

4   what time / you / go to work / tomorrow / ?
    ....
    ....

5   when / you / have / your exam / ?
    ....
    ....

6   we / get married / next Saturday / .
    ....
    ....

7   I / see / the optician / at half past ten / tomorrow / .
    ....
    ....

8   they / leave / for New York / next week / .
    ....
    ....

9   who / you / meet / at ten o'clock / ?
    ....
    ....

10 where / he / have lunch / today / ?
    ....
    ....

3 Read and write P for actions in the present and F for actions in the future.

1. I'm not going to school tomorrow. ......
2. We're having a great time on this island. ......
3. Are you going to basketball practice this afternoon? ......
4. Not all of my friends are coming to the party tonight. ......
5. He isn't reading, he's sleeping. Look, his eyes are closed. ......
6. The train's arriving. Hurry up! ......
7. We're having a short break next week. ......
8. Hey, you two! What are you doing? Copying? ......

The future expressed with the *present simple*

The **present simple** is sometimes used as future tense, although this is more unusual. We can find it in particular

- for scheduled events, for example to accompany a travel itinerary
- for events that happen at fixed times, such as arrivals and departures.

It's used especially with the verbs **leave** / **arrive**, **open** / **close**, **start** / **finish** and similar verbs, with the mention of a precise time.

VISITING HOURS
MONDAY- FRIDAY
9 am - 1 pm
SATURDAY - SUNDAY
9 am - 1 pm
4 pm - 6 pm

Tomorrow's Saturday, so visiting hours start at four.

4 A guide is describing an itinerary to a group of tourists in Berlin. Complete the text with the verbs below.

meet (x2)   get   visit   walk   have (x3)

'May I have your attention, please? Let me tell you what is happening today. We ¹............................ to the Siegel Hotel tonight at seven and we ²............................ dinner at the hotel. Tomorrow, we ³............................ after breakfast at 9.30 and ⁴............................ to the Pergamon Museum. It's not far from the hotel. We ⁵............................ the museum in the morning and afterwards ⁶............................ lunch in a restaurant nearby. Then you ⁷............................ a free afternoon. We ⁸............................ again in front of the museum at six to go back to the hotel together. Any questions?'

We arrive in Berlin at about 6 and check in at the hotel soon after.

5 Complete the sentences with the present simple or the present continuous of the verbs in brackets.

1. Do you know that the yoga course .... on March 1st? (start)
2. I .... on a trip to Bath next weekend. I want to see the Roman baths. (go)
3. We .... at Victoria Station at 7.50 pm. Will you be there to meet us? (arrive)
4. 'What .... you .... tomorrow?' 'I don't know. I don't have any plans.' (do)
5. Tomorrow I .... the house at 9 am because the bus .... at quarter past. (leave / leave)
6. Louise .... in the school choir tonight. I'm going to see her! (sing)
7. I .... a party on Saturday. Would you like to come? (have)
8. We .... a couple of days in Brighton next week. We've just booked the hotel. (spend)

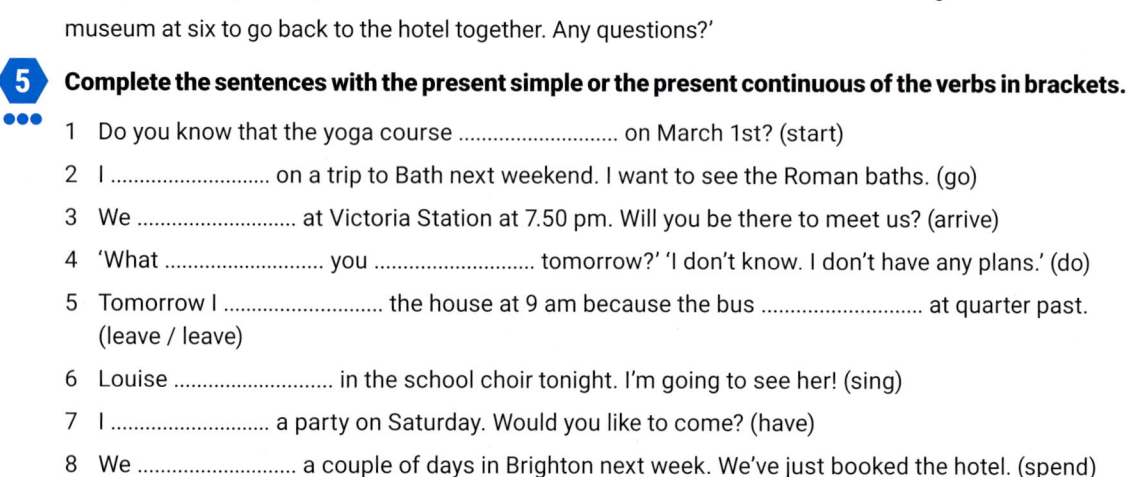

LESSON 2 The future with *going to*...

Another way of expressing the future is with the expression **be going to**... It is used in particular to talk about what we are intending to do, and talk about projects that depend on us in order to become reality.

Positive:

subject + **am** / **is** / **are** + **going to** + main verb

I am going to help him.
Short form: **I'm going...**

Negative:

subject + **am** / **is** / **are not** + **going to** + main verb

I am not going to help him.
Short form: **I'm not going...**

Interrogative:

(**Wh−** word) + **am** / **is** / **are** + subject + **going to** + main verb + ?

Short answers:

Yes, + subject pronoun + **am** / **is** / **are**.
No, + subject pronoun + **'m not** / **isn't** / **aren't**.

'Are you going to help him?' 'Yes, I am.'
'Aren't you going to help him?' 'No, I'm not.'
'Who are you going to help?' 'All of them, if I can.'

Short forms, both for the positive and the negative are the ones that are mainly used. →
She's going to talk to him.
We aren't going to read all of these books!

! In informal American English, we can find the contracted form **gonna**, short for **going to** → *It's gonna be hard!*, but this is a non standard form, like **gotta** (**got to**) and **wanna** (**want to**).

The future with **going to** is used mainly to talk about

- things we intend to do but which we haven't yet planned in any detail, or which are not yet in 'our diaries' → *I'm going to take courses in economics next year.* (I intend to take the courses, but I haven't enrolled yet.) Compare with: *I'm taking a course in economics in September. I start on the second.* (I've already enrolled, it's a firm date in my diary, so I use the **present continuous**).

- long-term life plans → *I'm going to be a pilot when I grow up.* (Also: *I want to be a pilot.* See page 240)
  I'm not going to live in this town forever. (Also: *I don't want to live...*)

In these cases, we will usually find a time expression in the sentence, for example:

this coming spring, **in two hours**, **soon**, **next year**, **when I grow up**, **when I go to England** and similar → *Are you going to find a job when you go to London?*
I'm going to be a pilot when I grow up.

FAQ

Q: Is it possible to say **I'm going to go to university**? It doesn't seem to sound right...

A: Yes, it's possible, although verbs of movement and **go** in particular, are used more with the **present continuous**.

1 Complete the sentences with the correct form of *going to* of the verb in brackets.

1 We .... in the same office. (not work)
2 I .... a qualification as a nurse. (get)
3 He .... a Spanish course in the summer. (take)
4 .... you .... her a present? (buy)
5 They .... to a bigger house soon. (move)

6 When .... you .... this film? (watch)
7 She .... for that job. (not apply)
8 Where .... you .... when you grow up? (live)

2 Read sentences a and b. Complete one with the *going to* future and the other one with the present continuous of the verbs in brackets.

1 (get married)
   a We're .... this coming spring. In March maybe, or in April. We'll see.
   b We're .... on 8th May. We've already sent invitations to everyone.

2 (not work)
   a I'm .... this weekend. The boss told me they don't need me to. Good news!
   b I'm .... at the weekend. The project I'm working on is nearly finished and I need to take a break.

3 (bring)
   a I'm .... a packed lunch on tomorrow's trip.
   b I'm .... sandwiches, crisps and a juice. I've already bought them.

The future with **going to** is also used to
- talk about something that is imminent, that will certainly happen in the immediate future. In this case there isn't usually a time expression, we understand the meaning as 'now', 'immediately'. → *Shhh…The film's going to start. Step back. The train's going to arrive.*
- communicate what we are going to cover in a lesson, conference or similar situation → *We're going to revise the use of the article. Today I'm going to deal with the problem of cyber-bullying.*

To talk about something that is going to happen, we can also use the expression **be about to…**, but this is less common → *My mother is about to retire from work.*

The future with **going to** is also used
- to make predictions, when these are based on factual evidence or when we are sure that things will happen in a certain way → *I'm sure it's going to be a great party. Things aren't going to change, that's for certain.* To make a prediction, however, the future with **will** is in all cases the most frequently-used verb tense (see page 270).

---

3 🎧13 Complete the dialogue with the correct form of *be going to* and the verbs below. Then listen and check.

take   not change   be   not do   tell

Luke Are you ready? The headmaster [1] .... here in a minute.
Debbie Good! I [2] .... him why we aren't happy with the new school rules.
Luke There's no point! He knows and he [3] .... anything about it.
Debbie Isn't he? Well, if nobody speaks up, things [4] ....
Luke I don't think we can do much, anyway.
Debbie You're always so negative. When [5] .... you .... some action?
Luke Alright. I'll be on your side this time. There! He's coming.

4 Rewrite the sentences using *going to*. Remember to keep the meaning of the original sentence.

1 He wants to be an engineer when he grows up.
....
2 Get an umbrella. It's about to rain. ....
3 I want to plant some fruit trees in my garden this coming spring.
....
4 We want to clean out the garage at the weekend.
....
5 Stop chatting! The lesson is about to start. ....
6 Look at those grey clouds. I'm sure it will rain soon.
....
7 Today I want you to work in pairs. ....

LESSON 3 The future with *will*

The future with **will**, sometimes called **will future** or **future simple**, is the most widely-used future form. It is constructed with the modal verb **will**, which is the same for all persons, and followed by the base form of the main verb.

Positive:

subject + **will** (contracted to **'ll**) + main verb

I will be there./ I'll be there.

Negative:

subject + **will not** (contracted to **won't**) + main verb

I will not be there. / I won't be there.

Interrogative:

(**Wh– word**) + **will** / **won't** + subject + main verb + ?

Short answers:

Yes, + subject pronoun + **will**.
No, + subject pronoun + **won't**.

'Will you be there?' 'Yes, I will'.
'Won't you be there?' 'No, I won't'.
'When will you be there?' 'Tomorrow at 11'.

The most common form is the contracted form, but it is not used in **positive short answers** → **Yes, they will.** NOT Yes, ~~they'll~~.

In the first person singular and plural, **will** can be replaced by **shall** → **I shall be there / We shall be there**, but this is not a common form in today's English (see page 255).

1 Reorder the words and write sentences.

1 get / She / will / by / there / noon / .
....
2 It / not / will / again / happen / .
....
3 will / The / set / sun / 7.30 / at / tonight / .
....
4 with / I / always / be / will / you / .
....
5 will / It / cloudy / be / and / tomorrow / cold / .
....
6 will / We / survive / not / on / money / this / for / whole / a / week / .
....
....
7 ahead / Go / , / I / you / follow / will / .
....
8 ready / Everything / be / o'clock / by / will / three / .
....
....

2 Complete the questions with the *will* future form of the given verbs, then complete the answers.

work   find   win   like   be   make   have   stay

1 'What do you think? .... I .... a good job?' 'Yes, I'm sure .... !'
2 '.................. they .... on Saturday?' 'No, ... , they'll go home.'
3 '.................. it .... a hot weekend?' 'No, ... It will be quite cold.'
4 '.................. you .... here a bit longer?' 'Yes, ... I can stay until five.'
5 '.................. you .... time to finish everything by Friday?' 'No, ... , I'm afraid.'
6 '.................. she .... this book?' 'Yes, I think .... She said she likes fantasy.'
7 '.................. they .... the Cup Final?' 'I'm not sure ....'
8 '.................. they .... a sequel of this action movie?' 'I hope .... It's fantastic.'

The future with **will** is used mainly to

- talk about inevitable facts, which will happen independently of our will → *I will be 50 next year. It will soon be winter.*
- make predictions, ask or say how we think things will go. The future sentence is often introduced by **I think…, I don't think…, I guess…, I expect…, I'm sure…, I wonder…** and similar expressions. → *I think we'll win the championship this year. We have a good chance.* *'What will you do now?' 'I guess I'll just wait and see what happens.'*

The sentence may include adverbs that express the degree of certainty of the prediction, for example **definitely, certainly, probably**. These adverbs usually come after **will** → *This match will definitely end in a draw.*

> ! For predictions which we consider to be quite certain, given the evidence, we also use the future with **going to…** (see page 268) → *We're going to have a great time.* = *I'm sure we'll have a great time.* For events that are probable or possible, we also use the modal **may / might** (see page 235). → *They may arrive soon.* = *They will probably arrive soon.*

3 Circle the correct option.

1 The weather **probably will** / **will probably** change soon.
2 I'm **think** / **sure** you will understand.
3 I don't think I **will** / **won't** apply for that job.
4 The bank will **be** / **have** closed tomorrow.
5 I wonder who the new headmaster **will be** / **was**!
6 My sister will **to start** / **start** university next week.
7 I **sure** / **hope** you'll have a nice journey.
8 She will certainly **get** / **gets** the promotion.
9 How long will **the game last** / **last the game**?
10 I don't think we'll **have** / **having** enough time.

The future with **will** is also used to express

- promises → *I'll come and see you next year. I promise.*
- resolutions → *I know I haven't worked hard enough. I'll try and work harder next term.* *'What are your New Year resolutions?' 'I'll do more physical exercise and I'll eat healthier food.'*
- hopes → *We hope we'll be able to see you before you leave.*

> ! After the verb **hope**, we can also find the **present simple** → *I hope you come.* = *I hope you will come.*

Future time expressions

In future time expressions using **will**, we often have fixed or indefinite time expressions like the following:

Fixed time expressions	Indefinite time expressions
Tomorrow / The day after tomorrow	In the (near) future
Next month / Next year	Soon
In four days	Later
In three years' time	Sooner or later
In (the year) 2050	Forever

4 Write these predictions in the correct column.

In 50 years' time…

Unemployment will be higher than now.
Unemployment will be lower.
Everybody will have enough to eat.
There will still be wars.
Air pollution will be worse.
There will still be hunger and poverty.
There will be no more wars.
There will be less air pollution.
There will be a cure for most illnesses.
There will be new diseases.

Pessimistic predictions	Optimistic predictions

5 Match the sentence halves.

1 I expect the children
2 It will soon be summer
3 I hope you will all come
4 We'll do our best
5 The room you've booked
6 Yes, Mum. I will walk
7 I'll call around nine
8 My mother will be 60 in May,
9 In case of emergency
10 I'll have a cup of tea

A and the days will get longer.
B will be ready at 12 pm.
C and feed the dog every day!
D and I'll phone my sister for a chat.
E will behave well.
F to our housewarming party.
G to check if there's anything you need.
H to meet your expectations.
I but she looks much younger.
J I will call the police.

1 ….. 2 ….. 3 ….. 4 ….. 5 ….. 6 ….. 7 ….. 8 ….. 9 ….. 10 …..

6 Circle the errors in each sentence, then rewrite them correctly.

1 I'll always am on your side. You can be sure of this.
....
2 I don't think it will to rain today.
....
3 Between five days we'll be at the seaside. I can't wait!
....
4 We'll be best friends for always.
....
5 I'm busy now. I'll talk to you next.
....
6 The climate will get probably warmer in the future.
....
7 I willn't fight with my brother again, I promise!
....
8 Where I will meet Mr Johnson?
....
9 Don't worry. They'll arrive soon or later.
....
10 Do you think you'll be free the day next tomorrow?
....

The future with **will** is also used to express

- spontaneous decisions taken at the moment of speaking → *'So. Who's driving? You, John?' 'Okay. I'll drive as far as the next service station.'* (I hadn't thought about it before, I decided just when I was talking)

    Compare with: *I am going to drive tonight. I'm the only one who doesn't drink!* (I decided beforehand, so I use the future with **going to**.) (See page 267)
    If we decide not to do something, we use **won't** → *I won't go!*

FAQ

Q: In a marriage proposal, we say **Will you marry me?** And the answer is **Yes, I will**. Isn't it - or at least shouldn't it be! - a decision taken beforehand? So why don't people say **Are you going to marry me?**

Will you marry me?

A: As we saw in Unit 13, Lesson 3, remember the modal verb **will** expresses willingness, so we should understand it as 'Do you want to marry me?' 'Yes, I want to', so as a result, I will. The concepts of volition and promising are both expressed with the modal **will**.

Another use of the future with **will** is to express 'what will happen if...' in the main clause of a first conditional sentence → *If we have time, we'll visit the British Museum.* We will see this structure in Unit 16 Lesson 2, page 292.

7 Match the sentences on the left to the answers on the right, then underline the intentions in blue and the decisions made at the moment of speaking in red.

1 I'm going to help them. They really need it.
2 Hi! Welcome back. I'll help you with your bags.
3 I'm going to buy you all a drink tonight.
4 How much do we have to pay?
5 Are we going to get a taxi to the station tomorrow?
6 Oh dear! We're late for the meeting…
7 We're going to a Japanese restaurant tonight.
8 Here's the menu. What will you have?

A Never mind. I'll pay for everyone.
B We'll get a taxi then.
C Good idea. I'll help too.
D That's great! I'm going to have sushi.
E Really? How come? Is it your birthday?
F Oh, thanks. That's so kind of you.
G Er… I think I'll have the fish.
H Yes, I think that's the best thing to do.

1 ….. 2 ….. 3 ….. 4 ….. 5 ….. 6 ….. 7 ….. 8 …..

LESSON 4 Future continuous; future perfect

The progressive form of the future is called the **future continuous** and it is the same for all persons, as follows:

Positive:

> subject + **will be ('ll be)** + **–ing** form of the verb

I'll be waiting for you.

Negative:

> subject + **will not be (won't be)** + **–ing** form of the verb

I won't be working at this time tomorrow.

Interrogative:

> (**Wh– word**) + **will / won't** + subject + **–ing** form of the verb + ?

Will you be waiting for me when I come home?

The **future continuous** is used

- to say what will be happening or what we will be doing at a certain moment of the future. As always with continuous forms, its use underlines the fact that an action will still be in progress.
  → *You'll be travelling to Spain at this time tomorrow. Don't call me between 3 pm and 5 pm this afternoon. I will be taking my exams at that time.*

We can use it as an alternative to the **present continuous**

- for planned actions that are scheduled in a diary → *I'll be attending a conference at nine o'clock tomorrow. = I'm attending a conference…*
- to ask about another person's plans → *What will you be doing at the weekend? = What are you doing…? Will you be studying tonight? = Are you studying tonight?*

1 You are thinking about a friend who is in the Bahamas. Complete the text with the future continuous.

I wish I could go on holiday with my friend Stephanie. Next week she ¹……………………… (lie) on a beach in the Bahamas. She ²……………………… (relax) and ³……………………… (enjoy) the sunshine, while I will be here in England in the cold rainy weather. Next week I ⁴……………………… (work) eight hours a day every day including Saturday. And, on Sunday, I ⁵……………………… (clean) the house and ⁶……………………… (cook) for the following week as usual. Who wouldn't want a break?

2 Complete the questions with the future continuous of the verbs below, then match them to the correct answers.

have   do   leave   go   use   travel   go out

1 .... (you) a night shift this week?
2 .... (you) with your new boyfriend tonight?
3 Where .... (they) to on holiday in the summer?
4 What time .... (you) tomorrow morning?
5 When .... (Robert) his next piano lesson?
6 .... (you) to Leeds on the coach?
7 .... (you) the car today, Dad?

A We'll be leaving quite early.
B He'll be having it at four this afternoon.
C No, I'll be doing one next week.
D No, I won't be going anywhere in the car today.
E They'll be going to the Lake District as usual.
F No, we'll be going by train.
G No, we'll be having a quiet evening at home.

1 ..... 2 ..... 3 ..... 4 ..... 5 ..... 6 ..... 7 .....

Future perfect simple and continuous

The **future perfect simple**, is formed as follows:

Positive:

subject + **will have ('ll have)** + past participle of the verb

Negative:

subject + **will not have (won't have)** + past participle of the verb

Interrogative:

(*Wh–* word) + **will / won't** + subject + **have** + past participle of the verb + ?

It is used to express what will have already happened at a time in the future → *By the time you get up, the sun will have risen.*

The **future perfect continuous** is formed with **will have been** + **–ing** form of the verb. It expresses a prolonged action which will have been completed within a certain period of time. Its use is not very common. → *I will have been watching three movies by the time we land in Los Angeles.*

The **future perfect** is often accompanied by expressions of time like **by two o'clock, by the time you come back, in three weeks' time** and other expressions of this kind.

3 Complete the sentences with the future perfect simple of the verbs in brackets.

1 By the time you come back, your parents .... (leave)
2 I hope I .... my degree by this time next year. (take)
3 In ten years' time, I .... very rich! (become)
4 You .... to speak German fluently in two years' time. (learn)
5 I .... making dinner by the time you arrive. (finish)
6 By the time you count to 20 everyone .... ! (disappear)

4 Complete the sentences with the future continuous or the future perfect.

read   eat   recover   finish   use   feel

1 By six tomorrow morning, I .... my night shift.
2 You .... a bit confused about the state of our relationship, I'm sure.
3 .... you .... the documents later?
4 I'm sure he .... from his cold in a week's time.
5 Nobody .... this computer this morning.
6 I .... certainly .... my lunch by two o'clock.

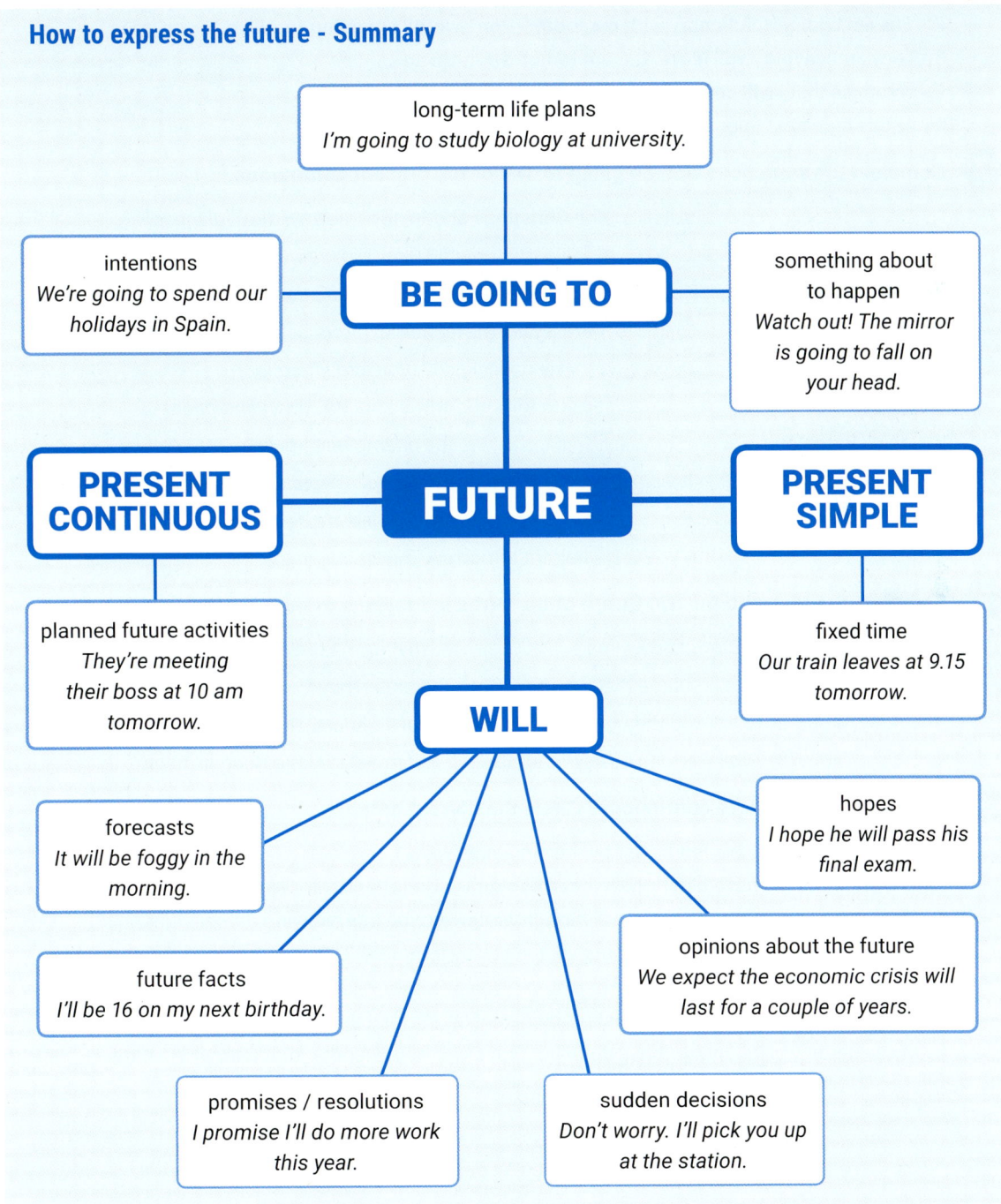

How to express the future - Summary

FUTURE

BE GOING TO
- long-term life plans
  I'm going to study biology at university.
- intentions
  We're going to spend our holidays in Spain.
- something about to happen
  Watch out! The mirror is going to fall on your head.

PRESENT CONTINUOUS
- planned future activities
  They're meeting their boss at 10 am tomorrow.

PRESENT SIMPLE
- fixed time
  Our train leaves at 9.15 tomorrow.

WILL
- forecasts
  It will be foggy in the morning.
- future facts
  I'll be 16 on my next birthday.
- promises / resolutions
  I promise I'll do more work this year.
- sudden decisions
  Don't worry. I'll pick you up at the station.
- opinions about the future
  We expect the economic crisis will last for a couple of years.
- hopes
  I hope he will pass his final exam.

ROUND UP 15

1 **Circle the correct option.**

1. We think our team **will win** / **is winning** the competition tomorrow.
2. 'Mum's case is heavy.' '**I'm carrying** / **I'll carry** it for her.'
3. The sun **is going to set** / **will set** at 5.37 tomorrow afternoon.
4. 'What time **do you meet** / **are you meeting** Mr Norton?' 'We **meet** / **are meeting** at 9.30 tomorrow morning.'
5. Dan! The buzzer went! **Will you open** / **Are you opening** the door, please?
6. I don't think computers **are going to** / **will** replace teachers in the future.
7. 'I haven't got my dictionary with me today.' 'Don't worry! **I'm going to** / **I'll** give you mine.'
8. They **are leaving** / **will leave** at 8 am tomorrow morning.
9. I promise that I **will come** / **am coming** and see you soon.
10. At this time next Sunday, we will **lie** / **be lying** on a beach in Greece.

2 **Complete the sentences with *be going to*, *will* or the present continuous.**

1. I .... the Christmas shopping tomorrow. (do) *[planned]*
2. .... at the party tonight? (you, be) *[intention]*
3. It .... later this evening. (rain) *[prediction]*
4. I .... here again. (never come) *[promise]*
5. What .... next weekend? (you, do) *[intention]*
6. I .... tickets for tomorrow's concert. (buy) *[intention]*
7. I think Barcelona .... the championship. (win) *[prediction]*
8. Jane .... to Rio for the holidays. (fly) *[planned]*
9. I .... you at 5 pm. (meet) *[immediate decision]*
10. I .... a haircut tomorrow. (have) *[planned]*

3 **Complete the text with the *will* future of the verbs in brackets in the simple or continuous form.**

Tomorrow at this time, Steve and Emma ¹.................... (fly) from London to Hong Kong. It ².................... (be) the first time that they have been to China. They ³.................... (leave) Heathrow Airport at 10 am and they ⁴.................... (fly) for 12 hours. At 11 am, they ⁵.................... (fly) over Germany. They ⁶.................... (arrive) in Hong Kong at 10 pm.

4 **Future perfect or future continuous? Circle the correct option.**

1. Will I **be feeling** / **have felt** better by this time next week?
2. The students will **have used** / **have been using** the computer lab for two hours by ten o'clock.
3. The human resources manager will **have interviewed** / **be interviewing** James right now.
4. 'Will you **have finished** / **be finishing** your essay by tomorrow?' 'Yes, I'll hand it in tomorrow morning.'
5. The kids won't **be eating** / **have eaten** their lunch at 11 am. Lunch break starts at 12 pm.
6. My daughter will **be doing** / **have done** her first exam at university tomorrow at this time.

5 Circle the correct option.

1. There's no milk left, Paul. ……… some when you're in town?
   A Are you getting   B Will you get   C Are you going to get

2. Here are the tickets. We have to run. The train ……… in two minutes.
   A will have left   B is going to leave   C is leaving

3. I've got an appointment with the dentist. I ……… him at ten o'clock tomorrow morning.
   A am going to see   B am seeing   C will see

4. I talked to the manager last week, and we ……… again tomorrow.
   A talk   B will have talked   C are going to talk

5. ……… to Australia, or haven't they decided yet?
   A Do they move   B They will move   C Are they going to move

6. It's nice weather, so I think we ……… to the beach next weekend.
   A will go   B would go   C are going

7. I must go. The children ……… home from school soon.
   A will have come   B are going to come   C will be coming

8. I ……… some food for you in the fridge.
   A will leave   B will have left   C will be left

9. Please call back after 11. He ……… before then.
   A will be back   B won't be back   C is not being back

10. He needs to go to bed early. He ……… for at least 12 hours tomorrow.
    A will have driven   B will be driven   C will be driving

6 Write a dialogue following the instructions below.

You	………………………………………………………………………………
	Ask Susan what she's going to do next summer.
Susan	………………………………………………………………………………
	Go to Cannes and attend a French course.
You	………………………………………………………………………………
	Ask how long she's going to stay there.
Susan	………………………………………………………………………………
	Three weeks. Suggests going too.
You	………………………………………………………………………………
	You can't. Working this summer.
Susan	………………………………………………………………………………
	Asks you what you're going to do and where.
You	………………………………………………………………………………
	Receptionist in a hotel in Geneva.
Susan	………………………………………………………………………………
	Says she will bring a present from Cannes.

MATRIX +

Future in the past: was / were going to

The **future in the past** is used to express a past intention that was either not realised, or about which we don't know whether it was realised or not → *I was going to sell my house last year, but then I changed my mind. When I last saw you, you were going to move to London. Have you moved there yet?*

The negative form (**wasn't / weren't going to**) expresses the idea that we weren't intending to do something or we didn't want to do something which then happened anyway → *I wasn't going to see her again, but she insisted on getting together one more time.*

When we ask about someone else's intentions, we can use the negative-interrogative form → *'Weren't they going to leave yesterday?' 'Yes, they were. But they didn't. They're leaving today.'*

> We can also use **would** + base form of the verb to express **future in the past** in indirect speech
> *They said they would leave the next day. = They said they were going to leave the next day.*
> (see page 351)

7 Write the second sentence so that it has the same meaning as the first one. Use *was / were going to*.

1 Sarah wanted to be an actress when she was younger.
....

2 I did not intend to study abroad.
....

3 They wanted to share their flat with a friend.
....

4 We had an appointment for the next day, but he didn't turn up.
....

5 We wanted to have the party at the local Youth Club, but it was not available.
....

6 It looked as if it would rain last night, but it didn't .
....

8 Read the text and circle the correct option.

Sometimes I look at my two teenage children and I wonder what they will [1] **do / be doing** in ten years' time. Will they [2] **have worked / be working** or will they [3] **be / being** unemployed? [4] **Will / Are** they still be living in England or will they [5] **have moved / have been moved** to some other country? [6] **Will they be / Are they** married? And [7] **are they having / will they have** any children? In about five years' time, they will [8] **be finishing / have finished** secondary school and they will [9] **be thinking / have thought** about their future. Will they look for a job or will they go to university? I hope at least one of them [10] **will decide / is deciding** to study medicine, but I don't think either will [11] **want / be wanting** to follow their father's example. The important thing is that they [12] **will / want** realize their dreams, whatever they are. And what about me? What will I [13] **be / have** doing in ten years' time? I hope I will [14] **have worked / be working** less than now. And I hope I [15] **will / won't** have time to travel to America, just like I was going to do when I was young. But then I got married and had two children... and all the big travelling plans had to be postponed!

FAQ

Q: I heard the expression It's gonna be alright in a song. What does it mean?

A: **Gonna** is a non-standard form of American English used in place of **going to...**, so the sentence means 'everything will be OK, it will work out fine'. Contractions like **gonna**, **wanna** (**want to**) and **gotta** (**have got to**) should, however, be avoided in writing.

9 Four of these sentences contain a mistake. Find them and rewrite them correctly.

1 Tomorrow at this time I'll hiking in the Alps.
   ....
2 You needn't worry. Whatever will be, will be.
   ....
3 I hope my children will have been leaving in a peaceful world.
   ....
4 The sea level will be steadily risen in the next fifty years.
   ....
5 The glaciers will melt if the temperature keeps rising.
   ....
6 'Are you taking an early train tomorrow morning?' 'Yes, I'm leaving at 6.30.'
   ....
7 'What will you have done in ten years' time?' 'I hope I'll be working in the marketing field.'
   ....
8 'Are all your students going to study Art next year?' 'No, some are going to take up a musical instrument.'
   ....

Reflecting on grammar

Reflect on the rules and say whether the following statements are true or false.

		True	False
1	The future can be expressed both with the **present continuous** and the **present simple**, but only in certain cases.		
2	Future intention is expressed with **be going to...** + base form of the verb.		
3	The word order in the sentence *He probably will come with me* is correct.		
4	The negative form of **I will pay** is **I willn't pay** or **I'll not pay**.		
5	To express a promise or our own opinion or prediction about the future, we usually use the **will future**.		
6	The sentence *We will have finished our report between three weeks' time* is correct.		
7	*I will be having dinner in Madrid tomorrow at this time* is a sentence with the **future perfect**.		
8	For a spontaneous decision taken at the moment of speaking, we usually use the **will future**.		
9	The sentence *Our coach leaves at 7 tomorrow morning* is correct.		
10	**Shall** can replace **will** in the third person singular of the future, but this is not a common use in today's English.		

MODALS AND OTHER VERBS: COMMUNICATIVE FUNCTIONS

Revision table

obligation or necessity	lack of necessity	prohibition
We must study hard. We have to study hard. We've got to study hard. We need to study hard. We had to study hard last year. We'll have to study hard next year.	We don't have to study hard. We don't need to study hard. We needn't study hard. We didn't have to study hard last year. We won't have to study hard next year.	You mustn't talk in the library. You can't talk in the library. Don't talk in the library. No talking in the library.
advice	**deduction**	**requests for instructions**
You should study hard. You ought to study hard. You had better study hard. You shouldn't worry about the exam.	It must be late. It can't be late. It should be easy. It ought to be easy. It might be easy.	What shall I do? What should I do? What can we do? Shall we turn right or left?
offers of help	**ability**	**possibility**
Shall I help you? Can I help you? Could I help you? I'd like to help you. Do you want me to help you? Let me help you! I'll help you!	I can ski. I could ski when I was young. I can't ride a horse. I couldn't ride a horse last year. I wasn't able to break his record. I'm afraid I won't be able to break his record.	I can go out tonight. (there's no problem) I may go out tonight. (it's possible) I might go out tonight. (I'm not sure) I'm likely to go out tonight. (it's probable) The odds are that I'm going out tonight. (colloquial)
permission	**requests (to have something)**	**requests (for others to do something)**
Can I go now? Could I go now? May I go now? You can go now. You may go now. I wasn't allowed to go. They didn't let me go. I'm sure I will be allowed to go. I'm sure they will let me go.	Can I have a cola, please? Could I have a cola, please? I'd like (to have) a cola. I want a cola.	Will you come here, please? Can you come here? Could you come here? Do you mind coming here? Would you mind coming here? I'd like you to come here. I want you to come here right now!
offers	**suggestions and proposals**	**wants and preferences**
Will you have a cola? Would you have a cola? Would you like a cola? Do you want a cola? How / What about a cola? Have a cola!	Shall we go to the park? Should we go to the park? Let's go to the park. How / What about going to the park? Why don't we go to the park? Would you like to go to the park?	I want to go home. I'd like to go home. I wish I could go home. If only I could go home. I'd prefer to go home. I'd rather go home (than stay here).

MODALS AND OTHER VERBS: TENSES

Revision table

can, could, be able to (ability)

Present simple	Past simple	Future
can / can't am / is / are able to 'm not / isn't / aren't able to	could / couldn't was / were able to wasn't / weren't able to	will be able to won't be able to
Present perfect have / has been able to haven't / hasn't been able to	**Past perfect** had been able to hadn't been able to	**Future perfect** will have been able to won't have been able to
Conditional could / couldn't would / wouldn't be able to	**Past conditional** could have / couldn't have would have / wouldn't have been able to	

may, might, be allowed to (possibility, permission)

Present simple	Past simple	Future
may / may not am / is / are allowed to 'm not / isn't / aren't allowed to	was / were allowed to wasn't / weren't allowed to	will be allowed to won't be allowed to
Present perfect have / has been allowed to haven't / hasn't been allowed to	**Past perfect** had been allowed to hadn't been allowed to	**Future perfect** will have been allowed to won't have been allowed to
Conditional might / might not would / wouldn't be allowed to	**Past conditional** might have / might not have would have been / wouldn't have been allowed to	

must, have (got) to, need, be compelled to, be obliged to, should (obligation, necessity, advice)

Present simple	Past simple	Future
must / mustn't need / needn't don't / doesn't need to have / has (got) to haven't / hasn't got to don't / doesn't have to	had to didn't have to didn't need to was / were compelled / obliged to wasn't / weren't compelled / obliged to	will have to won't have to will be compelled / obliged to won't be compelled / obliged to
Present perfect have / has been compelled to have / has been obliged to haven't / hasn't been compelled to haven't / hasn't been obliged to	**Past perfect** had been compelled to had been obliged to hadn't been compelled to hadn't been obliged to	**Future perfect** will have had to won't have had to will have been compelled / obliged to won't have been compelled / obliged to
Conditional should / shouldn't would have to wouldn't have to	**Past conditional** should have / shouldn't have would have had to wouldn't have had to	

Revision and Exams 5 (UNITS 13 – 14 – 15)

1 Complete the text with the verbs below.

wouldn't like   studying   needs   would like   wants to   be allowed   she's going to apply
has   she's going to learn   would prefer   she'd rather go   would like her

Jeanine ¹.................................. to work for a charity after university. That's why she's currently ².................................. at the faculty of International Studies in Aberdeen, Scotland. She's in her second year. This year ³.................................. for a scholarship to spend six months in another country. She ⁴.................................. to go to an English-speaking country because she ⁵.................................. learn a new language; ⁶.................................. to East Asia, possibly Japan, because she loves Japanese culture and ⁷.................................. Japanese. If she can't go to Asia, her second choice is America – she ⁸.................................. to go to South America rather than North America. And if she ⁹.................................. to stay in Europe, she hopes she'll ¹⁰.................................. to study in Greece. Jeanine's parents ¹¹.................................. to continue her studies in Scotland near home, but she really ¹².................................. to be independent.

2 🎧14 Complete the dialogue with the future *will* or *going to* form of the verbs in brackets. Then listen and check.

Nicole Guess what! I ¹.................................. (have) a job interview tomorrow morning at ten.
Lindsey Really? Where?
Nicole At Debenhams – you know, the big department store in the centre of town.
Lindsey Great! Have you thought about the questions they ².................................. (ask) you?
Nicole Not really, but I ³.................................. (answer) them honestly.
Lindsey They ⁴.................................. (probably – ask) you why you want the job.
Nicole Well, that's okay. I ⁵.................................. (tell) them I want the job because I like selling things. I'm the right person for them.
Lindsey Good! It sounds as if you ⁶.................................. (be) fine. I'm sure you ⁷.................................. (get) the job!

3 🎧15 This is part of the interview Nicole had. Complete the dialogue with the verbs in brackets following the indications. Then listen and check.

Manager You know you ¹.................................. (deal – **will** *future continuous*) with customers, so you ².................................. (have to – **will** *future simple*) be polite and patient with all of them.
Nicole Sure, I know. ³.................................. (I – have to – **will** *future*) wear a uniform?
Manager Yes, you ⁴.................................. (have to – **will** *future*) wear a suit.
Nicole ⁵.................................. (I – have to – **will** *future*) buy it myself?
Manager No, we'll buy it for you, but you will need to try it on.
Nicole ⁶.................................. (I – have to – **will** *future*) work at weekends?
Manager You ⁷.................................. (have to – **will** *future*) work only one weekend per month. ⁸.................................. (you – work – *past simple*) weekends in your previous job?
Nicole Yes, I ⁹.................................. (work – *past simple*) every second Sunday, but I didn't mind it.

4 Read this conversation between two colleagues. Complete the dialogue with the appropriate form and tense of *must*, *have*, *need* or *want*.

Ryan ¹............................ you .... to go to Bristol again on Friday, Patricia?

Patricia No, I ²............................ to relax a bit, so I'm taking Friday off. But Mr Paisley ³............................ me to go to New York for the annual conference next week, so I ⁴............................ prepare for that.

Ryan I've prepared most of the documents. ⁵............................ you .... me to prepare the slides for you?

Patricia You ⁶............................ to. The presentation is ready. What I still ⁷............................ to do is to get some dollars from the bank.

Ryan And you ⁸............................ forget your passport! Last time you went to the States, I ⁹............................ to rush to the airport to bring it to you.

Patricia You're right. And I ¹⁰............................ to get a visa too. By the way, ¹¹............................ I .... to sign the documents before I leave?

Ryan Yes, but you ¹²............................ to do it now.

Preliminary (PET) | Reading Part 1

5 Look at the text in each section. What does it say? Mark the correct letter A, B or C.

ALL VISITORS
You must return your headphones to the counter at the end of the tour.

1. A Visitors can take the equipment home.
   B Visitors have to give the equipment back when they've finished using it.
   C Visitors must return to the hall after the tour.

This car park is for use on weekdays only during the bank working hours.

2. A Cars can be parked here on Sunday mornings.
   B This car park is locked at night.
   C This car park can be used only by the bank staff.

ROADWORKS AHEAD
Take the first road on the right and follow the arrows.

3. A You must follow the road ahead of you.
   B You must keep to the right side of the road.
   C You are obliged to make a detour because of roadworks.

The elevator to the roof garden is out of order. Please use the next free one to the 19th floor, then climb the last flight of stairs.

4. A You must use the stairs from the ground floor to go to the roof garden.
   B There's only one lift going straight to the roof garden and it doesn't work.
   C There's only one lift in this place.

Doug, Peter and I must finish some urgent work tonight. Can we play squash on Saturday? Could you tell Dave too?
Larry

5. A Larry can't play squash today, but Peter can.
   B Doug would like to play squash on Saturday.
   C Larry was supposed to play with Doug and two more people.

Preliminary (PET) | Reading Part 5

6 Read the text and choose the correct word (A, B, C or D) for each space.

From next week, life⁰..C.. very different for Mark Lampard. On Monday, he ¹...... his new job as a stunt man. Mark's really excited, even if he knows it's ²...... a dangerous job. Mark knows he ³...... nervous at first, but he ⁴...... to it. In a few weeks, he ⁵...... to start work on film sets – he could soon be the man you ⁶...... flying through a window or jumping from an aeroplane wearing James Bond's clothes! In September, he ⁷...... in a TV series, so you ⁸...... definitely see him then. Mark has chosen a risky career – but he hopes it ⁹...... challenging and interesting. One thing he can probably be sure of is that the job ¹⁰...... boring.

0	A is going to be	B is being	C will be	D is
1	A start	B is starting	C going to start	D will starting
2	A being	B going to be	C will be	D is going to be
3	A feels	B is feeling	C to feel	D will be feeling
4	A will be look forward	B is looking forward	C look forward	D is look forward
5	A is going	B will be	C will be going	D will
6	A going to see	B are seeing	C see	D have seen
7	A will appearing	B is appearing	C is going appear	D appear
8	A are	B do	C have	D will
9	A is being	B will have been	C will be	D will going to be
10	A isn't	B won't be	C doesn't	D not

First (FCE) | Reading and Use of English Part 4

7 Complete the second sentence so that it has a similar meaning to the first using the given word. Do not change the given word. You must use between two and five words including the given word. Here's an example.

0 The train from Glasgow will arrive in ten minutes.

   DUE   The train from Glasgow .....*is due to*.................. arrive in ten minutes.

1 By this time tomorrow, he will be in hospital.

   GONE   By this time tomorrow, he .... into hospital.

2 My dentist's appointment is at 11 tomorrow.

   SEEING   I .... the dentist at 11 tomorrow.

3 Your temperature will have gone down to normal by this evening.

   HAVE   You .... a temperature by this evening.

4 You should wear warmer clothes. It's cold today.

   TO   You .... wear warmer clothes. It's cold today.

5 Shall I go to the market to buy some fruit, Jenny?

   WANT   .... go to the market to buy some fruit, Jenny?

6 Our bus won't arrive for another 20 minutes. Let's have some coffee while we're waiting.

   DUE   Our bus .... for another 20 minutes. Let's have some coffee while we're waiting.

7 You ought not to sunbathe in the middle of the day.

   BETTER   You .... in the middle of the day.

8 Accidents will happen for sure if people drive so fast on icy roads.
   BOUND   Accidents .... if people drive so fast on icy roads.

9 Jason used to organise trips out with his friends when he was a teenager.
   WOULD   Jason .... with his friends when he was a teenager.

10 I would prefer to stay at home tonight because I'm very tired.
   RATHER .... at home tonight because I'm very tired.

11 There's no need to go to work this coming Sunday.
   HAVE   We .... to work this coming Sunday.

12 Perhaps I'll visit my German friends next summer.
   MIGHT   .... my German friends next summer.

13 It's impossible that that girl is Tom's sister. She left for New York two days ago.
   BE   That girl .... sister. She left for New York two days ago.

14 That man's very likely to be Ben's father. He looks very much like him.
   MUST   That man .... He looks very much like him.

First (FCE) | Writing Part 1

8 You and a Swedish friend of yours are interested in a summer job abroad. A friend of yours in England has sent you an email with some information about a summer camp in the USA and you've found an advert about a summer camp in the south of France. Read both texts and, using all the information, write an email to your Swedish friend. Describe the differences between the two jobs, say what your preference is and ask for your friend's opinion.

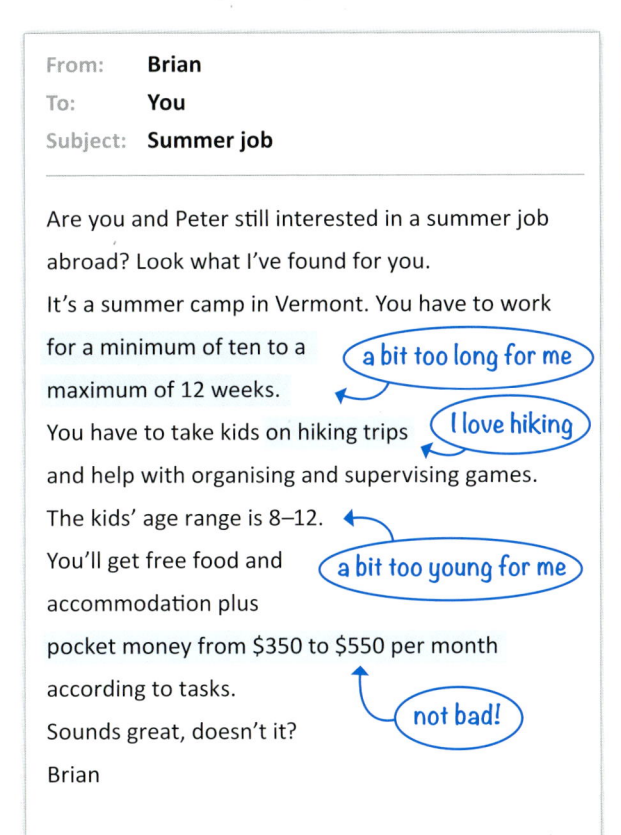

From: **Brian**
To: **You**
Subject: **Summer job**

Are you and Peter still interested in a summer job abroad? Look what I've found for you.
It's a summer camp in Vermont. You have to work for a minimum of ten to a maximum of 12 weeks. *(a bit too long for me)*
You have to take kids on hiking trips *(I love hiking)* and help with organising and supervising games.
The kids' age range is 8–12. *(a bit too young for me)*
You'll get free food and accommodation plus pocket money from $350 to $550 per month according to tasks. *(not bad!)*
Sounds great, doesn't it?
Brian

Le Pomier – Grenoble

Do you want to work during the summer and improve your French?

Do you like life in the open air? join us and pick fruit for six weeks. *(shorter period – better for me)* You'll get free food and accommodation on our farm, plus evening entertainment. *(good!)* 40€ pocket money per week. *(not much – but there aren't many expenses)* Free excursions on Sundays.

Towards Competences

1 You are part of the Students' School Council for your school. You have the job of writing the international section of your school's website and preparing a web page in English which gives a summary of your school rules. Write about 180 words.

2 To prepare for the school exchange, you need to explain to your partner school abroad what eco-behaviour rules students must observe in your school. Make a poster in which you list what you can and cannot do in terms of respect for the environment, for example, the separation of rubbish, energy-saving measures, etc.

Self Check 5

Circle the correct option. Then check your answers at the end of the book.

1 Students ……… park their cars in the teachers' car park.
  A might not   B can't   C don't are allowed

2 Jim ……… swim when he was four years old.
  A may have not   B could have not
  C couldn't

3 ……… to wear mini-skirts at your school?
  A Are you allowed   B Can you
  C Ought you

4 That woman ……… be the new receptionist. They said she was short with brown hair, like her.
  A can't   B must   C may not

5 Listen to this song. It ……… be an old Rolling Stones' song. This is Mick Jagger's voice.
  A can't   B mustn't   C must

6 You look very tired. You ……… go to bed earlier, Tom.
  A ought   B should   C may

7 This story ……… be true. There are too many strange coincidences.
  A must   B may   C can't

8 ……… we leave the room as soon as we finish the test?
  A May   B Ought   C Will

9 Join us for a pizza tonight, ……… ?
  A will you   B would you like
  C you would

10 ……… to watch an action film or the football match?
  A Would you   B Would you like
  C Will you

11 I wish ……… that girl's name.
  A I remember   B I was remembering
  C I could remember

12 I wish ……… so much time in my youth and studied more.
  A I wasted   B I hadn't wasted
  C I couldn't waste

13 Stop lying, John. You ……… tell her the truth!
  A have   B must   C will must

14 'What ……… for this exam?' 'Read ten novels by various authors.'
  A do we have to do
  B must we have to do
  C have we got do

15 You ……… bring your sleeping bags. There's bed linen at the hostel.
  A don't have to   B need   C don't have

16 You ……… play video games for such a long time. It's bad for your health.
  A don't have   B needn't to
  C shouldn't

17 You ……… bring so many clothes with you. We'll only be away for three days.
  A needn't   B mustn't   C don't need

18 He's ……… a great career. He's so clever!
  A bound to have   B due to have
  C forced to have

286

19 I .... Karen £20. I must remember to give it back to her.
   A due   B owe   C shall

20 You really .... read this novel. It's so gripping.
   A need   B are bound to   C must

21 The train to Glasgow is .... to arrive in 20 minutes.
   A owing   B due   C bound

22 The flood has caused a lot of damage. We .... to help the people in the village.
   A had better   B ought   C should

23 We .... finish this essay by tomorrow. The deadline is next Monday.
   A mustn't   B don't need
   C don't have to

24 Visitors .... have their mobiles on in the museum.
   A mustn't   B aren't due to
   C don't need

25 Only staff members .... beyond this door.
   A are bound   B are allowed
   C are due

26 My father .... 60 next November.
   A is going be   B going to be
   C will be

27 '......... work abroad after your degree?' 'I think so, but I' haven't planned anything yet.'
   A Are you going to   B Are you
   C Will you be

28 'What time .... the sales manager, Emma?' 'At 10.30, Ms Dell.'
   A am I meeting   B will I meeting
   C meet I

29 Watch out! That vase .... to fall off the shelf.
   A will   B ought   C is going

30 '......... early tomorrow?' 'Yes, my flight is at eight.'
   A Leave you   B Are you leaving
   C Do you leave

31 Look at those black clouds. ....
   A It will rain.   B It's going to rain.
   C It's raining.

32 .... write this essay. It's far too difficult for me.
   A I'm not going to   B I'm not able
   C I won't going to

33 I'm sure .... a great day out. The weather is gorgeous today.
   A it is being   B it won't be
   C it's going to be

34 I think .... record our next album in a couple of weeks.
   A we'll   B we're   C we'll be

35 We're so happy! Tomorrow at this time .... to the Caribbean.
   A we'll fly   B we're flying
   C we'll be flying

36 Tom .... his degree by this time next year.
   A will take   B will have taken
   C is going to take

37 By the time I finish work tomorrow, the shops ....
   A will close   B are going to close
   C will have closed

38 Next summer .... an English course in Cambridge. I need to improve my speaking.
   A I'm going to attend
   B I'm being attending
   C I'll have attended

39 Can you imagine? This time next Saturday, ... my favourite musical in Broadway.
   A I watch   B I'll be watching
   C I'll have watch

40 The Rolling Stones .... on tour in France next summer.
   A will may be   B are   C will be

Assess Yourself!

☐ **0 – 10**   Study harder. Use the online exercises to help you.

☐ **11 – 20**   OK. Use the online exercises to practise things you don't know.

☐ **21 – 30**   Good, but do some extra practice online.

☐ **31 – 40**   Excellent!

GRAMMAR MATRIX MAIN

UNIT 16 Conditional sentences and *if*-clauses

LESSON 1 Present and past conditionals

Present conditional

The **present conditional** is formed with the modal verb *would* and the base form of the verb.
Positive: *I would talk / I'd talk to him.*
Negative: *I would not talk / I wouldn't talk to him.*
Interrogative and short answers: 'Would you talk to him?' 'Yes, I would. / No, I wouldn't.'
Wh- questions: 'What would you tell him?' 'I'd tell him to be patient.'

1 Reorder the words and write sentences in the present conditional.

1 you / Would / go / swimming pool / the / me / with / to / ?
....
2 would / It / better / be / to / at / stay / today / home / .
....
3 try / white-water / would / rafting / Jim / not.
....
4 kayaking / I / go / in / wouldn't / weather / this / .
....
5 lay / you / me / the / table / Would / help / ?
....
6 really / steep / you / climb / Would / a / mountain face / ?
....

2 Complete the sentences with *would / wouldn't* and the verbs below. (+ positive sentences / − negative sentences).

do (x2)   help   be   accept   say

1 .... you .... me with this project? (−)
2 There's nothing I .... for you. (−)
3 I .... it's a good plan. (+)
4 .... you .... that for me? (+)
5 It .... better for you to learn a second language. (+)
6 I .... that job. (−)

Future in the past

Would + base form of the verb is often used in a secondary clause that follows a main clause with a verb in the **past simple**, for example: *I knew (that) he would come.*
This construction is referred to as **future in the past**. (See Unit 19 Lesson 3, page 351).
Compare:

Present + *will*... (future)	Past + *would*... (future in the past)
I hope it will be sunny.	I hoped it would be sunny.
She says she will help me.	She said she would help me.
I'm sure I'll have a good time.	I was sure I would have a good time.

See also page 278 for an alternative way of expressing the future in the past: **was / were going to...**
She said she was going to help me.

3 Change the tense of the sentences from present to past as in the example.

0 I'm sure Mum will like the idea of eating out.
   I was sure Mum would like the idea of eating out.

1 I hope they will arrive for the beginning of the film.
   ....

2 They promise they will call round this week.
   ....

3 Ann thinks she'll take up rowing.
   ....

4 They know they'll need a lot of training before going trekking in Nepal.
   ....

5 Tom says he will look for a new job soon.
   ....

6 We know they will fight for their rights.
   ....

7 Luke says he will invite us to try kayaking.
   ....

8 Jim promises he will have a haircut before the wedding.
   ....

Past conditionals

Past conditionals are formed with the modal verb *would* + *have* + the past participle of the verb.
Positive: *I would have gone. / I'd have gone.*
Negative: *I would not have gone. / I wouldn't have gone.*
Interrogative and short answers: *'Would you have gone?' 'Yes, I would. / No, I wouldn't.'*
Wh- questions: *'Where would you have gone?' 'To your house.'*

Conditional forms of modal verbs

The present conditional and the past conditional of modal verbs have the following constructions:

Present conditional	Past conditional
Could + base form	*Could have* + past participle
You could do better than this.	You could have done better than this.
Might + base form	*Might have* + past participle
They might arrive late.	They might have arrived late.
Should + base form	*Should have* + past participle
You should listen to me.	You should have listened to me.
Would like to + base form	*Would have liked to* + base form
I would like to see you.	I would have liked to see you.
	Also: *Would like to have* + past participle
	I would like to have seen you.

4 Rewrite the sentences using the past conditional.

1 We'd like to go shopping. ....
2 I might attend a German course. ....
3 Would you spend all that money on a pair of shoes? ....
4 You should be more careful. ....
5 They could run faster. ....
6 I wouldn't drive so fast. ....
7 We might buy a new car after the summer. ....
8 They could call after the match. ....

5 Complete the sentences with the correct form of the verbs below.

tell   take   like   arrive   put off   rest   be   go

1 I think my brother might .... paragliding. I'll tell him about the course.
2 I could have .... part in the tennis tournament because I play quite well.
3 They may .... the conference to next week.
4 You could have .... me that the bank had already closed.
5 I might .... to the beach next Sunday. Would you like to come?
6 You should .... more. You look very tired.
7 They must have .... late. I didn't see them before the show.
8 You should .... quite careful when going horseriding.

Modal verb + *be* + *–ing* form of the verb

We use this 'continuous' form to express what we could, might, must should or would be doing in a particular moment of the present or future:

Don't call her now. She might be working at this time.

Why are you standing out here? You should be having your history lesson.

What a noise! My brother must be playing the drums again.

If it weren't so cold, I would be swimming in the outdoor pool.

---

6 Complete the sentences with the continuous form of the verbs in brackets.

1 He should .... , not sleeping at this time. (work)
2 If she had taken my advice, she could .... abroad now. (study)
3 What's that you said? You must .... ! (joke)
4 They aren't here yet. That's strange. They should .... for us. (wait)
5 If I didn't have to work today, I would .... to London to meet my girlfriend. (travel)
6 They might .... the match. (win)
7 'Where's Jenny?' 'At work. She should .... coffee behind the bar at this time.' (serve)
8 There's nobody in the office. They must all .... lunch in the cafeteria. (have)

LESSON 2 Type 0 and Type 1 conditional sentences

To express the concept: 'What happens / will happen / would happen / would have happened, if…', we use a conditional sentence made up of a conditional subordinate clause, or *if* **clause**, and a **main clause**. We make a hypothesis in the *if* **clause**, and in the **main clause** we express the consequence of that hypothesis.

We use different tenses in both clauses according to the level of probability of the situation.

FAQ

Q: In a grammar lesson, the teacher had defined the subordinate clause and the main clause using terminology that I don't remember…

A: The protasis and the apodosis. The *if* **clause** is the protasis, the **main clause** is the apodosis.

There are four types of conditional sentence, conventionally called **Type 0**, **Type 1**, **Type 2** and **Type 3**.

Type 0

In a Type 0 conditional sentence, also called **zero conditional**, we give a condition which, when fulfilled, will have a consequence that is certain. In this case, the tense is the **present simple** in both parts of the sentence:

If clause	Main clause
If + present simple	present simple
If you book your flight in advance,	*you get a discount.*

> **!** If the *if* **clause** precedes the **main clause**, we usually insert a comma between the two clauses. Here's a good example: *If the 'if clause' comes first, you usually insert a comma between the two.*

The *if* **clause** can also follow the main clause: *You get a discount if you book your flight in advance.* In this case, there is no comma.

A zero conditional sentence is used:

- to express universal truths, rules and scientific laws

    The climate gets colder if you go north towards the Arctic Circle.

    If you add –ed to a regular verb, you get the past simple.

    In cases like these, the conjunction *if* can be replaced by **when**, precisely because we are talking about facts which have general validity, and occur each time: *The climate gets colder when you go north.*

    When you add -ed to a regular verb, you get the past simple.

- to give advice and say what to do if… In this case, the main clause has a verb in the imperative form or contains the modals **can** or **may**:

    Get something to eat if you're hungry. (Also: *You can / You may get something…*)

    If you see Ben, give him this book, please.

    You may stay here if you like.

1 Match the sentence halves.

1. Go to bed early
2. Don't eat too many sweet things
3. Don't stand under a tree
4. Don't behave like that
5. Buy a new squash racket
6. Watch this film
7. Wear a warm jacket
8. Meet us at 8 pm in the bus station

A if you want to lose weight.
B if you want to learn more about the war in Iraq.
C if your old one is broken.
D if you want to go hiking tomorrow morning.
E if you go out. It's cold!
F if you want to go to the cinema.
G if you're out in a storm.
H if you want to have a lot of friends.

1 ..... 2 ..... 3 ..... 4 ..... 5 ..... 6 ..... 7 ..... 8 .....

2 Complete the sentences with the verbs below in the present simple.

get   feel   tell   show   improve   buy   like   open

1. If you read a lot, your vocabulary .... and so does your mind!
2. If you cycle fast, the display .... how many calories you are burning.
3. Buy that funny hat if you really .... it.
4. If you .... two large tacos, you get a third one free.
5. If you key in your password, the program ....
6. If you buy the tickets online, you .... a 5% discount.
7. Go to bed if you .... tired.
8. If they ask you, you can .... them what happened.

Type 1

In a Type 1 conditional sentence, also called **first conditional**, we describe a real possibility: given a certain condition, it is certain or probable that a consequence will occur. In this case, the tenses are the **present simple** in the *if* clause and the future with *will* in the main clause:

If clause	*Main* clause
If + present simple	**will** future
If you study hard,	you will pass your exam.

Here are other examples, with the **main clause** before and after the *if* clause:

If you listen to this song, you will like it.
I'll go with him if he lets me.

Focus

In English, we must use the present tense in the *if* clause, and not the future with *will*. This is usually the present simple tense, although we can sometimes find the present continuous, too → *If you're staying overnight, I'll find you a room.*

In the **main clause**, instead of the *will* future, we can also find the modal verb **can** (if something is possible) or **may** (if something is probable but not certain) → *You can get anything you want if you work hard for it.   If you go on foot, you may arrive late.*

3 Complete the sentences with the correct form of the verbs in brackets.

1 If it .... , I .... to the shops. (rain, not go)
2 We .... a barbecue on Sunday if it .... (have, not rain)
3 Okay, I .... my hair cut short if you .... me to. (not have, not want)
4 He .... anything for you if you just .... him. (do, ask)
5 We .... on a cruise next summer if we .... a good offer. (go, find)
6 If you .... all your money on sweets, you .... any left to buy clothes. (spend, not have)
7 If you .... now, you .... home by ten. (leave, get)
8 If you .... , you .... to pass your test. (not study, not be able)
9 If they .... on time, we .... to the cinema together. (come, go)
10 The old apple tree .... on the house if the wind .... blowing like this. (fall, keep)

4 Type 0 or Type 1? Complete the sentences with the correct form of the verbs in brackets.

1 If you .... to bully your classmates, I .... to suspend you. (continue, be obliged)
2 If you .... me by your side, I .... right there! (need, be)
3 If she .... in the next race, I .... and see her. (compete, go)
4 If it .... hard tonight, we .... to school tomorrow. (snow, not go)
5 If you .... blue and yellow, you .... green. (mix, get)
6 Dad .... angry if I .... home late tonight. (be, get)
7 If it .... raining, we .... for a walk in the park. (stop, go)
8 Flowers .... if you .... them enough water. (die, not give)
9 If you .... at the sun without filtering lenses, your eyes .... damaged. (look, get)
10 You .... into trouble if you .... your homework. (get, not do)

LESSON 3 Type 2 and Type 3 conditional sentences

Type 2

In Type 2 conditional sentences, also called **second conditional**, we express an improbable condition, which is unlikely to come true, or an imaginary condition, which is different from the current situation or facts.
In this case, the tenses used are the **past simple** in the *if* clause and *would* + base form in the **main clause**.

If clause	Main clause
If + past simple,	**would** + base form
If we had more time,	*we would stop for a rest.*

The sentence above implies the fact that we do not have more time at present, therefore we will not stop for a rest.

Look at other examples:

'What would you do if you won ten million dollars?' (winning the money is a highly improbable hypothesis) *'I don't really know what I would do with all that money!'*

Your results would improve if you trained every day. (different conditions from factual reality: now you are not training every day)

> In a type 2 conditional sentence, the verb **be** has one form only, **were**, for all persons (If I / you / he / she / it / we / you / they were…). But in an informal register, we can use the form **was** with **I / he / she / it**, and **were** for the other persons → *She would be happier if she was at home with her children.* (or: *…if she were at home…*)
>
> The expression **If I were you…** is often used to give advice or warnings → *If I were you, I would*

1 Choose the correct option.

1. What **will / would / do** you do if someone left you in a dangerous situation?
2. You **wouldn't / didn't / hadn't** be happy if you knew the truth.
3. How would you travel to Edinburgh if your car **broke / will break / breaks** down?
4. We **could / will be able / can** invite all our friends if we had a bigger garden.
5. I **won't / wouldn't / didn't** be surprised if Tom got in some kind of trouble.
6. If my husband did more exercise, he **is / would be / will be** fitter.

2 Choose the correct option.

1. If you **tries / tried** parkour, I'm sure you'd **enjoy / enjoyed** it.
2. If you **lived / live** nearer London, I **would / had** come and see you more often.
3. Sue **would have / has** problems getting to work if she **wouldn't / didn't** have a car.
4. Mel certainly **didn't / wouldn't** go out with Jack if she **knew / will know** him better.
5. If you didn't **go / went** to bed so late, you **wouldn't be / weren't** so tired in the morning.
6. If they **studied / didn't study** so hard, they **won't / wouldn't** get such good marks.
7. I **wouldn't / didn't** ask the teacher to explain again if I **could / did** understand maths better.
8. If it **weren't / wouldn't be** so cold, we **would go / went** out for a walk.

3 Complete the sentences with the correct form of the verb in brackets.

1. Which places would you like to visit if you ………………… a week's holiday in the USA? (have)
2. I wouldn't have to get up so early if I ………………… nearer home. (work)
3. If he had a good plan, he ………………… me. (tell)
4. Would you buy this mini-skirt if your mum ………………… here? (be)
5. Kate would be cross if Tom ………………… on time. (not turn up)
6. If I had enough money, I ………………… around the world. (travel)
7. It would be great if we ………………… go skiing together. (can)
8. Amanda would go to the party if she ………………… better. (feel)
9. What ………………… if you found a gold necklace in the street? (you, do)
10. If John ………………… on time, he could see the presentation from the beginning. (arrive)

4 Complete the Type 2 sentences with the correct tense of the verbs in brackets.

1. My teacher .... (be) pleased if I .... (get) 10 out of 10 in the test.
2. I .... (dye) my hair green if my parents .... (allow) me to.
3. If you .... (improve) your IT skills, it .... (be) easier for you to find a job.
4. If I .... (not have) an Internet connection, what .... (I, do)?
5. .... (you, buy) these shoes if they .... (not cost) so much?
6. Oliver .... (not go) away on holiday if his neighbour .... (not look after) his dog.
7. If I .... (know) Simon's phone number, I .... (ring) him.
8. If Chris .... (win) the lottery, he .... certainly .... (give) some money to charity.
9. If I .... (be) you, I .... (not trust) him.
10. If he .... (find) the tickets, he .... (take) us to the rock concert.
11. I .... disappointed (be) if they .... (not invite) us to their party.
12. He .... a good career (have) if he .... (be) more ambitious.

Type 3

In the third type of conditional sentence, also called '**third conditional**', an impossible condition is expressed, because it refers to the past and therefore cannot come true: in reality things have gone differently, and we can only guess what would have happened if...

In this case, the tenses are: past perfect in the *if* clause, *would have* + past participle in the **main clause**.

If clause	Main clause
If + past perfect (**had** + past participle),	**would have** + past participle
If you had studied harder,	*you would have passed your exam.*

The sentence above implies the fact that you didn't study hard and therefore you didn't pass your exam. Here is an example of a question and a negative answer:
'*Would you have come to the concert if we had got tickets?*' '*No, I wouldn't have come anyway.*'

Focus

The **past perfect continuous** can also be used in place of the **past perfect simple** in a third conditional clause to underline the idea that the action lasted a longer period of time → *If it hadn't been snowing so hard, I would certainly have gone skiing.*

> ! We can also find a 'mixed conditional', which has the **past perfect** in the *if* clause, as in a **third conditional**, and the **present conditional** (*would* + base form) in the main clause, as in a **second conditional**. This happens when the result of the conditional action has a bearing on the present →
> *If I had followed his advice, I wouldn't be broke now.*
> *If they had left earlier, they would be here by now.*

FAQ

Q: I once found a series of contracted forms in a text: **If I'd seen her again, I'd have told her I was sorry. It would've been the best thing to do.** What are the full forms?

A: If I had seen her again, I would have told her I was sorry. It would have been the best thing to do.

As you can see, **'d** can be the contracted form of both **had** and **would**.

To distinguish between them, remember that **had** can only be followed by a past participle, whereas **would** can be only followed by the base form of a verb.

5 Match the two parts of the sentences, then decide if they are Type 1, Type 2 or Type 3.

1 If there isn't a bus she can get,
2 If they hadn't told me,
3 If Katie broke up with Charlie,
4 He would have tried bungee jumping
5 If there is some wind,
6 If Jim had had his boots,
7 She would do better at school
8 They would have arrived earlier

A he would easily forget her.
B we'll go sailing today.
C he would have come hiking with us.
D I'll drive her home in the car.
E if they had left on time.
F if he hadn't been so scared!
G I wouldn't have known about the accident.
H if she were more self-confident.

1 .... 2 .... 3 .... 4 .... 5 .... 6 .... 7 .... 8 ....

6 Complete the Type 3 sentences in the third conditional with the verbs below.

order   not make   wash   tell   choose   stay   read   not break   not order   get   wear   know

1 If she .... so many spelling mistakes, she .... a higher mark.
2 I .... casual clothes if you .... me that the party was a barbecue.
3 If we .... the portions were so big, we .... a starter.
4 Oh no! My jumper has shrunk. I .... it in cold water if I .... the label first.
5 Ted .... his leg if he .... on the easy ski slopes.
6 If everyone .... fish, we .... white wine, not red.

7 Rewrite the sentences as in the example using the correct conditional form.

0 I don't have a smartphone, so I can't send photos to you.
   If I had a smartphone, I could send photos to you.

1 I don't want my parents to be angry, so I won't go out tonight.
   If I went ....

2 I didn't have my car yesterday, so I couldn't go to the mall.
   If I ....

3 I'd love to have a tattoo, but my mum won't let me.
   If my mum ....

4 I don't get on with my brother. I never see him.
   If I ....

5 I'm not rich, so I can't buy a big house.
   If I ....

6 She went to the party and met her future husband.
   If she ....

296

LESSON 4 Use of modal verbs in conditional sentences

Modal verbs in the main clause

Type 1 sentences

In first conditional sentences, the use of **will** indicates with certainty that something will happen → *If you listen carefully, you will understand.*

As well as **will**, we can also find the following modals:

- **may**, to express that something will probably happen, but not with certainty → *You may meet Steve if you go to that new restaurant. He often goes there for dinner.*

- **can**, to indicate that something is possible → *If you like Mexican food, you can go to the new restaurant in Union Square.*

- **should**, to indicate that something is advisable or not advisable → *If you feel so tired, you shouldn't keep on driving, you should stop and relax for a while.*

1 Match the two halves of the sentences, then complete the main clause with *may* or *can*.

1. You .... have a room overlooking the sea
2. You .... get sunburnt
3. You .... see Tom if you go to the bar on North Street.
4. We .... easily find the way
5. I .... be able to join you at the restaurant
6. Mark .... have to work late tonight

A if you lie in the sun too long.
B if we look at Google Maps.
C if the meeting doesn't finish too late.
D if he doesn't finish his presentation this afternoon.
E if you ask for one when you book.
F He works there.

1 .....   2 .....   3 .....   4 .....   5 .....   6 .....

Type 2 sentences

In second conditional sentences, **would** expresses what we would do or what would happen if... → *I would wait a bit longer if I were you. She might still turn up.*

As well as **would**, we can also find the modals:

- **could**, to express possibility → *If I had a bigger car, I could take you all home.*

- **might**, to express probability → *If you tried skiing, you might like it.*

To express an obligation, we use **would have to** → *If I had to work full time, I would have to find someone to look after the children.*

To express a desire, we use **would like to** → *If I had enough money, I would like to buy a new car.*

2 Complete the sentences following the instructions in brackets.

1. If we had more time, we .... have one more go on the rides. (possibility)
2. If there was an earthquake, you .... get out of the house. (obligation)
3. If Karen knew about it, she .... decide to give up the idea. (probability)
4. If we rented a bigger flat, we .... pay more rent. (obligation)
5. If I could retire now, I .... go and live by the sea. (desire)
6. If you trained hard enough, you .... play in the main team. (possibility)
7. If you played an instrument, you .... join the band. (possibility)
8. If my husband tried Japanese food, he .... find that he likes it. (probability)

Type 3 sentences
In the third conditional, **would have** + **past participle** expresses what we would have done or what would have happened if... → *I would have waited for you if you had told me you were coming.*

As well as **would**, we can also find the modals **could**, **might** or **should**, with the same shades of meaning that we saw in the previous sections:

- *If I had brought my racket with me, I <u>could have played</u> a match with you.* (I would have had the possibility of doing it.)

- *They <u>might have got</u> here on time if they had left earlier.* (It's not certain, but it's probable.)
- *He <u>should have warned</u> us if he knew our flight would be delayed.* (This sounds like a reproach.)

For an obligation in the past → *I **would have had to** hire a pair of skis if I hadn't brought mine with me.*

For a desire or a wish in the past → *I **would have liked** to take a selfie with Bono if I had met him after the concert.*

It is also possible to say:
I would like to have taken a selfie with Bono...

3 Complete the sentences with the third conditional form of the verbs in brackets. In the main clause, use *would*, *could*, *might* or *should* on the basis of the meaning.

1 I .... to go on a cruise if I .... all that money on a new kitchen. (like, not spend)
2 If I .... my wallet at home this morning, I .... lunch in the restaurant! (not leave, have)
3 If we .... for you any longer in the street, we .... frozen! (wait, be)
4 We .... the new museum if there .... fewer people queuing up. (visit, be)
5 They .... the race if they .... harder. (win, train)
6 Carol .... us if she .... that the party had been cancelled. (tell, know)
7 I .... your behaviour to the headmaster if I .... that you were a bully. (report, know)
8 It .... possible to meet the actors if we .... the theatre so soon after the end of the show. (be, not leave)

Use of modal verbs in the *if*-clause

In second and third conditional sentences, we often find modal verbs and their replacement verbs in the subordinate clause with **if**.

Type 2	Type 3
If I could...	If I could have...
If I were able to... (ability)	If I had been able to...
If I wanted to...	If I had wanted to...
If I should... (eventuality)	If I should have...
If I had to... (obligation)	If I had had to...

If you should see Tom, please tell him I need to talk to him.
I wouldn't be very happy if I had to go to school in the summer.
I wouldn't have been very happy if I had had to go to school in the summer.

The expression **If you would...** is used to make a formal request very politely, especially in written language → *I would really be grateful if you would let me know as soon as possible.*

4 Match the sentence halves.

1. We would be grateful
2. If you should find something wrong with this new appliance,
3. If the company would accept our proposal,
4. If you wanted to start a new business,
5. If he should arrive earlier,
6. We would expand our business a lot

A could you meet him at the airport?
B if we could find a reliable partner in the UK.
C we would be able to give you some financial backing.
D you should report it to our customer service straight away.
E if you could send us your best quotations.
F we could develop an interesting product.

1 ..... 2 ..... 3 ..... 4 ..... 5 ..... 6 .....

5 Use these words to write third conditional questions and answers as in the example.

0. you / go / skiing / ?
   Yes / if / not / snowing / .
   Would you have gone skiing?
   Yes, if it hadn't been snowing.

1. he / pass / driving test / ?
   yes / if / practise / more often / .

2. they / enjoy / white-water rafting / ?
   yes / if / not be / so scared / .

3. the team / win / the competition / ?
   yes / if / one of them / not hurt / leg / .

4. you / sail / to the island / yesterday / ?
   yes / if / we / know / be windy / .

5. she / go / to Sally's party / ?
   yes / if / she / know / Peter was there / .

6 Complete the conditional sentences with the appropriate tense of the verbs in brackets.

1. If I .... talk to him, I .... him not to come. I knew the lecture .... quite boring. (be able to, tell, be) **Type 3**
2. If I .... work on Sundays, I .... this job, but luckily I only occasionally have to work on Saturdays. (have to, not accept) **Type 3**
3. I'm a lazybones. If I .... to do some sport, I think I .... football and I .... as a goalkeeper, so that I wouldn't have to run much! (be obliged, choose, play) **Type 2**
4. If I .... play the violin as well as you do, I .... to find a job in an orchestra. (be able to, try) **Type 3**
5. If I .... harder at school, I .... better marks. Now I realise how important it was. (work, get) **Type 3**
6. If I .... a better-paid job, I .... pay off my mortgage early. (find, be able to) **Type 2**

7 Match each text to the correct picture, then give an appropriate response.

1 **A:** Now go and explore! If any of you get lost, you should call me immediately on my phone! ☐
   B: ....
   ....
   ....

2 **A:** If I could sing, I would enter that talent competition.
   Why don't you? You've got a beautiful voice. ☐
   B: ....
   ....
   ....

3 **A:** If you would ask the manager to see me now, I would appreciate it. ☐
   B: ....
   ....
   ....

4 **A:** Sorry, Mum! If I could have helped you, I would have, but I had to go to Toby's house. ☐
   B: ....
   ....
   ....

5 **A:** I wouldn't have bought the dress if I had seen this!
   I'm very sorry. We'll give you a refund. ☐
   B: ....
   ....
   ....

8 Complete this table, which summarises the various types of conditional sentences.

	IF CLAUSE	MAIN CLAUSE
Type 0	**If** + present simple	Present simple
	If you book the hotel now,	*you get a discount.*
Type 1	**If** + present simple	Future (**will** + base form)
	If you [1].................... *the hotel now,*	*you* [2].................... *a discount.*
Type 2	**If** + past simple	First conditional (**would** + base form)
	If you [3].................... *the hotel now,*	*you* [4].................... *a discount.*
Type 3	**If** + past perfect (**had** + past participle)	Second conditional (**would have** + past participle)
	If you [5].................... *the hotel before,*	*you* [6].................... *a discount.*

9 **Complete the sentences with the appropriate modal in the affirmative or negative form:** *would / wouldn't, should / shouldn't, could / couldn't.*

1. If you feel depressed, you .... always stay at home. You .... go out and meet people.
2. We .... be so happy if we .... spend some time with you!
3. You are amazing! If I had done all that work, I .... be exhausted by now.
4. If I were you, I .... go to the Sahara with them. It might be a risky journey.
5. If it .... hail this week, the harvest .... be lost. Let's hope the weather does not change.
6. The situation .... be worse. If we had listened to your advice, we probably .... be in such big trouble now.
7. I .... be so happy if you .... come with me!

10 **Transform each of the following Type 1 *If* clauses into Type 2 and Type 3.**

1. If he goes to the opera, he will certainly enjoy it.
   ....
   ....
2. You won't spend too much if you buy things in the sales.
   ....
   ....
3. They will talk to him if they see him.
   ....
   ....
4. If you have a day off, we will go on a trip to the lake.
   ....
   ....
5. If she doesn't turn up on time, we will leave without her.
   ....
   ....
6. If you try hard, you will certainly succeed.
   ....
   ....

11 **Find the mistake in each of these sentences and correct them.**

1. You should have tell me that you were not coming.
   ....
2. If I have brought my packed lunch with me, I would have shared it with you.
   ....
3. If you like Japanese food, you would try the sushi in this restaurant. It's excellent!
   ....
4. What do you suggest I might do to improve my English?
   ....
5. If I had been more time, I would have prepared something special for dinner.
   ....
6. I was afraid she not might love me any more.
   ....
7. What would I do if I had been you? I just don't know! You should ask someone else.
   ....
8. I would had thanked them for their great hospitality if I had seen them.
   ....

ROUND UP 16

1 The following sentences refer to the present time. Rewrite them referring to the past, as in the example.

0   You must be joking!
    You must have been joking!

1   I wouldn't tell him a lie.
    ....

2   You should be more careful!
    ....

3   He could help you.
    ....

4   They can't be so silly!
    ....

5   She may know the truth.
    ....

6   I'd like to see them.
    ....

7   Which one would you choose?
    ....

8   They might be lucky.
    ....

9   It can't be Doug!
    ....

MATRIX +

In the **If** clauses of first conditional sentences, which are usually formed with **If** + present simple and **will** future in the main clause, we can also find:

- the **present continuous** in the subordinate clause:

    If <u>she's singing</u>, we'll be there to see her.

- other future forms (**going to** or **future continuous**) in the main clause:

    <u>I'm going to leave</u> for Thailand if I can find a cheap enough flight.
    Dad <u>will be painting</u> the fence if it doesn't rain on Saturday.

- a different conjunction to **if**, such as **provided** or **unless** (see page 370):

    You'll have a chance to win, **provided** you train regularly.
    I'm not going to go trekking this time, **unless** they need me as a guide.

2 Complete the sentences with the *going to* future or the future continuous – both are possible in some cases – and one of the verbs below:

read   leave   book   have   not read   build   melt   stop   not make   watch

1   If the weather gets warmer, the snow .... soon.
2   If the book is boring, I .... it.
3   If you stop the music, we .... dancing!
4   If I can find my glasses, I .... the instructions.
5   If this lecture doesn't finish soon, I ....
6   If the programme is interesting, we .... it.
7   If our friends come to see us tomorrow, we .... dinner with them.
8   If I get a pay rise, I .... a holiday straight away!
9   If we go to the beach this afternoon, we .... a huge sandcastle.
10 If I don't get a promotion at work this year, I .... a big fuss about it.

3 Complete the passage with the correct form of the verbs below:

melt (x2)   continue   become (x2)   rise (x2)   not limit   be   not be able
increase   not find

Global warming is a very serious problem for our environment. If the temperatures ¹................................, more land ²................................ desert and the ice of the polar caps ³................................. And if the ice of the glaciers ⁴................................, the sea level ⁵................................ and there ⁶................................ more floods. If we ⁷................................ alternative sources of energy and we ⁸................................ traffic in the cities, global warming ⁹................................ even more. And if global warming ¹⁰................................, a lot of animal species ¹¹................................ extinct because they ¹²................................ to find any more food or shelter. Governments must definitely take some action now and we must all do something about it – changing our habits a little bit may be a good start.

MATRIX +

The conjunction **If** can be omitted in second and third conditional sentences if **should** or **had** are included in the sentence. In these cases, the verbs take the first position in the sentence, followed by the subject:
If anything should happen, please call me immediately. → *Should anything happen….*
If he hadn't known, I would have excused him. → *Had he not known….*
This usage is quite formal and is rare in spoken language.

4 Rewrite the sentences without using the word *if*. Keep the same meaning.

1 If I should arrive late, please save a seat for me.
   ....

2 If I should decide to go, I'll let you know.
   ....

3 If we had enough money, we would buy this car.
   ....

4 If they had any children, they wouldn't be able to go out every evening.
   ....

5 If it should rain hard, we wouldn't go out.
   ....

6 If they had travelled more, they would be more open-minded.
   ....

303

5 Choose the correct option.

1 I will be very angry if you **won't / don't** come back on time.
2 Okay, do it if you really **want / wanted** to!
3 If you **are / will be** kind to other people, they will be kind to you.
4 If they hadn't cut down the tree, it **might / should** have fallen on the house.
5 It's a perfect moment. If it could only be just like this for ever, I **would / will** be the happiest person on earth.
6 If you **open / opened** the window, we'll be cold.
7 I was sure it would **be / have been** a great holiday!
8 Would you do anything different if you **would / could** rewind your life and start again?

6 Complete the *If* clauses with the correct form of the verbs below.

be   take   know   not pass   play   sleep   leave   choose

1 If he really wanted to leave, he .... by now!
2 If I could choose between going or staying, I .... staying. I really like being here.
3 If I should find a wallet on the street, I .... it to the police station.
4 If I had a kitten, I .... with it all day!
5 My parents would be very angry if I .... my exams.
6 If I worked in a circus, I .... a clown!
7 If there hadn't been so much noise, we .... much better.
8 If you had paid more attention during the lesson, you .... how to solve the problem now.

7 Complete the article with the correct tense of the verbs in brackets.

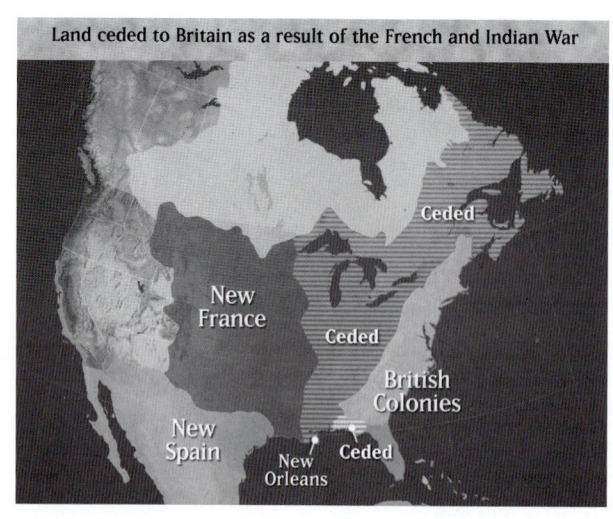

During an advanced course in American history, students were asked a few hypothetical questions, like 'What ¹................................. (happen) if France ²................................. (win) the Seven Years' War?' or '³................................. (American colonies, be) under a more absolutistic power if the kings of France ⁴................................. (rule) over them?' And again 'If North America ⁵................................. (be) under French control, what would have happened with the French Revolution?'

Here are some of the students' answers before they actually started a research project on the topic: If France ⁶................................. (win), all of North America ⁷................................. (speak) French by now. If North America had been under French rule, it ⁸................................. (back) the revolutionaries and ⁹................................. (gain) independence, but later than they did. ¹⁰................................. (the French Revolution, break out), without the American Revolution happening first?

Land ceded to Britain as a result of the French and Indian War

The questions and the first answers were just the starting point for a research project that went deeper into the roots of North American history and Europe as well. By trying to answer them, students had to examine lots of aspects of the history of Europe that they ¹¹... (study) otherwise. The project group is about to publish the results of their research on the university website. It ¹²... (be) interesting to read them, don't you think?

8 Complete these quotes with the suggested conditional of the verbs in brackets.

1 Type 0: 'All our dreams .... come true if we .... the courage to pursue them.' *Walt Disney* (can, have)

2 Type 1: 'If you never .... , you .... never ....' *Proverb* (try, know)

3 Type 1: 'If you .... a man a fish, he .... hungry tomorrow. If you .... a man to fish, he .... richer forever.' *Indian proverb* (give, be, teach, be)

4 Type 1: 'If you .... an apple and I .... an apple and we exchange these apples, then you and I .... still each .... one apple. But if you .... an idea and I .... an idea and we exchange these ideas, then each of us .... two ideas!' *George Bernard Shaw* (have x6)

5 Type 2: 'If I .... a physicist, I .... probably .... a musician. I often think in music.' *Albert Einstein* (be x 2)

6 Type 2: 'Everybody is a genius. But if you .... a fish by its ability to climb a tree, it .... its all life believing it is stupid.' *Albert Einstein* (judge, live)

Reflecting on grammar

Reflect on the rules and say whether the following statements are true or false.

		True	False
1	**Would**, abbreviated to **'d**, is used to form the conditional.		
2	The 'future in the past' is expressed with the past form of the conditional, that is **would have** + past participle.		
3	The sentence *She said she would come* is correct.		
4	There are three types of conditional sentence.		
5	In a conditional sentence, the main clause always precedes the **if** clause.		
6	In the **If clause** of a zero or first conditional sentence, we usually find a verb in the present simple.		
7	The sentence *Would you have been happy if they had called you on your birthday?* is correct.		
8	The sentence *If I didn't have to work, I would go with them* is a type 2 conditional and is correct.		
9	The verb in the **if** clause of a Type 3 conditional is in the **past perfect** (**had** + past participle).		
10	The sentence *If he's on WhatsApp, I would send him our photo* is correct.		

GRAMMAR MATRIX MAIN

UNIT 17 Passive forms

LESSON 1 The present passive

The passive form (or passive voice) is constructed as follows:

subject + auxiliary **be** + past participle of the main verb

- The auxiliary **be** takes the verb tense needed by the situation, as in the following table:

subject	present simple	present continuous	past simple	past continuous	present perfect	past perfect	will future	past participle
I	am	am being	was	was being	have been	had been	will be	
he / she / it	is	is being	was	was being	has been	had been	will be	called.
we / you / they	are	are being	were	were being	have been	had been	will be	

! It is only possible to use the passive form with transitive verbs, that is, verbs that are followed by a direct object, for example *make*, *build*, *write*, *use*, *call* ...

The passive form in the present simple

Affirmative: It is made of glass.
Negative: It isn't / It's not made of glass.
Interrogative: 'Is it made of glass?' 'Yes, it is. / No, it isn't.'
'What is it made of? Glass?' 'No, plastic!'

Note how we transform an active form into a passive form:

ACTIVE FORM			PASSIVE FORM		
subject	verb	direct object	subject	verb	agent
Laura Marston	presents	the new show.	The new show	is presented	by Laura Marston.

- The direct object of the active sentence (**the new show**) becomes the subject of the passive sentence.
- The subject of the active sentence (**Laura Marston**) becomes the agent of the passive sentence, and is preceded by the preposition **by**.
- The auxiliary **be** in the passive sentence stays in the same verb tense as the active sentence, in this case the **present simple**, and is followed by the past participle of the regular verb **to present** (...presents → ...is presented).

1 Rewrite the active sentences in the passive.

1. They sell sports equipment in this store.
   ....
2. They make designer clothes in this factory.
   ....
3. They don't produce cars here any more.
   ....
4. They play the national anthems before each game.
   ....
5. People speak French, German and Italian in Switzerland.
   ....
6. They give prizes to all winners.
   ....
7. They use computers in the marketing lessons.
   ....
8. A very young woman directs the orchestra.
   ....
9. They consider him a real maths genius!
   ....
10. Scotland, England, Wales and Northern Ireland make up the United Kingdom.
    ....

2 Transform the passive sentences into questions (?) or negative sentences (–).

1. The film is directed by Steven Spielberg. (?)
   ....
2. School uniforms are paid for by the families. (?)
   ....
3. The notice is written in my language. (–)
   ....
4. Dice are used for this game. (–)
   ....
5. Spanish is taught in their school. (?)
   ....
6. These sunglasses are made in Italy. (–)
   ....
7. The UNO Tower is made of glass and steel. (?)
   ....

The passive form is often used without including the agent:
- in notices and rules → *Heels are forbidden in the sports hall.* A comma is needed after Yes or No in short answers.
- in descriptions of production processes or experiments → *Crude oil is pumped into the fractioning column and then it is split into different hydrocarbons.*
- when we want to draw attention to the action that is taking place or to the results of that action, rather than who did the action → *Oranges are imported to our country from Spain or Morocco.* (We're not interested in who imports them.)

3 Rewrite the active sentences as passive. Omit the agent when it is not needed.

1. They grind coffee and then they pack it into tins.
   ....
2. They make these bags in Florence.
   ....
3. People celebrate Carnival in February.
   ....
4. Mrs Jones cleans the rooms every morning.
   ....
5. Where do they import these tomatoes from?
   ....

The passive form in the present continuous

The passive form in the **present continuous** is used to describe actions and processes that are taking place at or around the time of speaking: **Something is being done now / at the moment.**

Affirmative: Lunch is being served now.
Negative: Lunch is not / isn't being served now.
Interrogative: 'Is lunch being served yet?' 'Yes, it is. / No, it isn't.'
'When is lunch being served?' 'It's being served in about ten minutes, at 12.30.'

Compare the previous sentence with: *Lunch is served from 12.30 till 3.00.* → The **present simple** is used because we are talking about something that usually happens, not something that is happening at this exact moment in time or in the near future.

4 Complete the sentences with the present simple or present continuous of the verbs in brackets.

1 Rugby …………………………………… in both England and Wales. (play)
2 An important match …………………………………… tonight between the teams of Wales and England. (play)
3 Prices and conditions …………………………………… in our offer. (specify)
4 Some new cottages …………………………………… at the end of the road. They will be finished by the end of year. (build)
5 Delivery to your house …………………………………… in the price. (include)
6 That old building …………………………………… at the moment. It's going to be a four-star hotel. (refurbish)
7 Funds …………………………………… to help the people affected by the tsunami. (raise)
8 Breakfast …………………………………… in the cafeteria at the moment. (serve)

5 This is a paragraph on digestion taken from a biology book.
Complete it with the present simple passive form of the verbs below.

mix   call   not need   transform   expel   chew   swallow   complete

The food we eat [1]………………………… into energy through the process of digestion. Digestion begins in the mouth. Here the food [2]………………………… and becomes a bolus, then it [3]………………………… and goes down into the stomach, passing through the oesophagus.

In the stomach, the bolus [4]………………………… with gastric juices and forms a thick liquid which goes down into the small intestine.

Here, digestion continues. When the process of digestion [5]………………………… , the digested food goes into the blood, which carries it to the cells. This process [6]………………………… absorption. The substances that [7]………………………… by our body get into the large intestine. From here, they pass into the rectum and [8]………………………… through the anus in the form of faeces.

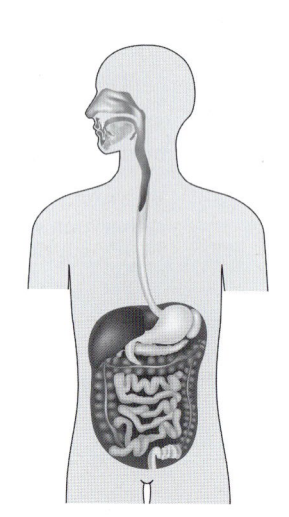

6 These are the rules of a school library. Complete the sentences with the passive form of the verbs below.

file   invite   borrow   forbid   fine   ask

1 Students ………………………………………… to join the library at the start of term.
2 Students ………………………………………… to be quiet in the library.
3 Books and periodicals ………………………………………… alphabetically.
4 It ………………………………………… to underline or write in books.
5 Books can ………………………………………… only after filling in a form.
6 Students ………………………………………… if they lose a book.

LESSON 2 The past passive

The passive form in the past simple

Affirmative: It was made in China.
Negative: It wasn't made in China.
Interrogative: 'Was it made in China?' 'Yes, it was. / No, it wasn't.'
'Where was it made? In China?' 'No, in Korea.'

As in the active form (see page 133), in the passive, the **past simple** is used for actions that are completely finished and have reference to a precise moment in the past. We find the **past simple passive** in past narrations, for example to talk about discoveries, inventions and similar topics.
Johannes Gutenberg introduced the printing press to Europe in 1439. (active form)
The printing press was introduced to Europe by Johannes Gutenberg in 1439. (passive form)
Remember! The agent is always preceded by the preposition **by**.

FAQ

Q: While I was listening to a programme on an English channel, I heard the sentence: **He got injured in the crash.** Did I hear that correctly? It seems like a passive sentence, so why does it include **got**?

A: You did hear correctly. In informal spoken English, the auxiliary **was / were** can be replaced by **got**, especially when describing unexpected actions. Here's another example:
He got fined for driving too fast.

1 Complete the sentences with the past simple passive of the verbs below.

conquer   name   create   write   design   invent   build   explore   defeat

1 *Romeo and Juliet* and *Hamlet* ………………………………… by William Shakespeare.
2 The capital of the USA ………………………………… after president George Washington.
3 Australia and New Zealand ………………………………… by Captain James Cook in the 18th century.
4 England ………………………………… by the Normans in 1066.
5 Anglo Saxon King Harold ………………………………… by William Duke of Normandy in the battle of Hastings.
6 The Shard Tower in London ………………………………… by Italian architect Renzo Piano.
7 The television ………………………………… by a Scottish engineer, John Logie Baird.
8 The mini-skirt ………………………………… by Mary Quant in the 1960s in London.
9 The Tower of London ………………………………… in the 11th century.

2 Write the question for each answer. Remember! The preposition goes at the end of the question.

0 Who was the telescope invented by?
   The telescope was invented by Galileo Galilei.

1 Who ....
   ....
   The Last Supper was painted by Leonardo da Vinci.

2 When ....
   ....
   The first Liverpool to Manchester railway was opened in 1830.

3 Who ....
   ....
   Mr Kent was replaced by Miss Ross in the English class yesterday.

4 What ....
   ....
   My first dog was called Sammy.

5 How many languages ....
   ....
   His novel was translated into ten languages.

6 How ....
   Where ....
   The glasses were packed in boxes and shipped to Africa.

7 Who ....
   Brick Lane was written by Monica Ali.

The passive form in the past continuous

The passive form in the **past continuous** is not used very much. It describes processes that were happening in a continuous way at a certain time in the past:

Innovative car models were being produced by FIAT at the time my father was employed there.

3 Transform the sentences from passive to active. If there is no agent, use *they* as the subject of the active sentence.

1 Mickey Mouse and Donald Duck were both created by the Walt Disney Company.

2 The light bulb was invented by Thomas Edison.

3 The main road was being repaired, so we came by a different route.

4 Higher walls were built in New Orleans after Hurricane Katrina destroyed part of the city.

5 Lots of cars were damaged by the storm last night.

6 The rock star was cheered by his fans all the way to his hotel.

7 Rosa Parks was arrested in Montgomery, Alabama, in 1955 because she had sat in a bus seat reserved for white people.

8 An ambulance was called immediately after the accident.

9 A mistake was made.

The passive form in the present perfect and the past perfect

Compare the differences between the active and passive forms of the present perfect:

Active: *The children have made this kite.*

Passive: *This kite has been made by the children.*

The passive form of the **present perfect** is used:

- to report events without saying when they happened → *He has been elected senator.*
- to ask whether something has ever happened → *Have you ever been invited to one of his parties?*
- to say that something has just / already been done or has not yet been done → *The room has just / already been cleaned. The room has not yet been cleaned.*

Compare the use of the present perfect and the past simple:

The new leisure centre has just been inaugurated. (The adverb **just** is present, we don't know when it happened → present perfect)

The new leisure centre was inaugurated last Sunday. (We know when it happened → past simple)

The passive form in the past perfect is used to say that something had just / already / not yet been done → *When we got to the hotel, our room had not been cleaned yet.*

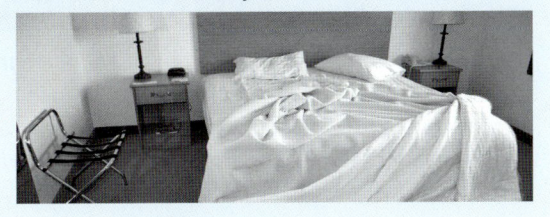

4 Complete the sentences with the past simple or the present perfect passive of the verbs in brackets.

1. The new library .... by the mayor. (inaugurate)
2. The Modern Art Gallery .... last Saturday. (open)
3. .... to his house? (ever, she, invite)
4. Peter .... as class head last week. (choose)
5. My car .... I can drive you to work now. (repair)
6. Your room .... It is ready for you now! (just, clean)
7. The itinerary for the Italian tour .... yet. (announce)
8. Their new album .... last week. (release)
9. My bike .... yesterday. (steal)

5 Complete the sentences with the present perfect or the past perfect passive of the verbs in brackets.

1. '............................. they ever .... here before?' 'No, never. It's the first time I've seen them here'. (be)
2. We had already packed our luggage when we heard our flight .... (cancel)
3. Sorry, your car .... yet. It will take a few more hours. (not repair)
4. Unfortunately an agreement .... yet. But they're still talking. (not reach)
5. Harriet .... as leader of the party. (announce)
6. Everything .... already .... by the time we got back: the food .... , the tables .... , and the room .... (do, cook, set, decorate)
7. Two tables .... for you and your family, sir. (reserve)
8. The arrangements for the concert .... before we arrived. (make)

LESSON 3 The passive form in the future and with modal verbs

The uses of the future passive are the same as those that we have seen for the active forms (see Unit 15), so we can choose the future with **will** or with **going to** according to the situation and the intention that we wish to communicate.
Both **will** and **going to** are followed by **be** + the past participle of the main verb.

The passive form in the future with *will*

Affirmative: It will be done by tomorrow. (It's a promise.)
Negative: It will not / won't be done by tomorrow, I'm afraid. (That's my prediction.)
Interrogative: 'Will it be done by tomorrow?' 'Yes, it will. / No, it won't.'
'When will it be done? By tomorrow?' 'No… in a couple of days.'

The passive form in the future with *going to*

Affirmative: He's going to be rewarded for what he's done. (This is something that is about to happen, a prediction that sounds certain.)
Negative: He isn't going to be rewarded, I'm afraid. (I don't believe that there is any intention to do it.)
Interrogative: 'Is he going to be rewarded?' 'Yes, he is. / No, he isn't.'
'How is he going to be rewarded? With some money?' 'No… with a smile! ☺'

The passive form with the future perfect

The future perfect is used to say within how long a certain action will have been completed.
Will is followed by **have been** + past participle and an expression of time with **by**. Its use is quite limited:
The winning numbers of the raffle will have been announced by this time tomorrow.
I'm sure Ms Rubens will have been appointed as Home Secretary by next week.

1 Complete the passive sentences with the future form indicated in brackets. Use one of the verbs below.

appoint   choose   ask   take   publish   release   hold   sell

1 She .... to the committee. She isn't very popular. (*not going to*)
2 I don't think his proposal .... seriously by the manager. (*will*)
3 I'm sure he .... as the new CEO by the end of the week. (*future perfect*)
4 You .... lots of questions in the interview. (*going to*)
5 Her new novel .... until early next year. (*will not*)
6 Their next album .... in two months. (*will*)
7 These beautiful prints .... in all the best art shops. (*going to*)
8 The next table-tennis tournament .... Dublin. (*will*)

2 Reorder the words to make sentences in the future passive.

1 certainly / You / be / will / innocent / declared / .
....

2 next / His / movie / going / to / New / is / be / in / Zealand / filmed / .
....

3 rooms / old / The / will / mansion / be / the / of / year / next / redecorated / .
....

4 exhibition / going / be / An / opened / this / interesting / month / to / is / later / .
   ....

5 be / A / will / organised / in / his / concert / memory / .
   ....

6 This / building / going / old / be / is / to / demolished / .
   ....

7 to / chosen / Who's / for / the / be / main / role / going / the / in / musical / ?
   ....

8 names / The / winners / the / of / be / will / tomorrow / announced / .
   ....

9 A / with / meal / traditional / wines / local / be / served / will / everyone / to / .
   ....

10 I / proposal / think / will / be / your / seriously / taken / .
   ....

The passive form with modal verbs

The passive form is often used after a modal verb (**can, could, must, may, would, should...**), referring either to the present or the past.

Note how an active sentence containing a modal verb is transformed into a passive sentence with the same meaning:

<u>You can solve this problem</u> in two different ways. → <u>This problem can be solved</u> in two different ways.

The structure of a passive sentence containing a modal is therefore as follows:

Present:

subject + modal + **be** + past participle of the main verb

Past:

subject + modal + **have been** + past participle of the main verb

It can / could be made easily. (It's possible.)

It may / might be made of aluminium. (It's probable.)

It must be made now. (It's an order.)

It has to be made / It needs to be made before noon. (It's necessary). Be careful: **have** and **need** do not behave like modal verbs, so they take **to**.

It should be made by you, not by your mum. (I'm giving advice that, in this case, also sounds like a reproach.)

It ought to be done soon. (I'm making a request.)

Remember: ought is also followed by **to**. (See page 297)

They said it would be done by the next day. (Indirect speech with the conditional, 'future in the past', see Unit 19, Lesson 3, page 351)

It can't / couldn't have been made by a kid! (I don't believe it.)

Your timetable may / might have been changed. (it's probable, I'm not certain about it.)

I should have been warned of the delay. (I'm expressing dissatisfaction.)

This car must have been used with very little care. (It's a deduction, the car is dirty and full of dents.)

3 Complete the sentences with the most appropriate modal verb. Choose from the verbs below.

must   must not   could   would   may   can   couldn't

1 The lift .... be used by children if not accompanied by an adult.
2 This dish .... be made only with vegetables, but I'm not sure which ones.
3 His latest song .... have been inspired by his new-born baby. It's so sweet.
4 The ball .... be touched with both hands and feet in rugby.
5 Only a monolingual dictionary .... be used in the exam.
6 This work .... have been done much better than this!
7 Treat people as you .... like to be treated.

4 Transform the sentences from active to passive. Keep the same modal verb as in the original sentence.

1 You should cut the apples into halves.
....

2 You need to wash the car today.
....

3 You can't touch the ball with the hands in soccer.
....

4 You should have informed me!
....

5 They might have lost your application form.
....

6 They ought to reach an agreement.
....

7 They might serve dinner in the garden this evening.
....

8 You can't have made it in three minutes!
....

5 Write questions for these answers. Use a modal verb and the passive.

1 ....
Yes, a boat can be hired for the lake.

2 ....
No, not all expenses must be paid in advance, luckily!

3 ....
Yes, a little butter can be added to the sauce if you like.

4 ....
No, not everyone should be punished. Only those who cause trouble.

5 ....
Yes, it can be cooked in the microwave. But not in that tin!

6 Transform the passive sentences from the present to the past.

1 Your essay should be written more carefully.
....

2 We might be invited to his party.
....

3 The onions should be chopped more finely.
....

4 They might be chosen for the part.
....

5 We should be informed about any problems.
....

7 Match the sentence halves.

1. Great photos can be
2. This logo will be
3. A new password has been
4. If your project is really innovative,
5. Earth is called "the blue planet"
6. Pluto was first photographed
7. Not everything can
8. This password is secure. It can't

A be done immediatly.
B used on all documents.
C from a short distance in July 2015.
D downloaded from this site.
E be easily guessed or hacked.
F because it looks this colour when seen from space.
G chosen. Do you know it?
H it might be crowdfunded.

1 ... 2 ... 3 ... 4 ... 5 ... 6 ... 7 ... 8 ...

LESSON 4 Personal and impersonal passive form; *have / get something done*

As we saw in Unit 7, Lesson 3 (see page 118), some verbs may be followed by two objects, one direct and one indirect, for example **give**, **lend**, **send**, **write** and several others. You will remember that the structure of the active sentence is as follows:

> subject + verb + person (to whom?) + object (what?)
> *They lent John a dictionary.*

In the passive voice, these verbs usually have the so-called personal form, that is, the person, not the thing, occupies the position of subject in the sentence.

> *John was lent a dictionary.* (*A dictionary was lent to John* is possible, but it's used much less frequently.)

Look at some more examples of a personal passive construction:

Active sentence	Passive sentence
They give young athletes prizes.	Young athletes are given prizes.
They offered me a big discount.	I was offered a big discount.
They will give Sharon a present.	Sharon will be given a present.

1 Tick (✓) the sentences that are correct or correct the mistakes.

1. The art gallery clients were all give a leaflet of the new exhibition. ....
2. My friend were given a super new mobile phone for his birthday. ....
3. On the farm, we were taught how to milk a cow. It was great! ....
4. Jean was offer a lot of money for her vintage fur coat. ....
5. They were told to park their car on the other side of the road. ....
6. I was shown a nice cottage, but the rent was too high. ....
7. When I had no money on my bank account, I was credit some by my dad. ....

2 Rewrite the sentences in the passive form.

1. Somebody sent her red roses.
   She was ....
2. They told Susan a nice story.
   Susan ....
3. They sent us an invitation to the opening of a new shop.
   We ....
4. The shop granted us a 30% discount on last year's clothes.
   We ....
5. The bishop showed Paul the cathedral.
   Paul ....
6. He asked Caroline to pick him up at the airport.
   Caroline ....
7. They gave the children some nice illustrated books.
   The children ....
8. Somebody taught me how to model clay.
   I ....

Declarative verbs or verbs of opinion like **believe, think, consider, know, find, report, say, suppose, warn** and a few others often express opinions that are widely shared.

In English, these are expressed using a passive construction, which may be:

- impersonal, with a declarative subordinate clause: **It is said (that) he owns a fortune.**
- personal, with **to** + base form: **He is said to own a fortune.**

The personal construction is the more common. Look at some more examples:
He is considered to be the best in his category.
They were found to be innocent. (also: *It was found that they were innocent.*)
He was reported to be missing. (also: *It was reported that he was missing.*)

If the opinion or the supposition refers to the past, we use **to have** + past participle:
They are supposed to have finished by now.
She is said to have won a big sum on the lottery.

> **!** Note the difference between a present opinion about a past fact:
> *People think she was a great dancer.* → *She <u>is thought to have been</u> a great dancer.*
> and a past opinion:
> *People thought she was a great dancer.* → *She <u>was thought to be</u> a great dancer.*

---

3 Complete the second sentence so that it has a similar meaning to the first using the given word. Do not change the given word. Use between two and five words including the given word.

0. He has always been known to be the greatest poet of his age.
   IT   *It has always been known* .... that he is the greatest poet of his age.
1. We were told a lot of lies.
   US   .... a lot of lies.
2. It was known that they were good singers.
   THEY   .... good singers.
3. It is supposed that you should be studying.
   ARE   .... studying.
4. It was found that he was guilty.
   BE   .... guilty.
5. This is considered to be an important painting.
   IS   This .... important.
6. It is said that this villa belongs to a famous billionaire.
   TO   This .... to a famous billionaire.

4 Read the sentences and decide if they refer to a judgement in the present (PR) or the past (PA).

1. He's thought to have been a genius. ....
2. They were believed to be the best painters of their time. ....
3. They are thought to have been robbed during the night. ....
4. She was considered to be the best fashion designer of the fifties. ....
5. Some hooligans are thought to have caused serious damage to the sculptures in Rome. ....
6. He's believed to have spent five years on a little island in the Pacific Ocean. ....
7. She's thought to be abroad. ....
8. He was believed to have been the best actor of his time. ....

5 Complete the text with the missing verbs below.

was devastated   was   had been taught   has been credited   was given   ran

10-year-old girl saves lives

A young New Zealand girl ¹.................................. with saving dozens of lives during last month's Samoan tsunami. Abby ².. on holiday with her family in the village of Lalomanu on Samoa's southern coast when she noticed the tsunami warning signs. She ³.. about them at school. She ⁴.................................. along the beach telling people to head for higher ground. Just minutes later, the entire area ⁵.. . Her warning ensured that many people reached safety in time. Back home, Abby ⁶.. a certificate of appreciation from the New Zealand Civil Defense Director in front of her impressed classmates in Wellington.

6 Rewrite these sentences in the passive form.

1. People think Martha Miller is an interesting artist.
   Martha Miller ....
2. They thought John Landis was a rich art dealer.
   John Landis ....
3. The police suppose that someone has already sold the stolen painting.
   The stolen painting ....
4. People know that their works are the most expensive in the gallery.
   Their works ....
5. Everybody knows that someone gave the painter a new canvas and some watercolours.
   The painter ....
6. They suppose that the fakers have moved to South America by now.
   The fakers ....
7. Everybody believes the owner of the art gallery is very wealthy.
   The owner ....

Have / Get something done

To express the idea that something (which is usually a service) is done for us by others, we use the passive construction: **have / get something done** → *I needed a certificate and I had it done in no time at all!* (Also: *...I got it done...*)

In most cases, the person carrying out the action or service is understood, as it's usually either obvious or not important.

If the person is expressed (the 'agent'), it is introduced with **by**.

Look at these examples:
Rob had his hair shaved by the new barber in King Street.
My cousin got his arm tattooed with his girlfriend's name.

> **!** Note the difference between: *We're going to paint our bedroom.* (We're going to do it ourselves) and *We're going to have our bedroom painted.* (Other people are going to do it for us).

The action may happen against our will, for example:
I had my bag stolen.

The following constructions are common: **I need to... / I want to... / I must... have something done**
→ *I need to have my car washed. It's really filthy!*

7 Match the sentence halves.

1 My sister had her bedroom   A repaired tomorrow.
2 You've just had your hair cut   B manicured one of these days.
3 My husband is getting his computer C by one of the top designers in London.
4 I'll have my nails   D painted white last month.
5 I had my wedding dress made   E our garden landscaped last year.
6 We had   F – it looks great!

1 ..... 2 ..... 3 ..... 4 ..... 5 ..... 6 .....

8 Use the given words and the verbs in brackets to write sentences, as in the example.

0 He / get / car / repair / after the accident (need)
He needs to get his car repaired after the accident.

1 I / get / these photos / print (want)
....

2 She / get / her jacket / dry-clean (must)
....

3 I / get / this shirt / iron (need)
....

4 We / get / our computer / repair (need)
....

5 My mum / have / the kitchen / extend (want)
....

6 My parents / have / new satellite dish / install (want)
....

7 Laura / have / nails / manicured / before the wedding (must)
....

8 She / have / a hole in her tooth / filled (must)
....

9 I / get / car / washed (need)
....

10 We / get / grass / cut / this weekend (must)
....

CONJUGATION OF A REGULAR VERB
Revision table

infinitive to check	past participle checked	present participle checking

ACTIVE FORM

present simple I / You / We / They check He / She / It checks	**present continuous** I am checking You / We / They are checking He / She / It is checking
past simple I / You / He / She / It / We / They checked	**past continuous** I / He / She / It was checking You / We / They were checking
present perfect simple I / You / We / They have checked He / She / It has checked	**present perfect continuous** I / You / We / They have been checking He / She / It has been checking
past perfect simple I / You / He / She / It / We / They had checked	**past perfect continuous** I / You / He / She / It / We / They had been checking
future simple I / You / He / She / It / We / They will check	**future continuous** I / You / He / She / It / We / They will be checking
future perfect simple I / You / He / She / It / We / They will have checked	**future perfect continuous** I / You / He / She / It / We / They will have been checking
***going to* future** I'm going to check You're / We're / They're going to check He's / She's / It's going to check	***going to* future in the past** I / He / She / It was going to check You / We / They were going to check
present conditional I / You / He / She / It / We / They would check	**past conditional** I / You / He/ She / It / We / They would have checked

PASSIVE FORM

present simple I am checked You / We / They are checked He / She / It is checked	**present continuous** I am being checked You / We / They are being checked He / She / It is being checked
past simple I / He / She / It was checked You / We / They were checked	**past continuous** I / He / She / It was being checked You / We / They were being checked
present perfect simple I / You / We / They have been checked He / She / It has been checked	**past perfect simple** I / You / He / She / It / We / They had been checked
future simple I/ You / He / She / It / We / They will be checked	**future perfect simple** I / You / He / She / It / We / They will have been checked
***going to* future** I'm going to be checked You're / We're / They're going to be checked He's / She's / It's going to be checked	***going to* future in the past** I / He / She / It was going to be checked You / We / They were going to be checked
present conditional I / You / He/ She / It / We / They would be checked	**past conditional** I / You / He/ She / It / We / They would have been checked

ROUND UP 17

MATRIX +

Look at the table showing the complete conjugation of the verb *to check* on the previous page. Each verb can be classified according to:

FORM or **VOICE**: active / passive (Remember: only transitive verbs can have a passive form!)

TENSE: present / past / future / present perfect / past perfect / future perfect / present conditional / past conditional (Remember: 'perfect' indicates completed or finished actions)

ASPECT: simple / continuous (or progressive)
The so-called 'aspect' is a peculiarity of the English language. 'Simple' indicates permanent situations. 'Continuous' or 'progressive' indicates actions in progress that are not yet finished or are temporary.

1 Analyze the underlined verbs. For each of them, give its form, aspect and tense as in the example.

0 She <u>was called</u> Mary, after her grandmother. → *passive, past simple*

1 They <u>were going</u> to school. ....

2 He <u>had been given</u> the house key. ....

3 They <u>will have been flying</u> for ten hours at this time tomorrow. ....

4 We <u>would have accepted</u> their proposal. ....

5 She <u>has been playing</u> since four o'clock. ....

6 They <u>had</u> very good results in their tests. ....

7 They <u>were going to be arrested</u>. ....

8 It <u>will be finished</u> soon. ....

2 What different forms can each of these verbs have? Note that some verbs are regular while others are irregular. Also remember any spelling variations. Do the same as in the examples.

LOOK – regular verb → *look**s*** (third person of the present simple) – *look**ing*** (gerund / present participle / noun verb) – *look**ed*** (past simple and past participle)

DO – irregular verb → *does* (third person of the present simple) – *doing* (gerund / present participle / noun verb) – *did* (past simple) – *done* (past participle)

1 WASH ....
2 CUT ....
3 LIVE ....
4 WRITE ....
5 ENJOY ....
6 CRY ....
7 COME ....
8 SPEND ....
9 SEE ....
10 SAY ....

3 **Complete the sentences with verbs in the passive. Use the verbs below and the tenses suggested in brackets.**

spend   reward   lose   serve   send   demolish

1 Lots of money .... by immigrants to their native countries. (present continuous)
2 My patience .... finally .... – a really big fish started pulling at my line. (past simple)
3 Everything .... ! We had nothing left. (past perfect)
4 Hopefully more money .... on health care by the government. (*will* future)
5 When we arrived, cocktails .... (past continuous)
6 Many old buildings in the city centre .... (present perfect)

4 **Change these sentences from active to passive. Keep the same tense. Remember: any preposition is put at the end of the passive sentence, as in the example.**

0 You don't have to pay <u>for</u> these brochures, they're free.
These brochures don't have to be paid for, they're free.

1 We will reply to all your emails.
....

2 A new babysitter will look after the children tonight.
....

3 They have played this song a hundred times on the radio today.
....

4 They might have changed the schedule.
....

5 They are going to sell their car.
....

6 They are building big dams in Venice.
....

7 Students must not use the equipment in the science lab without permission.
....

8 The club members have organised a charity concert.
....

5 **Change these passive sentences from the present to the past simple tense.**

1 Hot meals are served at all times in the restaurant.
....

2 The cake must be stored in a cool place.
....

3 Very good bargains can be found on Prime Day.
....

4 This dish is prepared the traditional way.
....

5 All of the carpets are hand-woven in Morocco.
....

6 The sauce needs to be prepared in advance.
....

7 The scarves in the shop window are all hand-painted.
....

8 The bags and belts are made of real leather.
....

6 Change each of these active sentences into two different kinds of passive sentences, as in the example.

0 They gave everyone a card.
   Everyone was given a card. / A card was given to everyone.

1 They offered him a film contract.
   ....

2 They will send you two copies of the contract.
   ....

3 They show new students the syllabus.
   ....

4 They are going to teach the children a nursery rhyme.
   ....

5 They have awarded her with an Oscar.
   ....

6 They passed each council member a folder of documents.
   ....

7 They have told Sara the story of this strange room.
   ....

8 They are giving the children some snacks for the break.
   ....

7 Write questions for these answers.

1 Can ....
   Yes, the oven can be switched off. The muffins are ready.

2 Who ....
   'Julius Caesar' was written by William Shakespeare.

3 Who ....
   This song was composed by John Lennon.

4 When ....
   She was given the prize last week.

5 What ....
   Nothing much can be done now, I'm afraid.

6 Which ....
   English, German and Spanish are spoken here.

7 Will ....
   Yes, his paintings will be sold at the next auction.

8 Is ....
   No, this flat is not going to be rented.

8 Complete the sentences with the past participle of the verbs below:

repair   wash   cut   devastate   restyle   do   iron   clean up   dye

1 It was terrible! They had their shop .... by the flood.
2 We had our car .... last week. It had a problem with the brakes.
3 She got her computer .... after it had caught a virus.
4 I'm going to have my hair .... , ... blond and .... I'm ready for a change!
5 If you use this software, you'll get your work .... in no time.
6 He hasn't got a washing machine so he usually gets his shirts .... and .... at a cleaner's.

9 Find the mistake in each sentence and correct it.

1 The students were gave some new books. ....
2 Have the stadium gates opened at 6 p.m. for the concert? ....
3 The Sagrada Familia were designed by Antoni Gaudi. ....
4 The film will be shooted in Central Italy. ....
5 The dog was supposed to missing. ....
6 A radio station has established by Marconi on the Isle of Wight. ....

Reflecting on grammar

Reflect on the rules and say whether the following statements are true or false.

		True	False
1	The auxiliary verb for the passive form is always **to have**.		
2	All verbs have an active and a passive form.		
3	The agent, which we can sometimes find after a passive form, is expressed by the preposition **from**.		
4	A modal verb in a passive sentence is followed by **be** + past participle if it refers to the present, and **have been** + past participle if it refers to the past.		
5	The sentence *He should be punished for what he's done* is correct.		
6	The sentence *He is said to have been very rich* refers to a judgement given in the present.		
7	The verb **have** can be replaced with **get** in sentences such as: *I had my hair cut very short*.		
8	The preposition in a **Wh- question** goes at the end in the passive, like in questions in the active form.		
9	The sentence *I was given a lot of presents on my birthday* is wrong. We should say *A lot of presents were given to me on my birthday*.		
10	The sentence *She is supposed to have finished by now* has a 'personal' construction while the sentence *It is supposed that she has finished by now* has an 'impersonal' construction.		

GRAMMAR MATRIX MAIN

UNIT 18 Relative clauses

LESSON 1 Relative pronouns in defining relative clauses

Relative clauses may be of two types: **defining** and **non-defining**.

Defining relative clauses complete a sentence, defining which thing or person we are talking about. If I said, for example: **'The film was good'**, you might ask **'Which film?' 'The film that we saw last night'**. By adding the relative clause, I specify which film I am talking about: the one we saw last night. Without the relative, the main clause would not have a proper meaning.

Remember:

- a **defining relative clause** is essential in order to identify the thing or person we are talking about
- since it is closely linked to the main clause, a **defining relative clause** is never separated from it by a comma.

Notice how it is possible to join two clauses, to avoid repetition and make the discourse flow better:

Santiago Calatrava is the famous Spanish architect. He designed this bridge. → *Calatrava is the famous Spanish architect **who** designed this bridge.*

That's the bridge. It was designed by Calatrava. → *That's the bridge **which** was designed by Calatrava.*

White is a colour. Calatrava prefers this colour for his buildings. → *White is the colour **that** Calatrava prefers for his buildings.*

Focus

As you can see, English has three different relative pronouns: **who**, **which** and **that**. Study how each is used:

	pronouns referring to people	pronouns referring to things and animals
subject	who or that	which or that
object	(who) or (whom) or (that)	(which) or (that)
after a preposition	(whom) or (that)	(which) or (that)
possessive case	whose	whose

The relative pronoun can function as the subject, direct or indirect object (with a preposition) of the sentence, or it can express possession.

- When the relative pronoun is the subject of the **defining relative clause**, it is always expressed:

  *Laura is the girl **who** sits next to me in the science class.*
  *The turtle is one of the animals **that** live the longest.*

- When the relative pronoun is the object of the **defining relative clause**, it is often understood, as shown by the brackets in the table:

  *The blonde girl **who(m)** / **that** you met at the party is my cousin.* → *The blonde girl you met...*
  *The story **which** / **that** you told me is very interesting.* → *The story you told me...*

FAQ

Q: It's not very clear to me when to use the pronoun **whom**.

A: **Whom** is a pronoun that refers to people, with the function of a complement. It is mainly used when there is a preposition, e.g. *The man to whom I was speaking was Mr Ross*. It belongs to a formal register and is not very common in speech. It is used more in **non-defining clauses** (see page 328).

- When a relative pronoun is accompanied by a preposition (indirect object), we can use three different constructions:
  - we can leave the preposition in front of the pronouns **which** or **whom**, but this cannot be done with **who** or **that** → *Is this the painting **for which** you paid ten thousand dollars?* (NOT ...*for that you paid...*)
  - we can move the preposition to the end of the relative clause, leaving the pronoun where it is, and in this case we can also use **that** → *The magazine **which / that** you're looking **for** is on your desk. The girl **whom / that** you were talking **to** is my sister.*
  - we can move the preposition to the end of the relative clause and omit the pronoun → *Tonight I'm going out with the boy I talked to you **about**. The parcel you were waiting **for** has just arrived.* This is the most common use in spoken language.
- To express possession in a relative clause, we always use the pronoun **whose**, which can't be omitted: *He's an artist. His work has been highly praised.* → *He's the artist **whose** work has been highly praised.*

1 Complete the sentences with *which* or *who*.

1 The man .... bought my car works in the same office as my son.
2 That's the mobile phone .... I'd like to have for my birthday.
3 The people .... have just come into the shop are from Sweden.
4 That woman .... is writing on her laptop looks like Marilyn Monroe.
5 The elephant .... is in that cage will be moved to a safari park soon.
6 Who is the person .... can fix computers in your company?
7 I like the white laptop .... is in that shop window.
8 The woman .... is responsible for the advertising department is my sister-in-law.

2 Correct the mistake in each sentence.

1 That is the lady who she owns the flower shop in the High Street.
   ....
2 Aren't these the earrings for that you've been looking for ages?
   ....
3 The doctor for who you're waiting has just arrived.
   ....
4 I'm sure this is the boy which father works in the bank next to my office.
   ....
5 Can't you see that car? The one who is parked in front of that gate?
   ....
6 Isn't he the artist which we met at yesterday's opening in Leo's art gallery?
   ....

3 Look at the sentences and put brackets around the relative pronouns that can be omitted.

1 The guy (who) I met on the plane was really nice.
2 The guy who was sitting next to me on the plane was very nice.
3 Your carbon footprint is the amount of carbon dioxide (that) you produce in your daily activities.
4 Emoticons are keyboard symbols that represent the expressions on somebody's face.
5 Emoticons are used in emails and text messages to show the feelings of the person who is sending the message.
6 A stepfamily is the family which is formed when somebody marries a person who already has children.
7 Parkour is a sport which you do in a city, running, jumping and climbing on roofs or walls.
8 The painting (that) we saw in the museum is a Rembrandt.

4 Complete the sentences with *who*, *which* or *whose*. Put brackets around the relative pronouns that can be omitted.

1 The guys (who) we met on holiday live in Finland.
2 The console (which) my parents gave me for Christmas has some great games.
3 The boy who was running with me in the park is my cousin Philip.
4 The woman whose laptop was stolen on the train is very upset.
5 The hedgehog (which) we saw in our garden last night looked really scared.
6 He's the actor whose interpretation of Hamlet was superb.
7 Do you like the electric bike which is parked outside the shop?
8 The graphic novel which has just been published is the best I've ever read.

5 Rewrite the sentences omitting the relative pronoun and moving the preposition to the end of the relative clause.

0 The holiday to which he was looking forward was cancelled.
   The holiday he was looking forward to was cancelled.

1 The friend with whom I usually play tennis has broken his arm falling off his bike.

2 The colleagues with whom my mother works gave her a necklace on her birthday.

3 The e-book about which we were talking yesterday got an important award.

4 The café to which we are going tonight was opened two hundred years ago!

5 Jack and Beatrix are going to buy the house of which they have been dreaming for a long time.

6 The document for which I had been looking for two days was in a drawer in my office.

7 The colleague with whom I travel to work every day is ill this week.

8 The large order to which we have been looking forward has finally arrived.

6 Rewrite the sentences, joining them with a relative pronoun. Omit the relative pronoun where possible.

1 That is the boy. His father is a renowned web designer.
....

2 The phone call came too late. I was waiting for it.
....

3 He's the man. You saw him at the pub last night.
....

4 This is the new scanner. I'm going to buy it.
....

5 That's the history teacher. He gives us a lot of homework.
....

6 This is the lady. She gave me her old digital camera.
....

7 The car was found near the park. It's Mr Beckett's.
....

8 The house is a really smart house. Carol lives in it.
....

7 Write sentences using the words below and the correct relative pronoun. In some sentences two different pronouns can be used.

0 A start-up / company / is just beginning to operate.
A start-up is a company that / which is just beginning to operate.

1 Comfort food / kind of food / makes you feel better, like chocolate and cookies.
....

2 Skydiving / sport / you jump from a plane and fall a long way down before opening your parachute.
....

3 A skydiver / person / does skydiving.
....

4 A segway / electric scooter / used in pedestrian areas.
....

5 A drone / aircraft without a pilot / controlled from the ground.
....

6 Paintball / game / people shoot balls of paint at each other.
....

7 A Q-R Code / type of matrix barcode / consists of black modules arranged in a square grid / can be read by a camera or a scanner.
....
....

8 A crocoburger / hamburger / made with crocodile meat.
....

LESSON 2 Relative pronouns in non-defining relative clauses

Non-defining relative clauses add some more information to what is said in the main clause, but this piece of information is not essential to identify who or what we are talking about. For this reason they are also called **extra-information clauses**. Look at this example, which contains a **non-defining clause**:

My parents, who have been married for 25 years, are celebrating their wedding anniversary next Sunday.

If I omit the underlined section, I still know who I'm talking about (**my parents**) and I still have a logical and coherent sentence: *My parents are celebrating their wedding anniversary next Sunday.* The non-defining clause adds a piece of information: *They have been married for 25 years.*

> ! Remember: a **non-defining relative clause** is always separated from the main clause by commas, or by a comma and the full stop at the end of the sentence → *Yesterday I met my old friend Jack, who used to go to my school.*

The relative pronouns used in non-defining clauses are as follows:

	pronouns referring to people	pronouns referring to things and animals
subject	who	which
object	who or whom	which
after a preposition	whom	which
possessive case	whose	whose or of which

Note that in this kind of sentence, unlike defining clauses:

- we never use the pronoun **that**, but only **who / whom** for people and **which** for things
- the relative pronoun is always included, even when it is the object of the sentence → *Meg and Tom, who(m) you met at my house last summer, are living in England now.*

When there is an indirect object, the preposition (**with**, **to**, **about**, **for**...) can:

- precede the relative pronoun → *This is Mr Rogers, with whom you will work during the next few weeks.*
- be at the end of the relative sentence but the pronoun cannot be omitted → *Yesterday I visited the Tate Modern Gallery, which I had never been to before.*

> ! The use of the comma is very important because it can change the meaning of the sentence. Look, for example, at the difference between a **defining** sentence without commas and a **non-defining** one with commas:
>
> *The students who had not received their exam results were feeling very anxious.* (only those who had not received them were anxious)
>
> *The students, who had not received their exam results, were feeling very anxious.* (all the students had not received them and they were all anxious.)

1 **Some of these sentences contain non-defining relative clauses. Identify them and insert commas in the correct place.**

1. The Sullivans who live opposite us have just bought a new car.
2. My washing machine which is quite old keeps breaking down.
3. The cordless phone that we have in our bedroom doesn't always work properly.
4. My son's friends who are often at our house are very pleasant young people.
5. The new app that I have just downloaded is very useful for my job.
6. The dilapidated building which is on the outskirts of the town has been chosen as the set for a film.
7. Do you know the technician who repairs all the computers in our office?

2 **Complete the sentences with the correct relative pronoun: *who*, *whom*, *which* or *whose*.**

1. My friend, ... father is a video-game designer, has lots of great video games.
2. Deborah, ... is my next-door neighbour, is a great cook and often invites me to dinner.
3. Steve, meet Dr Wells, ... works for AT&T.
4. Our French partners, ... we have signed a contract with, will receive the documents next week.
5. This contract, ... we signed last week, must be sent to the buyers immediately.
6. Our rep, ... you met yesterday, is one of the best salesmen in our company.
7. Luke, ... is the best in his class, is also very helpful with all his classmates.
8. *The Big Bang Theory*, ... is a successful TV series, tells the story of four young scientists.

3 **Rewrite the sentences, joining them with the correct relative pronoun. Some of the sentences have defining clauses.**

1. Our French teacher retired last month. We all liked her very much.
   ....
2. Mr and Ms Martin are a married couple. I met them in Spain last summer.
   ....
3. That is a self-portrait. My father painted it 20 years ago.
   ....
4. Do you know the name of that model? Her photo was on the front cover of *Vanity Fair* last week.
   ....
5. I work for Mr Owen. He's the financial manager of our company.
   ....
6. I've got two younger sisters. I get on well with them.
   ....
7. *Cats* is a very famous musical. It has been on in theatres all over the world for years.
   ....
8. I hate the novels. They tell silly love stories.
   ....
9. The friends are very good at maths and help me a lot. I study with them every day.
   ....
10. The desk is stacked with books and paper. I work at this desk.
    ....

LESSON 3 Other relative pronouns and adverbs: *what, all that, where, when...*

Other pronouns and relative adverbs are:

WHAT → *I didn't hear what she said.*

ALL / EVERYTHING → *This is all we need. They could have everything they liked.*
It's also possible to say: **all that / everything that**, but NOT ~~all what~~

WHICH, referring to the whole of the preceding sentence. Since this is a **non-defining** relative clause, it is added to the main clause after a comma → *We all went to see him off at the station, which made him very happy.* (= What we did made him very happy.)

THE REASON WHY or simply **WHY** → *I don't know (the reason) why she wouldn't tell me.*
It's also possible to say: **the reason for which...**, but NOT **the reason because...**

HOW or **THE WAY** → *This is how they make this dish.*
It's also possible to say: *This is the way they make this dish.*

WHERE → *The town where I was born is in the south of Scotland.*
It's also possible to say: *The town in which I was born is in the south of Scotland.*

WHEN → *Youth is the time of life when everything seems possible.*
It's also possible to say: *Youth is the time of life in which everything seems possible.*

> ❗ Be careful! With the expressions **the year..., the day..., the time...** we can find **when, in which / on which / at which** or no adverb:
>
> *2011 is the year when we got married. / ...the year in which we got married. / ...the year we got married.*
>
> *This is the day when everyone gets their exam results. / This is the day on which everyone... / This is the day everyone...*
>
> *One o'clock is the time when we usually meet. / ...the time at which we usually meet. / ...the time we usually meet.*

1 Choose the correct option.

1 '**All** / **That** you need is love' is a famous Beatles song.
2 Don't listen to **what** / **all what** she's saying!
3 I know it isn't much, but that's **all that** / **how** I can do for you.
4 Why are you so interested in **that** / **what** I'm doing?
5 There's no reason **how** / **why** we shouldn't go to that party.
6 You should teach me **all** / **how** to knit. You always make beautiful jumpers.
7 I like the smell of **how** / **what** you're cooking. What is it?
8 This is the place **when** / **where** we usually spend the weekend.
9 This is the year **when** / **which** Tom will get his degree at last.
10 Let's visit the village **whose** / **where** my parents met for the first time.
11 He never found out the reason **why** / **because** she had left him.
12 The office **in which** / **in where** I work has air conditioning.

2 Complete the sentences with *when, why, where, that* or *how*. Put brackets around the ones that can be left out.

1. Tell me .... you made these biscuits. They're delicious.
2. I'd like to know the reason .... you didn't come.
3. The country .... they come from is quite poor.
4. All .... you say from now on is going to be recorded.
5. This is the time .... they usually leave the office.
6. Tell me all .... you know about them.
7. Prime Day is .... the big sales start in the USA.
8. This is the hotel .... we spent our honeymoon.
9. A proverb says that 'Home is .... you belong'.
10. He didn't tell me .... he had to leave so early.

3 Join the sentences using *which*.

1. Everybody liked the food I had cooked. It was quite surprising.
   ....
2. Connie passed her driving test. She didn't quite expect it.
   ....
3. They didn't come to the concert. It was a shame.
   ....
4. Sam will have to work next Sunday. It's quite unusual.
   ....
5. A lot of students in our school do voluntary work. It is really admirable.
   ....
6. Quite a number of start-up companies have opened in our town. This is good news.
   ....

4 Find the mistakes in each sentence and correct them.

1. Why don't you tell me all what you know?
   ....
2. Give me one reason because I should help them.
   ....
3. This is the place on which I saw the accident.
   ....
4. An Indie Market is a place in where all the traders are independent.
   ....
5. Why don't you tell me way you solved the problem?
   ....
6. This is the time at when the ghost is said to appear in the Big Hall.
   ....
7. I couldn't see that she was wearing under her coat.
   ....

LESSON 4 Relative clauses expressed by the present or past participle; verbs of perception

The present participle of a verb, i.e. the *–ing* form, can function as a defining relative clause. This happens when the action described is in progress: *There are a lot of people who are running in the park.*
→ *There are a lot of people running in the park.*

1 Look at the picture and complete the sentences below using verbs in the *–ing* form.

1 There's a policeman .... at the gate.
2 There are .... along a path.
3 There are two women .... on a bench.
4 There's a child with .... from a kiosk.
5 There are some ....

Verbs of perception

The construction with the present participle is often found with verbs of perception.
I can see a lot of people running in the park.

The most common verbs of perception are those linked to seeing and hearing: **see**, **hear**, plus others like **listen**, **watch**, **notice**, **find**.

Other verbs of perception, linked to smell, touch and taste, are: **smell**, **feel**, **taste**.

Verbs of perception often appear with the modal verb **can**:

You can see the Royal Palace on your left.

Speak louder. I can't hear you.

2 Complete the sentences with the correct form of these verbs: *hear, smell, taste, feel, watch*.

1 .... how soft this woollen scarf is!
2 Can't you .... the birds singing?
3 This drink .... so bitter! I don't like it.
4 Yesterday I .... the kids playing football for an hour.
5 I can .... the alcohol on your breath. What have you been drinking?
6 I .... your phone ring a minute ago.

Perceiving active actions

We can often see or hear someone who is doing something.

- If the action is short in duration and we perceive the whole action, we use **see / hear someone do something**, with the base form of the verb → *I heard someone slam the door.*
- If the action is longer and therefore we cannot see it in its entirety, we can use:
  - a relative clause with a verb in the continuous form → *I heard someone who was crying.*
  - **see / hear someone doing something**, with the verb in the **–ing** form → *I heard someone crying.* This is the most common form.

Look at the difference between these two sentences:
I saw two people get off the train. (short action, started and finished)
I saw two people waiting for the train. (longer action which was still in progress when I stopped watching → **–ing** form)

> **!** In negative sentences and in those which contain an adverb of frequency like **always**, **never**, **usually**, we generally use the base form of the verb:
> *I didn't hear the phone ring. Did you?*
> *I've never seen that girl smile.*
> *I always hear dad sing in the bathroom in the morning.*

Perceiving passive actions

If we perceive a passive action which takes place over a longer time duration and therefore is not perceived in its entirety, we can use

- a relative clause with a passive verb in a continuous tense → *I saw a cyclist who was being chased by a dog.*
- the construction **see / hear something being done** → *I saw a cyclist being chased by a dog.*

If, on the other hand, we have a shorter action, which we perceive in its entirety, we can use:

- a relative clause with a passive verb in the simple form: *I heard my name that was called out.*
- the construction **see / hear something done**, with the past participle → *I heard my name called out.*

Focus

In English, we often use the past participle to replace a relative clause with a passive meaning, e.g.
A fanzine is a magazine written and read by the fans of a singer or a group. (instead of: …which is written…)
The information found on this website needs double-checking. (instead of: …that is found…)

Verbs of perception in the passive form

When the verb of perception is in the passive form, the verb which follows it can be with:

- **to + base form** (short action) → *He was seen to leave home at about three o'clock.*
- **–ing form** (longer action) → *They were heard shouting like mad.*

3 Rewrite the sentences as in the example.

0   The crocodile was moving. I saw it.   *I saw the crocodile moving.*
    The crocodile moved. I saw it.   *I saw the crocodile move.*

1   The kids were laughing. I heard them. ....

2   Something sweet was being baked. I smelt it. ....

3   Two men opened the door of the bank. I saw them. ....

4   A cold wind was blowing in the street. He felt it. ....

5   Two people left the room before the end of the lecture. I noticed them.
    ....

6   The waiter dropped a pile of plates. We saw him. ....

7   Somebody knocked at the door, but I didn't hear it. ....

8   The girl was playing the violin. I heard her. ....

4 Complete the sentences using the base form or –ing form of the verbs below.

burn   stand   fall   call   wait   gossip

1   We heard the sound of the glass .... onto the floor.

2   I saw a young man idly .... next to a lamppost.

3   We overheard two people .... about their colleagues.

4   I can smell something ....

5   Listen! I can hear somebody .... your name.

6   The witness saw the black car .... outside the bank.

5 Reorder the words to write sentences with the passive form of the verbs of perception.

1   throwing / He / was / stones / seen / .
    ....

2   heard / She / beautiful / was / a / song / singing / .
    ....

3   They / opening / were / the / door / heard / late / at / garage / night / the / .
    ....

4   noticed / Someone / walking / up / was / street / and / the / down / .
    ....

5   heard / He / to / was / whistle / .
    ....

6   been / You / seen / have / exam / during / copying / the / .
    ....

7   young / were / Some / hanging / people / noticed / late / night / last / around / .
    ....

8   was / to / Jack / get on / a / seen / the / train / at / station / .
    ....

9   baby / heard / at / The / was / crying / night / .
    ....

10 were / like / laughing / They / heard / mad / .
    ....

6 Rewrite the sentences, joining them with a past or present participle, as in the example.

0 The painting was a Gauguin. It was stolen from the art gallery.
   The painting stolen from the art gallery was a Gauguin.

1 Draw a picture of one of the animals. The animals are mentioned in the story.
   ....

2 The news was in an article. The article was published in a local magazine.
   ....

3 We're going to rent a flat. The flat is overlooking the sea.
   ....

4 The path leads to the waterfall. It's very steep.
   ....

5 My friend took some notes at the conference. They are very clear.
   ....

6 Try to explain the words. They are highlighted in the text.
   ....

7 A lady's sitting in the last row. Do you know her?
   ....

8 Do you know that girl? She's eating an ice cream.
   ....

7 Change the present participle or the past participle contained in these sentences into a relative clause, as in the example.

0 The free WI-FI area was full of people using their laptops.
   The free WI-FI area was full of people who were using their laptops.

1 This is the e-book illustrated by my father.
   ....

2 There were lots of kids playing games on the web.
   ....

3 There are more and more people using open-source software.
   ....

4 I met Linda looking for a new digital camera in the store.
   ....

5 There was a dark spot covering the PC screen.
   ....

6 He was looking at the images printed in colour.
   ....

7 They usually double-check the information found on Wikipedia.
   ....

8 This is the new software created by a group of students aged 16.
   ....

ROUND UP 18

1 **Join the two parts of the sentences.**

1 Colin has a computer game
2 This is the girl
3 Mark is the programmer
4 They are the founders of a firm
5 I bought the latest software
6 She's the computer graphics artist

A whose work has been greatly praised.
B which exports hi-tech products.
C which can take days to finish.
D which is on the market.
E who designed my website.
F who lent me her tablet.

1 ..... 2 ..... 3 ..... 4 ..... 5 ..... 6 .....

2 **Complete the sentences with the correct relative pronoun: *who*, *whom*, *which* or *whose*.**

1 Mr Gray, ... is a music teacher, is also a good sportsman.
2 My neighbour, ... I asked for help with my computer, works in an electronics store.
3 Laura, ... is the best at maths in our class, is also very good at playing chess.
4 My girlfriend, ... works in a pub, is looking for a better job.
5 This coffee machine, ... I bought last week, doesn't seem to work properly.
6 Your cousin, ... results in the test were outstanding, has joined my class.
7 Mark, ... I often play tennis with, has just bought a new racket.
8 These tennis balls, ... are quite expensive, do not seem to bounce very well.
9 You didn't tell me the truth, ... is quite bad of you.
10 He's the boy .... father is a web designer.

3 **Rewrite the sentences with the preposition at the end of the relative clause. Omit the relative pronoun.**

0 The holiday to which he was looking forward had to be cancelled.
  The holiday he was looking forward to had to be cancelled.

1 The text with which I was working suddenly vanished from the screen.
  ....

2 Who are the people for whom you are waiting?
  ....

3 The house in which they live is super technological.
  ....

4 The people with whom she went to the meeting went home early.
  ....

5 The e-book about which we were talking got an important award.
  ....

6 The music to which you are listening is played by the London Symphony Orchestra.
  ....

7 The kind of life to which they had got used was going to change.
  ....

8 The baby after whom I looked last summer is now nearly one year old.
  ....

4 Rewrite the sentences using *in / at / on / for + which* instead of *when / where / why*.

1 There are moments when I would like to live on a desert island.
....

2 This is the university where both my husband and I studied years ago.
....

3 I don't know the reason why she left her job. ....

4 Last Friday was the day when we moved to the new office.
....

5 Three o'clock is the time when you can meet the sales manager.
....

6 Unfortunately there isn't a place where you can camp near here.
....

7 The country where they speak Urdu is Pakistan. ....

8 Can you give me a good reason why I should have a healthier life?
....

5 You are showing your holiday photos to a friend. Describe them using the words suggested.

0 alpine star / we saw on a rock   *This is an alpine star that we saw on a rock.*

1 hut / we stayed there for the night
2 hot chocolate / we drank it to make ourselves warm
3 the view / we had it from the top of the mountain
4 a little lake / we stopped there for a picnic
5 my trekking boots / muddy at the end of the day
6 the mountain peak / we could reach it
7 our friends / they climbed the mountain with us
8 our guide / he led us to the top
9 a marmot / we saw it in a meadow

6 Insert the missing parts of the non-defining relative clauses in the text.

which usually come   who are always directed   which is accompanied
which are mostly composed   which are set   which is broadcast

The New Year's Concert from Vienna, ¹.. in most European countries, is a must in my family on New Year's Day. The Wiener Philharmoniker, ².. by one of the most famous orchestra directors in the world, play waltzes and polkas, ³.. by Johann Strauss father and son. The flowers on the stage, ⁴.. from Sanremo, Italy, are the most beautiful you've ever seen. The last piece that the orchestra play every year is the Radetzky March, ⁵.. by the hand clapping of the public. During the concert you can also see fantastic ballets, ⁶.. in the most amazing villas and parks of Austria.

7 Reorder the words to make meaningful sentences.

1 are / Things / always / like / done / not / the way / I / .
   ....
2 the one / who / I'm / yesterday / to you / on / the / spoke / phone / .
   ....
3 is / film / a / 'Goodbye Mr Holland' / good / came out / 1995 / in / which / .
   ....
4 who / is / A hero / does / day / his / duty / someone / every / .
   ....
5 is / painter / the / She / whose / girl / famous / mother / is / a / .
   ....
6 this / Is / the / which / present / for / you / Dad / bought / ?
   ....

8 Read the sentences and put into brackets the relative pronouns which can be omitted.

1 I've never met the girl who is going out with my brother.
2 It's the kind of game which I really like.
3 He's the man whom we saw at the cinema last night.
4 Have you ever visited the art gallery which is in Victoria Road?
5 The MP3 player which I found in the park belongs to my friend Julia.
6 The people who were at your party are really nice.
7 That is the bed which I would like to buy. It looks extremely comfortable.
8 The office which is for rent in this street could be suitable for our start-up.

9 These sentences have all got mistakes in them. Find the mistakes and rewrite correct sentences.

1 That was all what we could do. ....
2 I'm so curious. Tell me that you know. ....
3 He's the one which I was waiting for. ....
4 We're leaving tomorrow, that makes me very sad. ....

5 My house is the place at which I most like to be. ....
6 Come and see those girls which are dancing so well. ....
7 Cupertino is the town Apple has its headquarters. ....
8 Tigers are animals who are in danger of extinction. ....

10 Complete the quotes with an appropriate relative pronoun.

1 'A gentleman is one .... puts more into the world than he takes out.'
   George Bernard Shaw, Irish playwright
2 'Thinking is the hardest work there is, ... is probably the reason why so few engage in it.' *Henry Ford, American captain of industry*
3 'A soulmate is the one person .... love is powerful enough to motivate you to meet your soul.' *Kenny Loggins, American singer and songwriter*
4 'There are people .... the more you do for them, the less they will do for themselves.' *Jane Austen, English author*
5 'The love that lasts the longest is the love .... is never returned.'
   William Somerset Maugham, English author

11 Rewrite the sentences, joining them with the correct relative pronouns.

1 Our rep will offer you favourable contracts. You met him last week.
   ....
2 The technician is really good. He has repaired my computer.
   ....
3 Tom is a whizz at IT. I'm studying with him today.
   ....
4 The homepage is updated every week. It was created by one of our programmers.
   ....
5 The printer is also a scanner and a photocopier. We have it in our office.
   ....

Reflecting on grammar

Reflect on the rules and say whether the following statements are true or false.

		True	False
1	Non-defining relative clauses are separated by commas.		
2	Defining relative clauses are essential to the understanding of a sentence.		
3	**Whose**, the relative pronoun for possession, can be omitted.		
4	The relative pronoun **that** can replace both **who** or **which** in a defining relative clause.		
5	**Who** is used for animals and things, **which** for people.		
6	The sentence *This is the book I told you about* is wrong. We should say *This is the book about which I told you*.		
7	The relative pronoun relating to the object of a sentence must always be expressed.		
8	The sentence *This is all I have to tell you* is correct.		
9	The present participle of a verb, i.e. its **–ing** form, can replace a relative clause.		
10	If we perceive a short action in its entirety, we use a verb in the base form.		

Revision and Exams 6 (UNITS 16 – 17 – 18)

1 Complete the text with the correct tense of the verbs below.

get   buy   want   have   pay   manage   know

When I ¹..................... to have a good laugh, I go to a show in my town. In winter, there are quite a lot of shows with stand-up comedians. I love going and enjoy watching all kinds of shows: musicals, comedies, drama, classical plays. If I had more money and more time, I ²..................... a season ticket. If you buy a season ticket, you ³..................... less and you ⁴..................... a seat reserved for you. If you buy five tickets for the same show, you ⁵..................... a 20% discount. If I ⁶..................... about that last year, I would have saved a lot of money because I generally go with four or five friends. If I ⁷..................... to save some money, I would have been able to go more often!

2 Rewrite the text, changing the underlined phrases into the passive.

They teach three languages in my school: French, German and Spanish. I'm learning one, German. Ms Hofer, the German teacher, makes us work very hard: of course, we must speak only German during her lessons. She gives us lots of grammar exercises to do every day. She also asks us to read a new book and write a review of it every month, then we discuss each of our reviews in the class. You can obtain good results with Ms Hofer only if you study really hard. If you want to learn a language very well, the best thing to do is go to a country where they speak it. But you can learn a language quite well in school too, if you have a teacher like mine!

3 Complete the text using the base or –ing form of the verbs below.

lead   come   live   say   get (x2)   look   wait   sit

Lost and found

Tim Dalton, a six-year-old ¹..................... in a village near Ashdown Forest, disappeared on his way home last Friday afternoon. When his mum didn't see him ²..................... in at the usual time, she immediately called the local police and a group of friends and they all started searching the area. The boy had been seen ³..................... on the school bus with his little friends and ⁴..................... off at the bus stop near home. Somebody had heard him ⁵..................... that he wanted to find the home of Winnie-the-Pooh, a popular fictional bear, in the forest near his house. Tim's mother remembered seeing him ⁶..................... out of his bedroom window at the forest, so they all decided to start searching there before it got dark. Along the main path ⁷..................... into the forest, the police dogs smelt something and they followed the scent towards a clearing in the wood. Tim was there, ⁸..................... in the middle of the clearing, ⁹..................... for Winnie to come.

The next day, one of his mum's friends gave Tim a Winnie-the-Pooh bear.

Preliminary (PET) | Reading Part 5

4 Read the text and choose the correct word(s) (A, B, C or D) for each space.

When we think of rice, we imagine south-east Asian landscapes. However, we must remember that rice [1]...... in Europe too, and Italy is the largest European producer. The total Italian production amounts to about 1,200,000 tons, 90% of which [2]...... every autumn in the triangle formed by joining the towns of Novara, Vercelli and Pavia with an imaginary line. Smaller quantities of rice [3]...... in Sardinia and near the Po delta too. Rice [4]...... in April under irrigated conditions in large and highly mechanised farms. Today, less labour is needed than in the past: each hectare, [5]...... in 1939 required an average of 1,028 hours of work, now only needs an average of [6]...... 50 hours.

The earliest documents about rice cultivation date back to the late Middle Ages, notably to 1475 when rice [7]...... promoted by Galeazzo Maria Sforza, Duke of Milan. If he [8]...... the Duke of Ferrara one sack of rice which was of such high quality that it enabled the farmer to harvest 12 sacks in return, rice growing [9]...... as quickly in the fertile marshy plains between Piedmont and Lombardy. A system of canals was built and water was brought to flood the rice fields in the month of April [10]...... rice is sown. The Italians have a saying: 'Rice grows in water but dies in wine.'

The most famous Italian yellow rice dish [11]...... conceived during the construction of the famous Milan cathedral when saffron [12]...... introduced to colour the stained-glass windows of the cathedral and was added to rice as a joke.

1	A	are grown	B	has been grown	C	was grown	D	is grown
2	A	are harvested	B	is harvested	C	harvests	D	is harvesting
3	A	are grown	B	aren't grown	C	grows	D	don't grow
4	A	are planted	B	isn't planted	C	is planted	D	plants
5	A	which	B	who	C	whose	D	whim
6	A	less as	B	fewer than	C	as little than	D	as much as
7	A	has been	B	was	C	is	D	were
8	A	didn't give	B	has given	C	hadn't given	D	gave
9	A	wouldn't have spread	B	would spread	C	will have spread	D	won't spread
10	A	where	B	when	C	on which	D	which
11	A	is said to be	B	says to be	C	says to have been	D	is said to have been
12	A	has been	B	was	C	were	D	will be

5 **Complete the passage with the correct relative pronoun or adverb. You can omit the relative pronouns when they are not needed.**

Last Saturday, I didn't know ¹..................................... to do or ²..................................... to go. My friend Debbie, ³..................................... I had arranged to meet in town, had just rung to say she had to look after her little brother, and so I was on my own. There were two or three things ⁴..................................... I needed to buy – make-up and some toiletries – so I walked to the shops, ⁵..................................... I was sure I would find them. But the shop ⁶..................................... I usually buy these things was closed. A notice, ⁷..................................... was hung on the front door, said that the shop had moved to Burlington Street, but I didn't know ⁸..................................... that was. I realised I had left my mobile at home, so I couldn't search the Internet, and I had to do it the old-fashioned way: ask somebody. I walked up to a man ⁹..................................... was sitting on a bench under a tree and asked him, but he didn't know either, so I decided to walk back home. Suddenly, on my way back and not too far from home, I saw the shop ¹⁰..................................... I had been looking for. It was much bigger than it used to be and you should have seen the guy at the cash desk: one of the best-looking young men ¹¹..................................... I have ever seen. And guess what? We are going out together tomorrow, to the restaurant ¹²..................................... was opened a couple of weeks ago.

Preliminary (PET) | Writing Part 1

6 **Here are some sentences about the Eurotunnel. For each question, complete the second sentence so that it means the same as the first.**

1 France and Britain began the construction of the Eurotunnel in 1987. It was completed in 1994.

   The Eurotunnel construction, ...
   .... , was completed in 1994.

2 The Eurotunnel was finished in only seven years.

   It took ....

3 Queen Elizabeth II and French President François Mitterand officially opened it on 6th, May 1994.

   It was ....
   on 6th, May 1994.

4 First they started the international freight train in commercial service.

   The international freight train ....
   ....

5 The passenger shuttle service for cars came later that year. It was started on 22nd December, 1994.

   The passenger shuttle service for cars, ...,
   .... 1994.

6 In March 1999, they named the Eurotunnel 'Top Construction Achievement of the 20th Century'.

   The Eurotunnel ....
   ....

First (FCE) | Reading and Use of English Part 2

7 Read the text below and think of the word which best fits each gap. Use only one word in each gap.

I'm so glad that I did that computer course ⁰..*in*.. September. You see, the company was looking for someone ¹.................... knew most types of office software. If I hadn't ².................... good computer skills, I ³.................... have been right for the position I've got now.

When I started the course, I wasn't sure I would ⁴.................... able to complete it. I had three 90-minute lessons a week, ⁵.................... is quite a lot when you're working too, and the course lasted four months. On top of that, the lessons, ⁶.................... were from 7 to 8.30 pm, weren't always in the same school, so ⁷.................... I forgot to write the place in my diary, I could easily end up at the wrong school and miss the lesson!

Luckily the teacher was very good. If he ⁸.................... been, I would have probably given up after a while. He was very clear and patient. We ⁹.................... taught the most up-to-date versions of the most widely used software and we ¹⁰.................... given really challenging tasks, which had to be completed in groups. That way, I also made new friends during the course.

Towards Competences

Some of the grammar topics which we have looked at in these units are typical of formal written language, especially the passive form and non-defining relative clauses, which are used in narrative and descriptive text types. Put yourself to the test and use them as much as you can in the following texts.

1. As part of a cultural exchange programme in your school, your class has to carry out scientific experiments and write a detailed report to be published on the website. Your task is to write the report. Choose an experiment that you have carried out in the lab and describe it.

   REPORT SHEET
   Experiment:
   Date:
   Laboratory:
   Materials used and their quantities:
   Procedure:

2. For the website designed for the twinning of the place where you live, your task is to write an article about the main productive activities of your area. Do some appropriate research and write a text of about 300 words. Add some interesting and useful photos to it, too.

Self Check 6

Circle the correct option. Then check your answers at the end of the book.

1 You .... me that the meeting had been cancelled.
   A could have told
   B could told
   C had told

2 He .... very tired last night. He went to bed at 9.30.
   A had to have been
   B must have been
   C must had been

3 If you .... a little milk to the mixture, you get a softer cake.
   A will add
   B added
   C add

4 Get some bread if you .... to the supermarket.
   A will go
   B go
   C would go

5 .... too much time watching TV if you want to go out later.
   A You won't spend
   B Don't spend
   C Won't spend

6 If my favourite team .... tonight, I'll give up chocolate for a week!
   A wins
   B will win
   C could win

7 If you book your flight now, ... 30% less.
   A you'd pay
   B you'd paid
   C you'll pay

8 If I ...., I wouldn't spend my day watching videos on YouTube.
   A were you
   B be
   C would be you

9 If Mark .... arrived so late, he could have had lunch with us.
   A hadn't   B wasn't   C didn't

10 .... to work night shifts if they had accepted the job.
   A They would had have
   B They'd have
   C They would have had

11 Would you buy a new suit if they .... you to their New Year's party?
   A invited
   B had invited
   C would invite

12 If Alan Turing .... his data-processing device, we wouldn't have our personal computers today.
   A didn't develop
   B hadn't developed
   C don't develop

13 If he had asked, we .... him.
   A could have helped
   B had helped
   C must have helped

14 That vase on the shelf is .... of Bohemian crystal.
   A done   B built   C made

15 The best sports equipment can be .... in the shop in the mall.
   A find   B found   C finding

16 'Who .... ?' 'Picasso.'
   A was *Guernica* painted by
   B by was *Guernica* painted
   C was painted *Guernica* by

17 The story .... told with background music and photos.
   A have been   B was   C has

18 We discovered our flight .... cancelled when we got to the airport.
   A is just been
   B was just been
   C had just been

19 The new CEO will .... appointed in a few days.
   A have been   B be
   C have be

20 The winners of the competition .... by tomorrow evening.
   A will be announcing
   B will being announced
   C will have been announced

21 Dear me! This project .... before five this afternoon. It's far too long!
   A may finish
   B won't be finished
   C will have finished

22 They .... a wonderful Ferrari, but it was too expensive.
   A have been shown   B are shown
   C were shown

23 The best students in our school .... a scholarship every year.
   A are granting
   B have granted
   C are granted

24 We .... a very moving story during yesterday's reading meeting at the library.
   A have been told
   B were told
   C would tell

25 Ms Hogan .... the most skilled financial manager our company has ever had.
   A say to be
   B has said being
   C is said to be

26 This is considered .... one of the most beautiful portraits of our age.
   A being   B to be   C be

27 They were supposed .... in the warehouse, but they were actually taking a much longer break.
   A to be working   B work
   C they will work

28 Karen .... for the end-of-school party.
   A had her hair dyed blond
   B did her hair dyed blond
   C was dyed her hair blond

29 Could you tell me the name of the person .... car is parked next to mine?
   A which   B whom   C whose

30 This is the lady .... we met on the train.
   A which   B whose   C /

31 The model .... photo was on the cover of *Vogue* lives next door to my parents.
   A who her   B who's   C whose

32 The chair .... is in that corner is very old and valuable.
   A which   B who   C what

33 Jane and Tessa, ... are the friends I usually go on holiday with, aren't going to come with us this year.
   A how   B who   C that

34 September is the month .... the school year starts in most of Europe.
   A in which   B when   C where

35 Tell me the reason .... you gave up your job.
   A how   B because   C why

36 Do you know the restaurant .... they serve crocoburgers?
   A why   B on which   C where

37 November 15th was the day .... my mother retired.
   A at when   B on which
   C in which

38 This wine .... off. Throw it away.
   A tastes   B sounds   C looks

39 I didn't hear the front door bell .... Are you sure there was somebody there?
   A rung   B is ringing   C ring

40 She was seen .... some T-shirts from the market stall.
   A stolen   B stealing   C stole

Assess Yourself!

- 0 – 10   Study harder. Use the online exercises to help you.
- 11 – 20 OK. Use the online exercises to practise things you don't know.
- 21 – 30 Good, but do some extra practice online.
- 31 – 40 Excellent!

GRAMMAR MATRIX MAIN

UNIT 19 Direct speech and reported speech

LESSON 1 Verbs *say* and *tell*

The verb *say*

The verb **say** (past simple and past participle **said**) is used to:

- indicate who says the words reported in inverted commas (quotes) in direct speech. Often we find **say** at the end of the quotation, preceded by a comma. The name of the person who says the words is generally put after the verb, but it can also go before the verb → *'Everything's ready,'* <u>said Peter</u> / <u>Peter said</u>.
  The pronoun, however, always goes before the verb. → *'Help me, please!'* <u>he</u> <u>said</u>.

> **! Remember!** **Say** is followed by the pronoun **to** when we indicate the person we are talking to → *'You're right,' she said <u>to</u> me.* NOT ~~she said me~~.

- introduce indirect speech when we do not indicate the person to whom we are speaking → *He said he would come the following day.*

> **! Remember!** Between the main clause and the declarative clause that follows, there may be the conjunction **that**, or no conjunction → *The weather forecast says (that) it will rain tomorrow.*

Remember the personal passive construction: **Someone is said to be... / to have...** → *She is said to have a great talent.   He is said to have been a hero in time of war.*

The verb *tell*

The verb **tell** (past simple and past participle **told**) is used:

- to introduce reported speech, only when we have the name of the person to whom something is said. The person, name or pronoun, is not followed by any preposition → *I told Jane...   I told her...*
  The main clause with the verb **tell** can be followed by:
  - a declarative clause with or without the conjunction **that** → *He told me (that) he had just arrived.*
  - a verb with **to** → *I told him to keep calm.*
- in direct speech, after the words in inverted commas, only if the person we are talking to is mentioned → *'I'm ready to go,' she told him.* If the person is not mentioned, we use the verb **say**.

We can use the personal passive form with the verb **tell** as well: **Someone was told to do / not to do something** → *He was told to stay at home.   I was told not to go.*

Look at this summary table of the two structures.

Direct speech	Reported speech
'......,' he said / said Peter.	He said / Peter said (that)...
'......,' he said to me / he told me.	He told me (that)...
'......,' said my father / my father said.	My father told me (that)...
'......,' my father said to me / my father told me.	My father told me to...

Other uses of *say* and *tell*

The verbs **say** and **tell** are also used in the following expressions:

SAY	TELL
say yes, say no	tell the truth
say a word	tell a lie
say please	tell the time
say thank you	tell a story
say something, say nothing	tell jokes
say hello, say goodbye	tell someone your name
say a poem, say a prayer	tell someone about something

1 Complete the sentences with the correct form of *say* or *tell*.

1 .... me about your new school, Simon.
2 Don't .... a word. Someone may be listening.
3 .... thank you to Grandma, Carol.
4 I'm very bad at .... jokes.
5 Why don't you .... me the truth?
6 Did I .... something wrong?
7 .... yes, Mum. Please let me go to the party!
8 Excuse me, can you .... me the time, please?

2 Circle the correct option.

1 I told **her** / **to her** it was too late.
2 I said **him** / **to him** that I couldn't come before eight.
3 'Hurry up!' **said she** / **she said**.
4 They were told **not to be late** / **to be not late**.
5 'Wake up, lazybones!' my mother **says** / **tells** every morning.
6 He told **to me** / **me** that it was a lie.
7 They **told** / **said** goodbye and went away.
8 'Don't wait for me. I'll be late,' she **told** / **told us**.

3 Transform the sentences from active to passive.

1 They told me to wait until they came back.
   I was ....
2 They say she's a great artist.
   She is ....
3 They told us to reach the conference room before nine.
   ....
4 They say the lecturer is one of the best in his field.
   ....
5 They told the Board of Directors to meet in the afternoon.
   ....
6 They say that Serena Williams is one of the best tennis players ever.
   ....

LESSON 2 Indirect speech: giving orders and expressing statements in the present that are still true

Reporting commands or advice

Transformations from direct to indirect speech

Direct speech	Reported speech
Verbs in the imperative *My friend said to me:* *'Take a break and relax.'*	**to** / **not to** + base form of the verb *My friend told me to take a break and relax.* Or (**that**) + subject + **should** / **shouldn't** + base form of the verb *My friend told me (that) I should take a break and relax.*

Look at another example:

'Don't worry, everything will be alright,' his mother told him. → *His mother told him <u>not to worry</u> / (that) <u>he shouldn't worry</u>.*

As well as **tell** and **say**, we can find other verbs in the introductory clause in indirect speech, e.g. **order**, **remind**, **warn**, **ask**, **advise** → *She reminded me to lock the door.   They warned us not to drive on the icy road.*

1 Transform the sentences into indirect speech. Use both forms, as in the example.

The day before the school trip, the teacher said to the children:

0 'Don't be late for the trip.'
   → <u>The teacher told the children not to be late / they shouldn't be late for the trip.</u>

1 'Wait for the coach in the car park.'
   She told them ....

2 'Walk in a line while we are in town.'
   ....

3 'Hold your friend's hand when we cross the street.'
   ....

4 'Don't walk around on your own.'
   ....

5 'Bring your packed lunch.'
   ....

6 'Don't forget to bring an anorak and a hat.'
   ....

7 'Wear comfortable shoes.'
   ....

8 'Remind your parents to pick you up at 6 pm in front of the school.'
   ....

2 Complete the sentences with the correct form of the verbs below.

order   warn   remind   ask   advise

1 'Take some photos of the event, please.'
   I was .... to take some photos of the event.
2 'Remember to send the photos to the press.'
   They .... me to send the photos to the press.
3 'You shouldn't drive in this weather!'
   They .... us not to drive in that weather.
4 'Three coffees, please.'
   They .... three coffees.
5 'Keep away from the fire, Jack!'
   His mother .... Jack to keep away from the fire.

3 Rewrite the sentences using indirect speech. Use the verbs in brackets.

0 'Don't go out in the cold, Marion,' said her mother. (tell)
   Marion's mother told her not to go out in the cold.
1 'You should use sunscreen in this heat,' said Mike. (advise)
   ....
2 'Don't feed the animals,' the ranger said to the visitors. (remind)
   ....
3 'Stop making so much noise, children,' said the teacher. (tell)
   ....
4 'Don't drive up the mountain in this snow,' the police said to the drivers. (warn)
   ....
5 'Leave your valuables in the hotel safe,' said the receptionist to the hotel guests. (advise)
   ....

Reporting statements in the present: *He says that…*

If the introductory verb is in the present (**He says…**) and the facts that are reported have not changed compared to the present time, the tense of the verb in the direct speech does not change in indirect speech. However, the personal and possessive pronouns do change, according to the following tables:

Subject pronouns: I → he / she   you → I / we   we → they
Object pronouns: me → him / her   you → me / us   us → them

Possessive adjectives: my → his / her   your → my / our   our → their
Possessive pronouns: mine → his / hers   yours → mine / ours   ours → theirs

Look at this example:

Direct speech	Reported speech
Mum always says, 'I don't like the way you dress. Your clothes look so shabby!'	My mother always tells me that **she** doesn't like the way **I** dress and that **my** clothes look shabby, but I don't care!

As you can see, the **present simple** is used in both the direct and indirect speech, but the pronouns and possessives are different. These transformations occur in most other languages, too.

> When the introductory verb is in the past (**He said...**), and the fact that is reported is always true or is something that has not changed compared to the present time, the verb tense remains the same in indirect speech. Look at these examples:
>
> 'The museum <u>opens</u> at nine,' said the teacher. → *The teacher said that the museum <u>opens</u> at nine.* (This is still a true fact.)
>
> 'John<u>'s having</u> a great time in London,' his friend told me. → *His friend told me that John<u>'s having</u> a great time in London.* (The situation has not changed, John is still having a great time in London.)

4 **Complete the sentences with the verbs below.**

would like   says (x2)   will be   going   thinks   dates back   look   has passed

1 A survey .... teenagers .... at their cell phones up to 16 times an hour!
2 James says the exam was very hard, but he .... he .... it.
3 My daughter always says she .... to spend a semester studying abroad.
4 The weather forecast .... it .... overcast in the morning.
5 What does Tom say he's .... to do?
6 Our guide said that the castle .... to the 13th century.

5 **Rewrite the sentences in indirect speech.**

1 Robert says, 'I've just found a part-time job in a pub.'
   Robert says he .... a part-time job in a pub.
2 Laura always says, 'I want to go to the States when I finish studying.'
   Laura always says .... to go to the States when .... studying.
3 My dad often tells me, 'You need to work hard if you want your dreams to come true.'
   My dad often tells me .... to work hard if .... to come true.
4 Ryan says, 'I'm going to the Everglades this afternoon.'
   Ryan says .... to the Everglades this afternoon.
5 'The next test is on Monday 11th October,' says the teacher.
   The teacher says ....

6 a **Mr Ryder is speaking to his daughter, who is studying in Brighton, on Skype. Read the conversation.**

Dad   So, how is life in Brighton, Sarah?
Sarah I quite like it, Dad. I've made some new friends already. Oh, and I went to see Uncle Jack yesterday in Hove.
Dad   Good. What about the weather? Is it cold there?
Sarah Yes, it's quite cold. I've just been out shopping for some winter clothes.
Dad   What did you buy?
Sarah I've bought a jumper and an anorak because it's quite windy here.
Dad   Are you coming back home next weekend?
Sarah No, I'm not, I'm afraid. I've got to study. I think I'll come back in a fortnight.
Dad   Oh, no. I'll be away on business then. But Mum will be home. Well, bye, Sarah! I'll call you again in a couple of days.
Sarah Bye, Dad! And say hello to Mum.

b He then tells his wife about the conversation. Complete the text with the same verbs as in the dialogue. Use the same tenses, but change the pronouns.

'Sarah says ¹... life at college. She says that ²... some new friends and that ³... Uncle Jack yesterday. She says ⁴... just ⁵... shopping for some winter clothes because it's quite cold there. ⁶... a jumper and anorak because ⁷... . And she says that ⁸... home next weekend because ⁹... . She thinks ¹⁰... in a fortnight. Pity, because I ¹¹... on business but ¹²... home. Anyway, I ¹³... in a couple of days. Oh, and she says ¹⁴... .'

LESSON 3 Indirect speech: statements that were true in the past

Reporting a statement that was true in the past: *He said that...*

Transformation from direct to indirect speech

If facts or opinions that were true in the past are reported now, we use reported speech in the past, and the verb tenses change according to the following table:

Direct speech	Reported speech
Present simple: *'I like it.'*	Past simple: *He said **he liked it***.
Present continuous: *'I'm going.'*	Past continuous: *He said **he was going***.
Past simple: *'I saw John.'*	Past perfect: *He said **he had seen John***.
Present perfect: *'I've been there.'*	Past perfect: *He said **he had been there***.
Future simple: *'I will go.'*	Present conditional: *He said **he would go***.

In reported speech, as well as pronouns and possessives, as we have seen on page 349, there are changes to other parts of speech, in particular:

demonstratives
this → that *'Take this book!'* → *He told me to take that book.*
these → those *'Do like these paintings?'* → *He asked me if I liked those paintings.*

adverbs of place
here → there *'Come here!'* → *He told me to go there.*

adverbs and expressions of time
now → then *'Do it now!'* → *He asked me to do it then.*
today → that day *'I'm going shopping today.'* → *He said he was going shopping that day.*
tonight → that night / that evening *'I'm staying home tonight.'* → *He said he was staying home that night.*
yesterday → the day before / the previous day *'I saw her yesterday.'* → *He said he had seen her the day before.*
tomorrow → the next day / the following day / the day after *'I'm leaving tomorrow.'* → *He said he would leave the next day.*
last Saturday → the previous Saturday *'We arrived last Monday.'* → *They told me they had arrived the previous Monday.*
two weeks ago → two weeks before / earlier *'We were in Paris two weeks ago.'* → *They told us they were in Paris two weeks before.*
next week → the following week *'The games start next week.'* → *They said the games started / would start the following week.*

Direct speech	Reported speech
Ben said, 'I **can't** go skating tomorrow because I **have** some work to do.'	Ben said he **couldn't** go skating the following day because he **had** some work to do.
Danny said, 'My friend**'s helping** me a lot with my maths homework.'	Danny said his friend **was helping** him a lot with his maths homework.
Emma said, 'We **didn't play** the final of the tennis tournament yesterday because it **rained** all day.'	Emma said they **hadn't played** the final of the tennis tournament the day before because it **had rained** all day.
Alan said, '**I've been** here for two months, but I still **don't know** many people.'	Alan said he **had been** there for two months, but he still **didn't know** many people.
Georgia said, '**I'm going** on a trip to Yosemite National Park next week. I'm sure it **will be** a great experience!'	Georgia said **she was going** on a trip to Yosemite National Park the following week. She said she was sure it **would be** a great experience.

In addition to **say** and **tell**, we can use other introductory verbs in reported speech, e.g. **add**, **explain**, **remark**, **claim**, **state** (for formal use):

In 1956, the Supreme Court of the United States stated that segregation on buses was illegal.

1 **Complete the second sentence using indirect speech.**

0 'He's been waiting for an hour,' they said.
 They said ..*he had been waiting*.. for an hour.

1 'I won't be back from Chicago till tomorrow,' she said.
 She said .... from Chicago till ....

2 'Our next school trip will be in two weeks' time. We'll be going to Windsor,' said the teacher.
 The teacher said .... next school trip .... two weeks later and added .... to Windsor.

3 'I spent my holidays in Oslo three years ago,' she said.
 She said .... holidays in Oslo three years ....

4 'I'll phone you tomorrow when I arrive,' he said.
 He said .... when ....

5 'I booked my flight last week,' Ted said.
 Ted said .... flight ....

2 **Rewrite the sentences in indirect speech. Use the verbs *say* and *tell*.**

1 They said to us, 'We went to a new Thai restaurant last Saturday. It was really good.'
 They told us they .... and added it ....

2 Jane said to me, 'I always travel by myself. That way I'm more open to meeting new people.'
 ....

3 I said to my secretary, 'I'm going to leave earlier tomorrow.'
 ....

4 'We have been to the museum this morning,' they said.
 ....

5 'I'm afraid I won't be able to get seats for tonight's show,' the receptionist told us.
 ....

6 Mum said, 'I can't go to bed early tonight. I still have a lot of work to do.'
 ....

3 Complete the text with the correct tense of the verbs below.

sound   write   be (x3)   say   move   can   live   get

When my son ¹............................ in Thailand for the first time in 2012, he ²............................ me an email every day. He ³............................ enthusiastic about the place. He ⁴............................ the people ⁵............................ friendly and the food was superb. He also said there ⁶............................ fantastic sandy beaches and magnificent plants and flowers. And he said that if he ⁷............................ find a job, he would like to ⁸............................ there. And that's what he did! He ⁹............................ a job as a scuba-diving instructor on the island of Phuket and ¹⁰............................ there ever since.

4 Rewrite the sentences in indirect speech. Use the introductory verbs in brackets.

1 The law in 1865: 'Slavery is abolished all over the United States'. (state)

   ....

2 The suspect: 'I was at home all day on June 1st. I didn't see anyone except for my wife.' (claim – add)

   ....
   ....

3 The physics teacher yesterday: 'The speed of a body is the distance it covers over a period of time.' (explain)

   ....

4 Critics: 'The famous composer's new symphony is not very original.' (remark)

   ....

5 Read the dialogue from a managerial meeting about sportswear.

Sales Manager:	Some of our customers would like a new, more technological product. They are asking for an even lighter waterproof jacket.
Purchasing Manager:	In that case, we have to buy a different kind of fabric to meet their requirements.
Production Manager:	The machines should be updated too if we want to manufacture a new product.
Finance Manager:	I think we have to draw up a business plan. The costs can't exceed the benefits.
Sales Manager:	We also need to carry out a survey so that we have real data to analyse.
Finance Manager:	And the survey must be included in the costs. We can send questionnaires because interviews will be more expensive.

Now prepare a report about what was discussed.

This is the report of the March 15th meeting.
The Sales Manager stated that some of the customers would like…
The Purchasing Manager remarked that…

LESSON 4 Reported speech: questions

Reporting questions

Transforming questions in direct speech to questions in indirect speech

The verb that introduces a question is usually **ask**. It can be used in both the active form (**I asked him...**) and the passive form (**He was asked...**).

Other verbs that introduce reported questions are: **I want to know..., I'd like to know..., I wonder...**.

Reported questions:

- have the same construction as positive sentences, that is **subject** + **verb** (i.e. without the inversion of subject and verb): *'What time is it?'* → *She asked me what time it was.* (NOT ...what time ~~was it~~.)
- do not use the auxiliary **do**, which is found in direct questions: *'What kind of films do you like?'* → *He asked me what kind of films I like.*

Wh– questions

A **Wh– question** maintains the same **Wh–** word in indirect speech as it uses in direct speech (**what, where, how, how often...**). The tenses have the same variations as those we have seen for declarative clauses: *'How often do you train?' he asked me.* → *He asked me how often I trained.*
'Who did you see?' she asked him. → *She asked him who he had seen.*

Yes / No questions

Yes / No question in reported speech are introduced by the conjunction **if**: *'Do you often go skiing, Trish?' asked Oliver.* → *Oliver asked Trish if she often went skiing.*

We can also find the conjunction **whether... or...**: *'Did you do this puzzle by yourself or did someone help you, Julia?'* → *I asked Julia whether she had done the puzzle by herself or (whether) someone had helped her.*

FAQ

Q: We always talk about questions. What about answers? How do we report answers in indirect speech?

A: To introduce the answer, we can use the word **answer** or, more formally, **reply**. Here's an example: **'Do you like the film?' 'Yes, I do.'** → He asked me if I liked the film and <u>I answered that I did</u>. Another example: **'Do you know when we have our next school trip?' 'No, I don't.'** → My friend asked me if I knew when we had our next school trip and <u>I answered that I didn't</u>. We don't say '**I answered ~~yes / no~~**'!

Suggestions and proposals

Questions that contain suggestions or proposals (**How about...? What about...? Why don't you...?**) are usually reported using the introductory verb **suggest**, or **recommend** which is more formal, with the construction:

suggest to somebody **that** + subject + **should / could** + base form of the verb

'Why don't you go for a walk before dinner, Sam?' → *I suggested to Sam that he could go for a walk before dinner.*

Or: **suggest that** + subject + **past simple** form of the verb

'Why don't you go for a walk?' → *I suggested that they went for a walk.*

When the person making the suggestion to do something includes themselves in the suggestion (**Let's... / Why don't we...?**), we can use the construction:

suggest + **–ing** form of the verb   or

suggest + **we should** + base form of the verb

'Why don't we wait for them?' → *I suggested waiting for them. / I suggested we should wait for them.*

1 Complete the questions in indirect speech.

1. John: 'Where can I find the tickets for the show, please?'
   John asked me where ....
   ....

2. My friend: 'What time shall we meet?'
   My friend asked me what time ....
   ....

3. Peter: 'Why don't we play video games?'
   Peter suggested ....
   ....

4. Rachel: 'What about looking on Wikipedia?'
   Rachel suggested that we ....
   ....

5. Sammy: 'How much does this tablet cost?'
   Sammy asked the assistant ....
   ....

6. 'What does he have on his mind?'
   I still wonder ....
   ....

7. 'When are they coming?'
   I'd like to know ....
   ....

8. Suzanne: 'Why don't you take up a winter sport?'
   Suzanne suggested ....
   ....

2 Rewrite the questions in indirect speech.

0. 'Did you enjoy the trip, John?' she asked.
   She asked John if he had enjoyed the trip.

1. Amanda asked: 'What time is Jane coming tomorrow?'
   ....
   ....

2. Angela asked: 'Does Sammy like canoeing?'
   ....
   ....

3. Tom asked me: 'Why didn't you go swimming last night?'
   ....
   ....

4. Sally asked Kate: 'Is your brother working in Switzerland?'
   ....
   ....

5. I asked Sue: 'Can you lend me your pen, please?'
   ....
   ....

6. The teacher asked: 'Class, have you done your homework?'
   ....
   ....

3 🎧 16 Rewrite the dialogues in the reported speech. Then listen and check.

1. Grandma: 'What's your school like?' Me: 'It's great!'
   Grandma asked me .... and I answered ....

2. 'How long have you lived in Italy?' 'For two years.'
   I was asked .... and I answered ....

3. Dad: 'Did you know that more standing stones have been found near Stonehenge?' Me: 'No, I didn't.' Dad asked me if .... and I answered that ....

4. Pat: 'Have you ever been to Iceland?' Me: 'No, I've never been there. But I would like to go. I know it must be an amazing place.'
   Pat asked me if .... and I answered that I .... but .... and I added ....

5. Mum: 'Are you curious to know your exam results?' Me: 'I can't wait!'
   Mum asked me if .... and I answered that ....

4 Rewrite the sentences in direct speech.

1 Sarah told me she lived in a new house.
   Sarah: ....

2 Ben asked David where he had studied Italian.
   Ben: ....

3 Mum said she was very tired.
   Mum: ....

4 Mr Smith told Jason that he would arrive late the next day.
   Mr Smith: ....

5 Fiona asked me if Tom was working that afternoon.
   Fiona: ....

5 Rewrite the text as a dialogue, then listen and check.

Marco: 'I met an old friend, Julian, the other day. He asked me when we had last seen each other. I told him that I thought it had been two years earlier. Then he asked me if I still lived in the same house near the main street. I said no, I'd moved to a new house. He wanted to know where it was and I told him it was in the suburbs. He asked if I liked it and I told him I loved it because it had a big garden and a conservatory.'

Julian	Hi, Marco!
Marco	Hi, Julian! It's nice to see you again.
Julian	....
Marco	....
Julian	....
Marco	....
Julian	....
Marco	....
Julian	....
Marco	....

6 Write the Yes / No questions and answers in reported speech.

0 'Do you go skating every day, Lisa?' asked Ellen. 'Yes, I do,' Lisa answered.
   Ellen asked Lisa if / whether she went skating every day and Lisa answered that she did.

1 'Have you been to Athens before, Rick?' asked John. 'No, I haven't,' Rick answered.
   ....

2 'Are you having fun at the water park, children?' asked Emma. 'Yes, we are!' the children said.
   ....

3 'Is your husband happy with his new motorbike, Sarah?' asked Matt. 'Yes, he's very happy,' Sarah said.
   ....

4 'Did you come by train, Sylvia?' asked Mark. 'No, I didn't. I came in the car,' Sylvia answered.
   ....

5 'Have you got time to go for lunch, Julia?' asked Angela. 'Yes, I have,' Julia said. 'I suggest we go to the pub on the corner.'
   ....

7 Match the two parts of the sentences.

1	The doctor wanted to know	A	if they had all understood the new lesson.
2	The coach asked the team	B	where they could find a nice place for their tent.
3	The campers wondered	C	if they had been exercising lately.
4	The teacher asked the students	D	when I was going to come home from college.
5	The golf instructor wanted to know	E	how long I had had those symptoms.
6	My parents asked me	F	if I had ever played before.

1 ..... 2 ..... 3 ..... 4 ..... 5 ..... 6 .....

8 Write what they suggest in reported speech. Use the verbs *suggest* or *recommend*.

0 'Why don't we go fishing next weekend?' said Luke.
Luke suggested going / that they went fishing the following weekend.

1 'How about eating at the new Thai restaurant tonight?' said Lewis.
....

2 'You should go to Rhodes next summer,' said the tour operator.
....

3 'What about organising a garage sale to raise some money?' asked Marion.
....

4 'You'd better not go out today, Peter,' said his mother.
....

5 'Let's have a sleepover at my house on Saturday,' said June.
....

6 'You should have a long brisk walk at least twice a week,' said the therapist.
....

9 Change the *Wh–* questions into reported questions. In the main clause use the verbs in brackets in the past simple tense.

0 Linda: 'How are you going to travel to Portugal?' (ask)
Linda asked how we were going / would be going to travel to Portugal.

1 Ryan: 'Where will they go on holiday next summer?' (wonder)
....

2 Olivia: 'Who has booked the seats for the theatre?' (want to know)
....

3 Carl: 'What time are we meeting our guide for the city tour?' (ask)
....

4 Pamela: 'When is Nancy leaving for Rome?' (want to know)
....

5 Simon: 'Where would you like to go today?' (ask)
....

6 Mr Wilson: 'What is my son going to do when he leaves school?' (wonder)
....

ROUND UP 19

1 Write the following words in the correct column.

the time   hello   no   something wrong   a lie   the truth   a word
the difference   a joke   me about…   thank you   goodbye

SAY	TELL

2 Complete the sentences with the verbs *say* or *tell* in the correct tense.

1 You should always .... *please* and *thank you*.
2 Where's your mum? I want to .... goodbye to her.
3 They didn't .... me the truth about what had happened.
4 Vicky .... we were going to meet at 4.30.
5 Can you .... the difference between a bee and a wasp?
6 'Remember to take your keys,' she .... him.
7 Could you please .... me what time it is?
8 'Don't forget your packed lunch,' .... his mother.
9 My teacher always .... we must work hard for the exam.
10 Why didn't you .... me it was time to go?

3 Match the two parts of the sentences.

1 The science teacher told us
2 A police officer warned us
3 The doctor advised me
4 The zoo keeper reminded the children
5 The ranger warned
6 Rachel's mother warned her
7 The teacher asked the children
8 A life guard advised bathers

A not to drive on the icy road.
B visitors to the park to walk only along the path.
C not to come back late on Saturday night.
D to find information about global warming.
E to do physical exercise and lose some weight.
F not to swim far out to sea when it's rough.
G not to feed the monkeys.
H to stop making all that noise.

1 .....   2 .....   3 .....   4 .....   5 .....   6 .....   7 .....   8 .....

4 Complete the second sentence with the correct pronoun, demonstrative and time adverb.

0 Weather forecaster: 'There will be heavy rain tomorrow.'
   The weather forecaster said there would be heavy rain *the following day*.

1 Hilary: 'I will go skiing this afternoon if it doesn't snow too hard.'
   Hilary said that .... would go skiing .... afternoon if it didn't snow too hard.

2 Andrew: 'I can't come to see you next weekend. I'll be working.'
   Andrew said that .... couldn't come to see .... because .... would be working.

3 Danny: 'Dad, we haven't watched this film yet.'
   Danny told his dad that .... hadn't watched .... film yet.

4 Ruth: 'I really want to visit this art gallery. I like pop art.'

Ruth said that ……………… really wanted to visit ……………… art gallery. She also said ……………… likes pop art.

5 PE teacher: 'You aren't trying hard enough this term, Mike. Practice makes perfect.'

The PE teacher told Mike that ……………… wasn't trying hard enough ……………… term. He added that practice makes perfect.

6 Shop assistant: 'We don't have any blue jackets in stock. You should try again at the end of next week.'

The shop assistant said ……………… didn't have any blue jackets in stock. She added that ……………… should try again at the end of ……………… .

5 Write sentences in reported speech, making all the necessary changes.

0 My best friend told me, 'I'm happy to hear you are expecting a child!'
My best friend told me she was happy to hear I'm expecting a child.

1 Joan often says to her husband, 'I don't like you lying on the sofa all day on Sundays.'
……………………………………………………………………………………………

2 The science teacher said, 'Some dinosaures were herbivores, others were carnivorous.'
……………………………………………………………………………………………

3 The sales manager remarked, 'These data can't be correct! There must be a mistake!'
……………………………………………………………………………………………

4 Alan keeps telling Nicole, 'I want to find a better place to live and raise our children.'
……………………………………………………………………………………………

5 Mum always says, 'Patience is a great virtue. Never forget it!'
……………………………………………………………………………………………

6 My son sometimes tells me, 'You are a great cook, Mum!'
……………………………………………………………………………………………

7 Liza always says, 'I'll become a great singer.' And I think she will.
……………………………………………………………………………………………

6 In every reported sentence there is one mistake. Correct it.

1 He said: 'I will go to the mountains tomorrow.' → He said that I would go to the mountains the day after.
……………………………………………………………

2 She said: 'I am happy for you.' → She said she is happy for him.
……………………………………………………………

3 I told him: 'Don't play in your bedroom in those dirty shoes!' → I told him not play in his bedroom in those dirty shoes.
……………………………………………………………

4 Sam said: 'I met Jenny at the concert yesterday.' → Sam said he had met Jenny at the concert yesterday.
……………………………………………………………

5 Keira replied: 'I don't want to pay extra money for this service.' → Keira replied she doesn't want to pay extra money for that service.
……………………………………………………………

6 He asked her: 'Whose bike is it?' → He asked her whose bike was it.
……………………………………………………………

7 He told me: 'You and your family are very important to me.' → He told me that I and my family are very important to me.
……………………………………………………………

8 I said: 'I'm going home because I feel sick.' → I said I was going home because I feel sick.
……………………………………………………………

7 Rewrite the sentences in indirect speech. Choose the introductory verbs from the ones below and make all the necessary changes.

said (x2)   explained   told (x4)   suggested   answered   asked

1 Mum to the children: 'Stop making all that noise. I'm working.'
....
2 Ted to me: 'Let's meet at the station at eight tomorrow morning.'
....
3 The guide to the tourists: 'The stones used to build Stonehenge were taken from very far away.'
....
4 Sam to his friend Paul: 'I'd like to stay a little longer. You can go home if you want to.'
....
5 The teacher to her pupils: 'This Norman castle was built in the 12th century.'
....
6 My friend who lives in the USA to me: 'I'm going to visit Yellowstone National Park next summer.'
....
7 John to me: 'Can you let me have a look at your history project?'
  I to John: 'Sorry, I can't. I've already handed it in.'
....
....
8 The doctor to me: 'Eat less and do physical exercise regularly.'
....

8 Fill in the gaps with the past simple of the verbs below.

ask (x2)   say (x3)   remind   suggest   answer

My sister ¹.......................... me that tomorrow is Dad's birthday and ².......................... me if I was going to buy him a present. I ³.......................... yes and ⁴.......................... that we could buy a book or a classical CD. She ⁵.......................... it was a good idea and that we might buy both a book and a CD. I then ⁶.......................... who would go and buy them and guess what she ⁷..........................? She ⁸..........................: 'Here's my money. You go.' Typical of my sister! So I'll go to the shopping mall later. I hope she won't criticise what I choose.

9 Hilary works at a travel agency. When she goes home in the evening, she tells her husband, Fred, about her day at work. Read and turn the paragraph into a dialogue. Start like this:

Hilary: Do you know who came to the agency today, Fred?
Fred: Of course not. How should I?
Hilary: ....

Hilary went back in the evening and told her husband Fred that a schoolmate of theirs had come into to the travel agency that day. Fred asked who it was and Hilary said it was Albert Swanson. Fred commented that they hadn't seen him since they had left school and asked her what he was like. Hilary said that he was very elegant and looked even younger than he was when they were at school. He seemed to be very rich too because he was interested in very expensive holiday resorts. Fred reminded Hilary of how scruffy Albert had looked when he was a student and asked Hilary if she was sure it was really Albert. Hilary said that Albert had recognised her too. He had even suggested going out for a meal one day, the three of them and Albert's wife. Fred asked who Albert's wife was and Hilary answered that he would never guess. Albert's wife was Rose, the most beautiful girl in the school. Fred said he couldn't believe it because at that time Rose hadn't even wanted to sit next to Albert during lessons.

10 Rewrite the sentences into reported speech. Use the word given and don't change the meaning.

0   Arthur said to me: 'I can't come to the countryside with you tomorrow.'
    TOLD *Arthur told me he couldn't go to the countryside with me the next day.*

1   Rachel asked me: 'Do you want any more food for the picnic?'
    KNOW ....

2   Tony said to his father: 'I've had some trouble with my mountain bike recently.'
    SAID ....

3   Damien asked her: 'Are you happy with your new car?'
    WANTED ....

4   A friend asked me: 'Why did you give up fencing?'
    WONDERED ....

5   The ranger said to Don: 'Stay at home during the snowstorm.'
    WARNED ....

6   The instructor said to me: 'You should go waterskiing in the summer.'
    ADVISED ....

7   Andrew said to the children: 'Get out of that boat.'
    ORDERED ....

Reflecting on grammar

Reflect on the rules and say whether the following statements are true or false.

		True	False
1	The verb **tell** takes the preposition **to** before the name of a person or a pronoun, while **say** does not need any preposition.		
2	The expression *Tell thank you* is correct.		
3	The sentence *She asked me to wait for her* is correct.		
4	*He said: 'I'm leaving tomorrow'* becomes, in indirect speech *He said he's leaving tomorrow* (if I say this on the same day, when he has not yet left), or *He said he was leaving the next day* (if I say this some time later, when he has already left).		
5	The **present simple** in direct speech becomes the **past perfect** in indirect speech.		
6	The verb **suggest** can be followed by a verb in the **-ing** form when making a suggestion to do something together.		
7	In the sentence *He said he was tired*, the conjunction **that** is understood and not expressed.		
8	The auxiliary **do** is used in both direct and indirect questions.		
9	A **Yes** / **No** question is usually reported by using the conjunction **if**, for example: *He asked me if I wanted a cup of tea.*		
10	When we report a **Wh–** question, we put the verb first, then the subject, for example: *I asked him whose coat was it.*		

GRAMMAR MATRIX MAIN

UNIT 20 Connecting clauses

LESSON 1 Adversative and concessive clauses

Conjunctions and connectors have the function of joining together parts of a sentence or parts of a text. We have already seen the most common conjunctions on page 84: **and**, **but** and **or**, to join coordinating clauses, **because** and **so** to indicate cause and consequence. Here we will look at other types of conjunctions, as well as prepositions and adverbs, and what their functions are.

Adversative clauses

To introduce a clause that contrasts with another clause, we usually use the conjunction **but** → *I like this song, but it's not my favourite. I have no choice but to accept her offer.*

An adversative clause can also be introduced by:

- the adverb **however**, at the beginning or end of the sentence → *He finds maths very hard. However, he's trying his best to understand it.*
  I didn't feel very well this morning. I went to school, however.

- the adverb **though**, in informal use, placed at the end of the sentence → *It's a very nice dress. It's quite expensive, though.*

- the conjunction **yet** → *You have a good job, and yet you're always complaining.*

There are also correlating conjunctions: **on the one hand… (but) on the other (hand)…** introduce different points of view or contrasting ideas → *On the one hand, I think it would be a good idea to study abroad, but on the other it would be hard to leave my family and friends.*

1 **Join the two sentences using *but*. Keep the same meaning as the original.**

1. I studied hard. I didn't get a good mark, though.
   ....

2. He looks like a tough guy. He's very shy, however.
   ....

3. The film was good. It was a bit slow, however.
   ....

4. The T-shirt they gave me for my birthday is nice. It's too short, though.
   ....

5. Emma liked Tom. She didn't really trust him, though.
   ....

6. I thought it would be sunny in Sicily in May. We had lots of rain, however.
   ....

7. They've had a lot of problems recently, and yet they've never complained.
   ....

8. It's a very nice house. It's away from the centre, though.
   ....

2 Complete the text with these words: *because* (x2), *and* (x2), *but*, *or*, *so*, *however*.

Have you ever heard of a dodo or a quagga? Your answer could be no ¹.......................... these animals are now extinct. The dodo was a bird ².......................... the quagga a kind of zebra. A lot of different animal species no longer exist. Many disappeared a long, long time ago, ³.......................... others are in danger today ⁴.......................... people hunt them ⁵.......................... change their natural environment. The mountain gorillas of Zaire, for example, are in danger from the number of visitors coming to take photos of them. They disturb the primates and they don't reproduce, ⁶.......................... their number is decreasing each year. ⁷.........................., in some places things are changing for the better. Many animals are now protected ⁸.......................... there are special reserves where they can live safely.

Concessive clauses

Although and **even though** introduce a clause that makes the information in the main clause appear surprising or unexpected. The subordinate clause can precede or follow the main clause, from which it is separated by a comma → *Although he's only 22 years old, he's already a renowned chef.*
We won the match, even though we didn't play very well.

Though is often used with the same meaning in spoken language → *Though I studied hard, I didn't get a good mark.*

FAQ

Q: Is there a difference between even though and even if?

A: They both have a similar meaning, that we will do something no matter what. **Even though** refers to a real fact, for example: *I want to read this novel, even though my friend says it is quite boring.* **Even if** is used to talk about something that may or may not happen. *We'll go to the stadium even if it rains.*

The prepositions **despite** or **in spite of** also have a similar function to **although**. They are followed by a noun or the **–ing** form of the verb → *Despite making a big effort, he didn't manage to lift the heavy case. Despite being so young, she's already a famous singer. He is still very active despite his age.*
It's also possible to say: *In spite of the fact (that) she is so young, she's already a famous singer.*

However is used in front of an adjective or an adverb → *However late it is, it's never too late. She always wears a T-shirt, however cold it is. However carefully the teacher explains physics, I still don't understand.*

3 **Complete the text with *even though*, *despite*, *although*, *in spite of* or *however*. In some cases, two choices are possible.**

1　I'm going for a walk, ... it's raining.
2　... studying so little, he usually manages to get good marks.
3　She bought the leather bag, ... it was expensive.
4　... our room was quite small, it was neat and tidy.
5　... hard he tries, he will never do it!
6　... the fact it's a cheap restaurant, the food isn't bad.
7　I enjoyed my holiday .... the bad weather.
8　... early they leave, they won't get there on time.

4 **Match the sentence halves.**

1　The restaurant has changed the menu,　　A　you would have to anyway.
2　Although you might have to pay a bit more,　　B　everything I told you is true.
3　Although it may seem incredible,　　C　even though the old one was very popular.
4　Even if you didn't want to go,　　D　it will certainly be worth it to have a better room.
5　In spite of the fact he's nearly fifty,　　E　but on the other I find it really hard to do.
6　On the one hand I would like to forgive her,　　F　he's very fit and looks like someone in his thirties.

1 .....　2 .....　3 .....　4 .....　5 .....　6 .....

5 **Rewrite the sentences using the word given. Do not change the meaning of the sentences.**

1　Jane got home late but she prepared dinner for everybody.
　ALTHOUGH
　..

2　The waiter was very kind. The food wasn't that good, though.
　BUT
　..

3　I don't have an English / French dictionary but I can look words up in the Internet.
　THOUGH
　..

4　I don't know his wife, but I know his children.
　HOWEVER
　..

5　We had a great time although the weather wasn't very nice.
　EVEN THOUGH
　..

6　We got lost despite having a map of the city.
　ALTHOUGH
　..

7　No matter how good it may be, I will never be able to eat sushi.
　HOWEVER
　..

LESSON 2 Reason, consecutive and purpose clauses

Reason clauses

To introduce a sentence that explains the reason for something, we generally use **because** (see page 84). → *He arrived at work late because he had missed the bus.*

A reason clause can be introduced by the conjunctions **since**, **as** or **for**, all of which are quite formal. → *Since I lost my passport, I had to change my return flight.   As my computer wasn't working, I couldn't finish my report.*
I can't call her as I don't have her number.   I'm not going to pay him for he didn't do a good job.

1 Use the words in brackets and write sentences with the same meaning.

1. Since the weather is so bad, the barbecue has been cancelled. (as)
2. We didn't buy that computer because it was too expensive. (since)
3. As we didn't have any money for a taxi, we walked back home. (because)
4. As it was raining, we decided not to play tennis. (since)
5. Since our grandparents live there, we often go to Barcelona. (because)
6. We couldn't get there on time because there was a bus strike. (as)

Consecutive clauses

To introduce a clause that explains the result or consequence of an action, we generally use **so** (see page 84). → *I didn't feel very well, so I didn't go to school.*
Compare this with the reason clause, where the concepts are expressed in the opposite order: *I didn't go to school because I didn't feel very well.*

Other ways of introducing a consecutive clause:

- **as a result, for this reason, therefore, consequently** (the latter have quite a formal use) → *The theme park was very crowded. As a result, we had to queue up for each ride.*
- **so** + adjective / adverb + (**that**)... → *The line for the tickets was so long that we gave up and went home.*
- **so as to... / not to...** → *They were quiet so as not to wake everybody up.*
- **such a / an** + adjective + noun + (**that**)... → *It was such a great trip that nobody wanted to go home.*

2 Complete the second sentence so that it means the same as the first. Use the given word.

1. I couldn't wait any longer because it was too late.

   SO   It was too late ....

2. I didn't have any money so I couldn't buy anything.

   BECAUSE   I couldn't ....

3. We didn't have a good time at the party because we didn't know many people.

   SO   We didn't ....

4. My car broke down, so I went to work on my bike yesterday.

   BECAUSE   I went to ....

5. I'm going to eat less sugar because I want to lose weight.

   THEREFORE   I want to ....

6. His parents were furious with him because his school report was bad.

   THAT   His school report ....

3 Complete the sentences with the words below.

so good   such a great   so often   so badly   so boring   so long   so lucky   so much

1 He eats .... that he's putting on weight.
2 She's .... singer! Everybody loves her voice.
3 He's .... at chess. He often wins a lot of money.
4 My friend is .... – he always wins things on the lottery.
5 The flight took .... that I had watched all the films available by the time we landed.
6 My mother cooks fish .... that I'm getting fed up with eating it.
7 He played .... that he lost the match in less than half an hour.
8 The film was .... that I fell asleep after a quarter of an hour.

Purpose clauses

To introduce a sentence that explains the outcome or the aim of an action, we usually use **to** + base form of the verb → *I'm going to go to London to improve my English.* (NOT ... ~~for improve~~ *my English*).
Other ways of introducing a purpose clause:

- **in order to...** (more formal than simply **to** by itself) → *In order to preserve the quality of the garment, dry-clean it only.*
- **so that....** This expression introduces a clause that usually contains a modal verb → *I'll use the big screen for my PowerPoint presentation so that everybody can see it.*
- **so as (not) to....** → *They finished all their work in the evening, so as to be free the next day.*

4 Match the sentence halves.

1 I'm going to enrol on a creative writing course
2 She bought all the ingredients
3 She left her country
4 In order to qualify for the next Olympic Games,
5 I will take a lot of photos during the trip
6 She was ill and

A you'll have to improve your own personal record.
B therefore she had to cancel her holiday.
C so that I can improve my writing skills.
D to make an apple pie.
E to look for better opportunities and a new life.
F so that I will be able to show all the places I visited to my friends.

1 .....   2 .....   3 .....   4 .....   5 .....   6 .....

5 Circle the correct option.

1 The cafeteria was closed, **so** / **because** we couldn't get a drink.
2 Try to do your best **such** / **so as** to please your parents.
3 Ring the bell **for call** / **to call** room service.
4 They took the underground **because** / **so** they didn't want to walk.
5 **Therefore** / **Since** you have come late, you'll have to wait longer.
6 I always keep the TV volume low **so as not** / **in order** to disturb my neighbours.
7 I'm saving some money **so as to** / **so that** I can buy a motorbike.
8 John couldn't come with us **as a result** / **because** he was at home with flu.
9 They're working quite hard **therefore** / **in order to** pass the exam with a good mark.
10 Your company failed to send the offer by the fixed deadline, **consequently** / **because** we couldn't even examine it.

6 Complete the sentences with the appropriate connectors.

1 I've decided to become a vegetarian .... vegetables and cereal are a healthier diet.
2 I want to keep fit .... I work out in the gym every day.
3 .... I'm really interested in modern art, I'll visit the Tate Modern tomorrow.
4 I was very hungry last night .... I had skipped lunch.
5 I'll write him an email every day .... he'll remember me.
6 It's .... hot day today .... I won't go out till sunset.
7 The holiday in Kenya was .... adventurous .... everybody decided to go back there next year.
8 He did the washing up after dinner .... leave any mess for the morning.

LESSON 3 Time clauses; sequencing adverbs; linking words to build an argument

The main conjunctions which introduce time clauses are:

- **when**. Be careful! The verb that follows can be in the **present simple**, **past simple**, **present perfect** or **past perfect**, but not in the future with **will**. This is also true for the other time conjunctions. → *When you see him, tell him I've gone to hospital.* (NOT *When you will see him…*) *When I was young, I often went dancing.*

- **while**. We usually find it with the **present continuous** or the **past continuous**. → *While I'm writing this email, you can start making dinner. I broke my ankle while I was skiing.*

> ! The –ing form of the verb can also follow **when** and **while**: *You have to be careful when writing in English. I saw a fox while cycling in the country.*

- **as long as** → *I will love you as long as I live.* (NOT *…as long as I will live*)
- **until / till** → *I worked until it was dark.*
- **as soon as** → *I'll let you have the contract as soon as I get it signed.* (NOT *…as soon as I will get it…*)
- **before**. It's followed by the **–ing** form of the verb or by a phrase containing a finite verb: subject + **present** or **past simple** form of the verb. → *He does a paper round before he goes to school in the morning.* (also: *…before going to school…*) *He used to do a paper round before he went to school.*
- **after**. It's also followed by the **–ing** form or by a phrase containing a finite verb. → *He goes to school after he has done a paper round.* (also: *…after doing…*)

1 Circle the correct option.

1 **Before / Until / After** leaving for the weekend, I watered the plants.
2 Come on! You're always late! We must get to the cinema **while / before / until** the film starts.
3 Don't worry! You can stay here **while / as long as / when** you like.
4 Can you help me tidy up **before / as long as / as soon as** the party has finished?
5 Let's go for a walk in the park **until / while / after** the sun is still shining.
6 I can't go out **when / until / while** the cake is ready and out of the oven.
7 **Until / As soon as / Before** deciding what food to buy for the party, the girls had read a lot of recipes.
8 **After / Until / While** Rose was peeling the apples, her sister was whipping the cream.

2 Complete the sentences with the words below.

until   while   when   as soon as   after   as long as

1 I like working in the garden .... I'm on holiday. I find it relaxing.
2 I'll wait .... half past ten. Mr Brosnan should arrive then.
3 Please call me .... you get this message. It's urgent.
4 I cut my finger .... chopping parsley.
5 We can help you with the organisation of the conference for .... you need us.
6 .... watching the film, we went to bed.

Sequencing adverbs and expressions

To show a chronological sequence of events in a story, or to express the order to follow in a series of instructions, we use the following adverbs and time expressions:

first or **at first**

then

after that (not **after** by itself, because it's a preposition not an adverb!)

finally / in the end

3 Complete the recipe with the correct adverbs.

To make a Caesar salad, [1].......................... roast a chicken breast, [2].......................... cut it into strips and put it into a bowl. [3].......................... , add some lettuce and some pieces of toasted bread, and [4].......................... season with salad cream to taste.

FAQ

Q: What's the difference between **finally**, **at last** and **eventually**?

A: **Finally** has the meaning 'as the last in a list' or 'as the last thing to say'. **Eventually** means 'at the end of a period of time or a series of reasons'. **At last** is used when something happens after a long period of time, especially when there has been a delay or some difficulties.

Linking words to build an argument

When we list a series of arguments for or against something, especially in a piece of written work, we use the following adverbs:

firstly

secondly

another point is...

in addition (to that) (also: **on top of that**, in informal language)

finally / lastly / in conclusion

> **!** To conclude an argument, the expression **last but not least** is very widely used. For example, at the end of a congratulatory speech you may hear: *And, last but not least, let me mention his merits as a benefactor.*

4 Complete the text with the connecting words below.

last but not least   before   Firstly   Another point   because   In addition   Secondly

Our club would like to start a new course. Since a lot of people are now interested in healthy food, we are planning to organise a few evening classes on this topic. ¹.. , we need to find an expert who can talk about organic food. ².. , we have to find at least two chefs who can teach us how to cook healthy recipes. ³.. , we need a place with a big kitchen ⁴.. our premises don't have the necessary equipment. ⁵.. is the fee. We should decide how much the course should cost ⁶.. advertising it. And ⁷.. , we have to discuss whether to advertise it in the local newspapers or on the radio as well.

To add weight to an argument by adding further information or ideas, we can use the expressions:
moreover (formal) → *This is healthy food, and moreover it's organic.*
what's more… (informal) → *The hotel was very nice. What's more, it had a large pool.*
also → *If you want to lose some weight, you shouldn't just eat less, you should also do some exercise.*
besides + –ing form of the verb → *Besides being very helpful, she's also a great friend.*

5 Circle the correct option.

1 **Besides / Also / What's more** being good for you, bananas are also cheap.
2 I'm not very hungry. **Lastly / What's more / Finally**, this spaghetti is overcooked.
3 That restaurant is very expensive and **in addition / besides / firstly** the service is very slow.
4 I don't feel like going out tonight. I'm quite tired. **Firstly / What's more / Lastly**, I have to get up early tomorrow morning.
5 You forgot to put the documents for the meeting in my folder. **Secondly / Moreover / Finally**, you gave me the wrong address.
6 **Moreover / Besides / Also** winning the match, my favourite team played incredibly well yesterday.

6 Complete the sentences with the linkers or sequencers in the box.

as soon as (x2)   first of all   before   until   secondly   while

1 .... deciding what slides to prepare for the presentation, we had looked for a lot of images.
2 I was drawing the graphs .... the secretary was keying in the figures referring to the sales.
3 We won't be able to go home .... we have finished analysing these data.
4 We'll switch on the projector .... all the guests have taken their seats.
5 .... we have to find a room big enough for all the participants; .... we'll have to rent the conference equipment.
6 .... the presentation is over, the participants will move on to the garden to listen to a concert.

LESSON 4 Other conjunctions; causative verbs

Conditional clauses

As well as **if** (see page 291), we can also find the following conjunctions in conditional clauses:

- **provided** / **providing** (that) or **as long as** → *I'll let you go out tonight provided that you are at home before midnight.*
- **unless** introduces a subordinate clause with a positive verb, which follows or precedes a negative main clause → *I won't go unless you allow me to.   I don't watch TV unless there's something really interesting on.*
- **in case** → *Here's my phone number in case you need help.*
- **if only** in exclamatory sentences, with a **Past simple** verb or the modals **would** / **could**, is used to express a desire or regret about something → *If only I had a little more time!   If only she would give me another chance!* (also: *I wish I had… / I wish she would give me…* See page 240). With a **Past perfect** verb, it expresses regret about a past event → *If only I had told her!* (also: *I wish I had told her.* See page 241)
- **as if** or **as though** → *He started shouting as if he were mad.   Her voice sounded as though she had been crying.*

1 Match the sentence halves.

1 I can't help you   A provided you are back before midnight.
2 Don't watch this film   B in case we have to go for lunch.
3 You can go out with your friends   C as if he had never tasted food before.
4 Let's take some extra money   D if you don't like horror films.
5 He kept eating   E as if he was upset with us.
6 Tom behaved strangely   F unless you show me exactly what you have to do.

1 .....   2 .....   3 .....   4 .....   5 .....   6 .....

2 Complete the sentences with the words below.

if only   as long as   provided   as if (x2)   in case (x2)   unless

1 I'll drive ………………………… you tell me the way.
2 We can't come with you ………………………… we get back before dinner.
3 You look ………………………… you're going to starve.
4 ………………………… we hadn't agreed to go! I'm so tired I just want to stay at home!
5 Pack some warm clothes ………………………… the temperature drops.
6 She danced and danced ………………………… there were no tomorrow.
7 Just ………………………… you couldn't come, give me a ring.
8 The company can increase the sales ………………………… they start selling on line as well as in traditional shops.

Comparative clauses

Comparative clauses can be introduced by:

- **as** + adjective or adverb + **as…** → *It wasn't as difficult as I thought it would be.* (See page 194, **Comparisons with** *as … as*)
- **as / like** (informal use) → *Do as you like!   No one plays the violin like she does!*
- **than** preceded by comparative adjectives or adverbs → *The exam was easier than we expected.* (See page 191)

3 Complete the sentences with *than*, *as* or *as... as*.

1. The exhibition was much more interesting .... we expected.
2. It must be a very rich area. There are .... many jewellery shops in this one street .... in my whole town.
3. Nobody understands her .... I do.
4. They behaved .... if nothing had happened.
5. When you go to another country, eat .... the locals do.
6. The local university is offering a much wider choice of courses .... before.

Declarative and explanatory clauses

That is the most commonly-used declarative conjunction, but it is often simply understood in the clause, rather than actually used. → *I thought (that) he was coming. He promised (that) he would come. Did you know that she got married last month?*

That is to say, and its abbreviated form **i.e.** in formal written language (from the Latin *id est*), is used to specify the meaning of something more clearly → *You can arrive any time before noon, that's to say from eight to twelve.*

4 Complete the text with *that*, *than* or *if*.

Karen said ¹.................... she was going to do her Master's in Tokyo. Janet wanted to know ².................... she had to learn Japanese. Karen answered ³.................... she spoke Japanese much better ⁴.................... French. She promised ⁵.................... she would invite Janet to stay with her. Janet thanked her and told her ⁶.................... she had always wanted to visit Japan, but it was always more expensive ⁷.................... she could afford.

Causative verbs

There are various ways of expressing the idea of 'getting something done'. We can summarise these as follows:

- **make sb do sth** has either a 'neutral' meaning or an element of constraint → *Her story made me cry. The teacher makes us stay at school after classes if we misbehave.* (Also in the passive form: *We are made to stay at school...*)
- **let sb do sth** or **allow sb to do sth** → *My parents don't let me go camping with my friends – that's not fair! The teacher allowed us to use calculators during the test.* (Also in the passive form: *We were allowed to use...* See page 234)
- **get sb to do sth** has the sense of convincing someone to do something → *My friend got me to buy an automatic transmission car and I'm happy with it.*
- **compel sb to do sth** or **force sb to do sth** have the sense of obligation or being strongly constrained to do something. They are often used in the passive form (see page 258) → *A lot of people were forced to leave their jobs because of the crisis. They will be compelled to stay at home.*
- **cause sth (to happen)** often contains a negative idea → *The heat and winds of the last few days have caused the woods to catch fire.*

For the passive construction **get something done** or **have something done** see page 318.

5 **Complete the sentences with the correct form of the verb *make*.**

1 I .... the kids tidy their room yesterday.
2 Jack often .... me miss the bus in the mornings. He's always late.
3 My wife .... me paint the kitchen last week. My back is still aching.
4 Having a big breakfast in the morning .... me feel energetic all day.
5 Will your manager .... you prepare next week's presentation?
6 Are you really going to .... me speak in public during the meeting?
7 My parents .... me go to piano lessons when I was little. I didn't enjoy them!
8 Don't .... me laugh!
9 Are you really .... him go to that party with people he can't stand?
10 The boss .... me attend a German course before sending me to the Bremen branch.

6 **Complete the sentences with the correct form of *let*, *get* or *cause*.**

1 My husband .... me use his brand new car yesterday. It was great!
2 My sister .... the accident. She dropped a heavy pan on my foot!
3 The frost .... the lake to freeze.
4 The salesman .... us to buy a new dishwasher. He said ours couldn't be fixed.
5 The heavy rain .... the river to flood the village.
6 Will your brother .... you play with his new video game?
7 The principal .... me to attend this course on evaluation but I find it boring and useless.
8 Liza's parents .... her go on holiday on her own for the first time.

7 **Complete the sentences with the verbs below in the correct tense.**

let   make   allow   get   cause   oblige

1 Her parents .... her to stay out until midnight last Saturday.
2 I .... to go. It was a work dinner with our German partners. I couldn't miss it.
3 My mum .... her hair done at the hairdresser's every week.
4 Our maths teacher .... us do a test every week.
5 Why don't you .... them go? It's going to be a nice trip.
6 The freezing weather .... some of the plants in my garden to die.

8 **Use the prompts to write sentences with an appropriate causative verb.**

1 My parents / not go out / in the evening. / That's not fair. *(simple present)*

....

2 This film / very moving. / The ending / me cry. *(simple past)*

....

3 Mr Basset / us go into his lab / next week. *(future)*

....

4 I / you to come / swimming pool / with me / after work. / It's so relaxing! *(future)*

....

5 We / Tom sing a song / at the party / he didn't want to. *(simple past)*

....

6 This is music / that / everybody dance! *(simple present)*

....

> **Remember!** As well as the verbs **get**, **compel**, **oblige**, **allow**, **cause**, verbs of volition like **want** and **would like** and the verbs **ask** and **expect** all also take the construction: object + infinitive with **to** → **want somebody to do something / would like somebody to do something** (see page 240).
>
> As well as the verbs **let** and **make**, verbs of perception such as **see** and **hear** are also followed by an object + base form of the verb, when the perception refers to something instantaneous, which is perceived in its entirety → **hear somebody do something / see somebody do something** (see page 333).
>
> In the passive form, on the other hand, the verb that follows is in the infinitive with **to**: *I was made <u>to do</u> something / He was seen <u>to do</u> something* (it's also possible to say *He was seen <u>doing</u> something*, if the action is more prolonged).

9 Complete the sentences with the base form, the *-ing* form, or the infinitive with *to* of these verbs.

clean   take   have   ring   make   phone   go   load   leave   run   learn

1. The market is closing. I can see the greengrocer .... his van.
2. I'd like my daughter .... her hair cut.
3. I'd like you .... part in the next meeting. We have .... some important decisions.
4. Sometimes we are made .... our classroom at the end of the lessons.
5. Mum expected us .... her as soon we got to the airport.
6. Our friends wanted us .... to the theatre with them, but we couldn't.
7. They were seen .... the restaurant at about ten last night.
8. The teacher made me .... the poem by heart.
9. I always let my dog .... freely on the hillside.
10. Sorry, I didn't hear the phone ....

10 Complete the sentences with the missing connectors.

1. Yes, you can buy those shoes, ... they don't cost more than £50.
2. I don't usually ask for help with my homework, ... it's a really difficult task.
3. Take your anorak with you .... it gets colder.
4. He was behaving .... he was a little child.
5. .... I could play the piano like you!
6. This exercise is easier .... I thought.
7. He said .... he was going to help you .... you were in trouble.
8. No one makes a better apple pie .... you do.
9. .... hard I try, my English teacher is never satisfied with my work.
10. Switch on the oven .... you get home or the cake will never be ready for dinner.

ROUND UP 20

MATRIX +

Here is a summary of the main **connectors** (conjunctions and adverbs) listed according to their function.

Coordinating conjunctions

- **and** (addition)
- **nor** (exclusion)
- **but** (contrast)
- **for** (cause)
- **or** (alternative)
- **so** (consequence)
- **yet** (contrast)

In order to remember them, think of the letters of the word FANBOY, they are the initials of these conjunctions: **f**or **a**nd **n**or **b**ut **o**r **y**et

We use coordinating conjunctions to join together two clauses of equal importance. The sentence structure with coordinating clauses is as follows:

MAIN CLAUSE + coordinating conjunction + **MAIN CLAUSE**.

The conjunctions **yet** and **for** are usually preceded by a comma.

Subordinating conjunctions

- **as, because, for, since** (cause)
- **so, so that** (purpose)
- **although, though** (contrast)
- **after, before, until, while, when, as, as soon as** (time)
- **if, whether, unless, as long as, provided, whenever, whatever** (conditional, indirect question)
- **that** (reported speech, indirect statement, consequence)

We use subordinating conjunctions when a main clause is followed, or sometimes preceded, by a secondary clause. The sentence structures with subordinating conjunctions are as follows:

MAIN CLAUSE + **SECONDARY CLAUSE** with or without a comma between them **SECONDARY CLAUSE** + **MAIN CLAUSE** always with a comma between them.

Correlative conjunctions

- **both...and** (including)
- **either...or** (alternative)
- **whether...or** (alternative)
- **not only...but also** (including)
- **neither...nor** (excluding)
- **as...as** (comparing, equality)

We use correlating conjunctions to join together equal elements in a sentence. They are always made up of two parts.

Linking adverbs and transition words

- **accordingly consequently therefore thus** (consequence)
- **still nevertheless however otherwise instead** (contrast)
- **also besides moreover furthermore** (addition)
- **firstly secondly then next meanwhile finally** (time sequence)
- **indeed** (reinforcing)

We use these adverbs within a text to connect sentences or parts of sentences and to increase the fluency of the discourse. These words are considered to be 'transitional' between the different parts of a sentence.

1 Complete the sentences with the coordinating conjunctions below.

so   yet   nor   and (x2)   for   or   but

1 I love him .... I don't want to marry him.
2 I have some more free time this week, ... I'm going to play some sports.
3 It's a small car, ... it's very spacious.
4 I won't buy it, ... it's far too costly.
5 You can spend £500 .... have this TV set .... you can spend a little more .... have that one – it's much better!
6 She didn't want any fruit, ... would she eat the dessert.

2 Complete the sentences with the subordinating conjunctions below.

as long as   that   if   though   so   until   so…that   because

1 I'm going to London .... I've found a good job there.
2 This novel is quite good, ... some descriptions in it are rather boring.
3 I've set the alarm for six o'clock .... I won't oversleep.
4 They say .... the concert will be broadcast live tomorrow evening.
5 This cake is .... good .... everyone wants another slice.
6 I asked a passer-by .... he knew a good restaurant in that area.
7 They couldn't export any of their products .... they started selling them on the e-market.
8 You won't have any problems in high school .... you work hard enough.

3 Change the position of the main and subordinate clauses. Remember to adjust punctuation.

0 As it's raining, I'm going to the cinema this afternoon.
   I'm going to the cinema this afternoon as it's raining.

1 He didn't want anything else because he had eaten enough.
   ....

2 I went straight home after I finished school yesterday.
   ....

3 If you see anything strange, call me at once.
   ....

4 You can join us on our boat trip provided you don't suffer from seasickness.
   ....

5 I won't try this dish whatever they say.
   ....

6 I went jogging for an hour before I went to the office this morning.
   ....

7 As long as it doesn't rain, I'll go for a bike ride later.
   ....

4 Read the text and insert the missing connectors (conjunctions, adverbs or pronouns).

If only   who   to   before   also   that   so   which (x2)

Two years ago, a friend of mine, ¹............ pretended to be very well informed about financial matters, got me ²............ invest some of my money in certain funds ³............ apparently rewarded you with very high interest rates. ⁴............ I hadn't followed his advice! I've lost all the money I had invested that way. Luckily I hadn't put all of my money in those rotten funds, I had ⁵............ invested part of it in shares ⁶............ have performed very well on the stock market in the last few months, ⁷............ I have partly covered the losses. The lesson I've learnt is ⁸............ you must be very well informed ⁹............ you do any kind of investment.

5 Read the procedure to make custard cream and insert the sequencers.

first   finally   after that   then   until   next

Do you want to make proper custard?
Just follow these instructions.

Ingredients
1 pint of milk   4 egg yolks
2 fl. oz. of cream   2 spoonfuls of cornflour
1 oz. of sugar   ½ teaspoon of vanilla extract

¹............ bring the milk and the cream to simmering point. ²............ whisk the egg yolks with the sugar and the cornflour.
³............ , pour the hot milk and cream onto the eggs and sugar, whisking all the time.
⁴............ return to the pan and add the vanilla extract. Keep stirring with a wooden spatula ⁵............ thickened. ⁶............ , pour the custard into a jug and serve at once.

6 Read the article and insert the missing words.

as a result   and   which   however   if   although   in spite of

The San Andreas Fault

The San Andreas Fault, ¹............ extends for more than 600 miles (970 km) from Point Arenato to the Colorado Desert, is the most active fault in California.

But what exactly is a fault? The Earth's surface consists of about 20 rigid plates of rock that move slowly past one another. This motion squeezes ²............ stretches the rocks at the edge of these plates. ³............ the force is too great, the rocks break and shift and an earthquake is caused ⁴............ .

The energy created travels away from the fault in seismic waves. In 1906, a horizontal movement of the earth's crust caused the terrible earthquake in the city of San Francisco.

⁵............ the number of studies on the matter, the reliable prediction of earthquakes is not possible yet. ⁶............ , scientists study history to try and guess how often a certain region can expect a catastrophe.

For example, California may expect a catastrophic earthquake once every 50 to 100 years. And, ⁷............ there was a quake in 1989, Californians are still on the alert, waiting for 'the Big One'.

7 **Complete the text with the appropriate form of the verbs *make*, *get* or *let*.**

When it's sunny, my parents ¹............................ my brother and me help them in the garden – I hate it! The front garden is small and has some flowers, so it's not that bad, but the back garden is very big and my parents ²............................ us to grow vegetables there. We also have some apple and pear trees, my mother ³............................ us to pick the fruit for the family. Dad ⁴............................ us mow the lawn once a month and mum ⁵............................ us to weed the flower beds at the front. When she's too busy with her job, mum ⁶............................ us water the plants – indoor and out – and dad ⁷............................ my brother trim the hedge with him. Sometimes dad ⁸............................ me drive his car - I much prefer this to doing gardening.

8 **Complete the passage with the verbs below in the correct tense.**

make   allow   hear   force   see   need   oblige   get

1 Mum .... me to learn the piano even though I had no musical talent.
2 The maths teacher .... us do a test every day. That's hard!
3 Mrs Durrell .... her hair done in London every month.
4 Brian's parents .... him to stay out until midnight. He's so lucky!
5 I .... people buying the latest digital products at the fair yesterday.
6 David .... to get his suit dry-cleaned for tomorrow's meeting.
7 Ben felt .... to go. It was a work dinner and he couldn't miss it.
8 We .... the street sellers shouting on the market square early this morning.

Reflecting on grammar

Reflect on the rules and say whether the following statements are true or false.

		True	False
1	**And**, **nor** and **or** are subordinating conjunctions.		
2	**On the one hand...** must be followed by **on the other...**		
3	**Although** introduces a concessive clause (sometimes called a contrastive clause).		
4	A purpose clause is usually expressed with **for** + base form of the verb.		
5	**Since**, **for**, **as** and **because** are all conjunctions expressing reason.		
6	A subordinate clause cannot precede a main clause, so we never begin a sentence with a subordinating conjunction.		
7	The sentence *I'm going to tell him as soon as I'll see him* is correct.		
8	**Before** and **after** can be followed by a phrase containing a finite verb but also by the **–ing** form of the verb.		
9	The last point in an argument or a sequence of events is usually introduced by the adverb **first**.		
10	Causative verbs (**make**, **get**, **let**, **cause**) used in the active form all have the same construction: object + base form of the verb.		

GRAMMAR MATRIX MAIN

UNIT 21 Word order, phrasal verbs, word formation

LESSON 1 Word order in positive and negative sentences; inversion of verb and subject

Positive sentences

Positive sentences typically have the structure **subject** + **verb** + **objects**.
The verb **be** and linking verbs like **become**, **feel** and **look** can be followed by an adjective or a nominal phrase that add information to the subject. These are called **complements** → They are very nice.
He became a great chef.

Transitive verbs are followed by a **direct object** and then by other **indirect objects** → I met John at the shopping mall yesterday.

FAQ

Q: Our teacher told us to use the acronym **SVOMPT** to remember the order of words in a sentence, but I don't remember exactly what it means...

A: The acronym **SVOMPT** stands for the sequence of words in a positive sentence, i.e.
SUBJECT + VERB + OBJECT (what or who) + MANNER (how) + PLACE (where) + TIME (when)
Of course, not all the kinds of indirect objects may be present, but we follow this order for those that are present in the sentence, e.g.
I (subject) have (verb) a quick lunch (object) in the school cafeteria (place) on Mondays (time).

Intransitive verbs, like verbs of movement **go**, **come**, **drive** and similar, follow the **SVPMT** order:
SUBJECT + VERB + PLACE + MANNER + TIME

My parents (subject) went (verb) to London (place) in their friends' car (manner) last Sunday (time).

Alternatively, the complement of time can be placed in the final position → Last Sunday, my parents went to London in their friends' car.

1 Reorder the words and write sentences. Then say if the verbs are transitive, intransitive or linking verbs. Write T, I or L in the boxes.

1 leaving / He's / college / in / for / a / time / week's / . ☐
....

2 I / today / great / feel / . ☐
....

3 last / They / way / all / drove / the / Portugal / to / summer / . ☐
....

4 bought / I / a / pretty / skirt / very / in / the / shop / little / in / mall / the / . ☐
....

5 famous / They / very / became / their / last / after / album / .

....

6 watch / We / on / videos / YouTube / often / .

....

7 the / We / to / shop / in / went / the / High / lunch / fish-and-chip / Street / for / .

....

8 holiday / They / are / on / Holland / a / cycling / going / in / .

....

9 silly / at / night / party / last / He / very / trousers / the / looked / in / those / .

....

10 went / a / bikes / on / We / for / our / ride / .

....

Inversion of subject and verb

If there is an adverb or an adverbial expression at the beginning of the sentence which has a negative or restrictive meaning, such as **never, seldom, rarely, hardly ever, nowhere, not only…, no sooner…than…, only in this way…, by no means**, the construction will be the same as an interrogative sentence, i.e. **auxiliary verb** or **modal verb + subject**.

Rarely <u>have I listened</u> to such great music.
Not only <u>can you come</u> and see us any time, but you can also bring your brother.

If there is no auxiliary or modal verb, we insert the auxiliary **do** in the required tense, just as we do in a question → Hardly ever <u>does she arrive</u> on time.   Never <u>did they go</u> abroad for work.

> ❗ If there is a subordinate clause at the beginning of the sentence which starts with **not until** or with the adverb **only** (**only when…, only if…, only by doing so…**), it will be the main clause that has the inversion of the subject and the verb → Only if you work really hard, <u>will you be able</u> to achieve your goals.   Not until he spoke, <u>did I realise</u> who he really was.

Other cases of inversion of the subject and the verb:

- when a sentence starts with an adverb of place or an adjective. In this case, we don't need the addition of an auxiliary verb → Here comes the bride!   Awful was his anger.
- to introduce a conditional sentence when the conjunction **if** is omitted → Should I decide to go, I'll let you know. (= If I decided to go…) (See page 303)

2 Match the sentence halves.

1 Nowhere was a police officer
2 Never have I seen
3 No sooner had she got her degree
4 Only in this way will
5 Rarely in modern times
6 Only if everybody pays their taxes
7 Only by joining the club
8 Hardly ever

A than she was offered a job.
B have so many people migrated to Europe.
C to be seen.
D can social welfare be sustained.
E will you have the opportunity of meeting new people.
F the problem be solved.
G have I seen such a beautiful landscape.
H such a beautiful sea.

1 .....   2 .....   3 .....   4 .....   5 .....   6 .....   7 .....   8 .....

Negative sentences

In a negative sentence, an auxiliary or a modal verb must necessarily be present so that we can add the adverb **not** → *They were not / weren't at home.* (auxiliary **be**) *I could not / couldn't hear what they said.* (modal verb **could**)

If there is no auxiliary or modal verb, we insert the auxiliary **do / does** in the present or **did** in the past → *He does not / doesn't like drawing.* (third person singular of the present simple of **like**)
I did not / didn't know. (past simple of the verb **know**)

FAQ

Q: Is it possible to use do even in positive sentences? I once heard the sentence I do like it.

A: Yes, in order to emphasise the verb. **I do like it** has the same meaning as **I really like it**. Here are some other examples: *She does look nice today! You did buy that dress after all.   We do want to see it.*

3 Rewrite the sentences in the negative form. Make any necessary changes.

0   There was someone in the room. — *There wasn't anyone in the room.*
1   The man was standing near the shop door.
2   There was something strange about him.
3   They discovered a Neolithic site in this area.
4   Tina looks happy today.
5   I'm thirsty. I need something to drink.
6   I have to work at weekends this month.
7   The visitors left the museum before five.
8   Karen will arrive at the end of December.
9   We could see the entrance of the building on the screen.
10 She went out with her boyfriend last night.
11 I have played tennis a lot recently.
12 They had already left the office.

LESSON 2 Questions and short answers; question tags; *So do I / Neither do I*

Interrogative sentences: *Yes / No* questions

Yes / No questions always begin with an auxiliary or a modal verb followed by a subject or by other parts of the sentence (main verb, objects...). If there are no modal or auxiliary verbs present, we fall back on the use of **do / does** in the present, and **did** in the past for questions.
We usually use a short answer to respond, i.e.

> **Yes** or **No** + subject pronoun + the same auxiliary or modal verb that is in the question.

'Have you got any pets?' 'No, I haven't.'
'Can Janet speak Spanish?' 'Yes, she can.'
'Did you get there on time?' 'Yes, I did.'

Remember! After **Yes / No**, we always need a comma.

FAQ

Q: Why are they called **short answers**, when they aren't short at all? Wouldn't a simple **Yes** or **No** be enough?

A: They are called that because they are shorter than a full answer. In spoken language, we sometimes just say **Yes** or **No**, but in general we use the pronoun and the auxiliary to confirm the positive or negative answer.

! If the question asks for an opinion or a prediction e.g. **Do you think she will come?**, the answer can be: **I think so.** / **I don't think so.** Other possible responses are:

I expect so.	I expect not.
I guess so / I believe so.	I guess not / I believe not.
I hope so.	I hope not.
I suppose so.	I suppose not. / I don't suppose so.
I'm afraid so.	I'm afraid not.

To respond to invitations with **Would you like…?**, we usually use **Yes, please** to accept or **No, thank you** / **No thanks** to refuse.

To respond to requests with **Can I have…?**, we usually say, for example **Yes, sure** or **No, sorry**.

---

1 Reorder the words and write questions. Then write positive or negative short answers.

1 like / do / painting / you / ? (+)

....

2 play / does / in / the / school / Rebecca / team / volleyball / ? (−)

....

3 the / are / going / home / boys / ? (−)

....

4 like / would / to / her / meet / you / ? (+)

....

5 did / boyfriend / present / your / you / give / a / ? (+)

....

6 laptop / got / has / with / Marion / her / her / ? (−)

....

2 Answer the questions using the verbs in brackets in the positive or negative form.

1 Do you think she'll like our present? (hope / +) ....
2 Do you think the test will be difficult? (hope / −) ....
3 Will we really have to do all this work by tomorrow? (am afraid / +) ....
4 Are we going to have a longer holiday this year? (am afraid / −) ....
5 Is she coming tomorrow? (think / −) ....
6 Are they going to win the match? (guess / +) ....
7 Are we going to leave the office earlier tomorrow? (suppose / −) ....
8 Will Mr Dreier join the meeting later today? (believe / +) ....

Interrogative sentences: *Wh–* questions

Wh– questions begin with an interrogative word like **what**, **where**, **when**, **why** and similar words, followed by an auxiliary or modal + subject + main verb and any other complements in the sentence. As before, where there is no auxiliary or modal verb present, we insert **do / does** or **did** before the subject.

To respond, we give the information needed, with a full sentence or a short answer, without repeating the subject and the verb:
'What are you doing?' 'I'm working.'
'Where should I go?' 'To the bank.'
'What time does the film on Screen 3 start?' '(It starts) at nine.'

FAQ

Q: Why do we insert the word **do** in a question? What has **doing** got to do with it?

A: As a main verb, **do** has its own intrinsic meaning, which it loses when it is used as an auxiliary verb. The use of **do** is simply a kind of signal: for example, if I use **does** at the beginning of a question, I signal that I'm about to ask something about the present in the third person singular. If I start the question with **did**, it's a signal that I'm about to ask about the past. Look at the question **What do you do?** The first **do** is a signal, the second is the main verb.

> If there is a preposition in a **Wh– question**, it is placed at the end. → What are they talking <u>about</u>? (NOT ~~About what~~ are they talking?)   Where do they come <u>from</u>? (NOT ~~From where~~ do they come?).
> When **who**, **what** or **which** are the subject of the question, the structure is the same as a positive sentence, i.e. subject + verb → Who knows?   What happened?   Which is yours?

3 Reorder the words to make questions. Then match them to the correct answer.

1 station / do / to / we / how / get / the / ?
....
2 buy / when / you / your / did / car / ?
....
3 when / come / you / could / house / to / my / ?
....
4 laughing / why / you / were / ?
....
5 you / buy / which / of / T-shirts / those / did / ?
....
6 long / how / did / wait / them / you / for / ?
....
7 you / sell / to / flat / your / going / are / ?
....
8 time / brother / home / what / did / your / night / last / get / ?
....

A I can come tomorrow, if that's okay with you.
B The striped one.
C Because I heard a good joke on the radio.
D I bought it last year.
E Just after midnight, I think.
F For over an hour.
G Go down this road and then turn right.
H Yes, I want to buy a bigger one.

1 .....   2 .....   3 .....   4 .....   5 .....   6 .....   7 .....   8 .....

4 Write questions using elements from the table below.

Wh- word	Auxiliary	Subject	Verb	Complement	Preposition	
Where	are	you	get	to the cinema	to	
What	is	they	come	to school	for	
Who	was	he	go	the guitar course	at	?
When	were	Josh	start	in the holidays	from	
Why	do	your friends	running	last night	with	
How	does	Martina	going to do			
	did	your family	looking			
			waiting			
			going			

Question tags → Visual Grammar page 417

To ask for confirmation about something, we use the so-called **question tags**, i.e. a short question at the end of a sentence, separated from it by a comma.

In **question tags**, we repeat the auxiliary or modal verb used in the main sentence, and follow it with the subject pronoun → It's raining, <u>isn't it</u>?

The response will be a **short answer**: Yes, it is. (to confirm) / No, it isn't. (to deny)

If there is no auxiliary or modal verb, we use **do / does** or **did** → You like Italian food, <u>don't you</u>?

Remember!
Positive sentence, negative tag
You <u>like</u> fantasy films, <u>don't you</u>?
Ben <u>can</u> swim, <u>can't he</u>?

Negative sentence, positive tag
You <u>didn't</u> get a bad mark, <u>did you</u>?
I <u>can't</u> be in two places at once, <u>can I</u>?

Sometimes, the first part of the sentence is understood and not expressed → Great match, isn't it? (understood: It's a...)

In informal language, to ask for confirmation we also use the expression **Right?** → This is yours, right?

Look too at the rather formal **question tags** used with imperatives: Let's go, shall we? Pass the salt, will you?

Short questions

To show interest or surprise about what someone has just said, we can use short questions formed with the auxiliary or modal from the preceding sentence + subject pronoun, sometimes with the addition of the adverb **Really?** → 'You know, <u>Peter is</u> in my class.' '<u>Is he</u>? That's great!' (also: 'Is he really?' Or only: 'Really?')

'<u>I've</u> nearly finished the book!' 'Oh... <u>Have you really</u>? You're a quick reader.'

5 Complete the dialogues with question tags. Then listen and check.

ON THE BUS

A Excuse me, this is the right stop for Piccadilly Circus, [1]...........................

B Yes, it is. Piccadilly Circus is just over there.

A Thank you very much.

B You aren't British, [2]...........................

A No, I'm Australian, from Melbourne!

AFTER A PARTY

David Fabulous party, ³...........................

Megan Yes, it was great.

David Er... can I take you home?

Megan Yes, that'd be nice.

David You live in Weybridge, ⁴...........................

Megan No, in Walton, actually. You've got a car, ⁵...........................

David Well, no. You don't mind going on my motorbike, ⁶...........................

Megan Not at all. I love riding on motorbikes!

6 Complete the sentences with question tags.

1 Today is October 2nd, ...
2 Miss Johnson is the Sales Manager, ...
3 You've got a brother called Jack, ...
4 It wasn't such a long flight, ...
5 You don't mind walking, ...
6 Your guests arrived this morning, ...
7 You didn't call me earlier, ...
8 Max can play the guitar, ...
9 Let's order now, ...
10 He drives a taxi, ...

7 Write short questions for these statements.

0 James is a very good mechanic. _Is he?_
1 Daisy wants to become a web designer. ....
2 Do you know Tom is in India? .... I didn't know.
3 Dan would never behave like that. ....
4 I have never been here before. ....
5 He'll buy me some new clothes. ....
6 I can't go to the cinema tonight. ....
7 I've already watched this film. ....

Agreeing and disagreeing → Visual Grammar page 415

To express **agreement** about:

a positive statement	a negative statement
So + auxiliary or modal + subject	**Neither / Nor** + auxiliary or modal + subject

'I'm taking this course.' 'So am I.'
'I like rap.' 'So do I.'

'I'm not taking this course.' 'Neither am I.'
'I don't like jazz.' 'Neither do I.' / 'Nor do I.'

To express **disagreement** with or **opposition** to:

a positive statement	a negative statement
subject + negative auxiliary or modal	subject + positive auxiliary or modal

'I'm happy with the exam results.' 'I'm not.'
'I like this song.' 'Really? I don't.'

'I'm not happy with the exam results.' 'I am.'
'I don't like this song.' 'Really? I do.'

Look at some more examples:
'<u>We're</u> going out for dinner tonight.' '<u>So are we</u>. Let's go together, shall we?' / '<u>We aren't</u>. We're having dinner at home.'
'<u>Jack wasn't</u> on the school trip.' '<u>Neither was his sister</u>.' / 'Really? <u>His sister was</u>.'

8 Circle the correct option to express agreement.

1 I don't think it's a good idea.
   A Neither do I.
   B Neither don't I.
   C Nor I do.

2 I can't wait any longer.
   A Nor can I.
   B Nor could I.
   C So can I.

3 I'd like to work in a foreign country.
   A So I would.
   B So I'd like.
   C So would I.

4 I think you're right.
   A So am I.
   B So do I.
   C So did I.

5 I loved the concert!
   A So do we.
   B So loved we.
   C So did we.

6 Rick wants to learn French.
   A So does Eliza.
   B Nor does Eliza.
   C Neither does Eliza.

9 Match the statements (1–6) to the expressions of disagreement (A–F).

1 I would like to have a part-time job.
2 She likes to upload her photos on Facebook.
3 I don't cook at the weekend. My husband does.
4 I think he's the greatest rapper ever!
5 We didn't enjoy the cruise on the Nile.
6 We're ready to go. Are you?
7 We thought the film was really boring.

A I wouldn't. I'd rather work full time!
B I don't. He's not a good singer.
C Sorry, we aren't. We've just got up.
D My husband and I did! We loved it!
E We didn't. We thought it was good.
F Does she? Her boyfriend doesn't.
G Lucky you! Mine never does.

1 .....   2 .....   3 .....   4 .....   5 .....   6 .....   7 .....

10 Express agreement (=) or disagreement (≠). Use the subject in brackets.

0 I'm going to bed now.
   (=) (we) *So are we.*
   (≠) (we) *We aren't.*

1 They would like to leave early.
   (≠) (their friends) ....

2 We often travel abroad for work.
   (=) (we) ....

3 I'll give Kate a present for her birthday.
   (=) (I) ....

4 My daughter loves ballet!
   (≠) (my daughter) ....

5 I went to Brazil last year.
   (=) (my son) ....

6 My teachers are quite nice.
   (≠) (mine) ....

7 We've never been to Brazil.
   (=) (we) ....

LESSON 3 Word formation; prefixes and suffixes

Formation of compound nouns

Many compound nouns are made up of two words, either joined together, as in **weekend**, or separate, as in **school year**: the first part of the compound noun functions as an adjective and specifies or qualifies the second, as in **safety belt**. (What kind of belt? One meant for safety.)

Focus

Be careful of the difference between **a tea cup** (= the empty container) and **a cup of tea** (= the liquid inside the container).

Compound nouns (**noun + noun**) form the plural by adding **–s** to the second word, for example **tea bags**, **tennis rackets**. However, if the compound word is formed by a noun + an adverb or a preposition, the plural **–s** is always added to the noun part of the expression: **passers-by**, **brothers-in-law**...

Many compound nouns are used to indicate:

- a relationship of belonging → *the kitchen table   the school car park   the London Underground*
  Be careful! This is not a 'possessive' relationship, so we do not use the **possessive case 's** (NOT ~~London's~~ *Underground*)
- the use that we make of an object → *football boots   wallpaper   bathtub*
  The first word is often the **–ing form** of a verb: *frying pan   shopping bag   fishing rod*
- the material the object is made of → *a straw hat   rubber boots   a silk scarf*
- literary, music or movie genres → *crime stories   rock music   war films*
- espressions of time or festivals → *the summer holidays   a weekend trip   an end-of-school party*

We often find groups of three or more nouns together:
a science-fiction film   the World Football Championship   the UK Energy Resource Centre

1 Match the words 1-12 to the words A-L to produce compound nouns. Sometimes there is more than one possible combination.

1 washing	7 alarm	A pool	G office
2 swimming	8 front	B accident	H mall
3 weather	9 contact	C machine	I door
4 post	10 shopping	D clock	J station
5 railway	11 table	E cards	K lenses
6 road	12 Christmas	F forecast	L tennis

1 ..... 2 ..... 3 ..... 4 ..... 5 ..... 6 ..... 7 ..... 8 ..... 9 ..... 10 ..... 11 ..... 12 .....

2 Rewrite the expressions with nouns that can be used as adjectives. Remember: a noun used as an adjective is always in the singular form.

1 The team from the school
....

2 A holiday in the summer
....

3 A shelf for books
....

4 A magazine about fashion
....

5 A garden where vegetables are grown
....

6 Vegetables from the garden
....

7 A glass for drinking wine
....

8 A room for conferences
....

9 A shop where shoes are sold
....

10 Boots to use when you ski
....

11 A resort where you go in the winter
....

12 A story that talks about love
....

13 A court where you play tennis
....

14 Music in the rock style
....

15 A screen you use with your computer
....

16 The door of your car
....

Formation of adjectives

Many qualifying adjectives are really present participles, which end in **–ing** (**a marching band**), or past participles, which end in **–ed** for regular verbs (**a satisfied customer**) or have an irregular form (**a broken arm**). Remember! If an adjective ends in **–ing**, it has an active meaning, whereas if it ends in **–ed**, it has a passive meaning.

Verbs	Adjectives ending in *–ing*	Adjectives ending in *–ed*
interest	*interesting*	*interested*
relax	*relaxing*	*relaxed*
satisfy	*satisfying*	*satisfied*
tire	*tiring*	*tired*

Note: *Her story touched us all very deeply.   Hers was a touching story.   We were all touched by her story.*

The three sentences have a similar meaning.

Focus

Some adjectives are formed by adding **–ed** not to a verb but to a noun (e.g. parts of the body or items of clothing), which is preceded by another adjective or noun to which it is joined by a hyphen
→ *a dark-haired man, a blue-eyed girl, a long-legged dog*

FAQ

Q: I saw the expression **a ten-year-old boy. Shouldn't this be a ten-years-old…, in the plural?**

A: No, nouns used as adjectives do not take the plural form. Look too at: *a ten-pound note* (NOT *a ten-pounds note*). Some adjectives are used as collective nouns, to indicate a whole category. In this case too, they do not take the plural **–s**, e.g. *the young, the rich, the poor*.

3 Complete the sentences as in the example.

0   A shirt with short sleeves is a *short-sleeved shirt* .
1   A man with a big nose is a ....
2   A dog with short legs and a long tail is a ....
3   A girl with long hair is a ....
4   A hat with a wide brim is a ....
5   Shoes with high heels are ....
6   A baby who has just been born is a new- ....
7   A country that has been torn by war is a ....
8   A canal made by man is a ....

4 Complete the sentences with an adjective in the *–ing* or *–ed* form of the word in brackets.

1   I was really .... when most of my students didn't have their books with them. (annoy)
2   Your disruptive behaviour during the lesson was really .... (annoy)
3   The directions we were given were so .... that we couldn't find our way to the hotel. (confuse)

4 The action film I saw last night was really .... (excite)
5 We had a .... day yesterday. We were so .... in the evening! (tire)
6 My friend is very .... in Irish folk music and dance. (interest)
7 He's really .... when he tells his jokes. He makes everybody laugh. (entertain)
8 Look at the .... sun. What a majestic sight! (rise)
9 We had a really .... evening, just chilling out with a takeaway and a movie. (relax)
10 I was really .... by what you said. I couldn't understand your point at all. (confuse)

Words with prefixes and suffixes

A word can be modified by **prefixes** or **suffixes**, i.e. groups of letters placed either at the beginning or the end of a word. The word that is produced changes in meaning compared to the original **root word**, e.g. the prefix **mis** + verb **understand** → **misunderstand**.

Often the word modified by a suffix also has a different grammatical function, e.g. a noun can become an adjective: **beauty** + suffix **ful** → **beautiful**.

Prefixes

Here is a list of the main prefixes, subdivided by function:

- **Negative prefixes, which make words with the opposite meaning**
  dis– (dishonest, disappear)
  il– / ir– (illegal, irregular)
  im– / in– (imperfect, inhospitable)
  un– (unbelievable)
- **Prefix that indicates repetition**
  re– (rebuild, repay)
- **Prefix that indicates commonality or cooperation**
  co– (cooperation, coexist)
- **Prefix that indicates a decrease or deprivation**
  de– (deforestation, defrost)
- **Prefixes that indicate that something is done badly or is incorrect**
  mis– (misbehaviour, misfortune)
  ill– (ill-equipped)
- **Prefixes that indicate an excess or a defect**
  over– (overestimate, overpopulated)
  under– (underestimate, underweight)
- **Prefix that indicates anticipation or prediction**
  fore– (foresee, foretell)
- **Prefixes that indicate quantity or number**
  mono– (monotheistic)
  bi– (bicentennial)
  tri– (tricycle)
  poly– (polysyllabic)
  multi– (multipurpose)

5 Underline the prefixes and match the words to their definition.

1 multitasking   A have a different idea
2 forecast   B treated badly
3 polytheistic religion C put things in a different way
4 oversleep   D make dry by removing the water
5 dehydrate   E doing more than one thing at a time
6 disagree   F get up later than usual
7 unfriendly   G in three parts
8 undernourished   H not very sociable
9 trilogy   I not well fed
10 ill-treated   J say what the future will be like
11 rearrange   K someone who speaks many languages
12 polyglot   L more than one god is worshipped

1 ...... 2 ...... 3 ...... 4 ...... 5 ...... 6 ...... 7 ...... 8 ...... 9 ...... 10 ...... 11 ...... 12 ......

Suffixes that form nouns
- **Abstract nouns**

  –ness (happiness), **–ship** (friendship), **–hood** (childhood), **–ment** (disappointment), **–ance / –ence** (performance, difference), **–y / –ity / –iety** (jealousy, immunity, variety), **–tion / –ation** (connection, combination), **–dom** (boredom)

- **Nouns that indicate profession, human activity or the function of an object**

  –er / –or (employer, calculator), **–ress** for the feminine form of some professions (waitress), **–ee** (employee), **–ist** (novelist), **–ian** (politician), **–ant / –ent** (assistant, superintendent)

Suffixes that form adjectives
- **Adjectives that indicate a quality or characteristic**

  –able / –ible (reliable, convertible), **–ive** (attractive), **–ous** (dangerous), **–y** (noisy)

- **Nationality adjectives (always starting with a capital letter)**

  –an / –ian (Mexican, Canadian), **–ish** (Polish), **–ese** (Portuguese)

- **Adjectives with reductive or derogatory connotations**

  –ish (childish). Also used for colours that are not well defined: *reddish, yellowish…*

- **Adjectives that indicate abundance**

  –ful (hopeful)

- **Adjectives that indicate deprivation**

  –less (hopeless)

- **Adjectives that belong to technical, scientific or cultural language**

  –al (cultural, central), **–ar** (molecular), **–ic / –ical** (atomic, historical)

- **Adjectives derived from cardinal points**

  –ern (northern, southern, eastern, western, north-eastern, south-western…)

Suffixes that form verbs
Verbs that indicate 'make', 'become'

–ize / –ise (modernize, legalise), **–ify** (purify), **–en** (strengthen, widen, shorten)

Suffixes that form adverbs
–ly (mainly, generally)
Many of these adverbs are adverbs of manner (softly, gently).
(See page 174)

---

6 Write the names of professions or activities by adding the appropriate suffix to the word in brackets.

1. A great .... is someone whose work never dies. (art)
2. Most .... think that human events go in cycles. (history)
3. The .... said that sales should increase. (direct)
4. Picasso is one of the greatest .... of all times. (paint)
5. The .... made all the children laugh with his tricks. (magic)
6. He's the .... in the band and she's the .... (drum / sing)

7 Underline the prefixes and suffixes of the words below and write if they are a noun (N), verb (V), adjective (AD) or adverb (ADV).

0. <u>UN</u>FAVOUR<u>ABLE</u>   *(AD)*
1. PEACEFUL ....
2. REWIND ....
3. IMPATIENTLY ....
4. REORGANISATION ....
5. UNFORTUNATELY ....
6. DISADVANTAGE ....
7. INSECURITY ....
8. LEADERSHIP ....
9. LONELINESS ....

8 Complete the sentences with adjectives using *–ful* or *–less*. Use the words in brackets.

1 Not answering her emails is ………………… . (point)
2 The sunset is always a ………………… sight. (wonder)
3 There are lots of ………………… people sleeping on the park benches. (home)
4 This pocket calculator has proved to be very ………………… . (use)
5 Talking so loudly is really ………………… . We can hear you very well when you talk normally. (use)
6 Be very ………………… when driving in the fog. (care)
7 He's a ………………… writer. He makes lots of spelling mistakes. (care)
8 Our company's CEO is a ………………… woman. (power)
9 Patricia will never learn French. She's ………………… at foreign languages. (hope)
10 We hope this will be the start of a ………………… business relationship. (fruit)

9 Complete the second sentence so that it has the same meaning as the first. Use adjectives formed from the underlined words.

1 These jeans are in <u>fashion</u>. They're ………………… jeans.
2 He thinks only about him<u>self</u>. He's a ………………… person.
3 There's a lot of <u>noise</u> in here. It's a very ………………… place.
4 This drink has got <u>alcohol</u> in it. It's an ………………… drink.
5 What you said doesn't <u>mean</u> anything. What you said is ………………… .
6 Such protests are without <u>precedent</u>. Such protests are ………………… .
7 It's a night <u>without clouds</u>. It's a ………………… night.
8 Sara is a girl you can <u>rely</u> on. Sara is a ………………… girl.
9 It's <u>not possible</u> to climb that mountain. Climbing that mountain is ………………… .
10 It's <u>difficult to predict</u> what he's going to do next. He's very ………………… .

LESSON 4 Phrasal verbs

Phrasal verbs are composed of a main verb plus one or two adverbial or prepositional particles which give the verb a particular meaning, e.g. *Get on with your work* (= Continue...)

These verbs are used a lot in spoken language. Sometimes it is easy to guess their meaning by considering the meaning of the verb and the particle, e.g. **give back** or **go around**. In other cases, it's very difficult for a non-native speaker to guess because the meaning changes completely, e.g. **put up with** means 'tolerate' and **give in** means 'admit defeat'. So it's nothing to do with **put** or **give** taken alone.

FAQ

Q: I find it really difficult to remember **phrasal verbs**. Is there any alternative to using them?

A: There are almost always synonyms, verbs that express the meaning with a single word rather than a phrasal verb, and in English these longer words are often cognates from Latin: **tolerate** rather than **put up with**, **arrive** instead of **get to**, **enter** instead of **go in**, or **return** instead of **go back**. Words of Latin origin sound quite formal in English, so you will sound like a very well-educated if you use them a lot!

Phrasal verbs can be:
- intransitive, i.e. verb + preposition or adverb, without a direct object → They all <u>stood up</u> when the principal <u>came in</u>.
- transitive, i.e. followed by a direct object → <u>Wake up</u> the kids.
  Many of these verbs can be separated, i.e. the direct object may be placed either after the particle or between the verb and the particle → <u>Tidy up</u> your room. / <u>Tidy</u> your room <u>up</u>.
- If the object is a pronoun, it is always placed between the verb and the particle → He read the book and then he <u>brought it back</u> to the library. (NOT …he <s>brought back it</s>…).
  Be careful! If the particle is a preposition (**for**, **at**, **to**, **into**…), the verb cannot be separated into two parts → I ran into Kate this morning. (NOT I <s>ran Kate into</s>…)

FAQ

Q: Can a phrasal verb have more than one meaning?

A: Yes, this happens a lot. For example, **take off** used intransitively is the action of a plane when it departs (*My plane takes off in a few minutes*), while as a transitive verb it means **remove** (*Take off your coat*). Another example: **go off** can mean **go away**, **explode**, **stop working**, **fall asleep** and also **go bad**! Only the context can help you to understand which meaning is the correct one.

It's not possible to list all the **phrasal verbs**, there are simply too many. The lists that follow include only the most common ones.

Intransitive verbs

break out = begin suddenly (of unpleasant things)
call in = visit briefly
come in / go in = enter
come out / go out / get out = leave (a building or a room)
come up = ascend, approach, begin to grow
get off = leave (a public vehicle)
get on (well) with… = be friendly with
get on with… / carry on with… = proceed with sth
get up = arise from bed
give in = admit defeat, surrender

go away / get away from… = leave, escape
go back / come back / get back = return
go off = leave, explode, deteriorate
lie down = be in a horizontal position, rest
look out / watch out = be careful
stand up = get to your feet when sitting
sit down = move from a standing position to a sitting position
take off = rise into the air (aeroplane)
wake up = stop sleeping
wash up = wash the dishes

A few **phrasal verbs** can be followed by the **–ing form** of the verb → *My father gave up smoking a couple of months ago.*

FAQ

Q: What's the difference between **come out** and **go out**?

A: Both **come out** and **go out** have the meaning 'leave a place'. **Come out** is used by the person who is already outside, whereas **go out** is used by the person who is inside. The same thing for **come in** and **go in**. **Come in** is used by the person who is inside, while **go in** is used by the person who is outside. And so on for **come up / go up** and **come down / go down**.

1 Complete the sentences with an appropriate verb or adverbial particle.

1 Come .... , please. The door is open.
2 Let's .... in! It's cold outside.
3 Call .... tonight and we'll have a nice chat.
4 Never .... in without fighting!
5 I don't get .... very well with my new colleague.
6 You can't .... on like this. You should sleep more.
7 Wake .... ! It's late!
8 I sometimes wash .... after dinner.
9 We usually .... up at half past six a.m. on weekdays.
10 Please sit .... here, next to me.
11 If you have a headache .... down on the sofa and get some rest.
12 Let's go .... now. We can take a walk to the beach.
13 Bye, Sam. Come .... soon!
14 The Second World War .... out in 1939.
15 Take .... your coat. It's quite warm in here.
16 Our plane .... off at eight. We have to be at the airport two hours before.
17 Go .... and leave me alone!
18 There's a lot of traffic. .... out before crossing the street!
19 Thank you for the nice presentation. You can go .... to your seat now.
20 The yoghurt will go .... if you don't put it in the fridge.
21 I don't always wake up when my alarm goes ....
22 .... out, everybody! There's a bull in that field!
23 You should .... up when the principal walks into the classroom.
24 Dave ran .... a rabbit by mistake while he was driving to work.

Transitive verbs (that can be separated by an object)

bring about = cause sth to happen
bring back = return s.o. / sth
     return with sth for s.o. (a present)
bring up = rear, educate, bring to notice
carry out = put in practice, complete a task
cut down = reduce
cut out = remove by cutting, cut into a desired shape, omit, leave out
fill in = complete (a form)
get across = make sth understood
give out = distribute
give up = stop, abandon
hand in = give sth to a person in authority
make up = invent (excuses, stories)
pick up = collect s.o., lift sth from the ground
put away = put or store things tidily in their place
put off = postpone

put on = dress oneself in, put clothes on
put out = extinguish (a fire)
put up = provide lodging for
switch off = prevent electricity from flowing by turning a switch
switch on = allow electricity to flow by turning a switch
take off = remove (clothes)
take up = begin to follow (a profession, a hobby)
try on = put on clothes to find out if they fit
turn off = prevent water or electricity to flow by turning a tap or a switch
turn on = allow water or electricity to flow by turning a tap or a switch
turn down = reduce or make lower (volume, thermostat)
turn up = increase (volume, thermostat)

Verbs with two particles

catch up with = reach s.o. who is ahead, reach the same level with s.o. who is more advanced
do away with = remove, abolish
get away with = achieve sth wrong without being caught
get by on/with = manage to live using the money, knowledge or things that you have
get through with = finish with sth
go down with = be ill with
keep up with = make progress at the same rate as sth
look forward to = think with pleasure about sth that is going to happen
put up with = tolerate, bear
run out of = use up or finish a supply of sth
stand back from = move back from a place, be located away from sth
stand in for = substitute (for)

2 Write sentences with the same meaning by moving the particle after the object.

0 What has **brought about** this misunderstanding?
   *What has **brought** this misunderstanding **about**?*

1 **Bring back** the newspaper, will you?
2 **Fill in** this form, please.
3 **Hand in** your project by tomorrow.
4 It's cold. **Put on** your pullover.
5 Can I **try on** this coat, please?
6 **Switch on** the lights, it's dark.
7 **Put away** the glasses, please.
8 **Turn down** the TV. It's too loud.

3 Write sentences with the same meaning using a phrasal verb.

1 Return as soon as you can! — Come .... !
2 Something's happened at work. — Something's come ....
3 I told them to enter. — I told them to come ....
4 However hard I try, I can't stop smoking. — I can't give ....
5 He invented a good story. — He made ....
6 Do you know what caused her depression? — Do you know what brought .... ?
7 My grandparents raised eight children. — My grandparents brought ....
8 How can you tolerate his behaviour? — How can you put ....

4 Add the correct particle to complete the sentences. Choose from the ones below.

away   with   down   forward   up (x2)   on   of

1 Keep up .... the good work!
2 We're looking .... to seeing him!
3 I'm running out .... petrol, I'm afraid.
4 I have to catch .... with some work that I didn't get finished today.
5 How are you getting .... with your French?
6 They cheated during the test, but didn't get .... with it.
7 Last week she went .... with flu.
8 I can't keep .... with you. You're running too fast.

393

ROUND UP 21

1 In each of these sentences, one or more words are out of place. Rewrite the sentences with the words in the correct order.

1 He doesn't like at all horror films.
   ....
2 He didn't go last summer on holiday to the usual place.
   ....
   ....
3 Your sister speaks very well Spanish.
   ....
4 We thanked them for being to us so nice.
   ....
5 They spent in Africa two months last year.
   ....
6 What did you have yesterday for lunch?
   ....

7 They haven't been before to Turkey.
   ....
8 We spend usually our free time at the youth club or at the mall.
   ....
   ....
9 I today don't feel very well.
   ....
10 We're having in a week's time an exam.
   ....
11 What time does leave the next train?
   ....
12 From what platform does it leave?
   ....

2 These sentences are not correct. They need inversion of subject – verb. Write them the correct way.

0 You shouldn't smoke, nor you should drink alcohol.
   You shouldn't smoke, nor should you drink alcohol.
1 Not only she was a great singer, she was also a fantastic dancer.
   ....
2 No sooner he had arrived than he started chatting and never stopped.
   ....
3 Only if you train hard you will have a chance of winning the match.
   ....
4 Not until I got home in the evening I realised that my friend had left.
   ....
5 Never I have met such a silly boy as Tom.
   ....
6 Hardly ever they help with the housework. Their parents are really annoyed.
   ....
7 They came to the mountains, but not even once they tried to ski.
   ....
8 Only if you are nice to others, others will be nice to you.
   ....

3 Rewrite each of these sentences in the positive (+), interrogative (?) or negative (−) form.

1 This isn't my first time in New York. (+)
   ....
   ....

2 They've got a lot of friends here. (?)
   ....
   ....

3 We enjoyed the trip very much. (−)
   ....
   ....

4 The children have to be at school earlier tomorrow. (?)
   ....
   ....

5 The bus leaves on the half hour. (?)
   ....
   ....

6 They could find the answers to all of my questions. (−)
   ....
   ....

7 Tom and Lucy had dinner at home last night. (?)
   ....
   ....

8 There was a long queue at the post office. (?)
   ....
   ....

9 My mum doesn't know my friend John. (+)
   ....
   ....

10 We didn't get up late this morning. (+)
   ....
   ....

4 Add question tags to these statements.

1 You could have left before, ...
2 They've already had dinner, ...
3 You can't be sure of that, ...
4 You didn't study much yesterday, ...
5 Your parents don't speak German, ...
6 Your cousin Samantha lives near here, ...
7 That's her house, ...
8 They were all happy with their accommodation, ...
9 You've been to New York, ...

5 Agree (=) or disagree (≠) with what is said.

0   We will be leaving soon.   (=) *So will I*........................ . It's time for me to go home too.
1   I like this song.   (≠) .... I prefer the other one.
2   We went shopping yesterday.   (=) .... We bought some nice shirts.
3   I didn't stay till the end.   (≠) .... I thought it was a great conference.
4   We don't play hockey in my school.   (=) .... We play volleyball.
5   I don't like hipster jeans.   (=) .... I think they're horrible.
6   I couldn't help laughing!   (=) .... I thought it was so funny!
7   My brother goes to primary school.   (=) .... my brother. He's in Year 3.
8   My mother has retired from work.   (≠) Mine .... She still works as a nurse.
9   Jack sings so well!   (=) .... Steve. They both have great voices.
10 I didn't pay much for the flight.   (≠) .... ! I paid nearly £200.

6 Add suffixes to these words to form abstract nouns. Make the necessary spelling adjustments.

−ness   −ship   −hood   −ment   −ation   −ance   −ity   −dom

	Abstract noun		Abstract noun		Abstract noun
sweet	sweetness	establish		liberate	
educate		possible		kind	
enjoy		credible		endure	
friend		hard		free	
leader		sister		excite	
perform		real		happy	

MATRIX +

Here are other **phrasal verbs** that are commonly used, in addition to the ones in Lesson 4.

be off = go away, be free from duty
be on = being broadcast on TV or shown at the cinema
be over = be finished
be up to = be doing (implying mischief), be able to or fit for (a task)
break down = stop functioning, collapse through great emotion

call off = cancel
come back = return
come up with = find or produce an answer, suggest a solution
cut off = disconnect
drop in at = visit (casually) a place
drop in on = visit (casually) a person
hang around = wait or stay near a place without doing much

hang out = spend a lot of time at a place
hang on = ask s.o. to wait for a short time or stop what they are doing
hang on to = hold sth tightly, stick to sth, keep sth
set off = start on a journey
shut up = close doors and windows, stop talking
work out = do physical exercise

7 Change the underlined verb in each sentence to one of the phrasal verbs above with the same meaning.

1 The meeting has been <u>cancelled</u>. ....
2 The car engine <u>stopped all of a sudden</u>. ....
3 They had been together for two years when they <u>parted</u>. ....
4 Will they <u>be able to do</u> this task? ....
5 What <u>are</u> you <u>doing</u>, children? Leave the cat alone! ....
6 Okay. I must <u>be going</u> now. ....
7 Mr Romney is busy now. <u>Return</u> tomorrow, please. ....
8 We had a big problem, but our friends <u>found</u> a good remedy. ....
9 They <u>left</u> for Australia two days ago. ....
10 <u>Be quiet</u>, you two. Stop chatting. ....
11 I <u>do some exercise</u> in the gym once a week, doing weights and things like that. ....
12 <u>Hold</u> the rope tightly. ....
13 We like <u>spending our time</u> at the mall on Saturdays. ....
14 I saw a couple of boys <u>going up and down</u> the street. ....
15 It'<u>s</u> all <u>finished</u>! We won't have to think about it any more. ....

MATRIX +

Learn these expressions too, with **be** + past participle + particle:

be done away with = to be finished
be done in = be exhausted
be done for = be in a very bad situation, be certain to fail
be done with (+ noun or *–ing* form) = finished, completed
be fed up with (+ noun or *–ing* form) = be bored or unhappy with sth
be worn out = look or feel very tired

8 Change the underlined words to one of the expressions above with the same meaning.

1 I'll be happy when this job is over and <u>finished</u>. ....
2 I'm <u>too tired</u>, I can't work any longer today! ....
3 My shoes were <u>no longer useful</u> after I had walked all the way to Santiago de Compostela. ....
4 I <u>can't bear</u> my sons hanging around all day. ....
5 He's <u>exhausted</u> after a day's hard work! ....
6 Unless your school report is better this term, you'll be <u>in big trouble</u>. ....
7 All this paperwork should be <u>abolished</u>. ....
8 I <u>can't stand</u> this boring job. ....

Reflecting on grammar

Reflect on the rules and say whether the following statements are true or false.

		True	False
1	**SVOMPT** is an acronym that helps you remember the order of words in a positive sentence. The first three are **subject**, **verb**, **object**.		
2	In a positive sentence, we usually position the place reference after the time reference.		
3	A negative **question tag** usually follows a positive sentence and vice versa.		
4	If you agree with someone who says *I love ballet*, you say: *So am I*.		
5	The question *When does the next bus leaves?* is correct.		
6	In a compound noun made of **noun + noun**, such as **waterproof jacket**, the first noun, which has the function of an adjective, specifies or defines the second.		
7	**Underestimated** is an adjective containing a prefix and a suffix.		
8	**–hood** and **–ness** are suffixes used to form nouns that express professions or human activities.		
9	A sentence that begins with a word with a negative meaning, e.g. **never**, needs to be inverted: first the auxiliary then the subject.		
10	Transitive phrasal verbs are always separated from their particles when the object is a pronoun.		

Revision and Exams 7 (UNITS 19 – 20 – 21)

1 🎧 **Fill in the gaps in the dialogue. Then listen and check.**

Neil So, ¹.......................... was your holiday in Ireland?

Ellen Great! We really enjoyed ourselves!

Neil ².......................... were you exactly?

Ellen We were in Galway for two weeks.

Neil Galway? It's on the west coast, ³.......................... it?

Ellen Yes, exactly. It's a beautiful place. There are a lot of things going ⁴.......................... in the summer.

Neil What was the weather ⁵.......................... ? Windy and rainy, I guess.

Ellen Well, I was told the weather in that area was usually rainy, but in fact we had two weeks of sun.

Neil That was lucky! Did you go to the Aran islands?

Ellen Yes, absolutely. We hired two bicycles and we went ⁶.......................... a trip around the island of Inishmore. We also had a swim in the sea, even ⁷.......................... the water was very cold!

Neil How I would have liked to have been with you! I love Ireland. Have you been there before?

Ellen No, this was our first time, but we want to go ⁸.......................... there next year.

2 **When Neil gets to the office, he tells a colleague, Steve, about his chat with Ellen and reports the conversation above. Write what he says.**

Neil Hi, Steve. Guess who I've just met. Ellen, do you remember her? She used to work in the Accounts Department. I asked her what her holiday in Ireland was like and she said …

3 **Complete the dialogue with the phrasal verbs below.**

get across   done in   come on   run out   give in   put up (x2)   make out

Paul Don't ¹.......................... now, we're nearly there.

Dave But I'm ².......................... . I can't walk any more.

Paul Can't you see the top? One more effort and we'll be there. ³.......................... !

Dave I can't even ⁴.......................... the top in this mist.

Paul Stop complaining. You must learn to ⁵.......................... with difficulties.

Dave But I can ⁶.......................... with difficulties. I realise now that I'm not trained. How can I ⁷.......................... it .... to you?

Paul Okay, I see, but I know you can make it. Let's have some chocolate. It will help.

Dave Er… I didn't want to tell you, but we've ⁸.......................... of comfort food.

Paul Oh no! Do we have any water left?

Dave Yes, we've still got some water at least.

4 **When Dave gets home, he tells his brother about his climbing trip to the mountains and reports the conversation above. Write what Dave says.**

Dave You can't even imagine how difficult it was for me to get to the top. I thought I would give in…

5 **Complete the rules for the chemistry lab in a school using the words below.**

but   if (x3)   after (x2)   or (x3)   before   and   when

Chemistry Lab Regulations

- The chemistry lab assistant will prepare the instruments you need for all experiments, ¹.................. you must wash ².................. clean them ³.................. use ⁴.................. return them to their shelves or cupboards.
- You must wear an overall ⁵.................. doing experiments in the lab. You don't have to wear one ⁶.................. you are attending a plenary lesson.
- You are allowed in the laboratory only ⁷.................. a teacher or the lab assistant is present.
- You must handle all instruments with care.
- You must tell the lab assistant ⁸.................. you find anything broken, missing ⁹.................. in the wrong place ¹⁰.................. you start working.
- You have to write a report ¹¹.................. each experiment and hand it in to the chemistry teacher.
- You can't eat or drink ¹².................. chew gum in the lab.

6 **Complete the passage with the correct alternatives.**

I had never realised how odd English may sound to foreigners learning it ¹....... I had to learn a foreign language ²....... . I studied some French ³....... I was at school, but I didn't really learn it, ⁴....... I never picked up the differences between English and a Latin language.

I've recently taken ⁵....... an Italian course because I need it for my job, and one of the strangest things I'm learning is the order of words in a sentence. Adjectives often go ⁶....... nouns in Italian but not always, and sometimes you can find a noun 'surrounded' by adjectives, that is one adjective before it and a couple of adjectives after the same noun. Why is it so? I don't know. I'm going to buy a grammar book to see ⁷....... I can find any explanations.

Another point is compounds. There aren't so many compounds in Italian ⁸....... there are in English; for example, the word for *post office* sounds like 'office postal', *mail box* is 'the box of the mail', *racing car* is 'a car to race' and so on. It drives me crazy! To translate from English into Italian, I have to sort of 'undo' every compound and swap the position of the words, which slows me ⁹....... quite a lot. I guess ¹⁰....... an Italian person learning English will have to do the same, only vice versa.

1	A as long as	B until	C when
2	A myself	B my own	C me too
3	A until	B where	C when
4	A so	B if	C but
5	A off	B up	C over
6	A over	B under	C after
7	A when	B how	C if
8	A that	B as	C than
9	A down	B through	C over
10	A if	B that	C whether

Preliminary (PET) | Reading Part 5

7 Read the text and choose the correct word (A, B, C or D) for each gap.

Last night I went to a Bob Dylan concert. I was there ⁰..*B*.. 4 pm, well ¹....... the concert started, ²....... I wanted to be near the stage, ³....... the stadium was already crowded. ⁴....... Bob started singing 'Blowing in the Wind', his most famous hit, the audience started clapping ⁵....... everybody started singing along. ⁶....... he sang his 'evergreen' songs, thousands of lights from mobile phones appeared all over the stadium. ⁷....... Bob Dylan was famous in the 1970s ⁸....... I thought there wouldn't be a lot of young people at the concert, ⁹....... there were thousands of teenagers! ¹⁰....... being a great singer, Bob Dylan is also a cultural icon for all time.

0	A	on	B	at	C	until	D	till
1	A	after	B	before	C	until	D	soon
2	A	if	B	though	C	because	D	only if
3	A	but	B	case	C	unless	D	as soon as
4	A	Until	B	Unless	C	When	D	No sooner
5	A	however	B	though	C	but	D	and
6	A	When	B	However	C	But	D	Before
7	A	However	B	Even though	C	No sooner	D	Only if
8	A	and	B	but	C	as	D	like
9	A	secondly	B	firstly	C	until	D	in fact
10	A	Besides	B	When	C	As	D	Moreover

Preliminary (PET) | Writing Part 1

8 Complete the second sentence with a phrasal verb so that it means the same as the first one. Use no more than three words.

1 I can't stand people smoking while driving.

   I can't .... people smoking while driving.

2 The annual conference has been postponed.

   The annual conference has ....

3 Make sure that the children stay away from my flower beds.

   Make sure that the children .... my flower beds.

4 We have no more paper for the photocopier. I must go and buy some immediately.

   We have .... paper for the photocopier. I must go and buy some immediately.

5 Please complete this form if you want to apply for this job.

   Please .... this form if you want to apply for this job.

6 I want to stop eating meat.

   I want to .... meat.

7 Call in to see me next time you come to town!

   .... see me next time you come to town!

8 We can execute your order by the end of the month.

   We can .... your order by the end of the month.

First (FCE) | Reading and Use of English Part 2

9 Complete the text below with the word which best fits each gap. Use one word only in each gap.

A ⁰ *lot* of European students spend their summer picking fruit in farms all over the world. ¹........................... being a healthy open-air activity, it is ²........................... an excuse to go ³........................... for some time and have a holiday with other people. ⁴........................... of the time, they live in a big group and learn to put ⁵........................... with each other and become more tolerant. They have to adapt to things ⁶........................... queuing up for the shower, sleeping in uncomfortable beds and working long hours. Some can't do ⁷........................... their creature comforts and give ⁸........................... after a few days. ⁹........................... fruit picking is hard work, about half of the students decide to go ¹⁰........................... to the same farm the following year.

First (FCE) | Reading and Use of English Part 3

10 Read the text. Use the word given in capitals at the end of the lines to form a word to fill the gap in that line.

It is quite normal that there are ⁰ *disagreements* in families and that there are	**AGREE**
regular ¹................................. between family members, as everyone has their own ideas	**UNDERSTAND**
about what should happen when and how. In fact, it's almost ².................................	**BELIEVE**
that most families actually manage to live together relatively happily. It is normal	
for teenagers to fight for their ³................................. and for parents to feel very	**DEPEND**
⁴................................. towards them. Each family deals with the situation in a	**PROTECT**
⁵................................. way.	**DIFFER**

11 You ordered a waterproof jacket, but from an online catalogue you were not happy with it when it arrived for a number of reasons. Below is part of the catalogue on which you have written some notes. Write a letter of between 120 and 150 words in an appropriate style.

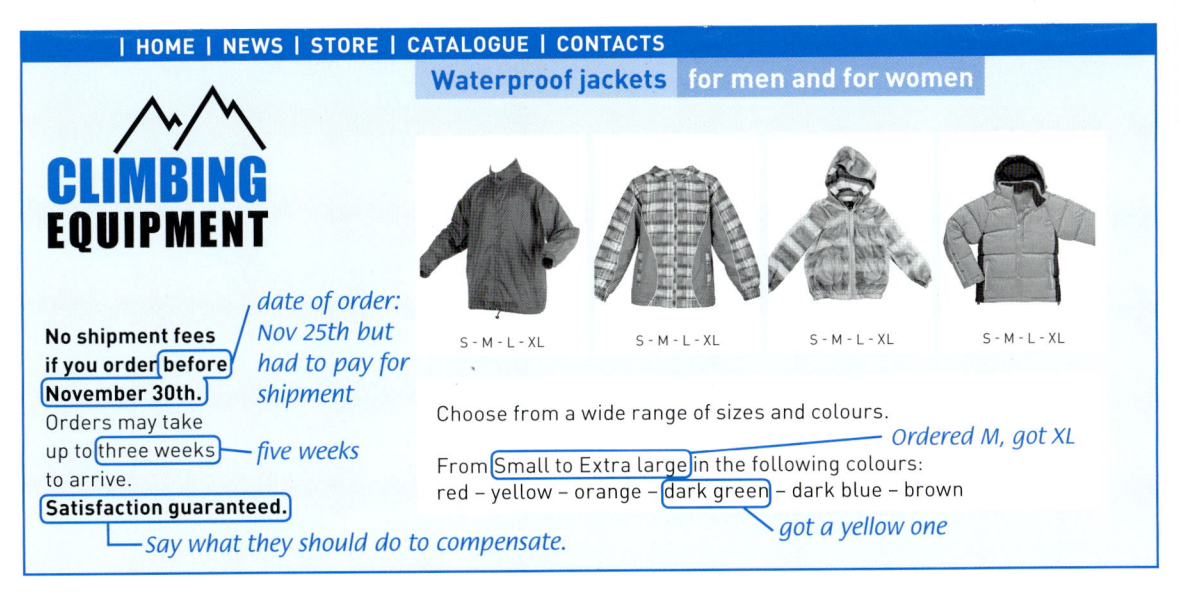

| HOME | NEWS | STORE | CATALOGUE | CONTACTS |

Waterproof jackets for men and for women

CLIMBING EQUIPMENT

S - M - L - XL   S - M - L - XL   S - M - L - XL   S - M - L - XL

No shipment fees if you order before November 30th.
— date of order: Nov 25th but had to pay for shipment

Orders may take up to three weeks to arrive.
— five weeks

Satisfaction guaranteed.
— Say what they should do to compensate.

Choose from a wide range of sizes and colours.
From Small to Extra large in the following colours:
— Ordered M, got XL
red – yellow – orange – dark green – dark blue – brown
— got a yellow one

401

Towards Competences

You've been asked to write a 'for and against' composition about the advantages and disadvantages of living in your area. The text will be published in the section 'International Exchanges' on your school website. Write a cohesive composition, using suitable connectors. Write about 200 words.

Self Check 7

Circle the correct option. Then check your answers at the end of the book.

1 You ……… me that the meeting was at three o'clock. Don't you remember?
   A said   B told   C told to

2 If you ……… me another lie, I won't talk to you any more.
   A say   B said   C tell

3 ……… thank you to your aunt. She's brought us a wonderful present.
   A Say   B Tell   C Give

4 Don't forget ……… goodbye to the manager when you leave the office.
   A to say   B to tell   C to give

5 He told me ……… for him in the hall.
   A waiting   B to wait   C wait

6 They ……… us to go to the lecture the following day.
   A warned
   B suggested
   C reminded

7 She suggested ……… together for the exam.
   A to revise
   B us to revise
   C revising

8 The farmer ……… us not to touch the electrified fence.
   A warned   B suggested   C said

9 She said she ……… her holidays in Greece the year before.
   A is spending
   B had spent
   C would spend

10 Why didn't you tell them that you ……… for Peru the next day?
   A were going to leave
   B have been going to
   C would going to leave

11 Mark told us he would arrive late the ……… day.
   A after   B previous   C following

12 They asked me why ……… to work night shifts.
   A did I accept
   B had I accepted
   C I had accepted

13 I asked him if ……… waterskiing.
   A he did like   B he liked   C did he like

14 Mandy asked Jim why he ……… her the night before.
   A wouldn't phone
   B hadn't phoned
   C wouldn't have phoned

15 Terry asked Sara what she ……… looking up in the dictionary.
   A will be   B would be   C was

16 Margaret wanted to know why Bob had arrived late at work the day ……… .
   A previous   B before   C following

17 ……… he is quite young, he has already gained lots of experience in his field.
   A But   B In spite   C Although

18 On the one hand, going jogging every day is healthy, but ……… it could be risky if you suffer from heart disease.
   A on the next
   B on the other
   C on another

19 ……. I had forgotten my wallet, Sam had to pay for my train ticket.
   A As   B So as   C Though

20 We're going out ……… some food for dinner.
   A to buying
   B for buy
   C to buy

21 Sara's going to attend evening classes ……… she can improve her Chinese.
   A in order   B so that   C so as

22 When you ………, make sure you have all your documents with you.
   A will come
   B come
   C will be coming

23 Switch off the TV ……… the film is over.
   A until
   B as long as
   C as soon as

24 I'm really tired! ……… , I have a terrible headache.
   A What's more
   B In addition to
   C Finally

25 Many animals are hunted for their skins. ……… , they've become very rare.
   A Accordingly
   B Therefore
   C So why

26 You can have the afternoon off, ……… you finish all your work by the end of the week.
   A unless   B provided   C as though

27 They ……… us stay at school after classes when we need to use the media lab.
   A let   B make   C cause

28 Did they go ……… ?
   A yesterday in the car to Glasgow
   B to Glasgow in the car yesterday
   C in the car yesterday to Glasgow

29 I like ……… .
   A very much reading detective stories
   B very much read detective stories
   C reading detective stories very much

30 'Do you think they'll increase our salaries?' 'I hope ……… .'
   A yes   B so   C they are

31 Pass me the mint sauce, ……… ?
   A shall I   B shall you   C will you

32 They don't belong to our sports club, ……… ?
   A do they   B don't they   C they do

33 Let's go to the cinema, ……… ?
   A let we   B shall we   C do we

34 You haven't seen her, ……… ?
   A haven't you   B do you   C have you

35 Look at that set of ……… . Aren't they beautiful?
   A cups for tea
   B cups of tea
   C tea cups

36 It's ……… to drive through a red light.
   A unlegal   B dislegal   C illegal

37 I'm afraid you're ……… about the matter.
   A disinformed
   B misinformed
   C uninformed

38 Please tell Ms Tyrrell that the meeting has been ……… .
   A put on   B put off   C put away

39 Oh dear! I forgot to put the meat in the fridge and now it's ……… .
   A gone out   B gone away   C gone off

40 I don't know what happened to him. He just didn't turn ……… .
   A up   B on   C off

Assess Yourself!

☐	0 – 10	Study harder. Use the online exercises to help you.
☐	11 – 20	OK. Use the online exercises to practise things you don't know.
☐	21 – 30	Good, but do some extra practice online.
☐	31 – 40	Excellent!

VERB BE | Present simple

Complete the charts with the missing elements.

not   am   they   Sheila and I   she   Tom and Susan
the dog   the children   it   the kitchen

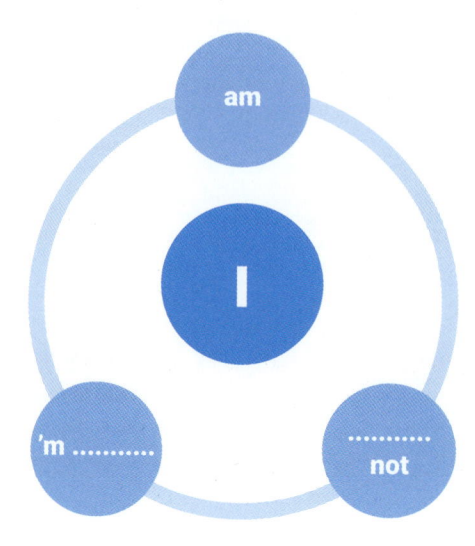

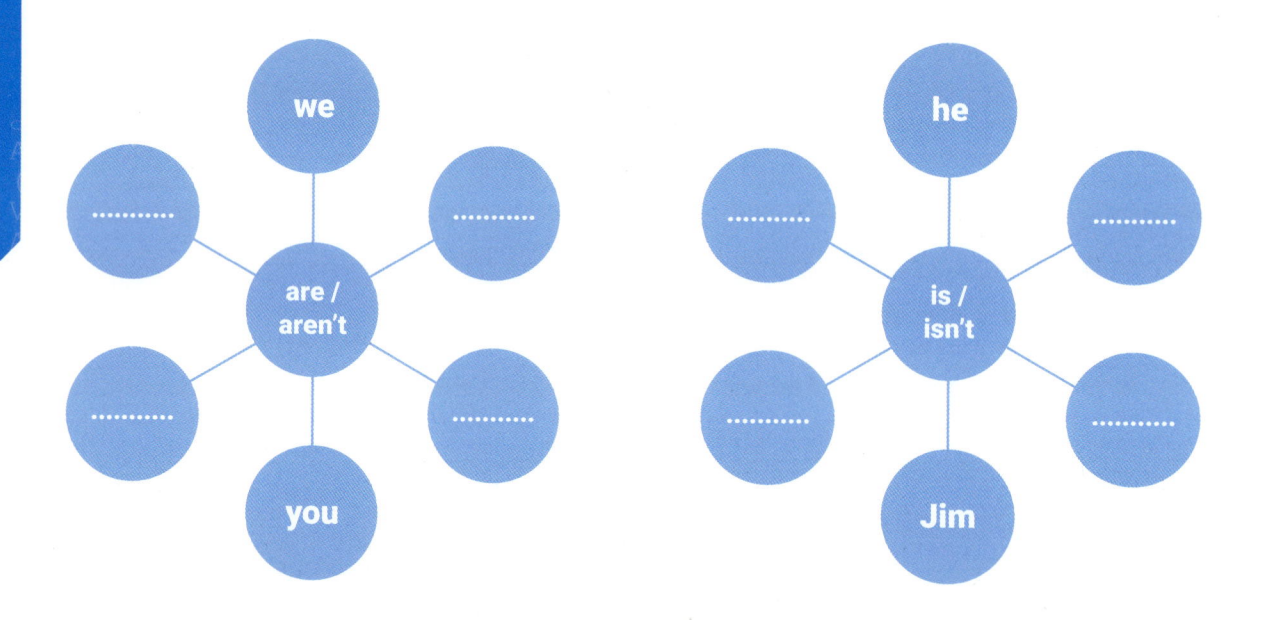

- am
- I
- 'm ....
- .... not

(we, ..., ..., ..., ..., you) — are / aren't

(he, ..., ..., ..., ..., Jim) — is / isn't

And the questions?

You are a doctor.   It is late.

Are you a doctor?   .... late?

404

VERB *HAVE GOT* | Present simple

Complete the charts with the missing elements.

they   we   it   you and Sally   the house   the children   she   the cat

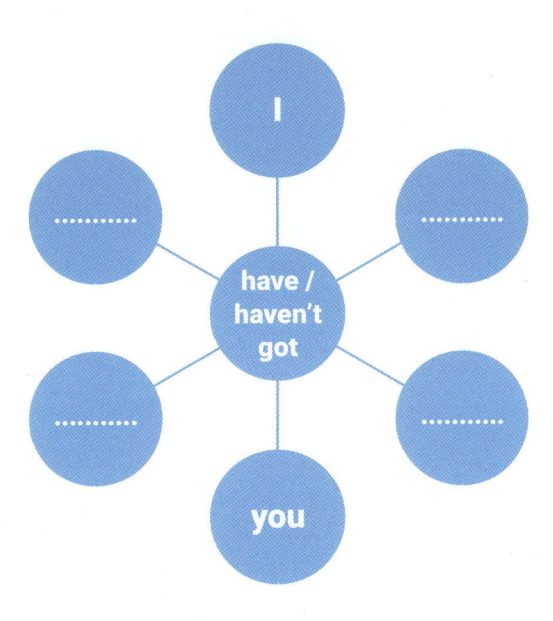

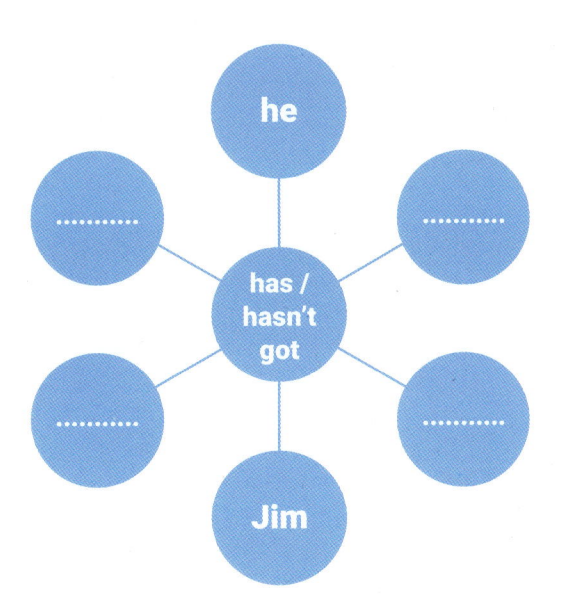

Chart 1 (centre: **have / haven't got**):
- I
- you
- ....
- ....
- ....
- ....

Chart 2 (centre: **has / hasn't got**):
- he
- Jim
- ....
- ....
- ....
- ....

And the questions?

You have got a car.   He has got a dog.

Have you got a car?   .... got a dog?

405

PRESENT SIMPLE | positive form

Complete the charts with the missing elements.

they   we   it   Jim and I   the secretary   the clerks   she   the lift

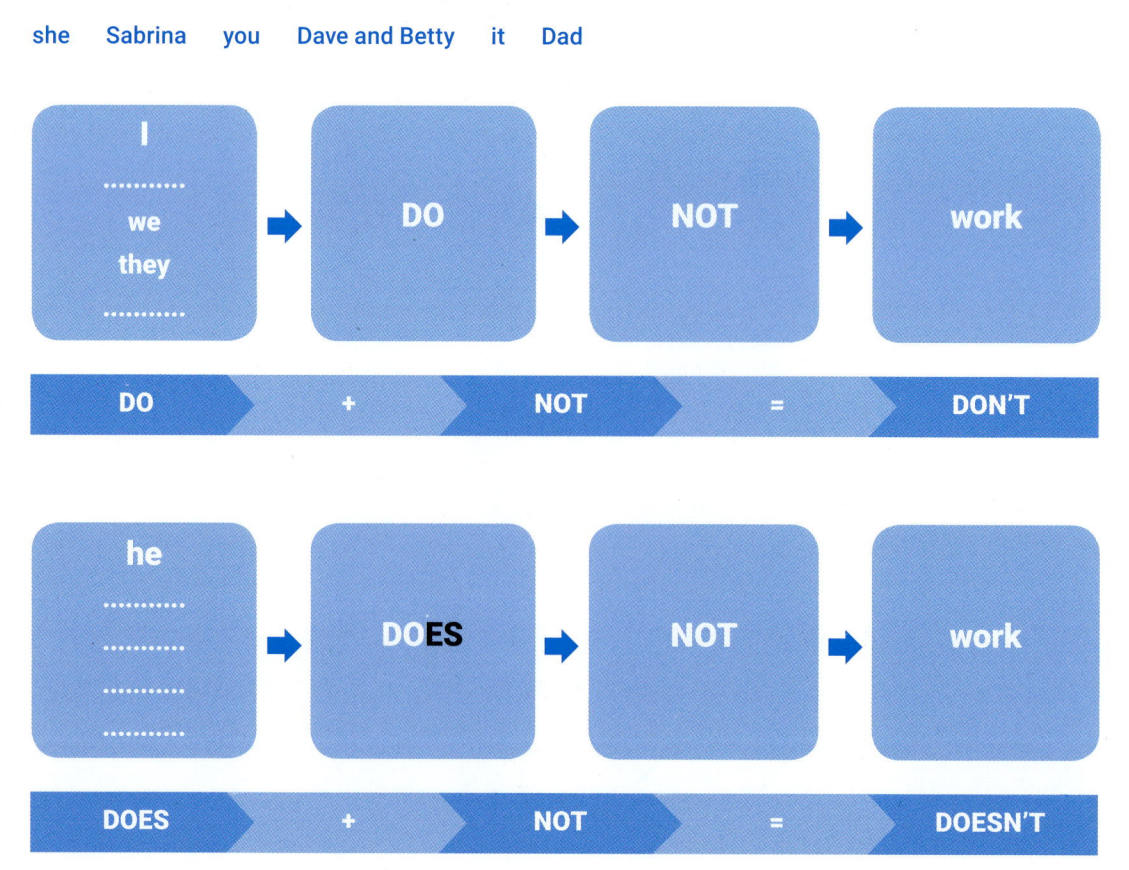

(Diagram 1: central "work" connected to I, You, and four blanks)

(Diagram 2: central "works" connected to he, Tim, and four blanks)

PRESENT SIMPLE | negative form

Complete the charts with the missing elements.

she   Sabrina   you   Dave and Betty   it   Dad

| I / ……… / we / they / ……… | → DO → NOT → work |

DO + NOT = DON'T

| he / ……… / ……… / ……… | → DOES → NOT → work |

DOES + NOT = DOESN'T

PRESENT SIMPLE | interrogative form

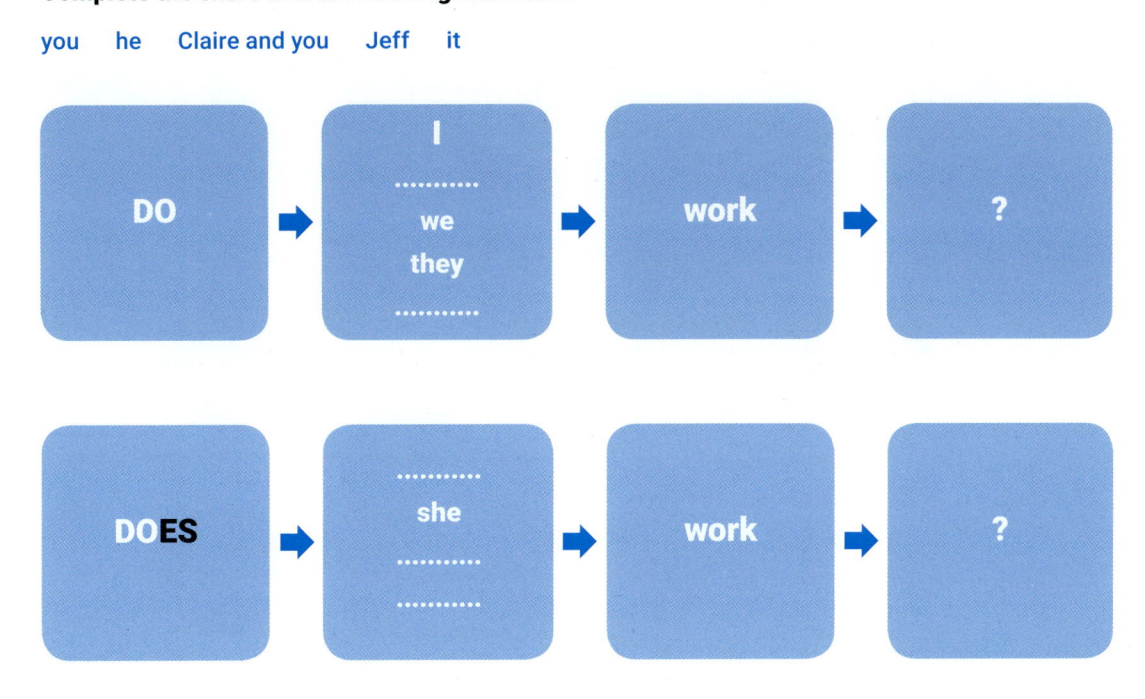

Complete the chart with the missing elements.

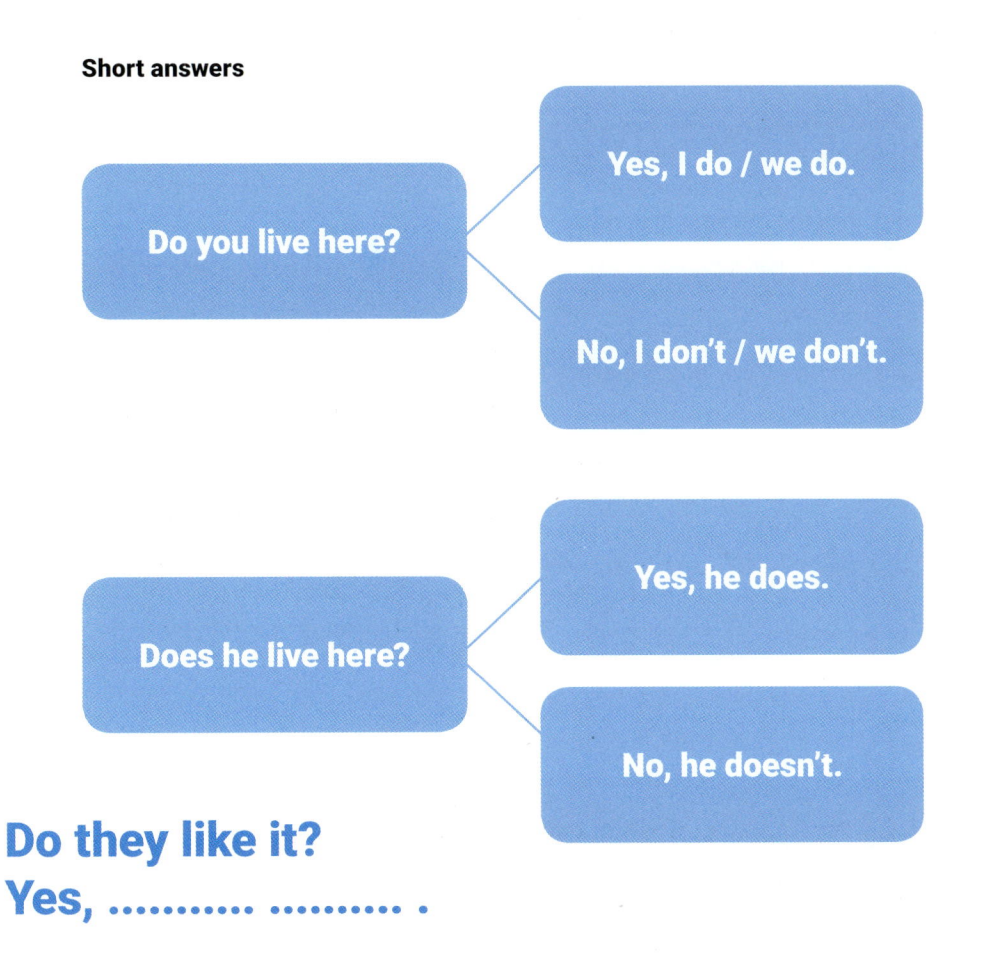

you   he   Claire and you   Jeff   it

DO → I / we / they / .... → work → ?

DOES → .... / she / .... → work → ?

Short answers

Do you live here?
- Yes, I do / we do.
- No, I don't / we don't.

Does he live here?
- Yes, he does.
- No, he doesn't.

Do they like it?
Yes, ...

PRESENT CONTINUOUS | positive form

Complete the charts with the missing elements.

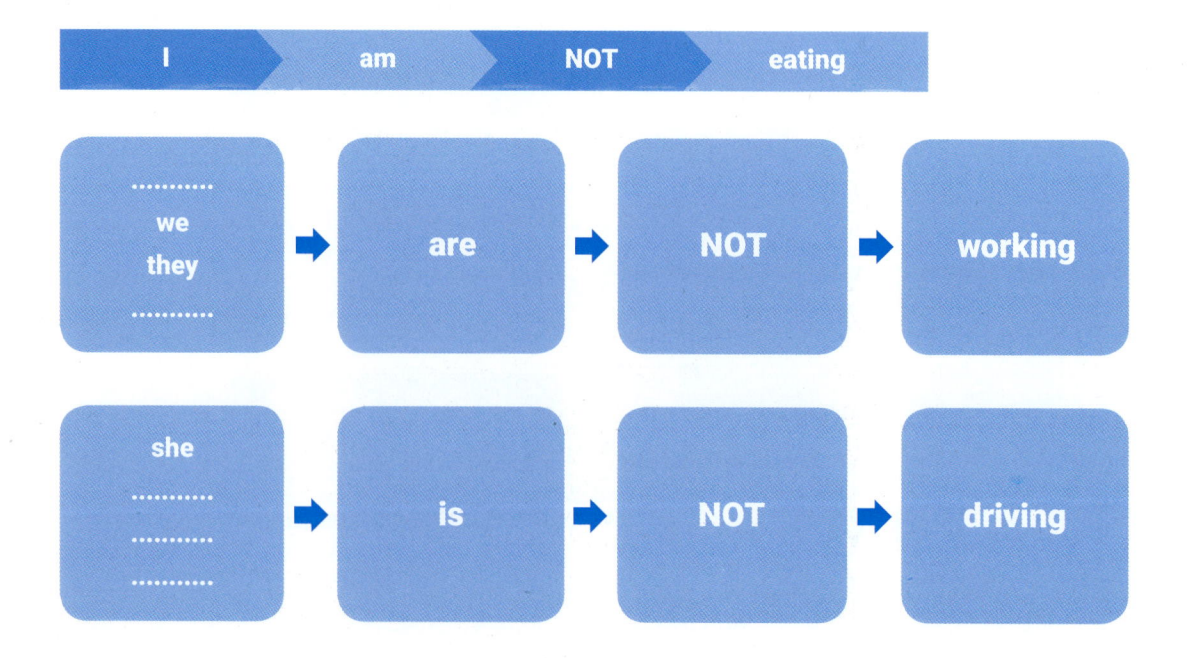

are   she   we   it   the dog   I   is

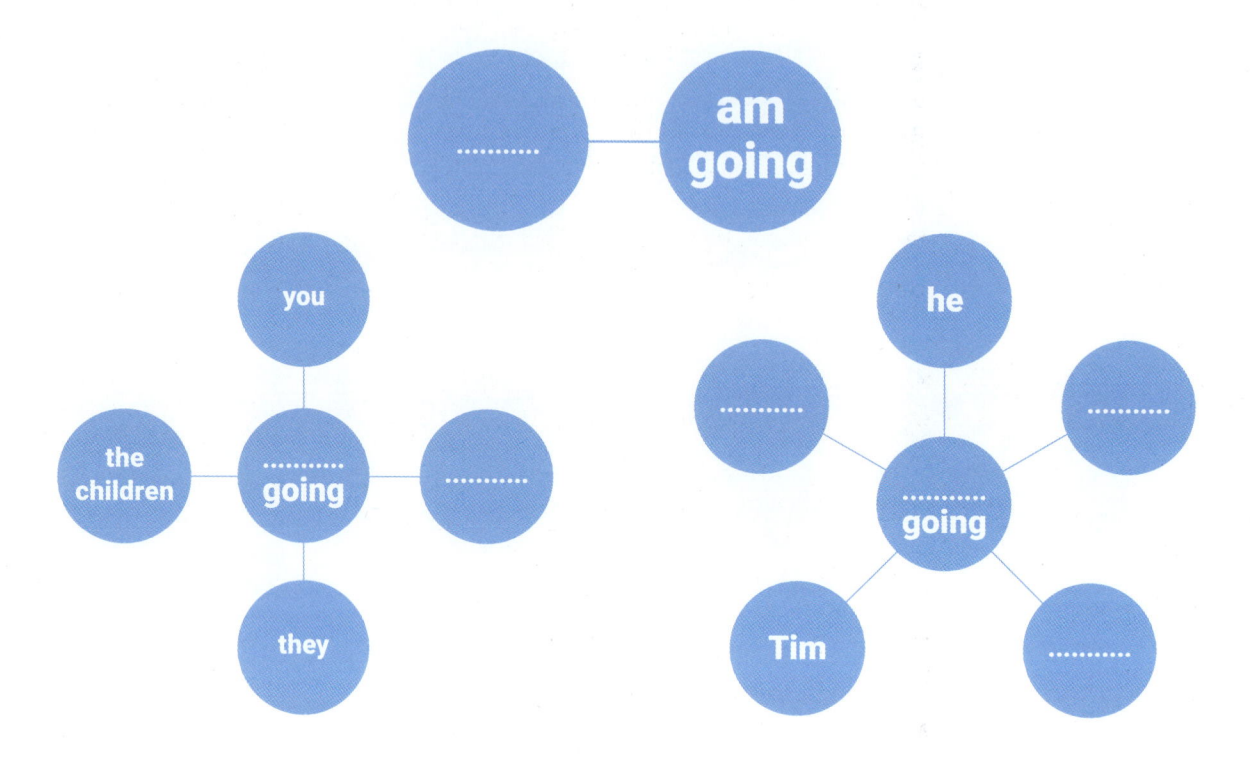

- .... — am going
- you / the children / .... / they → going → ....
- he / .... / .... / Tim / .... → going

PRESENT CONTINUOUS | negative form

Complete the chart with the missing elements.

you   it   the machines   he   Chuck

I → am → NOT → eating

.... / we / they / .... → are → NOT → working

she / .... / .... / .... → is → NOT → driving

PRESENT CONTINUOUS | interrogative form

Complete the charts with the missing elements.

you   they   the students   Paul   it   the dog

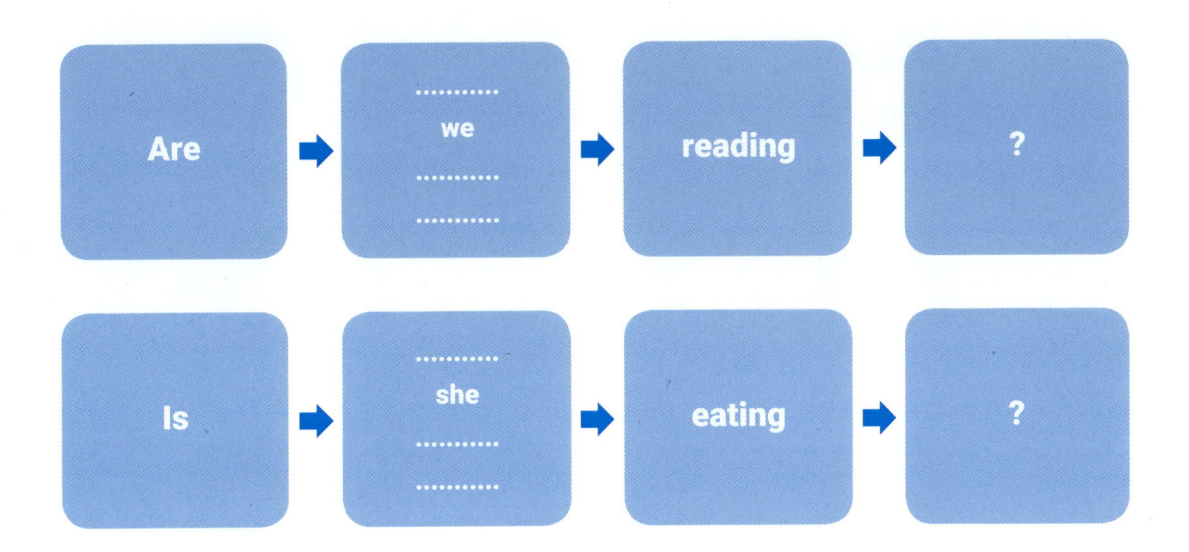

Are → .... / we / .... → reading → ?

Is → .... / she / .... → eating → ?

Short answers

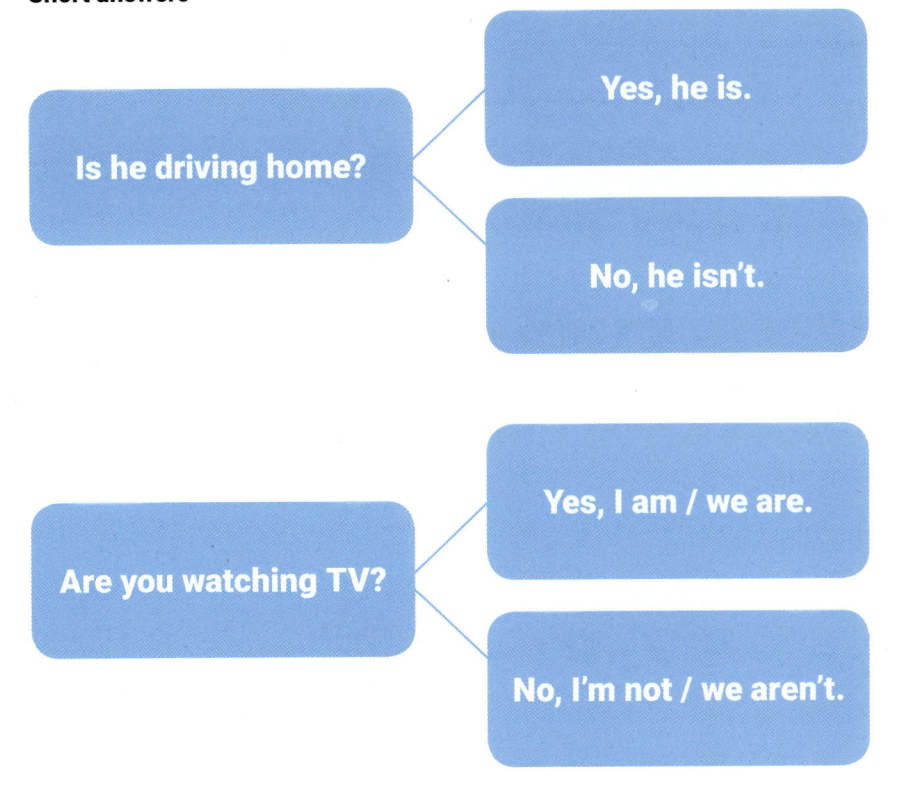

Is he driving home?
- Yes, he is.
- No, he isn't.

Are you watching TV?
- Yes, I am / we are.
- No, I'm not / we aren't.

Are they going out?
No, ...

VERB BE | past simple

Complete the charts with the missing elements.

they   Dad and I   she   Tom and Susan   the web designer   the children   it   the town

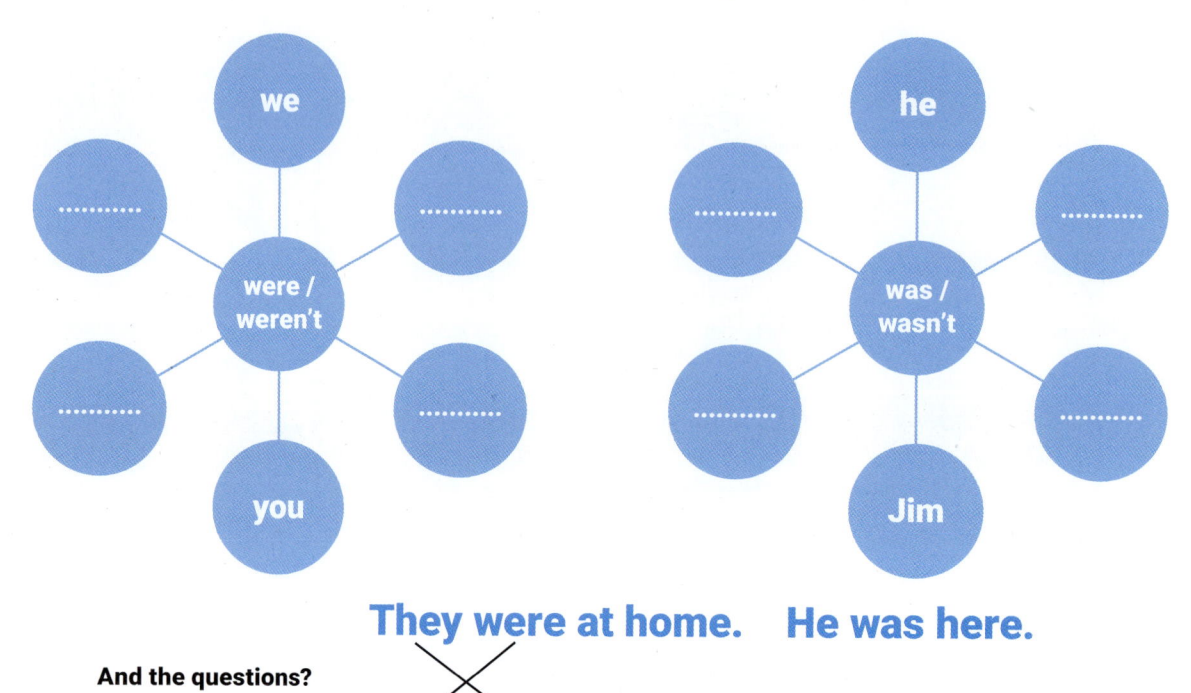

- we
- were / weren't
- you

- he
- was / wasn't
- Jim

And the questions?

They were at home. → Were they at home?

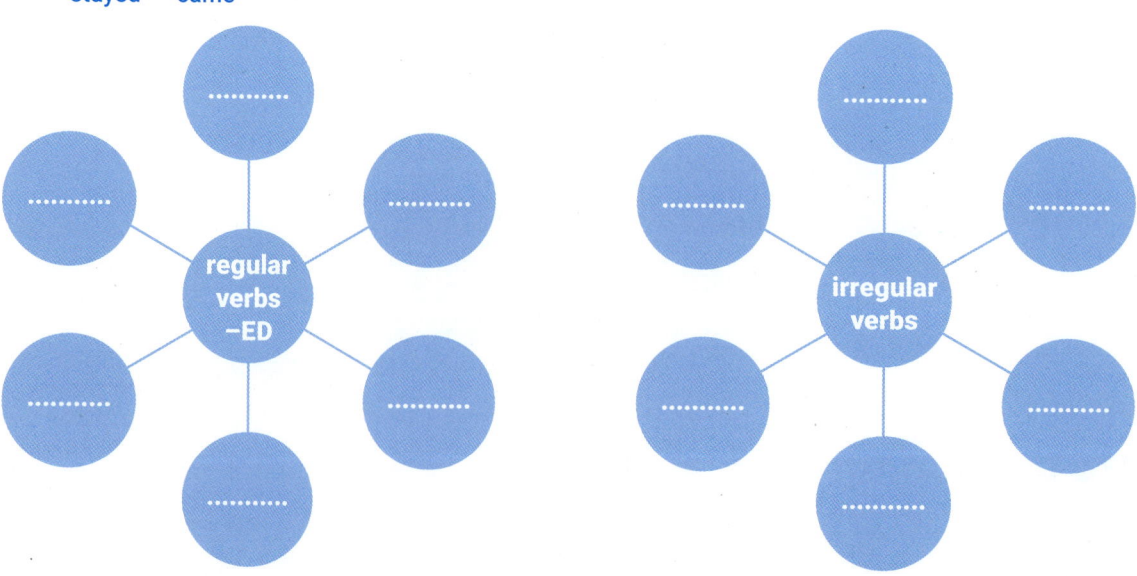

He was here. → .... here?

PAST SIMPLE | positive form

Complete the charts with the missing elements.

went   arrived   talked   drank   sat   watched   brought   did   lived   imagined   stayed   came

- regular verbs –ED
- irregular verbs

PAST SIMPLE | negative form

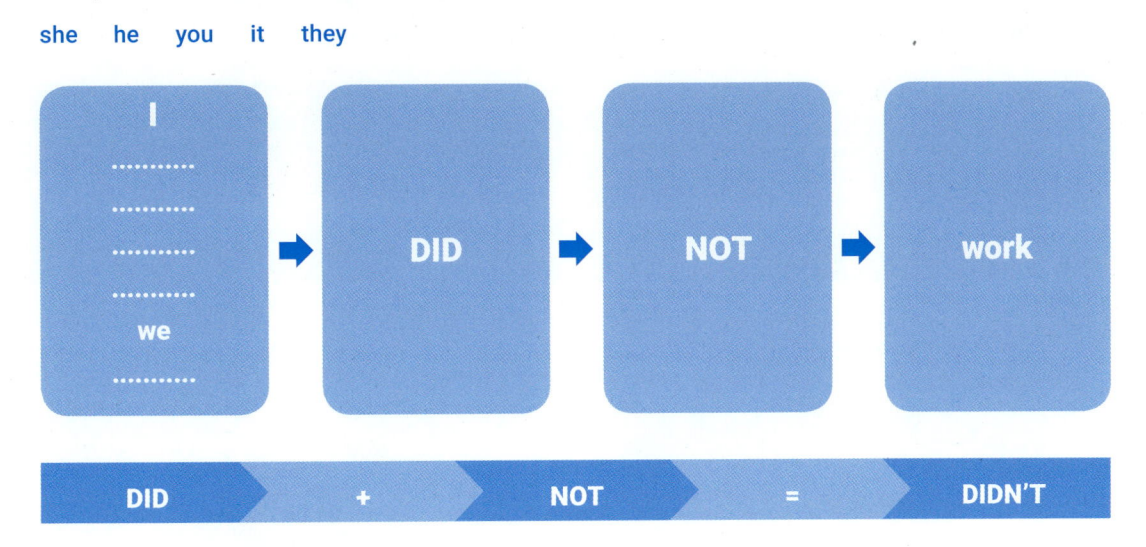

Complete the chart with the missing elements.

she   he   you   it   they

I			
....			
....	DID → NOT → work
....			
we			
....			

DID + NOT = DIDN'T

PAST SIMPLE | interrogative form

Complete the chart with the missing elements.

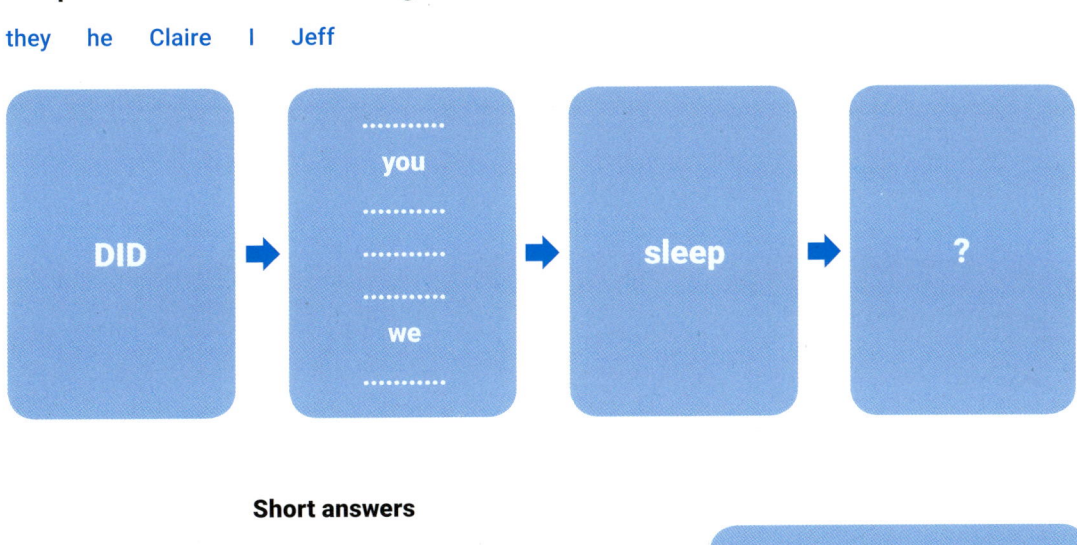

they   he   Claire   I   Jeff

| DID → | .... you .... we .... | → sleep → ? |

Short answers

Did he live here? → Yes, he did. / No, he didn't.

Did she go with you?
Yes, ...

PRESENT PERFECT | positive and negative forms

Complete the charts with the missing elements.

she   you   it   they

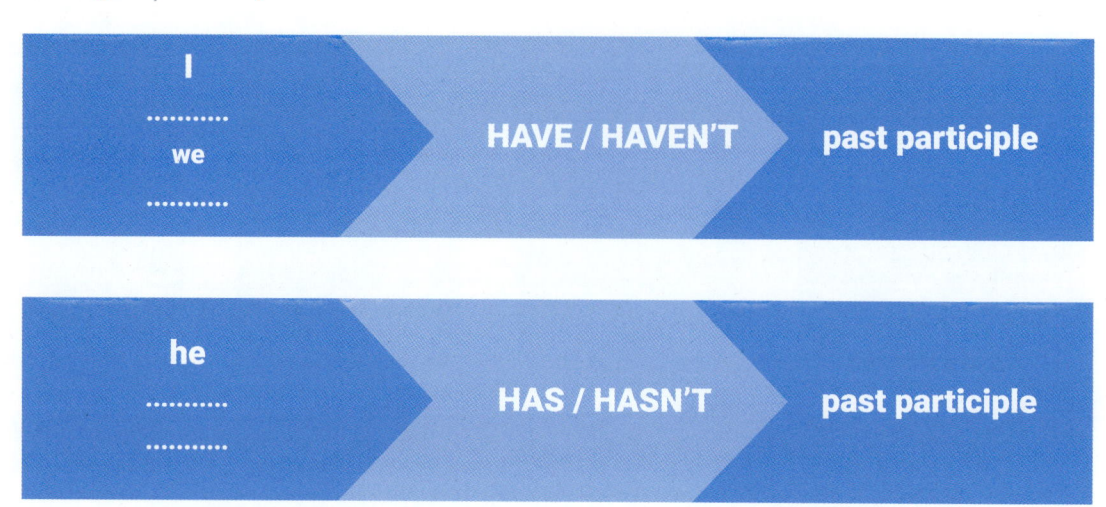

| I |
| .... |
| we |
| .... |

HAVE / HAVEN'T — past participle

| he |
| .... |
| .... |

HAS / HASN'T — past participle

I .... finished. (+)   He .... gone! (−)

PAST PARTICIPLE

Complete the charts with the missing elements.

gone   washed   dictated   eaten   sat   looked   bought   done   stayed   cleared   listened   written

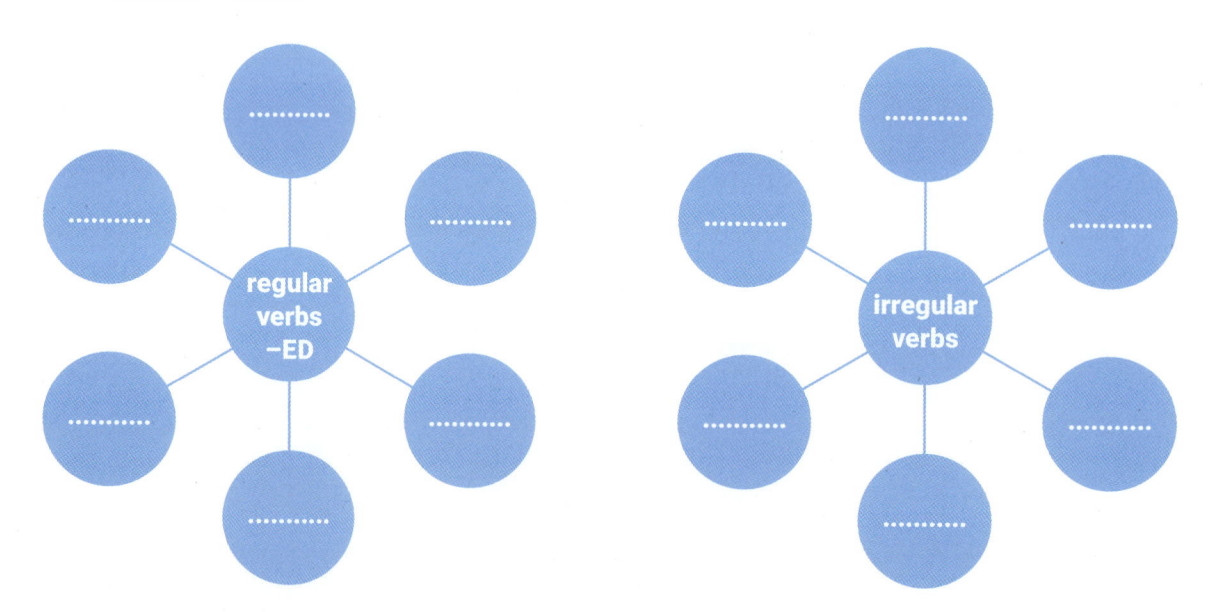

regular verbs −ED

irregular verbs

412

PRESENT PERFECT | interrogative form

Complete the charts with the missing elements.

it   they   he   you

| HAVE | I / we / .... | SLEPT | ? |

| HAS | .... / she / .... | COME | ? |

Short answers

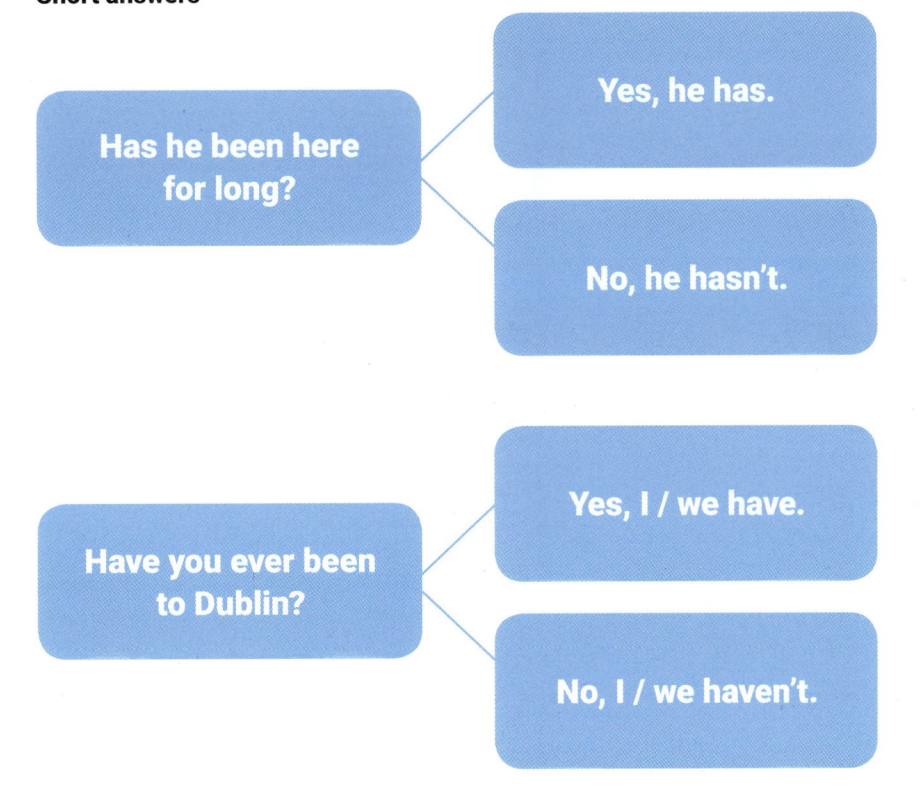

Has he been here for long?
- Yes, he has.
- No, he hasn't.

Have you ever been to Dublin?
- Yes, I / we have.
- No, I / we haven't.

Have they seen the film?
No, ...

THERE IS / THERE ARE
THERE WAS / THERE WERE

Complete the chart with the words below.

a double bed   two bedside tables   a big French window   nice pictures   a mirror
some shelves   a small wardrobe
some food   a DJ   lots of drinks   nice decorations   very good cocktails

PRESENT

In the hotel room

THERE ARE...

two chairs

....
....
....

THERE IS...

a desk

....
....
....
....

PLURAL | **SINGULAR**

At last night's party

THERE WERE...

a lot of people

....
....
....

THERE WAS...

good music

....
....

PAST

AGREEING / DISAGREEING

Look at the chart.
Complete the chart with phrases for agreeing or disagreeing.

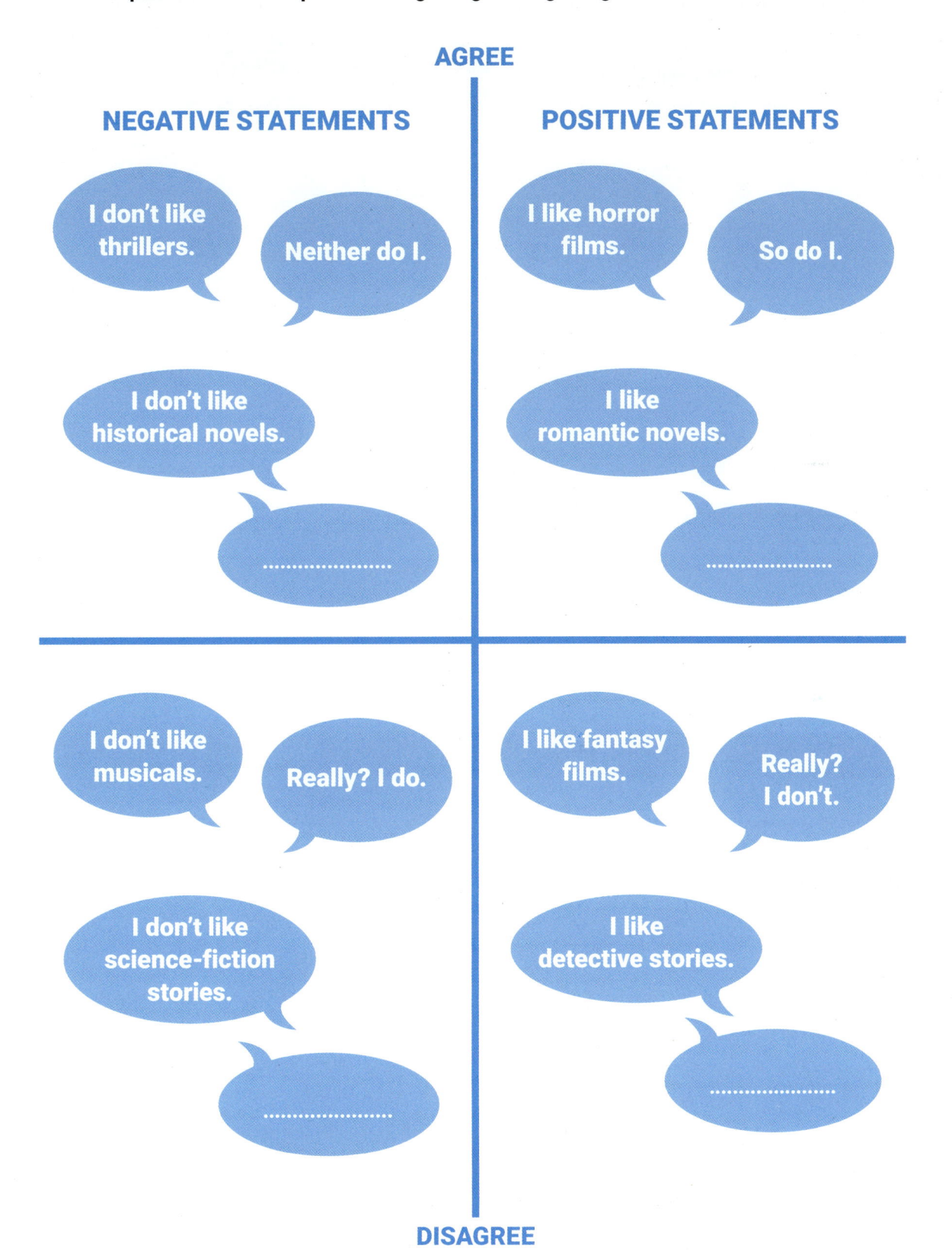

AGREE

NEGATIVE STATEMENTS

- I don't like thrillers.
- Neither do I.
- I don't like historical novels.
- ....

POSITIVE STATEMENTS

- I like horror films.
- So do I.
- I like romantic novels.
- ....

- I don't like musicals.
- Really? I do.
- I don't like science-fiction stories.
- ....

- I like fantasy films.
- Really? I don't.
- I like detective stories.
- ....

DISAGREE

INDEFINITE ADJECTIVES AND PRONOUNS | some / any / no

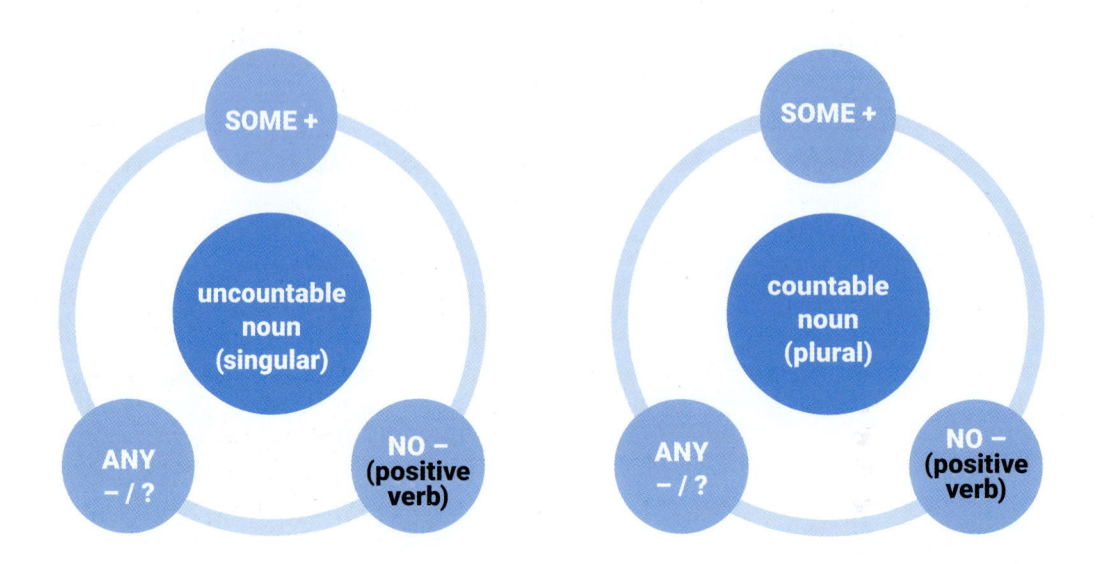

SOME + / **ANY − / ?** / **NO − (positive verb)** — uncountable noun (singular)

SOME + / **ANY − / ?** / **NO − (positive verb)** — countable noun (plural)

Complete the charts with the missing elements.

| We | have | ………… | paper | and | ………… | pens. | (+) |

| They | have | ………… | sugar | and | ………… | cherries. | (−) |

| There | isn't | ………… | ink | in | the | cartridge. | (−) |

| There | aren't | ………… | students | in | the | classroom. | (−) |

| Are | there | ………… | theatres | in | your | town? | (?) |

| Have | you | got | ………… | questions | to | ask | me? | (?) |

| Would | you | like | ………… | coffee? | (+) |

→ Offers and requests can be treated as positive forms.

| Can | I | have | ………… | staples, | please? | (+) |

INDEFINITE PRONOUNS | Compounds with *some–, any–, no–, every–*

Complete the chart.

		PEOPLE	THINGS	PLACES
		–body / –one	–thing	–where
+	some	somebody / someone		
–	no			
– / ?	any			
+ / – / ?	every			

QUESTION TAGS

Look at the examples and complete the tags.

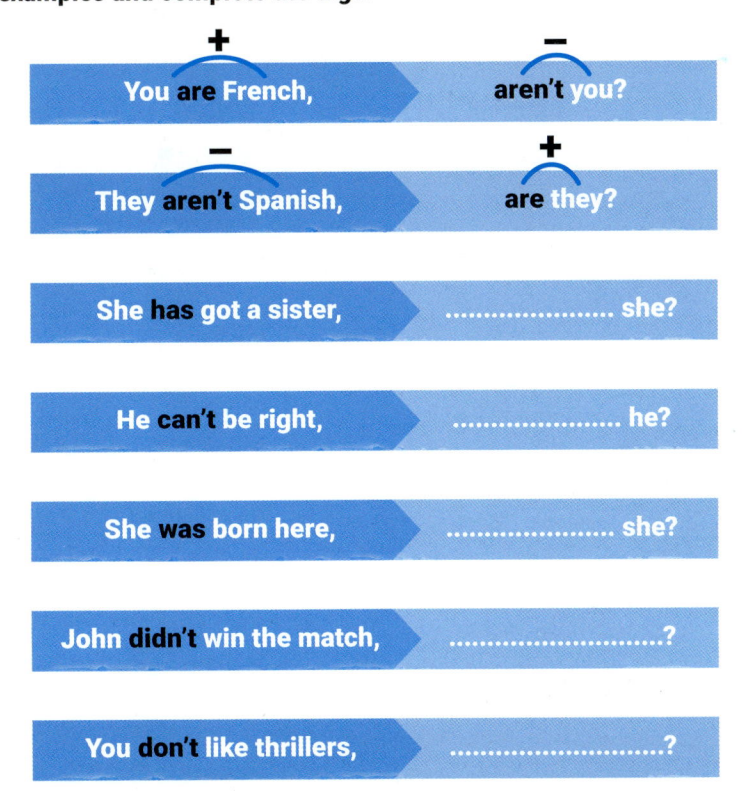

+	–
You are French,	aren't you?

–	+
They aren't Spanish,	are they?

She has got a sister,	.... she?
He can't be right,	.... he?
She was born here,	.... she?
John didn't win the match,	.... ?
You don't like thrillers,	.... ?

COMPARATIVES

Complete the charts with the comparative forms of the adjectives below.

easy fast busy comfortable cheap warm expensive pretty early fat
thin nice coarse intelligent young hot wide gentle flat familiar

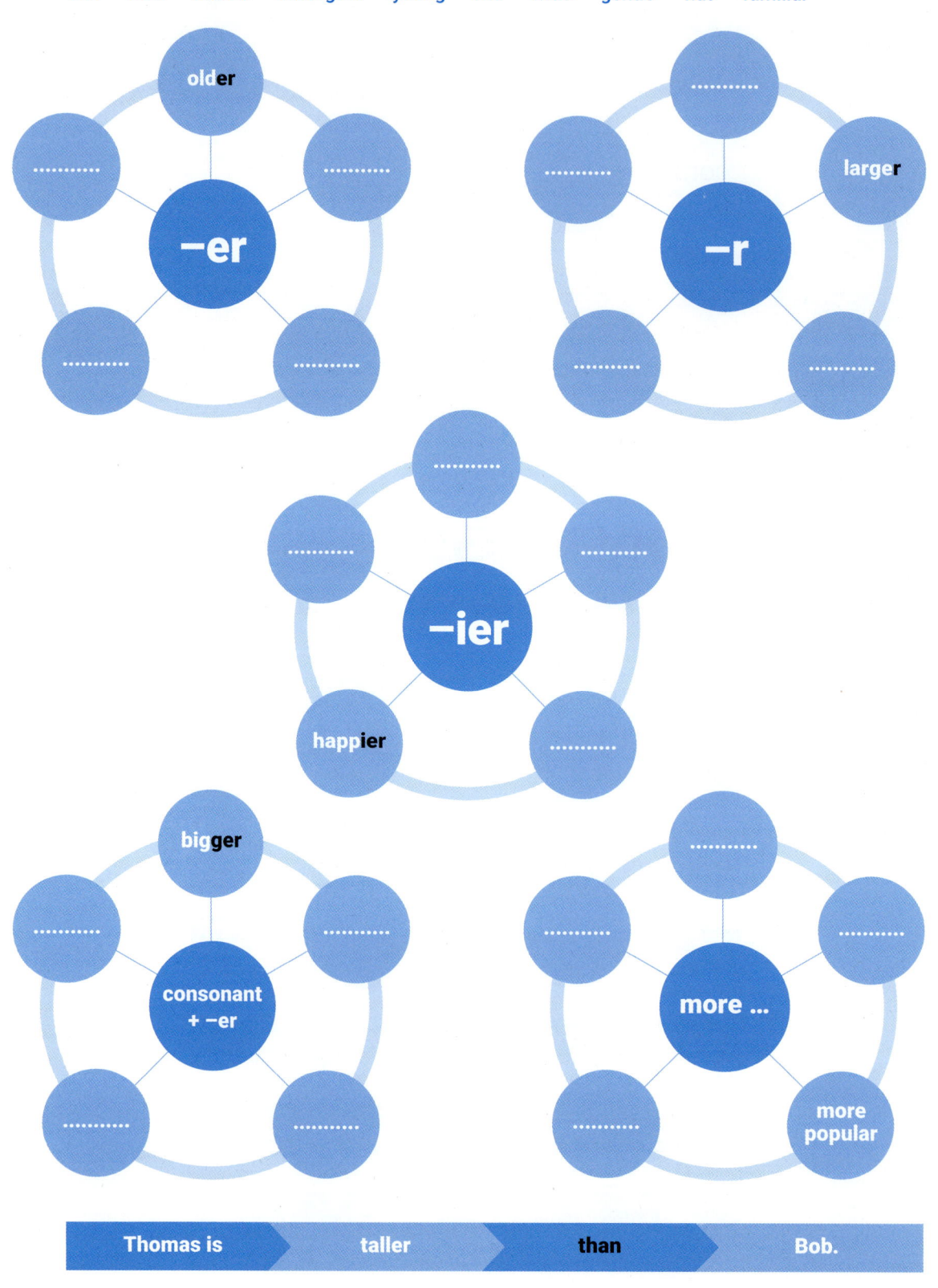

-er: older, ..., ..., ..., ...

-r: ......, larger, ..., ..., ...

-ier: ......, ..., ..., happier, ...

consonant + -er: bigger, ..., ..., ..., ...

more ...: ......, ..., ..., more popular, ...

Thomas is → taller → than → Bob.

SUPERLATIVES

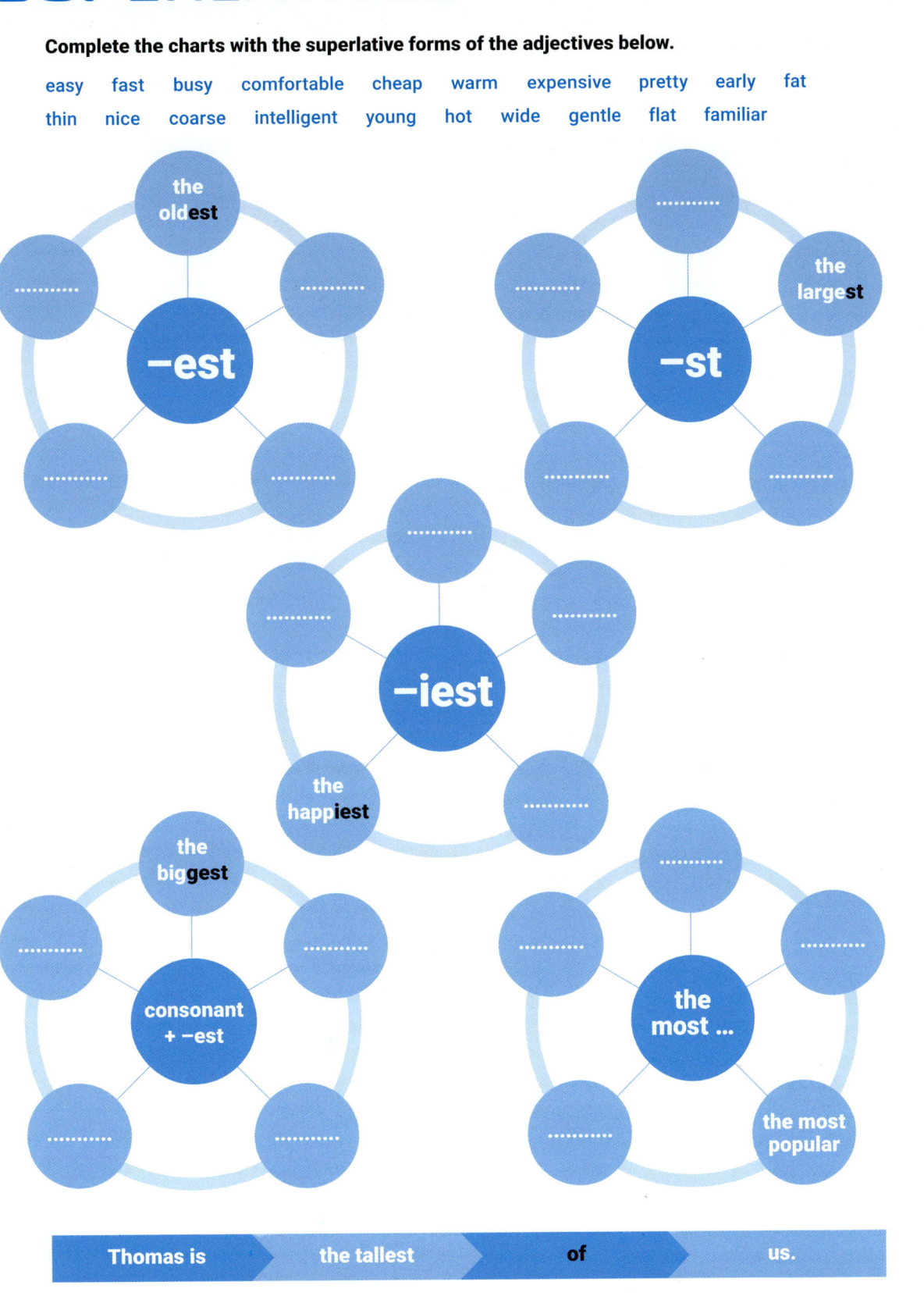

Complete the charts with the superlative forms of the adjectives below.

easy fast busy comfortable cheap warm expensive pretty early fat
thin nice coarse intelligent young hot wide gentle flat familiar

–est: the oldest, ..., ..., ..., ...

–st: ...., the largest, ..., ..., ...

–iest: ...., ..., ..., the happiest, ...

consonant + –est: the biggest, ..., ..., ..., ...

the most ...: ...., ..., ..., the most popular, ...

| Thomas is | the tallest | of | us. |

| The Po is | the longest | river in | Italy. |

ANSWER KEYS

VERB BE | Present simple page 404
not, am
they, Sheila and I, Tom and Susan, the children
she, it, the dog, the kitchen
Is it late?

VERB HAVE GOT | Present simple page 405
they, we, you and Sally, the children
it, the house, she, the cat

PRESENT SIMPLE | positive form page 406
they, we, Jim and I, the clerks
it, the secretary, she, the lift

PRESENT SIMPLE | negative form page 406
you, Dave and Betty
she, Sabrina, it, Dad

PRESENT SIMPLE | interrogative form page 407
you, Claire and you
he, Jeff, it
Yes, they do.

PRESENT CONTINUOUS | positive form page 408
I
are, we
she, it, the dog, is

PRESENT CONTINUOUS | negative form page 408
you, the machines
it, he, Chuck

PRESENT CONTINUOUS | interrogative form page 409
you, they, the students
Paul, it, the dog
No, they aren't.

VERB BE | Past simple page 410
they, Dad and I, Tom and Susan, the children
she, the web designer, it, the town
Was he there?

PAST SIMPLE | positive form page 410
arrived, talked, watched, lived, imagined, stayed
went, drank, sat, brought, did, came

PAST SIMPLE | negative form page 411
you, she, he, it, they

PAST SIMPLE | interrogative form page 411
I, he, Claire, Jeff, they
Yes, she did.

PRESENT PERFECT | positive and negative forms page 412
you, they
she, it
have, hasn't

PAST PARTICIPLE page 412
washed, dictated, looked, stayed, cleared, listened
gone, eaten, sat, bought, done, written

PRESENT PERFECT | interrogative form page 413
you, they
he, it
No, they haven't.

THERE IS / THERE ARE, THERE WAS / THERE WERE page 414
two bedside tables, nice pictures, some shelves
a double bed, a big French window, a mirror, a small wardrobe
lots of drinks, nice decorations very good cocktails, some food, a DJ

AGREEING / DISAGREEING page 415
Neither / Nor do I.
So do I.
I do.
I don't.

INDEFINITE ADJECTIVES AND PRONOUNS | some / any / no page 416
some, some   any
no, no   any
any   some
any   some

INDEFINITE PRONOUNS | Compounds with some–, any–, no–, every– page 417
somebody /someone, something, somewhere
nobody / no one, nothing, nowhere
anybody / anyone, anything, anywhere
everybody /everyone, everything, everywhere

QUESTION TAGS page 417
hasn't   did he
can   do you
wasn't

COMPARATIVES page 418
–er: faster, cheaper, warmer, younger
–r: nicer, coarser, wider, gentler
–ier: easier, busier, prettier, earlier
consonant + –er: fatter, thinner, hotter, flatter
more…: more comfortable, more expensive, more intelligent, more familiar

SUPERLATIVES page 419
-est: the fastest, the cheapest, the warmest, the youngest
-st: the nicest, the coarsest, the widest, the gentlest
-iest: the easiest, the busiest, the prettiest, the earliest
consonant + -est: the fattest, the thinnest, the hottest, the flattest
the most…: the most comfortable, the most expensive, the most familiar, the most intelligent

INTERNATIONAL PHONETIC ALPHABET KEY page 422

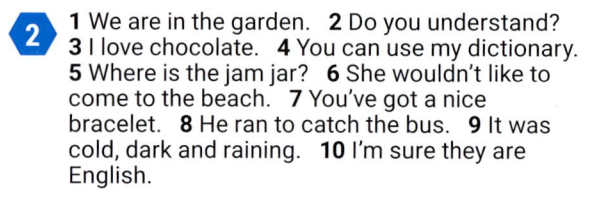

1 1 thing 2 thin 3 seen 4 since 5 find 6 fine 7 pot 8 port 9 fire 10 fear 11 boot 12 but

2 1 We are in the garden. 2 Do you understand? 3 I love chocolate. 4 You can use my dictionary. 5 Where is the jam jar? 6 She wouldn't like to come to the beach. 7 You've got a nice bracelet. 8 He ran to catch the bus. 9 It was cold, dark and raining. 10 I'm sure they are English.

BRITISH ENGLISH / AMERICAN ENGLISH MAIN GRAMMATICAL DIFFERENCES

There are various differences between British English and American English: differences in vocabulary, pronunciation and spelling, which are pointed out in dictionaries, and a few grammatical differences. The following list shows some of the most significant of these.

- In American English, the **past simple** is used more than in British English. For example, it is used instead of the **present perfect** when there isn't a specific time reference and with the adverbs **just, already, yet, ever, never**.

  BrE
  'Have you seen Jane?' 'Yes, I've seen her.'
  Has he arrived yet?
  I've never tried Thai food.

  AmE
  'Did you see Jane?' 'Yes, I saw her.'
  Did he arrive yet?
  I never tried Thai food.

- The form **have got / haven't got** isn't used very often in American English.

  BrE
  Have you got a pen?
  I haven't got many friends here.

  AmE
  Do you have a pen?
  I don't have many friends here.

- **Question tags** aren't used as often in American English as they are in British English.

  BrE
  You're 16, aren't you?
  Don't be late, will you?

  AmE
  You're 16, right?
  Don't be late, okay?

- The verb **need**, often used in British English as a semi-modal, is always used as an ordinary verb in American English.

  BrE
  You needn't wait for me.

  AmE
  You don't need to wait for me.

- In American English, it's more common to use the modal **should**, rather than **shall**.

  BrE
  What shall we do tonight?
  Shall I go now?

  AmE
  What should we do tonight?
  Should I go now?

- Collective nouns such as **family, team** and **government**, which in British English can be singular or plural, are always singular in American.

  BrE
  John's family is / are leaving tomorrow.

  AmE
  John's family is leaving tomorrow.

- The past participle of **get** is **got** in British English and **gotten** in American.

  BrE
  Your Spanish has got much better.

  AmE
  Your Spanish has gotten much better.

- In American English, the verb **take** is used instead of **have** in expressions such as **take a bath / a shower / a break…**

  BrE
  I have a shower every morning.

  AmE
  I take a shower every morning.

- Americans use the forms **go get, go see…**, whilst English people say **go and get, go and see…**

  BrE
  Go and get the newspaper, please.

  AmE
  Go get the newspaper, please.

- In colloquial American, some adverbs ending in **–ly** lose the suffix when they precede an adjective.

  BrE
  She's really crazy.

  AmE
  She's real crazy.

- In American English, the verb **help** isn't followed by **to**.

  BrE
  Can you help me to do my homework?

  AmE
  Can you help me do my homework?

INTERNATIONAL PHONETIC ALPHABET (IPA)

The following table lists the symbols that represent the sounds of British English.
Go to **www.helbling-ezone.com** to listen to the pronunciation.

Vowel sounds

ɪ	s<u>i</u>t, cr<u>i</u>cket, b<u>i</u>scu<u>i</u>t, th<u>i</u>s	ɔː	fl<u>oo</u>r, m<u>o</u>re, th<u>ou</u>ght
iː	s<u>ee</u>, m<u>ea</u>n	ʊ	f<u>oo</u>t, p<u>u</u>t
e	p<u>e</u>n, spr<u>ea</u>d, <u>e</u>dge, s<u>ai</u>d	uː	m<u>oo</u>n, s<u>ui</u>t, thr<u>ou</u>gh
æ	s<u>a</u>d, <u>a</u>dd, <u>a</u>dapt	ʌ	b<u>u</u>s, t<u>ou</u>ch, t<u>ou</u>gh, bl<u>oo</u>d, <u>u</u>pset
ɑː	f<u>a</u>ther, c<u>a</u>r, gl<u>a</u>ss, c<u>a</u>lm	ɜː	g<u>i</u>rl, b<u>u</u>rn, w<u>o</u>rk
ɒ	st<u>o</u>p, g<u>o</u>lf, r<u>o</u>ck, c<u>o</u>ntinent	ə	<u>a</u>dopt, numb<u>e</u>r, act<u>o</u>r, actr<u>e</u>ss, bish<u>o</u>p

Diphtong sounds

eɪ	t<u>a</u>ke, r<u>ai</u>n, d<u>ay</u>	aɪ	fl<u>y</u>, k<u>i</u>te, r<u>i</u>ght	ɔɪ	b<u>oy</u>, b<u>oi</u>l	eə	h<u>air</u>, wh<u>ere</u>
əʊ	f<u>o</u>ld, sh<u>ow</u>, th<u>ough</u>	aʊ	n<u>ow</u>, m<u>ou</u>se, sh<u>ow</u>er	ɪə	n<u>ear</u>, h<u>ere</u>	ʊə	s<u>ure</u>, p<u>oor</u>

Consonant sounds

b	<u>b</u>ad, tu<u>b</u>	dʒ	<u>j</u>am, fri<u>dg</u>e	ŋ	so<u>ng</u>	ʒ	vi<u>s</u>ion, mea<u>s</u>ure
k	<u>c</u>at, <u>k</u>it, a<u>c</u>t	h	<u>h</u>ouse	p	<u>p</u>ost, u<u>p</u>	t	<u>t</u>ree, sui<u>t</u>
tʃ	<u>ch</u>air, crun<u>ch</u>	j	<u>y</u>ou	r	<u>r</u>un, ba<u>rr</u>ier	θ	<u>th</u>in, ba<u>th</u>
d	<u>d</u>o, <u>d</u>id	l	<u>l</u>ast, a<u>ll</u>	s	<u>s</u>it, ri<u>c</u>e, cro<u>ss</u>	ð	<u>th</u>is, wi<u>th</u>
f	<u>f</u>ast, rou<u>gh</u>	m	<u>m</u>ust, roo<u>m</u>	z	<u>z</u>oo, ro<u>s</u>e, day<u>s</u>	v	<u>v</u>an, star<u>v</u>e
g	<u>g</u>et, pi<u>g</u>	n	<u>n</u>o, te<u>n</u>	ʃ	<u>sh</u>arp, ca<u>sh</u>	w	<u>w</u>ell

Accents

If the word has more than one syllable, the syllable on which the stress falls is preceded by an accident in the phonetic alphabet, e.g. /ɪnˈtelɪdʒənt/, /nəˈsesəti/, /fəˈget/, /ˈhʌŋgri/, /ˈmɑːvələs/.

1 Read the phonetic transcriptions and write the words.

1 /θɪŋ/ ....
2 /θɪn/ ....
3 /siːn/ ....
4 /sɪns/ ....
5 /faɪnd/ ....
6 /faɪn/ ....
7 /pɒt/ ....
8 /pɔːt/ ....
9 /ˈfaɪə/ ....
10 /fɪə/ ....
11 /buːt/ ....
12 /bʌt/ ....

2 Read the phonetic transcription and write the sentences.

1 /wi ɑː ɪn ðə ˈgɑːdn/
....

2 /duː ju ʌndəˈstænd/
....?

3 /aɪ lʌv ˈtʃɒkələt/
....

4 /ju kən juz maɪ ˈdɪkʃənəri/
....

5 /weər ɪz ðə dʒm dʒɑː/
....?

6 /ʃi ˈwʊdnt laɪk tə kʌm tə ðə biːtʃ/
....

7 /juv gɒt ə naɪs ˈbreɪslət/
....

8 /hi ræn tə kætʃ ðə bʌs/
....

9 /ɪt wəz kəʊld, dɑːk ənd ˈraɪnɪŋ/
....

10 /aɪm ʃʊə ðeɪ ɑːr ˈɪŋglɪʃ/
....

PUNCTUATION MARKS

. **full stop / period (AmE)**
at the end of a sentence: *He arrived yesterday.*

, **comma**
- separates the different elements of a list: *He had ham, salad, apple pie and a cup of tea.*
- separates clauses, comments:
  My father, who works in Bristol, comes home at the weekend.
- after introductory subordinate sentences: *When it stops raining, I'll go out to play.*
- with direct speech: *'Come and see me,' said Pete, 'I'll show you my new flat.'*

: **colon**
introduces an explanation, a list or a quotation:
For the trip you need: an anorak, walking boots, a rucksack and a cap.
Martin Luther King started his famous speech with the words: 'I have a dream...'

; **semicolon**
- is placed between two main clauses that are related in meaning:
  I don't like eating in restaurants; I prefer cooking my own meals.
- separates elements of a list if these elements are long and complex:
  The characters in the play include Dennis, a London teenager; Debbie, his girlfriend; Mr Johnson, Debbie's stepfather; and Ms Ross, Dennis's mother.

? **question mark**
at the end of a direct question: *How long will you be away?*

! **exclamation mark**
to give particular emphasis: *What a lovely day!*

... **dots / ellipsis**
to show that a sentence, quotation or list is incomplete:
I think I'll have roast beef, salad, some cake...

– **dash**
is used in check-lists, defines a non-essential clause or adds information.
Spend a weekend in San Francisco – the liveliest city of the Bay Area!

/ **slash / stroke**
to provide an alternative: *Part–time / Full–time jobs as waiters / waitresses. Apply inside.*

- **hyphen**
- in compound nouns and adjectives: *My mother-in-law is a bit absent-minded.*
- after prefixes, when the word starts with the same vowel:
  Co-operation is essential to get good results.
- to split a word that continues in the next line.

( ) **brackets / parentheses**
contain extra-information, especially when cross-references are used:
Study the verb forms (see page 43).

" " **inverted commas / quotation marks (double or simple)**
' '
mark a quotation or direct speech:
'A witty portrait of literary life in New York' Sunday Telegraph

' **apostrophe**
in short forms and the possessive case: *That isn't James's car.*

A **capital letter / upper-case letter**
in English, the following are always written with a capital letter:
- proper nouns: *Paul Smith, my dog Rex, the Statue of Liberty, Mount Etna, Lake Erie*
- titles and professions: *Mr Bell, Ms Derrick, Professor Dawson, Queen Elizabeth II*
- the days of the week, the months and festivities: *Sunday, August, Easter*
- adjectives and nouns indicating nationality and languages: *Brazilians speak Portuguese.*
- nouns indicating family members when they are used alongside proper nouns or instead of them:
  Are you ready, Mum? Uncle Jim is waiting for us.
- titles of books, films, newspapers, etc.: *'The Good Life' by Jay McInerney is a moving novel.*

a **small letter / lower-case letter**

new line / new paragraph

MOODS, TENSES AND ASPECTS

MOOD	TENSE	ASPECT	
Indicative	present	simple	I **call** him every day.
	past	simple	I **called** him yesterday.
	future	simple	I **will call** him tomorrow.
	present	continuous	I**'m callin**g him right now.
	past	continuous	I **was calling** him when you arrived.
	future	continuous	I **will be calling** him tomorrow at this time.
	present	perfect	I **have** just **called** him.
	past	perfect	I **had called** him some time before you arrived.
	future	perfect	I **will have called** it by this time.
	present	perfect continuous	I **have been calling** him for an hour.
	past	perfect continuous	I **had been calling** him for an hour when ...
	future	perfect continuous	By 5 pm I **will have been calling** him for an hour.
Imperative			**Come** here! **Don't talk**!
Conditional	present		I **would take** an umbrella if it rained.
	past		I **would have taken** a taxi if I had been late.
Subjunctive			If I **were** you, I would accept that job.
Infinitive		simple	It is impossible **to save** money now.
		continuous	He seems **to be following** us.
Participle	present		I heard a girl **singing** in the next room.
	past		He came in, **followed** by his big dog.
Gerund		simple	I often spend my free time **reading**.
		perfect	He denied **having been** there.

MODAL VERBS – TENSES

can, could, be able to

Present simple	Past simple	Future
can / can't am / is / are able to 'm not / isn't / aren't able to	could / couldn't was / were able to wasn't / weren't able to	will be able to won't be able to
Present perfect	**Past perfect**	**Future perfect**
have / has been able to haven't / hasn't been able to	had been able to hadn't been able to	will have been able to won't have been able to
Conditional	**Past conditional**	
could / couldn't would / wouldn't be able to	could have / couldn't have would have / wouldn't have been able to	

may, might, be allowed to

Present simple	Past simple	Future
may / may not am / is / are allowed to 'm not / isn't / aren't allowed to	was / were allowed to wasn't / weren't allowed to	will be allowed to won't be allowed to
Present perfect	**Past perfect**	**Future perfect**
have / has been allowed to haven't / hasn't been allowed to	had been allowed to hadn't been allowed to	will have been allowed to won't have been allowed to
Conditional	**Past conditional**	
might / might not would / wouldn't be allowed to	might have / might not have would have been / wouldn't have been allowed to	

must, have (got) to, need, be compelled to, be obliged to, should

Present simple	Past simple	Future
must / mustn't need / needn't don't / doesn't need to have / has (got) to haven't / hasn't got to don't / doesn't have to	had to didn't have to didn't need to was / were compelled / obliged to wasn't / weren't compelled / obliged to	will have to won't have to will be compelled / obliged to won't be compelled / obliged to
Present perfect	**Past perfect**	**Future perfect**
have / has been compelled to have / has been obliged to haven't / hasn't been compelled to haven't / hasn't been obliged to	had been compelled to had been obliged to hadn't been compelled to hadn't been obliged to	will have had to won't have had to will have been compelled / obliged to won't have been compelled / obliged to
Conditional	**Past conditional**	
should / shouldn't would have to wouldn't have to	should have / shouldn't have would have had to wouldn't have had to	

CONDITIONAL SENTENCES

Conditional sentences – Type 1

IF clause	Main clause
If I can…	I will…
If I want to…	I will…
If I must / have to…	I will…

If I can stay one more day, I will be able to go on a sightseeing tour of the city.
If I want to play in the final, I will have to train hard.
If I must / have to wait so long, I will just go home and come back tomorrow.

If clauses – Type 2

IF clause	Main clause
If I could… If I were able to…	I could… I would be able to… I might… (maybe)…
If I wanted to… If you would…	I would like to…
If I were to… (eventuality) If I should… (eventuality) If I had to… (obligation)	I should… (personal obligation) I ought to… (personal obligation) I would have to… (obligation deriving from external circumstances or people)

If I could find a better-paid job, I would be able to pay off my mortgage earlier.
If I should win the race, I should thank the coach for his help.
If I had to work at the weekend, I would have to ask someone to come and look after the kids.
If you wanted to start a new business, we might be able to give you some financial backing.
If he were to arrive earlier, could you please meet him at the airport?

If clauses – Type 3

IF clause	Main clause
If I could have… If I had been able to…	I could have… I would have been able to… I might have… (maybe)…
If I had wanted to…	I would have liked to… (*also:* I'd like to have + *past participle*)
If I should have… If I had had to…	I should have… I ought to have… I would have had to…

If I had had to pay a higher rent, I would have had to find a smaller flat.
If I had been able to ski, I would have liked to spend a holiday in the Swiss Alps.
If I had had to wait for you any longer in the street, I might have frozen to death!
If I had really wanted to reach the top, I could easily have done so.

CONJUGATION OF AN IRREGULAR VERB

infinitive to choose	past participle chosen	present participle choosing

ACTIVE FORM

present simple	present continuous
I / You / We / They choose	I am choosing
He / She / It chooses	You / We / They are choosing
	He / She / It is choosing
past simple	**past continuous**
I / You / He / She / It / We / They chose	I / He / She / It was choosing
	You / We / They were choosing
present perfect simple	**present perfect continuous**
I / You / We / They have chosen	I / You / We / They have been choosing
He / She / It has chosen	He / She / It has been choosing
past perfect simple	**past perfect continuous**
I / You / He / She / It / We / They had chosen	I / You / He / She / It / We / They had been choosing
future simple	**future continuous**
I / You / He / She / It / We / They will choose	I / You / He / She / It / We / They will be choosing
future perfect simple	**future perfect continuous**
I / You / He / She / It / We / They will have chosen	I / You / He / She / It / We / They will have been choosing
***going to* future**	***going to* future in the past**
I'm going to choose	I / He / She / It was going to choose
You're / We're / They're going to choose	You / We / They were going to choose
He's / She's / It's going to choose	
present conditional	**past conditional**
I / You / He / She / It / We / They would choose	I / You / He / She / It / We / They would have chosen

PASSIVE FORM

present simple	present continuous
I am chosen	I am being chosen
You / We / They are chosen	You / We / They are being chosen
He / She / It is chosen	He / She / It is being chosen
past simple	**past continuous**
I / He / She / It was chosen	I / He / She / It was being chosen
You / We / They were chosen	You / We / They were being chosen
present perfect simple	**past perfect simple**
I / You / We / They have been chosen	I / You / He / She / It / We / They had been chosen
He / She / It has been chosen	
future simple	**future perfect simple**
I / You / He / She / It / We / They will be chosen	I / You / He / She / It / We / They will have been choosen
***going to* future**	***going to* future in the past**
I'm going to be chosen	I / He / She / It was going to be chosen
You're / We're / They're going to be chosen	You / We / They were going to be chosen
He's / She's / It's going to be chosen	
present conditional	**past conditional**
I / You / He / She / It / We / They would be chosen	I / You / He / She / It / We / They would have been chosen

MAIN IRREGULAR VERBS

Base form	Past simple	Past participle
be	was, were	been
beat	beat	beaten
become	became	become
begin	began	begun
bend	bent	bent
bet	bet	bet
bind	bound	bound
bite	bit	bitten
blow	blew	blown
break	broke	broken
bring	brought	brought
broadcast	broadcast	broadcast / broadcasted
build	built	built
burn	burnt / burned	burnt / burned
burst	burst	burst
buy	bought	bought
catch	caught	caught
choose	chose	chosen
come	came	come
cost	cost	cost
cut	cut	cut
deal	dealt	dealt
dig	dug	dug
do	did	done
draw	drew	drawn
dream	dreamt / dreamed	dreamt / dreamed
drink	drank	drunk
drive	drove	driven
eat	ate	eaten
fall	fell	fallen
feed	fed	fed
feel	felt	felt
fight	fought	fought
find	found	found
fly	flew	flown
forecast	forecast	forecast
foresee	foresaw	foreseen
forget	forgot	forgotten
freeze	froze	frozen
get	got	got / gotten
give	gave	given
go	went	gone
grow	grew	grown
hang	hung / hanged	hung / hanged
have	had	had
hear	heard	heard
hide	hid	hidden
hit	hit	hit
hold	held	held
hurt	hurt	hurt
keep	kept	kept
kneel	knelt	knelt

Base form	Past simple	Past participle
know	knew	known
lay	laid	laid
lead	led	led
learn	learnt / learned	learnt / learned
leave	left	left
lend	lent	lent
let	let	let
lie	lay	lain
light	lit	lit
lose	lost	lost
make	made	made
mean	meant	meant
meet	met	met
pay	paid	paid
put	put	put
quit	quit	quit
read /ri:d/	read /red/	read /red/
ride	rode	ridden
ring	rang	rung
rise	rose	risen
run	ran	run
say	said	said
see	saw	seen
seek	sought	sought
sell	sold	sold
send	sent	sent
set	set	set
shake	shook	shaken
shine	shone	shone
shoot	shot	shot
show	showed	shown
shrink	shrank	shrunk
shut	shut	shut
sing	sang	sung
sit	sat	sat
sleep	slept	slept
smell	smelt / smelled	smelt / smelled
speak	spoke	spoken
spend	spent	spent
stand	stood	stood
steal	stole	stolen
swim	swam	swum
take	took	taken
teach	taught	taught
tell	told	told
think	thought	thought
throw	threw	thrown
understand	understood	understood
wear	wore	worn
win	won	won
write	wrote	written

GRAMMAR WORDS

A **NOUN** is a word indicating
- a person (*student, friend, man, woman*)
- a thing, a substance or an animal (*computer, sugar, dog, lion*)
- an idea or a quality (*imagination, hope, peace*)

- Nouns can be **proper** nouns, written with a capital letter (*Paul Smith, my dog Rex, the Statue of Liberty, Mount Etna*), or **common** nouns (*animal, earth, science, intelligence, children, teachers*).

- **Compound** nouns are formed by two words, usually two nouns: *piano player, bank robber, road sign*.

- Most English nouns can be **singular** (*a table*) or **plural** (*tables*).
- **Countable** nouns have both a singular and a plural form (*car – cars, party – parties*). Some nouns are only plural, e.g. *trousers, glasses, earnings, remains, contents*.
- **Uncountable** nouns are only singular (*gold, water, fear, imagination*). Some nouns are uncountable in English, but not in other languages, e.g. *furniture, hair, homework, information, money, luggage, news, business, advice*.

- English nouns do not have a specific ending for feminine or masculine.

A **DETERMINER** is a word introducing a noun. Determiners can be:
articles
- The indefinite article is **a / an**:
  *I spoke to **a** receptionist.*
  *I had **an** appointment.*
- The definite article is **the**:
  ***The** receptionist I spoke to was very polite.*
  ***The** appointment was at ten o'clock.*

demonstratives
- *this these that those*
  *I like **this** T-shirt and **these** jeans.*
  *I don't like **that** hoodie or **those** boots.*

possessive adjectives
- *my, your, his, her, its, our, their*
  *She is **my** friend. She writes with **her** left hand.*

quantifiers
- *some, any, much, many, most, all, (a) little, (a) few, lots of, every, each, enough*
  *Have we got **any** sugar? We've got **some**, but not **much**.*
  *I would like **a little** milk and **a few** biscuits.*

An **ADJECTIVE** is a word describing a noun.
- English adjectives have one form for singular and plural, masculine and feminine.
- Qualifying adjectives precede the noun or follow the verb *be*.
  *I saw a **beautiful modern** <u>building</u>.*
  *The <u>mountain</u> **was** high and **inaccessible**.*

Adjectives can have a comparative and a superlative form.
Comparative: *He is **more** intelligent **than** me.*
Superlative: *They are **the most** intelligent students **in** the school.*

430

A **PERSONAL PRONOUN** is a word replacing a noun that has already been mentioned. According to their role in a sentence, they are called:
- **subject pronouns:** *I, you, he, she, it, we, you, they*
- **object pronouns:** *me, you, him, her, it, us, you, them*
- **possessive pronouns:** *mine, yours, hers, his, ours, yours, theirs*
- **reflexive pronouns:** *myself, yourself, himself, herself, itself, ourselves, yourselves, themselves.*

Other common PRONOUNS are:
- **relative:** *who, which, that, whose* – I met the girl **who** lives next door.
- **interrogative:** *who, what, whose, which* – **What** did you get for your birthday?
- **indefinite:** *someone/body, something, anyone/body, anything, no-one/nobody, nothing, everyone/everybody, everything* – I didn't speak to **anybody** at the party.
- **reciprocal:** *each other, one another* – How long have they known **each other**?
- **distributive:** *each, either, neither* - Take one each.

A **VERB** is a word indicating
- an action: *She **texts** me every evening.*
- a situation: *It **is** a beautiful day.*
- an event: *The war **broke out**.*
- a perception: *He **seems** a nice person.*

A verb together with a subject and one or more complements forms a **sentence**:
She (subject) *gave* (verb) *presents* (direct object) *to all of us* (indirect object).

A **transitive verb** can be followed by an object. An **intransitive verb** cannot have an object.
- transitive: *I **met** John in the market square.*
- intransitive: *We **went** to London by train.*

A transitive verb can be **active** or **passive**:
- active form: *The earthquake **killed** more than two hundred people.*
- passive form: *More than two hundred people **were killed** by the earthquake.*

Verbs have **MOODS**, **TENSES** and simple, continuous and perfect **ASPECT**.

Indicative mood:	the present simple: *I **call** him every day.*
	the past simple: *I **called** him yesterday.*
	the future with *will*: *I **will call** him tomorrow.*
continuous tenses	the present continuous: ***I'm calling** him right now.*
	the past continuous: *I **was calling** him when you arrived.*
	the future continuous: *I **will be calling** him tomorrow at this time.*
perfect tenses	the present perfect: *I **have** just **called** him.*
	the past perfect: *I **had called** him some time before you arrived.*
	the future perfect: *I **will have called** it by this time.*
perfect tenses continuous	the present perfect continuous: *I **have been calling** him for an hour.*
	the past perfect continuous: *I **had been calling** him for an hour when …*
	the future perfect continuous: *By 5 pm I **will have been calling** him for an hour.*
Imperative mood:	***Come** here! **Don't talk**!*
Conditional mood:	*I **would take** an umbrella if it rained.*
	*I **would have taken** a taxi if I had been late.*
Subjunctive mood:	*If I **were** you, I would accept that job.*

The VERBAL FORMS called **gerund, infinitive, present participle** and **past participle** are not used as action words in sentences, so they do not have a subject. They usually function as nouns.

The **gerund** ends in *–ing*: ***Dancing** is a favourite pastime of mine. Do you enjoy **skiing**?*

The **infinitive** is the base form of a verb with *to*: *I started **to learn** some Chinese.*

A **participle** ends in *-ing* (present participle) or *-ed* (past participle).

An **AUXILIARY VERB** is a verb used to form the tenses, moods, and voices of other verbs.
The auxiliary verbs in English are **be**, **have** and **do**.
- The auxiliary **be** is used
  to form continuous tenses: He**'s watching** the news. I **was cooking**. I**'ll be arriving** by train.
  to form the passive voice: This vase **is made** of glass. He **was named** after his dad.
- The auxiliary **have** is used to form the perfect tenses:
  She **has** just **arrived**. How long **have** you **lived** here? We **hadn't seen** New York before.
- The auxiliary **do/does/did** is used
  to make negative statements: He **doesn't work** here.
  to make questions: **Did** you **forget** your keys?
  to make negative questions: **Don't** you **understand**?
  for emphasis: We **do** know him. She **did** tell me but I forgot.

A **MODAL VERB** is an auxiliary verb that expresses
- ability, possibility, permission and volition: **can/could, may/might, will/would**

  He **can** drive very well.   **May** I ask you a question?
  I **can** come tomorrow.   She **might** not like this T-shirt.
  Could we have some sandwiches?   **Will** you dance with me?

- obligation and necessity: **must, need, ought to, shall/should**

  You **must** be punctual for your appointment.   We **needn't** go if it rains.
  She **ought to** apologise.   What **shall** we do at the weekend?
  We **should** visit the newly opened museum.

A **PHRASAL VERB** is a verb followed by one or two particles (i.e. prepositions or adverbs) which change its meaning.
  They **stood up** when the teacher **came in**. (you can't separate the particle from its verb)
  Take off your coat. **Take** your coat **off**. (you can separate the particle from its verb)
  Keep up with the good work. (two particles, they can't be separated)

A passive **CAUSATIVE CONSTRUCTION** is used to show that something is done for us by somebody else:
- **have / get something done**
  She had her hair cut yesterday. I have my car washed every Saturday.

An active **CAUSATIVE CONSTRUCTION** is used to show that somebody caused or allowed something to happen:
- **make / have somebody do something** (also: get / compel / force / cause somebody **to** do something)
  She made me cry. I had the mechanic repair my car. The frost caused the lake to freeze.
- **let / allow / help somebody do something** (also: help somebody **to** do something)
  Her parents let her stay out until midnight. Can you help me do this maths exercise?

A **PREPOSITION** is a word describing the position or movement of something or the time when something happens, or the way something is done. Prepositions are followed by a noun or pronoun.
- Prepositions of time: *at, in, on, during, since, for, till, until, before, after*
- Prepositions of place: *at, in, on, under, below, over, above, in front of, behind, between, near to*
- Prepositions of movement: *to, from, into, out of, past, over, towards, along, through, up, down*
- Others: *with, without, by, for, of, about*

A preposition can be part of a phrasal verb, and can sometimes appear at the end of the sentence.
*I ran **into** Kate this morning. He tidied his room **up**.*

An **ADVERB** is a word describing a verb, an adjective or another adverb.
- Adverbs of manner often end in **–ly**. They can have a comparative and a superlative form.
  *He plays the cello **beautifully**.* (describes the verb *plays*)
  *They are **greatly** admired.* (describes the adjective *admired*)
  Comparative: *He is driving **more carefully than** usual.*
  Superlative: *Who can run **the fastest**?*
- Adverbs of frequency: *Men and women haven't **always** had the same rights.*
- Adverbs of degree are used with an adjective or another adverb: *The film was **extremely** long. Today's test was **fairly** easy. We don't understand **very** well.*
- Adverbs of time: *What did you do **yesterday**?*
- Adverbs of place: *The children were playing **outside**.*
- Interrogative adverbs: ***Where** did you go? **How** did you travel? **When** did you arrive? **Why** didn't you tell me?*
- Sequencing adverbs: ***First** mix flour and butter, **then** add two tablespoons of water and mix to firm dough. **After that** knead the dough briefly on a floured surface. **Finally** wrap in cling film and chill.*
- Linking adverbs: *The hotel had a large pool and it **also** had a golf course. This is healthy food, and **moreover** it's organic.*

A **CONJUNCTION** is a word used to connect phrases, clauses and sentences. There are coordinating conjunctions and subordinating conjunctions.
- Coordinating conjunctions: **and, or, but, so, therefore**
  *We can visit the park **and** the zoo at the same time.*
  *Would you like tea **or** coffee?*
  *The journey was very long **but** interesting.*
- Subordinating conjunctions:
  as, because, for, since (cause), *so, so that* (purpose), *although, though* (contrastive), *after, before, until, while, when, as, as soon as* (temporal), *if, whether, unless, as long as, provided, whenever, whatever* (conditional, indirect question), *that* (reported speech, indirect statement, consequential)
- Correlative conjunctions:
  both ... and (including), **either ... or** (alternative), **whether ... or** (alternative), **not only ... but also** (including), **neither ... nor** (excluding), **as ... as** (comparing, equality)

An **EXCLAMATION** is a word or phrase that expresses surprise, pleasure, anger or other emotions.
Great! Well done! Ouch! Oh dear! What a beautiful day! What bad luck! How clever! How awful!

BASIC ELEMENTS OF A SENTENCE
A CLAUSE is a group of words consisting of: subject + verb (+ complements).
A SENTENCE is made up of a main clause followed by one or more coordinate or subordinate clauses.

I'm late	because I missed the bus.
main clause	subordinate clause
When I was young,	I lived in Scotland.
subordinate clause	main clause
I did my homework,	then I went out with my friends.
main clause	coordinate clause

The SUBJECT is the person or thing performing the action. ***She** bought a T-shirt. Did **you** by anything?*
The OBJECT is the thing on which the subject acts. *She bought **a T-shirt**. Did you by **anything**?*
The INDIRECT OBJECT is the receiver of the action. *She bought a T-shirt **for Jim**. She bought **Jim** a T-shirt.*
The PREDICATE is the verb in the sentence. *Jeremy **plays** rugby every Saturday.*

INDEX

A

a / an 14, 16-18
(be) able to 234, 280, 281
about 117, 119, 121
(be) about to 268
above 114
across 116
adjectives:
- followed by prepositions 119, 125
- formation of adjectives 387
- nationality 47
- order of adjectives 47
- possessive 66
- qualifying 46-48
- 'strong' 179
- suffixes that form adjectives 389
- used as nouns 19
see also *comparative* and *superlative*
adverbs:
- degree 177-179
- frequency 81
- interrogative 34-37
- manner 174-175
- place 33
- position in the sentence 81, 175
- relative 330
- time 95, 134, 146-148
- to build an argument 368
see also *comparative* and *superlative*
after
- conjunction 367
- in sequences 134, 374
- preposition of time 113
agreeing 384, 415
all (of) 187, 211
all that 330
allow sb to do sth 371
(be) allowed to 234, 280, 281
along 115
already 148
also 369, 374
although 363, 374
always 81
American English 421
among 115
and 27, 84, 374
any 44-45, 53, 416

- compounds: *anybody, anyone, anything, anywhere* 208-209, 417
around 115
articles:
definite article *the* 19-20
- with geographical names 21
- with uncountable nouns 25
- other uses 25
indefinite article *a / an* 16-18
- with countable nouns 14
- in exclamatory sentences 179
as
- in reason clauses 365, 374
- in time clauses 138
as... as 194, 374
as a result 365
as far as 116
as if 370
as long as 367, 374
as soon as 367, 374
as though 370
as well 237
as well as 200
at
- preposition of place 114-116
- preposition of time 112
away from 115

B

be
- past simple 128, 410
- present simple 28-31, 404
be to 254
be used to 123
because 34, 84, 374
before
- in time sequences 134
- preposition of time 112-113
- conjunction 367
behind 115
below 114
beside 115
besides 369
between
- preposition of time 113
- preposition of place 115
(a) bit 186
both (of) 211
both... and 215, 374
(be) bound to 258

British English / American English 421
but 27, 84, 117, 362
by
- as agent in passive sentences 117, 306
- preposition of time 112-113
- with means of transport 117
- with reflexive pronouns used as emphasising pronouns 219

C

can 232-234, 280, 281
- in conditional sentences 291, 292, 297
- can't help +-ing 246
cause sth to happen 371
close to 115
comparative of adjectives:
- as... as 194
- intensifiers 192
- irregular 193
- less than 194
- majority 190-191, 205, 418
- special types 192
comparative of adverbs 200
comparative with nouns 201-202, 204
comparative with verbs 202
compel sb to do sth 371
(be) compelled to 258, 281
compounds with –ever 216
compounds of *some, any, no* 208-209, 417
compound nouns see nouns
conditional
- modal verbs 297
- past 289
- present 288
conjunctions
- adversative 362
- comparative 370
- concessive 363
- conditional 291, 302, 303
- consecutive 365
- declarative and explanatory 371
- purpose 366
- reason 365
- time 367
consequently 365, 374

434

correlatives
- conjunctions 374
- pronouns 215,
could 232-234
- conditional 289
- in if-clauses 297-298
countable nouns see *nouns*

D
date 50
despite 363
demonstrative, adjectives and pronouns 42-43
distributive, adjective and pronouns 211
disagreeing 384, 415
double genitive 70
during 112, 113
duration form
- with *past perfect simple* and *continuous* 162, 163
- with *present perfect simple* and *continuous* 151-155

E
each (of) 211
each other 214
either (of) 211
either... or 215
else 209
enough 177, 178, 182
even if / even though 363
ever 81, 146
- compunds with *–ever* 216
every 211
- compounds *everybody, everyone, everything, everywhere* 212-213, 417
except (for) 117

F
fairly 177
far 177
(by) far 197
(a) few 183-184
fewer / the fewest 201-202
finally 134, 368, 374
firstly 374
(at) first / first of all 134, 368
for
- preposition of movement 116
- preposition of time (duration) 112-113, 151-153

- various meanings 117
force sb to do sth 371
(be) forced to 258
fractions see *numbers*
frequency adverbs see *adverbs*
from
- preposition of movement 115
- preposition of time 112, 113
future 264, 275
- with *going to* 267-268
- with the *present continuous* 265
- with the *present simple* 266
- with *will* 269-270, 272
future continuous 273
future in the past 278
future perfect 274
future time expressions 271

G
get
- causative verb 371
- *get sth done* 318
- in passive sentences 309
going to 267-268
gonna 267
gotta 267

H
had better 257, 280
hardly 175
have (got) 62-65, 73, 405
have sth done 318
have (got) to 250-251, 280, 281
here is / are 33
how
- interrogative and compounds 35
how long 35, 153
how much / many 35, 181
however 216, 362
how often 82

I
if 291, 303, 354, 374
if clauses
- type 0 / zero conditional 291
- type 1 / first conditional 292, 302
- type 2 / second conditional 293-294, 303
- type 3 / third conditional 295-296, 303
- use of modal verbs 297-298
if only 370

imperative 76, 86
in
- after superlative 197
- preposition of place 114, 124
- preposition of time 112, 113
in case 370
indirect speech see *reported speech*
in front of 115
in order to 366
in spite of 363
indefinite adjectives and pronouns 44-46, 52, 53, 180-184, 187, 416
infinitive
- after verbs 100, 123
- other uses 102
-ing form
- after adjectives 119
- after verbs 100, 120
- after verbs of perception 332-333
- form and uses 90-91, 103
International Phonetic Alphabet 422
intensifiers 186, 192
interrogative adjectives and pronouns 34, 382
into 115
inversion of subject and verb 379
it's, impersonal use 40

J
just 147-148

L
last 199
lately 146
least 199, 202
less 194, 202
let's 76, 86
let sb do sth 371
like (preposition) 36, 117
(a) little 183-184, 187
(a) lot / lots (of) 180-181

M
main clause 374
make sb do sth 371
many 180-181, 184, 202
may 235-237, 246, 270, 280, 281
- in conditional sentences 291, 292, 297
might 235-237, 289

- in conditional sentences 297, 298

modals and other verbs
- to express ability and possibility 232-237
- to express obligation and necessity 250-259
- to express volition 238-245
- communicative functions (revision table) 280
- in present and past conditional 289-290
- in if-clauses 297-298
- tenses (revision table) 281

more 190, 201, 202
(the) most (of) 196, 197, 200, 201, 202, 211
much 177, 179, 180-181, 184, 202
must / mustn't 250-251, 280, 281

N

near 115
need / needn't / don't need to 253, 280, 281
neither (of) 211
neither... nor 215
neither do I 384, 415
never 81, 146
next 271
next to 115
no 44-45, 53, 416
- compounds *nobody, no one, nothing, nowhere* 208-209, 417

none 44-45
none of 52
nor do I 384
nouns
- collective 13
- compounds 385-386
- countable and uncountable 14-15, 24
- in comparisons 201-204
- irregular plural 12, 23
- only plural 13
- plural 11
- suffixes to form nouns 389

numbers
- cardinal 48-49
- decimal 49
- fractions 49
- ordinal 49

O

object pronouns see *pronouns*
(be) obliged to 258, 281
of 69, 117
- after adjectives and verbs 119, 121, 125
- after superlative 197
off 115
on
- after adjectives and verbs 119, 121, 125
- preposition of place 114, 117
- preposition of time 112
one 18
one / ones 43, 219
one another 214
only if / only when 379
opposite 115
or 27, 84, 374
otherwise 374
ought to 256-257, 280
out of 115, 116
over 113, 114, 115
owe 259
own 66, 218

P

passive form
- conjugation (revision table) 319
- *have / get sth done* 318
- in the future 312
- in the past 309-311
- in the present 306-308
- with modal verbs 313
- with two objects 315-316
- with verbs of perception 333
past (preposition) 115
past conditional 289, 295
past continuous 136-137, 295
past participle 144, 412
past perfect continuous 161, 162, 163
past perfect simple 159-160, 162, 163
past simple
- *be* 128, 410
- form, regular and irregular verbs 129-131, 410-411
- uses 133-134
- versus *present perfect* 150
perhaps 236
(be) permitted to 234
phrasal verbs 390-393, 396-397

plenty (of) 180
plural of nouns see *nouns*
possessive adjectives 66
possessive case 68-70, 75
- with reciprocal pronouns 214
possessive pronouns 67
prefixes 388
prepositional verbs 120-121, 125
prepositions
- after adjectives 119, 125
- after verbs 120-121, 125
- of movement 115-116
- of place 114-115
- of time 112-113
- position in questions 35
- position in relative sentences 325
- various uses 117
present conditional 288-289
present continuous
- for the future 265, 275
- form 91-93, 408-409
- uses 94-95, 99
- versus *going to* and *will* 264
- versus *present simple* 96
present participle 332 see also –*ing form*
present perfect continuous 154, 158, 165
- duration form 155
present perfect simple
- duration form 151-153, 155
- form 144, 412-413
- uses 146, 147-148, 158
- versus *past simple* 150
present simple
- for the future 266, 275
- form 77-79, 406-407
- uses 80
- versus *present continuous* 96
pronouns
- correlative 215
- distributive 211-212
- indefinite 180-182, 183-184, 187, 208-209, 416-417
- object 83
- possessive 67
- reciprocal 214
- reflexive 217-218
- relative 324, 328, 330
- subject 26-27
provided / providing 302, 370
punctuation marks 423

Q

questions:
- wh- questions 382
- yes / no questions 380-381

question tags 383, 417
question words 34-37
quite 177-178, 179

R

rather 177-178, 179, 186
reflexive pronouns see pronouns
relative adverbs 330
relative pronouns 324, 328, 330
reported speech:
- introductory verbs 346, 348, 352
- with changes to various parts of speech 351
- with commands or advice 348
- with questions 354
- with statements in the present 349-350
- with statements true in the past 351-352

S

say 346-347
secondly 368
sequencing adverbs, prepositions and expressions 134, 368
sentence structure
- inversion of subject and verb 379
- negative 380
- word order in positive sentences 378
- Wh- questions 382
- Yes / No questions 380-381

shall 255
short answers
- with be 31
- with can / could 233
- with did 131
- with do / does 79
- with had 159
- with have 65
- with will / would 238

should 255, 289, 297-298
should have 289, 297-298
since 113, 151-153, 365
so (that) 84, 365
so as to 365
so do I 384, 415
some 44-45, 53, 416

- compounds somebody, someone, something, somewhere 208-209, 417

still 148, 467
subject pronouns see pronouns
such a 17, 365
suffixes 389
suggest 262, 354
superlative of adjectives
- intensifiers 197
- irregular 198
- majority 196-197, 205, 419
- with least 199

superlative of adverbs 200
superlative with nouns 201-204

T

tell 346-347
time expressions for
- the future 265, 267, 271, 274
- the past 133
- the present 82, 95

than 191
that
- declarative conjunction 371
- demonstrative 42-43
- relative pronoun 324-325

the 19-21
then 134, 368, 467
there is / there are 32-33, 414
there was / there were 128, 414
therefore 365, 374
though 363, 374
through 116
till 112
to
- after adjectives 119, 123
- after verbs 120-121
- indirect object 118
- movement 115, 123
- purpose conjunction 366
- various meanings 123

too 177, 179
towards 116

U

uncountable nouns see nouns
under 114
unless 302, 370, 374
until 112
used to 123, 135

V

verbs
- action 97-98, 153
- causative 371
- conjugation (revision table) 319
- declarative 352
- followed by –ing form 100
- followed by infinitive 100
- followed by prepositions 120-121, 125
- in comparative structures 202
- irregular 129, 428-429
- modal 232-239, 250-257
- perception 373
- phrasal 390-393, 396
- regular 129
- state 97-98, 153
- to express wants or preferences 243-244
- volition, desire 240-241
- with double object 118

very 177, 179

W

want 240
what
- in exclamations 17
- interrogative 34, 36
- relative 330

whatever 216
when
- conjunction 138, 367
- interrogative 34
- in conditional clauses 291
- relative 330

whenever 216
where
- interrogative 34
- relative 330

wherever 216
whether 354, 374
which
- interrogative 34
- relative 324, 328, 330

whichever 216
while 138, 367, 374
who
- interrogative 34
- relative 324, 328

(the) whole 187
whom 324, 325, 328
whose
- interrogative 34, 68

- relative 324-325, 328
why 34, 330, 354
will 238-239, 269-272, 275, 280, 292
wish 240-241
with 117, 119, 121, 467
within 113
without 117
word formation see *prefixes* and *suffixes*
word order in sentences 378-379
would 141, 238-239, 293-294
would like 243
would prefer / would rather 244

Y

yet / not... yet 148

INDEX OF TABLES

- The Words of Grammar. Nouns, Articles and Verb Cluster — 8
- The Words of Grammar. Adjectives and Pronoun Cluster — 9
- The Words of Grammar. Adverbs, Connectors, Linkers and Preposition Cluster — 10
- Present Tenses: Uses of the present simple and the present continuous – Summary — 99
- Uses of the -ing form – Summary — 103
- Present Perfect: Uses of the present perfect simple and continuous – Summary — 158
- Past Tenses: Use of the past tenses – Summary — 163
- Comparative and superlative with nouns – Summary — 204
- How to express the future – Summary — 275
- Modals and other verbs: Communicative functions – Revision table — 280
- Modals and other verbs: Tenses – Revision table — 281
- Conjugation of a regular verb: active and passive form – Revision table — 319

STUDENT'S BOOK ANSWER KEYS

UNIT 1

LESSON 1

1

-s	-es	-ies	-ves
boys	branches	strawberries	shelves
volcanos	wishes volcanoes	countries	halves
oranges	matches	parties	calves
roofs	glasses	lorries	wives
novels	echoes	ladies	lives
drinks	foxes	libraries	thieves
earphones		babies	
rays			

2 1 Schools are closed today. 2 They're old churches. 3 Those cliffs are dangerous. 4 The shops are open now. 5 Where are my / our keys? 6 They're great cities. 7 These stories are true. 8 Two cars are parked in the street(s).

3 1 shelves 2 books 3 wall 4 bed 5 posters 6 singer(s) / actor(s) 7 actor(s) / singer(s) 8 sofa 9 armchairs 10 table 11 chairs 12 meals

4 1 cliffs 2 tomatoes / potatoes 3 potatoes / tomatoes 4 cherries 5 strawberries 6 cities 7 buses

5 1 children 2 pence 3 people 4 women 5 Geese 6 Mice 7 means 8 dice 9 fish 10 feet

6 1 are 2 are 3 are, is 4 is 5 are 6 is / are 7 is / are 8 are 9 are 10 is 11 are 12 is 13 are 14 are

LESSON 2

1
wool U	lemon C	egg C	ice U
window C	butter U	bottle C	beauty U
sandwich C	snow U	chair C	wine U
silver U	tea U	rain U	juice U
peace U	plastic U	biscuit C	gold U

2 some oil, some butter, an apple, some onions, some bread, an artichoke, a banana, some food, some sweets, some tomato sauce, some mayonnaise, some sugar

3 1 D 2 H 3 A 4 B 5 F 6 C 7 E 8 G

4
a jar of — sweets, tomato sauce, mayonnaise
a bottle of — oil, tomato sauce
a kilo of — bread, butter, artichokes, apples, onions, sugar, bananas
a bag of — food, sweets, sugar
a packet of — sweets, sugar
a slice of — bread, apple, onion

5 1 hair is 2 homework is 3 information, is 4 luggage, is 5 news is 6 furniture is 7 Business is 8 are, teas

LESSON 3

1 1 an 2 a 3 an 4 a 5 a 6 a 7 an 8 a 9 an 10 a 11 an 12 an 13 an 14 a 15 a 16 a 17 a 18 an 19 a 20 an 21 an

2 1 a 2 an 3 a 4 a 5 an 6 a 7 a, an 8 a, the 9 a 10 The 11 a 12 a 13 a 14 an 15 an 16 a

3 1 a 2 one 3 one, an 4 one / a 5 a, a 6 an 7 an / one 8 One 9 A 10 an

4 1 Correct 2 It's a beautiful day. 3 Serena is at home because she's got a cough. 4 Do you have ~~an~~ a high temperature? 5 Correct 6 Correct 7 What ~~an~~ a horrible day! 8 Mike, ~~a your friend's~~ a friend of yours is / one of your friends is on the phone! 9 Sheila has got ~~a~~ brown hair and ~~a~~ brown eyes. 10 Correct

5 1 a 2 an 3 a 4 a 5 a 6 one

LESSON 4

1 1 the 2 a 3 a 4 the 5 the 6 an 7 a 8 the 9 a 10 the 11 the 12 the 13 the 14 the 15 an 16 the

2 1 The, a 2 a, a, The, a, the, an 3 a, the, the 4 the 5 The 6 the 7 the, the, a 8 the 9 the 10 A, a

3 1 //, //, // 2 The, the 3 the 4 //, // 5 the, the 6 The 7 //, the 8 //, the 9 //, // 10 //, //, the, the

4 1 A / The, an 2 An / The, an / the 3 A / The 4 A / The, a 5 A / The, a

5 1 the, // 2 The, the, the 3 The, the, the, the, the 4 //, //, the, // 5 The, the, the 6 the, // 7 //, the, // 8 The, //

6 1 ~~The~~ mathematics is my favourite subject. 2 There's a good film on at **the** cinema this week. 3 The quiz starts at ~~the~~ 7.30. 4 Jason plays **the** drums. 5 Eleanor loves ~~the~~ nature. 6 I don't like ~~the~~ tennis. 7 These are ~~the~~ your sandwiches. 8 Sardinia is **a** beautiful island.

ROUND UP 1

1 1 wives 2 leaves 3 knives 4 lives 5 loaves 6 shelves 7 halves 8 thieves

2 1 is / are 2 are 3 are 4 are 5 are 6 is 7 is 8 are 9 is 10 is 11 are 12 is

439

3 1 P 2 P 3 S 4 S 5 S 6 P

4 1 fungi / funguses 2 hypotheses 3 analyses
4 criteria 5 media

5 1 much, 2 much, 3 many, 4 many, 5 A, 6 some

6 1 a cup of 2 a jar of 3 paper 4 bread
5 a slice of 6 a bottle of 7 beer 8 chocolate
9 a drop of 10 a box of

7 1 experience, experiences 2 business,
businesses 3 damages, damage 4 fish, fishes
5 coffees, coffee 6 glass, glasses

8 1 the 2 a 3 a 4 the 5 the 6 an 7 the 8 the
9 a 10 the 11 a 12 the 13 an 14 an 15 an
16 the 17 the 18 the 19 a 20 a

9 1 the, the 2 The, a 3 a, a, The, the 4 the
5 the 6 The 5 a 6 the 7 a 8 the

Reflecting on grammar
1 F 2 T 3 F 4 T 5 F 6 F 7 F 8 T 9 F 10 T

UNIT 2

LESSON 1

1 1 She 2 He 3 We 4 They 5 you, It, it
6 you 7 They 8 It 9 They 10 You

2 1 She, she 2 They, They 3 I, I 4 They
5 You / We 6 they 7 He 8 We 9 You 10 He
11 She 12 you 13 we 14 you

3 1 D 2 H 3 G 4 F 5 A 6 C 7 B 8 E

4 1 My dad ~~he~~ always gets back home very late.
2 Ann likes cooking but (she) hates cleaning the kitchen.
3 On Saturdays they go shopping or (they) see their friends.
4 John and Kylie ~~they~~ have a lot of common interests.
5 Marion plays computer games or (she) reads a book in her spare time.
6 The film ~~it~~ starts at 8.30 and (it) ends at eleven o'clock.
7 I love Japanese food but (I) don't like Indian food. It's too hot and spicy.
8 Mr Ross leaves home at 7.30 every morning and (he) takes a bus to his office.
9 Jason ~~he~~ is late as usual.
10 Karen doesn't play the piano, but (she) sings beautifully.
11 The children ~~they~~ go to the playground every afternoon.

5 1 It's 2 is 3 You're 4 It's 5 Who's, He's 6 I'm

LESSON 2

1 1 Camilla is / 's a nice old lady.
2 Brian is / 's thirsty.
3 Jack and Debbie are our next-door neighbours.
4 The dog is / 's outside in the garden.
5 Mark and I are cousins.
6 My parents are on holiday in Spain.
7 I am / 'm very tired tonight.
8 You are / 're really funny.

2 1 're 2 's 3 are 4 's 5 's 6 's, 's 7 're 8 're
9 'm 10 are

3 1 thirsty 2 in a hurry 3 right 4 cold
5 scared 6 hungry 7 sleepy 8 hot

4 1 is / 's 2 am / 'm 3 is / 's 4 are / 're 5 is / 's
6 am / 'm 7 is / 's 8 is 9 are 10 are / 're

5 1 We aren't ready for the test. / We're not ready for the test.
2 They aren't at home now. / They're not at home now.
3 It isn't too late! / It's not too late.
4 Aman isn't at school today. / Aman's not at school today.
5 I'm not afraid of the dark.
6 She isn't 17 years old. / She's not 17 years old.
7 My parents aren't at work.
8 I'm not very good at maths.

6 1 aren't / 're not 2 aren't 3 'm 4 're
5 aren't 6 isn't / 's not 7 aren't 8 're

7 1 are 2 is / 's 3 is / 's 4 are not / aren't / 're not
5 is / 's 6 is / 's 7 am / 'm 8 am / 'm not
9 are / 're

8 1 Is 2 Are 3 Are 4 Am 5 Is 6 Are

9 1 Are, aren't / 're not 2 Is, is 3 Are, aren't / 're not 4 Am, are 5 Is, is 6 Is, isn't / 's not

10 1 Is Matthew Susan's cousin? Yes, he is.
2 Isn't he a good singer? Yes, he is.
3 Are your children at school today? No, they aren't / they're not. They're on holiday.
4 Is your sister's name Claire? Yes, it is.
5 Are Chris and Daniel twins? No, they aren't / they're not. Chris is older than Daniel.
6 Aren't Bob and Edward good friends? Yes, they are.

11 1 'Am I short?'
2 'Is it warm/hot in here?' / 'Are you warm/hot in here?'
3 'Are you afraid of the dark?'
4 'Is your sister good at maths?'
5 'Are you and Claire sisters?'
6 'Is Peter's office on the first floor?'
7 'Is Mark John's brother?'
8 'Are you hungry?'

LESSON 3

1
1 There's 2 There isn't 3 There's 4 There are
5 There isn't 6 There aren't
7 There's, there isn't 8 There aren't

2
1 Are there, there are 2 Is there, there isn't
3 Are there, there are 4 Is there, there isn't
5 Is there, there is 6 Are there, there aren't

3
1 there 2 here 3 there 4 Here 5 here 6 here

4
1 ~~Here's~~ a great match tomorrow.
  There's a great match tomorrow.
2 There ~~are~~ one table and four chairs in the kitchen.
  There **is / 's** one table and four chairs in the kitchen.
3 'Is ~~there~~ your brother?' 'No, he's at work.'
  '**Is your brother there / here?**' 'No, he's at work.'
4 '~~There is~~ a room for tonight?' 'Yes, there is.'
  '**Is there** a room for tonight?' 'Yes, there is.'
5 Here ~~it is~~ your bill.
  Here's your bill.
6 How many of you ~~there are~~?
  How many of you **are there**?
7 ~~There are~~ any tickets left?
  Are there any tickets left?
8 ~~There's~~ two bags on the table.
  There are two bags on the table.

LESSON 4

1
1 E 2 H 3 A 4 G 5 C 6 B 7 F 8 D

2
1 How old 2 How long 3 How many
4 How much 5 Why 6 How far
7 When 8 How 9 Where 10 How often

3
1 What's your house like?   D
2 Who are you talking to?   H
3 What's the weather like?   A
4 How is Peter now?   B
5 What's your sister like?   C
6 Where are you from?   E
7 What are you talking about? F
8 Who is this present for?   G

Suggested answers:

4
1 What's your family like? 2 When is John at home? 3 Where's the party? 4 Who's Mr Blackwell? 5 What's your favourite food?
6 What's your telephone / mobile number?
7 Where's Silvia from? 8 How many people are there? 9 How much (money) have you got in your wallet? 10 Which car does Carol prefer?

5
1 How high is Mount Everest?
2 How long is the Mississippi River?
3 How deep is Loch Ness?
4 How big is the Isle of Wight?
5 How tall is your brother?
6 How wide is this table?

6
1 F 2 E 3 C 4 B 5 D 6 A

ROUND UP 2

1
1 They are both from Newcastle.
2 She is 16 years old. 3 It is a big school.
4 He is Swedish. 5 We are friends.

2
1 It 2 she 3 she 4 She 5 they
6 It 7 you 8 I 9 I 10 It

3
1 There is a lamp and a book on my bedside table.
2 There are three cans of orangeade in the fridge.
3 There is a new boy in my class this year.
4 There are a lot of books in your rucksack!
5 There are only 12 students in the class today.
6 There are a lot of good songs on my MP3 player.

4
1 are 2 is / 's 3 is 4 are not / aren't / 're not
5 is 6 is / 's 7 am / 'm 8 am / 'm not 9 are / 're

5
1 is 2 it is / 's 3 be 4 is / 's 5 are 6 you are / 're
7 you are / 're 8 is / 's 9 is / 's 10 you are / 're
11 are

6
1 Susan and I ~~am~~ **are** students in this school.
2 Janet is 15 and her twin brothers ~~is~~ **are** 20.
3 – Who ~~are~~ **is** that man?
   – ~~She~~ **He**'s my uncle.
4 – ~~Is~~ **Are** you a member of the drama club?
   – Yes, ~~I'm~~ **I am**.
5 Thomas and his friend ~~is~~ **are** taking part in the school tennis tournament.
6 The student's room ~~are~~ **is** on the first floor.
7 I know that policeman. ~~She's~~ **He**'s a friend of my brother's.
8 ~~Is~~ **Are** we going to the cinema tonight?

7
1 There is / There's 2 you are 3 Are there 4 are
5 Here 6 It is / It's 7 here is / here's 8 It is / It's
9 you are 10 here is / here's

8
1 he 2 Is, isn't 3 far 4 isn't, she 5 She's / She is
6 Are, not 7 like 8 How

9
1 D 2 A 3 F 4 E 5 C 6 B

10
1 it is / it's not a good 2 it is / it's very upsetting to 3 because it is / it's Mum's 4 it is / it's okay by / with 5 it is / it's good for me 6 That's / That is the nicest thing

11
1 It's 2 It's, That's 3 That's 4 it's 5 It's, That's
6 That's 7 It's, That's 8 It's

12
1 How much 2 How many 3 How old
4 Why 5 Where 6 When 7 How 8 Who
9 Which 10 How tall

Reflecting on grammar

1 T 2 F 3 T 4 F 5 F 6 F 7 T 8 F 9 F 10 F

UNIT 3

LESSON 1

1 🎧02 1 those 2 these 3 those 4 that 5 that

2 1 That 2 this 3 that 4 that 5 This
6 this / that 7 This 8 that

3 1 He's a new student in this school.
2 This is good news!
3 These are our mobile phones.
4 That's a great idea!
5 Give me those magazines, please.
6 That's all I need.
7 This is my best friend.
8 Who are those two guys over there?

4 1 Those 2 those / these 3 These 4 these / those, these 5 that, This 6 these, that

LESSON 2

1 1 any, any 2 some 3 a 4 some 5 a 6 an
7 any 8 some

2 *Possible answers*
There's an important meeting this morning.
There's some good news in today's paper.
There's some fruit in the kitchen.
There's a post office just round the corner.
There are some children in the playground.
There are some fantastic beaches on this island.

3 1 R some 2 O some 3 R some
4 I any 5 I any 6 O some

4 1 any 2 no 3 any 4 none 5 no 6 any, none
7 no 8 any

5 🎧03 1 1 some 2 any
2 1 any 2 some 3 some 4 some
5 some 6 any 7 Any
3 1 Any
4 1 any 2 some 3 any 4 some

LESSON 3

1 1 It's a <u>hot</u> day today.
2 There is a <u>small</u> church in my village. / There is a church in my <u>small</u> village.
3 Are these chairs <u>comfortable</u>?
4 The <u>big</u> house in the square looks abandoned.
5 There are some <u>young</u> children in the park.
6 The view from the tower is <u>fantastic</u>.
7 Is this <u>famous</u> restaurant <u>expensive</u>? / Is this <u>expensive</u> restaurant <u>famous</u>?
8 There is a <u>new</u> clothes shop on the <u>main</u> street.

2 1 There are two ~~bigs~~ **big** computer labs in our school.
2 Is ~~ready~~ your brother **ready** for his final exam?
3 Correct
4 Correct
5 Are ~~happy~~ your parents **happy** with your school results?
6 Mr Ross always gives **interesting** speeches ~~interesting~~.
7 Some ~~youngs~~ **young** boys are playing in the park.
8 Correct

3 1 A blue and white, Chinese, porcelain fruit bowl
2 An abstract, large oil painting
3 A neoclassical, French, wooden chest of drawers
4 Five old, Italian, silver coffee spoons
5 A white and violet, Venetian, glass paperweight

4 1 The girls are wearing expensive, black, American, leather jackets.
2 Here's a valuable, old, African, ebony elephant for your collection.
3 Why don't you buy that simple, green, cotton dress?
4 Let's sit around this oval, dark green, plastic table.
5 The new teacher is a handsome, young, tall, Canadian man. Everyone likes him!
6 His girlfriend has got long, straight, blonde hair.
7 There's a horrible, big, black spider in my bedroom.

LESSON 4

1 1 F 2 B 3 E 4 C 5 A 6 D

2 1 two hundred and twenty-five 2 hundreds
3 thousand 4 Thousands 5 million
6 two hundred and five pounds
7 hundred and thirty-three 8 two point five five
9 Thousands 10 Two thousand and seven

3 1 twentieth 2 fifth 3 thirteenth 4 sixteenth
5 twelfth 6 second 7 forty-ninth, fiftieth

4 1 1st January, 2000 (Br.)
2 23rd April, 2005 (Br.)
3 March 17th, 1969 (Am.)
4 July 4th, Independence Day (Am.)
5 9th November, 2011 (Br.)
6 30th January, 2014 (Br.)
7 January 1st, New Year's Day (Am.)

5 1 $^2/_9$ 2 $^4/_7$ 3 $^4/_{15}$ 4 $^7/_{18}$ 5 $^5/_8$ 6 $^3/_5$ 7 $^6/_{17}$ 8 $^2/_{11}$

6 1 zero 2 love 3 nil 4 oh 5 zero 6 nought
7 oh 8 nought 9 oh

ROUND UP 3

1 1 These are my friends. 2 Those are his dogs.
3 These are our sisters. 4 Those are your students. 5 Those are their cars.

2 1 any, some 2 some 3 any 4 Some 5 any
6 any 7 any, some 8 any 9 any, some 10 any

3 1 none 2 no 3 no 4 None 5 no 6 No
7 None 8 None

4
1 No shops <u>aren't</u> open today. It's a holiday.
   No shops are open today. It's a holiday.
2 I haven't <u>no</u> homework to do for tomorrow.
   I haven't any homework to do for tomorrow.
3 'No, there aren't <u>none</u>.'
   'No, there aren't any.'
4 <u>Not any</u> patients are allowed in this area.
   No patients are allowed in this area.
5 <u>None</u> journalists can get into the room.
   No journalists can get into the room.
6 It's no <u>any</u> use crying over spilt milk.
   It's no use crying over spilt milk.
7 The airport must be <u>any</u> 20 miles from here.
   The airport must be some / about 20 miles from here.
8 We're <u>some</u> good at painting.
   We're no good at painting.

5
1 Finnish, Latvian 2 Canadian 3 Thai
4 German 5 Belgium, Europe 6 Holland / the Netherlands

6
1 B 2 A 3 C 4 A 5 A 6 C 7 B 8 C 9 A
10 B 11 C 12 A 13 B 14 C

Reflecting on grammar
1 F 2 T 3 F 4 F 5 F 6 F 7 F 8 T 9 T 10 F

REVISION AND EXAMS 1

1
1 the 2 // 3 // 4 the 5 // 6 // 7 an 8 the
9 a 10 // 11 // 12 a 13 a 14 // 15 the

2
1 are 2 am / 'm 3 am not / 'm not 4 are
5 is / 's 6 are 7 are / 're 8 is / 's

3
1 oxen 2 sheep / cows 3 cows / sheep 4 are
5 ducks / geese 6 geese / ducks 7 deer
8 bushes 9 is 10 Are

4
1 B 2 C 3 C 4 C 5 A 6 B 7 C 8 B 9 B
10 A 11 A 12 A

5
Suggested answers
1 great, trendy 2 popular 3 colourful, eco-leather
4 cheap 5 long-sleeved, black or white, cotton
6 incredible 7 short, tight, denim 8 long, low-necked, blue 9 fantastic 10 long, glittery, evening

6
1 has 2 be 3 is 4 has 5 is 6 are 7 are

7
1 are 2 the 3 the 4 is 5 the 6 the 7 The 8 an
9 The 10 is 11 the 12 is

8
1 B 2 B 3 B 4 A 5 A 6 D 7 B 8 C 9 A 10 D

9
1 the 2 It 3 Some / Many 4 the 5 some
6 their 7 they 8 a 9 the 10 the

SELF CHECK 1
1 B 2 C 3 B 4 B 5 B 6 A 7 B 8 C 9 A
10 C 11 C 12 A 13 C 14 B 15 C 16 C 17 B
18 B 19 C 20 C 21 A 22 C 23 B 24 A 25 A
26 A 27 B 28 A 29 B 30 C 31 B 32 C 33 B
34 C 35 A 36 A 37 C 38 B 39 C 40 B

UNIT 4
LESSON 1

1
1 My mother's got a part-time job.
2 They've got some relatives in Australia.
3 *The contracted form can't be used in this sentence.*
4 You've got great talent!
5 My brother's got a degree in physics.
6 She's got a very large house.
7 We've all got black hair in my family.
8 Julie's got a fantastic voice.

2
1 My sister has long, straight hair.
2 I've got a very bad headache.
3 I have a tattoo on my left arm.
4 We've got two tickets for the concert.
5 Our hotel has got an indoor pool.
6 Your dad has a good sense of humour.
7 We have got a big, black dog.
8 I've got your phone number.

3
1 Adam's **got** spiky hair.
2 *This sentence is correct.*
3 She<s>'s got</s> **has** a shower every morning.
4 The children<s>'ve</s> **have (got)** blue eyes.
5 Dad<s>'s got</s> **has** a rest in the afternoon.
6 Have <s>got</s> a good time at the party!
7 *This sentence is correct.*
8 *This sentence is correct.*

LESSON 2

1
1 hasn't got 2 haven't got 3 has got
4 hasn't got 5 has got 6 have got 7 have got
8 has got, hasn't got

2
1 I haven't got any warm clothes with me.
2 She hasn't got a present for you.
3 The students don't have a break at 11 o'clock in the morning.
4 He hasn't got a lot of contacts on social media.
5 They don't have a holiday in July.
6 She doesn't usually have tea for breakfast.
7 My mother hasn't got blue eyes.
8 We haven't got tickets for the match.

3
1 My bedroom doesn't have a balcony, but it does have French windows. / My bedroom hasn't got a balcony, but it has got French windows.
2 The village has a post office, but it doesn't have a bank. / The village has got a post office, but it hasn't got a bank.
3 I don't have any trees in my garden, but I have lots of flowers. / I haven't got any trees in my garden, but I've got lots of flowers.
4 We don't have enough money for a pizza, but we have enough for a couple of sandwiches. / We haven't got enough money for a pizza, but we've got enough for a couple of sandwiches.

4
1 D 2 E 3 A 4 B 5 F 6 C

5
2 Does Ben have any good video games?
3 It's heavy! What do you have in your bag?
4 Do we have time to catch the next train?
5 Do you have any good music on your MP3 player?
6 Do you have any pink clothes?

6
1 My house has got solar panels on the roof.
2 I haven't got time to chat. I'm busy at the moment.
3 'Has Peter got a big family?' 'Yes, he's got four children.'
4 'What car have you got?' 'I've got a hybrid car. It's very cheap to run.'
5 London has got a population of over 8.3 million.
6 We haven't got much money. We must find an ATM.
7 'Have you got any preferences for your room?' 'I'd like a non-smoking one, please.'
8 'Has your school got a big playground?' 'No, but it's got a very big gym.'
9 'Have you got any hand luggage, madam?' 'I've only got this handbag.'
10 We haven't got any bread, but we've got some breadsticks.

LESSON 3

1
1 E you, your 2 A Zimbabwe, Its
3 G Mr Johnson, His 4 F Kate, Her
5 D We, Our 6 B My uncle and aunt, their

2
1 their 2 your 3 its 4 her 5 my 6 his 7 our 8 your

3
1 **His** house is on Darwin Road.
2 Emma's got a little brother. **His** name's Harry.
3 This farm belongs to my grandparents. It's **their** farm.
4 She's wearing **her** new red dress.
5 The hamster isn't in **its** cage!
6 My diary has got flowers on **its** cover.
7 I often have sleepovers at **my** friend's house.
8 John and Simon have **their** own fitness instructor.
9 Karen's got a sister. **Her** name is Davina.

4
1 yours 2 your, mine 3 His, his 4 theirs
5 hers 6 yours 7 ours 8 their

LESSON 4

1
1 Whose are those scooters? / Whose scooters are those?
2 Whose is that coat? / Whose coat is that?
3 Whose is this telephone number? / Whose telephone number is this?
4 Whose are those suitcases? / Whose suitcases are those?
5 Whose is this magazine? / Whose magazine is this?
6 Whose is that idea? / Whose idea is that?

2
3, 1, 4, 2, 6, 5

3
1 a week's holiday
2 your brother's email address
3 my brothers' bedroom
4 one of Amy Winehouse's best songs
5 The clowns' tricks
6 Van Gogh's paintings
7 The principal's office

4
1 the kitchen walls 2 the laptop charger
3 the pen cap 4 the book cover
5 the door handle 6 the table legs
7 the computer screen
8 the TV remote control 9 the tree top

5
1 bicycle is white. 2 my father's computer.
3 eyes are beautiful. 4 the guides' backpacks.
5 smartphone is new. 6 computer is very good.

6
1 Rino's 2 chemist's 3 St Peter's 4 doctor's
5 my friend's 6 baker's 7 dentist's
8 greengrocer's

7
1 Two of the Smiths' neighbours 2 One of my brother's colleagues 3 Many of John's selfies
4 One of the Browns' friends 5 Four of my cousin's birthday presents 6 One of Peter's cousins 7 Some of the stamps of my father's collection

8
1 Albert and Maddie's 2 Albert and Daphne's
3 Joe and Alice's 4 Albert and Maddie's
5 Joe and Alice's 6 Joe and Alice's
7 Maddie and Jack's 8 Ann and Mark's
9 Maddie's 10 Jack's

9
1 Correct
2 I usually have two **weeks'** holiday in July.
3 Correct
4 Where are the **children's** backpacks?
5 Is James's brother a friend of **Thomas's**?
6 This isn't today's newspaper. It's **yesterday's**.
7 Correct
8 Two **of the** UK's top attractions are the Tower of London and Windsor Castle.
9 My office is five **minutes'** walk from the bus station.
10 Correct
11 Correct
12 Knockin' on Heaven's Door is **one of** Bob Dylan's most famous songs.

10
1 Mrs 2 house 3 car 4 girlfriend 5 students'
6 bicycles 7 son 8 Mary and Lucy's
9 Peter's and John's 10 one of 11 Some of
12 your father's

ROUND UP 4

1
Possible answers
I have got six hundred names in my contact list. / I have got big responsibilities in my new job. We have got some crisps in our packed lunch. / We have got a lot of homework for tomorrow. They have got three sons but no daughters. Wimbledon Centre Court has got a movable roof.

Robert has got a funny hat.
The black rhino has got a gigantic horn.
That girl has got a new email address.
That man has got a beard and a moustache.
This mini-van has got eight seats.
A dice has got six faces.
The Statue of Liberty has got a torch in her hand.

2 1 is 2 has (got) 3 is 4 is 5 is 6 is
7 have (got) 8 has (got) 9 have 10 have (got)

3
1 They don't have lunch at home on weekdays.
2 I haven't got / don't have a new car. This is my old one.
3 Sheila hasn't got / doesn't have an umbrella with her.
4 The company hasn't got / doesn't have a new sales manager. Mr Jones is still the Chief Buyer.
5 We don't have a sandwich for lunch at the weekend.
6 That man hasn't got / doesn't have a pass. Stop him!
7 My parents don't have a walk in the evening. They're far too lazy.
8 I haven't got / don't have a cold. Why are you asking?
9 Mark doesn't have breakfast at home. He usually goes to a café next to his office.
10 Oh dear! I haven't got / don't have my wallet with me. Can you lend me some money?

4 1 O 2 P 3 G 4 P 5 A 6 P

5
1 Do you usually have a bath?
2 Have a nice stay
3 Has Gwen got measles?
4 What have you got in your packed lunch?
5 Have some more biscuits / another biscuit.
6 Are you having a break?
7 Let's have a walk.
8 Are you having a rest?

6 1 your 2 mine 3 mine 4 Whose 5 Hers 6 her
7 your 8 mine / his 9 his / mine 10 your
11 yours 12 ours 13 Our 14 our 15 your

7
1 <u>Has Pat usually</u> a snack during the break?
Does Pat usually have a snack during the break?
2 This is not <u>mine</u> tablet. It's Peter's.
This is not **my** tablet.
3 Jason must be at home. That's <u>her</u> bicycle in the garden.
That's **his** bicycle in the garden.
4 Don't wait for me. I'm going to the <u>dentists'</u> and I'll come back late.
I'm going to the **dentist's** and I'll come back late.
5 Let's print the <u>students's</u> reports before the end of the lessons.
Let's print the **students'** reports before the end of the lesson.
6 Why don't we read <u>a Dickens' novel</u> this year, Miss Pearson?
Why don't we read **one of Dickens' novels** this year, Miss Pearson?
7 'Whose <u>those cars are</u>?' 'I don't know. But they're parked outside our house.'
'Whose **are** those cars?' / 'Whose cars **are** those?'
8 <u>Some my</u> friends are coming for dinner tonight.
Some of my friends are coming for dinner tonight.

8
1 tie of your father's
2 of my nephews is moving
3 walls bright yellow
4 of my sister's neighbours has a beautiful German shepherd
5 the children's toys are still in the
6 of the room was locked
7 (best) friend of his
8 of Thomas's are having a barbecue in the garden

9 1 ours 2 Their 3 his 4 His 5 Hers 6 their
7 their 8 their 9 Their 10 her

10 1 dentist's 2 greengrocer's 3 baker's
4 butcher's 5 chemist's 6 hairdresser's

11 1 Sophocles' plays 2 St James's Park
3 Dickens' biography 4 Prince Charles's residence 5 Mr Fox's desk 6 Douglas's son

Reflecting on grammar

1 F 2 T 3 F 4 F 5 F 6 T 7 F 8 T 9 T 10 T

UNIT 5

LESSON 1

1 1 give 2 sit 3 Wait 4 have 5 Let's 6 Don't
7 Enjoy 8 Let's not go

2 1 Sit, don't jump 2 Don't lie 3 Walk, turn
4 Read, write 5 Don't tell 6 Don't be, remember

3 1 Let's make 2 Let's work
3 Let's not buy, Let's go 4 Let's not watch
5 Let's play 6 Let's have

LESSON 2

1

–s	–es	–ies
plays	kisses	cries
likes	does	studies
prefers	washes	marries
finds	watches	tidies
asks	mixes	replies
says	passes	hurries

2
1 Thomas studies Russian, too.
2 I go to university, too.
3 My cousin lives in Manchester, too.
4 I love antique furniture, too.
5 I get up at seven o'clock, too.
6 He misses his friends, too.
7 My boyfriend watches a lot of TV, too.

3
1 tidies 2 plays 3 washes 4 does
5 goes 6 misses 7 arrives 8 stays

4
1 check 2 doesn't wear 3 don't go
4 don't study 5 doesn't get

5
1 Frances doesn't dance very well.
2 She doesn't like romantic novels.
3 We don't have lunch at school.
4 They don't work in a hospital.
5 Catherine doesn't play the violin.
6 We don't go shopping on Mondays.
7 The film doesn't start at 9.00.
8 He doesn't go to work by car.

6
1 doesn't have 2 doesn't go 3 doesn't play
4 don't, watch 5 don't work 6 don't go, don't work

7
1 Do, I / we do 2 Does, he doesn't 3 Do, they do
4 Does, he does 5 Do, we do 6 Does, she doesn't
7 Do, I / we don't 8 Do, they don't

8
1 When do you do your homework?
2 Where does your best friend come from?
3 What kind of music do they like?
4 How much does that smartphone cost?
5 Which song do you like best?
6 What do you have for breakfast?

9
6 A 3 B 1 C 5 D 2 E 4 F

10
1 time do you (usually) get up 2 do you go to work 3 does, help 4 do you (usually) meet your friends 5 do you go 6 does she live

11
1 ✗ Water ~~freeze~~ **freezes** at 0°C and ~~boil~~ **boils** at 100°C. 2 ✓ 3 ✗ The match doesn't ~~starts~~ **start** at three o'clock. 4 ✗ This laptop ~~don't belongs~~ **doesn't belong** to the teacher. 5 ✗ What **do** you think of this plan? 6 ✓ 7 ✗ I ~~doesn't~~ **don't** agree with you. 8 ✓ 9 ✓ 10 ✗ He doesn't ~~believes~~ **believe** his team can win today. 11 Does he ~~wants~~ **want** to go to the cinema with us? 12 ✓

LESSON 3

1
1 We occasionally meet for a drink after work.
2 My brother is never at home in the evening.
3 Where do you usually have lunch?
4 He sometimes listens to classical music. / Sometimes he listens to classical music. / He listens to classical music sometimes.
5 I don't often go to the theatre.
6 They are always at school in the morning.
7 My friend rarely eats meat.
8 We never see each other at weekends.

2
Possible answers
1 I always go to the market on Saturday morning.
2 I am / I'm never at home in the mornings.
3 I rarely play tennis at the weekend.
4 I usually sleep till late on Sunday morning.
5 I sometimes go to the theatre with my friends.

3
1 They seldom have piano lessons in the morning.
2 Greg often surfs the Internet in the evening.
3 This train is usually on time.
4 Does Mum ever come back late from work?
5 Jill sometimes works at the weekend. / Jill works at the weekend sometimes / Sometimes Jill works at the weekend.

4
1 E 2 A 3 C 4 B 5 F 6 D

5
Possible answers
1 Where do your parents work?
2 How much does this book cost?
3 How does this machine stop?
4 What time do the shops open?
5 When does the yoga course start?
6 How often do you practise?

6
1 five days a week / on weekdays 2 twice a year
3 once a year 4 every day 5 twice a day
6 three times a year 7 four times a month

LESSON 4

1
1 it 2 them 3 us 4 him 5 her 6 you
7 them 8 me

2
1 Are you talking to me?
2 Here's a present for you, Dad!
3 I don't know her very well.
4 I like it very much.
5 They are coming with us.
6 Can you wait for me, please?

3
1 She, him 2 us 3 it, her 4 He, it 5 him, He
6 her, She 7 they, them 8 them, They

4
1 because 2 so 3 and 4 or 5 so 6 or 7 and
8 because

5
1 and 2 but 3 so 4 or, and 5 or 6 and
7 because 8 so

6
1 Go to the science lab quickly because your teacher is waiting for you.
2 Would you like / prefer an apple or an orange?
3 Come before five so we can have a nice chat.
4 Steve is a nice boy, but he's a bit lazy.
5 My son helps me at home, but he can't cook (though).

7
1 them 2 him 3 me 4 because 5 and 6 them
7 But 8 So 9 them 10 and 11 them 12 them
13 And 14 or

8 1 but 2 she 3 because 4 at 5 her 6 because 7 Their 8 in 9 and 10 and 11 them 12 Her 13 because 14 and 15 and 16 but 17 their 18 but 19 them 20 them

ROUND UP 5

1
1 Always wear gloves and a mask. / It is important that you always wear gloves and a mask. / It is important for you to always wear gloves and a mask. / It is essential that you always wear gloves and a mask.
2 Don't park your car here. / You mustn't park your car here.
3 Have some coffee. / Would you like some coffee? / Do you want some coffee? / How about some coffee?
4 Let's go to the leisure centre. / Why don't we go to the leisure centre? / What about going to the leisure centre? / Shall we go to the leisure centre?
5 Let's have an ice cream. / How about having an ice cream? / What about having an ice cream? / Shall we have an ice cream?
6 Read this novel. It's really good.
7 Read the instructions before you start. / You must read the instructions before you start. / It is important for you to read the instructions before you start. / It is essential that you read the instructions before you start.
8 Let's talk about it. / How about talking about it? / What about talking about it? / Shall we talk about it?
9 Never give up.
10 Come here, please.

2 1 E 2 A 3 F 4 G 5 H 6 B 7 C 8 D 9 J 10 I

3 1 P 2 A 3 S 4 OF 5 O 6 OF 7 S 8 P 9 A 10 OF 11 O 12 S

4 1 c 2 j 3 h 4 d 5 a 6 i 7 f 8 e 9 g 10 b

5
1 Do you have piano lessons (every Monday)?
2 Does she (ever) eat meat?
3 Do they like the mountains? / Do they spend any time in the mountains? / Do they ever go to the Alps / mountains?
4 What language(s) do you study (as a foreign language)?
5 How often do you have basketball practice?
6 Which dress do you prefer?
7 Where does your sister work? / What does your sister do?
8 Where do your parents live?
9 What do you do at the weekend? / When do you go jogging?
10 Do you (ever / often) go to the theatre?
11 Do you ever go to the mountains in summer?
12 Where's the Sales Manager's office? / Which floor is the Sales Manager's office on?
13 What does your grandfather do in the evening?
14 How often do you go to the cinema? / What do you do once a week?

6 1 Get me 2 Get me 3 go and see 4 can sign 5 you say 6 Turn down 7 give me 8 Why don't you

7 1 says 2 catches 3 sleep 4 catch 5 like 6 go 7 work 8 finish 9 gets up 10 goes 11 prefer

8 1 it / them 2 they 3 me 4 us 5 I 6 you 7 you

Reflecting on grammar

1 T 2 F 3 F 4 T 5 F 6 T 7 F 8 T 9 F 10 T

UNIT 6

LESSON 1

1 putting watching leaving writing entering answering reading asking lying dancing hitting thinking living trying behaving staying marveling (USA) working transmitting committing suffering referring waiting stopping dyeing typing changing playing painting copying rising getting shouting

2
1 Playing tennis is one of his favourite activities. N
2 I'm having a geography lesson in a few minutes. V
3 She really loves working out in the gym. N
4 Oh dear! That's such a heartbreaking story! A
5 We're leaving for Paris next week. V
6 That is shocking news. A
7 Congrats! You're doing a really great job. V
8 Most people are interested in learning English. N

3
1 Dad is cooking an exotic meal tonight.
2 Knitting is Rachel's favourite hobby.
3 I enjoy drawing and painting / painting and drawing.
4 Her performance was so disappointing!
5 Learning Japanese is really challenging.
6 This is a deeply moving film.

LESSON 2

1 1 are doing 2 is wearing 3 is / 's having 4 are walking 5 is / 's watching 6 are playing 7 is / 's getting 8 am / 'm writing 9 are / 're buying 10 is / 's texting

2 1 's filing 2 's studying 3 's talking 4 are running 5 's leaving 6 're lying 7 are staying 8 is having 9 's having 10 's working

3
1 The secretary isn't filing some / any documents.
2 My brother isn't studying at San Francisco State University.
3 The President isn't talking to Congress right now.
4 The students aren't running to their class because they're early / they aren't late.
5 The ship isn't leaving New York harbour.
6 We aren't lying in the sun.

7 My friends aren't staying at a four-star hotel by the sea.
8 Ms Sunis isn't having lunch at the moment.
9 Dad isn't busy right now.
10 Sam isn't working on the roof.

4
1 Julie isn't reading a magazine.
2 My parents aren't meeting their friends.
3 You aren't studying history.
4 They aren't drinking tea.
5 Ben isn't playing football.
6 I'm not going to the park this afternoon.
7 They aren't filing documents.

5
1 am not / 'm not studying, am / 'm studying
2 is not / isn't playing **3** are cooking
4 am not / 'm not enjoying **5** are sleeping
6 am not / 'm not playing, am / 'm, writing
7 are not / aren't going, are coming

6 **1** E **2** D **3** A **4** F **5** B **6** C

7
1 Is your brother sleeping on the sofa? Yes, he is.
2 Are Jo and Tamsin acting in the school play? Yes, they are.
3 Isn't she watching TV tonight? Yes, she is.
4 Are they having breakfast now? No, they aren't. / No, they're not.
5 Isn't Tom ironing his shirts? No, he isn't. / No, he's not.
6 Aren't you studying for your test tomorrow? Yes, I am / we are.
7 Is the train leaving in ten minutes? No, it isn't. / No, it's not.
8 Is Rob taking part in the tennis tournament? Yes, he is.

8
1 Aren't / Are you staying at home (this afternoon)?
2 Are you going out?
3 Are you listening to your favourite rock band?
4 Aren't / Are you chatting with Tom?
5 Why aren't you doing any / your homework (today)?
6 Why are they running?
7 Who are you playing with? / What are you doing with your little sister?

9 **1** F **2** C **3** E **4** A **5** B **6** D

10
1 always **2** tonight **3** these **4** this / next
5 right **6** next / this **7** nowadays **8** tomorrow

11
1 is / 's, waiting **2** is / 's talking **3** is / 's sitting
4 (is) drinking **5** is / 's carrying **6** walking
7 isn't / is not, walking **8** is / 's running
9 is / 's calling

LESSON 3

1
1 I'm spending **2** Do you collect **3** You're always making **4** is not going **5** are visiting
6 usually eat **7** works **8** is watching

2
1 read, am / 'm reading **2** does, is / 's cooking
3 cycles, is / 's raining, is / 's driving **4** shines
5 is / 's setting

3 🎧 **04** **1** Do, live **2** live **3** do you do **4** run **5** grow
6 'm staying **7** are opening **8** 're having

4
1 can't hear **2** is enjoying **3** hate **4** doesn't mind
5 are seeing **6** Do you like **7** Do you think
8 is having **9** knows **10** Do you want
11 Do you remember **12** I'm hating **13** I enjoy
14 are you thinking

5
1 are you thinking **2** do you remember
3 don't know **4** lives **5** 're / are cooperating
6 Don't you usually work **7** 's / is enjoying

LESSON 4

1
1 to eat **2** smoking **3** getting **4** talking
5 moving **6** eating **7** working **8** to have
9 driving **10** helping

2
1 eating **2** to have **3** to meet
4 to meet / meeting **5** watching **6** washing
7 skiing **8** to learn / learning **9** singing
10 drinking

3
1 Keep ~~to work~~ **working** and you'll get a promotion.
2 I'd love ~~touring~~ **to tour** the Australian outback.
3 He denied ~~to steal~~ **stealing** the gold necklace.
4 I'd like ~~talking~~ **to talk** to the manager, please.
5 My son always avoids ~~to help~~ **helping** with the housework!
6 Don't forget ~~buying~~ **to buy** some bread for tonight.
7 Do you miss ~~to live~~ **living** in a big city?
8 I always stop ~~buying~~ **to buy** the newspaper on my way to work.
9 I often fancy ~~to tour~~ **touring** Iceland in the summer.
10 Why don't we stop here ~~having~~ **to have** breakfast?

4
1 telling **2** to wake up **3** running **4** running
5 to be **6** to avoid **7** doing **8** to say

ROUND UP 6

1
1 to find **2** to talk **3** to abandon **4** to go
5 to buy **6** to play **7** to do **8** to give **9** to leave
10 to become **11** to get up **12** to see

2
1 crying **2** smoking **3** acting, dancing / dancing, acting **4** Cooking **5** rising **6** bullying **7** raising
8 talking

3
1 working **2** cooking **3** cleaning **4** to help
5 helping **6** to help **7** to stop **8** to employ
9 to help **10** paying

4
1 am staying **2** go **3** lie **4** don't swim
5 am going **6** am looking **7** are you doing
8 Are you studying

5 1 lives 2 works 3 gets 4 starts 5 finishes 6 gets 7 goes 8 meets 9 is / 's looking 10 is / 's staying 11 does not / doesn't have 12 is / 's having / has 13 is / 's getting up 14 is / 's going 15 is / 's dating 16 are / 're going back 17 wants

6 1 NV 2 NV 3 PP 4 G 5 PP 6 G

Reflecting on grammar
1 T 2 T 3 F 4 F 5 T 6 F 7 T 8 T 9 F 10 T

REVISION AND EXAMS 2

1 1 Discover / Admire 2 Rent 3 admire / discover 4 Ride 5 observe 6 Finish 7 don't forget

2 1 Keep 2 Don't leave 3 Remember / Don't forget 4 Use 5 take 6 Put 7 Don't smoke 8 Don't forget / Remember

3 1 Are you having 2 keep 3 remember 4 learn 5 write 6 Write 7 helps 8 am / 'm trying 9 am / 'm writing 10 am / 'm talking 11 do 12 are / 're using 13 are / 're 14 are / 're saying

4 1 lives 2 work 3 send 4 pass 5 organise 6 do 7 starts 8 sleeps 9 has 10 goes 11 meet 12 go

5 1 is / 's getting up, is / 's, sleeping 2 is / 's having, is / 's starting 3 are, working, is / 's , is / 's 4 are / 're having 5 is / 's going, is / 's, working 6 are meeting, are / 're looking

6 1 span 2 offers 3 offers 4 are teaching 5 enrol 6 opens 7 closes 8 're / are carrying out 9 is 10 Visit

7 Students' own answers

8 1 Do 2 it / them 3 but 4 take / share 5 because 6 don't 7 do 8 because / as 9 so 10 and

SELF CHECK
1 B 2 B 3 C 4 A 5 B 6 A 7 B 8 A 9 A 10 C 11 B 12 C 13 B 14 C 15 B 16 C 17 A 18 C 19 B 20 C 21 A 22 B 23 C 24 B 25 A 26 A 27 B 28 C 29 C 30 C 31 B 32 C 33 B 34 A 35 C 36 A 37 C 38 B 39 C 40 B

UNIT 7

LESSON 1

1 1 in 2 at 3 on 4 in the 5 In, at 6 at 7 at 8 at

2 1 on 2 at 3 on 4 in 5 in 6 in 7 at 8 on 9 on 10 in 11 in 12 in, in

3 1 In, for 2 after 3 in, Till 4 from 5 for, until 6 during, at 7 by 8 over 9 within 10 until

4 1 for 2 between 3 from, to 4 during 5 since 6 by 7 in 8 before

5 1 I often study **at** night.
2 Are you free on Monday **between / from** five **and / to** six?
3 What do you usually do **on** Christmas Day?
4 We have to hand in our essays **by** next Monday.
5 We like sleeping until late **on** Sundays.

LESSON 2

1 1 on 2 on, at 3 in 4 in, at 5 on 6 over / on, over 7 in, in

2 1 next 2 along 3 from 4 in front 5 around 6 off 7 between 8 opposite 9 behind 10 among

3 1 to 2 on, to 3 to 4 past 5 for 6 - - - 7 along 8 off

4 1 from 2 at 3 for 4 along 5 into, through 6 up to 7 away from 8 out of 9 to 10 as far as

5 1 down, as far as 2 into, on 3 at, across 4 off, at, along 5 past, on 6 to 7 up, from 8 to, in 9 along 10 towards

LESSON 3

1 1 by, on 2 of, of 3 on 4 about 5 like 6 of 7 with 8 by 9 without 10 for

2 1 Show me your notebook, will you? ✓
2 Can you lend ~~to~~ me your credit card, Dad?
Can you **lend me** your credit card, Dad?
3 Dave gave a present to each of his nephews. ✓
4 Samantha explained ~~me her plans~~.
Samantha explained **her plans to me**.
5 'Take this basket to your grandmother,' said Little Red Riding Hood's mother to her daughter. ✓
6 She introduced the new assistant to the manager. ✓
7 Can you give him this document, please? ✓
8 They offered ~~to~~ us a very good meal.
They **offered us** a very good meal.
9 Why don't you dictate this letter to your secretary? ✓
10 We will deliver ~~our customers the goods~~ in two weeks.
We will deliver **the goods to our customers** in two weeks.
11 We must report ~~the manager the theft~~.
We must report **the theft to the manager**.
12 Could you bring me a glass of water, please? ✓

3
1 Can you give my friend a lift, please?
2 Can you lend me this book? I'd like to read it.
3 *This sentence can't change.*
4 Give your sister this paper, please.
5 If you like, I'll show you my photos.
6 They offered all the ladies a red rose.
7 *This sentence can't change.*
8 Have you sent Mr Wayne an email yet?
9 My neighbour told everybody the news.
10 The coach asked the players their names.

LESSON 4

1 1 keen 2 Sorry 3 surprised 4 angry 5 popular
6 bored 7 afraid / scared, scared / afraid
8 interested 9 good 10 happy

2 1 about 2 with 3 to 4 on 5 with 6 from / to
7 with 8 with

3
1 Aren't you surprised **to** see me here?
2 My father is interested **in learning** how to surf.
3 Mr Higgins is really angry **with** his son because he has just broken the kitchen window.
4 I am very keen **on** English.
5 I am quite worried **about** the Spanish test. I haven't studied much.
6 I'm not very happy **with** my job. I would like a change.
7 Is she married **to** the new doctor?
8 Come on! You can't be scared **of** bugs. They're harmless.
9 She's always been very fond **of** her grandmother. She visits her every day.
10 We are really disappointed **by / at / with** the quality of this project.
11 Are you aware **of** all the risks involved in using chemicals?
12 He's responsible **for** the whole marketing department.

4 1 H 2 A 3 F 4 B 5 D 6 E 7 C 8 G 9 J 10 I

5 1 on 2 of 3 from 4 about 5 in 6 about
7 for 8 for 9 for 10 after

6 1 about 2 about 3 after 4 with, about / on
5 in 6 from 7 about 8 for 9 for 10 to, about

7 1 ask 2 apologise 3 agree 4 get used
5 complain 6 borrows 7 arguing 8 looking
9 shouting 10 thank

8 1 look round 2 look after 3 look up
4 looking into 5 looked at 6 looked for

9 1 having 2 get 3 waiting 4 going 5 seeing
6 be 7 meet 8 find 9 be 10 play 11 go
12 working 13 tell 14 being

ROUND UP 7

1 1 at / on 2 in, in 3 at 4 on 5 on 6 on
7 on 8 in, in 9 in 10 on

2 1 without 2 on, to / from 3 about / on
4 for / from 5 by 6 to 7 to 8 at 9 in 10 on

3
1 I was born ~~in~~ **on** 8th October 2005.
2 I don't like being home alone ~~in the~~ **at** night.
3 We usually go ~~in~~ **to** the mountains for a week ~~on~~ **in** August.
4 *No mistakes in this sentence.*
5 *No mistakes in this sentence.*
6 I will be at home between four ~~to~~ **and** five in the afternoon tomorrow.
7 *No mistakes in this sentence.*
8 Go ~~until~~ **up to / as far as** the traffic lights and then turn ~~to~~ left.
9 *No mistakes in this sentence.*
10 Do you often go jogging ~~at~~ **in the** morning?

4
1 He lent his son his mobile.
2 Can you bring me that magazine, please?
3 Give my secretary your email address, will you?
4 They sent us a lot of photos when they were in Australia.
5 Will you please give your teacher this book?
6 We showed our friends our new car.
7 He sent his girlfriend a beautiful present for her birthday.
8 Take your dad the paper.

5 1 A 2 D 3 B 4 B 5 C 6 D 7 D 8 A 9 A 10 C

6 1 for 2 by 3 for 4 of 5 on 6 to, about 7 at
8 like 9 of 10 with

7 1 accusing 2 on 3 embarrassed 4 feel
5 on 6 of 7 for 8 of / about 9 for 10 protect

Reflecting on grammar

1 F 2 T 3 T 4 F 5 T 6 T 7 F 8 F 9 T 10 T

UNIT 8

LESSON 1

1
1 There were two (great) playgrounds.
2 There wasn't a restaurant.
3 There was a (beautiful) beach.
4 There were lots of tourists.
5 There were lots of camper vans.
6 There weren't any tents. / There were no tents.

🎧 05 **Tapescript**
A So, what was the campsite like? Was it good?
B Yes, it was great. There was a mini-market and there were two great playgrounds for the kids.
A Was there a restaurant?
B No, there wasn't. The best thing was the beautiful beach nearby – you walked along a path for two minutes and you were there, by the sea.
A Were there many tourists there?
B Yes, the campsite was nearly full. There were lots of camper vans but no tents when we were there!

2 1 was not / wasn't 2 was, was
3 was not / wasn't 4 were not / weren't
5 Was, was 6 was, was not / wasn't
7 was, were, were 8 Were, were

3 1 D 2 H 3 A 4 F 5 B 6 C 7 E 8 G

LESSON 2

1

Regular verbs		Irregular verbs	
Base form	Past simple	Base form	Past simple
stop	stopped	have	had
help	helped	know	knew
play	played	leave	left
shout	shouted	meet	met
work	worked	go	went
try	tried	tell	told
refer	referred	take	took
quarrel (UK)	quarrelled	read	read
submit	submitted	come	came
move	moved	speak	spoke

2 1 played 2 met 3 quarrelled / shouted
4 worked, moved 5 read 6 tried, tried 7 took
8 had 9 helped 10 submitted

3 1 had 2 took 3 had 4 got 5 felt 6 spent
7 saw 8 drove 9 saw 10 flew
11 crossed over *This is the only regular verb in the exercise.* 12 came across 13 was

4 a 1 stayed, didn't meet 2 had, didn't go
3 watched, didn't go 4 went, didn't stay up
b 1 Mr and Ms Steel didn't stay at home last night, they met their friends.
2 They didn't have dinner at home, they went to a restaurant.
3 They didn't watch a film on TV, they went to the cinema.
4 They didn't go to bed early, they stayed up late.

5 1 Did, enjoy, I / we did 2 Did, play, he didn't
3 Did, travel, they didn't 4 Did, work, she did
5 Did, have, I / we didn't 6 Did, come, he did

6 1 We didn't like the film at all.
2 Did you buy a return train ticket?
3 Didn't you check your emails this morning?
4 She didn't go out with Thomas last night.
5 Did she get up late on Sunday?
6 We didn't do our homework yesterday.
7 Did he repeat the same story over and over again?
8 They didn't want to leave the party so early.

7 06 1 Where did you buy, How much did you pay
2 What did you do, Who with 3 How did you, When did you get here 4 Where did you study, What did you study 5 What did you do, How did you book

LESSON 3

1 1 last 2 give 3 opens, opened 4 on
5 last 6 last 7 ago 8 this 9 before yesterday
10 last night

2 *Possible answers*
1 in March 2 in 2015 3 two days ago
4 last month 5 yesterday 6 at four o'clock
7 last week 8 when I was 15 9 in 2010
10 three months ago

3 1 After 2 First 3 then 4 After 5 then
6 first 7 After 8 Finally

4 *Possible answer*
Last Saturday, we went on a trip to Canterbury. First, we visited the cathedral. Then we had lunch in a fast-food restaurant. After that, we went around the shops and bought gifts. Finally, we had coffee and drove back home.

5 1 First pre-heat the oven to 180°C.
2 To make the dough, mix the butter and sugar together.
3 When the butter and sugar mixture is light and fluffy, beat in the egg and slowly add the flour.
4 Then break up the chocolate into small pieces and put them into the mixture.
5 After greasing a baking sheet, put about 20 teaspoonfuls of the mixture onto it.
6 Then bake in the oven for 15 to 20 minutes until the cookies are golden brown.
7 Finally, put them on a wire rack to cool.

6 1 Did your brother use to be a boy scout?
2 Jane used to dye her hair red when she was younger.
3 I used to study long hours when I was at college.
4 We didn't use to have mobile phones or MP3 players.
5 My family used to run a youth hostel in the town centre.
6 Where did you use to go dancing in the old days?

7 1 used to have 2 did not / didn't use to buy
3 used to make 4 used to hang up 5 did not / didn't use to sleep 6 did not / didn't use to have
7 used to act 8 used to sing

8 1 There used to be a fountain in this park.
2 We used to wear a uniform when we were in / at primary school.
3 I went out after closing all the windows and switching off the lights.
4 Before going skateboarding in the park, I helped my grandma with the shopping.
5 My husband drove for five hours before stopping at a service area.
6 My father used to help me with my homework when I was little.
7 The last time I missed a day's work was two years ago.
8 I was last in bed with flu during the Christmas holidays three years ago.

LESSON 4

1 1 H 2 E 3 I 4 F 5 C 6 G 7 A 8 D 9 J 10 B

2 🎧 07 1 Were - wearing, was wearing 2 Was - driving, was studying 3 were - doing, was working 4 arguing, was making, was watching 5 wasn't driving, were going

3 1 D 2 A 3 C 4 F 5 B 6 G 7 E

4
1 While I was walking in the street, I saw a bad accident.
2 While we were all cheering, a group of hooligans invaded the football pitch.
3 While they were going home, they saw an old friend getting off the bus.
4 While the actors were getting ready for the shoot, the director suddenly left.
5 While I was doing my homework, my friend was waiting for me in the hall.
6 While I was talking to the English teacher, the principal came into the library.
7 While we were having a drink, a band started playing folk music.
8 While the exam students were still writing, the final bell rang.

5
1 was cycling, saw
2 came / was coming, was baking
3 was trying, went off
4 opened, heard
5 was dreaming, jumped, woke (her) up

ROUND UP 8

1 1 was 2 were 3 was 4 was 5 were 6 weren't 7 was 8 were 9 weren't 10 was 11 wasn't 12 was 13 wasn't 14 wasn't

2 1 was born 2 studied 3 didn't go 4 was 5 married 6 had 7 left 8 became 9 started 10 wrote 11 started 12 bought 13 retired 14 died

3
1 I cycled to my grandma's every Sunday.
2 We (always) learnt / learned nursery rhymes by heart when we were in primary school.
3 He worked six days a week for his former company.
4 My mother cooked fresh vegetables every day.
5 They (always) went to an organic market to buy local cheeses when they lived in Lincoln.
6 I walked a lot when I was younger.
7 She never took / didn't take her sister with her.
8 Did you have a red motorcycle years ago?

4 1 Five minutes ago 2 Three hours ago 3 Last night 4 Yesterday morning 5 Last week 6 Two months ago 7 Last year

5 1 were watching TV 2 was going back home 3 was waiting 4 went out 5 was 6 lasted 7 got back home 8 went to bed

6 1 spread 2 didn't reach 3 came 4 began 5 spread 6 grew 7 developed 8 started 9 became

7 1 Were (you) sleeping 2 was checking 3 did (you) get 4 got 5 Did (you) enjoy 6 had 7 met 8 did (you) meet 9 was walking 10 saw 11 was 12 knew 13 was 14 was 15 left 16 heard 17 was (he) doing

8 1 to 2 were 3 had 4 was 5 used 6 lot 7 While 8 After 9 As / Since / Because 10 danced

9 1 was sleeping 2 rang 3 answered 4 didn't hear 5 put 6 tried 7 rang 8 decided 9 was dialling 10 saw 11 was walking 12 (was) searching 13 answered 14 whispered 15 tried 16 was happening 17 was waiting 18 hid 19 was doing 20 was getting 21 heard

10 *Possible answer*
I was very scared, but I opened the door. My neighbour stood there with a torch in his hand and his cat under his arm. 'I'm so sorry,' he said. 'I lost my cat and my mobile phone. I just found them both in your garden shed ... and I think my cat pressed the speed-dial number for your house by mistake. Did you get some strange phone calls?' I was very relieved, but it took quite a lot of explaining when the police arrived ...

Reflecting on grammar

1 T 2 T 3 F 4 F 5 F 6 T 7 F 8 F 9 T 10 F

UNIT 9

LESSON 1

1 1 've lost 2 haven't planted 3 've tried 4 's moved 5 haven't done 6 've had 7 haven't watered 8 've, liked 9 haven't washed 10 Have you ordered, haven't brought

2 🎧 08 1 Have, checked B 2 have, bought C 3 Has, arrived D 4 Have, built F 5 Have, seen A 6 has, cooked E

3 1 been 2 been 3 gone 4 been 5 gone 6 gone 7 gone 8 gone 9 been 10 been

4 1 ever 2 ever 3 ever 4 never 5 never 6 never

5
1 My son has never lived on his own before.
2 Have you ever thought of moving abroad?
3 I've never seen such a beautiful picture!
4 Have you done any research so far?
5 It's been hot and sunny all day today.
6 We have never been there.
7 Has your team won a match so far this year?
8 She has never worked in a restaurant before!

6 1 F 2 D 3 A 4 G 5 E 6 B 7 H 8 C

452

LESSON 2

1
1 just 2 still 3 just 4 yet, yet 5 just
6 just / already, yet 7 yet, still 8 already
9 already

2
Possible answers
1 We have never tried bungee jumping.
2 They have already seen this film.
3 I have just written my history project.
4 My sister has already read this novel.
5 He has just booked a flight to New York.
6 She has never played the xylophone.

3
1 She has already bought some bags of sweets for the kids.
2 She hasn't decorated the birthday cake yet.
3 She hasn't put the marquee up in the garden yet.
4 She has already organised some games.
5 She hasn't asked Martha for some more chairs yet.
6 She has already bought some balloons and party hats.

4
1 G 2 D 3 J 4 A 5 I 6 C 7 H 8 E 9 F 10 B

5
1 lived, came 2 have been 3 got up, didn't have
4 have lived 5 have read 6 hasn't been
7 have had, haven't found 8 stayed
9 didn't have, were 10 Have you ever been

6
1 I haven't tidied my bedroom yet. PP
2 She tidied her bedroom last Saturday. PS
3 Has Louise got back from France yet? PP
4 When did Louise get back from France? PS
5 Guess who I have just seen in town! PP
6 I saw an old friend of mine at the theatre last night. PS
7 My brother has already graduated from high school. PP
8 I graduated from high school last year. PS

7
1 had, was, Have you ever tried
2 've already done, went, saw, haven't visited
3 've just got back
4 Have you booked, did
5 've already bought, still haven't bought
6 didn't go, 've already been
7 've never been
8 's just phoned, arrived

8
1 Mark Have you ever visited the Tate Modern? / Have you visited the Tate Modern yet?
Julie Yes, I have.
Mark When did you go?
Julie I went yesterday afternoon.
2 Adam Have you ever been camping?
Rick Yes, I have.
Adam Did you like it?
Rick Yes (, I did). It was a great experience.
3 Brad Have you ever been to Australia?
Frances Yes(, I have). I've been twice.
Brad Did you stay long?
Frances I stayed for two weeks the first time and three weeks the second time.
Brad Which cities did you visit?
Frances I visited Sydney and Melbourne.

LESSON 3

1

FOR	SINCE
ten minutes	yesterday
two years	March 2015
an hour	last month
centuries	last week
a long time	five o'clock
ages	1998

2
1 have lived, since 2 has been, since
3 have known, for, since 4 have wanted, since
5 have lived, since 6 has owned, for
7 have / 've been, since, have / 've taught, for
8 have worked, for, since

3 🎧 09
1 have you known 2 have / 've known
3 did you, see 4 saw 5 came 6 did he get married 7 have they known 8 met 9 have been 10 have you heard 11 haven't heard
12 has / 's been

4
1 I haven't been to New York for ten years.
2 We haven't had dinner in a restaurant since my birthday.
3 The last time I had a long holiday was the summer of 2016.
4 I bought this Harley Davidson three years ago.
5 I've been a Manchester City fan since I was five years old.
6 They became best friends a long, long time ago.
7 He was in a club for three hours last night, from 11 to 2 am.
8 We haven't had a heavy snowfall since the winter of 2014.
9 Carol and Richard met in 2011 and (they) got married in 2012.
10 They last played tennis together last year.

5
1 Mr Reed has been teaching Class 3. They have designed a school web page.
2 The students in Class 2 have been reading their study notes. They have revised things for their exams.
3 The ICT teacher has been tutoring a small group. They have learnt / learned InDesign.
4 Our English class has been looking at the present perfect. I / We have done this exercise.
5 The headteacher has been writing end-of-term reports. He / She has nearly finished all the reports.
6 Mrs Seath has been revising French irregular verbs. She has read out a list of difficult verbs.

6 1 A 2 A 3 B 4 B 5 A 6 A 7 B 8 B

7
1 have / 've been learning — D
2 have / 've been working — F
3 have / 've been waiting — A
4 have / 've been walking — H
5 has been teaching — B
6 have / 've been trying — C
7 has / 's been playing — E
8 have / 've been practising — G

8
1 [Since when] have you been singing in the school choir?
2 [Has] it been raining all afternoon [there]?
3 [How long] have [the kids] been playing?
4 Have [you] been studying [chemistry]?
5 [How long] have you been eating [for]?
6 [What kind of music] have [you] been listening [to]?
7 [What] have you been doing [this afternoon]?
8 [Since when] have you been working [on your computer]?

9
1 I've been working on this project for five days.
2 Peter has / 's been working out in the gym for two hours.
3 I've been telling you over and over again how to behave. Why don't you ever listen to me?
4 It's been snowing for three hours, since 9 pm.
5 The boys have been swimming for an hour to train for their next event.

10 🎧10 1 Have, ordered; have, ordered 2 have, been doing; have been sleeping; reading; watching; have you been watching; have been watching 3 's been cooking; has, been cooking; has made 4 haven't looked up; have, been reading; have, finished 5 Have - tried

LESSON 4

1 1 A 2 A 3 B 4 A 5 A 6 B

2
1 had, begun 2 got, had, gone
3 had eaten, walked 4 opened, had drunk
5 had, bought 6 came, had not / hadn't seen
7 had, got 8 had not / hadn't studied

3
1 had been looking for — D 2 had done — A
3 had had — H 4 had been — B 5 had met — G
6 had attended — C 7 had been watching — E
8 had been driving — F 9 had been tidying — J
10 had already finished — I

4
1 had been 2 had been 3 went 4 had
5 had been shouting 6 had been hoping
7 have 8 had been 9 got 10 had been

5
1 had not / hadn't been 2 had 3 'd / had been looking forward 4 visited 5 'd / had never met
6 (had) organised 7 stayed 8 was 9 'd / had missed 10 was

ROUND UP 9

1 1 B 2 C 3 A 4 C 5 B 6 A 7 B 8 C

2
1 have / 've been 2 has not / hasn't disappointed
3 have / 've been 4 have already seen
5 have / 've just come back 6 built 7 got 8 was
9 ate 10 bought 11 have not / haven't had
12 have / 've always found / always find
13 have / 've been teaching 14 have / 've never felt 15 got 16 gave up 17 have / 've ever done 18 has / 's already got 19 has / 's been telling me / has / 's told me / tells 20 have / 've booked

3
1 lived 2 was looking 3 came 4 'd / had found
5 (had) lived 6 couldn't / could not 7 asked
8 were imagining / imagined 9 broke 10 had thrown

4
1 started studying / to study three hours
2 While we were standing
3 I've / I have / I'd / I had ever walked
4 's / has been working on her project since
5 When we got, were already open
6 we got to the theatre, had already started.
7 's / has (only) been waiting for a short time
8 've / have (only) worked out little

5
1 got 2 realised 3 had happened 4 had broken
5 opened 6 had moved 7 'd / had left 8 was
9 'd / had cleared up 10 left 11 phoned
12 'd / had been

6
1 decided 2 did not / didn't have 3 went
4 bought 5 had 6 decided 7 went 8 asked
9 could not / couldn't 10 searched 11 said
12 have / 've lost 13 said 14 came 15 left
16 found 17 caught 18 went 19 asked
20 was 21 told 22 'd / had lost
23 (had) had 24 said 25 have / 've found

7
1 'd / had had 2 ('d / had) interviewed
3 received 4 'd / had been looking 5 arrived
6 took 7 did not / didn't show 8 felt
9 have / 've been working 10 have / 've been

8
1 arrived 2 had already closed 3 had 4 was
5 were waiting 6 was 7 was going 8 had told
9 'd / had wanted 10 hadn't / had not left

9
1 danced / were dancing
2 'd / had been practising 3 took part 4 were
5 were waiting 6 talked / were talking 7 was
8 'd / had never seen 9 had never danced
10 had performed 11 announced 12 had won
13 'd / had never been

Reflecting on grammar

1 F 2 F 3 F 4 T 5 T 6 T 7 T 8 F 9 F 10 T

REVISION AND EXAMS 3

1 1 into 2 to 3 down 4 to 5 into 6 at 7 on 8 to 9 out of

2 Roy Brooks ~~gets~~ **got** up at 9.00 on Monday 11th May 2015 and ~~has~~ **had** breakfast on the terrace of his penthouse overlooking the bay. He usually has a big breakfast, but ~~this~~ **that** morning he only ~~has~~ **had** a cup of green tea.
He ~~feeds~~ **fed** his dogs, two giant black Schnauzers, and plays **played** with them for half an hour. After ~~washing and getting dressed~~ he **had washed** and **(he had) got dressed**, he ~~leaves~~ **left** home at about 11.00 and ~~drives~~ **drove** to his office downtown. At 11.30, he ~~parks~~ **parked** his car in his office parking lot and ~~takes~~ **took** the elevator to the 27th floor, where his secretary ~~greets~~ **greeted** him with a cup of coffee.
He ~~doesn't~~ **didn't** have any lunch ~~today~~ **that day**. At 3.00, a South-American man ~~goes~~ **went** into Roy's office and they ~~talk~~ **talked** for about an hour. Just before the man ~~leaves~~ **left** the office, Roy ~~is shouting~~ **had been shouting** some words in Spanish. When the man ~~leaves~~ **left**, Roy ~~is~~ **was** visibly upset and ~~makes~~ **made** a few telephone calls.
At 6.00, he ~~takes~~ **took** a taxi to The Fox and Hunter, a fashionable bar on Columbus Avenue, where his girlfriend Linda ~~is waiting~~ **had been waiting / was waiting** for him. They ~~have~~ **had** a Martini, ~~leave~~ **left** the bar and ~~walk~~ **walked** to a nearby Chinese restaurant, Chow Mei. They ~~have~~ **had** dinner there and Roy ~~talks~~ **talked** to the Chinese restaurant manager for quite a long time. At 10.30, a driver they ~~have~~ **had** never seen before picks **picked** them up and ~~drives~~ **drove** them towards the harbour.

3 1 had been sitting 2 had 3 was 4 had been 5 has always been 6 reminded 7 were chatting

4 1 became 2 established 3 housed 4 withdrew 5 fell 6 became 7 were 8 gave 9 invaded 10 established 11 flourished 12 declined 13 entered 14 became 15 helped

5 1 B 2 A 3 B 4 A 5 B 6 B 7 A 8 A 9 A 10 A

6 1 B 2 A 3 C 4 B 5 A 6 D 7 A 8 B 9 A 10 C

7 1 have been our 2 used to be 3 've / have been sitting 4 had been cooking for 5 his favourite cartoons for hours 6 've / have known Susan for ten 7 have / 've already tidied my 8 have / 've just seen your sister

SELF CHECK 3

1 B 2 B 3 C 4 B 5 C 6 C 7 A 8 C 9 B 10 C
11 B 12 A 13 C 14 B 15 A 16 B 17 B 18 A
19 B 20 A 21 C 22 B 23 A 24 B 25 B 26 B
27 A 28 A 29 C 30 C 31 B 32 B 33 B 34 A
35 B 36 C 37 B 38 C 39 A 40 C

UNIT 10

LESSON 1

1

smartly	hungrily	notably	ideally	truly
softly	angrily	possibly	politically	idly
quickly	easily	comfortably	beautifully	
cheaply	lazily	probably	socially	
freely	luckily	honourably	practically	
impressively				incredibly

2 1 well, quickly 2 correctly, perfect 3 good 4 simple 5 beautiful 6 delicious 7 hard, hardly 8 wonderfully

3 1 The computer system was seriously damaged by a virus.
2 Harrison Ford is totally unrecognisable in this film.
3 Your lasagne is good. You always cook it incredibly well. / Your lasagne is incredibly good. You always cook it well.
4 It's highly improbable that they will be here tomorrow.
5 Dear me! It's terribly late. I must hurry up.
6 They have been happily married for over 20 years.

4 1 quietly 2 hard 3 carefully 4 well 5 easily 6 fast

5 1 Luckily 2 different, hardly 3 angrily 4 Lately, well 5 friendly 6 easily 7 carefully 8 correctly 9 delicious

LESSON 2

1 1 I had quite a good result in yesterday's test.
2 Their performance was absolutely perfect.
3 We watched quite an enjoyable film last night.
4 It's rather late, but the shop is still open.
5 They can dance pretty well.
6 Were there enough chairs for everybody?
7 The hotel was a fairly modern building.
8 This package holiday is way too expensive for what it offers.

2 1 extremely 2 not very 3 not at all 4 rather 5 too 6 fairly 7 too 8 enough

3 **normal** ugly, happy, excited, scared, nice, sad cold, nervous, angry, afraid
strong marvellous, astonishing, furious freezing, fantastic, frantic

4 1 so 2 really 3 quite 4 quite a hard 5 absolutely 6 really 7 such a 8 long enough

5
1 We had a really nice holiday last summer.
2 The palace was so big that we got lost.
3 He is quite a good actor.
4 It isn't warm enough to swim in the lake.
5 It's such a cute little dog.
6 It's rather a dull autumn day.

6
1 He's <u>enough old</u> to cook his own meals.
   He's **old enough** to cook his own meals.
2 It's <u>a so exciting</u> thriller. It keeps you on edge until the end.
   It's **such an exciting** thriller. It keeps you on edge until the end.
3 I could <u>hard</u> understand what she was saying.
   I could **hardly** understand what she was saying.
4 The view from the hotel terrace is <u>very amazing</u>.
   The view from the hotel terrace is **absolutely amazing**.
5 We bought <u>a quite cheap</u> dishwasher but it broke after a couple of years.
   We bought **quite a cheap** dishwasher but it broke after a couple of years.
6 My son <u>likes a lot</u> cooking.
   My son **likes cooking a lot**.

7 1 too 2 so, hardly 3 really 4 quite 5 much

LESSON 3

1 1 a lot of 2 many, a lot of 3 much
4 many, many 5 a lot of 6 much

2 1 Too 2 too 3 many 4 much 5 too 6 many
7 too 8 much 9 much 10 much 11 too busy
12 too

3 1 many 2 many 3 much 4 many 5 plenty of
6 All 7 Most 8 enough 9 loads of 10 enough

4
1 There aren't enough sandwiches for all these people.
2 The room isn't big enough for the party.
3 We have seen enough of this film.
4 He hasn't studied enough to pass this test.
5 Harry isn't old enough to have his own credit card.

5 1 many / enough 2 many / most 3 enough
4 much 5 many, enough 6 most, all

LESSON 4

1 1 little 2 a little 3 a few 4 a few 5 a few
6 few 7 a little 8 little

2 1 a few, none 2 much 3 hardly any 4 few
5 a little 6 a lot of 7 a few 8 Not many
9 hardly any 10 none

3 1 B 2 D 3 B 4 C 5 B 6 C 7 B

4 1 much information 2 warm enough
3 a few ethnic restaurants 4 much traffic
5 much traffic at this time 6 take no risks
7 such an irresistible rhythm that everyone started

5 1 a little 2 few 3 a little 4 very little 5 many
6 much 7 many 8 a few 9 very little

ROUND UP 10

1 1 too / very / really 2 really / very 3 absolutely
4 quite 5 such, really / very 6 so 7 at all
8 slightly / a bit 9 slightly / a bit
10 really / rather / very / so / quite / slightly / a bit
11 just / absolutely / really, so

2 1 quietly 2 straight 3 fluently 4 beautifully
5 Luckily 6 well 7 hard 8 enthusiastically
9 unfortunately

3 1 all the 2 the whole 3 all 4 All of 5 all of / all
6 all 7 all / all of 8 The whole

4
1 It's too good to be true.
2 There's too much salt in the soup.
3 There isn't enough sugar in my coffee.
4 There's too much noise in this room.
5 The shops are too crowded on the first day of the sales.
6 There are too many people here today.
7 I haven't got enough money for the ticket.
8 This table isn't large enough.

5 1 some 2 some 3 How much 4 enough
5 any 6 How many 7 some 8 a little 9 finely
10 slowly 11 gently 12 delicious

6 1 very 2 (very) much 3 a few 4 fairly 5 any
6 (very) much 7 very / fairly 8 a few 9 actually
10 a little

7 1 a few 2 quite a 3 All of us 4 the most
5 all 6 quite 7 rather 8 so few 9 a bit
10 especially 11 whole 12 completely
13 slightly 14 definitely

8 1 Unfortunately 2 unpredictable 3 amazing
4 glowing 5 commonly 6 mainly

Reflecting on grammar

1 F 2 F 3 T 4 F 5 T 6 F 7 F 8 T 9 F 10 T

UNIT 11

LESSON 1

1

Adjective + –er	Adjective + –ier	More + adjective
taller	healthier	more intelligent
slimmer	drier	more dangerous
smarter	heavier	more interesting
cheaper	trendier	more successful
hotter	luckier	more important
brighter	prettier	more beautiful

2
1 This building is tall. The other one is taller.
2 This suitcase is heavy. The other one is heavier.
3 This T-shirt is cheap. The other one is cheaper.
4 Yesterday was hot. Today is hotter.
5 This boy is clever. The other one is cleverer / more clever.
6 This land is dry. The other (land) is drier.

3
1 cheaper than   2 cleverer / more clever than
3 more difficult than   4 more careful
5 more successful than   6 healthier, healthier
7 warmer, than   8 nicer, than   9 faster
10 kinder, kinder

4
1 far / a lot / much more exciting
2 far / much / a lot quieter   3 darker, darker
4 much / a lot / far more expensive, much / a lot / far more comfortable
5 much / a lot / far hotter   6 thinner, thinner

5
Possible answers
1 I think living in a big city is more exciting than living in the country, but living in the country is much cheaper.
2 I think adventure films are far more exciting than comedies, but comedies are nicer.
3 I think cycling is a lot more tiring than walking, but cycling is much healthier.
4 I think travelling by train is more expensive than travelling by car, but travelling by car is far easier.
5 I think working in an office is more boring than working in the open air, but working in the open air is far more tiring.
6 I think doing yoga is a lot more relaxing than going jogging, but going jogging is much healthier.
7 I think golf is far more relaxing than football, but football is much better.

LESSON 2

1
1 Mr Johnson's lessons are usually less boring than Mr Riley's.
2 The blue coat is less expensive than the brown one.
3 My suitcase is less heavy than yours.
4 This building is a less modern style than the other one.
5 Today it's less warm than yesterday.
6 This TV series is less exciting than the one on Channel 4.
7 It's less likely to rain this afternoon.

2
1 She's just as beautiful as her sister.
2 Luckily I'm not so/as busy today as I was yesterday.
3 Bob Dylan is as famous as Bruce Springsteen.
4 This article is not so/as interesting as the one in *TIME* magazine.
5 The show was as exciting as a cold rice pudding!
6 Their latest concert was just as good as last year's.
7 The Rolling Stones were as popular as The Beatles in the 1960s.

3
1 Claire is as old as Karen.
2 Today is as hot as yesterday.
3 The blue jacket is not as expensive as the black jacket.
4 Their flat is not as large as our flat.
5 The history book is not as big as the grammar book.
6 The Ohio river is not as long as the Mississippi.
7 The Breithorn is not as high as Mont Blanc.
8 Oxford is as far from here as Salisbury.

4
1 Cross-country skiing isn't as risky as alpine skiing or snowboarding.
2 A small tent isn't as comfortable as a campervan.
3 This song isn't as famous as the others on her latest album.
4 Baseball isn't as popular in Italy as football.
5 She hasn't been as successful in her career as her sister.
6 My scooter isn't as sporty as your motorbike.

LESSON 3

1
1 the largest   2 the oldest   3 newest
4 the busiest   5 the most careful
6 the most exclusive   7 the most exciting
8 the smallest

2
1 in   2 of   3 in   4 of   5 of   6 in   7 in   8 of   9 in

3
1 This is one of the most exciting football matches we have ever seen.
2 Mrs Ray is the most competent teacher I've ever met.
3 This is by far the best career opportunity Jack has ever had.
4 It's one of the most moving stories I've ever read.

4
1 G Last night's fireworks display was the most spectacular we had / 'd ever seen.
2 A This is the biggest pumpkin they have / 've ever grown.
3 F This is the most comfortable armchair I have / 've ever tried.
4 B I have / 've ever heard.
5 C That was the steepest path we had / 'd ever walked up.

6 E I'm having fun in Ibiza. It's the most exciting holiday I have / 've ever had.
7 H George thought that was the hardest exam he had / 'd ever taken.

5 1 best 2 worst 3 oldest 4 farthest / furthest
5 best 6 latest 7 eldest 8 last 9 worst
10 farthest / furthest

6 1 the least useful thing 2 the least exciting match 3 the least amusing programme
4 the least complicated person 5 the least interesting place 6 the least popular resort
7 the least expensive bag 8 the least relevant thing 9 the least flattering 10 the least impressive attempt

LESSON 4

1 1 as 2 longest 3 more 4 later, longer 5 more
6 better 7 higher 8 less, than 9 more, more
10 further, smaller

2 1 I'm sure I can run as fast as you.
2 This term I haven't studied as hard as last term.
3 Paula always works harder than everyone else.
4 The film festival started later this year.
5 They climbed higher than ever before.
6 The last journey took us longer than usual.
7 He speaks the most quickly when he's nervous.
8 The earlier you leave, the less traffic you'll find.

3 1 Today we have as many guests in our restaurant as we had yesterday, 20. / Yesterday we had as many guests in our restaurant as we have today, 20.
2 We took as much time to clean the house as (we did) to prepare dinner.
3 The conference room on the first floor has as many seats as the one on the ground floor, 50. / There are as many seats in the conference room on the first floor as there are in the one on the ground floor, 50.
4 There are as many fish in the aquarium as (there are) in the pond, 12.
5 Italy got as many gold medals as Belarus in the Baku 2015 European Games, ten.
6 Paul has as many elephants as Lawrence in his collection, 550.

4 1 less 2 more / better than, best 3 less, than, least 4 as much, as 5 as many, as 6 less, than
7 more than 8 less, less, than 9 as much as, more 10 more, than 11 more, than, the most
12 the least

5 1 more, than 2 more, more / less 3 less than
4 a lot more 5 harder / more, than 6 as much as

ROUND UP 11

1 1 many, the most 2 lots of, the most
3 a few, fewer 4 little 5 The less, the more
6 More and more 7 less 8 the most 9 few
10 less

2 1 most shaken 2 most harmless
3 most hidden 4 more bent 5 most renowned
6 best known 7 most hopeless 8 more helpful

3 1 A 2 B 3 C 4 A 5 B 6 C 7 A 8 C

4 1 Who jumped the farther **the furthest / farthest** in the last event?
2 Your girlfriend was the most elegant in **of** all the girls at last night's party.
3 The most **Most / More** people communicate through social networks these days.
4 Please drive more carefuller **carefully** than usual. There's a baby in the car.
5 Why didn't you study as hard than **as** usual?
6 Always try to do your better **best**.
7 I like this song as **more** than the other one.
8 Their later **latest** CD is much better than the previous one.
9 Which was the worse **worst** experience you've ever had, if I may ask?
10 Don't go any farthest **farther / further**. It could be dangerous.
11 The more people there are, the loudest **louder** you'll have to shout.
12 As harder **hard** as it seems, it will be worth it in the end.

5 1 the best 2 latest 3 eldest 4 youngest
5 later 6 longer

6 1 A 2 B 3 B 4 A 5 D 6 B 7 C 8 D 9 C
10 B 11 D 12 A

Reflecting on grammar

1 F 2 F 3 F 4 T 5 T 6 F 7 T 8 F 9 F 10 T

UNIT 12

LESSON 1

1 1 anything 2 anything / anything, Anything
3 nothing 4 something, something 5 nothing
6 something 7 something 8 something / anything
9 nothing 10 anything

2 1 someone 2 anyone 3 somebody 4 no one
5 anyone 6 anybody 7 anything 8 Nothing
9 Somebody, something 10 nothing
11 anything, nothing 12 something

3 1 John didn't tell me anything about what happened last night.
2 There wasn't anybody who knew the right answer.
3 If we don't have a car, there's nowhere we can go.
4 We've bought nothing for Emily's birthday yet.
5 I don't have anything new to tell you.
6 I didn't see anybody in town yesterday.
7 We didn't go anywhere at the weekend, we stayed at home.
8 Sorry, there's nothing else I can do for you.

458

4
1 Nothing 2 anywhere 3 Nobody / No one
4 nowhere 5 someone / somebody
6 somewhere 7 anything 8 anyone / anybody
9 anywhere, somewhere 10 something
11 No one / Nobody 12 anyone / anybody

5
1 something of wrong → something wrong
2 aren't doing nothing → aren't doing anything
3 wasn't someone → wasn't anyone / anybody
4 anywhere interesting → anything interesting
5 anything → anyone / anybody
6 Anything other? → Anything else?
7 Let's go anywhere → Let's go somewhere
8 don't want nothing → don't want anything

LESSON 2

1
1 either 2 Most of, were 3 all 4 either
5 Neither 6 both 7 either 8 all 9 both
10 Either 11 all 12 all

2
1 each 2 both 3 Each 4 Neither, either
5 Either, both 6 both 7 either 8 Neither
9 either 10 Neither

3
1 every 2 everyone / everybody
3 Everyone / Everybody 4 everywhere
5 Everything, everything 6 everyone / everybody
7 everything 8 everywhere 9 Every
10 Everyone / Everybody

4
1 ✗ Everyone I know **likes** reading. 2 ✓
3 ✗ **All** of them went to the same place for their holidays. 4 ✓ 5 ✗ There's free WiFi in every **room** of the hostel. 6 ✗ If you want everything, you may end up with **nothing**. 7 ✓ 8 ✓

5
1 everywhere 2 everyone / everybody
3 everything 4 both games 5 Most 6 All
7 Neither of us 8 anywhere 9 Both of them
10 Neither of them

LESSON 3

1
1 Simon and Rachel often help each other.
2 They didn't listen to each other. Both of them just went on talking.
3 Sally and I have been sending / have sent each other birthday cards for many years.
4 My neighbour and I often look after each other's cats when we're away.
5 Mark and Fiona are madly in love with each other.
6 When we met at the airport, we gave each other a big hug.

2
1 F 2 D 3 J 4 A 5 C 6 B 7 I 8 H 9 G 10 E

3
1 wherever 2 Whoever 3 whatever 4 whatever
5 Wherever 6 whenever 7 Whoever 8 Whatever

4
1 Anywhere you go on this island, you find people enjoying themselves.
2 You can go into any bars or restaurants wearing whatever you like.
3 Just call me any time you want.
4 Anything I cook, he finds something wrong with it.
5 Whoever touches my computer wouldn't dare do so again.
6 Whichever of you who wants to work on this project should come to tomorrow's meeting.
7 Some cause happiness wherever they go, others whenever they go.
8 I take my tablet with me anywhere I go.
9 Tell whoever comes that I'm very busy these days.
10 Here's some money for your birthday. Buy whatever you like.

LESSON 4

1
1 C 2 H 3 F 4 A 5 G 6 B 7 D 8 E

2
1 yourself 2 myself 3 herself 4 themselves
5 ourselves 6 himself 7 itself 8 yourselves
9 ourselves 10 yourself

3
1 cut himself 2 enjoyed ourselves
3 washed itself 4 bought herself
5 ask yourself 6 found themselves
7 tied himself 8 hurt myself 9 scared themselves 10 cheered herself up

4
1 your 2 by 3 themselves 4 myself
5 himself 6 on 7 herself 8 yourself 9 own
10 herself

5
1 He was by himself all weekend.
2 They did it by themselves.
3 You can work by yourself today.
4 I travelled around France by myself.
5 I have never sung by myself before.
6 You can't leave a baby by itself in the house!
7 He was able to run the firm by himself.
8 I don't mind living by myself in my new flat.
9 Don't worry. She's used to staying at home by herself.
10 Look at this beautiful cake I decorated it by myself.

6
1 one 2 one 3 ones, ones 4 one 5 ones
6 one, one 7 one 8 one, ones

7
1 ✗ Lisa must learn to control **herself**. 2 ✓
3 ✗ 'I like those boots.' 'Which **ones** do you mean?' 4 ✗ I always tell the children to wash **their hands** before eating. 5 ✓ 6 ✓ 7 ✗ We really enjoyed **ourselves** at the barbecue party. 8 ✗ Help **yourselves**, guys! There's food for everyone. 9 ✗ The twins hurt themselves when their treehouse fell down. 10 ✓

8
🎧 11 1 jacket 2 one 3 one 4 size 5 trousers
6 ones 7 trousers 8 cake 9 one 10 one 11 one

9
🎧 12 1 the best one 2 a new one 3 A French one
4 Which one 5 another one 6 a similar one

ROUND UP 12

1
1 some 2 all 3 someone 4 anyone 5 No one
6 any 7 someone 8 everybody's 9 anyone
10 anyone 11 some 12 all

2
1 Both... and 2 Most 3 every 4 Each
5 neither... nor, something 6 each other
7 Nothing 8 Each

3
1 either 2 neither 3 either 4 Neither
5 Neither 6 Either

4
1 **Each** of these sentences contains a mistake. Find it and correct the sentences.
2 Most of the tourists who visit Juliet's house in Verona **leave** a love message.
3 He's new here. He doesn't know **anybody** yet.
4 Everybody **likes** this cake. It's very popular with my family.
5 **Everybody / Everyone**, clap your hands and give our host a warm welcome.
6 Either John **or** Jack must have left his coat behind.
7 You can have **whatever** you like, it's all free.
8 Whoever **wants** to join me on my adventure is welcome.

5
1 wherever 2 Whoever 3 whenever
4 whatever 5 Wherever 6 however

6
1 F 2 D 3 A 4 B 5 C 6 E

7
1 D 2 A 3 C 4 A 5 B 6 D 7 B 8 C 9 B 10 C

8
1 Every 2 whatever 3 something
4 whoever 5 each 6 own 7 any more

9
1 everywhere, somewhere 2 Most 3 own
4 someone, where 5 Wherever 6 another
7 both 8 somewhere 9 anything
10 anything, nothing

10
1 C 2 A 3 C 4 A 5 D 6 C

Reflecting on grammar

1 F 2 T 3 F 4 T 5 T 6 T 7 F 8 F 9 T 10 F

REVISION AND EXAMS 4

1
1 none 2 Both 3 and 4 quite 5 many
6 Neither 7 nor 8 such a 9 both

2
1 the most exclusive 2 hotter than
3 so/as cold 4 milder 5 farther / further
6 darker / longer 7 longer / darker 8 tastier
9 fewer 10 the best

3
1 everyone 2 whenever 3 myself 4 somewhere
5 nothing 6 something 7 herself 8 anything

4
1 anyone 2 either 3 faster 4 very 5 best
6 more 7 herself 8 anything 9 both 10 all
11 anything 12 ones 13 one 14 How many
15 Anything 16 much 17 many 18 How much

5
1 each other 2 Everybody 3 lots of 4 both
5 Neither 6 each other 7 Neither 8 each other
9 everybody 10 himself

6
1 Both 2 all 3 quite / very / extremely / rather / really 4 Most 5 most 6 someone 7 All
8 as 9 Everyone / Everybody 10 best

7
1 A 2 C 3 C 4 D 5 B 6 C 7 A 8 C 9 D 10 A

8
1 last day of the crew / film crew's last day
2 the best in the class
3 the fastes driver 4 is nothing John
5 haven't (got) anything 6 mind either English cheddar 7 lot of free / empty 8 Each / Every student 9 isn't enough space / room
10 such a funny

SELF CHECK 4

1 B 2 C 3 B 4 A 5 B 6 B 7 C 8 A 9 C 10 B
11 C 12 A 13 C 14 B 15 C 16 B 17 B 18 A
19 B 20 A 21 C 22 A 23 A 24 C 25 B 26 C
27 B 28 A 29 C 30 C 31 C 32 A 33 B 34 A
35 B 36 C 37 B 38 A 39 B 40 C

UNIT 13

LESSON 1

1
1 Sam ~~cans~~ **can** ski well because his father is a ski instructor.
2 They might ~~to~~ arrive a bit late tonight.
3 ~~Does he will~~ **Will he** go to university after secondary school?
4 You ~~don't should~~ **shouldn't** go to bed so late every night!
5 ~~Do we may~~ **May we** hand in our assignment next week, Miss?
6 Joe can ~~drives~~ **drive** us to the restaurant. His car's bigger than ours.

2
1 can't 2 Could, could 3 couldn't
4 Can / Could, can't 5 can / could
6 can't, couldn't / can't 7 Could, Could 8 Couldn't
9 can't 10 Can / Could 11 Could

3
1 Can / Could you look after my dog today?
2 Could he walk when he was (13) months old?
3 Can / Could you help me paint the kitchen?
4 Can / Could I have a coffee and some milk, please?
5 Can I drive your car?
6 Can you close / shut the door, please?
7 Can / Could you tell me the way to Euston Station?
8 Could they go on holiday last summer?

4 1 I 2 P 3 R 4 A 5 R 6 A 7 P 8 I

5
1 I'm sorry I won't be able to come to the conference next week. I'll be away on business.
2 I didn't manage to get to the top of the mountain. It was too hard for me.
3 We aren't / We're not allowed to park on this side of the road.
4 Students aren't / are not permitted to smoke in the school grounds.
5 Have you been able to talk to the manager?
6 Will it be possible see the house later this afternoon?
7 We won't be allowed to enter the club. We aren't dressed properly.

LESSON 2

1
1 My favourite basketball team may win the championship this year.
2 They may arrive any minute now.
3 We might not go on holiday with our parents next summer.
4 I may not be able to come to your graduation next week.
5 The local council might not organise a summer festival this year.
6 We may not join the drama club this year.

2
1 Maybe your brother knows our new colleague.
2 Perhaps they will / they'll spend next weekend in Paris.
3 It's likely that Tom will leave early tomorrow morning. / Tom is / Tom's likely to leave early tomorrow morning.
4 Maybe Mary will want to go to the zoo next Sunday.
5 It's unlikely that Melanie will go to John's party if you're not going. / Melanie is / Melanie's unlikely to go to John's party if you're not going.
6 Perhaps Jim and I will visit the new museum on Saturday morning.
7 It's likely that we will / we'll join the carnival tomorrow if it's sunny. / We're / We are likely to join the carnival tomorrow if it's sunny.
8 Ben will probably decide to retire next year.
9 Maybe we will not / won't have time to go.
10 My sister is likely to join the yoga club.

3 1 I 2 Pr 3 Pr 4 I 5 W 6 Pr 7 Pe 8 W 9 Pr 10 W

4
1 My friends might organise a barbecue in their garden next Sunday.
2 Peter may not marry Jane. They're so different.
3 Ted and Sue may enjoy their holiday in Florida.
4 Greg may / might buy a new suit for the wedding.
5 We may join our friends in the pub tonight.
6 Lily might not leave Marshall. She still loves him.
7 My father may / might give me some money to buy a present for Jenny.
8 The tourist guide may organise an excursion to the island.
9 Mr Ross may put off his lesson to next week.
10 The twins might not wear the same clothes at the wedding tomorrow.

LESSON 3

1
1 Will you have lunch with me today?
2 Would you like a sandwich, Jack?
3 Would you bring me the menu, please?
4 Will / Would you pass the salt, please, Susan?
5 Will you help me make dinner, please, Harry?
6 Would you like a drink?

2 1 C 2 D 3 B 4 A 5 E

3
1 Mr Hanley wants Ms Dell to make an appointment with Ms Bradley on Tuesday morning.
2 Tom and Claire's parents don't want them to get back late tonight. / Our parents don't want Tom and Cliare to get back late tonight.
3 John's mother doesn't want him to play video games all afternoon.
4 Tess wants Nella to invite David to her party.
5 My brother wants me to lend him ten pounds.

4
1 I wish it would stop raining.
2 I wish it wasn't / weren't so hot.
3 I wish I was / were lying on a beach.
4 I wish I / we had some snow.
5 I wish I could paint better.
6 I wish I could sing like her.

5
1 We wish our favourite team would win the championship.
2 I wish I was / were 10 cm taller.
3 We wish our neighbours were not / weren't so noisy.
4 Dan wishes he had a brand new car.
5 I wish my husband had more free time.
6 Our teacher wishes he / she could retire at the end of this school year.

6
1 I / We wish we had been luckier!
2 Ben and Karen wish they hadn't gone out trekking in the bad weather.
3 Dinah wishes she hadn't worn her gold necklace last night. / Dinah wishes she hadn't lost her gold necklace last night.
4 Mike wishes he had gone to university after secondary school.
5 I wish I hadn't forgotten the appointment with an important customer.
6 I wish they had gone to the club with me. / I wish I had gone to the club with them. / I wish they hadn't gone to the club without me.

7 1 D 2 A 3 F 4 B 5 C 6 E

8 *Suggested answers*
1 I wish my girlfriend was / were here.
2 I wish I could go out with my friends tonight.
3 I wish I hadn't eaten raw fish last night.
4 I wish I'd learned / learnt to ski when I was young.
5 I wish I could be a pop singer.

LESSON 4

1 1 G 2 F 3 E 4 D 5 B 6 A 7 C

2 1 like 2 would like 3 Would, like 4 would like
5 like 6 Do, like

3 1 would prefer 2 would rather 3 would rather
4 would rather 5 would prefer 6 would prefer
7 would rather 8 would prefer

4 1 D 2 F 3 G 4 A 5 B 6 H 7 C 8 E

5
1 I'd like ~~that~~ James ~~washes~~ **to wash** my car. It's so dirty!
2 They would rather ~~spending~~ **spend** the weekend in London than at home doing gardening.
3 He would prefer **to** go to a rock concert. He doesn't like house music very much.
4 Would you like ~~coming~~ **to come** to my birthday party next week?
5 'What would you like to drink?' 'I **'d / would** like a soft drink.'
6 Do we really have to go out with Ben and Louise? I ~~had~~ **would** rather eat out you and me alone.'
7 Our instructor would like ~~we trained~~ **us to train** three times a week.
8 It's so cold that I ~~had~~ **'d / would** prefer **to** stay at home tonight.
9 'Would you like ~~sitting~~ **to sit** on the terrace?' 'Oh yes, that would be nice.'
10 'Do you want a drink of water?' 'Well, er ... I'd rather ~~to~~ have some juice.'

ROUND UP 13

1 1 can 2 couldn't 3 can't 4 can't 5 can't
6 could 7 can't 8 can 9 can / could 10 can

2 1 can't have been 2 may have gone
3 can't have been 4 can't have been
5 may have arrived 6 can't have been
7 may have finished 8 may have had
9 can't have run 10 may have handed in

3
1 The film was so moving I couldn't help but cry most of the time.
2 He couldn't help telling her, although it was a secret.
3 They might be able to help you, but I'm not sure.
4 I may visit my American cousins next summer.
5 The witness can't have recognised the thieves. They were wearing masks.
6 Dinah would rather buy a notebook instead of a tablet.
7 I wish I could have more money!
8 Jane wishes (that) she'd learned / learnt to play an instrument when she was young.
9 Terry may be at home. That's her car over there.
10 Lucy would prefer to call a wedding planner to organise the ceremony.

4
1 Will you be able to do it?
2 You won't be allowed to come back after midnight.
3 They haven't been allowed to go.
4 You may not be allowed to use your calculator.
5 She has managed to get here on time.
6 It's likely that it will snow tonight.
7 I don't know if I will be able to come.
8 She will probably be late.
9 Could you talk to him about his horrible behaviour?
10 They might be able to help organise the catering for your garden party.

5
1 He will be able to leave early tomorrow because there's a train at 6.30 am.
2 Visitors were only allowed to see / could only see the rooms on the ground floor.
3 I was able to fix my bike on my own eventually
4 I won't be allowed to stay out late in the evening.
5 I won't be able to come, I'm sorry.
6 I see you have manged to make this elaborated chocolate cake.
7 'Have you been able to talk to Mr Bailey yet?' 'No, I haven't.'
8 I won't be able to park my car in front of the restaurant.
9 We won't be able to go to Sally's wedding next month.
10 We were likely to go to the Halloween party. / It was likely that we went to the Halloween party

6
1 Will you dig the garden, please?
2 Would you mind telling me / tell me where Castle Street is?
3 Would you wait / mind waiting in the queue, please?
4 Would you fasten your seat belts, please?
5 Would you follow me to the lift, please?
6 Will you go to the football match with me?
7 Will / Would you go to the art exhibition with me, please?
8 Would you sign at the bottom of the form, please?

7
1 She 'd like her mum to make her a big chocolate cake for her birthday.
2 I'd like my parents to book me on a cruise.
3 Bill wants his friends to organise a fancy-dress party.
4 My son would like the university to give him a grant to study in Berlin.
5 My brother wants me to lend him my new laptop.
6 The citizens want the city council to build a new indoor swimming pool.

Reflecting on grammar

1 F 2 T 3 T 4 F 5 T 6 F 7 T 8 T 9 F 10 F

UNIT 14

LESSON 1

1 1 B 2 D 3 E 4 A 5 F 6 C

2 1 to get up early 2 mustn't talk in the library
3 don't have / need to bring 4 don't have to tell
5 mustn't bring 6 have to hand in your essays

3 1 We had to carry a lot of books to classes.
2 They didn't have to hurry to catch their train.
3 She will / 'll have to work very hard to prepare for the exam.
4 I will / 'll have to buy a new car; mine is very old now.
5 It must have been love!
6 He has had to study all the irregular verbs for the test.

4 1 F 2 E 3 A 4 G 5 C 6 D 7 B

5 *Suggested answers*
1 Do you have to work on / at weekends?
2 Must I cut / mow the grass / lawn?
3 Do you have to wear a uniform at work?
4 When do I / we have to hand in my / our project(s)?
5 Can / May I / we sit on these sofas?
6 Do you have to buy / get a new computer?

LESSON 2

1 1 needs 2 don't need 3 Do, need 4 need
5 needs 6 needn't 7 didn't need 8 needed
9 Do, need 10 needn't 11 will need / need
12 need

2 1 You may need to reserve a table.
2 They don't need to / needn't go.
3 This coat needs to be dry-cleaned.
4 You don't need to / needn't be there before nine o'clock.
5 All passengers need to be informed about the safety rules.
6 We didn't need to call / needn't have called the doctor for our mother.

3 1 are to show 2 is to talk 3 is to be signed
4 are to vote 5 is to meet 6 Am I to get out

4 1 have to, has to 2 don't need 3 is 4 need
5 must / has to 6 needs

LESSON 3

1 1 D 2 E 3 A 4 C 5 B

2 1 Take the number 15. It's quicker.
2 Let's get some drinks and snacks.
3 No, I've got some. Get some crisps.
4 Let's go to the Multiplex.
5 Would three o'clock be okay?
6 You needn't cook tonight. I'll get pizza.

3 1 Shouldn't you be working at the moment?
2 Should I bring a bag?
3 Shall we watch this DVD?
4 Should I / we bring some flowers?
5 Shall we ask Mark to our party?
6 Should they walk or (shlould they) take the bus?

4 1 ought 2 should 3 'd better 4 shouldn't
5 should 6 Shall I

5 1 had better 2 had better 3 ought
4 had better not 5 had better not
6 had better 7 ought not 8 had better

LESSON 4

1 1 was due 2 is obliged 3 was forced 4 is due
5 is / was due 6 'm / am forced / obliged

2 1 owe 2 owed / owes 3 was bound
4 owe 5 are bound 6 are / were bound

3 1 due 2 alerted 3 compelled to
4 been forced 5 take off 6 will be obliged

4 1 F 2 E 3 H 4 D 5 B 6 C 7 A 8 G

ROUND UP 14

1 1 Make a suggestion
2 Absence of obligation
3 Deduction (in the present based on fact)
4 Ask permission
5 Ask for instructions
6 Give advice
7 Say what you want someone else to do
8 Obligation (imposed by someone else)
9 Prohibition
10 Make a request (formal)

2 1 mustn't tell 2 must fasten 3 must win
4 mustn't forget 5 must drive 6 must book
7 must be 8 mustn't leave 9 must tidy
10 must hurry

3 1 has to 2 had to 3 didn't / did not have to
4 Do / Did, have to 5 had to 6 didn't / did not have to

4 1 must D 2 should / must C 3 must F
4 must / should A 5 should / must E
6 don't have B

5 1 can, mustn't 2 mustn't, can
3 must, don't have to

6 1 doesn't have to drive 2 mustn't walk
3 doesn't have to wear / must wear
4 mustn't leave 5 don't have to wash

7 1 must have won 2 must have been
3 must have had 4 must have been
5 must have got up 6 must have cost

463

8
1 You can't have gone on holiday with no money?
2 There must be a report on yesterday's athletics competition in the local newspaper.
3 He can't be over 65. He's still working!
4 He must be fit, as he is a PE teacher.
5 There must be some coffee left. I bought it yesterday.
6 You can't have recharged the mobile phone battery last night: it's gone flat already.
7 She can't be her mother: she's far too young.
8 That must have been the manager who just left.

9
1 ought 2 owe, owe 3 should / ought to / must
4 better, should / ought to / must
5 forced / obliged / compelled 6 ought
7 don't have 8 due 9 supposed / allowed
10 shall 11 should, should 12 obliged / forced

10
1 C 2 C 3 A 4 B 5 A 6 A 7 B 8 C 9 C 10 B

11
1 must 2 have to 3 have to / must
4 have to / must 5 don't have to
6 should / must 7 must 8 due

12
1 Our bus is due **to arrive** in the next few minutes. Hurry up!
2 They were forced **to** leave their home because of the flood.
3 'How much **do I owe** you?' 'Eight pounds.'
4 You'd better ~~to~~ come to work on time if you want to keep your job.
5 Tess suggested **having** lunch together tomorrow. / Tess suggested **that we / they (should) have** lunch together tomorrow.
6 You look tired. Shall I ~~to~~ cook for you tonight?

Reflecting on grammar
1 F 2 T 3 T 4 T 5 F 6 F 7 T 8 F 9 T 10 T

UNIT 15

LESSON 1

1
1 B/C 2 C 3 B/C 4 C 5 A 6 A

2
1 We are / 're visiting the Tate Gallery at three o'clock.
2 Are you going shopping this afternoon?
3 I am /'m having dinner at a Greek restaurant tonight.
4 What time are you going to work tomorrow?
5 When are you having your exam?
6 We are / 're getting married next Saturday.
7 I am / 'm seeing the optician at half past ten tomorrow.
8 They are / 're leaving for New York next week.
9 Who are you meeting at ten o'clock?
10 Where are you having lunch today?

3
1 F 2 P 3 F 4 F 5 P 6 P 7 F 8 P

4
1 get 2 have 3 meet 4 walk 5 visit 6 have
7 have 8 meet

5
1 starts / is starting 2 am / 'm going
3 arrive / are / 're arriving 4 are, doing
5 am / 'm leaving, leaves 6 is singing
7 am / 'm having 8 are / 're spending

LESSON 2

1
1 are not / aren't going to work 2 am / 'm going to get 3 is / 's going to take 4 Are, going to buy
5 are / 're going to move 6 are, going to watch
7 is not / isn't going to apply 8 are, going to live

2
1 a) going to get married b) getting married
2 a) not working b) not going to work
3 a) going to bring b) bringing

3 🎧 13 1 is going to be 2 'm going to tell
3 isn't going to do 4 aren't going to change
5 are, going to take

4
1 He is / 's going to be an engineer when he grows up.
2 Get an umbrella. It is / 's going to rain.
3 I am / 'm going to plant some fruit trees in my garden this coming spring.
4 We are / 're going to clean out the garage at the weekend.
5 Stop chatting! The lesson is / 's going to start.
6 Look at those grey clouds. It is /'s going to rain soon.
7 Today you are / 're going to work in pairs.

LESSON 3

1
1 She will get there by noon.
2 It will not happen again.
3 The sun will set at 7.30 tonight
4 I will always be with you.
5 It will be cold and cloudy / cloudy and cold tomorrow.
6 We will not survive on this money for a whole week.
7 Go ahead, I will follow you.
8 Everything will be ready by three o'clock.

2
1 Will, find, you will 2 Will, work, they won't
3 Will, be, it won't 4 Will, stay, I will
5 Will, have, I won't 6 Will, like, she will
7 Will, win, they will 8 Will, make, they will

3
1 will probably 2 sure 3 will 4 be 5 will be
6 start 7 hope 8 get 9 the game last 10 have

4

Pessimistic predictions	Optimistic predictions
Unemployment will be higher than now.	Unemployment will be lower.
There will still be wars.	Everybody will have enough to eat.
Air pollution will be worse.	There will be no more wars.
There will still be hunger and poverty.	There will be less air pollution.
There will be new diseases.	There will be a cure for most illnesses.

5 1 E 2 A 3 F 4 H 5 B 6 C 7 G 8 I 9 J 10 D

6
1 I'll always **be** on your side. You can be sure of this.
2 I don't think it **will** rain today.
3 **In** five days we'll be at the seaside. I can't wait!
4 We'll be best friends for **ever**.
5 I'm busy now. I'll talk to you **later**.
6 The climate will **probably get** warmer in the future.
7 I **won't** fight with my brother again, I promise!
8 Where **will** I meet Mr Johnson?
9 Don't worry. They'll arrive **sooner** or later.
10 Do you think you'll be free the day **after** tomorrow?

7 1 C 2 F 3 E 4 A 5 H 6 B 7 D 8 G
Red: 2, 8, A, B, C, G
Blue: 1, 3, 5, 7, D

LESSON 4

1
1 will / 'll be lying 2 will / 'll be relaxing
3 enjoying 4 will / 'll be working
5 will / 'll be cleaning 6 cooking

2
1 Will you be doing   C
2 Will you be going out   G
3 will they be going   E
4 will you be leaving   A
5 will Robert be having   B
6 Will you be travelling   F
7 Will you be using   D

3
1 will have left 2 will / 'll have taken
3 will / 'll have become
4 will / 'll have learned / learnt
5 will / 'll have finished 6 will have disappeared

4
1 will / 'll have finished 2 will / 'll be feeling
3 Will, be reading 4 will / 'll have recovered
5 will be using 6 will / 'll, have eaten

ROUND UP 15

1
1 will win 2 I'll carry 3 will set 4 are you meeting, are meeting 5 Will you open 6 will
7 I'll 8 are leaving 9 will come 10 be lying

2
1 am / 'm doing 2 Are you going to be
3 will rain / is / 's going to rain
4 will / 'll never come 5 are you going to do
6 am / 'm going to buy 7 will win 8 is / 's flying
9 will / 'll meet 10 am / 'm having

3
1 will be flying 2 will be 3 will leave
4 will be flying 5 will be flying 6 will arrive

4
1 be feeling 2 have been using
3 be interviewing 4 have finished
5 be eating 6 be doing

5 1 B 2 C 3 B 4 C 5 C 6 A 7 C 8 A 9 B 10 C

6
You   What are you going to do next summer?
Susan I'm going (to go) to Cannes to take a French course.
You   How long will you / are you going to stay / there in Cannes?
Susan Three weeks. Would you like to go / come with me?
You   I'd like to, but I have to work this summer.
Susan What are you going to work as, and where are you going to work?
You   I'm going to work as a receptionist in a hotel in Geneva.
Susan I'll bring you a present from Cannes.

7
1 Sarah was going to be an actress when she was younger.
2 I wasn't going to study abroad.
3 They were going to share their flat with a friend.
4 We were going to have an appointment for the next day, but he didn't turn up.
5 We were going to have the party at the local Youth Club, but it was not available.
6 It looked as if it was going to rain last night, but it didn't .

8
1 be doing 2 be working 3 be 4 Will
5 have moved 6 Will they be 7 will they have
8 have finished 9 be thinking 10 will decide
11 want 12 will 13 be 14 be working 15 will

9
1 By this time tomorrow, I'll **be** hiking in the Alps.
2 Correct
3 I hope my children **will be leaving** in a peaceful world.
4 The sea level **will be steadily rising** / **will steadily rise** in the next fifty years.
5 Correct
6 Correct
7 'What **will you be doing** in ten years' time?'
8 Correct

Reflecting on grammar

1 T 2 T 3 F 4 F 5 T 6 F 7 F 8 T 9 T 10 F

REVISION AND EXAMS 5

1
1 would like 2 studying 3 she's going to apply
4 wouldn't like 5 wants to 6 she'd rather go
7 she's going to learn 8 would prefer 9 has
10 be allowed 11 would like her 12 needs

2
1 am / 'm going to have 2 will / 'll ask
3 am / 'm going to answer / will / 'll answer
4 will / 'll probably ask 5 am / 'm going to tell / will / 'll tell 6 will / 'll be 7 will / 'll get

3
1 will / 'll be dealing   2 will / 'll have to
3 Will I have to   4 will / 'll have to
5 Will I have to   6 Will I have to   7 will / 'll have to
8 Did you work   9 worked

4
1 Do, have   2 want   3 wants / needs   4 must
5 Do, want / need   6 don't / do not have
7 have / need   8 mustn't / must not   9 had
10 need / have   11 do, have / need
12 don't / do not have / need

5
1 B   2 C   3 C   4 A   5 C

6
1 B   2 B   3 D   4 B   5 A   6 C   7 B   8 D   9 C   10 B

7
1 will / 'll have gone   2 am / 'm seeing
3 will not / won't have   4 ought to
5 Do you want me to   6 is not / isn't due
7 had / 'd better not sunbathe
8 are bound to happen   9 would organise trips out
10 I'd / I would rather stay
11 We don't / do not have   12 I might visit
13 can't be Tom's   14 must be Ben's father

8
Student's own answer

SELF CHECK 5

1 B   2 C   3 A   4 B   5 C   6 B   7 C   8 A   9 A   10 B
11 C   12 B   13 B   14 A   15 A   16 C   17 A   18 A
19 B   20 C   21 B   22 B   23 C   24 A   25 B   26 C
27 A   28 A   29 C   30 B   31 B   32 A   33 C
34 A   35 C   36 B   37 C   38 A   39 B   40 C

UNIT 16

LESSON 1

1
1 Would you go to the swimming pool with me?
2 It would be better to stay at home today.
3 Jim would not try white-water rafting.
4 I wouldn't go kayaking in this weather.
5 Would you help me lay the table?
6 Would you climb a really steep mountain face?

2
1 Wouldn't you help me with this project?
2 There's nothing I wouldn't do for you.
3 I would say it's a good plan.
4 Would you do that for me?
5 It would be better for you to learn a second language.
6 I wouldn't accept that job.

3
1 I hoped they would arrive for the beginning of the film.
2 They promised they would call round this week.
3 Ann thought she would / 'd take up rowing.
4 They knew they would / 'd need a lot of training before going trekking in Nepal.
5 Tom said he would look for a new job soon.
6 We knew they would fight for their rights.
7 Luke said he would / 'd invite us to try kayaking.
8 Jim promised he would / 'd have a haircut before the wedding.

4
1 We would have liked to go shopping. / We would have liked to have gone shopping.
2 I might have attended a German course.
3 Would you have spent all that money on a pair of shoes?
4 You should have been more careful.
5 They could have run faster.
6 I wouldn't have driven so fast.
7 We might have bought a new car after the summer.
8 They could have called after the match.

5
1 like   2 taken   3 put off   4 told   5 go   6 rest
7 arrived   8 be

6
1 be working   2 be studying   3 be joking
4 be waiting   5 be travelling / traveling
6 be winning   7 be serving   8 be having

LESSON 2

1
1 D   2 A   3 G   4 H   5 C   6 B   7 E   8 F

2
1 improves   2 shows   3 like   4 buy   5 opens
6 get   7 feel   8 tell

3
1 rains, will not / won't go
2 will / 'll have, doesn't rain
3 will not / won't have, do not / don't want
4 will / 'll do, ask
5 will / 'll go, find
6 spend, will not / won't have
7 leave, will / 'll get
8 don't study, will not / won't be able
9 do not / don't come, will not / won't go
10 will fall, keeps

4
1 continue, will / 'll be obliged   2 need, will / 'll be
3 competes, will / 'll go   4 snows, will not / won't go   5 mix, get   6 will be, get   7 stops, will / 'll go   8 die, don't / do not give   9 look, get   10 will / 'll get, don't / do not do

LESSON 3

1
1 would   2 wouldn't   3 broke   4 could
5 wouldn't   6 would be

2
1 tried, enjoy   2 lived, would   3 would have, didn't
4 wouldn't, knew   5 go, wouldn't be
6 didn't study, wouldn't   7 wouldn't, could
8 weren't, would go

3
1 had   2 worked   3 would tell   4 was / were
5 didn't turn up   6 would / 'd travel   7 could   8 felt
9 would you do   10 arrived

4
1 would be, got   2 would dye, allowed
3 improved, would be   4 didn't have, would I do
5 Would you buy, didn't cost
6 wouldn't go, didn't look after
7 knew, would / 'd ring   8 won, would / 'd give
9 were, wouldn't trust   10 found, would / 'd take
11 would / 'd be, didn't / did not invite
12 would / 'd have, was / were

5
1 D Type 1 2 G Type 3 3 A Type 2 4 F Type 3
5 B Type 1 6 C Type 3 7 H Type 2 8 E Type 3

6
1 hadn't made, would / 'd have got
2 would / 'd have worn, had / 'd told
3 had / 'd known, would not / wouldn't have ordered
4 would / 'd have washed, 'd / had read
5 would not / wouldn't have broken, had 'd stayed
6 had ordered, would / 'd have chosen

7
1 If I went out tonight, my parents would be angry.
2 If I had / 'd had my car yesterday, I could have gone to the mall.
3 If my mum (would) let me, I would / 'd love to have a tattoo.
4 If I got on with my brother, I would / 'd see him.
5 If I was / were rich, I could buy a big house.
6 If she hadn't / had not gone to the party, she would not / wouldn't have met her future husband.

LESSON 4

1
1 E can 2 A may 3 F may 4 B can 5 C may
6 D may

2
1 could 2 would / 'd have to 3 might
4 would / 'd have to 5 would / 'd like to
6 could 7 could 8 might

3
1 would 'd have liked, hadn't / had not spent
2 hadn't / had not left, would / 'd have had
3 'd / had waited, 'd / would have been frozen
4 might / would have visited, had been
5 could / might / would have won the race, 'd / had trained
6 should have told, if she knew
7 'd / would have reported, 'd / had known
8 might have been, hadn't / had not left

4
1 E 2 D 3 F 4 C 5 A 6 B

5
1 'Would he have passed his driving test?' 'Yes, if he'd practised more often.'
2 'Would they have enjoyed white-water rafting?' 'Yes, if they hadn't been so scared.'
3 'Would the team have won the competition?' 'Yes, if one of them hadn't hurt his / her / their leg.'
4 'Would you have sailed to the island yesterday?' 'Yes, if we'd known it would be windy. / was going to be windy.'
5 'Would she have gone to Sally's party?' 'Yes, if she'd known (that) Peter was there.'

6
1 If I had been able to talk to him, I would have told him not to come. I knew the conference would be quite boring.
2 If I had had to work on Sundays I wouldn't have accepted this job, but luckily I only occasionally have to work on Saturdays.
3 I'm a lazybones. If I was / were obliged to do some sport, I think I would choose football and I would play as a goalkeeper, so that I wouldn't have to run much!
4 If I had been / were able to play the violin as well as you do, I would have tried to find a job in an orchestra.
5 If I had worked harder at school, I could have got better marks. Now I realise how important it was.
6 If I could have found a better-paid job, I would / might have been able to pay off my mortgage early.

7
1 E 2 D 3 B 4 C 5 A

8
1 book 2 will get 3 booked 4 would get
5 had booked 6 would have gott

9
1 shouldn't, should 2 would, could 3 would
4 wouldn't 5 should, would / could
6 could, wouldn't 7 would, could

10
1 If he went to the opera, he would certainly enjoy it.
If he had gone to the opera, he would certainly have enjoyed it.
2 You wouldn't spend too much if you bought things in the sales.
You wouldn't have spent too much if you had bought things in the sales.
3 They would talk to him if they saw him.
They would have talked to him if they had seen him.
4 If you had a day off, we would go on a trip to the lake.
If you had had a day off, we would have gone on a trip to the lake.
5 If she didn't turn up on time, we would leave without her.
If she hadn't turned up on time, we would have left without her.
6 If you tried hard, you would certainly succeed.
If you had tried hard, you would certainly have succeeded / have certainly succeeded.

11
1 You should have <u>told</u> me that you were not coming.
2 If I <u>had</u> brought my packed lunch with me, I would have shared it with you.
3 If you <u>liked</u> Japanese food, you would try the sushi in this restaurant. / If you like Japanese food, you <u>should</u> try the sushi in this restaurant. It's excellent!
4 What do you suggest I <u>could</u> do to improve my English?
5 If I had <u>had</u> more time, I would have prepared something special for dinner.
6 I was afraid she <u>might not</u> love me any more.
7 What would I <u>have done</u> if I had been you? / What would I do if I was / were you? I just don't know! You should ask someone else.
8 I would <u>have</u> thanked them for their great hospitality if I had seen them.

ROUND UP 16

1
1 I wouldn't have told him a lie.
2 You should have been more careful!
3 He could have helped you.
4 They can't / couldn't have been so silly!
5 She may have known the truth.
6 I'd have liked to see them / I'd like to have seen them.
7 Which one would you have chosen?
8 They might have been lucky.

2
1 is going to melt
2 am not going to read / won't be reading
3 are going to stop
4 am going to read
5 am leaving / am going to leave
6 are going to watch / will be watching
7 are having / are going to have
8 am going to book / will be booking
9 are going to build
10 am not going to make / will not be making

3
1 rise 2 will become 3 will melt 4 melts
5 will rise 6 will be 7 don't find 8 don't limit
9 will increase 10 continues 11 will become
12 won't be able

4
1 Should I arrive late, please save a seat for me.
2 Should I decide to go, I'll let you know.
3 Had we enough money, we would buy this car.
4 Had they any children, they wouldn't be able to go out every evening.
5 Should it rain hard, we wouldn't go out.
6 Had they travelled more, they would be more open-minded.

5
1 don't 2 want 3 are 4 might 5 would
6 open 7 be 8 could

6
1 would have left 2 would choose 3 would take
4 would play 5 didn't pass 6 would be
7 would have slept 8 would have known / would know

7
1 would have happened 2 had won
3 Would the American colonies have been
4 had ruled 5 had been 6 had won
7 would have been speaking
8 would have backed
9 would have gained
10 Would the French Revolution have broken out
11 wouldn't have studied 12 will be

8
1 can come, have 2 never try, 'll never know
3 give, will be, teach, will be
4 have, have, will, have, have, have, will have
5 wasn't / weren't, would, be 6 judged, would live

Reflecting on grammar

1 T 2 T 3 T 4 F 5 F 6 T 7 T 8 T 9 T 10 F

UNIT 17

LESSON 1

1
1 Sports equipment is sold in this store.
2 Designer clothes are made in this factory.
3 Cars aren't produced here any more.
4 The national anthems are played before each game.
5 French, German and Italian are spoken in Switzerland.
6 Prizes are given to all winners.
7 Computers are used in the marketing lessons.
8 The orchestra is directed by a very young woman.
9 He is considered a real maths genius!
10 The United Kingdom is made up of Scotland, England, Wales and Northern Ireland.

2
1 Is the film directed by Steven Spielberg?
2 Are school uniforms paid for by the families?
3 The notice is not / isn't written in my language.
4 Dice are not / aren't used for this game.
5 Is Spanish taught in their school?
6 These sunglasses are not / aren't made in Italy.
7 Is the UNO Tower made of glass and steel?

3
1 Coffee is ground and then (it is) packed into tins.
2 These bags are made in Florence.
3 Carnival is celebrated in February.
4 The rooms are cleaned by Mrs Jones every morning.
5 Where are these tomatoes imported from?

4
1 is played 2 is being played 3 are specified
4 are being built 5 is included
6 is being refurbished 7 are being raised
8 is being served

5
1 is transformed 2 is chewed 3 is swallowed
4 is mixed 5 is completed 6 is called
7 are not / aren't needed 8 are expelled

6
1 are invited 2 are asked 3 are filed
4 is forbidden 5 be borrowed 6 are fined

LESSON 2

1
1 were written 2 was named 3 were explored
4 was conquered 5 was defeated
6 was designed 7 was invented 8 was created
9 was built

2
1 Who was *The Last Supper* painted by?
2 When was the first Liverpool to Manchester railway opened?
3 Who replaced Mr Kent in the English class yesterday?
4 What was your first dog called?
5 How many languages was his novel translated into?
6 How were the glasses packed? Where were they shipped to?

3
1. The Walt Disney Company created both Mickey Mouse and Donald Duck.
2. Thomas Edison invented the light bulb.
3. They were repairing the main road, so we came by a different route.
4. They built higher walls in New Orleans after Hurricane Katrina destroyed part of the city.
5. The storm damaged lots of cars last night.
6. The rock star's fans cheered him all the way to his hotel.
7. They arrested Rosa Parks in Montgomery, Alabama, in 1955 because she had sat in a bus seat reserved for white people.
8. They called an ambulance immediately after the accident.
9. They made a mistake.

4
1 has been inaugurated 2 was opened
3 Has she ever been invited 4 was chosen
5 has been repaired 6 has just been cleaned
7 has not / hasn't been announced
8 was released 9 was stolen

5
1. Have, been
2. had been cancelled
3. has not / hasn't been repaired
4. has not / hasn't been reached
5. has been announced
6. had, been done, had been cooked, had been set, had been decorated
7. have been reserved
8. had been made

LESSON 3

1
1 is not / isn't going to be appointed
2 will be taken 3 will have been chosen
4 are / 're going to be asked
5 will not / won't be published 6 will be released
7 are going to be sold 8 will be held

2
1. You will certainly be declared innocent.
2. His next movie is going to be filmed in New Zealand.
3. The rooms of the old mansion will be redecorated next year.
4. An interesting exhibition is going to be opened later this month.
5. A concert will be organised in his memory.
6. This old building is going to be demolished.
7. Who's going to be chosen for the main role in the musical?
8. The names of the winners will be announced tomorrow.
9. A traditional meal with local wines will be served to everyone.
10. I think your proposal will be taken seriously.

3
1 must not 2 can / could 3 must 4 may / can
5 can / could / may 6 couldn't 7 would

4
1. The apples should be cut into halves.
2. The car needs to be washed today.
3. The ball can't be touched with the hands in soccer.
4. I should have been informed!
5. Your application form might have been lost.
6. An agreement ought to be reached.
7. Dinner might be served in the garden this evening.

5
1. Can a boat be hired for the lake?
2. Must all expenses be paid in advance?
3. Can a little butter be added to the sauce?
4. Should everyone be punished?
5. Can it be cooked in the microwave?

6
1. Your essay should have been written more carefully.
2. The armchair was too big to have been taken in the car.
3. The onions should have been chopped more finely.
4. They might have been chosen for the part.
5. We should have been informed about any problems.

7
1 D 2 B 3 G 4 H 5 F 6 C 7 A 8 E

LESSON 4

1
1 ~~invite~~ invited 2 ~~were~~ was 3 ✓
4 ~~offer~~ offered 5 ✓ 6 ✓ 7 ~~credit~~ credited

2
1. She was sent red roses.
2. Susan was told a nice story.
3. We were sent an invitation to the opening of a new shop.
4. We were granted a 30% discount on last year's clothes.
5. Paul was shown the cathedral by the bishop.
6. Caroline was asked to pick him up at the airport.
7. The children were given some nice illustrated books.
8. I was taught how to model clay.

3
1 They told us 2 They were known to be
3 You are supposed to be 4 He was found to be
5 painting is considered to be
6 villa is said to belong

4
1 PR 2 PA 3 PR 4 PA 5 PR 6 PR 7 PR 8 PA

5
1 has been credited 2 was 3 had been taught
4 ran 5 was devastated 6 was given

6
1. Martha Miller is thought to be an interesting artist.
2. John Landis was thought to be / have been a rich art dealer.
3. The stolen painting is supposed (by the police) to have already been sold.
4. Their works of art are known to be the most expensive in the gallery.
5. He has / 's been given a new canvas and some watercolours.
6. The fakers are supposed to have moved to South America by now.
7. The owner of the art gallery is believed to be very wealthy.

7 1 D 2 F 3 A 4 B 5 C 6 E

8
1 I want to get these photos printed.
2 She must get her jacket dry-cleaned.
3 I need to get this shirt ironed.
4 We need to get our computer repaired.
5 My mum wants to have the kitchen extended.
6 My parents want to have a new satellite dish installed.
7 Laura must have her nails manicured before the wedding.
8 She must have a hole in her tooth filled.
9 I need to get the car washed.
10 We must get the grass cut this weekend.

ROUND UP 17

1
1 active, past continuous
2 passive, past perfect simple
3 passive, future perfect continuous
4 active, past conditional, simple
5 active, present perfect continuous
6 active, past simple
7 passive, *going to* future in the past
8 passive, future simple

2
1 washes, washing, washed
2 cuts, cutting, cut
3 lives, living, lived
4 writes, writing, wrote, written
5 enjoys, enjoying, enjoyed
6 cries, crying, cried
7 comes, coming, came, come
8 spends, spending, spent

3
1 is being sent   2 was finally rewarded
3 had been demolished   4 will be spent
5 were being served   6 have been demolished

4
1 All your emails will be replied to.
2 The children will be looked after by a new babysitter tonight.
3 This song has been played a hundred times on the radio today.
4 The schedule might have been changed.
5 Their car is going to be sold.
6 Big dams are being built in Venice.
7 The equipment in the science lab must not be used by students without permission.
8 A charity concert has been organised by the club members.

5
1 Hot meals were served at all times in the restaurant.
2 The cake had to be stored in a cool place.
3 Very good bargains could be found on Prime Day.
4 This dish was prepared the traditional way.
5 All of the carpets were hand-woven in Morocco.
6 The sauce needed to be prepared in advance.
7 The scarves in the shop window were all hand-painted.
8 The bags and belts were made of real leather.

6
1 He was offered a film contract. / A film contract was offered to him.
2 You will be sent two copies of the contract. / Two copies of the contract will be sent to you.
3 New students are shown the syllabus. / The syllabus is shown to new students.
4 The children are going to be taught a nursery rhyme. / A nursery rhyme is going to be taught to the children.
5 She has been awarded with an Oscar. / An Oscar has been awarded to her.
6 Each council member was passed a folder of documents. / A folder of documents was passed to each council member.
7 Sara has been told the story of this strange room. / The story of this strange room has been told to Sara.
8 The children are being given some snacks for the break. / Some snacks are being given to the children for the break.

7
1 the oven be switched off?
2 was 'Julius Caesar' written by?
3 was this song composed by?
4 was she given the prize?
5 can be done now?
6 languages are spoken here?
7 his paintings be sold (at the next auction)?
8 this flat going to be rented?

8
1 devastated   2 repaired   3 cleaned up
4 cut, dyed, restyled   5 done   6 washed, ironed

9
1 The students were ~~gave~~ **given** some new books.
2 ~~Have~~ **Were** the stadium gates opened at 6 p.m. for the concert?
3 The Sagrada Familia ~~were~~ **was** designed by Antoni Gaudi.
4 The film will be was ~~shooted~~ **shot** in Central Italy.
5 The dog was supposed to **be** missing.
6 A radio station ~~has~~ **was** established by Marconi on the Isle of Wight.

Reflecting on grammar

1 F 2 F 3 F 4 T 5 T 6 F 7 T 8 T 9 F 10 T

UNIT 18

LESSON 1

1
1 who 2 which 3 who 4 who 5 which 6 who
7 which 8 who

2
1 That is the lady who ~~she~~ owns the flower shop in the High Street.
2 Aren't these the earrings **(that) you've been looking for** for ages? / Aren't these the earrings for **which you've been looking** for ages?
3 The doctor for **whom** you're waiting has just arrived. / The doctor **(whom) you're waiting for** has just arrived.

4 I'm sure this is the boy **whose** father works in the bank next to my office.
5 Can't you see that car? The one **which / that** is parked in front of that gate?
6 Isn't he the artist **(that / whom / who*)** we met at yesterday's opening in Leo's art gallery?
* Although whom is correct here, who would be used in most colloquial situations.

3
1 (who) **2** – **3** (that) **4** – **5** – **6** –, –
7 (which) **8** (that)

4
1 (who) **2** (which) **3** who **4** whose **5** (which)
6 whose **7** which **8** which

5
1 The friend I usually play tennis with has broken his arm falling off his bike.
2 The colleagues my mother works with gave her a beautiful necklace on her birthday.
3 The e-book we were talking about yesterday got an important award.
4 The café we are going to tonight was opened two hundred years ago!
5 Jack and Beatrix are going to buy the house they have been dreaming of for a long time.
8 The document I had been looking for for two days was in a drawer in my office.

6
1 That is the boy whose father is a renowned web designer.
2 The phone call I was waiting for came too late.
3 He's the man you saw at the pub last night.
4 This is the new scanner I'm going to buy.
5 That's the history teacher who gives us a lot of homework.
6 This is the lady who gave me her old digital camera.
7 The car which / that was found near the park is Mr Beckett's.
8 The house Carol lives in is really smart.

7
1 Comfort food is a kind of food that / which makes you feel better, like chocolate and cookies.
2 Skydiving is a sport in which you jump from a plane and fall a long way down before opening your parachute.
3 A skydiver is a person who does skydiving.
4 A segway is an electric scooter that / which is used in pedestrian areas.
5 A drone is an aircraft without a pilot that / which is controlled from the ground.
6 Paintball is a game in which people shoot balls of paint at each other.
7 A Q-R Code is a type of matrix barcode that / which consists of black modules arranged in a square grid that / which can be read by a camera or a scanner.
8 A crocoburger is a hamburger that / which is made with crocodile meat.

LESSON 2

1
Non-defining clauses:
1 The Sullivans, who live opposite us, have just bought a new car.
2 My washing machine, which is quite old, keeps breaking down.
4 My son's friends, who are often at our house, are very pleasant young people.
Sentences 3, 5, 6 and 7 are defining clauses and do not need commas.

2
1 whose **2** who **3** who **4** whom / who
5 which **6** whom / who **7** who **8** which

3
1 Our French teacher, who / whom we all liked very much, retired last month
2 Mr and Ms Martin, who / whom I met in Spain last summer, are a married couple.
3 That is a self-portrait which / that my father painted 20 years ago.
4 Do you know the name of that model whose photo was on the front cover of *Vanity Fair* last week?
5 Mr Owen, who I work for / for whom I work, is the financial manager of our company. / I work for Mr Owen, who is the financial manager of our company.
6 I've got two younger sisters who I get on well with / with whom I get on well.
7 *Cats*, which has been on in theatres all over the world for years, is a very famous musical. *Cats*, which is a very famous musical, has been on in theatres all over the world for years.
8 I hate novels which / that tell silly love stories.
9 The friends I study with every day are very good at maths and help me a lot. / The friends with whom I study every day are very good at maths and help me a lot. / The friends whom I study with every day are very good at maths and help me a lot.
10 The desk I work at is stacked with books and papers. / The desk at which I work is stacked with books and papers. / The desk which I work at is stacked with books and papers.

LESSON 3

1
1 All **2** what **3** all that **4** what **5** why **6** how
7 what **8** where **9** when **10** where **11** why
12 in which

2
1 how **2** why **3** (that / where) **4** (that)
5 (when / that) **6** (that) **7** when **8** where
9 where **10** why

3
1 Everybody liked the food I had cooked, which was quite surprising.
2 Connie passed her driving test, which she didn't quite expect.
3 They didn't come to the concert, which was a shame.
4 Sam will have to work next Sunday, which is quite unusual.
5 A lot of students in our school do voluntary work, which is really admirable.

6 Quite a number of start-up companies have opened in our town, which is good news.

4
1 Why don't you tell me ~~all~~ what you know?
2 Give me one reason ~~because~~ why I should help them.
3 This is the place ~~on~~ in which / where I saw the accident.
4 An Indie Market is a place ~~in~~ where all the traders are independent.
5 Why don't you tell me ~~way~~ how you solved the problem?
6 This is the time ~~at~~ when / at which the ghost is said to appear in the Big Hall.
7 I couldn't see ~~that which~~ what she was wearing under her coat.

LESSON 4

1
1 There's a policeman standing .
2 There are two people cycling along a path.
3 There are two women sitting on a bench.
4 There's a child with his mum buying something from a kiosk.
5 There are some boys playing football on the grass.

2
1 Feel 2 hear 3 tastes 4 watched 5 smell
6 heard

3
1 I heard the kids laughing.
2 I smelt something sweet baking / being baked.
3 I saw two men open the door of the bank.
4 He felt a cold wind blowing in the street.
5 I noticed two people leave the room before the end of the lecture.
6 We saw the waiter drop a pile of plates.
7 I didn't hear anyone / anybody knock at the door.
8 I heard the girl playing the violin.

4
1 crash 2 standing 3 gossiping 4 burning
5 call / calling 6 waiting

5
1 He was seen throwing stones.
2 She was heard singing a beautiful song.
3 They were heard opening the garage door late at night.
4 Someone was noticed walking up and down the street.
5 He was heard to whistle.
6 You have been seen copying during the exam.
7 Some young people were noticed hanging around late last night.
8 Jack was seen to get on a train at the station.
9 The baby was heard crying at night.
10 They were heard laughing like mad.

6
1 Draw a picture of one of the animals mentioned in the story.
2 The news was in an article published in a local magazine.
3 We're going to rent a flat overlooking the sea.
4 The path leading to the waterfall is very steep.
5 My friend'a notes, taken at the conference, were very clear.
6 Try to explain the words highlighted in the text.
7 Do you know the lady sitting in the last row?
8 Do you know that girl eating an ice-cream?

7
1 This is the e-book that / which was illustrated by my father.
2 There were lots of kids who were playing games on the web.
3 There are more and more people who are using open-source software.
4 I met Linda when / while she / I was looking for a new digital camera in the store.
5 There was a dark spot that / which was covering the PC screen.
6 He was looking at the images that / which were printed in colour.
7 They usually double-check the information that / which is found on Wikipedia.
8 This is the new software that / which was created by a group of students aged 16.

ROUND UP 18

1
1 C 2 F 3 A 4 B 5 D 6 E

2
1 who 2 whom / who 3 who 4 who 5 which
6 whose 7 who / whom 8 which 9 which
10 whose

3
1 The text I was working with suddenly vanished from the screen.
2 Who are the people you are waiting for?
3 The house they live in is super technological.
4 The people she went to the meeting with went home early.
5 The e-book we were talking about got an important award.
6 The music you are listening to is played by the London Symphony Orchestra.
7 The kind of life they had got used to was going to change.
8 The baby I looked after last summer is now nearly one year old.

4
1 There are moments in which I would like to live on a desert island.
2 This is the university at which both my husband and I studied years ago.
3 I don't know the reason for which she left her job.
4 Last Friday was the day on which we moved to the new office.
5 Three o'clock is the time at which you can meet the sales manager.
6 Unfortunately there isn't a place in / at which you can camp near here.
7 The country in which they speak Urdu is Pakistan.
8 Can you give me a good reason for which I should have a healthier life?

5
1 This is a hut we stayed in for the night / where we stayed for the night.

2 This is a hot chocolate (which / that) we drank to make ourselves warm.
3 This is the view (which / that) we had from the top of the mountain.
4 This is a little lake where we stopped for a picnic.
5 These are my trekking boots, which were muddy at the end of the day.
6 This is the mountain peak (that / which) we were able to reach.
7 These are our friends who climbed the mountain with us.
8 This is our guide, who led us to the top.
9 This is a marmot (which / that) we saw in a meadow.

6
1 which is broadcast
2 who are always directed
3 which are mostly composed
4 which usually come
5 which is accompanied
6 which are set

7
1 Things are not always done the way I like.
2 I'm the one who spoke to you on the phone yesterday.
3 'Goodbye Mr Holland' is a good film which came out in 1995.
4 A hero is someone who does his duty every day.
5 She is the girl whose mother is a famous painter.
6 Is this the present which Dad bought for you?

8
1 –   2 (which)   3 (whom)   4 –   5 (which)   6 –
7 (which)   8 –

9
1 That was all (that) we could do.
2 I'm so curious. Tell me what you know.
3 He's the one (that / who / whom) I was waiting for.
4 We're leaving tomorrow, which makes me very sad.
5 My house is the place in which / where I most like to be.
6 Come and see those girls who / that are dancing so well.
7 Cupertino is the town Apple has its headquarters / in which Apple has its headquarters. / where Apple has its headquarters.
8 Tigers are animals which / that are in danger of extinction.

10
1 who   2 which   3 whose   4 who / whom
5 which / that

11
1 Our rep, whom / who you met last week, will offer you favourable contracts.
2 The technician who has repaired my computer is really good.
3 Tom, who I am studying with today, is a whizz at IT!
4 The homepage which was created by one of our programmers is updated every week.
5 The printer (that) we have in our office is also a scanner and a photocopier.

Reflecting on grammar
1 T   2 T   3 F   4 T   5 F   6 F   7 F   8 T   9 T   10 T

REVISION AND EXAMS 6

1
1 want   2 would / 'd buy   3 pay   4 have   5 get
6 'd / had known   7 had / 'd managed

2
Three languages are taught in my school: French, German and Spanish. I'm learning one, German. **We are made to work very hard by Ms Hofer, the German teacher**: of course, **only German must be spoken** during her lessons. **We are given lots of grammar exercises** to do every day. **We are also asked** to read a new book and write a review of it every month, then **each of our reviews is discussed** in the class. **Good results can be obtained** with Ms Hofer only if you study really hard. If you want to learn a language very well, the best thing to do is go to a country where **it is spoken**. But **a language can be learned / learnt** quite well in school too, if you have a teacher like mine!

3
1 living   2 come   3 getting   4 getting
5 say / saying   6 looking   7 leading   8 sitting
9 waiting

4
1 D   2 B   3 A   4 C   5 A   6 B   7 B   8 C   9 A
10 B   11 D   12 B

5
1 what   2 where   3 who / whom
4 – / that / which   5 where   6 where   7 which
8 where   9 who   10 – / that / which
11 – / that   12 which / that

6
1 which was begun by France and Britain in 1987
2 only seven years to finish the Eurotunnel.
3 officially opened by Queen Elizabeth II and French President François Mitterand
4 in commercial service was started first
5 which came later that year, was started on December 22,
6 was named 'Top Construction Achievement of the 20th Century' in March 1999.

7
1 who   2 had   3 wouldn't   4 be   5 which
6 which   7 if   8 wasn't   9 were   10 were

SELF CHECK 6
1 A   2 B   3 C   4 B   5 B   6 A   7 C   8 A   9 A   10 C
11 A   12 B   13 A   14 C   15 B   16 A   17 B   18 C
19 B   20 C   21 B   22 C   23 C   24 B   25 C   26 B
27 A   28 A   29 C   30 C   31 C   32 A   33 B   34 A
35 C   36 C   37 B   38 A   39 C   40 B

UNIT 19

LESSON 1

1 1 Tell 2 say 3 Say 4 telling 5 tell 6 say 7 Say 8 tell

2 1 her 2 to him 3 she said 4 not to be late 5 says 6 me 7 said 8 told us

3 1 I was told to wait until they came back.
2 She is said to be a great artist.
3 We were told to reach the conference room before nine.
4 The lecturer is said to be one of the best in his field.
5 The Board of Directors was / were told to meet in the afternoon.
6 Serena Williams is said to be one of the best tennis players ever.

LESSON 2

1 1 She told them to wait for the coach in the car park. / (that) they should wait for the coach in the car park.
2 She told them to walk in a line while they were in town. / (that) they should walk in a line while they were in town.
3 She told them to hold their friend's hand when they crossed the street / (that) they should hold their friend's hand when they crossed the street.
4 She told them not to walk around on their own. / (that) they shouldn't walk around on their own.
5 She told them to bring their packed lunch. / (that) they should bring their packed lunch.
6 She told them not to forget to bring an anorak and a hat. / (that) they shouldn't forget to bring an anorak and a hat.
7 She told them to wear comfortable shoes. / (that) they should wear comfortable shoes.
8 She told them to remind their parents to pick them up at 6 pm in front of the school / (that) they should remind their parents to pick them up at 6 pm in front of the school.

2 1 asked 2 reminded 3 advised 4 ordered 5 warned

3 1 Mike advised me / us to use sunscreen in this heat.
2 The ranger reminded the visitors not to feed the animals.
3 The teacher told the children to stop making so much noise.
4 The police warned the drivers not to drive up the mountain in that snow.
5 The receptionist advised the hotel guests to leave their valuables in the hotel safe.

4 1 says, look 2 thinks, has passed 3 would like 4 says, will be 5 going 6 dates back

5 1 's / has just found 2 she wants, she finishes 3 I need, I want my dreams 4 he's / he is going 5 the next test is on Monday 11th October

6 1 she quite likes 2 she's / she has made 3 she went to see 4 she's / she has 5 been out 6 She's / She has bought 7 it'a / it is quite windy there 8 she isn't / is not coming back 9 she's / she has got to study

LESSON 3

1 1 she wouldn't / would not be back, the next / following day
2 their, would be, (that) they'd / would be going
3 she had spent her, earlier / before
4 he would phone me the following / next day, he arrived
5 he had booked his / the previous week / the week before

2 1 They told us they had been to a new Thai restaurant the Saturday before and added it had been really good.
2 Jane said to me she always travels by herself and added that way she's more open to meeting new people.
3 I told my secretary I was going to leave earlier the following / next day.
4 They said they had been to the museum that morning.
5 The receptionist told us she was afraid she wouldn't be able to get seats for that night's show.
6 Mum said she couldn't go to bed early that night and added she still had a lot of work to do.

3 1 was 2 wrote 3 sounded 4 said 5 were 6 were 7 could 8 move 9 got 10 has lived

4 1 The law in 1865 stated that slavery was abolished all over the United States.
2 The suspect claimed that he was at home all day on June 1st and added that he hadn't seen anyone except for his wife.
3 The physics teacher explained yesterday that the speed of a body is the distance it covers over a period of time.
4 Critics remarked that the famous composer's new symphony was not very original.

5 *Possible answer*
This is the report of the March 15th meeting. The Sales Manager stated that some of the customers would like a new, more technological product. They were asking for an even lighter waterproof jacket. The Purchasing Manager remarked that, in that case, they had to buy a different kind of fabric to meet their requirements. The Production Manager suggested that the machines should be updated too if they wanted to manufacture a new product. The Finance Manager said that he / she thought they had to draw up a business

plan. He / She added that the costs couldn't exceed the benefits. The Sales Manager remarked that they also needed to carry out a survey so that they had real data to analyse. The Finance Manager explained that the survey had to be included in the costs. He added they could send questionnaires because interviews would be more expensive.

LESSON 4

1
1. he could find the tickets for the show.
2. we should meet.
3. that we (should / could) play video games. / playing video games.
4. (could) look on Wikipedia.
5. how much the / that tablet cost.
6. what he has / had on his mind.
7. when they are / they're coming.
8. taking up a winter sport / that I / we took up a winter sport

2
1. Amanda asked what time Jane was coming the following / next day.
2. Angela asked if / whether Sammy liked / likes canoeing.
3. Tom asked me why I hadn't gone swimming the night before.
4. Sally asked Kate if / whether her brother was working in Switzerland.
5. I asked Sue if / whether she could lend me her pen.
6. The teacher asked the class / whether they had done their homework.

3 🎧 16
1. Grandma asked me what my school was like and I answered that it was great.
2. I was asked how long I had lived in Italy and I answered for two years.
3. Dad asked me if I knew that more standing stones had been found near Stonehenge and I answered that I didn't.
4. Pat asked me if I'd ever been to Iceland. I answered that I'd never been there and I added that I'd like to go because I knew it must be an amazing land.
5. Mum asked me if I was curious to know my exam results and I answered that I couldn't wait.

4
1. Sarah — 'I live in a new house.'
2. Ben — 'Where did you study Italian, David?'
3. Mum — 'I'm / am very tired.'
4. Mr Smith — 'Jason, I will / I'll arrive late tomorrow.'
5. Fiona — 'Is Tom working this afternoon?'

5 🎧 17
Julian Hi, Marco!
Marco Hi, Julian! It's nice to see you again.
Julian When did we last see each other?
Marco I think it was two years ago.
Julian Do you still live in the same house near the main street?
Marco No, I've moved to a new house.
Julian Where is it?
Marco It's in the suburbs.
Julian Do you like it?
Marco I love it because it has a big garden and a conservatory.

6
1. John asked Rick if / whether he had been to Athens before and Rick answered that he hadn't.
2. Emma asked the children if / whether they were having fun at the water park and they answered that they were.
3. Matt asked Sarah if / whether her husband was happy with his new motorbike and she answered that he was.
4. Mark asked Sylvia if / whether she had come by train and she answered that she hadn't, she'd come in the car.
5. Angela asked Julia if / whether she had time to go for lunch and she answered she had. She suggested going / that they go to the pub on the corner.

7
1 E 2 C 3 B 4 A 5 F 6 D

8
1. Lewis suggested eating / that they ate at the new Thai restaurant that night.
2. The tour operator recommended going / that they / we go to Rhodes the following summer.
3. Marion suggested organising / that they / we organised a garage sale to raise some money.
4. Peter's mother suggested (to him) that he shouldn't / had better not go out that day.
5. June suggested having / that we had a sleepover at her house the following Saturday.
6. The therapist recommended having / that he / she / we / I should had a long brisk walk at least twice a week.

9
1. Ryan wondered where they would go / would be going on holiday the following summer.
2. Olivia wanted to know who had booked the seats for the theatre.
3. Carl asked what time we were meeting our guide for the city tour.
4. Pamela wanted to know when Nancy was leaving for Rome.
5. Simon asked where I / we would like to go that day.
6. Mr Wilson wondered what his son was going to do when he left school.

ROUND UP 19

1
SAY: hello, no, something wrong, a word, thank you, goodbye
TELL: the time, a lie, the truth, the difference, a joke, me about…

2
1 say 2 say 3 tell 4 said 5 tell 6 told 7 tell 8 said 9 says 10 tell

3 1 D 2 A 3 E 4 G 5 B 6 C 7 H 8 F

4 1 she, that 2 he, me / us the following weekend / he 3 they, that 4 she, that, she 5 he, that 6 they, I / we, the following week

5
1 Joan often says to her husband that she doesn't like him lying on the sofa all day on Sundays.
2 The science teacher said that some dinosaurs had been herbivores, others had been carnivorous.
3 The sales manager remarked that those data couldn't be correct. There must have been a mistake.
4 Alan keeps telling Nicole that he wants to find a better place to live and raise their children.
5 Mum always says that patience is a great virtue. We should never forget it.
6 My son sometimes tells me that I am a great cook.
7 Liza always says that she will / she'll become a great singer. And I think she will.

6
1 He said that ~~I~~ **he** would go to the mountains the day after.
2 She said she ~~is~~ **was** happy for him.
3 I told him not **to** play in his bedroom in those dirty shoes.
4 Sam said he had met Jenny at the concert ~~yesterday~~ **the previous day / the day before**.
5 Keira replied she ~~doesn't~~ **didn't** want to pay extra money for that service.
6 He asked her whose bike ~~was it~~ **it was**.
7 He told me that I and my family are very important to ~~me~~ **him**.
8 I said I was going home because I ~~feel~~ **felt** sick.

7
1 Mum told the children to stop making all that noise. She was working.
2 Ted suggested meeting / that we met at the station the next / following morning at eight.
3 The guide told the tourists that the stones used to build Stonehenge had been taken from very far away.
4 Sam told his friend Paul that he'd like to stay a little longer, but that he could go home if he wanted to.
5 The teacher explained to her pupils that that Norman castle had been built in the 12th century.
6 My friend who lives in the USA told me he / she was / is going to visit Yellowstone National Park next / the following summer.
7 John asked me if he could have a look at my history project. I answered that he couldn't because I'd already handed it in.
8 The doctor advised me to eat less and do physical exercise regularly.

8 1 reminded 2 asked 3 said 4 suggested 5 said 6 asked 7 answered 8 said

9
Hilary Do you know who came into the agency today, Fred?
Fred Of course not. How should I?
Hilary It was a schoolmate of ours.
Fred Who was it?
Hilary It was Albert Swanson.
Fred We haven't seen him since we left school. What's he like?
Hilary He's very elegant and looks even younger than he was when we were at school. He seems to be very rich, too, because he's interested in very expensive holiday resorts.
Fred Do you remember how scruffy Albert looked when he was a student? Are you sure it was really Albert?
Hilary Albert recognised me too. He suggested going out for a meal one day, the three of us and his wife.
Fred Who's Albert's wife?
Hilary You'll never guess. His wife is Rose, the most beautiful girl in the school.
Fred I can't believe it! Rose didn't even want to sit next to Albert during lessons then.

10
1 Rachel wanted to know if / whether I wanted any more food for the picnic.
2 Tony told his father that he'd had some trouble with his mountain bike a short time before.
3 Damien wanted to know if she was happy with her new car.
4 A friend wondered why I had given up fencing.
5 The ranger warned Don to stay at home during the snowstorm.
6 The instructor advised me to go waterskiing in the summer.
7 Andrew ordered the children to get out of the boat.

Reflecting on grammar

1 F 2 F 3 T 4 T 5 F 6 T 7 T 8 F 9 T 10 F

UNIT 20

LESSON 1

1
1 I studied hard, but I didn't get a good mark.
2 He looks like a tough guy, but he's very shy.
3 The film was good, but it was a bit slow.
4 The T-shirt they gave me for my birthday is nice, but it's too short.
5 Emma liked Tom, but she didn't really trust him.
6 I thought it would be sunny in Sicily in May, but we had lots of rain.
7 They've had a lot of problems recently, but they've never complained.
8 It's a very nice house, but it's a long way from the centre.

2 1 because 2 and 3 but 4 because 5 or
6 so 7 However 8 and

3 1 even though 2 Despite / In spite of 3 even though / although 4 Although / Even though
5 However 6 Despite 7 despite / in spite of
8 However

4 1 C 2 D 3 B 4 A 5 F 6 E

5 1 Although Jane got home late, she prepared dinner for everybody.
2 The waiter was very kind, but the food wasn't that good.
3 I don't have an English–French dictionary. I can look words up on the Internet, though.
4 I don't know his wife, however I know his children.
5 We had a great time, even though the weather wasn't very nice.
6 We got lost, although we had a map of the city.
7 However good it may be, I will never be able to eat sushi.

LESSON 2

1 1 As the weather is so bad, the barbecue has been cancelled.
2 We didn't buy that computer since it was too expensive.
3 We walked back home because we didn't have any money for a taxi.
4 Since it was raining, we decided not to play tennis.
5 We often go to Barcelona because our grandparents live there.
6 We couldn't get there on time as there was a bus strike.

2 1 It was too late, so I couldn't wait any longer.
2 I couldn't buy anything because I didn't have any money.
3 We didn't know many people, so we didn't have a good time at the party.
4 I went to work on my bike yesterday because my car isn't working.
5 I want to lose weight, therefore I'm going to eat less sugar.
6 His school report was so bad that his parents were furious with him.

3 1 so much 2 such a great 3 so good
4 so lucky 5 so long 6 so often 7 so badly
8 so boring

4 1 C 2 D 3 E 4 A 5 F 6 B

5 1 so 2 so as 3 to call 4 because 5 Since
6 so as not 7 so that 8 because 9 in order to
10 consequently

6 1 because 2 so 3 As / Since / Because
4 because 5 so (that) 6 such a, that 7 so, that
8 so as not to

LESSON 3

1 1 Before 2 before 3 as long as 4 as soon as
5 while 6 until 7 Before 8 While

2 1 when 2 until 3 as soon as 4 while
5 as long as 6 After 7 before

3 1 first 2 then 3 After that 4 finally

4 1 Firstly 2 Secondly 3 In addition 4 because
5 Another point 6 before 7 last but not least

5 1 Besides 2 What's more 3 in addition
4 What's more 5 Moreover 6 Besides

6 1 Before 2 while 3 until 4 as soon as
5 First of all, secondly 6 As soon as

LESSON 4

1 1 F 2 D 3 A 4 B 5 C 6 E

2 1 provided 2 unless 3 as if 4 If only 5 in case
6 as if 7 in case 8 as long as

3 1 than 2 as, as 3 as 4 as 5 as 6 than
7 as, as 8 than

4 1 that 2 if 3 that 4 than 5 that 6 that 7 than

5 1 made 2 makes 3 made 4 makes 5 make
6 make 7 made 8 make 9 making 10 made

6 1 let 2 caused 3 caused 4 got 5 caused 6 let
7 got 8 let / will let

7 1 allowed 2 was obliged 3 gets 4 makes
5 let 6 caused

8 1 My parents do not / don't me go out in the evening. That's not fair!
2 This film was very moving; the ending made me cry.
3 Mr Basset is going to / will let us go into his lab next week.
4 I will / 'll get you to come to the swimming pool with me after work. It's so relaxing!
5 We made Tom sing a song at the party, although he didn't want to.
6 This is music that makes everybody dance!

9 1 loading 2 to have 3 to take, to make
4 to clean 5 to phone 6 to go 7 leaving
8 learn 9 run 10 ring

10 1 as long as 2 unless 3 in case 4 as if 5 If only
6 than 7 that, as / because / since
8 than 9 However 10 as soon as

ROUND UP 20

1 1 but 2 so 3 yet 4 for 5 and, or, and 6 nor

2 1 because 2 though 3 so 4 that 5 so, that 6 if 7 until 8 as long as

3
1 Because he had eaten enough, he didn't want anything else.
2 After I finished school yesterday, I went straight home.
3 Call me at once if you see anything strange.
4 Provided you don't suffer from seasickness, you can join us on our boat trip.
5 Whatever they say, I won't try this dish.
6 Before I went to the office this morning, I went jogging for an hour.
7 I'm going for a bike ride later, so long as it doesn't rain.

4 1 who 2 to 3 which 4 If only 5 also 6 which 7 so 8 that 9 before

5 1 First 2 Then 3 After that / Next 4 Next / After that 5 until 6 Finally

6 1 which 2 and 3 If 4 as a result 5 In spite of 6 However 7 although

7 1 make 2 get 3 gets 4 makes 5 gets 6 makes 7 makes 8 lets

8 1 forced 2 makes 3 gets 4 allowed / allow 5 saw 6 needs 7 obliged 8 heard

Reflecting on grammar

1 F 2 T 3 T 4 F 5 T 6 F 7 F 8 T 9 F 10 F

UNIT 21

LESSON 1

1
1 He's leaving for college in a week's time.
2 I feel great today.
3 They drove all the way to Portugal last summer.
4 I bought a very pretty skirt in the little shop in the mall.
5 They became very famous after their last album.
6 We often watch videos on YouTube.
7 We went to the fish-and-chip shop in the High Street for lunch.
8 They are going on a cycling holiday in Holland.
9 He looked very silly in those trousers at the party last night.

2 1 I 2 I 3 I 4 T 5 I 6 T 7 I 8 I 9 L

3 1 C 2 H 3 A 4 F 5 B 6 D 7 E 8 G

4
1 The man wasn't / was not standing near the shop door.
2 There wasn't / was not anything strange about him.
3 They didn't / did not discover a Neolithic site in this area.
4 Tina doesn't / does not look happy today.
5 I'm / I am not thirsty. I don't / do not need anything to drink.
6 I don't / do not have to work at weekends this month.
7 The visitors didn't / did not leave the museum before five.
8 Karen won't / will not arrive at the beginning of December.
9 We couldn't / could not see the entrance of the building on the screen.
10 She didn't / did not go out with her boyfriend last night.
11 I haven't / have not played tennis a lot recently.
12 They hadn't / had not left the office yet.

LESSON 2

1
1 'Do you like painting?' 'Yes, I / we do.'
2 'Does Rebecca play in the school volleyball team?' 'No, she doesn't.'
3 'Are the boys going home?' 'No, they aren't. / No, they're not.'
4 'Would you like to meet her?' 'Yes, I / we would.'
5 'Did your boyfriend give you a present?' 'Yes, he did.'
'Did you give your boyfriend a present?' 'Yes, I did.'
6 'Has Marion got her laptop with her?' 'No, she hasn't.'

2 1 I hope so. 2 I hope not. 3 I'm afraid so. 4 I'm afraid not. 5 I don't think so. 6 I guess so. 7 I suppose not. / I don't suppose so. 8 I believe so.

3
1 How do we get to the station?   G
2 When did you buy your car?   D
3 When could you come to my house?   A
4 Why were you laughing?   C
5 Which of those T-shirts did you buy? B
6 How long did you wait for them?   F
7 Are you gong to sell your flat?   H
8 What time did your brother get home last night? E

4 *Possible answers*
Where did you go in the holidays?
What were your friends going to do last night?
Who is Martina looking for?
When does he start the guitar course?
Why are they running?
How did you get to the cinema?

5 🎧 18 1 isn't it? 2 are you? 3 wasn't it? 4 don't you? 5 haven't you? 6 do you?

6 1 isn't it? 2 isn't she? 3 haven't you? 4 was it? 5 do you? 6 didn't they? 7 did you? 8 can't he? 9 shall we? 10 doesn't he?

7
1 Does she? 2 Is he really? 3 Wouldn't he?
4 Haven't you? 5 Will he? 6 Can't you?
7 Have you?

8
1 A 2 A 3 C 4 B 5 C 6 A

9
1 A 2 F 3 G 4 B 5 D 6 C 7 E

10
1 Their friends wouldn't. 2 So do we. 3 So will I.
4 My daughter doesn't. 5 So did my son.
6 Mine aren't. 7 Neither / Nor have we.

LESSON 3

1
1 C 2 A 3 F, J 4 E, G 5 B, J 6 B 7 D 8 I
9 K 10 H 11 L 12 E

2
1 The school team 2 A summer holiday
3 A book shelf 4 A fashion magazine
5 A vegetable garden 6 Garden vegetables
7 A wine glass 8 A conference room
9 A shoe shop 10 Ski boots 11 A winter resort
12 A love story 13 A tennis court
14 Rock music 15 A computer screen
16 Your car door

3
1 big-nosed man 2 short-legged, long-tailed dog
3 long-haired girl 4 wide-brimmed hat
5 high-heeled shoes 6 new-born baby
7 badly done exercise 8 man-made canal

4
1 annoyed 2 annoying 3 confusing 4 exciting
5 tiring, tired 6 interested 7 entertaining
8 rising 9 relaxing 10 confused

5
1 multitasking E 2 forecast J 3 polytheistic religion L 4 oversleep F 5 dehydrate D
6 disagree A 7 unfriendly H 8 undernourished I
9 trilogy G 10 ill-treated B 11 rearrange C
12 polyglot K

6
1 artist 2 historians 3 director(s) 4 painters
5 magician 6 drummer, singer

7
1 PEACE<u>FUL</u> (AD)
2 <u>RE</u>WIND (V)
3 IM<u>PATIENT</u>LY (ADV)
4 <u>RE</u>ORGANI<u>SATION</u> (N)
5 <u>UN</u>FORTUNATE<u>LY</u> (ADV)
6 <u>DIS</u>ADVANTAGE (N)
7 <u>IN</u>SECUR<u>ITY</u> (N)
8 LEADER<u>SHIP</u> (N)
9 LONELI<u>NESS</u> (N)

8
1 pointless 2 wonderful 3 homeless 4 useful
5 useless 6 careful 7 careless 8 powerful
9 hopeless 10 fruitful

9
1 fashionable 2 selfish 3 noisy 4 alcoholic
5 meaningless 6 unprecedented 7 cloudless
8 reliable 9 impossible 10 unpredictable

LESSON 4

1
1 in 2 go 3 in 4 give 5 on 6 carry / go 7 up
8 up 9 wake / get 10 down 11 sit / lie 12 out
13 back 14 broke 15 off 16 takes 17 away
18 Watch 19 back 20 off 21 off 22 Look
23 stand 24 over

2
1 Bring the newspaper back, will you?
2 Fill this form in, please.
3 Hand your project in by tomorrow.
4 It's cold. Put your pullover on.
5 Can I try this coat on, please?
6 Switch the lights on, it's dark.
7 Put the glasses away, please.
8 Turn the TV down. It's too loud.

3
1 Come back as soon as you can!
2 Something's come up at work.
3 I told them to come in.
4 I can't give up smoking.
5 He made up a good story.
6 Do you know what brought about / on her depression?
7 My grandparents brought up eight children.
8 How can you put up with his behaviour?

4
1 up 2 forward 3 of 4 up 5 on 6 away
7 down 8 up

ROUND UP 21

1
1 He doesn't like horror films at all.
2 Last summer, he didn't go on holiday to the usual place. / He didn't go on holiday to the usual place last summer.
3 Your sister speak Spanish very well.
4 We thanked them for being so nice to us.
5 Last year, they spent two months in Africa. / They spent two months in Africa last year.
6 What did you have for lunch yesterday?
7 They haven't been to Turkey before.
8 We usually spend our free time at the youth club or at the mall.
9 I don't feel very well today.
10 We're having an exam in a week's time.
11 What time does the next train leave?
12 What platform does it leave from?

2
1 Not only was she a great singer, she was also a fantastic dancer.
2 No sooner had he arrived than he started chatting and never stopped.
3 Only if you train hard will you have a chance of winning the match.
4 Not until I got home in the evening did I realise that my friend had left.
5 Never have I met such a silly boy as Tom.
6 Hardly ever do they help with the housework. Their parents are really annoyed.
7 They came to the mountains, but not even once did they try to ski.
8 Only if you are nice to others will others be nice you.

3
1 This is my first time in New York.
2 Have they got a lot of friends here?
3 We didn't enjoy the trip very much.
4 Do the children have to be at school earlier tomorrow?
5 Does the bus leave on the half hour?
6 They couldn't find the answers to all of my questions.
7 Did Tom and Lucy have dinner at home last night?
8 Was there a long queue at the post office?
9 My mum knows my friend John.
10 We got up late this morning.

4 1 couldn't you? 2 haven't they? 3 can you? 4 did you? 5 do they? 6 doesn't she? 7 isn't it? 8 weren't they?

5 1 I don't 2 So did we 3 I did 4 Neither / Nor do we 5 Neither / Nor do I 6 Neither / Nor could I 7 So does 8 hasn't 9 So does 10 I did

6

	Abstract noun
educate	education
enjoy	enjoyment
friend	friendship
leader	leadership
perform	performance
establish	establishment
possible	possibility
credible	credibility
hard	hardship, hardness
sister	sisterhood
liberate	liberation
kind	kindness
endure	endurance
free	freedom

7 1 called off 2 broke down 3 broke up 4 be up to 5 are, up to 6 be off 7 Come back 8 came up with 9 set off 10 Shut up 11 work out 12 Hang on to 13 hanging out 14 hanging around 15 is / 's, over

8 1 done with 2 worn out / done in 3 worn out 4 am / 'm fed up with 5 worn out / done in 6 done for 7 done away with 8 am / 'm fed up with

Reflecting on grammar
1 T 2 F 3 T 4 F 5 F 6 T 7 F 8 F 9 T 10 T

REVISION AND EXAMS 7

1 🎧19
Neil So, **how** was your holiday in Ireland?
Ellen Great. We really enjoyed ourselves!
Neil **Where** were you exactly?
Ellen We were in Galway for two weeks.
Neil Galway? It's on the west coast, **isn't** it?
Ellen Yes, exactly. It's a beautiful place. There are a lot of things going **on** in the summer.
Neil What was the weather **like**? Windy and rainy, I guess.
Ellen Well, I was told the weather in that area was usually rainy, but in fact we had two weeks of sun.
Neil That was lucky! Did you go to the Aran Islands?
Ellen Yes, absolutely. We hired two bicycles and we went **on** a trip around the island of Inishmore. We also had a swim in the sea even **if / though** the water was very cold!
Neil How I would have liked to have been with you! I love Ireland. Have you been there before?
Ellen No, this was our first time but we want to go **back** there next year.

2 **Neil** Hi, Steve. Guess who I've just met. Ellen, do you remember her? She used to work in the Accounts Department. I asked her what her holiday in Ireland was like and she said that they really enjoyed themselves. She explained that they were in Galway for two weeks, on the west coast, and said that it's a beautiful place and that there are a lot of things going on in the summer. I asked her what the weather had been like and she replied that she had been told the weather in that area was usually rainy, but in fact they had had two weeks of sun. I asked her if they had been to the Aran Islands, and she said that they had. She added that they had hired two bicycles and had been on a trip around the island of Inishmore. She said that they had even swum in the sea, even if / though the water had been very cold. I told her I would have liked to have been with them because I love Ireland. I asked her if they had been there before, and she answered that it had been their first time, but they wanted to go back there next year / the following year.

3 1 give in 2 done in 3 Come on 4 make out 5 put up 6 put up 7 get, across 8 run out

4 You can't even imagine how difficult it was for me to get to the top. I thought I would give in, but Paul told me not to give in then, as we were nearly there. I told him that I was done in and I couldn't walk any more, but he asked me if I couldn't see the top. He said that with one more effort, we would be there, and told me to come on. I complained that I couldn't even make out the top in that mist, but he told me to stop complaining and said that I should learn to put up with difficulties. I said that I could put up with difficulties, but I realised then that I wasn't trained. I asked him how I could get that across to him. He said that he saw, but added that he knew I could make it. He suggested we had some chocolate and said it would help, but I said that I hadn't wanted to tell him, but we'd run out of comfort food. He asked if we had any water left, and I replied that we did still have some water at least.

5 1 but 2 or 3 after 4 and 5 when 6 if 7 if
8 if 9 or 10 before 11 after 12 or

6 1 B 2 A 3 C 4 A 5 B 6 C 7 C 8 B 9 A 10 B

7 1 B 2 C 3 A 4 C 5 D 6 A 7 B 8 A 9 D 10 A

8 1 put up with 2 been put off 3 keep off
4 run out of 5 fill in 6 give up eating
7 Pop / Drop in to 8 carry out

9 1 Besides 2 also 3 away / abroad 4 Most
5 up 6 like 7 without 8 up 9 Although
10 back

10 1 misunderstandings 2 unbelievable
3 independence 4 protective 5 different

11 Students' own answers

SELF CHECK 6

1 B 2 C 3 A 4 A 5 B 6 C 7 C 8 A 9 B 10 A 11 C 12 C 13 B 14 B 15 C 16 B 17 C 18 B 19 A 20 C 21 B 22 B 23 C 24 A 25 B 26 B 27 A 28 B 29 C 30 B 31 C 32 A 33 B 34 C 35 C 36 C 37 B 38 B 39 C 40 A

Grammar Matrix + Answer Keys
Lucy Becker, Carol Frain, Karen Thomas

ISBN 978-85-469-0196-8

First published 2018

© HELBLING LANGUAGES 2018

All right reserved. No part of this publication may be reproduced, stored in a retrieval system, or transmitted in any form or by any means, electronic, mechanical, photocopying, recording, or otherwise without the prior written permission of the publisher.

Acknowledgements
The authors would like to thank Professor Jerome Su and Satoshi Saito for their inspiring ideas and valuable consultancy.
The publisher would like to thank the following for their kind permission to reproduce the following photographs and other copyright material:
© Alexander Pladdet p23 (cup of coffee), Libux77 p23 (jar of marmalade), Paul Cowan p23 (bar of chocolate), Adogslifephoto p30, Tim Hester p37 (Mount Everest), Drekasami p48 (teapot), Foto21293 p48 (chest of drawers), Vickie Priestley p48 (paperweight), Design56 p51 (keys), Infomods p57 (pub) Alexander Limbach p57 (online shop), Wmj82 p60 (Australia flag), Jagodka p72, Rhbabiak13 p74, Kadettmann p85, Jaroslaw Baczewski p86, Udo Schotten p87 (no overtaking sign), Dimitrios Kaisaris p87 (no stopping sign), Nikolai Sorokin p87 (no entry sign), Arkadi Bojaršinov p87 (no cycling sign), Rademakerfotografie p89, Cupertino10 p109 (smartphone), Oleg Dudko p110, Richard Jemmett p140 (Tudor cottage), Olena Yakobchuk p145, Oleg Mashkov p172, nullplus p250, Zygotehasnobrain p272, 1000words p303 (traffic), Shchipkova Elena p303 (polar bear), Mark Eaton p306 (vase), irur p306 (presenter), Eveleen007 p308 (anatomy), Karkas p308 (restaurant), Simonekesh p324 (Calatrava bridge), 2happy p363, jennagenio p383, Graphic Symbol Photo p384, Garsya p385, Michael Kraus p387 (hat), MaleWitch p387 (shoes) | **Dreamstime.com**; ©iStock.com/JackJelly p23 (biscuits), matt_benoit p28, Hong Li p48 (fruit bowl), kolae p51 (thermometer), Georgo p51 (umpire), sd619 p51 (test), IGphotography p85 (shopping centre), Sezeryadigar p106, Lexa11 p107 (shoes), thehague p108, Juanmonino p126 (child), Milenko Bokan p126 (mother and son), Lexa11 p131, Neustockimages p147, retroimages p153, Di Andy-pix p167, Ionut David p169, Savas Keskiner p181 (cars), Alfonso Cacciola p206, skynesher p222, Victor Maschek p225, Firina p226, gorica p228, Yuri_Arcurs p229, Zygotehasnobrain p257, Chris Bernard Photography Inc. p305 (kids), ElementalImaging p311 (kite), Phototreat p311 (bedroom), andeva p337 (lake), RapidEye p337 (boots), Lya_Cattel p356, EmirMemedovski p363; Andrey Armyagov (background), Robin Crossman p29 (spider), wavebreakmedia p29 (Sam), Dorothy Gaziano p48 (painting), Dr.Margorius p48 (teaspoons), JuliusKielaitis p56 (cathedral), rickyd p56 (farm), Sigitasd p58 (Snowdonia National Park), fredex p58 (British Isles), Di Bernd Rehorst p59, alessandro0770 p87 (speed limitation road sign), Sergey Sikharulidze p87 (give way sign), Jojoo64 p87 (no motor vehicles allowed), Jojoo64 p87 (no right turn traffic sign, no U-turns sign), ronnarid p87 (turn left ahead sign), wavebreakmedia p104, Angela Aladro mella p107 (woman), Patryk Kosmider p109 (Santorini), Merydolla p132, Moving Moment p135, michaeljung p137, Georgios Kollidas p140 (William Shakespeare), fztommy p141, amenic181 p142 (coffee beans), Paul Lesser p142 (Barbecue), Michiel de Wit 143, filipw p148 (man), Valua Vitaly p148 (woman), Dorothy Gaziano p148 (British flag), Dr. Margorius p148 (USA flag), FenlioQ p170, Sergio33 p188 (mother and daughter), Iakov Filimonov p188 (woman at the door), Kathy Hutchins p221 (Brad Pitt), PHILIPIMAGE p221 (cheese), Nataliass p221 (bag), Karkas 243, Pixel Embargo p265 (Post-it), Roman Sotola p265 (ticket), Alexander Lukatskiy p305 (fisherman), Sergiy Kuzmin p327 (segway), Arina P Habich p328, Robert Adrian Hillman p333, Miroslav Hlavko p337 (alpine star), Shaiith p337 (hut), RTimages p337 (hot chocolate), davide guidolin p337 (mountains), Daniel Prudek p337 (mountain peak), Dmitry Molchanov p337 (friends), disq p337 (guide), Przemyslaw Wasilewski p337 (marmot), Vira Mylyan-Monastyrska

p338 (orchestra), Jimmy Tran p341 (rice fields), Roberto Lo Savio p341 (risotto), gpointstudio p342, Goodluz p343, luminaimages p348 (teacher), Andrey Armyagov p373, keko64 p376 (custard), Everett Historical p376 (earthquake), sanddebeautheil p377 (gardening tool), Fathur Rahman p389, Vixit p398, Africa Studio p399, p401 **/ Shutterstock.com**; **Wikimedia Commons** p37 (Eurotunnel), p113, John Bites p304, p342 (Euro Tunnel logo).

Illustrated by Sergio Cingolani, Doriano Strologo.
Editing and language consultancy by Pat Bulhosen, Michela Calore, Jenny Newton, Paola Tite, Oonagh Wade, Dona Velluti, Catriona Watson-Brown.
Designed by Gianluca Armeni, Amanda Hockin, Pixarte.
Cover by Capolinea
Printed by Athesia, Italy

Every effort has been made to trace the owners of any copyright material in this book. If notified, the publisher will be pleased to rectify any errors or omissions.